HANDLING, TRANSPORTATION AND STORAGE OF FRUITS AND VEGETABLES

VOLUME 1, SECOND EDITION

Vegetables and Melons

TYPICAL WHOLESALE MARKET SCENE

HANDLING, TRANSPORTATION AND STORAGE OF FRUITS AND VEGETABLES
Volume 1, Second Edition
Vegetables and Melons

A. Lloyd Ryall, M.S.
U.S. Department of Agriculture (Retired)
Formerly, Chief, Horticultural Crops
Research Branch, Agricultural
Research Service

Werner J. Lipton, Ph.D.
Principal Plant Physiologist,
Market Quality Research Division,
Agricultural Research Service,
U.S. Department of Agriculture,
Fresno, California

avi

AVI PUBLISHING COMPANY, INC.
Westport, Connecticut

Library of Congress Cataloging in Publication Data (Revised)

Ryall, Albert Lloyd, 1904-

    Handling, transportation, and storage of fruits and
vegetables.

    Vol. 1 by A. L. Ryall and W. J. Lipton
    Includes bibliographies and index.
    CONTENTS: v. 1.   Vegetables and melons.—v.
2.   Fruits and tree nuts.
    1. Fruit—Marketing.   2.   Vegetables—Marketing.
I.   Lipton, Werner J., 1928-   joint author.
II.   Pentzer, Wilbur Tibbils, 1901-   III. Title.
SB360.R85   634'.04'6   75-188035
ISBN 0-87055-115-9(v. 1, 1st ed.) .

Printed in the United States of America

Preface to the Second Edition

This Second Edition of Volume 1 is a substantially revised version of the 1972 original. Change is a continuous process in the produce industry. The changes are partly the result of innovations introduced by industry and are partly an outgrowth of information developed by State, Federal and foreign researchers.

We have included significant recent developments in the biological and physical aspects of produce marketing. Also, in recognition of universal acceptance, we have added metric units for essentially all measurements.

Despite the trend to increased consumption of frozen and heat-processed vegetables over the last twenty years, we see ample evidence that fresh vegetables and melons hold a secure place in the market. Since 1973 "fresh" has shown a gradual increase in per capita consumption. This trend likely will continue as nutritional values receive more emphasis and understanding among all segments of the population. We hope that this edition will aid in the attempt to provide consumers with fresh vegetables and melons that please the eye and the palate while satisfying nutritional needs.

Finally, we thank those individuals and organizations who kindly provided the new illustrations. We acknowledge Arlene Hoeppner and Barbara Flouton, AVI Publishing Co., for their editorial assistance in bringing out this new edition.

A. L. RYALL, LAS CRUCES, N.M.
W. J. LIPTON, FRESNO, CALIF.

September 1978

Preface to the First Edition

Despite increased production and consumption of frozen and heat-processed vegetables over the past years, we see ample evidence that fresh vegetables and melons are here to stay. Most producers and marketers are now aware that "fresh" creates the image that sells the "processed." It is significant that although 52% of commercial vegetable acreage was grown for processing in the 1964-1967 period, the 48% grown for the fresh market provided 71% of total farm value. The grower who sees profit in "fresh," the consumer who prefers to use "fresh," and those who pack, move and distribute vegetables all have a stake in the produce market.

In this book we intend to cover biological and physical aspects of marketing fresh vegetables, including potatoes and melons. The economics of marketing will be left to those better qualified in that field.

Over the years substantial research has been done on harvesting, preparation, packaging, transportation, and storage of horticultural crops. Considerable effort has also been devoted to control of post-harvest diseases and disorders, and to physiological changes that occur in harvested crops.

Much of this research has been conducted in some dozen State Experiment Stations that are located in States with important horticultural industries. Substantial contributions to post-harvest research with horticultural crops have also been made at various laboratories of the Agricultural Research Service of the United States Department of Agriculture and specialized post-harvest laboratories in other parts of the world, particularly in western Europe. Important additions, principally to applied research and development, have come from those associated industries whose efforts extend beyond the art of salesmanship.

The findings of much of this research have been published. However, the bits and pieces are scattered through innumerable state, federal, and foreign bulletins, circulars, and progress reports. Additionally, many papers appear in professional journals, industry magazines, and trade papers. We have attempted to assemble pertinent and reasonably current information from these various sources into a useful reference for research and extension workers, teachers, storage operators, packaging and transportation personnel, as well as shippers, receivers, and distributors of fresh vegetables.

Past emphasis in most of the State Experiment Stations and in the U.S. Department of Agriculture has been heavily oriented to production research. Reference books covering propagation, breeding, nutrition, and cultivation of all the commonly-grown horticultural crops are available. However, no commercial crop is of real value at the completion of production. It must be marketed to have economic value. Getting a vegetable crop to market involves harvesting, sorting, grading, packaging, and provision of a suitable environment for the product during transport, possible storage, and wholesale-retail distribution. This book provides information for these phases of the vegetable industry.

Our background and the majority of our sources of information naturally cause us to emphasize crops, practices, and technology prevalent in North America and Europe. However, the discussions of biological principles and processes, as involved in post-harvest problems of vegetables, apply to any crop or geographic area. Thus, our efforts hopefully will encourage education and investigations in the biological and physical aspects of marketing fresh vegetables in regions where physical and nutritional losses negate much of the effort expended in production.

We appreciate the cooperation of various individuals and organizations who generously furnished illustrative or tabular material for our use. Their specific contributions are identified by means of credit lines.

A. L. RYALL, LAS CRUCES, N.M.
W. J. LIPTON, FRESNO, CALIF.

January 1972

Contents

To the many scientists whose research in horticulture, physiology, pathology, and engineering during the last three-fourths of a century laid the foundation upon which this book is built.

Vegetables as Living Products—Respiration and Heat Production

THE PROCESS OF RESPIRATION

Respiration, the process whereby organisms convert matter into energy, concerns us because it is one of the basic processes of life, and all fresh vegetables and melons are living organisms. However, we will confine ourselves to those aspects of respiration that are directly related to the handling, transportation, or storage of fresh commodities.

In plants, respiration principally involves the enzymatic oxidation of sugars to carbon dioxide (CO_2) and water, accompanied by a release of energy. However, other substances, such as organic acids and proteins, also enter the respiratory chain. Consequently, we will be concerned with the loss of these principal food reserves of plants, with the need for oxygen (O_2), and with the disposition of the CO_2 and energy that are produced. The water derived from respiration has no significance in the context of this discussion. A further important concern will be the rate at which this process occurs.

First, let us consider the quantities of the various components that are involved in respiration. The basic equation states that for every 180 g (1 mole) of glucose (the substrate) respired, 192 g (6 moles) of O_2 are consumed and 264 g (6 moles) of CO_2, 108 g (6 moles) of water and 673 kcal of energy are produced. The plant or plant part provides the substrate, the air furnishes the O_2 and receives the CO_2 and energy that are liberated, although some of the end-products may be retained by the plant.

Substrate Consumed

The quantity of substrate consumed is minor, about 1 g for each gram of CO_2 produced. Since most vegetables produce no more than 0.1 g of CO_2 for each kilogram of plant material per hour at usual temperatures, the loss of substrate would be only 0.01% per hour, or less. Consequently, even for crops stored 6 or 8 months, such as potatoes, onions or cabbage, the weight loss due to respiration usually is no more than 2 or 3% because these crops have low respiration rates when stored at recommended temperatures.

Availability of Oxygen

The supply of O_2 for normal respiration is generally adequate unless access to air is accidentally or intentionally restricted. Under such circumstances, fermentation may take place. This usually is accompanied by the production of undesirable odors or flavors. Fermentation can readily be avoided by packing produce only in adequately ventilated containers (see Chapter 5) or by proper design and maintenance of controlled atmosphere storages.

Disposition of Carbon Dioxide

The disposition of the respiratory CO_2 generally requires more attention than the supply of O_2, because CO_2 may be in excess even when the supply of O_2 is adequate. A 3% reduction in O_2 concentration (e.g., from 21 to 18%) would have no adverse effect on a product, whereas a comparable increase in CO_2 (e.g., from 1 to 4%) could completely ruin some vegetables in a few days. Consequently, uncontrolled accumulation of respiratory CO_2 in the air surrounding the vegetables must be avoided, and its concentration should never exceed 1% unless higher concentrations are known to be harmless.

Disposition of Heat

While the supply of O_2 or the dispersal of CO_2 occasionally may require special care, the disposition of respiratory heat always needs close attention during all phases of marketing vegetables and melons. Because the disposition of respiratory heat is of such fundamental importance, the sections on precooling and refrigeration will deal with the subject in detail.

Rate of Respiration

The rate of respiration is of concern, because it determines the quantity of O_2 that must be available per unit time and the quantities of CO_2 and heat that must be disposed of at the same time. Further, the rate of respiration is a good indicator of the rates at which other reactions proceed, such as the conversion of sugar to starch in sweet corn or peas, the loss of vitamins, such as ascorbic acid, or deterioration caused by physiological changes or diseases.

Definition of Terms

To properly discuss various aspects of the rate of respiration, we first have to exactly define the terms to be used.

Rate of Respiration   The weight of CO_2 produced per unit fresh weight and time (mg CO_2 per kg-hr). The rate also may be expressed in ml CO_2 per kg-hr, or any other convenient unit, such as the quantity of O_2 taken up rather than that of CO_2 produced. Many favor the first expression, although for calculations involving volumes, such as encountered in controlled atmosphere storage, ml CO_2 per kg-hr is more convenient.

Initial Rate of Respiration   The rate prevailing immediately after harvest, or within a few hours thereafter, depending upon the crop and temperature.

Average Rate of Respiration   The average rate prevailing during the storage period considered. It is determined by measuring the rate at definite time intervals, summing the rates thus determined, and dividing by the number of intervals involved.

Respiratory Drift   The change in the rate of respiration with time. Unlike a rate, drift is not a quantitative expression, but is depicted graphically (Fig. 1.1) as a line of drift. Its direction is indicated by such terms as downward, upward, or constant.

Effect of Temperature on Rate

The rate of respiration generally increases as the temperature of the vegetable increases from just above its freezing point up to temperatures that induce heat injury. At such high temperatures the rate then decreases until respiration ceases at the thermal death point (Fig. 1.2). While vegetables and melons can reach this point, our discussion will be confined to the range of increasing rates, because this range is of greatest concern during the marketing of most commodities.

Effect of Chemical Composition and Botanical Structure on Rate

Initial rates of respiration are of greatest interest because they largely determine the refrigeration requirements of crops during pre-cooling and early storage, and because they indicate the magnitude of the average rate during prolonged storage. Initial rates vary tremendously among vegetables held at the same temperature. They range from about 10 mg CO_2 per kg-hr for potatoes held at 15° C (59° F) to nearly 30 times that for broccoli. The actual rates for a variety of vegetables held at various temperatures are given in Table 1.1. From

FIG. 1.1.   SCHEMATIC REPRESENTATION OF LINE OF RESPIRATORY DRIFT FOR A VEGETABLE

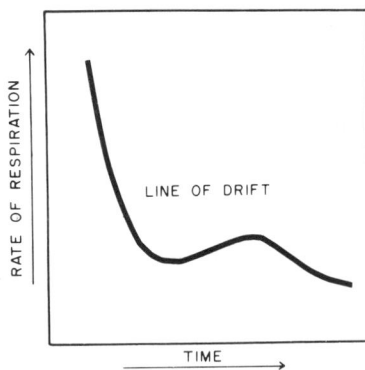

FIG. 1.2.   SCHEMATIC REPRESENTATION OF CHANGE IN INITIAL RATE OF RESPIRATION WITH TEMPERATURE FROM FREEZING POINT TO THERMAL DEATH POINT

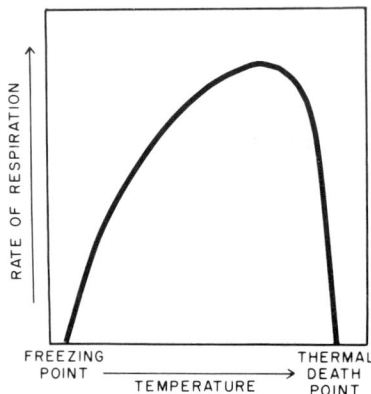

this table we note that the rate of respiration and the quantity of food reserves in the crop are not related, e.g., at 15° C (59° F) sweetpotatoes, which are very high in carbohydrates, respire at about half the rate of head lettuce, which is over 90% water, and at only about ⅛ the rate of sweet corn, which is comparatively high in carbohydrates. If, however, we classify the crops by botanical structure, we find such a close relationship between structure and rate of respiration, that we can class the rate as high, low, or intermediate simply by knowing the type of tissue to be stored. High rates are characteristic of young tissue, such as growing points (asparagus), partly developed flower buds (broccoli), and developing seeds (green peas), or immature fruits (sweet corn, okra). Low rates are typical of storage organs, such as roots (sweetpotatoes), stems (potatoes), bulbs (onions), and mature fruits (pumpkins). Intermediate rates occur in unripe fruits (cucumbers) and most leafy vegetables, although the latter range widely, with spinach approaching the highest rate and cabbage the lowest.

Ripening fruits, such as tomatoes, exhibit a still different characteristic, the so-called climacteric pattern of respiration. Prior to ripening, the rate of respiration decreases to the pre-climacteric minimum; as ripening starts it increases to a maximum, the climacteric. In tomatoes this stage coincides with a light pink color. The rate of respiration then gradually decreases as ripening proceeds further. In Fig. 1.3 the pattern for tomatoes is contrasted with that of several vegetables not showing a climacteric. Some fruits, among them cantaloups, show the climacteric considerably before the fruits normally are harvested, and thus the climacteric is not of direct concern during marketing of such fruits. The phenomenon of the climacteric has been widely investigated and more detailed information can be found in texts on plant physiology or in review articles (e.g., Biale 1975).

Rate as an Index of Storage Life

The rate of respiration often is a good index to the storage life of a crop: high rate, short life; low rate, long life (Fig. 1.4). However, this relation mainly holds when the entire range of rates is considered. Once a rate of about 100 mg CO_2 per kg-hr is exceeded, storage life, expressed as time required to reach an unsalable condition, decreases little. Since subjective judgment enters any such determination of storage life, the durations given are not precise. Further, the relationship between rate of respiration and storage life holds mainly when different crops are compared; it does not necessarily hold in a comparison of two samples of the same crop that somehow have been treated differently. For example, if

TABLE 1.1. RATES OF CO_2 PRODUCTION OF VEGETABLES AT VARIOUS CONSTANT TEMPERATURES—INITIAL RATES AND, IN PARENTHESES, APPROXIMATE EQUILIBRIUM RATES.[1]
(To convert to BTU per ton-day[2], multiply by 220; to convert to kcal per 1000 kg-day multiply by 61.2)

Mg CO_2 per kg-hr at Temperatures[3] Given

Vegetable	°C 0 / °F 32	5 / 41	10 / 50	15 / 59	20 / 68	25 / 77	Source
Artichokes, globe	45 (23)	60 (32)	98 (54)	145 (77)	233 (136)	301 (150)	Rappaport and Watada (1958)
Asparagus, green	80 (27)	136 (55)	304 (90)	327 (160)	500 (275)	600 (500)	Lipton (1957)
Beans, snap	20 (23)	35 (34)	58 (54)	93 (85)	130 (118)		Watada and Morris (1966)
Bean Sprouts, mung	23	42	96				Lipton et al. (1981)
Beets, red, roots	7 (5)	10 (9)	14 (12)	23 (17)			Smith (1957)
Broccoli[4]		34	81	174	299		Scholz et al. (1963)
		73 (41)		292 (182)			Rappaport et al. (1957)
Brussels sprouts	24 (15)	49 (32)	85 (63)	107 (96)			Smith (1957)
Cabbage spring		11	18	23	43	56	Scholz et al. (1963)
	14 (9)	21 (18)	33 (29)	57 (54)			Smith (1957)
savoy[5]	19	28	57	94	140		Intern. Inst. Refrig. (1967)
Carrots		19	32	40	70		Scholz et al. (1963)
Cauliflower		20	34	46	80		Scholz et al. (1963)
	24 (8)	27 (20)	49 (41)	81 (67)			Smith (1957)
Celery[5]				37	64		Lutz and Hardenburg (1968)
	7	11	27 (20)				Smith (1957)
Celeriac[5]	7	13	23	36	46		Intern. Inst. Refrig. (1967)
Cucumbers	5 (5)	9 (13)		33 (24)	48 (32)		Eaks and Morris (1956)
Endive[5]	41	47	66	90	120		Intern. Inst. Refrig. (1967)
Garlic[6]	3 (11)	6 (26)	9 (32)	11 (27)	10 (18)	181	Mann and Lewis (1956)

Commodity							Reference
Horseradish	(8)	(14)	(26)	(33)	(44)		Pieh (1965)
Kale	(20)	(40)	(80)	(140)	(230)		Hruschka (1971)
Kohlrabi	(10)	(16)	(31)	(49)			Pieh (1965)
Leek	16	29	68	117			Smith (1957)
Lettuce, crisphead	(10)	(20)	(54)	(83)	60		Pratt et al. (1954)
	17	20	40	41			
leaf	(9)	(13)	(27)	(39)	(57)	82	Scholz et al. (1963)
	14	22	36		100	146	Scholz et al. (1963)
	29	39	63	67			Smith (1957)
	26	49	67				
Romaine	18	(13)	(24)	(40)	69	108	Scholz et al. (1963)
Mushrooms[5]	(11)	20	35	44	316		Lutz and Hardenburg (1968)
	44	71	(148)	(230)			Pieh (1965)
	(24)	(90)					
Muskmelons							
Cantaloups	9	15	36	48	67		Scholz et al. (1963)
Honey Dew	8	14	24	30	33		
	4		(13)		(22)		Pratt and Morris (1958)
Okra	3	90	146	261	345		Scholz et al. (1963)
Onions, dry	19	7	11	17	28		Scholz et al. (1963)
green[8]	(16)	28	52	89	126	175	Hardenburg (1970)
	(25)	65	(47)	(81)	(111)	(122)	
	17						
Parsley	37	100	43				Apeland (1971)
Parsnips	15	26	(32)				Smith (1957)
	(9)	(20)					
	(12)						
Peas, unshelled	39	117		295			Tewfik and Scott (1954)
	36	(68)					Smith (1957)
	(29)						
shelled	75						
Pepper, sweet	10	15	23	395			Tewfik and Scott (1954)
Potato[7,9], immature	12	21	31	44			Scholz et al. (1963)
	(12)	(14)	(18)	45			Morris (1970)
mature	6	10	12	16			
	(7)	(7)	(7)				
very mature	5	7	10	12			
	(7)	(7)	(9)	58			
Radishes[5], topped	10	13	42	58	89		Lutz and Hardenburg (1968)
with tops	17	21	78	136	193		
Rhubarb, stalk	15	25	40	48			Hruschka (1967)
Rutabagas[5]	5	9	14	38			Intern. Inst. Refrig. (1967)

TABLE 1.1. (Continued)

Vegetable	°C 0 / °F 32	5 / 41	10 / 50	15 / 59	20 / 68	25 / 77	Source of Data
	Mg CO_2 per kg·hr at Temperatures[3] Given						
Spinach							
Spinach, summer	21	46	110	179	230		Scholz et al. (1963)
winter	(12) 25 (18)	32 (27) 58 (34)	75 (58) 103 (68)				Smith (1957)
Squash, summer[5]	13	19		90	97		Lutz and Hardenburg (1968)
Sweet corn, with husk		78	112	162	288	407	Scholz et al. (1963)
Sweetpotatoes, cured			(14)	(23)			Lewis and Morris (1956)
non-cured				29		73	Lutz and Hardenburg (1968)
Tomatoes,							
mature-green		7	15	20	34	43	Scholz et al. (1963)
ripening			14	27	40	48	Workman et al. (1957)
Turnips, roots	6 (4)	15 (7)	20 (13)	22 (15)	32		Smith (1957)
tops[9]	28 (18)	(59)	68				Morris (1970)
Watercress	26	49 (44)	92 (83)	204 (165)	(139)	(266)	Smith (1957)
Watermelon	(19)	4	7	21			Scholz et al. (1963)

[1] Equilibrium rates are representative of the values during the usual storage life at a given temperature; e.g., for asparagus at 0° and 30° C (32° and 86° F), the approximate rates after 2 weeks and 14 hr, respectively, were used.

[2] Ton = 2000 lb.

[3] The rates are for the temperatures cited ±1° C (±2° F). Those given for 0° C (32° F) include a few for −0.5 and 0.5° C (31° and 33° F). Rates in italics are for rates in the chilling range.

[4] Large difference in initial rate at 5° C may be due to difference in proportion of flower heads and stem tissue in sample.

[5] No indication whether initial or equilibrium rates are given.

[6] The equilibrium rates are higher than the initial rates because the degree of rest decreased during storage.

[7] Initial rate, 2 days, equilibrium rate 8 days after harvest; maximum storage period used was 10 days. Cultivar: White Rose. Immature, mature, and very mature refer to harvest 98, 126, and 141 days after planting, respectively.

[8] Hardenburg (1970).

[9] Morris (1970).

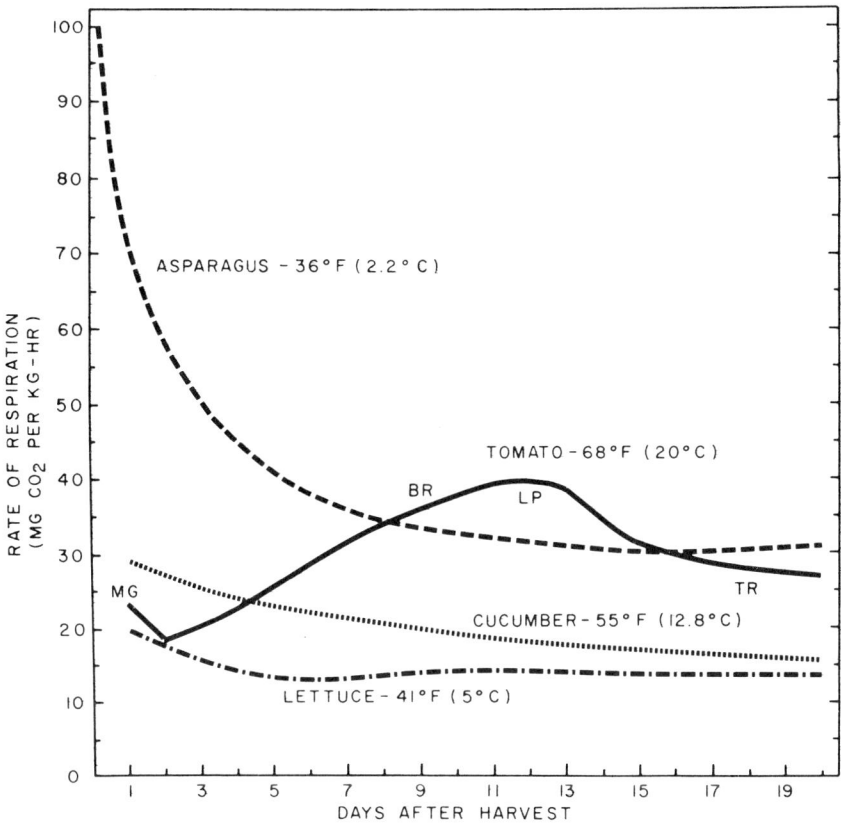

From Lipton (1957), Pratt et al. (1954),
and Workman et al. (1957), respectively

FIG. 1.3.   RATE OF RESPIRATION OF A SHOOT (ASPARAGUS), A LEAFY VEGETABLE (HEAD LETTUCE), A NON-RIPENING FRUIT (CUCUMBER), AND OF A RIPENING FRUIT (TOMATO) AT TEMPERATURES COMMONLY ENCOUNTERED DURING THEIR MARKETING
(For Tomato: MG—mature-green; BR—breaker; LP—light pink; TR—table ripe).

one sample was sprayed with a senescence retardant it may show an increased rate of respiration, but still remain longer in usable condition than the nontreated lot. In contrast, normal respiration is depressed in an atmosphere seriously deficient in oxygen, while the storage life is drastically shortened. Consequently, any claim that a product lengthens storage life *because* it reduces the rate of respiration must be suspect.

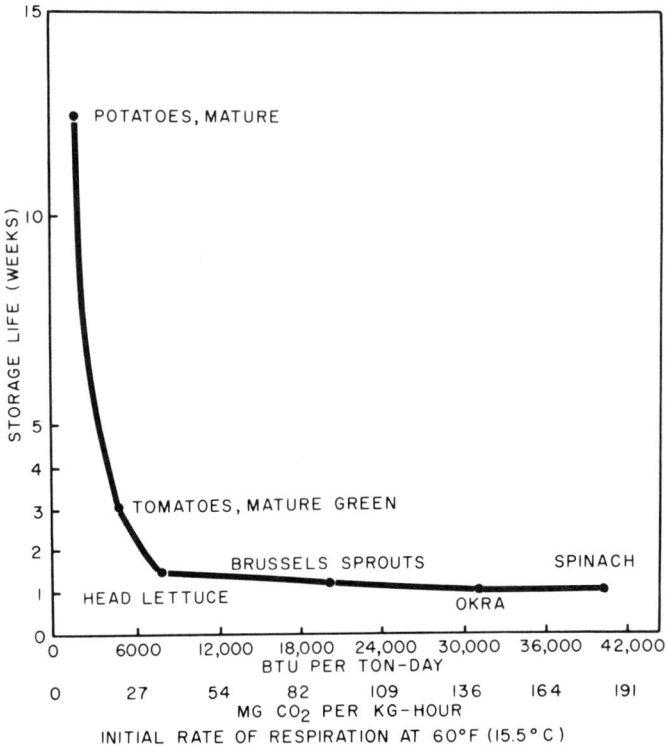

FIG. 1.4.   RELATION BETWEEN INITIAL RATE OF RESPIRATION AND STORAGE LIFE (TO UNSALABLE CONDITION) OF SELECTED VEGETABLES HELD AT 15.5° C (60° F)

Interconversion Between Respiratory Units

While the rate of respiration conventionally is expressed in units involving CO_2 liberated or O_2 taken up, we have noted earlier that these quantities are directly related to the amount of energy liberated when sugars are respired. Quantities of energy are expressed in calories (cal), kilo calories (kcal, equal to 1000 cal), or in applied work in the United States, in British Thermal Units (Btu). Since practical applications usually involve large quantities of a commodity stored for days or weeks, the respiratory energy produced is expressed in terms of kcal per metric ton (1000 kg) per day or in Btu per short ton (2000 lb) per day (2000 lb = 908 kg). However, since respiratory rates usually are determined on small quantities and in terms of the amount of CO_2 released, interconversion between quantities of CO_2 and of energy involved is essential for many practical uses. If mg CO_2 per kg-hr is multiplied by 61.2 the product is in kcal per metric ton-day. If, instead, the multiplier is 220, the product is in Btu per short ton-day (see Appendix for derivations). For example, when asparagus is held at 2.5° C (36° F) it respires at a rate of about 50 mg CO_2 per kg-hr and thus produces 3060 kcal per metric ton-day or 11000 Btu per short ton-day. These conversion factors are useful in calculating refrigeration requirements for any commodity with a known rate of respiration. If the rate is given in ml CO_2, the quantity must be multiplied by 1.9 before conversion, because 1 ml CO_2 weighs about 1.9 mg.

The factor 220 is derived from the basic respiration equation where sugar is respired and where 1 mole of O_2 (32 g) is taken up for every mole of CO_2 (44 g) produced. However, the heat production thus calculated may be higher than justified if the ratio of moles CO_2 produced to moles O_2 consumed is greater than one (Haller *et al.* 1945). Such an error could be significant if substantial quantities of organic acids, such as citric or malic acids, are respired, or if fermentation takes place. However, the errors induced by the breakdown of acids would be negligible for most vegetables. Fermentation does not normally occur in properly stored vegetables. Consequently, the factor 220 can be used for all practical applications.

Temperature Quotient (Q_{10}) of Respiration

The rate of respiration is known for many vegetables at various temperatures. Relatively simple laboratory methods are available to measure the rate at any desired temperature within the biological range. However, the ability to predict the rate at a given temperature from a few determinations at lower and higher temperatures would save time and money, and would permit rapid access to the needed information. Such prediction is possible, and with reasonable precision, by use of the temperature quotient, or Q_{10}. This concept, named after the Dutch chemist van't Hoff, states that the rate of a chemical reaction approximately doubles for each 10° C (18° F) rise in temperature, which is abbreviated as:

$$Q_{10} = R_2/R_1 = \text{a constant, about 2}$$

where R_1 represents the rate of a process at a given temperature and R_2 represents its rate at a temperature 10° C higher.

However, a more general form of the van't Hoff rule, applicable to temperature intervals other than 10° C, states:

$$Q_{10} = (R_2/R_1)^{10/(t_2 - t_1)} = \text{constant, about 2}$$

where t_2 and t_1 are any temperatures in $^\circ$ C and R_2 and R_1 are the respective rates.

This formula permits calculation of either the Q_{10} or an unknown rate for any temperature difference, but the difference should not exceed 10° C, or else the result may be too far from the true value. Sample calculations are given in the Appendix.

Use of Q_{10} Values

Since van't Hoff's time scientists have found that the Q_{10} is not constant for many biological processes, including respiration. The Q_{10} usually ranges from 1 to about 5, although higher values may occur. Q_{10} values are highest between 0° and 10° C (32° and 50° F). They are commonly between 2 and 3 between 10° and 32° C (50° and 90° F) and then they approach 1.

Q_{10} of 1 indicates that the rate does not change with a change in temperature, and a Q_{10} below 1 shows that the rate is decreasing as the temperature rises.

Q_{10} values are useful, even though they change with temperature, because if the rate of respiration of a crop is known at 10° C (18° F) intervals between 0° and about 40° C (32° and about 104° F), any intermediate rates can be calculated with sufficient accuracy for prediction of refrigeration or ventilation requirements. However, Q_{10} values should be based on initial respiration rates, because after storage at different temperatures the vegetables would no longer be of the same physiological age and the results would be misleading.

Q_{10} Values for Respiratory Rates of Various Crops

Q_{10} values differ widely among vegetables over a given temperature range as seen in Table 1.2. A high rate of respiration (Table 1.1) does not necessarily imply a high Q_{10} or vice versa.

Conclusion

Respiration and its consequences obviously must be considered by all concerned with the marketing of fresh produce, simply because this process is basic to life. Any fresh vegetable or fruit is living and must be treated as such. Disregard of this fact has led to much waste during marketing of fresh produce.

WATER LOSS

All vegetables continue to lose water vapor after they are harvested. If this water loss, or transpiration, is not retarded, the produce can rapidly become wilted, tough or mushy, and eventually inedible. These symptoms of water loss become objectionable when vegetables have lost between 5% and 10% of their weight due to transpiration, the exact percentage depending upon their structure. The structure and condition of the vegetable also strongly influence the rate of water loss, which, however, also depends on (1) the moisture content and temperature of the air in contact with the vegetable, (2) air movement, and (3) atmospheric pressure.

Structure and Condition of Vegetable

Leafy vegetables lose water vapor principally through stomata, minute openings in the epidermis, which are the same pores through which other gases (such as O_2 and CO_2) are exchanged. Other natural avenues of water loss are stem scars, lenticels, or the waxy surface of the vegetable. In general, the larger the surface to volume ratio, the more readily the vegetable loses moisture in a given environment. Consequently, spinach and leaf lettuce, which have all leaves exposed, wilt more rapidly than head lettuce, where the exposed surface is relatively small. Stem scars are an important avenue of water loss in tomatoes, whereas lenticels provide the path in potatoes.

These differences in the tendency of vegetables to lose moisture have been measured and quantified by van den Berg and Lentz (1971) and termed the Coefficient of Transpiration. The coefficient is a measure of the rate of moisture loss per unit weight per unit water vapor pressure difference (mg/kg-hr-mmHg). The coefficient ranges from about 20 to 80 for uncured potatoes and from about 15 to 30 for cured potatoes. For trimmed cabbage it ranges from 115 to 130 and for carrots it is about 800.

Water is also lost from vegetables via small surface cracks that develop during growth or are the result of mechanical handling of the produce. Abrasions, bruises and other injuries that remove or weaken the protective outer layers, such as the skin of potatoes, also can in-

TABLE 1.2. TEMPERATURE QUOTIENTS (Q_{10}) FOR RATES OF RESPIRATION OF VARIOUS VEGETABLES

Vegetable	Temperature Range (°C and °F)[1]						Source[2]
	0 to 5 / 32 to 41	5 to 10 / 41 to 50	10 to 15 / 50 to 59	15 to 20 / 59 to 68	20 to 25 / 68 to 77	25 to 30 / 77 to 86	
Artichoke, globe	1.8	2.7	2.2	2.6	1.7		Rappaport and Watada (1958)
Asparagus	3.3	4.2	1.2	2.3	1.5	2.0	Lipton (1957)
Beans, snap		2.7	2.6	1.9	2.2		Watada and Morris (1966)
Beet, red	1.9	1.8	2.6				Smith (1957)
Broccoli	5.2	4.6	3.9	2.7			Scholz et al. (1963)
Brussels sprouts	4.9	2.7	1.5				Smith (1957)
Cabbage	2.5	1.5	3.2	1.6			Scholz et al. (1963)
Cabbage, spring	2.8	2.2	2.7				Smith (1957)
Cabbage, winter	4.7	2.5					Smith (1957)
Carrot, roots	2.0	2.3	1.5	2.8			Scholz et al. (1963)
Cauliflower	1.8	2.4	1.7	2.7			Scholz et al. (1963)
Cauliflower	1.2	2.8	2.5				Smith (1957)
Celery	3.5	4.0	1.7				Smith (1957)
Cucumber	4.0	2.2		2.1	1.3	2.3	Eaks and Morris (1956)
Garlic	3.7	4.6	1.5				Mann and Lewis (1956)
Leek	1.7		2.6				Smith (1957)
Lettuce, head	2.0	2.5	2.4	2.1	1.8		Pratt et al. (1954)
head	2.0	1.7	2.3	2.3	1.9[3]		Scholz et al. (1963)
leaf	2.5	3.0	1.8	2.3	2.0[3]		Scholz et al. (1963)
leaf		2.7	1.5				Smith (1957)
Romaine		2.5	4.6	2.2	2.3[3]		Scholz et al. (1963)
Muskmelons, cantaloup	5.2		1.5	1.7	1.8[3]	1.7[4]	Scholz et al. (1963)
Honey Dew			2.4	2.7	1.6[3]	1.1[4]	Scholz et al. (1963)
Okra				2.8	1.6[3]	1.8[4]	Scholz et al. (1963)
Onions, dry	1.6	2.4	2.1	2.1	2.5[3]		Scholz et al. (1963)
green	2.4	3.9	2.6	1.9	1.8[3]		Hardenburg (1970)
Parsnip	1.3	3.0	2.4				Smith (1957)
Peas, in pod	2.8[5]	2.2[6]					Tewfik and Scott (1954)
shelled	2.1[5]	1.8[6]					Tewfik and Scott (1954)

Commodity							Source[2]
Peppers, sweet	2.2		2.2	3.2			Scholz et al. (1963)
Potatoes	2.1	1.3	1.3				Smith (1957)
Potatoes		1.7	2.9	1.9			Morris (1970)
Radishes		3.4	2.5	2.1			Lutz and Hardenburg (1968)
Rhubarb		2.6	2.3	1.4			Hruschka (1967)
Spinach, summer		4.8	2.4	1.6			Scholz et al. (1963)
Spinach, summer	2.5	4.6	3.6				Smith (1957)
Spinach, winter	6.8	2.8	2.8				Smith (1957)
Sweet corn, with husks	6.0	1.9	2.0	2.8	1.9[3]	1.3[4]	Scholz et al. (1963)
Tomatoes, mature-green				2.6	1.5[3]	1.2[4]	Scholz et al. (1963)
ripening				2.1	1.4[3]	1.8[4]	Scholz et al. (1963)
Turnips, roots	8.2	1.7	1.3				Smith (1957)
tops	2.5[7]		2.0[8]	3.7			Morris (1970)
Watercress	4.1	3.2	4.2				Smith (1957)
Watermelon		3.5	2.6[8]	1.9[9]			Scholz et al. (1963)

[1] Some respiration rates were determined at intermediate temperatures. The relevant Q_{10} values are listed under the temperature that is within 1° C (about 2° F) of them.

[2] Source of data refers to respiration rates.

[3] Actual range for Q_{10} determination: 21° to 27° C

[4] Actual range for Q_{10} determination: 27° to 32° C

[5] Actual range for Q_{10} determination: 0° to 3° C

[6] Actual range for Q_{10} determination: 3° to 7° C

[7] Actual range for Q_{10} determination: 0° to 10° C

[8] Actual range for Q_{10} determination: 10° to 20° C

[9] Actual range for Q_{10} determination: 21° to 32° C

crease the rate of water loss. Thus, gentle handling not only reduces direct losses, but the indirect ones caused by rapid drying.

Relative Humidity and Temperature

Water loss, as is universally known, is rapid at low, and slow at high relative humidity (RH). It is rapid at low RH because the air in the room contains less water vapor than it can hold at the temperature of the room. Thus, water vapor is readily transferred from the humid interior of the leaf or fruit to the relatively dry air. In contrast, if RH in the room is 100% (a water-saturated atmosphere), the air in the room and that in the vegetable are balanced in respect to moisture content, the gradient between the two is low, and moisture loss is nil, when air and vegetable are at the same temperature.

The amount of moisture the air can hold before it is saturated rises as the temperature rises. That is, more water is required to saturate air at 15° C (59° F) than at 5° C (41° F). Accordingly, a room at 15° C and 90% RH is drier than a room at 5° C and 90% RH, and dehydration would be more rapid in the room held at 15° C. Further, water has a greater tendency to evaporate as its temperature rises. Thus, if a vegetable is at 15° C, the water it contains has a greater tendency to evaporate than if it were at 5° C. This means that water will be lost more rapidly from a warm than from a cool vegetable at a given air temperature and RH, which, in turn, points to the need for rapid cooling of vegetables to the temperature of the surrounding air. Rapid cooling thus not only reduces the danger of decay but also of wilting.

We have seen that RH is not an entirely satisfactory indicator of likely water loss, because a given RH level is "drier" at a high than at a low temperature. This limitation of relative humidity is particularly evident when we need to choose between two sets of conditions. For example, in which of the following environments will water loss be higher, 84% RH at 2° C (35° F) or 90% RH at 5° C (41° F)? Such questions can be resolved most readily by taking advantage of the facts that water vapor, like all gases, exerts pressure and that, at a given atmospheric pressure, the amount of vapor pressure depends only on temperature. Knowledge of the vapor pressure under two conditions permits determination of the vapor pressure differences (VPD) between them, which in turn tells in which of the two atmospheres moisture loss will be greater. This task has been greatly simplified by the development of a nomogram (Fig. 1.5) that relates VPD to temperature and RH (Williams and Brochu 1969).

For the conditions given in the first example, simply connect 2 on the

TEMPERATURE

°F   °C
95 ┬ 35

90

85   30

80   25

75

70   20

65

60   15

55

50   10

45

40   5

35

        0

30

28

NOMOGRAM
BY
J. BROCHU
AND
G.D.V. WILLIAMS

RELATIVE
HUMIDITY
(%)
99.0

98.5
98.0
97.5
97.0
96.0
95.0
94.0
92.0
90.0
88.0
84.0
80.0
75.0
70.0
60.0
50.0
40.0
20.0
0.0

VAPOR
PRESSURE
DEFICIT(mbs)
0.05

0.10

0.15

0.2

0.3
0.4

0.6

0.8
1.0

1.5

2.0
2.5
3.0
3.5
4.0

5.0

7.0

10.0

15.0

20.0

30.0

40.0
50.0
57.0

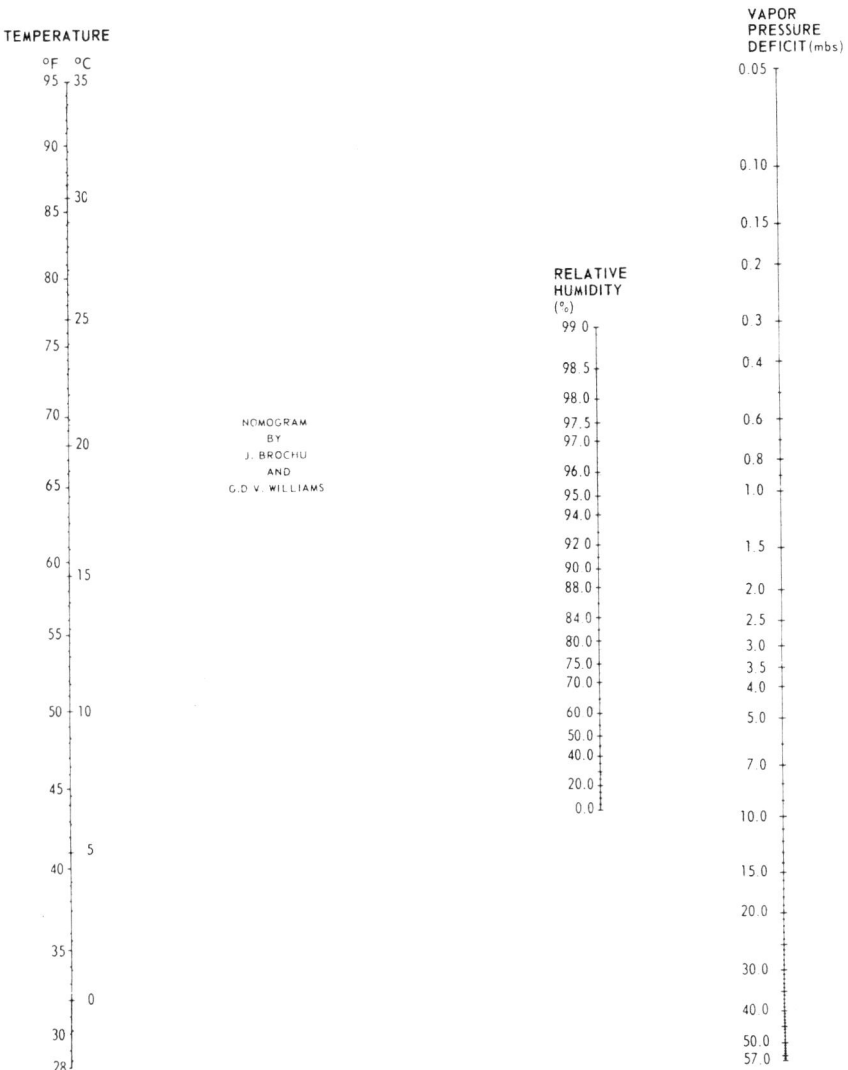

Courtesy of G. D. V. Williams, J. Brochu, and Le Naturaliste Canadien (1969)

FIG. 1.5. NOMOGRAM FOR FINDING VAPOR PRESSURE DEFICIT (VPD) FROM RELATIVE HUMIDITY AND TEMPERATURE
For explanation, see text.

temperature scale with 04 on the RH scale and read the value where the straight edge intersects the VPD scale: about 1.1 mb (millibars; 1 mb =0.03 in. of Hg or 0.74 mm of Hg or 1.02 g/cm²). For the second example VPD is about 0.85 mb. Consequently, water loss will be greater under the conditions given first. Further, by dividing 1.1 mb by 0.85 mb we find that water loss will be 1.3 times as fast in the drier air. Thus, we know not only under what conditions water loss will be greater, but also how much greater. Although the nomogram was developed for meterological applications, it will be equally useful in the context of storage.

A third measure of the moisture status of air is the absolute, or specific, humidity. This measure is expressed in terms of the concentration of water vapor in dry air, e.g., g water vapor/kg dry air. Knowledge of the specific humidity in a room is essential if one has to calculate the energy that is required to cool or warm a room to which moisture is added for humidification, because more energy is required to cool or warm moist than dry air. Specific humidity also is useful in determining whether moisture will move into or out of a storage room as produce is being added or taken out. The results of such calculations will determine whether moisture needs to be added to restore a high RH or whether the split should be increased to dry the atmosphere.

All three of these quantities, RH, vapor pressure, and specific humidity are interrelated and their equivalent values can be determined by means of psychrometric charts. These are illustrated in the Appendix and sample calculations are provided.

Air Movement

The more rapidly air of a given RH moves across the surface of a vegetable, the more rapidly it will lose moisture, unless the moving air is water-saturated. High velocity air causes rapid water loss because it continuously removes the extremely thin layer of saturated air that envelops a leaf or fruit. Consequently, there exists a gradient which impels moisture to move from the humid interior of the tissue to the relatively dry room. As a result, air velocity should be just sufficient to effectively remove respiratory heat from the product after it has been cooled to the temperature of the room, trailer or rail car. However, if air velocity through a load, a stack or a bin is too low, the product may warm up toward the center due to insufficiently rapid removal of respiratory heat. Under such conditions water loss will increase because the VPD between produce and air will increase.

These precautions regarding *air velocity* should be carefully distinguished from recommendations regarding *air volume,* as pointed out by Grierson and Wardowski (1975). Circulation of a high volume of air (within limits dictated by cost and engineering considerations) is desirable, because such a practice results in a minimal temperature difference between air blast and return air, and thus assures a high RH.

Atmospheric Pressure

Water, as all liquids, evaporates more readily at low than at high atmospheric pressure, all other factors being constant. The rate of evaporation of water is inversely proportional to air pressure, i.e., for every 10% decrease in pressure, water loss will increase 10%. This physical fact is of concern in air transit of produce because the planes are pressurized to an elevation of about 1500 m (5000 ft) rather than to sea level, where the air pressures are about 63 cm (25 in.) and 76 cm (30 in.) of mercury, respectively. Thus the rate of water loss in a plane can exceed that on the ground by about 20%, due to the difference in pressure alone. Then, should the lower air pressure be coupled with low RH and relatively high temperature, a significant amount of water can be lost from produce during air transit.

Minimizing Water Loss

Basically, there are two ways to reduce dehydration of vegetables. First, we can minimize the difference between the humidity that exists inside the vegetable and between that of the surrounding air. Secondly, we can protect the vegetable from relatively dry air.

The first goal can be achieved by having the RH of the storage space as close to saturation as possible. This is done by minimizing the temperature difference between the cooling surface and the air in the room. With these two close together, little moisture will condense out on the cooling surface. Ideally this difference (called the "split") should not exceed 1° C (2° F) (Guillou 1967). With a small split a greater volume of air will have to be circulated than with a larger split to maintain a constant temperature. However, a large volume of air flowing over a cooling surface at −1° C (30° F) will cause less dehydration in a room held at 0° C (32° F) than a smaller volume of air passing over a coil at −3° C (27° F). For example, when the air that returns to the cooling surface has a RH of 95% and the split is 1° C, about 1.7 liters of water will condense out for each 100,000 kcal of refrigeration. However, if the split is 3° C the amount of condensate increases to 2.5 liters. The approximately equivalent values in British units are 0.3 gal. for a 2° F split and 0.5 gal. for a 5° F split per ton of refrigeration (Guillou 1965).

Moisture can be added to the air by water sprays or by fogging devices. These methods, which are described in detail by Guillou (1960, 1967), are particularly useful during precooling when moisture loss is highest, and when dry containers literally can draw moisture from their contents. For long-term storage of initially cool or for well precooled vegetables the jacketed room system, in which all walls are the cooling surface, minimizes moisture loss (Jorgensen 1974). Similar results are achieved with air-water counter flow systems (Meredith 1974). Both of these systems are discussed in greater detail in Chapter 12.

Vegetables can be protected from dry air by packaging in various plastic bags or film wraps, by providing moisture in the form of ice or by hydrocooling, or by covering the vegetable with a water impermeable coating, such as a wax. Care must be taken, however, that the bags or wraps are perforated or that the layer of wax is thin enough to permit adequate gas exchange. Otherwise, serious injury may result from insufficient O_2 or excess CO_2. Bags or films that hold 500 g (1 lb) of spinach, or its equivalent in other produce, should be perforated with about a dozen 3 mm (⅛ in.) holes. The ventilation thus provided will not permit any significant moisture loss under normal conditions.

While perforated films provide excellent protection against moisture loss, they can minimize it only under nearly constant air temperatures. If air temperature fluctuates even a few degrees, the produce will cool more slowly than the film and moisture drawn from the produce will condense on the film. If this pumping action is repeated sufficiently, wilting may follow.

High Relative Humidity in Relation to Decay Development

Research conducted primarily in Canada during the recent decade has shown the popularly held notion that high RH almost inevitably engenders a high level of decay to be questionable. Van den Berg and Lentz (1973A,B, 1974, 1977A, B) have repeatedly shown that during long-term storage decay is usually less serious when RH is 98 to 100% than when it is lower, and that condensation is not necessarily harmful as long as storage is at the temperature recommended for the commodity. For most of the vegetables tested that was 0° to 2° C (32 to 36° F) during storage lasting up to several months. Other researchers have obtained similar results (as will be discussed under specific vegetables).

ETHYLENE IN THE POSTHARVEST LIFE OF VEGETABLES AND MELONS

Ethylene is one of the most active plant hormones known and is produced by most (possibly all) higher plants, as well as by some fungi and bacteria. Ethylene is of great importance in postharvest physiology, because it is intimately involved in the ripening of fruits and because it can cause serious disorders in leafy vegetables and flowers at very low concentrations, in the range of about 0.05 to 10 ppm (10 ppm equals 0.001%).

The literature on ethylene as a factor in the biology of plants in general, and in postharvest physiology in particular, is vast and has been summarized by Abeles (1973). We will confine ourselves to practical aspects of involvement of ethylene in the postharvest life of vegetables and melons.

Beneficial Effects

The beneficial aspects of ethylene are related to its effect on ripening; hence it is sometimes called the "ripening gas." While ethylene is produced by ripening fruits (such as tomatoes or Honey Dew melons), applying supplementary ethylene early during ripening or to initiate ripening can speed up the process and increase the uniformity of ripening in a given lot of fruit. Consequently, ethylene has been used extensively to ripen Honey Dews and, to a lesser extent, to attain uniform coloration of tomatoes. Although fruits respond to a concentration of 10 to 20 ppm or even less, usually 200 ppm (1 part in 5000), or even more, is used to assure an adequate concentration throughout the storage room, rail car, or truck trailer, and within the containers. Concentrations in excess of 5000 ppm (0.5%) should be avoided, because gas is wasted and because a highly explosive concentration, that ranges from about 3% to 30%, accidentally may be reached.

Ethylene treatment is most effective when the fruit is between 21° C (70° F) and 24° C (75° F), and when the humidity is about 85% to 95%. The minimum effective temperature is about 15° C (59° F). Exposure for 24 hr usually is optimal at the most effective temperature range, although longer exposures are harmless. Between 15° and 21° C, ethylene treatment may have to last 48 to 72 hr to be effective.

Can ethylene be used to defraud by causing softening and coloration of immature fruits of inferior quality? Ethylene can induce some signs of ripening, such as softening and color changes in small, immature fruits, but the potential for fraud depends on the fruit being considered. In cantaloups the danger is nil because only softening and yellowing would take place. Their small size or lack of net would make them unmarketable if treated sooner than about 3 weeks after bloom (McGlasson and Pratt 1964A). If ethephon were used to accelerate ripening, application any time prior to the last few days before normal harvest could result in substantially lower sugar content, because almost half is accumulated during the terminal week of maturation (Bianco and Pratt 1977).

On tomatoes, which turn red under the influence of ethylene or when sprayed with a chemical that releases ethylene, 2-chloroethyl-phosphonic acid (ethephon), the chance of fraud exists, because color change is the only sign of ripening for the consumer and a red tomato is assumed to be ripe. The possibility of fraud is greater in areas where small fruits are marketed because fruits smaller than about 5 cm (2 in.) in diameter, depending on cultivar, are not likely to ripen to satisfactory quality, even though they may be red (Bondad and Pantastico 1973).

Ethephon and ethylene also have been shown to aid in the coloration of tomatoes that have been subjected to chilling exposures without, however, negating any other aspect of chilling damage (Buescher 1974; Saimbhi et al. 1975). Consequently, tomatoes with chilling injury could be ripened and sold to purchasers who would unwittingly assume the risk involved in buying inferior tomatoes.

Detrimental Effects

The universality of ethylene production by plants is at the root of its potential for causing injury. While the acceleration of aging induced by ethylene in respect to ripening is often considered beneficial, it is un-questionably harmful when it results in early senescence of vegetative tissue. This occurs, for example, when head lettuce is exposed to minute amounts of ethylene (1 ppm or even less). Thus exposed, lettuce shows reddish-brown or olive spots within a few days, an occasionally serious disorder termed russet spotting. Ethylene exerts these deleterious effects even at low temperatures, near 5° C (41° F), unlike those related to ripening, which require moderate temperatures (Rood 1956; Lipton 1961). Consequently, commodities sensitive to ethylene should never be held for more than a few hours in the same storage room, conveyance, or even the vegetable compartment of a home refrigerator with products that emit much ethylene, such as apples or cantaloups. If such mixing is unavoidable, the danger can be minimized by holding the items between 0° and 1° C (32° and 34° F), by adequate ventilation (which wastes refrigeration), or by forcing the air through filters of brominated acti-vated charcoal or alkaline potassium permanganate (Purafil), both of which are commercially available. If air is filtered with brominated charcoal, it must then be passed through non-brominated activated charcoal to prevent escape of bromine into the air. The action of ethylene also can be inhibited by enriching the atmosphere with about 5% or more of CO_2 or by lowering its O_2 level to 5% or less. However, this method can be used only when such conditions are known not to injure the crops involved.

Particular caution must be exercised so that seedlings are not exposed to excessive amounts of ethylene during transport or storage. Pepper transplants, for instance, are seriously defoliated and subsequent growth is retarded when the ethylene concentration in the surrounding air exceeds about 0.5 ppm for 48 hr (Kays *et al.* 1976).

Table 1.3 lists the rates of ethylene production of various crops that sometimes are shipped or held in the same vehicle or room with vegetables that may be harmed by ethylene. Although the data mostly are for moderate temperatures, the ranking of crops normally held at lower temperatures is likely to remain the same. The large differences in rates of ethylene production for a given crop at the same or a similar temperature may be due to differences in the physiological state of the product when measurements were taken. Caution suggests that the highest rate listed for a given temperature be accepted when decisions are made as to whether a vegetable that may be damaged by exposure to ethylene should be stored with a product that emits a substantial amount of ethylene.

Finally, storage of diseased or mechanically injured specimens should be avoided, because infections and wounds can substantially increase ethylene production, thus causing excessively rapid ripening of fruits, or senescence in vegetative tissues.

CHILLING INJURY

Definition of Terms

Chilling injury is a disorder induced by low, but nonfreezing temperatures in susceptible plants or parts of plants. The injury may be induced before or after harvest, or during both periods. While the disorder also has been termed low-temperature injury, chilling injury seems preferable, because this term is concise, not readily confused with freezing injury, and has historical precedence as the term ("Erfrieren") first applied to this disorder in 1897 by Molisch. Further, following the suggestion of Eakes and Morris (1957), we will use the term "chilling injury" to refer to the physiological damage done at low temperatures, whereas the term "chilling" will refer to the exposure to low temperature.

Types of Crops Affected

Chilling injury affects only certain vegetables, mainly those which had their origins in the tropics or in the subtropics. Susceptible plants that

TABLE 1.3.   APPROXIMATE MAXIMUM RATES OF ETHYLENE PRODUCTION BY VARIOUS CROPS

Crop	Temperature (° C)	(° F)	Ethylene (μl/kg-hr[1])	Source
Apple				
Rome Beauty	20	68	50	Brown et al. (1966)
Royal Red Delicious			75	
Ruby			125	
Gravenstein	18	64	12	Biale et al. (1954)
Cox's Orange Pippin	3	38	41	Fidler and North (1969)
Newton Wonder			2	
Avocado	15	59	9	Biale (1950)
	20	68	88	
Banana	20	68	4	Biale et al. (1954)
Citrus	none unless injured or decayed			Eaks (1970)
Muskmelon				
Cantaloup	20	68	16–33	Lyons et al. (1962)
Honey Dew	20	68	3	Kasmire et al. (1970)
Papaya	25	77	37	Biale et al. (1954)
Peach (Hale)	20	68	36	Biale et al. (1954)
Pear				
Anjou	18	64	30	Biale (1950)
Bartlett			222	
	20	68	122	Biale et al. (1954)
Bosc			29	
Plum				
Beauty	13	55	54	Uota (1955)
Duarte	10	50	17	
	21	70	142	
Santa Rosa	10	50	25	
	21	70	192	
Tomato	20	68	22	Lieberman and Mapson (1962)
	20	68	3	Lyons and Pratt (1964)

[1]μl/kg-hr $\times$ 0.91 = ml/ton-hr (1 ton = 2000 lb).
[2]Values given are for 2 fruits of same age and general appearance.

originated in temperate zones (such as asparagus) are dormant during the cold season. Chilling injury affects roots (sweetpotatoes) and stems (potatoes), but fruits are most commonly affected, while none of the leafy vegetables commonly grown in temperate climates are susceptible. The susceptibility to chilling injury of all tropical vegetables is assumed, although specific information on many of them is nonexistent.

Factors Involved

Three factors, acting together, determine the extent of chilling injury: temperature, duration of exposure to a given temperature, and the chilling sensitivity of the crop.

The upper temperature limit for the induction of chilling injury frequently is cited as 10° C (50° F), although for some vegetables it is about 13° C (55° F) and for others below 4° C (40° F). Further, the lower the temperature within the chilling range, the sooner injury will be evident. For example, sweetpotatoes are injured after 1 day at 0° C (32° F) but not until 4 days at 7° C (45° F) (McClure 1959). Similarly, 4 days at 10° C do not injure the roots significantly, whereas 10 days at 10° C causes serious damage, as measured by the incidence of decay after 4½ months' storage (Lutz 1945).

Susceptible crops, and even cultivars of a given crop, differ greatly in their sensitivity to chilling injury. Asparagus is relatively insensitive, sweet peppers are moderately sensitive, and sweetpotatoes are highly sensitive. These roots also are a good example of differences that exist among cultivars in respect to chilling sensitivity; Yellow Jersey is much more sensitive than Porto Rico (Lewis and Morris 1956). The chilling sensitivity of various crops and their cultivars is detailed in Table 1.4.

TABLE 1.4.   SUSCEPTIBILITY OF VARIOUS VEGETABLES AND MELONS TO CHILLING INJURY

Crop and Cultivar[1]	Degree of Susceptibility[2]
Asparagus	low
Bean, lima	
in pod	moderate
shelled	low
Bean, snap	
Romano	low
Bountiful	moderate
Wade	
Black Valentine	
Tendergreen	
Top Crop	
Contender	
Kentucky Wonder	
Cucumber	high
Eggplant	high
Ginger	high
Muskmelon	
Cantaloup	
Hard ripe	low
Eastern choice	low
Western choice	none
Casaba and Crenshaw	
Mostly green	high
Firm ripe	low
Honey Dew[3]	
Ripeness classes 1 or 1–2	high
Higher ripeness classes	low
Okra	moderate

(Continued)

TABLE 1.4.   (Continued)

Crop and Cultivar[1]	Degree of Susceptibility[2]
Pepper, bell	
green	moderate
ripe	probably low
Potato	
Katahdin	low
Kennebec	
Pumpkin and winter squash	moderate
Sweetpotato	high
Porto Rico	
Ranger[4]	
Yellow Jersey[4]	
All Gold[4]	
Goldrush[4]	
Tomato	
Ripe	low
Pink	
Mature-green	high
Manapal	
Homestead[5]	
STEP 434[5]	
Grothen	
Watermelon	moderate
Yam	high

[1]When cultivars are listed, they are arranged in increasing order of susceptibility.
[2]The approximate upper limits for induction of chilling injury are below 5° C (41° F), between 5° and 10° C (41° and 50° F), and above 10° C (50° F) for low, moderate or high susceptibility, respectively. Lowest safe storage temperature within each group depends on duration of storage. For details, see *Recommended Condition for Individual Crops*.
[3]See definition of ripeness classes, p. 187.
[4]Proper location of All Gold and Goldrush among these four not clear, because information from sources with different criteria of evaluation.
[5]Proper location for Grothen not clear for same reason as in footnote 4.

Interrelation of Factors

The relationship between sensitivity to chilling injury, storage life, and temperature was well illustrated by Tomkins (1966) who based his figure, which is here reproduced with some changes (Fig. 1.6), on one drawn by Kidd *et al.* (1927). Curve A represents crops that are not chilling sensitive, such as cabbage, and whose storage life is longest just above their freezing point. B would apply to asparagus, whose storage life is longest at about 2° C (36° F), whereas curve C is representative of the most chilling sensitive crops, which can be stored longest at about 13° C (55° F). Many moderately chilling sensitive crops lie somewhere between curves B and C, their maximum storage life lying between about 5° C (41° F) and 10° C (50° F). Further, the peak for curve C may be nearer 10° C (50° F) for certain crops, such as beans.

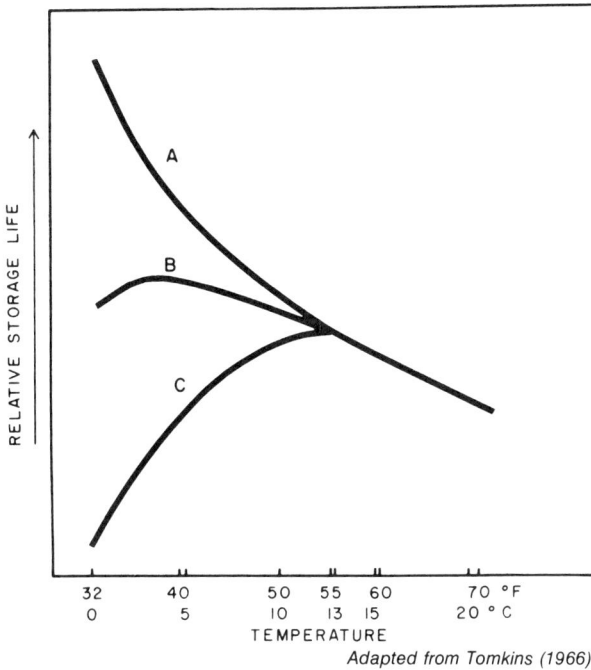

Adapted from Tomkins (1966)

FIG. 1.6.   CHANGE IN RELATIVE LENGTH OF STORAGE LIFE
AT VARIOUS TEMPERATURES OF CROPS WITH NO (A),
SLIGHT (B), OR HIGH (C) SENSITIVITY TO CHILLING INJURY

Symptoms

The symptoms of chilling injury of direct concern are those that
reduce the quality of the injured product. However, before any visible
damage occurs, substantial changes have taken place on the cellular
level. Consideration of these changes in membrane structure and
metabolism is beyond the scope of this discussion, but these subjects
have been clearly and thoroughly explained by Lyons (1973).

Visible symptoms of chilling injury are elusive as well as conspicuous.
They are elusive because they may not be evident while the vegetable is
held at chilling temperatures, only to become noticeable after transfer
to room temperature. They are conspicuous because the chief symptoms,
singly or in combination, are decay, discoloration, pitting, and the loss of
the ability to ripen normally, depending upon the vegetable involved.

Decay   Chilled vegetables decay readily because the low temperatures reduce the resistance of cells to invasion by pathogens. In addition,

they prevent wound healing in such crops as sweetpotatoes, thus enhancing the chance of decay. In severely chilled vegetables, decay can spread rapidly, particularly at room temperature, because the pathogens are growing on dead or dying tissue.

Discoloration   Discoloration is nearly as serious as decay, "nearly" because some crops, such as cucumbers, readily decay but do not discolor when chilled. The discoloration may occur externally, as in beans, or internally, as in eggplant. The spots or areas may be tan, brown or black. They may become evident while the product is at low temperature or show primarily after transfer of the vegetable to a non-chilling temperature, depending on the severity of the injury. Further, internal discoloration may be noticeable immediately upon cutting the vegetable, or only after the injured tissue has been exposed to air.

Pitting   Pitting of the surface is another nearly universal and early symptom of chilling injury. The severity of pitting depends not only on the severity of chilling, but also on the relative humidity of the atmosphere. Pits develop more readily in low than in high relative humidity (Morris and Platenius 1939). Under relatively dry conditions, the injured cells apparently lose moisture more rapidly than it can be transported to them. Desiccation then results in the collapse of the cells and the formation of pits. As chilling progresses, the pits may coalesce to form large shallow depressions. While high humidity reduces or even prevents pitting in chilled vegetables, it does not prevent the injury itself.

Abnormal Ripening   The prevention of normal ripening due to chilling is shown most conspicuously in mature-green tomatoes and Honey Dew melons. In the former, coloration is uneven, desirable softening is delayed in both, and severe chilling may prevent the fruit from ever reaching an edible stage even if decay is absent. However, sensitivity to chilling decreases progressively in some fruits as they ripen, so that ripe tomatoes can tolerate low temperatures more readily than pink fruits and, in turn, the pinks can tolerate low temperatures better than mature-green fruits.

Texture Changes   A symptom of chilling injury only recently fully described is the development of "hardcore" in sweetpotatoes (Daines *et al.* 1974). This defect is characterized by the development of a mass of tissue that does not soften even upon cooking and is discussed more fully under disorders of sweetpotatoes.

Rapidity of Symptom Expression

Chilling injury is induced rapidly at 0° C (32° F), as has been noted, but the symptoms of chilling injury described may appear earlier at 2° or 3° C (36° or 38° F) than at 0° C (32° F). This phenomenon was explained by van der Plank and his associates (1937) on the basis of the operation of two processes in chilling injury. The first is the induction of chilling injury, and the second is its visible expression. Near 0° C the injury is rapidly induced, but its expression is retarded because visible changes occur slowly near the freezing point. At 2° or 3° C the injury is less rapidly induced, but the resulting changes are noticeable earlier, because the effects of more rapid aging at the higher temperatures are added to those of chilling.

Chilling not only may cause the conspicuous injuries discussed, but it also can reduce the nutritive value in some crops. Carotene, the precursor of vitamin A, increases in sweetpotatoes stored at 13° C (55° F) or above, but not when stored at 10° C (50° F), which is in the chilling range (Ezell and Wilcox 1952). Chilling reduces the ascorbic acid (vitamin C) content of some vegetables, but not of others. The influence of chilling on other nutritionally important constituents of vegetables has received almost no attention in research, most likely because the obvious symptoms of chilling injury are economically much more important than the invisible, and possibly minor, changes in nutritive value.

Preharvest Chilling

While our chief concern is the response of vegetables to conditions existing after harvest, we must be concerned with chilling injury that occurs before harvest, because it affects the storage life of vegetables and because chilling is cumulative. For example, mature-green tomatoes chilled before harvest will not ripen properly even if they are protected from chilling after harvest (Morris 1954). Further, tomatoes that are, for example, chilled for 5 days before harvest and 6 days after harvest behave like fruit chilled 11 days after harvest. Ignorance of, or disregard for, these facts had added to the large losses caused by postharvest chilling in tomatoes until research explained their cause.

Combatting Chilling Injury

The best method of combatting chilling injury is the obvious one of holding chilling sensitive crops only at noninjurious temperatures.

However, should chilling occur inadvertently, or unavoidably, before harvest, the injury may be reduced by exposure to warm temperatures after harvest. Curing sweetpotatoes 8 days at 30° C (86° F) can negate 1 day's chilling at 0° C (32° F) or 4 days of exposure to 7° C (45° F). In tomatoes 2 to 3 days at 20° C (68° F) can counteract an equal number of days at 0° C. In potatoes periodic interruption of low temperatures by intermediate ones eliminates symptoms of chilling injury (McClure 1959; Lewis 1956; Hruschka et al. 1967).

While the above procedures are feasible for reducing injury in crops that do not deteriorate rapidly at moderate or high temperatures, they probably would be unsuitable for crops that are normally highly perishable, such as okra.

Controlled atmospheres have been shown to reduce symptoms of chilling injury in a few fruits (Spalding and Reeder 1975; Wardowski et al. 1975) and similar claims have been made for hypobaric storage. However, so far there exists no convincing evidence that application of high CO_2 or low O_2 (at normal or low pressure) would help in the amelioration of chilling injury in vegetables.

DEVELOPMENT, MATURATION, RIPENING, SENESCENCE AND DETERIORATION

Explanation of Terms

Discussions of development, maturation, ripening and senescence of horticultural crops frequently have become snarled by differences over terminology. Clarity of usage is lacking even with fruits that pass through readily identifiable stages, such as tomatoes. Consider a mature-green tomato. It is generally considered to be fully mature if it will ripen properly. What then is a pink tomato? Certainly not over-mature. What about a cucumber? Is it immature or mature when normally eaten? It definitely is not ripe. Head lettuce popularly is considered to be mature when it has reached sufficient density for marketing, although, being a vegetative structure, it does not exhibit any stages comparable to a tomato or cucumber during its maturation. Should fruits and vegetative structures even be covered by the same terminology? Should such terms as mature or ripe be defined according to the physiological state of the vegetable, or from the viewpoint of man, who coined these terms long before they were given imprecise scientific meanings? If the answers to such questions could be brought into a logical, easily understood framework, discussions of the subject would be less confusing. Gortner *et al.* (1967) took a valuable step in this direction, although their article dealt only with fruits. A graphical scheme developed in 1962 by members of the Department of Vegetable Crops of the University of California covers fruits and vegetative structures but was presented only informally. The scheme to be used by us borrows heavily from both proposals, but is intended to apply to all horticultural crops that are marketed fresh, whatever their botanical structure. Our scheme also is compatible with the terminology recently advocated by Coombe (1976) for ripening of fleshy fruits.

Our point of view is that of consumers, as they see the stages in the life of the edible part, be it vegetative or reproductive. Our scheme is relative rather than absolute. That is, it is based on the interval between the visible appearance of the edible part and the end of its usefulness as a human food. Under this nomenclature, a green cucumber is just as *harvest-mature* as a red tomato, because *relative* to their life as a consumable vegetable, both are at the same stage even though they are physiologically at dissimilar stages. Further, a cucumber 8 cm (3 in.) long is in prematuration if intended for slicing, but is harvest-mature if used for pickling; or a green tomato 5 cm (2 in.) across is harvest-mature for frying, but certainly not for postharvest ripening.

The names of the stages are those suggested by Gortner and co-workers: development, prematuration, maturation, ripening, and senescence (Fig. 1.7), although their scope has been widened to accommodate vegetative and reproductive structures. Development starts with the formation of the edible part, such as the setting of a fruit, the emergence of a seedling, the swelling of a root, tuber, or bulb, or the elongation of a stalk or petiole. Development ceases with the termination of desirable or natural enlargement, or with a change in growth pattern of the edible part. Development occurs largely before harvest and includes prematuration and part of maturation. Prematuration starts with development and lasts until the edible portion reaches a usable, but not particularly desirable condition. Maturation overlaps prematuration and is followed by senescence; it begins before harvest, but may continue after harvest. Ripening, where applicable, usually comes late during maturation but may begin during development. The terminal phase of maturation is the period of maximum usefulness of the structure and may last a few hours or several months. Senescence follows maturation, but may overlap it slightly, and it may start before or after harvest. This stage is characterized by the dominance of degradative changes. Relative to suitability of the product for human

DEVELOPMENT

PREMATURATION

MATURATION

RIPENING*

SENESCENCE

PASSAGE OF TIME

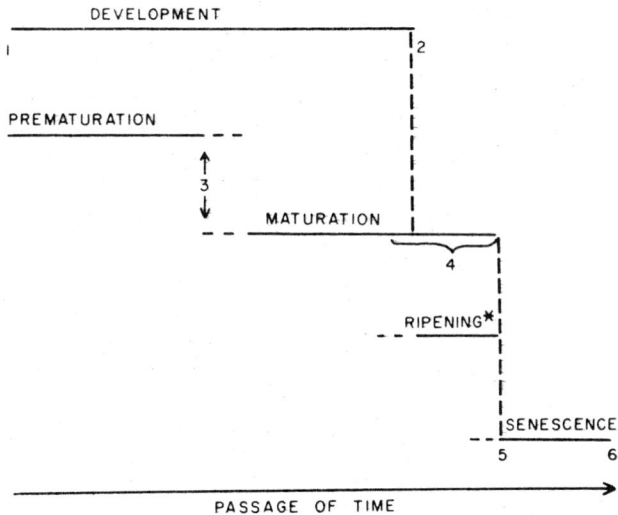

FIG. 1.7. STAGES DURING LIFE SPAN OF FRESH VEGETA-
BLES AND FRUITS
1—Initiation of edible part. 2—Termination of natural or desirable
growth in size or type. 3—Start of period of usefulness, but too
immature for most users. 4—Period of maximum usefulness.
5—Degradative changes become predominant. 6—End of usefulness for human consumption.
*In this context applies only to some fruits.

consumption, senescence ends when the product is no longer usable as a
food. Botanically, however, senescence ends only with death of the
organ (Sacher 1973). Thus, by our scheme, a green bean has reached the
end of senescence when it is too tough to eat; botanically, its senescence
ends only when cellular breakdown has resulted in death of the pod.

Deterioration, inevitably associated with the life span of a fresh fruit
or vegetable, must be distinguished from senescence. Senescence
applies only to normal physiological changes, such as changes in composition, flavor, texture, color, or mode of growth, whereas deterioration
encompasses all aspects of quality loss: senescence, physiological disorders, diseases induced by fungi, bacteria, or viruses, wilting, freezing, or
the aftermath of mechanical injury. Further, deterioration can start
any time during senescence and continue beyond the end of usefulness
of the food for human consumption.

Application of Terms to Specific Crops

How does this scheme fit specific crops, tomatoes, for example? Visible development and prematuration start soon after pollination. However prematuration and maturation grade into each other because the mature-green state still cannot always be precisely determined. The period of maximum usefulness is determined by the intended use; for example, mature-green for frying, firm-red for table use, and soft-red for processing. For the first use, senescence begins before the fruit is ripe; for the second, it begins with excessive softness; and for the last with disintegration of cells. With tomatoes, a month or two may elapse from the first to the last stage.

A zucchini squash as used in the United States, in contrast, may pass from development through senescence within the span of a few days, without, however, having shown any signs of ripening.

The development of lettuce begins with emergence of a seedling, prematuration ends, and maturation begins as the head is being formed, and its period of maximum usefulness may be fairly long as in head lettuce, or rather short, as in bibb lettuce. Excessive hardness of head lettuce or the growth of a seedstalk are signs of senescence that occur before harvest, whereas normal yellowing of the green leaves and other deterioration are postharvest symptoms.

In green asparagus all stages are greatly compressed in time, the period from initial development (emergence of the shoot) to senescence (feathering) may encompass only 2 or 3 days, while the period of maximum usefulness may be counted in hours when temperatures are high.

Sweet corn has a fairly long period of prematuration, but at summer temperatures maturation and the period of maximum usefulness are extremely compressed, the latter lasting a few hours. Further, in sweet corn the transitions from prematuration to maturation to senescence chiefly are characterized by the change of sugar to starch, unlike in most other crops, where color or structure changes perceptibly.

Deterioration—the Major Concern

While clarification of the terms related to development and senescence of vegetables or fruits helps in describing the current stage of a given specimen in research, or of a shipment during its journey from field to consumer, the overriding practical concern is with deterioration.

Deterioration is of great concern because all vegetables and melons deteriorate, because its economic implications are readily apparent, and because the rate and mode of deterioration generally can be controlled to a greater extent than any phase of development.

The rate of deterioration is subject to various environmental influences, such as relative humidity, light, composition of the atmosphere in respect to CO_2, O_2, ethylene and other volatiles, but with temperature exceeding all others in importance.

Deterioration, like respiration, proceeds slowly at low temperature (except for crops subject to chilling injury, or when freezing inadvertently occurs), and rapidly at high temperature. Spinach, for example, becomes unsalable 13 times as rapidly at 27° C (80° F) as at 2° C (35° F), or expressed differently, a delay of only 1 hr before precooling costs as much shelf-life as half a day of storage after precooling. Further, the rate of deterioration (as that of respiration) does not increase uniformly with temperature, but at a greater rate at low temperatures than at high temperatures. Consequently, the temperature quotients (Q_{10}) decrease with a rise in storage temperature. Platenius (1939), one of the pioneers in the study of postharvest physiology of vegetables, determined the Q_{10} of deterioration for various crops from the time they were field fresh to the time they were judged to be unsalable (Table 1.5), except for peas, where sugar loss was the criterion of change. When this chemical change was considered, the Q_{10} for the range from 0° to 10° C (32° to 50° F) was nearly ten times that for visual deterioration, indicating that appearance is not necessarily the only, or even the best, way to judge quality in crops where flavor or texture deteriorate more rapidly than appearance.

Various Factors in Deterioration

Factors that can contribute to rapid deterioration, other than temperature, are here noted only briefly because they are discussed in detail under their own headings.

Relative humidity can affect the rate of deterioration by being too low or too high. Dry air leads to rapid wilting, whereas air near water saturation tends to encourage growth of microorganisms in some vegetables.

Low O_2 or excessive CO_2 in the storage atmosphere can directly injure crops or aggravate disorders, such as chilling injury, whereas ethylene may cause discoloration or premature yellowing of green vegetables.

Light contributes to deterioration by inducing greening in potatoes displayed in supermarkets, and this greening is enhanced as temperature rises.

TABLE 1.5. TEMPERATURE QUOTIENT (Q_{10}) FOR RATE OF DETERIORATION OF VARIOUS VEGETABLES FOR TEMPERATURES BETWEEN 0° AND 30° C (32° AND 86° F) AT 10° C (18° F) INTERVALS

Temperature Range		Asparagus			Brussels Sprouts	Celery	Head Lettuce	Peas		Radish	Spinach	Sweet Corn
°C	°F	Q_{10}[1]	Q_{10}[2]	Q_{10}[3]	Q_{10}[1]	Q_{10}[1]	Q_{10}[1]	Q_{10}[1]	Q_{10}[2]	Q_{10}[1]	Q_{10}[1]	Q_{10}[2]
0–10	32–50	2.7	5.8	10	3.8	4.1	2.5	3.3	27.5	2.9	3.3	3.9
10–20	50–68	2.4	2.7	2	2.7	2.3	2.2	2.8	2.6	2.3	2.5	3.6
20–30	68–86	1.8	1.4	2	1.9	1.9	1.9	2.0	1.5	1.6	1.8	1.5

[1] Based on time required for vegetable to reach an unsalable condition as judged by appearance (Platenius 1939).
[2] Based on time required for vegetable to lose 30% of sugar initially present (Platenius 1939).
[3] Based on time required for a 50% increase in weight of fiber (Lipton 1957).

The rate of deterioration, then, is influenced by the interaction of various environmental factors, but with temperature exceeding all others in importance. Temperature not only directly affects the rate, but also modifies the effects of the other factors.

Types of Deterioration

Types of deterioration vary so much with the commodity considered and with the physical handling it receives that this subject is deferred to the consideration of individual crops.

Practical Considerations

The above use of the terminology for the stages in the life span of fresh vegetables and fruits lends itself to practical application by avoiding confusion between popular and scientific terms. While precise, physiologically-based definitions are essential for the characterization and understanding of the various stages from prematuration through senescence, such definitions should be in terms that reflect specific biochemical changes rather than popular usage. Separation of terminology will better serve the layman and the plant scientist than present usage that is partly popular and partly scientific.

REFERENCES

Respiration

APELAND, J. 1971. Factors affecting respiration and color during storage of parsley. Acta Hort. No. 20, 43–52.

BIALE, J. B. 1975. Synthetic and degradative processes in fruit ripening. *In* Postharvest Biology and Handling of Fruits and Vegetables. N. F. Haard and D. K. Salunkhe (Editors). AVI Publishing Co., Westport, Conn.

EAKS, I. L., and MORRIS, L. L. 1956. Respiratory response of cucumbers to chilling and nonchilling temperatures. Plant Physiol. *31*, 308–314.

HALLER, M. M., ROSE, D. M., LUTZ, J. M., and HARDING, P. L. 1945. Respiration of citrus fruits after harvest. J. Agr. Res. *71*, 327–359.

HARDENBURG, R. E. 1970. Personal communication. Beltsville, Maryland.

HRUSCHKA, H. W. 1967. Storage and shelf-life of packaged rubarb. U.S. Dept. Agr. Mktg. Res. Rept. *771*.

HRUSCHKA, H. 1971. Storage and shelf life of packaged kale. U.S. Dept. Agr. Mktg. Res. Rept. *923*.

INTERN. INST. REFRIG. 1967. Recommended Conditions for Cold Storage of Perishable Produce, 2nd Edition. International Institute of Refrigeration, Paris.

LEWIS, D.A., and MORRIS, L. L. 1956. Effect of chilling storage on respiration and deterioration of several sweetpotato varieties. Proc. Am. Soc. Hort. Sci. *68*, 421–428.

LIPTON, W. J. 1957. Physiological changes in harvested asparagus *(Asparagus officinalis)* as related to temperature. Ph.D. Thesis. Univ. Calif., Davis.

LIPTON, W. J., ASAI, W. K., and FOUSE, D.C. 1981. Deterioration and CO_2 and ethylene production of stored mung bean sprouts. J. Am. Soc. Hort. Sci. *106*, 817–820.

LUTZ, J. M., and HARDENBURG, R. E. 1968. The commercial storage of fruits, vegetables, and florist and nursery stocks. U.S. Dept. Agr. Handbook *66*.

MANN, L. K., and LEWIS, D. A. 1956. Rest and dormancy in garlic. Hilgardia *26*, 161–189.

MORRIS, L. L. 1970. Personal communication. Davis, Calif.

PIEH, K. 1965. Cooling of fruits and vegetables. Deut. Gartenbau *13*, 136–140. (German)

PLATENIUS, H. 1942. Effect of temperature on the respiration rate and the respiratory quotient of some vegetables. Plant Physiol. *17*, 179–197.

PRATT, H. K., and MORRIS, L. L. 1958. Physiological aspects of vegetable and fruit handling. Food Technol. Austral. *10*, 407–417.

PRATT, H. K., MORRIS, L. L., and TUCKER, C. L. 1954. Temperature and lettuce deterioration. Proc. Conf. Transport. Perishables. Univ. Calif., Davis. 77–83.

RAPPAPORT, L., LIPTON, W. J., and WATADA, A. E. 1957. Differential deterioration of broccoli varieties. Univ. Calif. Veg. Crops Rep. *1653*.

RAPPAPORT, L., and WATADA, A. E. 1958. Effect of temperature on artichoke quality. Proc. Conf. Transport. Perishables. Univ. Calif., Davis. 142–146.

SCHOLZ, E. W., JOHNSON, H. B., and BUFORD, W. R. 1963. Heat evolution of some Texas-grown fruits and vegetables. J. Rio Grande Valley Hort. Soc. *17*, 170–175.

SMITH, W. H. 1957. The production of carbon dioxide and metabolic heat by horticultural produce. Modern Refrig. *60*, 493–496.

TEWFIK, S., and SCOTT, L. E. 1954. Respiration of vegetables as affected by postharvest treatment. J. Agr. Food Chem. *2*, 415–417.

WATADA, A. E., and MORRIS, L. L. 1966. Effect of chilling and nonchilling temperatures on snap bean fruits. Proc. Am. Soc. Hort. Sci. *89*, 368–378.

WORKMAN, M., PRATT, H. K., and MORRIS, L. L. 1957. Studies on the physiology of tomato fruits. I. Respiration and ripening behavior at 20°C as related to date of harvest. Proc. Am. Soc. Hort. Sci. *69*, 352–365.

Water Loss

CLAYPOOL, L. L., MORRIS, L. L., PENTZER, W. T., and BARGER, W. R. 1951. Air transportation of fruits, vegetables and cut flowers; temperature and humidity requirements and perishable nature. U.S. Dept. Agr. H. T. & S. Office Rept. *258*.

GRIERSON, W., and WARDOWSKI, W. F. 1975. Humidity in horticulture. HortScience *10*, 356–360.

GUILLOU, R. 1960. Design for fog sprays for produce storage. Univ. Calif., Davis, Dept. Agr. Eng. Unnumbered mimeo.

GUILLOU, R. 1967. Problems in perishables handling—the engineer's view. Proc. Fruit and Vegetable Perishables Handling Conf., Univ. Calif., Davis. 5–9.

GUILLOU, R., and RICHARDSON, H. B. 1965. Humidity's valuable role in keeping produce cool. Produce Marketing *8*, No. 2, 37–39.

JORGENSEN, E. G. 1974. Jacketed fruit and vegetable storages in Canada— design and operating experience. *In* Relative Humidity and the Storage of Fresh Fruits and Vegetables—Recent Research Results and Developments. Symp. ASHRAE Semi-annual Meet. Chicago, 1973.

LENTZ, C. P., VAN DEN BERG, L., and MCCULLOUGH, R. S. 1971. Study of factors affecting temperature, relative humidity and moisture loss in fresh fruit and vegetable storages. Can. Inst. Food Technol. J. *4*, 146–153.

MEREDITH, D. 1974. The humi-fresh system—design and operating experience. *In* Relative Humidity and the Storage of Fresh Fruits and Vegetables—Recent Research Results and Developments. Symp. ASHRAE Semi-annual Meet. Chicago, 1973.

SZULMAYER, W. 1969. Humidity and moisture measurement. Food Preserv. Quart. *29*, 27–35.

VAN DEN BERG, L., and LENTZ, C. P. 1971. Moisture loss of vegetables under refrigerated storage conditions. Can. Inst. Food Technol. J. *4*, 143–145.

VAN DEN BERG, L., and LENTZ, C. P. 1973A. Effect of relative humidity, temperature, and length of storage on decay and quality of potatoes and onions. J. Food Sci. *38*, 81–83.

VAN DEN BERG, L., and LENTZ, C. P. 1973B. High humidity storage of carrots, parsnips, rutabagas, and cabbage. J. Am. Soc. Hort. Sci. *98*, 129–132.

VAN DEN BERG, L., and LENTZ, C. P. 1974. High humidity storage of some vegetables. Can. Inst. Food Sci. Technol. J. *7*, 260–262.

VAN DEN BERG, L., and LENTZ, C. P. 1977A. Effect of relative humidity of storage life of vegetables. Acta Hort. No. 62, 197–208.

VAN DEN BERG, L., and LENTZ, C. P. 1977B. Study of rate of air change, condensation, and mixed commodities in high humidity vegetable storage. Acta Hort. No. 62, 209–215.

WELLS, A. W. 1962. Effects of storage temperature and humidity on loss of weight by fruit. U.S. Dept. Agr. Mktg. Res. Rept. *539*.

WILLIAMS, G. D. V., and BROCHU, J. 1969. Vapor pressure deficit vs. relative humidity for expressing atmospheric moisture content. Naturaliste Can. *96*, 621–636.

Ethylene

ABELES, F. B. 1973. Ethylene in Plant Biology. Academic Press, New York.

ANON. 1961. Matheson Gas Data Book. Matheson Co., East Rutherford, N.Y.

BIALE, J. B. 1950. Post-harvest physiology and biochemistry of fruits. Ann. Rev. Plant Physiol. *1*, 183–206.

BIALE, J. B., YOUNG, R. E., and OLMSTEAD, A. J. 1954. Fruit respiration and ethylene production. Plant Physiol. *29,* 158–174.

BIANCO, V. V., and PRATT, H. K. 1977. Compositional changes in musk-melons during development and in response to ethylene treatment. J. Am. Soc. Hort. Sci. *102,* 127–133.

BONDAD, N. D., and PANTASTICO, E. B. 1973. Ethrel-induced ripening of immature and mature-green tomato fruits. Econ. Bot. *26,* 238–244.

BROWN, D. S., BUCHANAN, J. R., and HICKS, J. R. 1966. Volatiles from apple fruits as related to variety, maturity and ripeness. Proc. Am. Soc. Hort. Sci. *88,* 98–104.

BUESCHER, R. W. 1974. Ethylene and ethephon effects on chilled tomato fruits. Arkansas Farm Res. *23,* No. 2, 12.

EAKS, I. L. 1970. Respiratory response, ethylene production, and response to ethylene of citrus fruits during ontogeny. Plant Physiol. *45,* 334–338.

FIDLER, J. C., and NORTH, C. J. 1969. Production of volatile organic com-pounds by apples. J. Sci. Food Agr. *20*, 521–526.

GRIERSON-JACKSON, W. 1951. Air purification for fruit storages. Agr. Inst. Rev. (Canada), No. 6, 14–16, 18.

HEINZE, P. H., and CRAFT, C. C. 1953. Effectiveness of ethylene for ripening tomatoes. Proc. Am. Soc. Hort. Sci. *62,* 397–404.

KASMIRE, R. F., PRATT, H. K., and CHACON, F. 1970. Honey Dew melon maturity and ripening guide. Univ. Calif. Agr. Ext. Serv. *MA-26.*

KAYS, S. J., JAWORSKI, C. A., and PRICE, H. C. 1976. Defoliation of pepper transplants in transit by endogenously evolved ethylene. J. Am. Soc. Hort. Sci. *101,* 449–451.

LIEBERMAN, M., and MAPSON, L. W. 1962. Inhibition of the evolution of ethylene and the ripening of fruit by ethylene oxide. Nature *196,* 660–661.

LIPTON, W. J. 1961. Anatomical observations on russet spotting and pink rib of lettuce. Proc. Am. Soc. Hort. Sci. *78,* 367–374.

LYONS, J. M. MCGLASSON, W. B., and PRATT, H. K. 1962. Ethylene produc-tion, respiration, & internal gas concentrations in cantaloupe fruits at vari-ous stages of maturity. Plant Physiol. *37,* 31–36.

LYONS, J. M., and PRATT, H. K. 1964. Effect of stage of maturity and ethylene treatment on respiration and ripening of tomato fruits. Proc. Am. Soc. Hort. Sci. *84,* 491–499.

MCGLASSON, W. B., and PRATT, H. K. 1964A. Effects of ethylene on can-taloupe fruits harvested at various ages. Plant Physiol. *39,* 120–127.

MCGLASSON, W. B., and PRATT, H. K. 1964B. Effects of wounding on respira-tion and ethylene production by cantaloupe fruit tissue. Plant Physiol. *39,* 128–132.

PRATT, H. K., and RAPPAPORT, L. 1956. Using ethylene to ripen honey dew melon. Proc. Conf. Transport. Perishables. Pacific Grove, Calif. 124–127.

RADSPINNER, W. A. 1954. Commercial aspects of ripening mature-green tomatoes with ethylene gas. Pre-Pack-Age *8*, No. 4, 20–21.

ROOD, P. 1956. Relation of ethylene and post-harvest temperature to brown spot of head lettuce. Proc. Am. Soc. Hort. Sci. *68*, 296–303.

SAIMBHI, M. S., KANWAR, J. S., and NANDPURI, K. S. 1975. Artificial ripening of mature green tomatoes with two-chloroethylphosphonic acid. J. Res. Punjab Agr. Univ. *12*, 128–130.

UOTA, M. 1955. Effect of temperature and ethylene on evolution of carbon dioxide, ethylene, and other oxidizable volatiles from three varieties of plum. Proc. Am. Soc. Hort. Sci. *65*, 231–243.

UOTA, M. 1970. Sleepiness of carnation blooms—how much ethylene does it take? Florists' Rev. *146*, No. 3772, 35, 65–67.

Chilling

DAINES, R. M., CEPONIS, M. J., and HAMMOND, D. F. 1974. Relationship of chilling to development of hardcore in sweetpotatoes. Phytopathology *64*, 1459–1462.

EAKS, I. L., and MORRIS, L. L. 1956. Respiratory response of cucumbers to chilling and non-chilling temperatures. Plant Physiol. *31*, 308–314.

EAKS, I. L., and MORRIS, L. L. 1957. Deterioration of cucumbers at chilling and non-chilling temperatures. Proc. Am. Soc. Hort. Sci. *69*, 388–399.

EZELL, B. D., and WILCOX, M. E. 1952. Influence of storage temperature on carotene, total carotenoids and ascorbic acid content of sweetpotatoes. Plant Physiol. *27*, 81–94.

EZELL, B. D., WILCOX, M. S., and CROWDER, J. N. 1952. Pre- and post-harvest changes in carotene, total carotenoids and ascorbic acid content of sweetpotatoes. Plant Physiol. *27*, 355–369.

HRUSCHKA, H. W., SMITH, W. L., JR., and BAKER, J. E. 1967. Chilling-injury syndrome in potato tubers. Plant Dis. Reptr. *51*, 1014–1016.

HRUSCHKA, H. W., SMITH, W. L., JR., and BAKER, J. E. 1969. Reducing chilling injury of potatoes by intermittent warming. Am. Potato J. *46*, 38–53.

HUELIN, F. E. 1962. Chilling injury in stored fruits and vegetables. Food Preserv. Quart. *22*, 63–64.

KIDD, F., WEST, C., and KIDD, M. N. 1927. Gas storage of fruit. Gt. Brit. Dept. Sci. Ind. Res. Food Invest. Spec. Rept. No. *30*.

KUSHMAN, L. J., and DEONIER, M. T. 1957. Effects of storage temperatures on Porto Rico, Allgold and Goldrush sweetpotatoes. Proc. Am. Soc. Hort. Sci. *70*, 425–431.

KUSHMAN, L. J., and WRIGHT, F. S. 1969. Sweetpotato storage. U.S. Dept. Agr. Handbook *358*.

LEWIS, D. A. 1956. Physiological studies of tomato fruits injured by holding at chilling temperatures. Ph.D. Thesis. Univ. Calif., Davis.

LEWIS, D. A., and MORRIS, L. L. 1956. Effect of chilling storage on respiration and deterioration of several sweetpotato varieties. Proc. Am. Soc. Hort. Sci. *68*, 421–428.

LIPTON, W. J. 1958. Effect of temperature on asparagus quality. Proc. Conf. Transport. Perishables. Univ. Calif., Davis. 147–151.

LUTZ, J. M. 1945. Chilling injury of cured and noncured Porto Rico sweet-potatoes. U.S. Dept. Agr. Circ. *729.*

LYONS, J. M. 1973. Chilling injury in plants. Ann. Rev. Plant Physiol. *24,* 445–466.

MCCLURE, T. T. 1959. Rhizopus decay of sweetpotatoes as affected by chilling, recuring, and hydrowarming after storage. Phytopathology *49,* 359–361.

MOLISCH, H. 1897. Investigations on the chilling injury of plants. Fischer, Jena, Germany. (German)

MORRIS, L. L. 1947. The use of ice on cantaloupes and other melons. Univ. Calif. Truck Crops Mimeo No. *38.*

MORRIS, L. L. 1954. Field and transit chilling of fall-grown tomatoes. Proc. Conf. Transport. Perishables. Univ. Calif., Davis. 101–105.

MORRIS, L. L., and PLATENIUS, H. 1939. Low temperature injury to certain vegetables after harvest. Proc. Am. Soc. Hort. Sci. *36*, 609–613.

NELSON, R. 1926. Storage and transportational diseases of vegetables due to sub-oxidation. Mich. Agr. Expt. Sta. Tech. Bull. *81.*

PENTZER, W. T., and HEINZE, P. H. 1954. Postharvest physiology of fruits and vegetables. Ann. Rev. Plant Physiol. *5,* 205–224.

RASMUSSON, L. 1957. Metabolic disturbances in fruits and vegetables at low temperatures. Kältetechnik *9,* No. 9, 293–294. (German)

SHICHI, H., and URITANI, I. 1956. Alteration of metabolism in plants at various temperatures. Part I. Mechanism of cold damage of sweetpotato (sic.) Bull. Agr. Chem. Soc. Japan *20* (Suppl.), 284–288.

SPALDING, D. H., and REEDER, W. F. 1975. Low-oxygen high-carbon dioxide controlled atmosphere storage for control of anthracnose and chilling injury of avocados. Phytopathology *65,* 458–460.

TOMKINS, R. G. 1966. The choice of conditions for the storage of fruits and vegetables. Ditton Lab. Mem. No. *91.*

VAN DER PLANK, J. E., and DAVIES, B. 1937. Temperature-cold injury curves of fruit. J. Pomol. Hort. Sci. *15,* 226–247.

WARDOWSKI, W. F. *et al.* 1975. Chilling injury and decay of grapefruit as affected by thiabendazole, benomyl, and CO_2. HortScience *10,* 381–383.

WHEATON, T. A., and MORRIS, L. L. 1967. Modification of chilling sensitivity by temperature conditioning. Proc. Am. Soc. Hort. Sci. *91,* 529–533.

Maturation

ADDICOTT, F. T. 1969. Aging, senescence, and abscission in plants: phytogerontology. HortScience *4,* 114–116.

CLAYPOOL, L. L. 1953. Why are fresh fruits and vegetables perishable? Proc. Conf. Transport. Perishables. Univ. Calif., Davis. 24–31.

COOMBE, B. G. 1976. The development of fleshy fruits. Ann. Rev. Plant Physiol. *27,* 207–228.

GORTNER, W. A., DULL, C. G., and KRAUSS, B. H. 1967. Fruit development, maturation, ripening, and senescence: a biochemical basis for horticultural terminology. HortScience *2,* 141–144.

LEOPOLD, A. C. 1961. Senescence in plant development. Science *134,* 1727–1732.

LIPTON, W. J. 1957. Physiological changes in harvested asparagus (*Asparagus officinalis*) as related to temperature of holding. Ph.D. Thesis. Univ. Calif., Davis.

MORRIS, L. L., and SOMMER, N. F. 1961. Packing, cooling and loading. Biological factors in product handling. Proc. 5th Conf. Transport. Perishables. Univ. Calif., Davis. 30–39.

PATTERSON, M. E. 1970. The role of ripening in the affairs of man. HortScience *5,* 30–33.

PLATENIUS, H. 1939. Effect of temperature on the rate of deterioration of fresh vegetables. J. Agr. Res. *59,* 41–58.

PRATT, H. K., and MORRIS, L. L. 1958. Some physiological aspects of vegetable and fruit handling. Food Technol. Australia. *10,* 407, 409, 411, 413, 415, 417.

SACHER, J. A. 1973. Senescence and postharvest physiology. Ann. Rev. Plant Physiol. *24,* 197–224.

2

Harvesting Practices and Equipment

Most vegetables grow near, on, or in the ground. Harvesting of these crops has never been one of the more popular forms of labor. It involves much manual effort, commonly referred to as "stoop" labor. With the decreasing availability of migrant farm labor, harvest labor for major vegetable areas sometimes reaches critical shortage. This, together with increasing cost of available field labor, has produced a major effort in research and development toward complete or partial mechanical harvest of many vegetable crops.

As of 1976, only a few of the vegetables sold in the fresh market are harvested mechanically. On the other hand, several vegetables grown for processing are now largely harvested mechanically. The list includes tomatoes, snap beans, green peas, cucumbers, and sweet corn, among others. Sweet corn and bush snap beans are now harvested to a limited extent for the fresh market, and tomato harvest for the fresh market appears to be ready, but not yet in use.

Most of the crops for processing, on which substantial progress has been made in harvest mechanization, will be among the first mechanized for the fresh market.

Further development of mechanical harvesters and picking aids is now and will increasingly result from team effort. This is a multi-discipline approach with teams assessing the crop requirements, conducting the research, evaluating the results in the light of commodity characteristics, environmental requirements, economic factors, and mechanical principles. Included on such teams are mechanical and industrial engineers, horticulturists, plant pathologists, soil scientists, food technologists, and economists. Progress to date with specific crops is discussed in the following sections.

LEAFY, IMMATURE FLOWER HEADS AND MISCELLANEOUS STRUCTURES

General

Those vegetables commonly classed as "leafy" include lettuce, spinach, endive-escarole, cabbage, Brussels sprouts, and celery. Often broccoli, cauliflower, sweet corn, and artichokes are included. Each of these has a high labor requirement for harvest and, except for spinach and sweet corn, multiple harvests are necessary for maximum yield of product for the fresh market. While research and development on mechanized harvest of these crops are underway in several commercial production areas, the widespread use of mechanization so far is confined to spinach, celery, sweet corn, and Brussels sprouts.

As with most vegetable crops, success in mechanization of harvest depends on three factors: (1) cultivars which will develop uniformly and with needed characteristics for machine harvesting and handling; (2) cultural practices designed for a weed-free, evenly-spaced, uniform crop; and (3) machines designed and developed for specific crops.

Leafy Vegetables

Brussels Sprouts   Brussels sprouts are largely harvested by hand and as many as ten pickings over several months are required before the harvest is completed. The introduction of the cultivar Jade Cross initiated development of mechanized harvest because hand harvest of the cultivar is very difficult. Machines have been developed which cut and convey the stalks to a stripping unit which removes the sprouts by a spring-held rotating knife. The stalks must be hand-fed to the stripping unit and for this reason most of the machine-cut product is carried to a stationary stripping unit rather than being stripped on a field combine unit.

Cabbage   Most cabbage is harvested by hand since selective cutting is necessary for maximum yield. Much of the commercial cabbage is now machine-harvested, but almost all of this is for processing. Cost of manual harvest of cabbage is several times the cost of production. This has encouraged research and development of mechanical harvesters and several are now in limited use. All are based on once-over harvest with lifting, stem cutting, and conveying equipment common to all. Physical damage to the heads, largely due to uneven sizes and heights, is delaying use for fresh market cabbage. Cultivars with greater size and growth uniformity together with perfection of precision planting technique will speed the development of mechanized harvest.

Celery   In the major celery growing areas of Florida and California the harvest is at least partly mechanized. Instead of the former hand cutting and trimming in the field, most of the crop is now cut from the root and topped by a one-row harvester which then elevates the stalks into a truck or trailer traveling beside the harvester. The celery is then transported to a stripping unit in the field and onto a field or warehouse packing sytem. Most of the trimming is still a hand operation, but machines that size by weight or diameter and automatic crate or carton closing machines are widely used to replace manual operations. When a machine is perfected for removing unwanted petioles from the stalks, the harvest and packing can be completely mechanized. The mobile field packing machine is also used to some extent. This involves manual

From Grizzell and Honry (1971)

FIG. 2.1.   A MOBILE UNIT FOR TRIMMING, WASHING AND PACKING FLORIDA CELERY IN THE FIELD

cutting and placement on extension conveyors which move the stalks to a washing unit and then to trimmers and packers on the moving unit.

Corn, Sweet   Sweet corn deteriorates so rapidly after harvest that the complete harvest, packing and refrigeration system must be geared to efficiency and speed.

The usual method of harvesting sweet corn involves pulling the ears by hand, which is followed by wagon or trailer transport to a packing shed where the corn is graded and packed. This method is gradually being replaced, particularly in southern Florida, by mechanical harvesters which cut the stalks near the ground, remove the ears, and convey them to a bin attached to the harvester or carried on a separate tractor-drawn trailer, which in turn carries the corn to the packing area. Another method involves the use of self-propelled packing units which move through the field where the hand-pulled ears are placed on conveyors for sorting, grading and packing by workers on the harvester.

The harvesting machine replaces many laborers for the ear removal step. However, some problems are created by mechanical separation of the ears. The main problem at packing is separation and disposal of small ears and other plant parts from the marketable ears. In a Florida study (Showalter 1967), immature ears, leaves, and stalk sections in machine-harvested Iobelle sweet corn ranged from 13 to 23% by weight in 1967 and from 18 to 30% in 1968. When machine-harvested corn is hauled to a packing area in the field or shed, disposal of the waste material from machine-harvested corn becomes a problem. Hand-harvesting leaves such material in the field.

Showalter (1974) states that an improved sweet corn harvester cuts the shanks from the stalk instead of pulling them. The pulled shanks accounted for 3 to 12% of the total ear weight and required much hand labor for trimming. The newer harvester cuts the shank and is adjustable for shank length. When the shanks were cut at least 6.5 cm (2.5 in.) long, kernel injury was minimal, the trash problem was reduced, but some hand trimming was still required.

A 1966 study in Massachusetts (Melnick 1966) showed a 90 to 95% recovery of marketable ears with a one-run harvester. The machine, with a crew of 3 men, harvested the same amount in 5 hr as a crew of 14 men by hand-pulling. Cost of picking and packing was reduced by almost half by operation of the mechanical picker.

Lettuce   Most of the commercial crop of head lettuce is now produced in California and Arizona. All is now hand cut and trimmed on a selective harvest basis. Commonly about one-third of a given crop is cut

Courtesy of FMC Corp.

FIG. 2.2.   TWO-ROW SWEET CORN HARVESTER LOADING BULK TRAILER IN THE FIELD

at first harvest with two or three successive cuttings, depending on market and weather conditions. Essentially all of the crop is now packed in cartons (1½ to 2½ dozen heads), usually in the field, but if a plastic film wrap is used it may be wrapped and packed in field or shed. Vacuum cooling is the exclusive method for removal of field heat before shipment.

A California study (Zahara *et al.* 1974) compared harvest costs for head lettuce by the usual manual method, with mechanized harvest with a one-bed unit. Even with the mechanical harvester labor was a major part of harvest costs. However, estimated cost per carton was about 55% less for mechanical than for manual harvest. Despite the testing of two once-over and four selective harvesters during the 1964–74 period, hand harvest crews have not been replaced.

Spinach   Spinach harvest is one of the most highly mechanized among vegetable crops. Since hand harvest requires a very high labor input over a short time and uniform growth of the crop enables once-over harvest, the mechanization of harvest is well advanced for both fresh and processing spinach. Fresh market spinach is cut below the lower leaves and elevated into bulk trucks or trailers. Since some dirt usually accompanies the spinach, it is taken to a central packing shed for washing, grading, bunching or bagging.

Immature Flower Heads

Artichokes   Globe artichokes are produced commercially only in a few coastal areas of California. One cultivar, Green Globe, is grown and it is variable in all characteristics which must be uniform for successful mechanized harvest. Buds which are ready for harvest are cut by hand and placed in containers carried by the laborers. These containers are emptied into bulk bins for transport to the packing shed. Mechanization of artichoke harvest will not be accomplished until new cultivars, which are more determinate in their bearing habits and have greater numbers of buds per bearing shoot, are developed. Modifications in cultural practices and plant spacings will probably also be necessary. As processing of buds and artichoke hearts increases, the possibilities for mechanized harvest will improve.

Broccoli and Cauliflower   Both broccoli and cauliflower are almost entirely hand harvested. The pickers select and cut prime heads and toss them into bulk trailers or bins. Both are trimmed and packed in a central shed. The broccoli heads, with some leaves attached, are usually tied into 1- and ½-lb bunches, whereas the leaves around the cauliflower head usually are trimmed back even with the curd and the heads packed individually, often with a plastic film wrapper over each head.

Miscellaneous Structures

Asparagus   Mechanical harvest of asparagus presents many unique problems because of the nature of its growth. White asparagus is cut 20 to 26 cm (8 to 10 in.) under the surface of the plant bed when just the tip is showing above the surface. Green asparagus, the greater portion of the crop, is cut or snapped above or just below the ground surface. Since new shoots are appearing daily over a harvest period of 6 to 10 weeks, a selective harvest is highly desirable. However, research and development of mechanical harvesters for asparagus have explored both selective cutting or snapping and set-level cutting which removes all spears that have developed above the cutting level of the harvester. Despite the commercial development of both selective and nonselective harvesters, almost all asparagus is still harvested by hand, principally because of decreases in yield and quality associated with machine harvest. Intensive research on machines and cultural practices is underway at the New Jersey and California Experiment Stations. It now appears that by 1980 a significant proportion of the asparagus crop will be harvested mechanically.

ROOTS AND TUBERS

Roots

Carrots   Until about 1950 almost all carrots harvested for immediate marketing were sold as bunched carrots with tops on. Harvesting and packing methods changed very rapidly about 1950 as a result of research which showed that topped carrots packed in ventilated plastic film bags holding about 0.5 to 1 kg (1 or 2 lb) retained quality for a longer period than bunched carrots and were more economical to prepare for market.

Machine-harvested carrots are loosened by a lifter device and elevated out of the row by belts which grasp the carrot tops. After the tops are mechanically cut or twisted off, they fall back on the field. The roots are elevated to bulk trucks or pallet bins on flat-bed trucks or trailers. The bulk loads are then transported to a packing shed where the roots are washed, sized and packed in plastic film bags for shipment.

Sweetpotatoes   The harvest of sweetpotatoes remains essentially a manual operation. Research on mechanization of sweetpotato harvest is underway at several southern and eastern experiment stations, but there is only limited commercial development to date.

Mechanization of sweetpotato harvest is complicated by heavy vines, a very tender, easily damaged root, and somewhat difficult separation of the root from the vine.

A vine cutter is described by O'Brien and Scheuerman (1969). Used as a separate operation before harvest it lifts the vines, cuts them at ground level and discharges them between rows. This step enabled reasonably efficient mechanical harvest with a machine combining a wide digger-lifter blade, a rod lifting conveyor, a manned sorting belt, and another conveyor to carry the sorted roots to field lugs or pallet bins.

Austin and Graves (1970) found that vine killing treatments applied several days before harvest facilitated mechanical harvest. However, vine killing early in the harvest season, or 2 weeks before harvest reduced yield.

Present practice involves cutting or beating the vines followed by digging with a tractor-drawn turning plow. The roots are hand picked from the ground and often have to be pulled from the attached vines. For many years the roots were picked into bushel baskets or hampers, which were then used as curing and storage containers. More recently, palletized wire-bound containers, which stack with less product damage, are increasingly used. There is also an interest in and some limited use of pallet bins. As mechanized harvest increases, pallet bins will be more widely used.

Miscellaneous Root Crops   Beets, turnips, and radishes are handled in and from the field much the same as carrots. Since beet and turnip tops are commonly used as greens, a larger proportion of these crops is bunched for market. The larger, more mature beets and turnips are commonly topped and packed in plastic film bags or in bulk containers. Some radishes are still sold with tops on, but an increasing quantity is field-topped and marketed in ventilated or nonventilated plastic bags. Equipment for harvesting and topping is essentially the same for all of these root vegetables.

Tubers

Potatoes.—Commercial application of mechanized potato harvest began about 1950. Twenty years later harvest was essentially completely mechanized in all of the major producing areas.

Harvesting equipment is manufactured by many companies, but the general operation of the harvesting machines is similar. They come in one-, two-, or four-row sizes with conventional diggers, rod conveyors, dirt and vine eliminators, and cross and extension conveyers for transfer of the tubers to the accompanying bulk trucks. Most of the larger harvesters provide space on the machine for several sorters so that obvious culls, clods and stones can be disposed of before the tubers move to the bulk hopper or dump trucks. Some have special equipment for separation of tubers from stones and clods.

The most serious problem encountered in mechanized harvest of potatoes is physical damage to the tubers, mostly bruising. Some of this has been due to faulty machine design, i.e., too many drops onto hard surfaces and too much travel on rough conveyors. Many of these defects have been corrected in present models. Current problems are largely caused by hard clods in areas of heavy soils or soil compaction and by stones in rocky soils such as those of northern Maine.

Paralleling research and development with mechanical equipment has been perfection of vine killers for maturation and skin-set of tubers

Courtesy of FMC Corp.

FIG. 2.3. MODERN TWO-ROW MECHANICAL POTATO HARVESTER LOADING HOPPER-TYPE BULK TRUCK IN THE FIELD

before harvest and many developments in bulk storage and handling of the potato crop. Some of these will be discussed in later sections on storage and transport.

Mechanization of potato harvest was born largely of the necessity to harvest crops in the absence of sufficient field labor to do the job. Cost of harvesting was not the primary concern. Cost studies have shown little difference in total cost of harvest for machine digging, hand picking into sacks, and manual loading of the sacks onto flat-bed trucks as compared with complete mechanization of digging, loading and hauling. Saving in labor costs with mechanization is largely or entirely offset by machine cost.

Bulbs

Onions   Some fall onions are now harvested mechanically by one of several available methods, including the mechanical potato harvester, a combination harvester which incorporates pinch roll equipment to remove tops and a harvester that includes an air blast to raise the tops so that rotating knives can cut them. However, the use of mechanical harvesters and bulk bins or trucks is limited to those areas and operators who have facilities for curing the onions after removal from the field.

The usual procedure for onion harvest involves three steps. (1) The onions are undercut or hand-pulled and allowed to dry for a period of 5 to 10 days before topping. (2) The bulbs are topped by hand or machine and placed in burlap bags for further curing in the field. (3) The bagged onions are loaded onto trucks and hauled to a building for storage or immediate packing for market. When the curing step can be incorporated into the harvesting machine or facilities are provided for rapid curing of the bulbs at the packing shed or storage house, the mechanization of onion harvest will become general.

Unripe Fruits

Beans, Snap   All beans for processing, except pole beans, have been harvested mechanically for many years. The method of snapping or raking bean pods from the plants is essentially unchanged from the earliest machines. Slender rotary metal fingers or tines on a reel work downward through the plants as the machine progresses down the row.

Courtesy of Gilroy Foods, Inc.

FIG. 2.4.   MECHANICAL ONION HARVESTER
Onions are undercut, topped and windrowed for field curing before this final harvest operation.

The harvested pods are then conveyed to a trailer or truck. Many different makes and sizes of machines are available, some self-propelled and some tractor-drawn.

The mechanical harvester has been successfully adapted to harvest of snap beans for the fresh market in Florida. Considerable amounts of leaves, stems and immature pods are included in the once-over machine harvest. Sorting, grading and sizing is done at a field or central packing unit. Even though much of this involves hand labor, studies in Florida have indicated that the market quality of machine-harvested beans is somewhat lower than of those hand-harvested. Nevertheless, the use of machines is increasing as labor becomes scarcer and more expensive.

Hoffman (1971) reported on the condition of machine- and hand-harvested snap beans. More weight loss and surface browning occurred after harvest in machine-picked than hand-picked pods. Of the several cultivars tested, Provider showed the least harvest injury. A possibility for reducing the symptoms of machine harvest injury has been reported by Isenberg and Sandsted (1969). A 1-min dip in an 0.8% solution of sodium dehydroacetate significantly reduced surface discoloration of the pods. The treatment had the added advantage of reducing mold and bacterial development during holding at 5° C (41° F). Potential users should inquire about approval for commercial use.

Cucumbers   Pickling cucumbers are widely harvested by machine on a once-over vine-destructive system. However, cucumbers for the fresh market are almost entirely hand-harvested. No machine is yet available which will make multiple harvests without excessive damage to the vines, and cultivars are not yet available which will produce a profitable yield on a once-over harvest.

Peas Garden.   Pea harvesting for processing involves three separate operations: (1) cutting and windrowing the vines; (2) loading and hauling to the stationary viner; and (3) separation of the pods and shelling of the peas in the viner. Some operations use a mobile viner, thus eliminating step two in the above sequence. Garden peas are seldom marketed now in the fresh form so harvest for the fresh market is of little importance.

Other Pod Vegetables   Harvest of lima beans and southern peas is mostly mechanical and with essentially the same equipment as for garden peas. A major part of each of these crops is marketed in canned, frozen or dried form.

Ripe Fruits

Cantaloups   Much of the same situation prevails with cantaloups as with cucumbers. Research is underway in several states on machines for once-over and selective, multiple pickings and on breeding cultivars which mature a substantial part of the crop at one time. It appears that hand harvest of Honey Dews and watermelons will prevail for some years to come, but machine harvest of cantaloups appears imminent.

The two basic systems for machine harvest of cantaloups are: (1) once-over harvest destructive to the vines; and (2) multiple harvest with the mature melons grasped or raked from the growing vines. In the first system the vines are cut at ground level and conveyed to a unit which shakes off full-slip melons. The less mature fruits are squeezed off between compression rollers (O'Brien and Zahara 1971). Vines are deposited behind the machine, and the separated melons are placed at the edge of the bed for later pickup.

Multiple harvest machines have been developed by Fairbanks and Hall (1976) and Harriot and Grounds (1972). In the former unit the cantaloups are grasped by a unique system of rotating split tires as the machine moves down the row. Released to a conveyor, the melons are carried to containers. Under good field and crop conditions 86% of harvest-mature melons were picked. The second machine (Harriot and Grounds 1972) serves both as a mechanical vine trainer during growth and a harvester when the melons are mature. A combing device separates melons from the vines and rolls them into the adjoining furrow. A separate pickup machine gathers the harvested melons and deposits them in padded bins. The authors report that melon damage was no greater with the machine than with hand harvest, and a saving in cost from both vine training and harvesting was possible.

Manually harvested cantaloups are commonly harvested from 5 to 10 times from any one field during a season. The largest single harvest usually occurs about the middle of the harvest season. Harvesting is entirely by hand labor. The pickers must be skilled in selection of melons for harvest. Cantaloup selection is based largely on size, ground color, and ease of separation from the stem. Complete separation of the stem (full slip) at the abscission layer is desirable for good market quality and required by some state codes. The melons are usually picked into bags carried on the back or side of the laborer. When 25 to 30 kg (60 or 70 lb) of melons are in the bag, the picker carries it to the field truck or trailer for emptying. An inclined plank is often used to enable the picker to enter the truck for unloading the melons.

Courtesy of Western Grower and Shipper

FIG. 2.5.   HAND-HARVESTING OF CANTALOUPS
Mature melons are picked into sacks, emptied into trucks and hauled to the packinghouse.

Harvest aids for cantaloups are used in some of the more concentrated production areas. The mobile field packing machine moves through the field covering 10 to 20 beds by means of conveyors extending from each side of the packing unit. Pickers select mature fruits and place them on the conveyors as the machine moves down the rows. The melons are carried to a packing area on the machine. After packing, the filled cartons or crates are loaded onto a following truck for transport to the precooling and loading shed. A little more damage to the vines occurs than without the machine, but only 5 to 10 pickings are usually made in the same field.

Large Melons   The large melons (Persian, Honey Dew, Crenshaw, Casaba, etc.) are harvested in essentially the same manner, but because these melons do not slip from the stem, indices of size, ground color, finish, and blossom end firmness are used by the pickers to determine suitability for harvest. Crenshaw melons are sometimes packed into shipping containers in the field because they are tender-skinned and susceptible to bruising.

Squash   Squash, both mature, as Butternut and Hubbard, and summer as Zucchini and Scallops, are entirely hand-harvested. Pumpkins and squash for processing are commonly lifted and broken from the vines with flat-tined forks and either placed directly into trucks or trailers or placed on inclined conveyors for loading.

Tomatoes   Harvest of tomatoes for the fresh market remains largely a manual operation. The nature of growth and the ripening pattern of the commonly grown cultivars of fresh market tomatoes requires repeated pickings for either mature-green or vine-ripe packs. This involves much hand labor over a period of several weeks for any one field in order to obtain profitable yields.

There are limiting factors in converting machines now widely used for the harvest of processing tomatoes. (1) Cultivars maturing a large proportion of the crop at one time are not yet available for the fresh market crop. (2) Mechanical damage from machine harvesting is more critical to acceptance of fresh market tomatoes than processing fruit. (3) Soil moisture, high humidity, and irregular temperature changes are more limiting in the harvest of fresh market tomatoes because days instead of hours elapse before use. (4) Staked or "pole" tomatoes would not lend themselves to mechanical harvest by any modification of present one-pick machines.

Research continues in several tomato growing areas, but, as of now, industry interest in mechanized harvest of fresh market tomatoes is at a low ebb. Cultivars developed for machine harvest are not widely grown for the fresh market, and favored cultivars are better adapted to manual harvest (Showalter 1976). Plant breeders continue the search for fresh market cultivars adapted to machine harvest.

REFERENCES

ANON. 1970. Reviews progress mechanical harvest fresh tomatoes. Packer 77, No. 23, 9B.

AUSTIN, M. E., and GRAVES, E. 1970. Preharvest treatments on skinning of sweetpotato roots. J. Am. Soc. Hort. Sci. 95, 754–757.

BEEMAN, J. F., DEEN, W. W., JR., and HALSEY, L. H. 1966. Development of a mechanical celery harvester. Florida Agr. Expt. Sta. J. Ser. 2298.

BINGLEY, G. W. 1962. Mechanized cucumber harvesting. Agr. Eng. 43, 22–25.

BROOKE, D. L., and SPURLOCK, A. H. 1967. Cost of harvesting snap beans by machine. Florida Agr. Expt. Sta. Agr. Econ. Mimeo. Rept. EC68–2.

CARGILL, B. F., and ROSSMILLER, G. E. 1969. Fruit and vegetable harvest mechanization—technological implications. (Report of a symposium with papers by leading authorities on mechanized harvesting.) Mich. State Univ., Rural Manpower Center Rept. *16.*

DAVIS, G. N., WHITAKER, T. W., BOHN, G. W., and KASMIRE, R. F. 1965. Muskmelon production in California. Calif. Agr. Expt. Sta. Circ. *536.*

FAIRBANKS, G. E., and HALL, C. V. 1976. Mechanical muskmelon harvesting. HortScience *11*, 608–610.

FINDLEN, H., and GLAVES, A. H. 1964. Vine killing in relation to maturity of Red River Valley potatoes. U.S. Dept. Agr. Tech. Bull. *1306.*

FINNEY, E. E., JR., and FINDLEN, H. 1967. Influence of preharvest treatments upon turgor of Katahdin potatoes. Am. Potato J. *44*, 383–386.

FRANKLIN, D. F., WORKS, D. W., and WILLIAMS, L. G. 1966. Experiments in harvesting, curing, and storing yellow Sweet Spanish onions. Idaho Agr. Expt. Sta. Bull. *479.*

FRENCH, G. W. 1967. An evaluation of cost factors in the production and harvesting of potatoes. U.S. Dept. Agr. Prod. Res. Rept. *98.*

FRENCH, G. W., and LEVIN, J. H. 1968. An evaluation of multirow methods of potato harvesting. U.S. Dept. Agr. *ARS 42–138.*

GREENE, E. E. L., KUSHMAN, L. J., and SPURLOCK, H. C. 1959. An analysis of quality and cost of harvesting and handling potatoes with mechanical equipment. Florida Agr. Expt. Sta. Bull. *612.*

HARRIOT, W., and GROUNDS, R. 1972. Machines for melons take big step forward. Western Grower and Shipper *43,* 18–19, 27.

HOFFMAN, J. C. 1971. Injury of snap bean pods associated with machine harvesting and handling. J. Am. Soc. Hort. Sci. *96,* 21–24.

ISENBERG, F. M., and SANDSTED, R. F. 1969. Results of using sodium dehydroacetate applications to reduce discoloration of snap beans damaged by machine harvesting. J. Am. Soc. Hort. Sci. *94,* 631–635.

KEITH, T. 1968. Machine harvesting—big strides in state vegetable production. Florida Grower, *Feb.,* 17–19.

LORENZ, O. A. 1969. The mechanized growing and harvesting of vegetable crops in the West. HortScience *4,* 238–239.

MELNICK, W. 1966. Machine harvesting of sweet corn. Veg. News and Notes, Univ. of Mass. Oct.

MILLER, C. H., SPLINTER, W. E., and WRIGHT, F. S. 1969. The effect of cultural practices on the suitability of cabbage once-over harvest. J. Am. Soc. Hort. Sci. *94,* 67–69.

MOORE, M. J. 1966. Mechanical harvesting of asparagus. Agr. Eng. *47,* 21–23.

O'BRIEN, M., and LINGLE, J. 1965. Mechanical harvesting cantaloupes. Agr. Eng. *46,* 74–77.

O'BRIEN, M., and SCHEUERMAN, R. W. 1969. Mechanical harvesting, handling, and storing sweetpotatoes. Trans. Am. Soc. Agr. Eng. *12,* 261–263, 269.

O'BRIEN, M., and ZAHARA, M. 1971. Mechanical harvest of melons. Trans. Am. Soc. Agr. Eng. *14*, 883–885.

SHOWALTER, R. K. 1967. Mechanizing the harvesting and postharvest handling of snap beans, celery and sweet corn. Proc. Florida State Hort. Soc. *80,* 203–207.

SHOWALTER, R. K. 1968. Mechanization after machine harvesting of celery and snap beans. Florida State Hort. Soc. *81,* 120–126.

SHOWALTER, R. K. 1969. Detachment force for harvesting snap beans. Proc. Florida State Hort. Soc. *81,* 115–118.

SHOWALTER, R. K. 1974. Mechanical harvesting and trimming of sweet corn. Proc. Florida State Hort. Soc. *87,* 252–254.

SHOWALTER, R. K. 1976. Personal communication. Gainesville, Florida.

SIMS, W. L., and SMITH, P. 1968. Mechanical system for market tomatoes. Western Grower and Shipper *39,* No. 4, 21–22, 28–29.

SIMS, W. L., ZOBEL, M., and KING, R. C. 1966. Growing tomatoes for mechanical harvest. Univ. Calif. Agr. Ext. Ser. *AXT 150.*

STOUT, G. J. 1967. Machine harvest of fresh market tomatoes. Am. Veg. Grower *15,* No. 7, 9–11.

STOUT, B. A., BAKKER-ARKEMA, F. W., and RIES, S. K. 1964. Developing a mechanical cabbage harvester. Trans. Am. Soc. Agr. Eng. *9,* 860–861.

WHITAKER, T. W., SHERF, A. F., LANGE, W. H., NICKLOW, C. W., and RADEWALD, J. D. 1970. Carrot production in United States. U.S. Dept. Agr. Handbook *375.*

WOOD, C. 1976. Mechanical harvesting of peppers. Florida Grower and Rancher, *Feb.,* 14.

WRIGHT, F. S., and SPLINTER, W. E. 1966. Development of a mechanical cabbage harvester. Trans. Am. Soc. Agr. Eng. *9,* 862–865, 871.

ZAHARA, M., JOHNSON, S. S., and GARRETT, R. E. 1974. Labor requirements, harvest costs, and potential for mechanical harvest of lettuce. J. Am. Soc. Hort. Sci. *99,* 535–537.

3

Preparation for Market

After horticultural crops are harvested they must be cleaned, sorted, sized and usually packaged if they are to be sold in the fresh produce market. Additional steps in preparation may involve use of a disinfectant in the wash water, or as a separate treatment, and the application of wax or other protective coating. Usually these procedures take place in a central packing house, but head lettuce, which does not require washing, is usually trimmed and packed in the field. Other crops, such as celery, sweet corn and cantaloups, are sometimes packed on portable packing line equipment which moves through the field as harvest proceeds.

CLEANING THE CROP

Adhering dirt, dust, insects and sometimes spray residues must be removed before produce is ready for the fresh market. Usually this involves washing, but occasionally dry brushing is sufficient. A heavy flood or force-spray of water is required, particularly for root and tuber crops which have tightly adhering soil. Rotary brushes, either longitudinal or crosswise, are usually used to ensure complete removal of foreign material.

Soak Tanks

Root and tuber crops are often emptied into soak tanks or vats from the bulk field trucks. Experiences in the early potato districts of

California during the 1940s showed that prolonged soaking of potatoes in dirty water, particularly in deep vats, substantially increased bacterial soft rot infections at lenticels (Dewey and Barger 1948). Hydrostatic pressure, exposure time in the vat, and sun injury before soaking were all factors in lenticel infection. Increasing depths from 0.3 to 3 m (1 to 10 ft) with exposures from ½ to 1 hr caused increased infections from both depth and time. Water tanks are still widely used for receiving potatoes and carrots from bulk loads. They also serve a useful purpose for loosening adhering soil. However, now shallow vats are used and frequently with a flow of water in a flume-type soak tank.

Disinfectants in Water

Low concentrations of chlorine are widely used in presoak or wash water for vegetables. Data on the effectiveness of chlorine and chlorine compounds for decay reduction are conflicting. Many studies show little or no effect from low concentrations of chlorine. Probably the best that can be expected is a reduction in total inoculum in water which is constantly receiving added loads of bacteria and fungi from the surface of the products being cleaned. Segall (1968) and others have shown that many factors, including concentration, solution temperature, exposure time, and pH affect the bactericidal action of chlorine solutions. It is also well known that organic matter combines with chlorine and the maintenance of desired concentration in dirty water requires frequent tests and chlorine additions.

A study was made in Michigan (Grigg and Chase 1967B) to compare the effects of a 30 sec exposure of potatoes to concentrations of chlorine from 50 to 10,000 ppm. Concentrations of 1000 ppm and above caused some surface darkening and cut surfaces turned black one day after treatment. No effect on subsequent tuber greening was observed. Concentrations of 100 ppm or above stimulated wound healing with an increasing effect at the higher (up to 5000 ppm) concentrations. Effects of chlorine concentration on decay development were not determined.

Chlorine has the advantage of leaving no chemical residue on the product. However, for the same reason it has no residual effect. If an effective concentration is maintained it will prevent buildup of contamination in hydrocooling water and it is useful for cleanup of rollers, brushes and conveyors at the end of a day's run. A study of the cause and control of black spot of radishes (Segall and Smoot 1962) showed that most of the bacterial infections responsible started at injuries caused during mechanical harvesting, washing and sizing. Satisfactory control of the disease was obtained by maintaining 40 to 60 ppm of chlorine in the wash water. Use of chlorine in the wash water is more effective against black spot than higher concentrations in the hydrocooler. Several other disinfectants are used before packing as fungicidal solutions for the control of specific diseases of vegetables. These are subject to change as new materials are tested and approved. Current information on effective and approved fungicides can be obtained from local authorities.

Scrubber Brushes

The scrubbing action in vegetable washers may be obtained by rotary brushes of natural or synthetic fiber, or strips of rubber with multiple small fingers called pintles. Abrasion-type washing is also possible in a rotating cylinder with a spiral flange on the inner surface to move the product through the wash water. This type is commonly used for topped carrots and other root crops. Damage to the product sometimes occurs from use of the wrong brush type or excessive speed. A pitting disorder found in Red River Valley potatoes several years ago was traced to the use of rubber pintle brushes that were too hard. Tests made at the Potato

Courtesy of American Machinery Corp.

FIG. 3.1.   COMBINATION WASHER AND HOT WAX APPLICATOR FOR ELONGATED VEGETABLES
Variation in brush diameter turns products parallel to brushes; wax applicator at discharge end.

Research Center (Claycomb and Hansen 1957) showed that either new or worn pintle brushes with a Durometer hardness of 60 caused pitting, whereas a softer material (Durometer 40) caused no damage. Speed of the brushes did not appear to be a factor in injury.

Drying After Washing

Since free moisture on vegetables tends to stimulate the growth of decay organisms, many types of driers have been used to remove water after washing. The commonest types use high velocity heated air, usually applied in a tunnel, or metal or fabric covered rollers with a squeegee to remove water from each roller. In harvest areas of high temperatures and low relative humidity, such as the San Joaquin Valley of California or the Columbia Basin of Washington State, moisture evaporates rapidly so that by the time the potatoes pass over the grading belt, sizer and bagger, very little free moisture is present. On the other hand, in moist, high-humidity areas some artificial drying may be desirable after washing. A series of tests made in the Red River Valley with a heated air drier indicated no need of drying after washing unless serious amounts of decay were present in the potatoes as they were removed from storage. Weight loss during shipment was greater in the dried potatoes, but one lot with severe late blight infection developed much less decay during marketing when dried.

Dry Brushing

Mature onions are never washed since added moisture is undesirable. Dry brushing to remove the outer loose, dry scales is common practice. This is often combined with an air blast to dry exposed scales, carry away the dry material, and assist the brush action. Cantaloups and other melons are also often dry-brushed to remove dry field dirt or dust.

Washing Before or After Storage

Root and tuber crops which are stored before marketing are generally washed as they are removed from storage if they are to be sold in the fresh market. Research in Maine and Minnesota has generally indicated that unwashed potatoes keep better in common storage than prewashed tubers. Studies with sweetpotatoes in Louisiana showed similar results. These roots kept best when cured and stored without washing. On the other hand, tests made in Michigan on seed potatoes stored washed and unwashed indicated some advantage in appearance and stand counts for those washed before storage.

CURING EARLY ONIONS

Early crop onions as produced in southern and southwestern states are seldom completely mature when harvested. Leaves are often green and if cut immediately are wet and susceptible to infection. The usual practice is to leave the onions in windrows a few days before topping and then lining or stacking the bagged or crated onions in the field for a few days before transfer to the packinghouse. This is a satisfactory procedure if the weather is dry and the relative humidity is low during field curing. When these conditions do not prevail, artificial curing is desirable.

Several methods of artificial curing have been tried, but the method most commonly used for early onions involves blowing heated air at 43° to 46° C (110° to 115° F) vertically through a grill on which the onions in mesh bags have been placed. Such treatment continued for a period of 8 to 12 hr usually provides satisfactory curing for either immediate shipment to market or storage for later sale. Some tests with onions grown in South Texas (Rosberg and Johnson 1959) showed that direct exposure to gas-fired infrared radiation for a period of 6 min gave better control of neck rot in freshly harvested onions than forced-air curing for 4 hr at 47° C (118° F). However, there has been no commercial use of the gas-fired curing system.

Garlic requires essentially the same type of postharvest treatment as onions. Most of the domestically-produced garlic is grown in California where field conditions are satisfactory for curing. In those instances when unfavorable field conditions prevail, garlic can be artificially cured the same as onions.

SORTING THE CROP

General

Sorting is almost entirely a manual operation because human sight and dexterity have not been satisfactorily replaced by machines. Sorting is generally accomplished in a central packing shed as part of a cleaning, sorting, sizing and packing line. The purpose is two-fold: (1) to remove items which are obviously unsuitable for sale, such as products with severe mechanical injury, decay, or atypical shape or color for the cultivar; and (2) to meet requirements of a grade established by federal, state or marketing agreement authority.

Sorting Equipment

The products for sorting generally move over a belt or roller conveyor. A roller conveyor which turns the product as it moves forward is preferable to a belt because it allows the sorters to see all sides of each item. Each sorter on the line picks out those products which are unsuitable for the top grade. Then, depending on the quality and grades to be marketed, these items may be placed on a separate belt for a lower grade or discarded completely in a cull chute.

Detailed studies are lacking on equipment for increasing the efficiency of manual sorting of vegetables and melons. However, several different types of sorting methods and equipment were tested for apples (Hunter *et al.* 1958) and the results should be applicable to most vegetables.

The three types of sorting tables studied included one with a flat belt, one with longitudinal spiral rolls, and one with reverse-rotating rubber rollers moving over a plywood frame. Modifications as the tests proceeded included addition of sorting lanes, variable forward speed of rolls, and ultimately a new design called the float-roll table. The surface of this table consists of small, rubber-covered rolls extending across the table. The forward motion is controlled by varying the speed at which the rolls move down the table; the rotating speed of the fruit is controlled by varying the rate at which the rolls rotate.

The cost of labor for sorting a given amount of fruit was lowest for the float-roll table and highest for the belt table. When sorting fruit of good quality, the relative efficiency of various types of equipment was apparent. The time required for visual inspection was a major factor and visual inspection was much easier on the tables which rolled the fruit.

Dividing the sorting tables into lanes and assigning a lane to each sorter improved sorter efficiency and responsibility. Without lanes many fruits were examined by several sorters, causing needless duplication.

Sufficient light above the sorting table is also essential for efficiency and the light should be of a quality approaching daylight, particularly if color of the product is a factor in selection. The U.S. Department of Agriculture Standardization and Inspection Service can recommend light intensities and color for sorting most vegetables. Some automated color sorting is now available. This is discussed under *Measurement of Quality, Light Reflectance.*

HARVEST CONTAINERS

General

Picking containers vary widely, depending on the crop harvested and the production area. They vary from tow sacks (large bags dragged or carried by the picker) as used for melons, to canvas buckets, metal pails, baskets, hampers and boxes. Often the container carried by the picker is emptied into a larger container, which may be a field box, barrel, trailer or bulk bin. Harvest of sweet corn, broccoli, cauliflower and cabbage often by-passes the small container entirely with the pickers tossing the items directly into the trailer, truck or bin as they are picked. This is also a common method of watermelon harvest, although melons must be caught by someone in the truck to prevent injury.

Bulk Containers

As increasing mechanization develops in the field and packinghouse, there is a corresponding increase in bulk handling. Potatoes and carrots are now largely moved from the field in bulk. Potatoes are transported in hopper body or dump trucks, but carrots are more commonly hauled from the field in pallet bins. Before lettuce packing moved to the field, almost all lettuce was hauled from the field to the packinghouse in large steel baskets, each of which held several hundred pounds of lettuce. Much of the shed-packed broccoli, cauliflower, celery and cabbage is still hauled from the field in these large baskets. Mature-green tomatoes are now commonly emptied into pallet bins in the field from the picking containers. Experience in central California indicates less physical damage to tomatoes hauled in bins holding about 150 to 300 kg (335 to 670 lb) than in the conventional field boxes. Tests with materials for pallet bin construction showed little difference in fruit damage between wire mesh, plastic, fiberboard and wood (Stout *et al.* 1968). The important factors were rigidity, life expectancy, and ease of cleaning. However, the depth of fruit in the pallet bin did affect the amount of damage after extended truck transport. Mature-green fruits loaded 300 kg (670 lb) to the bin graded only 57% number one at packing as compared with 82% number one for those loaded only 150 kg to the bin. A study

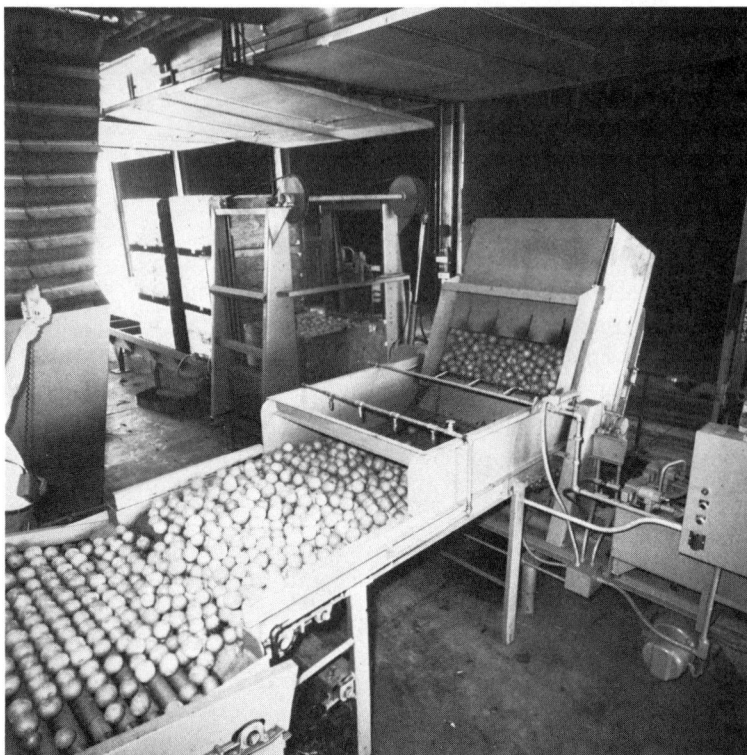

Courtesy of Brogdex Co.

FIG. 3.2. AUTOMATIC BULK BIN DUMPER WITH UNSTACKER IN BACKGROUND

comparing bulk handling of potatoes from harvester to packing line (Bowman *et al.* 1966) indicated that a bulk dumper truck was more economical and caused no more tuber damage than a hopper body or pallet bins on a flat-bed truck.

THE PACKING LINE

Dumping the Containers

Small picking containers, whether field boxes, baskets, bags or crates, are usually hand dumped onto the packing line. This step varies all the way from slinging the box and contents onto an unpadded roller or chain-conveyor to careful dumping by gradual release through a special container cover into a presoak tank or a padded receiving bin from which the products are conveyed to the washer, sorters and sizer. A vast amount of damage, much of which is not immediately evident, results from careless and poorly supervised dumping. Mechanical box and bin dumpers are commercially available and in use in many of the larger central packinghouses. Through various mechanical devices they tilt or roll the container gradually while at the same time limiting the flow onto the packing line. These devices are not only labor saving but handle the product better than all but the most conscientious laborer.

Careful Handling

Most packing lines are designed for efficiency and volume. Too often volume is attained by operating belts and conveyors at speeds inconsistent with careful product handling. High speeds along side rails or at sharp curves in the system will scuff and abrade even the hardiest product.

Drops from one section of the packing line to another are a common cause of physical damage to the commodity. (See *Disorders, Physical Injury*). Studies on causes of physical damage to tomatoes (McColloch 1962) showed that bruise damage to fruit locules after ripening increased more than four times from a 15 cm (6 in.) drop onto a hard surface, as compared with those not dropped. Even a 15 cm (6 in.) drop onto a 2.5 cm (1 in.) foam rubber almost doubled total injury as compared with no drop. Injury increased with each increment of drop until at a 46 cm (18 in.) drop to a hard surface 91% of the fruit showed locule damage after ripening.

All of the evidence for the handling of commodities from artichokes to zucchini indicates that impacts, wherever they occur, whether on harvester, packing line, or after packing, cause losses during marketing and decrease consumer satisfaction. The only remedy is properly designed handling equipment and constant attention to handling practices.

APPLICATION OF SURFACE COATINGS

Purpose of Coatings

Surface coatings, mostly waxes, are applied to certain vegetables primarily to reduce moisture loss, and thus shrivelling and wilting. The surface luster produced by brushing a waxed surface on such products as tomatoes, peppers and cucumbers improves sales appeal and further justifies the treatment. However, waxing is, at best, a useful adjunct to good handling. It cannot improve the quality of inferior produce.

While the three fruits noted have a natural wax coating over most of their surface, waxing still reduces moisture loss, because it seals off the stem scar or base of the petiole, the main routes for transpiration. Thus, water loss can be cut by about 50%. Similar reductions can be achieved for root crops like turnips and rutabagas. Cantaloups and sweetpotatoes also frequently are waxed.

Surface coatings as such do not generally reduce decay, they may even increase it by trapping spores in lenticels or minute injuries, thus providing a moist chamber. However, waxes containing disinfectants are available. They have some fungistatic properties but have not generally been proven as effective for decay control as a separate treatment with these chemicals.

Additives to Coatings

Sprout inhibitors also may be incorporated into waxes, but unless waxing independently benefits the crop, the material can be applied more cheaply as an aerosol or with water as the carrier.

Addition of dyes to wax, principally to enhance the color of red potatoes, is now prohibited or restricted by law, because the procedure was sometimes used fraudulently to conceal defects. Discoloration of utensils and hands during preparation was another drawback.

Types and Application

Waxes are the most commonly applied surface coatings by far. The formulations are mostly proprietary, but generally contain some combination of carnauba wax, beeswax, or paraffin and emulsifiers.

Waxes are applied by specialized equipment as water emulsions, solutions in solvents, or as foams. Some, particularly the solvent type, are applied at $38°$ C ($100°$ F) or higher. Waxing usually is followed by brushing to achieve a uniform, glossy coating and sometimes by a heated air blast to dry or set the wax.

Emulsions of plastics and pectin gels have been tested, but so far have not been commercially used on vegetables.

Precautions

Excessive applications of wax, although unlikely with modern equipment, may interfere with normal respiration. If CO_2 accumulates or O_2 becomes depleted, injury likely will follow and show up as uneven and delayed ripening in tomatoes, pitting of cucumbers, and increased decay in potatoes.

Leafy vegetables and bunched roots do not lend themselves to waxing because the material does not dry fast enough where leaves or roots touch each other.

STANDARDIZATION AND INSPECTION

Purposes of Standards

Almost all agricultural commodities are now marketed on the basis of official standards established under federal or state law. The role of official standards is particularly important in the case of such perishable commodities as fresh vegetables and melons. Such standards serve many purposes, the more important of which are: (1) They provide the first step in orderly marketing by providing a common language for producers, packers, buyers and consumers. (2) Precise standards are indispensable in the settlement of disputes between buyer and seller. (3) Standardized grades form the basis for prices published in Market News reports, and are necessary for a meaningful comparison of market prices. (4) They enable pooling of products with reimbursement to individual members on an equitable basis. (5) They are necessary as a basis for advertising, which is meaningless unless backed up by uniformly graded and packed products. (6) They provide a basis for financing an industry in which standardized grades are of great importance in establishing value.

Problems Before Standardization

The need for official standards for horticultural crops became apparent with the advent of transcontinental, refrigerated transport. Before this, buying was almost entirely local with the buyer purchasing on personal inspection. As production of vegetables expanded in the western states, the eastern buyer seldom visited the production areas and the grower even less frequently saw his products in the market. Business was conducted by telegraph and telephone and abuses abounded as unscrupulous buyers reimbursed the grower or packer on the basis of a destination count and quality assessment.

Origins of Standardization

Preceding any form of official grades, some growers and receivers took the first steps in standardization by building a personal reputation for a high-quality, honest pack. This practice gradually led to the use of trademarks and brands identified by special labels or stamps.

Government Action. Congressional action in 1912 and 1913 provided the legislation and funds for a real beginning of federal aid to the fruit and vegetable industry in the marketing of their products. Several years of intensive study in the formulation of standards, involving many meetings and conferences with growers, shippers and receivers, finally resulted in the establishment of grades for potatoes in 1917. This was fortunate timing since it coincided with United States entry into World War I and a heavy crop year during which the Federal Reserve Board authorized member banks to accept warehouse receipts as collateral security for loans.

During the same period authority was granted for federal operation of a terminal market inspection service. The Bureau of Markets immediately established inspection offices in 34 of the nation's markets. Several years later (1922) Congress gave the Department of Agriculture authority to conduct inspection services at shipping points. This service was immediately organized on a cooperative Federal-State basis in a number of states. Since 1942 practically all states have been parties to such agreements. With the addition of standards for new commodities each year and additional inspection points and personnel, shipping-point inspections grew from more than 72,000 in 1922 to approximately three-quarters of a million by 1956; by 1967 almost 1½ million carlot equivalents for fresh and processing markets were inspected.

Development of Standards

General   Most U.S. standards for horticultural crops are optional. However, there are mandatory grades for certain exported crops and the Marketing Agreement Act gives authority to restrict shipments of produce by grade, size or maturity, thus making grading and inspection compulsory for certain products in production areas which have adopted marketing agreements and orders.

Probably the most important principle in establishing a set of standards is recognition of definite gradations in quality of the entire supply. In such a development the standards for grades are the most important. However, U.S. standards also include requirements for factors other than grades, such as standards for bunching of certain vegetables, or for product arrangement in the container, uniformity of size, and tightness of pack. The highest grade represents the quality and condition of product most desired by the trade and which commands the highest price. The lower grades represent qualities not so desirable in appearance but which are merchantable and have good food value.

Industry Participation   The requirements of grades in U.S. standards are primarily the responsibility of members of the industry concerned, rather than of the technical employees of U.S. Department of Agriculture. The latter act only as referees during the numerous hearings and discussions in the principal production areas. Receivers are also consulted for ideas, as are vegetable specialists in the research and extension departments of universities and federal agencies. The latter are consulted as to frequency of defects and their causes. After all the points are agreed upon, a proposed grade standard is drawn up, reviewed by members of the technical staff, and often sent to trade representatives and inspection supervisors for suggestions before publication in the *Federal Register*. During the period between publication for rule making and final promulgation of the grade, there is additional opportunity for comments or objections from interested parties.

Language in Standards

There is purposely much uniformity in the wording of grade requirements for different commodities. This enables inspectors and industry people who use the grades to more readily understand the terms. Also, in formulating standards the same order of grade factors is generally used. Terms which must be defined in somewhat general descriptive terms are usually given first. These include color, shape, freshness and firmness. Following this, serious defects, the incidence of which can be given numerically, such as decay, insect damage, freezing injury, etc., are listed. Less serious defects are ordinarliy covered by expressions such as "free from damage" or "free from serious damage," depending on the grade designation used. Since it is not humanly possible to remove all defective specimens as a product moves over the sorting line, tolerances for grade defects are written into the grade standards. These vary from 5 to 10% for minor defects to only 1 or 2% for the more serious defects such as decay or freeze damage. Objective measurements of quality are used in the grade standards for those products and qualities for which such measurements have been developed. An example is the requirement that the juice of cantaloups contain a minimum percentage of soluble solids.

An example of an existing grade standard for a high-volume commodity is included in the Appendix.

MEASUREMENT OF QUALITY

Introduction

Most of the product characteristics which affect grade are determined subjectively by the inspector. He estimates color, shape, firmness and freshness largely by eye and touch. Based on the training and experience that an official inspector has, his judgment on these factors is usually quite accurate.

However, there is a real need for objective measurements of those product characters which affect appearance, sale value, and particularly internal quality.

Research on instrumentation and sensory methods for objective measurement of fruit and vegetable quality has been in progress for many years. Such methods are extremely valuable to the Inspection Service, particularly in those cases where the inspector's judgment is in question. Such instruments also provide the foundation for mechanical or electronic sorting of products on the basis of external or internal color, internal defects, or even physiological maturity.

Texture

Objective measurement of fruit and vegetable texture is critical to many research studies involving response of horticultural crops to post-harvest environments. Such measurements are vital also to relate the commonly used sensory indices of quality to objective tests. A detailed review of instrumental measurements of texture has been published by Szczesniak (1972).

Elasticity   The modulus of elasticity has been proposed (Finney and Norris 1967) to define the firmness of fresh plant tissues. This is influenced by at least three factors: (1) rigidity of cell walls; (2) stiffness of the intercellular bonding agents; (3) turgor pressure within the cells. Because changes in the modulus of elasticity of plant tissues are linearly and directly related to turgor pressure in the cells, it follows that changes in moisture content could influence flesh firmness. Crete *et al.* (1974) have described an objective method for measuring onion firmness. A constant pressure applied between 400 and 3200 g was timed electronically. This provides a direct measure of bulb deformation which relates well to cultivar, treatment effects, and storage environment. The results correlated well with human evaluations.

Pressure Tester A useful instrument for measuring flesh firmness was developed for apples and pears many years ago (Magness and Taylor 1925). It is widely used as a measure of harvest maturity in pears and peaches, and for determining the rate of flesh softening in apples after harvest. Various modifications of this instrument have been tested to measure skin puncture and indentation resistance of many horticultural products.

Shear Press The shear press (Kramer *et al.* 1951) is widely used for determining the toughness or fibrousness of sweet corn, southern peas, green peas, asparagus, and other vegetables. By measuring the force required to shear a measured volume of material in a standard cell, it produces a reproducible figure on texture. A number of attachments are available to adapt the instrument to different commodities. It is now used almost entirely for texture evaluation of processed vegetables or vegetables intended for processing. In common with the pressure and puncture testers, these texture measurements are destructive. This means that repeated readings over an interval of time cannot be made on the same object.

The Instron Universal Testing Instrument allows measurement of shear resistance, compressibility, extensibility (e.g., to measure fiber strength in celery), and deformation under a set load. However, the cost of the instrument makes it principally useful at research laboratories or in quality control sections of processing plants.

Specific Gravity

Specific gravity (the weight of a product in air divided by its weight in water) is widely used as a measurement of quality in potatoes. It is essentially a relationship between weight and volume of an object and, except where air voids, seeds or seed cavities exist in the product, is also a good measure of total solids. Certain cultivars of potatoes, such as Russet Burbank, are rather consistently high in specific gravity, while a few commonly grown cultivars are generally on the low side but are popular with growers for reasons such as high yield, sales appeal, or early maturity. Specific gravity varies with maturity, area of production, and water supply, as well as with cultivar. Buyers of potatoes for manufacture into chips now buy largely on the basis of specific gravity or total solids. Potatoes for baking or French fries also produce better quality products when specific gravity is high.

Plant breeders use specific gravity as an important index of quality in development of new potato varieties. Several methods of determining specific gravity are available, including weighing the tubers in air and water and the hydrometer method of the National Potato Chip Institute.

Specific gravity also provides a means of separating potatoes on a quality basis. The usual way is by flotation in saline solutions of different densities. This method has been recommended for commercial use for selection and premium pricing of consistently fine baking potatoes. However, its use is now limited to a few suppliers of luxury markets.

Studies on the relationship between intercellular space and specific gravity of sweetpotatoes (Kushman *et al.* 1966) during curing and storage showed that weight loss exceeded volume loss because of an increase in intercellular space. Specific gravity decreased in proportion to the weight-volume changes. Decreases in specific gravity were greater in those roots stored at 21° to 27° C (70° to 80° F) with 70% relative humidity than in those stored at 13° to 15° C (55° to 60° F) with 85% RH. Of the five cultivars tested, Centennial roots lost the least weight during curing and Gem roots lost the most.

Composition

Probably the easiest compositional value to measure is the percentage of soluble solids in the juice of the edible part of the product. With a hand refractometer and a small juice press, the percentage of soluble solids can be easily and quickly determined. The usual procedure for melons is to take several plugs from the equator of the melon, squeeze a few drops of juice from a small hand press directly onto the refractometer plate and read the concentration directly in percent soluble solids. Since these are primarily sugars, the reading is essentially for sweetness. An average temperature of the tested melons should be obtained if the instrument does not have built-in temperature compensation. For those not so equipped, the correction factors are given in instruction manuals supplied by the manufacturer.

Soluble solids content has been generally recognized as the best index of eating quality in cantaloups, watermelons, Honey Dews, and other large melons. The U.S. standards for cantaloups recognize this by defining "very good internal quality" as meaning that juice from a random sample of melons must contain not less than 11% soluble solids as determined by an approved hand refractometer. "Good internal quality" indicates a minimum of 9% soluble solids in the juice by the same method. A California study (Davis *et al.* 1964) of muskmelon quality indices showed a multiple regression coefficient of 0.766 between soluble solids content and the external characters of net tightness, background color, shape and firmness. This indicates a good degree of predictability of internal quality on the basis of these four external indices.

On the other hand, studies by Aulenbach and Worthington (1974) indicate that a soluble solids content above 8% was not always associated with sweetness or flavor in muskmelons. Neither was external color consistently related to soluble solids content. They suggest that sensory tests should be a part of any research on muskmelon quality.

Determinations of soluble solids in the flesh of three cultivars of Florida watermelons (Showalter 1975) show significant differences in content between stem, middle and blossom end, and between the heart section and other tissue. The distribution of soluble solids within different tissues varied among the cultivars tested.

Other compositional factors which are used, principally by plant breeders or in research on the effects of postharvest treatments, include pH, total acidity, and ascorbic acid and carotene content. Watada *et al.* (1976A) showed that ascorbic acid in five cultivars of tomatoes was not affected by harvest at the mature-green, breaker or ripe stage. Provitamin A was slightly higher in tomatoes harvested as ripe fruit than in ripe fruit harvested as mature-greens.

External and Internal Color

General   The color of vegetables is a highly significant factor in the salability and commercial value of the product. This may be amount or intensity of color natural to the product or some abnormal and undesirable color produced by disease, sunburn or functional disorder. The undesirable color may be external or internal, and, of course, is much more difficult to detect and quantify when it is internal. Until rather recently all color standards for grade or quality were based on visual estimation of color. This was true of both normal color and that due to defects. The inspector or research worker concerned with color sometimes has a color chart available for matching and definition of color, but his decision must be based on his ability to match product hues and intensities with the chart and to accurately estimate the percentage of the surface involved. Furthermore, figures for internal color or defects must be obtained by the destructive cutting of enough items to get a meaningful average.

Light Reflectance   One of the first efforts toward objective measurement of color involved the use of light reflectance. The measurement of light of known wavelengths reflecting from a product can determine the amount and quality of the color present. Since the normal color of fruit-vegetables, such as the tomato, is often produced by a combination of several pigments, a single wavelength will not provide the absorption necessary for an accurate reading. The tomato colorimeter (Hunter and Yeatman 1961) uses a trichromatic procedure for objective` measurement of raw tomato puree. The instrument uses the source-filter-phototube combinations and optical unit of the color difference meter (Hunter 1958) and readings are based on a formula developed by the U.S. Department of Agriculture which provides numbers for tomato puree colors (Yeatman *et al.* 1960). This instrument is now widely used by tomato processors for establishing the value of individual loads of tomatoes for processing into juice, ketchup, paste, or whole tomatoes. Raw tomato color is critical to value because the colors of the processed products depend upon the colors of the fruit from which they are made.

Objective measurements of the internal color of cut watermelons and the external color of tomatoes and other fruits are made by light reflectance. The principle has now been incorporated into commercial units for the separation of fresh market tomatoes on the basis of the amount of red surface color. The machines do a satisfactory job of color separation but are not widely used at present. Subjective sorting by color on the basis of human judgment is apparently less costly than machine sorting. Plant breeders and research workers concerned with the effects of various cultural practices or postharvest treatments on produce color use color reflectance widely for objective measurement of this quality.

Light Transmittance   The obvious advantage of being able to see through opaque objects has intrigued investigators for many years. The X-ray is one such tool and some research has been devoted to adapting the X-ray instrument to exploring the interior of plant tissues. However, the hazards of irradiation to workers and possible damage to the products being irradiated have restricted commercial use.

The use of transmitted light for nondestructive measurement of color and detection of certain internal defects in fruits and vegetables developed from a spectrophotometric method for detecting blood in intact eggs (Brant *et al.* 1953). An extension of this research led to the development of instrumentation and methods for recording the spectral transmittance curves of several agricultural products. This broader application required a more efficient light-measuring system because fruit and vegetable tissue generally transmits less than 0.1% of the light falling on it. Research at the Instrumentation Research Laboratory of the U.S. Department of Agriculture developed the "Difference Meter" (Birth and Norris 1965) and other special types of transmittance instruments. These are used to determine the internal color of such diverse products as tomatoes, cherries, peaches and apples. It is also practical to measure nondestructively hollow or black heart in potatoes, water core in apples, and other undesirable internal defects in horticultural products. Such instruments are valuable to inspectors for determination of both product maturity and internal defects. Additionally, the principles involved in the instruments have distinct possibilities for incorporation in automatic sorters for internal color or defects. Such equipment is now in pilot instrument form and nearing commercial adaptation.

Worthington (1974) demonstrated that chlorophyll in green tomatoes and carotenoids in ripening tomatoes can be estimated on the basis of light absorbance at a specified basis of light absorbance at specified wavelengths. A later study (Watada *et al.* 1976B) using several light absorbance and reflectance instruments showed that the chlorophyll and lycopene contents in whole tomatoes could be estimated rapidly by nondestructive optical methods when absorbance at wavelenths described earlier was used.

Sensory Evaluation

The rating of food products by organoleptic (taste, smell and touch) methods has received much attention for many years. The complex sensation that results from the interaction of these senses is used to measure food quality for quality control, new product development, evaluation of new cultivars, and to determine the effect of certain treatments on quality.

Some aspects of quality can be measured only by sensory panels. Even those aspects, such as texture, which can often be measured objectively by instrument, must initially depend on sensory evaluation to prove and standardize the objective tests.

People are used as measuring instruments in sensory evaluation. Since people vary widely in their sensory acuity, careful screening is essential for meaningful product evaluation. Much information has been published on sample preparation, selection of panelists, testing conditions, design of experiments, and analysis of data. An excellent source of such information is a publication by the Canada Department of Agriculture (Larmond 1967).

The two principal types of tests made by sensory panels are difference tests and preference tests. The former usually involves a small panel of trained people. They are merely asked to determine whether a difference exists between two or more samples. Individual likes and dislikes must be disregarded and each panelist must be objective. The preference tests are designed to determine preferences of representative populations. They are often conducted with large panels of 100 or more untrained persons. Such tests are sometimes conducted for large companies which wish to market new foods. However, even extensive tests with such products do not assure that the results will apply to the total population.

A detailed study of subjective tests for food texture, including sensory panels, preference-acceptance, discriminatory and descriptive methods is given in the review by Abbott (1972).

SIZING THE PRODUCT

Purpose

Most volume buying of vegetables is done on the basis of grade and size. Buyers for chain or service wholesalers want specified sizes and a uniform size within each container or lot. Size preferences vary with terminal markets and even within areas of one market. Buyers are aware of these preferences and purchase accordingly.

Manual Sizing

Sizing of many vegetables is based on human judgment and is a manual operation. It may be done by sorters who select specific sizes from a belt and place them on special conveyors to be carried to bins for the packers. This method is commonly used for cantaloups and large melons. For the smaller packing operations it may also be used for sweetpotatoes, celery, carrots and leafy vegetables.

Machine Sizing

Mechanical sizers are now commercially available for almost all vegetables and melons. Practically all fresh market tomatoes are mechanically sized, as are most peppers, cucumbers and sweetpotatoes that are packed in central facilities. Sizing by machine may involve only elimination of those units too small or too large for market acceptability, or it may be used to separate a number of sizes for special packs. Potatoes are usually marketed in mixed sizes with only very small and extra large tubers eliminated. However, some fancy packs, particularly for baking, are sized and sold by size.

Equipment for Sizing

Sizing by Weight. Mechanical sizing is done by weight, diameter or length. Excellent machines of many designs are available for each system. Weight sizers are used principally for long cultivars of potatoes, particularly for count packs of baking potatoes for restaurant and institutional trade. However, the equipment is suitable for other products which tend to be elongated, such as cucumbers and sweetpotatoes. Weight sizing, particularly with products of nonuniform shape, relates length to diameter more accurately than sizing based on length or

Courtesy of FMC Corp.

FIG. 3.3. MANUAL SIZING AND PACKING OF HONEY DEW MELONS

smallest diameter. Some weight sizers deliver products to the bins more gently than diameter sizers and for this reason are commonly used by packers of greenhouse tomatoes and cucumbers. A widely used weight sizer (Fig. 3.4) has a "turn and timing" table which aligns tubers or other products before delivering them into the weighing cups. After the tubers are in place, the cups are gently vibrated to ensure centering for accurate weighing. Each potato is weighed as it moves along the sizer assembly. As it reaches its weight area the cup is tripped and the tuber falls onto a side delivery belt for delivery to a packing bin. Each sizing section is adjustable to meet size requirements.

Sizing by Diameter   Diameter sizers are commonly fabric or steel mesh belts with holes for products of certain sizes to drop through. They may have only one size hole, as for the elimination of unsalable small sizes, or they may consist of several sections with the smallest holes in the first section and increasingly larger holes in succeeding sections. A cross belt conveyor under each sizing section carries the product to the packing bins. This type is commonly used for sizing mature-green or pink tomatoes.

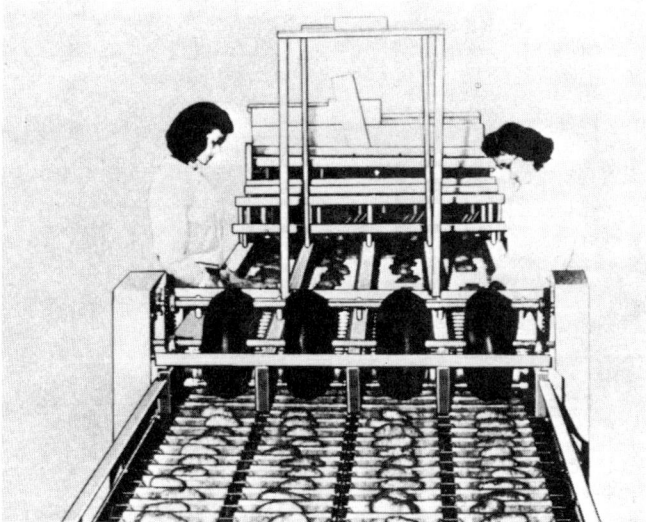

Courtesy of FMC Corp.

FIG. 3.4. WEIGHT SIZER FOR LONG PRODUCTS SUCH AS CUCUMBERS AND RUSSET BURBANK POTATOES
Includes a number of adjustable sizing sections, each removing products of predetermined weight.

Courtesy of American Machinery Corp.

FIG. 3.5.   MOVING CHAIN, DOUBLE BELT POTATO SIZER—INFEED
END
Small and medium sizes fall through and large sizes discharge at end.

Many diameter sizers use rollers, either longitudinal or crosswise, which either decrease in diameter (longitudinal rollers) with increasing distance from the intake end or rotate at increasing distances from each other as the product progresses. Most operate as conveyors as well as sizers with the smaller items dropping first and the larger going through as the distance between rollers increases. The rollers may be in the form of brushes or of solid wood or steel. One type of longitudinal roller operates independently of the conveyor but catches the product as it moves on narrow conveyors and rolls it into the right size receiver. Some of these diameter sizers have cross conveyor belts while others drop the product into chutes which feed directly into the packing bins.

Courtesy of American Machinery Corp.

FIG. 3.6. PUNCHED BELT SIZER FOR TOMATOES—INFEED END
Holes are punched progressively larger to separate fruit into three sizes.

REFERENCES

Preparation

BOWMAN, E. K., YOST, G. E., and GREENE, R. E. L. 1966. Bulk handling spring crop potatoes from harvester to packing line. U.S. Dept. Agr. Mktg. Res. Rept. *761.*

CLAYCOMB, R. S., and HANSEN, J. C. 1957. Potato pitting during washing. Am. Potato J. *34,* 230–234.

DAVIS, R. M., JR., BAKER, G. A., and KASMIRE, R. F. 1964. Muskmelon quality characteristics—their variability and interrelationships. Hilgardia *35,* 479–489.

DEWEY, D. H., and BARGER, W. R. 1948. The occurrence of bacterial soft rot on potatoes resulting from washing in deep vats. Proc. Am. Soc. Hort. Sci. *52,* 325–330.

GRIGG, G. T., and CHASE, R. W. 1967A. Pre-storage washing of potatoes. Am. Potato J. *44,* 232–235.

GRIGG, G. T., and CHASE, R. W. 1967B. The effect of washing potatoes with wash solutions containing chlorine. Am. Potato J. *44,* 425–428.

GULL, D. D. 1960. Artificially curing Florida onions. Proc. Florida State Hort. Soc. *73,* 153–156.

HATTON, T. T., JR., and REEDER, W. F. 1963. Effect of field and packing house handling on bruising of Florida tomatoes. Proc. Florida State Hort. Soc. *76*, 301–304.

HOYLE, B. J. 1948. Onion curing—a comparison of storage losses from artificial, field, and noncured onions. Proc. Am. Soc. Hort. Sci. *52*, 407–415.

HUNTER, D. L., KAFIR, F., and MEYER, C. H. 1958. Apple sorting methods and equipment. U.S. Dept. Agr. Mktg. Res. Rept. *230*.

LUTZ, J. M., RAMSEY, G. B., GLAVES, A. H., and STRAIT, J. 1953. Drying tests with washed late-crop potatoes in the Red River Valley. Am. Potato J. *30*, 179–184.

McCOLLOCH, L.P. 1962. Bruising injury of tomatoes. U.S. Dept. Agr. Mktg. Res. Rept. *513*.

ORR, P. H. 1971. Handling potatoes from storage to packing line—methods and costs. U.S. Dept. Agr. Mktg. Res. Rept. *890*.

ROSBERG, D. W., and JOHNSON, H. B. 1959. Artificial curing of Texas onions. Texas Agr. Expt. Sta. Misc. Publ. *395*.

SEGALL, R. H. 1968. Fungicidal effectiveness of chlorine as influenced by concentration, temperature, pH, and spore exposure time. Phytopathology *58*, 1412–1414.

SEGALL, R. H., and SMOOT, J. J. 1962. Bacterial black spot of radish. Phytopathology *52*, 970–973.

SPANGLER, R. L. 1956. Standardization and inspection of fresh fruits and vegetables. U.S. Dept. Agr. Misc. Publ. *604*.

STOUT, B. A., RIES, S. K., BAKKER-ARKEMA, F. W., and HERRICK, J. F., JR. 1968. Handling tomatoes in pallet boxes. U.S. Dept. Agr. Mktg. Res. Rept. *802*.

TERESHKOVICH, G., and NEWSOM, D. W. 1965. Some effects of date of washing and grading on keeping quality of sweetpotatoes. Proc. Am. Soc. Hort. Sci. *86*, 538–541.

Quality Measurement

ABBOTT, J. A. 1972. Sensory assessment of food texture. Food Technol. *26*, 40–49.

ABBOTT, J. A., and SAN ANTONIO, J. P. 1974. Compartive sensory evaluations of two cultivated mushrooms. J. Food Sci. *39*, 416–417.

AULENBACH, B. B., and WORTHINGTON, J. T. 1973. New portable colorimeter to evaluate external fruit color of tomato and peach. HortScience *8*, 92–94.

AULENBACH, B. B., and WORTHINGTON, J. T. 1974. Sensory evaluation of muskmelons: Is soluble solids content a good quality index? HortScience *9*, 136–137.

BASSETT, M. J. 1973. Relationship between core size, specific gravity, and soluble solids in carrots. HortScience *8*, 139.

BIRTH, G. S. 1960. A nondestructive technique for detecting internal discoloration in potatoes. Am. Pot. J. *37*, 53–60.

BIRTH, G. S., and NORRIS, K. H. 1965. The difference meter for measuring interior quality of foods and pigment in biological tissues. U.S. Dept. Agr. Tech. Bull. *1341.*

BIRTH, G. S., NORRIS, K. H., and YEATMAN, J. N. 1957. Nondestructive measurement of internal color of tomatoes by spectral transmission. Food Technol. *11,* 552–557.

BOURNE, M. C., MOYER, J. C., and HAND, D. B. 1966. Measurement of food texture by a universal testing machine. Food Technol. *20,* 170–174.

BOUWKAMP, J. C., SCOTT, L. E., and HARRIS, W. L. 1972. Rapid determination of "skin-toughness" in sweetpotato. HortScience *7,* 473–474.

BRANT, A. W., NORRIS, K. H., and CHIN, G. 1953. A spectrophotometric method for detecting blood in white shell eggs. Poultry Sci. *32,* 357–363.

CRETE, R., VOISEY, P. W., BERNIER, R., and LARMOND, E. 1974. A new technique for evaluating changes in onion firmness during storage and a comparison with sensory changes. HortScience *9,* 223–225.

DAVIS, R. M., JR., BAKER, G. A., and KASMIRE, R. F. 1964. Muskmelon quality characteristics—their variability and interrelationships. Hilgardia *35,* 479–489.

FINNEY, E. E., JR. 1969A. To define texture in fruits and vegetables. Agr. Eng. *50,* 462–465.

FINNEY, E. E., JR. 1969B. Objective measurements for texture in foods. J. Texture Studies *1,* 19–37.

FINNEY, E. E., JR. 1972. Elementary concepts of rheology relevant to food texture studies. Food Technol. *26,* 68–77.

FINNEY, E. E., JR., and NORRIS, K. H. 1967. Sonic resonant methods for measuring properties associated with texture of Irish and sweet potatoes. Proc. Am. Soc. Hort. Sci. *90,* 275, 282.

GAFFNEY, J. J., and JAHN, O. L. 1970. Photoelectric color sorting of vine-ripened tomatoes. U.S. Dept. Agr. Mktg. Res. Rept. *868.*

HICKS, J. R., HAYSLIP, N.C., and SHOWALTER, R. K. 1975. Consumer preferences in buying pink and red-ripe tomatoes. HortScience *10,* 11–12.

HUNTER, R. S. 1958. Photelectric color difference meter. J. Opt. Soc. Am. *48,* 985–995.

HUNTER, R. S., and YEATMAN, J. N. 1961. Direct-reading tomato colorimeter. J. Opt. Soc. Am. *51,* 552–554.

JAHN, O. L. 1975. Comparison of instrumental methods for measuring ripening changes of intact tomato fruit. J. Am. Soc. Hort. Sci. *100,* 688, 690.

KASMIRE, R. F., PRATT, H. K., and CHACON, F. 1970. Honey Dew melon maturity and ripening guide. Agr. Extn., Univ. Calif., Davis, *MA-26.*

KEE, W. E., and FISHER, V. J. 1976. Evaluation of quality measurement techniques for raw baby lima beans. HortScience *11,* 613–615.

KRAMER, A., BURKHART, G. J., and ROGERS, H. P., JR. 1951. The shear-press: a device for measuring food quality. Canner *112,* No. 5, 34–36, 40.

KUSHMAN, L. J., POPE, D. T., and MONROE, R. J. 1966. Estimation of intercellular space and specific gravity of five varieties of sweetpotatoes. N. Carolina Expt. Sta. Tech. Bull. *175.*

LARMOND, E. 1967. Methods for sensory evaluation of food. Can. Dept. Agr. Publ. *1284.*

MacKEY, A. C., HARD, M. M., and ZAERINGER, M. V. 1973. Measuring textural characteristics of fresh fruit and vegetables—apples, carrots, cantaloupes. Oregon Agr. Expt. Sta. Tech. Bull. *123.*

MAGNESS, J. R., and TAYLOR, G. F. 1925. An improved type of pressure tester for the determination of fruit maturity. U.S. Dept. Agr. Circ. *350.*

POWERS, J. B., GUNN, J. T., and JACOB, F. C. 1953. Electronic color sorting of fruits and vegetables. Agr. Eng. *34,* 149–154.

SHOWALTER, R. K. 1960. Watermelon color as affected by maturity and storage. Proc. Florida State Hort. Soc. *73,* 289–293.

SHOWALTER, R. K. 1975. Sampling watermelons for soluble solids. Florida State Hort. Soc. *88,* 272–276.

SZCZESNIAK, A. S. 1972. Instrumental methods of texture measurement. Food Technol. *26,* 50–56, 63.

VOISEY, P. W., KLOEK, M., and MacDONALD, D. C. 1964. A rapid method of determining the mechanical properties of fruits and vegetables. Proc. Am. Soc. Hort. Sci. *85,* 547–553.

VOISEY, P.W., and MacDONALD, D. C. 1964. An instrument for measuring the puncture resistance of fruits and vegetables. Proc. Am. Soc. Hort Sci. *84,* 557–563.

WATADA, A. E., AULENBACH, B. B., and WORTHINGTON, J. T. 1976A. Vitamins A and C in ripe tomatoes as affected by stage of ripeness at harvest and by supplementary ethylene. J. Food Sci. *41,* 856–858.

WATADA, A. E., NORRIS, K. H., WORTHINGTON, J. T., and MASSIE, D. R. 1976B. Estimation of chlorophyll and carotenoid contents of whole tomato by light absorbance techniques. J. Food Sci. *41,* 329–332.

WITZ, R. L. 1954. Measuring resistance of potatoes to bruising. Agr. Eng. *35,* 241–244.

WORTHINGTON, J. T. 1974. A light transmittance technique for determining tomato ripening rate and quality. Acta Hort. No. 38, Vol. *1,* 198–215.

YEATMAN, J. N., SIDWELL, A. P., and NORRIS, K. H. 1960. Derivation of a new formula for computing raw tomato juice color from objective color measurement. Food Technol. *14,* 16–20.

Surface Coatings

BEN-YEHOSHUA, S. 1967. Some physiological effects of various skin coatings on orange fruit. Israel J. Agr. Res. *17,* 17–27.

EMMERT, F. H., and SOUTHWICK, F. W. 1954. The effect of maturity, apple emanations, waxing, and growth regulators on the respiration and red color development of tomato fruits. Proc. Am. Soc. Hort. Sci. *63,* 393–401.

FINDLEN, H., HARDENBURG, R. E., and HRUSCHKA, H. W. 1956. Effect of waxing on weight loss, decay and appearance of potatoes. Proc. 7th Natl. Potato Utiliz. Conf. 29–36.

FRANKLIN, E. W. 1967. The waxing of turnips for the retail market. Can. Dept. Agr. Publ. *1120.*

HABEEBUNNISA, PUSHPA, M. C., and SRIVASTAVA, H. C. 1963. Studies on the effect of protective coating on the refrigerated and common storage of bell peppers (*Capsicum frutescense*). Food Sci. (Mysore) *12,* 192–196.

HALL, E. G., and TROUT, S. A. 1944. Some effects of waxing on weight loss from oranges and certain vegetables. J. Australian Inst. Agr. Sci. *10,* 80–82.

HARDENBURG, R. E. 1967. Wax and related coatings for horticultural products. A Bibliography. U.S. Dept. Agr. *ARS 51–15.*

HARDENBURG, R. E., FINDLEN, H., and HRUSCHKA, H. W. 1959. Waxing potatoes—its effect on weight loss, shrivelling, decay and appearance. Am. Potato J. *36,* 434–443.

HARTMAN, J. D., and ISENBERG, F. M. (undated) Waxing vegetables. Cornell Ext. Bull. *965.*

HOWARD, F. D., YAMAGUCHI, M., and TIMM, H. 1957. Effect of illumination and waxing on the chlorophyll development in scrubbed White Rose potato tubers. Am. Potato J. *34,* 324–329.

MACK, W. B., and JANER, J. R. 1942. Effects of waxing on certain physiological processes of cucumbers under different storage conditions. Food Res. *7,* 38–47.

PLATENIUS, H. 1939. Wax emulsions for vegetables. Cornell Univ. Agr. Expt. Sta. Bull. *723.*

4

Shipping Containers

GENERAL

A shipping container is primarily a handling unit to facilitate moving material from one location to another. It also provides some physical protection for the commodity, but such protection varies widely with the type of container. Burlap, mesh, or paper bags provide little protection from impact or pressure, whereas nailed wooden boxes or wirebound boxes with reinforced ends have sufficient rigidity to provide some protection from impacts and, unless packed with excessive bulges, can stack to any practical height without exerting harmful pressure on the product. Fiberboard boxes fall somewhere between bags and wooden boxes for product protection.

STANDARDS

A few states have established container standards through legislation. These regulations specify what types and sizes of containers can be used for specific vegetables. In some cases they also require approved containers for interstate shipment of produce, thereby prohibiting the movement of bulk produce. Other states do not have container specifications but do require that produce be shipped in containers recognized by the produce industry, and that such containers be marked to indicate the kind of produce, net weight, count, or volumetric measurement. Most states also require that the name and address of the grower or shipper be plainly marked on the shipping container.

The sizes, shapes, construction, and material of shipping containers are controlled principally by the railroads. These container tariffs are developed and enforced by the Transcontinental Freight Bureau of the Association of American Railroads. The published tariffs are complete with pictures, specifications, and sizes of approved shipping containers.

The tariffs not only specify what commodities may be packed in each container, but also how the containers are to be loaded in the rail car. There are procedures for obtaining experimental permits for new containers and for obtaining approval for the new container if it performs satisfactorily under the specified test conditions. Periodic checks of packed container weights are made by the same organization to determine if there is overpacking or serious deviation from the billing weights specified in the tariffs.

The vast proliferation of container sizes has become a major concern of trade associations, transportation companies and produce exporters. Increased interest in and use of palletization for handling and transport of fruits and vegetables has emphasized the need for containers which will achieve maximum utilization of the standard 120 × 100 cm (47.5 × 39.5 in.) pallet. A survey of produce shipping containers in 1965–1966 (Stokes and Woodley 1974) showed 547 types and sizes for 49 commodities. Of these, 371 differed in dimension. Based on outside dimensions many of the containers do not fit well on the standard pallet.

Obucina (1976) states that industry adoption of four standard containers is a "must" for the produce industry. Each of these must utilize 90% of the space when stacked on the standard pallet. Stokes (1976) urged the industry to standardize on a few containers designed to fit the internationally accepted 120 × 100 cm pallet.

The Organization for Economic Co-operation and Development (OECD) has published recommendations for international standardization of fruit and vegetable containers. The following four sizes are suggested: 40 × 30 cm (15¾ × 11¾ in.); 50 × 30 cm (19¾ × 11¾ in.); 50 × 40 cm (19¾ × 15¾ in.); and 60 × 40 cm (20¾ × 15¾ in.). Stokes and Woodley (1974) stress that limiting produce containers in this way would have added benefits of economies in manufacture, lower investment by the produce packer, more efficient packinghouse labor and greater utilization of space in storage and transport.

TYPES OF CONTAINERS

Needs and Uses

Shipping containers now vary widely within the regulations specified by the railroads, the several states, and the industry organizations. Sometimes economy or custom overrides the protective needs of the commodity.

Widely used shipping containers include burlap, cotton or plastic mesh, and ventilated plastic film bags; fiberboard boxes of full telescope (2-piece with top completely covering bottom piece when closed), partial telescope (top partially covering bottom piece), or flap-top types (1-piece); wirebound boxes of wood veneer or combinations of veneer and fiberboard; sawn and nailed wooden boxes; and more recently molded plastic or plastic foam boxes with plastic or fiberboard lids or with a wrap-around plastic shrink film cover. Details on types and capacities of shipping containers for vegetables are included in the Appendix.

Mesh Bags and Wirebound Crates

Vegetables which are usually top-iced for shipment are often packed in 23 kg (50 lb) capacity mesh bags. Cabbage and sweet corn are well adapted to such a container and, if precooled and stacked to allow good contact with crushed ice in the loaded vehicle, satisfactory temperatures can be maintained. Wirebound containers are also suitable for

Courtesy of Package Research Laboratory

FIG. 4.1. WIREBOUND VENEER CRATE, AS SHIPPING CONTAINER FOR CELERY

top-iced shipments. The substantial spaces between veneer slats allow good penetration of ice and water. Wirebounds are commonly used for sweet corn and cabbage. In addition, topped carrots in film bags, celery, globe artichokes, broccoli, cauliflower, bell peppers, cucumbers, eggplant, spinach and cantaloups are packed in wirebound crates. These are shipped with or without top ice, depending upon the requirements of the commodity.

Fiberboard Boxes and Paper Bags

Fiberboard boxes and multiwall paper bags are used most frequently for those commodities which have been precooled before packing or which require minimum refrigeration. Practically all commercial head lettuce is now field-packed in fiberboard boxes and vacuum cooled before loading. Hydrocooled carrots in consumer packages often move to market in ventilated boxes or multiwall paper bags. Many other hydrocooled or consumer-packaged vegetables now go to market in corrugated boxes, as well as substantial quantities of mature-green tomatoes, fresh market potatoes, and melons.

A well-known shortcoming of the conventional fiberboard box is its tendency to absorb moisture and lose strength as the moisture content increases. This prevents its use for commodities which are hydrocooled after packing. It also limits the height to which loaded containers can be stacked, particularly in areas where the relative humidity is high. Various methods are used to provide extra strength in corrugated boxes.

FIG. 4.2.   FULL TELESCOPE BOX WITH FIBERBOARD DIVIDERS FOR LARGE MELONS

Courtesy of American Forest Products Corp.

FIG. 4.3.   FIBERBOARD CONTAINER IN GENERAL USE FOR HEAD LETTUCE

These include extra fiberboard liners, cells, dividers, etc., as well as full telescope construction which provides two outer walls. Under low humidity conditions good stacking strength is provided by these innovations. A more recent development involves treatment of the fiberboard, either before or after manufacture, with waxes, oils or resins to provide moisture resistance. Depending on the material used and the method of application, such treatments can produce some reduction in moisture absorption for increased stacking strength or almost completely water-proof containers to withstand hydrocooling and even top-icing. Commodities, such as consumer-bagged carrots, must be thoroughly pre-cooled before packing when shipped in conventional boxes or multiwall paper bags. Since these containers cannot be top-iced, field heat must be removed before loading for transport.

Nailed Wood Boxes

Nailed wood boxes are constructed primarily of sawn lumber although the bottoms and lids are usually prefabricated from wood veneer with cleats to allow for slight top and bottom bulge. The principal merit of nailed wood boxes is rigidity. They have excellent stacking strength, maintain shape under moist conditions, and can be spaced in the transport vehicle with nailed wood strips. They are shipped from the mills as box shook and are quickly assembled on power nailing machines. For

Courtesy of International Paper Co.

FIG. 4.4.   CORRUGATED CONTAINER FOR CANTALOUP SHIPMENT
Listed as half-crate because it holds half the number of melons as the "Jumbo" wood crate.

many years nailed wood boxes, bushel baskets, and veneer hampers were the accepted shipping containers for most fresh fruits and vegetables. A substantial quantity of tomatoes, melons, celery, and other commodities continue to go to market in nailed wood boxes, but the trend for many products has been to fiberboard, veneer and plastic as container materials.

Plastic Containers

The most recent development in shipping containers is the molded sheet or foam plastic. These generally have and maintain good weight carrying strength for stacking but have a tendency to be brittle, particularly the foam plastic, which shatters quite readily when dropped or handled roughly. One advantage of the molded foam containers is that the user can manufacture the containers as needed, once equipped with the proper molds and foam mixer. A large investment is involved in equipment and materials for molded boxes, but the packer who uses large quantities of containers can probably justify the investment if the

Courtesy of American Forest Products Corp.

FIG. 4.5. NAILED WOOD TOMATO LUG FOR FANCY PLACE-PACKED TOMATOES

containers meet his needs. However, material disposal problems may develop as use of this container increases.

An innovation developed by a western celery packer adds strength, particularly against shatter or cracking, to the molded foam plastic container. After packing, usually in the field, the celery is hydrocooled in the molded, bottom-drain containers. After cooling, a plastic film sleeve is slipped over each container and the packed sleeved containers are conveyed through a short heat tunnel which shrinks the film tightly around the box. This serves the dual purpose of providing a moisture barrier while at the same time adding strength to the box.

Containers for Specific Crops

Potatoes Each type and design of container has its place in the movement of vegetables and melons from place of production to market. Until rather recently almost all potatoes were shipped to market in burlap bags holding 46 kg (100 lb) net. The present trend is to smaller containers which can be more easily handled during loading, unloading, and at the terminal markets. Bags holding 23 kg (50 lb) are increasingly used for shipment, and fiberboard boxes containing 23 kg (50 lb) net are popular, particularly for the fancier packs of sized potatoes.

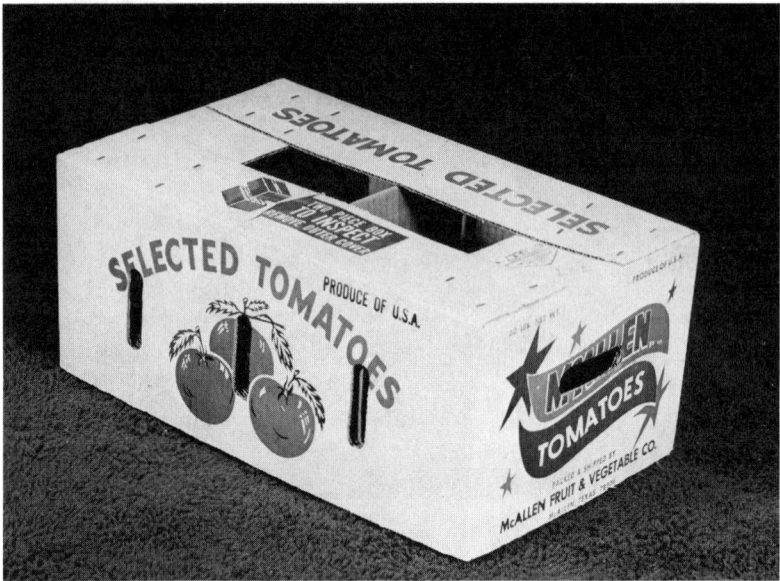

Courtesy of International Paper Co.

FIG. 4.6.   CORRUGATED CONTAINER FOR TOMATO SHIPMENT
For 13.6 kg (30 lb) net weight.

Tomatoes   Until the mid 1950s practically all mature-green tomatoes were shipped to market in nailed wood boxes called Los Angeles
lugs. Most of the fruits in these packs were individually wrapped in
tissue paper. Because of increasing labor costs, the wrap-pack has
largely disappeared for mature-green fruit. Shipments from the major
producing districts are now mostly jumble-packed in 27.5 kg (60 lb)
wirebound crates, 18.5 kg (40 lb) fiberboard boxes, or Los Angeles lugs.
Size designations in the jumble-pack remain largely those used in the
L. A. lug place pack. Since these refer to row counts in the lug as 5×5, 6
$\times$ 6, etc., they have no meaning in a jumble pack except to those in the
tomato industry.

One factor in the increasing use of the 18.5 kg (40 lb) corrugated box
for mature-green tomatoes is the dual-purpose role it fills as a shipping
container and as a container for the repacker to use in distributing
consumer packs to the retail store.

The so-called "vine-ripe" or pink tomatoes are mostly packed in nailed
wood flats or lugs with medium and large fruits packed in two layers,
and the smaller fruits in three layers. Hothouse tomatoes are largely
packed in wood or fiberboard flats or in veneer or fiberboard baskets.

MASTER CONTAINERS

Consumer-size quantities of vegetables are increasingly packaged at origin for direct movement to retail food outlets. Such consumer packages may be ventilated plastic or mesh bags as commonly used for potatoes, onions, carrots and others; individual wraps of plastic film as used for cauliflower, head lettuce and celery; or over-wrapped paper or plastic trays as sometimes used for bell peppers, cucumbers, sweetpotatoes and salad mixes. Shipment of these relatively small packages generally makes the use of a master container essential. Consumer bags of potatoes in 4.5 and 11.5 kg (10 and 25 lb) sizes are often shipped to market as individual units, but when 1.5 or 2.2 kg (3 or 5 lb) units are packed the labor required to handle these units would be prohibitive.

Master containers are usually corrugated boxes or multiwall paper bags, although wirebound boxes are commonly used for consumer packs of topped carrots. Master containers for trimmed and overwrapped cauliflower are one- or two-layer boxes with or without partial or complete dividers between heads. A California study on cauliflower shipment (Gin and Hale 1960) showed that fully trimmed, overwrapped cauliflower in one-layer fiberboard boxes arrived at market with less bruising and discoloration than untrimmed cauliflower in the conventional crate or trimmed cauliflower in wooden boxes. When head lettuce is shrink-film-wrapped at origin it may be packed in the regular carton or in a smaller carton designed for the shrink-wrapped heads. These are more compact than the nonwrapped heads, because the wrapper leaves have been removed.

Small consumer bags of potatoes and onions are generally packed for shipment in multiwall paper bags, with packed net weights of about 23 kg (50 lb). Overwrapped trays of vegetables such as peppers, cucumbers and sweetpotatoes are usually packed in boxes. Sometimes fiberboard dividers are used between layers of trays to reduce chafing or pressure bruising.

FILLING THE CONTAINERS

Type of Pack

The method of packing vegetables in shipping containers varies from manual place-packing, with each unit separately wrapped, to jumble-pack fill, either manually or by machine. Between these two extremes there is "face and fill," placement in preformed trays, and place-pack

From Hallee and Sides (1976)

FIG. 4.7. PALLETIZED MASTER CONTAINERS FOR
SHIPMENT OF POTATOES IN CONSUMER PACKS
Each 122 × 102 cm (48 × 40 in.) pallet holds four corrugated
bins, each with a net capacity of 182 kg (400 lb). The loaded
bins are also suitable for retail display.

without individual wraps. Another variant is a multi-layer place-pack
or tray-pack with only the top layer units individually wrapped. The
place-pack with each unit wrapped has largely disappeared from the
trade because of the high cost of the skilled labor required. Preformed
trays of molded pulp or plastic reduce labor requirements greatly for
place-packs and are now sometimes used for fancy packs of "vine-ripe"
tomatoes.

Modified Place-pack Face and fill is accomplished by place-
packing the top layer, either in a separate tray or form or by packing the
box upside down so that the layer packed in the bottom of the box
becomes the top layer when the box is righted. After the face is placed,
by whatever method, the remainder of the pack is jumbled in either to a
fixed count or net weight. If the product is presized, a count pack is often
used, but if the product is of mixed sizes, it is packed to weight or volume.

Jumble-pack A jumble-pack is exactly what the term implies. The
product is poured into a container from a diverter on the conveyor or
through a special side chute from the conveyor. When mechanically

FIG. 4.8. AUTOMATIC CONTAINER FILLER FOR JUMBLE PACKING
VEGETABLES
Box is automatically advanced by conveyor when predetermined weight
is reached.

filled, as is commonly practiced now, the box usually rests on a vibrating
platform which gently shakes the box and contents as the container is
filled. The box may be filled to count by a mechanical counter on the
filling unit or it may be filled to weight or volume. When weight is used a
scale is included either in the box filler or holder. When the predetermined weight is reached the flow of fruit is stopped. Volume fill, as to a
bushel or some other accepted volume measurement, usually requires an
operator to determine the right degree of fill for the vibrated container.

CLOSING THE CONTAINERS

Mechanical closing units are now available for all types of shipping
containers. Some are completely automatic, such as the case sealer for
flap-top cartons which conveys the filled cartons through a gluer, flap

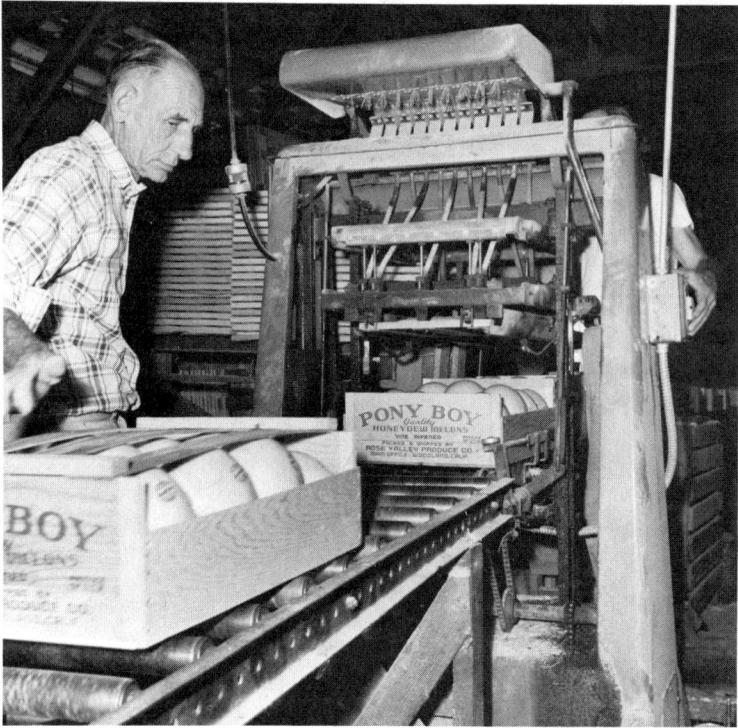

Courtesy of American Forest Products Corp.

FIG. 4.9.   NAILED WOOD HONEY DEW CRATES AND LIDDING MACHINE

closer and sealer. Semi-automatic machines nail lids on wood boxes and close the wire loops on wirebound boxes. Only the smaller packing-houses close cartons with hand staplers or stitchers, and few wood or wirebound boxes are now hand nailed or closed.

BULK CONTAINERS

Most shipments of vegetables move to market in bags, boxes, crates or cartons, but a small proportion are now transported in larger units such as pallet bins or even bulk trucks or rail cars. These large units are actually shipping containers since they contain the product during shipment from origin to destination.

Bulk containers serve processors and repackers for delivering prod-ucts which do not require small containers. These units reduce cost by eliminating the need for small shipping containers. The large units also provide great potential for completely mechanized loading and unloading which can greatly reduce labor costs.

Bulk shipment is now used principally for potatoes. Terminal repackers, who pack and distribute consumer packages to retailers, are interested in receiving onions and perhaps carrots in bulk. A few bulk shipments of onions have been successfully made and carrots in 1 lb bags were hauled in bulk from California to New York City.

Pallet bins lend themselves well to mechanized loading and unloading, but net load weight is usually reduced as compared with conventional shipping containers, because of the space occupied by the bins and pallets and the difficulty of fitting bins into the exact space available in a truck or rail car. Where per-car transportation rates prevail, less net weight per car increases unit costs. This, together with the problem of returning empty bins to shipping point, is delaying use of this method of bulk shipment.

Besides trucks or trailers for transport of bulk produced, there are several types of rail cars which have been modified or built for bulk movement of potatoes. This equipment is discussed in the section covering transportation equipment and services.

REFERENCES

ANON. 1967. Recommendations on the international standardization of packaging for fruits and vegetables. Organization for Economic Co-operation and Development, OECD Bureau of Publications, Paris.

BLACK, W. R., and BREAKIRON, P. L. 1961. New shipping containers for cantaloups. U.S. Dept. Agr. Mktg. Res. Rept. *459*.

ENGER, M. R., MYERS, K., BREAKIRON, P. L., and BARGER, W. R. 1958. Efficiency and potential economies of dual-purpose shipping containers for mature-green tomatoes. U.S. Dept. Agr. Mktg. Res. Rept. *257*.

GINN, J. L., and HALE, P. W. 1960. Packaging California cauliflower. U.S. Dept. Agr. Mktg. Res. Rept. *414*.

HALLEE, N. D., and SIDES, S. E. 1976. Retail shipping-display unit for Maine potatoes. Am. Soc. Agr. Eng. Paper *76-6508*. Dec. meeting, Chicago.

MASTERS, B. M., WINTER, J. C., and ROSANOFF, B. P. 1955. Potential savings by shipping cauliflower in double-layer packs. U.S. Dept. Agr. Mktg. Res. Rept. *78*.

MORRISON, W. W. 1962A. Preparing fresh tomatoes for market. U.S. Dept. Agr. Mktg. Bull. *19*.

MORRISON, W. W. 1962B. Fresh cabbage from grower to retailer. U.S. Dept. Agr. Mktg. Bull. *21*.

OBUCINA, J. D. 1976. Standardization a "must." *In* United Fresh Fruit and Vegetable Association Yearbook. pp 87–88. United Fresh Fruit and Vegetable Assoc., Washington, D.C.

PAWSKI, L., and FINDLEN, H. 1961. Handling and shipping potatoes to processing plants in pallet boxes and burlap bags. U.S. Dept. Agr. Mktg. Res. Rept. *495.*

STOKES, D. R. 1976. Palletization-unitization for fresh fruits and vegetables. *In* United Fresh Fruit and Vegetable Association Yearbook. pp. 145–160. United Fresh Fruit and Vegetable Assoc., Washington, D.C.

STOKES, D. R., and WOODLEY, G. W. 1974. Standardization of shipping containers for fresh fruits and vegetables. U.S. Dept. Agr. Mktg. Res. Rept. *991.*

THUERK, E. D., and OBUCINA, J. D. 1973. Unitization for industry: Challenge and solutions. *In* United Fresh Fruit and Vegetable Association Yearbook. pp. 123–124. United Fresh Fruit and Vegetable Assoc., Washington, D.C.

5

Consumer Packages

Packaging in "consumer size" units before final sale in the retail store is not of recent origin, as witness the millions of cans and bottles of preserved foods that have been used for generations. Even the packaging of fresh produce is not new, for most fresh fruits and vegetables have been packaged in some fashion, usually at the checkout counter, before the customer carried them home. However, prepackaging of fresh produce, which infers a "consumer size" package prepared prior to final sale, dates back only to the mid 1940's.

WHERE TO PACKAGE

Prepacking may be and is done by the original packer at point of production; by a repacker at a destination distribution area; by a chain store warehouse to serve a group of its own stores; or in the back room of a retail store. Countless words have been spoken and written as to where prepackaging should be done. The problem has no real resolution. Each commodity has a different degree of perishability, and shippers, receivers, and retailers, each of which has unique facility and economic considerations.

Packaging at Shipping Point

The case for prepackaging at shipping point has generally been made on the basis of: (1) the greater availability and lower cost of labor in production areas as compared with the urban areas where most of the large repackers and wholesalers are located; and (2) reduced shipping weight as a result of trimming unsalable parts of the product before shipment. However, the availability of equipment for automated weighing or counting and for container filling, overwrapping, and sealing reduces the validity of labor cost differences.

Savings in freight costs are substantial with such items as topped carrots and radishes, trimmed cauliflower, and husked sweet corn. A study with trimmed versus untrimmed cauliflower (Ginn and Hale 1960) showed a reduction in weight of 70% in full-trimmed cauliflower for overwrapping as compared with untrimmed heads as shipped for many years in bulk crates. Similar, but somewhat smaller, savings in transportation costs are attained through removal of carrot and radish tops or trimming inedible butts from fresh asparagus before packaging.

Added protection to the product may sometimes justify prepackaging at origin. Some types of small packages, such as overwrapped trays or cardboard boxes, provide better protection against physical damage than bulk packs in conventional shipping containers. However, the type of master container used for these prepacks will determine how much protection is provided. Master containers which contain separate support dividers between layers of packages usually provide excellent protection. Bags as prepacks do not usually provide added protection against physical damage to the contents and, unless very carefully packed into master containers, may increase damage as compared with regular jumble packs. Overwraps or sleeves for such items as head lettuce, cauliflower, celery, and asparagus give some protection from such physical damage as scuffing and loosening of leaves or buds.

Courtesy of Butler County Mushroom Farm, Inc.
FIG. 5.1. PREPACKAGED PENNSYLVANIA
MUSHROOMS BEING DISPLAYED IN RETAIL STORE
Also note tray-packed, overwrapped tomato and bell peppers.

Protection from excessive moisture loss is sometimes added justification for prepackaging at shipping point. Vegetables such as snap beans, asparagus, topped radishes, and carrots lose water readily when exposed to dry air. Packaging of such items in ventilated plastic film bags or tightly overwrapped, but vented, trays as soon as possible after harvest reduces the chance of shriveling or wilting.

Packaging at the Market

Many metropolitan areas have firms which specialize in prepackaging fresh fruits and vegetables for distribution to retail outlets in the market area. They receive products such as potatoes and onions in conventional shipping containers or in bulk and tomatoes in cartons or crates. With specialized and highly automated equipment these repackers may handle practically all produce items sold in the average food market or they may specialize in a few items which require minimum refrigeration, such as potatoes and onions.

The principal advantages of terminal prepackaging are: (1) efficiencies possible through high-volume operation with automated or semiautomated equipment; (2) freshness of the pack with little chance of deterioration or decay occurring during retail display and sale; (3) knowledge of the market with flexibility of supply possible to meet the requirements of the market; and (4) the opportunity for advertising and promotion of items in abundant supply.

The principal advantage of terminal prepackaging is also the greatest risk of origin prepacking: the chance that deterioration in the form of decay or breakdown will occur during the transportation and distribution period from point of production to the retail store. If one unit in a bag of potatoes or a tray of globe antichokes has seriously deteriorated, the whole lot may have to be repacked at substantial cost. The other alternative is unhappy customers and loss of confidence in the store and in prepackaging in general.

In the early days of prepackaging vegetables, much of the trimming and packaging was done in the back room of the grocery store. This practice has largely been abandoned due to excessive labor costs and space requirements. These stores now obtain prepacks through the original shipper or from a commercial prepacker in the market area.

INCENTIVES FOR PREPACKAGING

The principal incentives for the food retailer to display and sell prepackaged vegetables are: (1) the saving of checkout labor and time in preweighed and price-marked produce as compared with bulk; (2) the reduction in wastage from customer handling and selection of individual items from bulk displays; and (3) the essential elimination of litigation or customer dissatisfaction from loose produce on the floor with the hazard of slips or falls by shoppers.

Most of the labor cost in a modern self-service chain store or supermarket is for the workers who check out purchased items and receive payment from the store's customers. Prepackaged and prepriced produce speed checkout greatly as compared with the counting or weighing involved for each kind of produce when shoppers obtain their needs from bulk displays. While some large food chains, particularly in the Northeast, have converted their produce department entirely to prepackaged items, several studies by industry groups have shown clearly that produce sales are greatest in a given store when most of the commonly used items are displayed both in bulk and prepackaged. Some shoppers insist upon selecting the units they want from bulk displays while others like the convenience and sanitary features of prepacked vegetables.

PACKAGING MATERIALS

Plastic Films

The initial phases of prepackaging development for vegetables revolved largely around the use of cellulose acetate and several types of coated cellophanes. These were used as sealed bags or as sealed wrappers on small cartons or trays. The hope for these films was that they would provide good protection against moisture loss but have sufficient permeability to allow normal exchange of carbon dioxide and oxygen in the respiratory process.

As more sophisticated types and combinations of films were developed, much research was devoted to relating film permeability (Table 5.1) to commodity tolerances in the belief that modified atmospheres could be maintained in these small packages which would be beneficial to the market life of the commodity. However, the lack of complete uniformity within films of the same composition and gauge; the impossibility of controlling respiratory activity in the packed produce by maintenance of uniform temperatures; and the difficulty, under commercial operating conditions, of obtaining perfect seals on the packages has largely discouraged this approach to prepackaging.

Plastic films now available for packaging include cellulose acetate,

TABLE 5.1. CHARACTERISTICS OF CERTAIN FILMS USED FOR PRODUCE PACKAGING

Type of Film	Sealing Temperature[1] °C	°F	Permeability to[1] H₂O	CO₂	O₂	Remarks
Acetate	—	—	high	low	low	window cartons; tomato overwraps
Polyethylene, low density	149–260	(300-500)	very low	low	low	bags, liners
Polyethylene, oriented	121–193	(250-380)	very low	high	high	overwraps
Polystyrene, oriented	149–193	(300-380)	high	high	high	stiff, crisp
Polyvinyl chloride			low	interm	low	soft, clinging
Polyvinyl chloride, oriented	143–226	(290-440)	high	low	low	soft
Polypropylene, oriented	160–166	(320-330)	low	low	low	not shrunk for produce

Source: Adapted from Anon. (1965) and Scott (1966).
[1]There are large variations between and within brands.

rubber hydrochloride, polyester, oriented polystyrene, vinylidene chloride, irradiated polyethylene, nylon, vinyl, and polypropylene. These vary widely enough in characteristics so that almost any packaging need can be met. With volume production of these films, some are now the least expensive packaging materials made.

Other packaging materials used by prepackers include: trays of molded pulp, plastic or cardboard; hallocks or cups of veneer, plastic, or cardboard; and small cardboard boxes with windows of transparent material. Some of these containers are overwrapped with shrink film, others, particularly waxed paper cups for Brussels sprouts, have only film covers which are secured with rubber bands.

APPEARANCE OF PACKAGES

The interest of the consumer in prepackaged vegetables is not always the same as that of the prepackager or the retailer. The consumer wants assurance that the packaged produce is as good and as uniform in quality as one could obtain by selection from bulk displays. Consumers prefer a package which permits all items to be seen clearly. They like to

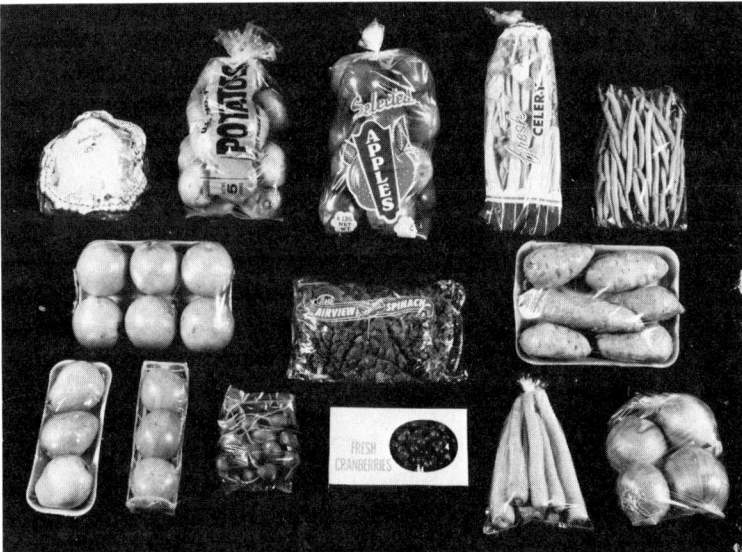

U.S. Dept. of Agriculture Photo

FIG. 5.2. THE DIVERSITY OF CONSUMER PACKAGES USED FOR FRESH PRODUCE

CONSUMER PACKAGES   107

have information on the package as to grade, net weight, or number of units contained. Unfortunately these conditions are not always met. Too often the shopper finds off-grade or unwanted-size items in the package when it is opened at home. When this happens all prepackaged items become suspect and the program loses ground.

The use of colored plastic films, which enhance the color of the packaged product, is deceptive. Some state laws now prohibit the use of orange-colored film for carrot bags, tan film for russet potatoes, red film for red potatoes and similar practices. However, the practice prevails in many states which do not specifically prohibit it.

The prepackager who is interested in building and maintaining a business must conscientiously supply the following services: (1) consistent good quality; (2) factual labelling and honest weighing; (3) maximum visibility from all angles of view; (4) aesthetically pleasing packages devoid of deceptive materials; and (5) some simple cooking instructions or basic recipes for items not widely used, such as globe artichokes or Brussels sprouts.

SHRINK-FILM PACKAGING

Certain plastic films, such as polyethylene, polystyrene, polyvinyl chloride, polyester, and rubber hydrochloride, can have heatshrink characteristics built into them during manufacture. This is accomplished by stretching the films under controlled temperature and tension to create molecular orientation and then locking the film in this stretched condition by cooling.

These films, when used as overwraps on trimmed lettuce, cabbage, or celery, or as sleeves or overwraps over consumer-size tray- or carton-packs, shrink when exposed to moderate heat and make a very tight package. Products packaged in this way are immobilized with the result that damage from rubbing or chafing during normal handling is reduced. Heat for shrinking the films after overwrapping is usually applied in a short tunnel which contains electric resistance coils as a heat source. A properly designed tunnel will supply just enough heat to shrink the film but not enough to harm the packaged product.

VENTILATION OF PACKAGES

Fresh vegetables and melons are composed of living tissue and must be kept alive to be marketable. In order to live, this tissue must have oxygen and in this process, called respiration, it gives off carbon dioxide and heat which must be removed (see section on respiration). Thus a package must provide for some gas and heat exchange.

Many of the plastic films used for prepackaging vegetables are rather impermeable to gases, so some ventilation must be provided. A few small openings will provide adequate carbon dioxide and oxygen exchange in a film of limited permeability so the decision for amount of ventilation must be based on the amount of moisture retention desired. Studies conducted by Hardenburg (1954A) showed that two 6.5 mm (¼ in.) holes in a sealed film bag holding 340 g (12 oz) of green beans or 285 g (10 oz) of spinach permitted maintenance of essentially normal atmospheres in these high respiration products at 21° C (70° F) (Table 5.2). This limited amount of ventilation would maintain very high RH within the package because of limited movement of moisture vapor from within. High RH is desirable for most of the green or leafy vegetables to prevent wilting, but it is not desirable for potatoes, dry onions and sweetpotatoes. Rooting of onions, sprouting of potatoes and sweetpotatoes, and decay of each of these products is stimulated by an environment of high RH. This factor can be controlled by adjusting the amount of ventilation in the package to the RH requirement and quantity of the commodity in the package. Thus two 6.5 mm (¼ in.) holes are adequate for polyethylene packages holding 0.9 kg (2 lb) or less of commodities requiring high RH. On the other hand, a polyethylene or Pliofilm bag holding 1.4 or 1.8 kg (3 or 4 lb) of onions (Table 5.3) needs 24 to 32 6 mm (¼ in.) holes; similar bags containing 1.8 or 2.2 kg (4 or 5 lb) of sweetpotatoes need 24 to 48 6 mm holes; and film bags of potatoes (Table 5.4) holding 4.5 kg (10 lb) need 32 to 48 6 mm holes to maintain the desired 70 to 75% RH. If small ventilation holes are used, correspondingly more of them will be required. Since heat sealing of shrink film is seldom perfect, extra ventilation is not required unless the film used is very impermeable, but is a desirable safety measure. Numerous pin holes made by a needle wheel revolving against a roll of film as it is used give adequate ventilation for film used on overwrap trays.

COMMODITY PACKAGING

Roots and Tubers

Carrots   Probably the outstanding example of prepackaging success is that of carrots. Before 1951 practically all fresh carrots were sold bunched with the tops on. They were shipped to market in large crates

TABLE 5.2 OXYGEN AND CARBON DIOXIDE CONCENTRATIONS IN CELLOPHANE 450-LSAT PACKAGES WITH TWO TYPES OF VENTILATION

Product	Size of Package	Days at 21° C (70° F)	Two 6 mm (¼ in.) Holes		Many 1.5 mm (¹/₁₆ in.) Flaps[1]	
			O_2 (%)	CO_2 (%)	O_2 (%)	CO_2 (%)
Tomatoes	4 fruits	4	19.9	0.7	20.0	0.2
Green beans	340 g (12 oz)	6	20.6	0.5	21.0	0.2
Spinach	285 g (10 oz)	1	15.0	3.8	16.8	1.7
Cauliflower	340 g (12 oz)	2	19.3	1.0	19.1	0.5
Cole slaw	225 g (8 oz)	2	18.4	1.9	19.6	0.4

Source: U.S. Dept. of Agriculture; Hardenburg (1954A).
[1]U-shaped flaps—from 80 to 120 per package.

TABLE 5.3   EFFECT OF NUMBER AND TYPE OF PERFORATIONS IN 1.4 KG (3 LB)
BAGS OF ONIONS ON RH, ROOTING AND WEIGHT AFTER 14 DAYS AT 24° C (75° F)

Type of Bag	Number and Type of Perforations		RH in Bag (%)	Onions Rooted (%)	Weight Loss (%)
Polyethylene 150		none	98	71	0.5
Polyethylene 150	36	1.5 mm (1/16 in.) flaps[1]	88	59	0.7
Polyethylene 150	40	3 mm (1/8 in.) flaps	84	40	1.4
Polyethylene 150	8	6 mm (1/4 in.) holes	—	24	1.8
Polyethylene 150	16	6 mm (1/4 in.) holes	54	17	2.5
Polyethylene 150	32	6 mm (1/4 in.) holes	51	4	2.5
Kraft paper with film windows		none	54	0	3.4

Source: Data from U.S. Dept. of Agriculture; Hardenburg (1954A).
[1]U-shaped flaps.

TABLE 5.4.   EFFECT OF NUMBER OF HOLES IN 4.5 KG (10 LB) BAG OF POTATOES ON
RH AND SURFACE MOLD AFTER 10 DAYS AT 21° C (70° F) AND 50%RH

Type of Bag	6 mm (1/4 in.) Holes per Bag (No.)	RH in Bag (%)	Surface Mold (%)
Polyethylene 150	0	99	extensive
Polyethylene 150	0[1]	98	extensive
Polyethylene 150	8	90	extensive
Polyethylene 150	32	86	slight
Polyethylene 150	48	67	0
Polyethylene 150	64	67	0
Polyethylene 150	80	69	0
Kraft paper	16	67	0

Source: Data from U.S. Dept. of Agriculture; Hardenburg (1954A).
[1]Perforated with 72   3 mm (1/8 in.) U-shaped flaps.

with crushed ice between layers and on top of the pack. The packed
crates weighed well over 46 kg (100 lb), were bulky, and difficult to
handle. However, most produce people felt that the green tops were
evidence of freshness and sales would suffer if tops were removed.

However, a study at Cornell (Platenius 1934) had shown that after
carrots are harvested, the green tops draw moisture from the roots and
hasten shriveling. Unless carrots with tops are kept continuously on ice
or frequently misted with water the roots quickly become flabby.

Further research showed that topped carrots in a perforated
polyethylene or other moisture resistant film bag lost substantially less
weight than carrots with tops when held under comparable conditions.

AVERAGE WEIGHT LOSS FROM 7 VEGETABLES
STORED II DAYS AT 34 F PLUS 4 DAYS AT 70 F

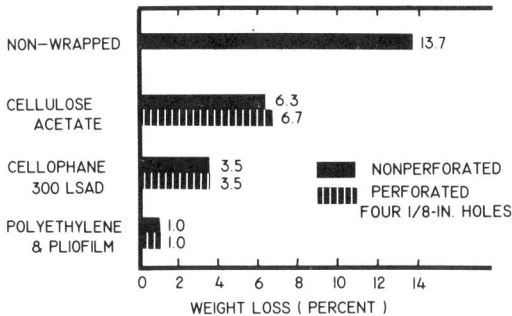

FIG. 5.3. EFFECTS OF PERFORATED AND NONPERFO-
RATED PLASTIC FILMS ON AVERAGE WEIGHT LOSS OF
VEGETABLES
Metric temperatures: 11 days at 1° C plus 4 days at 21° C.

Commercial prepackaging of carrots grew rapidly in the 1950s. No significant consumer resistance occurred as a result of the transition, so within a few years of the initial trials practically all fresh carrots were marketed as topped and prepackaged roots. Waste and spoilage losses are less in prepackaged carrots, principally because of less breakage of roots and because salability is not lost due to yellow or wilted tops. An added bonus accrues in saved freight charges because the inedible tops accounted for about 20% of the total weight.

Miscellaneous Root Crops Several other root crops are now marketed extensively as topped and bagged products. These include radishes, parsnips, beets and turnips. An interesting offshoot of this procedure is the modified atmosphere packing of topped radishes as developed by the Weasel Pre-Pak Corporation. The system includes holding the topped radishes under refrigeration in a low oxygen atmosphere for a week or more and then packaging them in sealed plastic film bags, each holding 170 g (6 oz) of radishes. The bagged radishes are packed into a master carton which is in turn overwrapped and heat sealed. With continuous refrigeration from packaging to final sale, which is essential for success, the radishes are said to maintain excellent crispness and flavor. However, if such packages are hermetically sealed and O_2 drops to 0.5% or less, there is acute danger of injury, followed by soft rot. This danger is greater as temperature increases.

Sweetpotatoes Before the development of satisfactory decay control treatments (sodium-o-phenylphenate and Botran washes) prepackaging of sweetpotatoes at origin usually ended in disaster due to excessive decay in the packaged product. Much of the commercial sweetpotato crop is stored for several months before marketing. After storage the roots must be washed and graded and during this process some physical injuries occur. These injured roots are very susceptible to soft rot caused by a species of the *Rhizopus* fungus. When packaged in ventilated film bags or overwrapped trays, the high relative humidity in the package favors decay development. Since sweetpotatoes are subject to chilling injury, they must be held at temperatures above 13° C (55° F). At these holding or transit temperatures, infected roots decay rapidly and the rot can spread to sound roots by contact.

Ceponis *et al.* (1973) conducted decay control experiments with three cultivars of New Jersey-grown sweetpotatoes. After several months of storage the roots were washed and graded in a commercial packinghouse. Part of each lot was spray treated with a 900 ppm solution of 2,6-dichloro-4 nitroaniline (DCNA). Both treated and untreated roots were then prepacked in overwrapped trays and in bulk cartons. After holding to simulate a wholesale period and retail display the untreated lots, both packaged and bulk, were essentially unmarketable because of Rhizopus soft rot. DCNA reduced decay in the prepackaged lots by about 90%. The best treatment was DCNA combined with a ventilated film overwrap on a molded pulp tray. Potential users should confirm local approval for use.

Kushman *et al.* (1964, 1965) have previously shown that treatment with a modified solution of sodium-o-phenylphenate (SOPP) or Botran (2,6-dichloro-4-nitroaniline) reduced soft rot sufficiently to permit origin prepackaging of North Carolina-grown sweetpotatoes.

Potatoes Potatoes were probably the first fresh produce item to be prepackaged for retail sale. Kraft paper bags, often filled to 2.2 or 4.5 kg (5 or 10 lb) weights in the back room of the grocery store, were widely used before prepackaging of other produce developed. Later, paper or cotton mesh bags and Kraft bags with mesh windows became popular. Plastic film bags came later, but those first used were not successful because they had little or no provision for ventilation. With present knowledge of venting for plastic film bags, an adequate number of holes can be provided to assure reduced relative humidity around the product (see *Ventilation of Packages*).

Ventilated polyethylene bags are now widely used for 2.2 or 4.5 kg (5 and 10 lb) consumer packs. However, mesh and paper bags retain a substantial part of this prepackage business.

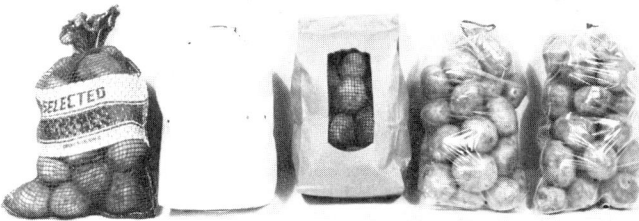

From Hardenburg (1954)

FIG. 5.4.   TYPES OF BAGS USED FOR RETAIL DISTRIBUTION OF POTATOES

The advantages of ventilated polyethylene bags over paper or mesh bags are: (1) increased visibility of all tubers in the bags; (2) somewhat less weight loss, particularly under adverse environments; and (3) somewhat less surface browning at skinned areas due to high RH. The case against polyethylene bags is based largely on a somewhat greater tendency to tuber decay and much less protection against tuber greening when the packs are exposed to intense light or extended periods in any light. The 4.5 and 11 kg (10 and 25 lb) packs in paper or mesh are often handled and loaded individually, whereas 2.2 and 4.5 kg (5 and 10 lb) packs in polyethylene bags are usually packed in multiwall paper master containers for shipment.

FIG. 5.5.   A CONSUMER PACKAGE COMMONLY USED FOR BRUSSELS SPROUTS AND MUSHROOMS

Courtesy of Produce Packaging and Marketing Assoc.

Brussels Sprouts   Almost all Brussels sprouts are now prepackaged for retail sale. The packaging may be done by the original packer at production point or by repackers or chain store warehouses at the terminal market. The commonest consumer package is a waxed-paper cup with a film top held in place with a rubber band. Some sprouts are prepackaged in overwrapped paper or plastic trays and occasionally paraffin-coated window cartons are used.

Asparagus   Most fresh asparagus is sold at retail in bulk or simply tied in bunches weighing 450 to 680 g (1 to 1.5 lb). Some prepackaging is done, principally because asparagus loses water rapidly and exposed stalks tend to wilt. One western shipper prepacks in open-face, moisture proof cartons, each holding 680 g (1.5 lb) of product. Each carton has a water soaked pad in the base to retard wilting. The display cartons are packed 16 to a master container and each stands upright to reduce broken tips during loading and transport.

Lettuce   Wrapping of individual heads of lettuce at shipping point for marketing increased quite rapidly in the early 1960s but has leveled off in more recent years. Wrapping of the trimmed heads is done either in the field on traveling packing units or in the packinghouse where somewhat more sophisticated equipment is available. Most of the wrapping is done with shrink films, which cling very tightly to the head after heating.

A considerable amount of lettuce wrapping is also done at terminal repacking facilities. The arguments for and against origin versus terminal wrapping are about the same as for other vegetables in which weight savings can be made by trimming and wrapping at origin. Labor and freight charge savings favor origin packaging while freshness of the product at retail display favors terminal trimming and packaging.

Many types of films have been tried experimentally for wrapping lettuce and several are satisfactory. Oriented polystyrene has been generally favored as a shrink wrap, primarily because of its permeability to respiratory gases and water vapor. However, some consumers object to the brittle feel of this film.

Controlled studies have generally shown little difference in market quality between wrapped and naked-pack lettuce when the lettuce moves through regular market channels (Stewart *et al.* 1967). However, studies involving lettuce for Navy supply ships (Parsons *et al.* 1960) showed that individual lettuce heads packed in polyethylene bags had significantly less weight loss and trimming waste after holding 3 to 7 weeks, as required in supply ships, than naked-pack lettuce stored in identical environment at 0.5° or 3°C (33° or 38°F).

Spinach and Salad Mixes   These highly perishable products are increasingly prepackaged. Almost all of this packaging is done by professional repackers at terminal distribution centers. Thorough washing of the leafy products is imperative and centrifugal drying is often used. This cleanliness together with the convenience of spinach ready for the cooking pot, or salad vegetables precut and premixed, are the principal selling points for these products. Continuous refrigeration near 0°C (32°F) from packaging to final retail sale is essential for success with these products.

Celery and Sweet Corn   Celery and sweet corn are also sold at retail largely from bulk displays. A limited quantity of celery is now being prepackaged at origin in shrink-film sleeves or in open-top plastic film bags. These provide some protection from moisture loss and abrasion injury and additionally permit brand identification. The latter advantage is of real interest to the packer of quality produce. Many attempts have been made to prepackage husked sweet corn, but there has been only limited success in the endeavor. The husks of sweet corn provide some protection to the kernels and with optimum refrigeration, which is essential to sweet corn marketing, quality can be maintained. However, trimming of the husks is desirable. Studies in Florida (Showalter 1963) show that trimming back the shanks and flag leaves soon after harvest reduces denting of kernels, which results from loss of moisture. Even though the closely trimmed husks show more wilting and discoloration than the nontrimmed, the kernels do not dent on the trimmed ears, while those on the nontrimmed ears lose enough moisture to cause denting. Apparently water moves from the kernels to the attached husks on the untrimmed ears. Some serious and potentially successful efforts are being devoted to prepackaging of completely husked sweet corn.

Packaging Machinery

There are a number of packaging machine companies in the United States and Europe which manufacture excellent machines to replace or supplement hand labor for prepackaging. The bagging machines vary from the sophisticated units which open bags, weigh and fill the contents, and then close them, to those which provide only conveyors and filling chutes for the bags. Automatic wrappers, sealers, and film shrink units are available for tray packs, but manual filling of the trays is still necessary. Machines to handle almost any size or type container or consumer package from the 0.5 kg (1 lb) carrot bag to the 11 kg (25 lb) potato bag are in use.

CURRENT STATUS

Since the late 1960s commercial interest in packaging vegetables in consumer-size units has levelled off. Some retail produce departments prepackage all vegetables on display, while others provide a choice of bulk or packaged for most of the more widely used vegetables. All of the larger markets offer topped carrots, turnips and parsnips in consumer-size packages, and potatoes are generally for sale in 2.2, 3.6 and 4.5 kg (5, 8 and 10 lb) bags.

Research on packaging fresh produce for retail display and sale was widespread from the late 1940s to the mid-1960s. As of 1978 essentially no new findings are being reported in the United States. Hardenburg (1971, 1974) has published useful reviews of previous findings, with emphasis on product precooling, refrigeration needs of each product and adequate package ventilation.

REFERENCES

ANON. 1965. Films for produce packaging. Produce Marketing 8, No. 11, 60–61.

ANON. 1966. CA for radish packaging. Am. Veg. Grower 14, No. 2, 30

BADGER, D. D. 1961. Consumer acceptance for prepackaged and bulk sweet-potatoes. Virginia Agr. Expt. Sta. Res. Rept. 56.

CEPONIS, M. J., and GRIFFIN, G. J. 1963. Effects of heat-tunnel temperatures on the quality of shrink-film-wrapped lettuce. U.S. Dept. Agr. Mktg. Res. Rept. 634.

CEPONIS, M. J., and KAUFMAN, J. 1968. Effect of relative humidity on moisture loss and decay of eastern lettuce pre-packaged in different films. U.S. Dept. Agr. ARS 51-18.

CEPONIS, M. J., KAUFMAN, J., and TIETJEN, W. H. 1973. Effects of DCNA and prepackaging on the retail quality of sweetpotatoes. HortScience 8, 41–42.

CHAPOGAS, P. G., and HALE, P. W. 1960. Pre-packaging early California potatoes at point of production. U.S. Dept. Agr. Mktg. Res. Rept. 401.

CHAPOGAS, P. G., and STOKES, D. R. 1964. Pre-packaging lettuce at shipping point. U.S. Dept. Agr. Mktg. Res. Rept. 670.

GINN, J. L., and HALE, P. W. 1960. Packaging California cauliflower. U.S. Dept. Agr. Mktg. Res. Rept. 414.

HALE, P. W., and MALLISON, E. D. 1966. Pre-packaging pole beans in trays and polyethylene bags. U.S. Dept. Agr. ARS 52-10.

HARDENBURG, R. E. 1954A. How to ventilate packaged produce. Pre-Pack-Age 7, No. 6, 14–17.

HARDENBURG, R. E. 1954B. Comparison of polyethylene with various other 10-pound consumer bags for Sebago, Katahdin, and Green Mountain potatoes. Am. Potato J. *31*, No. 2, 29–38.

HARDENBURG, R. E. 1955. Ventilation of produce. Mod. Packaging *28*, 140–144, 199–200.

HARDENBURG, R. E. 1960. What values accrue from pre-packaging fresh produce? Proc. Intl. Inst. of Refrig. Bull. Annex. *3*, 227–231.

HARDENBURG, R. E. 1966. Packaging and protection. *In* Protecting our Food. U.S. Dept. Agr. Yearbook, 102–117.

HARDENBURG, R. E. 1971. Effect on in-package environment on keeping quality of fruits and vegetables. HortScience *6*, 198–201.

HARDENBURG, R. E. 1974. Use of plastic films in maintaining quality of fresh fruits and vegetables during storage and marketing. ASHRAE Symposium on Relative Humidity and Storage of Fresh Fruits and Vegetables. Chicago, *CH-73-77*, 19–29.

KENDRICK, J. G., and SHERMAN, R. W. 1962. Effect of packaging produce on retail merchandising efficiency. Ohio Agr. Expt. Sta. *A. E. 338.*

KUSHMAN, L. J., HARDENBURG, R. E., and WORTHINGTON, J. T. 1964. Consumer packaging and decay control of sweetpotatoes. U.S. Dept. Agr. Mktg. Res. Rept. *650.*

KUSHMAN, L. J., WRIGHT, W. R., KAUFMAN, J., and HARDENBURG, R. E. 1965. Fungicidal treatments and shipping practices for controlling decay of sweetpotatoes during Marketing. U.S. Dept. Agr. Mktg. Res. Rept. *698.*

PARSONS, C. S., ATROPS, E. A., and STEWART, J. K. 1960. Effects of trimming and packaging methods on keeping quality of lettuce. U.S. Dept. Agr. *AMS-376.*

PARSONS, C. S., and WRIGHT, R. C. 1956. Effects of temperature, trimming, and packaging methods on lettuce deterioration. Proc. Am. Soc. Hort. Sci. *68*, 283–287.

PLATENIUS, H. 1934. Physiological and chemical changes in carrots during growth and storage. Cornell Univ. Agr. Expt. Sta. Mem. *161.*

SCOTT, C. R. 1966. Selecting the appropriate film for packaging of commodities. Down to Earth, Fall, 14–15. Material from Down to Earth used by permission of Dow Chemical Co.

SCOTT, C. R., BUTTS, F. J., and EICHHIRN, J. 1965. Evaluation of transparent films for the pre-packaging of lettuce. Mod. Packaging *38*, No. 6, 135–139, 212–213.

SHOWALTER, R. K. 1963. Shank and husk trimming effects on sweet corn storage life. Proc. Florida State Hort. Soc. *76*, 308–312.

STEWART, J. K., CEPONIS, M. J., and HARRIS, C. M. 1967. Market quality of film-wrapped and naked-packed head lettuce. U.S. Dept. Agr. *ARS 51–11.*

TOMKINS, R. G. 1962. The conditions produced in film packages by fresh fruits and vegetables and the effect of these conditions on storage life. J. Appl. Bact. *25*, 290–307.

6

Commodity Requirements—Leafy Vegetables and Immature Flower Heads

This and the next three chapters discuss in detail the conditions that will result in the least deterioration of a given commodity during transit or storage. These conditions include: (1) temperature, (2) relative humidity (RH), (3) air circulation, (4) packaging criteria, (5) permissible or advantageous atmosphere modifications, and (6) special treatments or precautions, such as are involved in curing or exposure to ethylene. Length of storage that can reasonably be expected under specific conditions also will be noted.

Since recognition of the results of good or poor shipping or storage practices presupposes recognition of good quality produce, we will cite readily recognized external or internal criteria of quality for various crops.

Crops will be divided into morphologically similar groups with similar requirements to avoid needless repetition. However, quality criteria and specific requirements will be given for individual crops. Requirements are given in Table 6.1 for quick reference. The members of each group will be listed by common and botanical names to avoid confusion. For this we have followed the nomenclature of Smith and Welch (1964).

Much helpful information for these chapters came from U.S. Department of Agriculture Handbook *66* (Lutz and Hardenburg 1968), but original sources were consulted whenever feasible. Quality criteria were largely from personal knowledge and experience, but "Tips on Selecting Fruits and Vegetables" (Morrison 1961) provided useful information.

LEAFY VEGETABLES

Members of Group

Vegetables included in this group consist exclusively or primarily of leaves and associated parts, such as petioles, and include the following crops:

Common Name	Botanical Name
Brussels sprouts	*Brassica oleracea,* gemifera
Cabbage	*Brassica oleracea,* capitata
Cabbage, Chinese	*Brassica campestris,* pekinensis
Celery⁄	*Apium graveolens,* dulce
Chard	*Beta vulgaris,* cicla
Chicory (witloof)	*Cicorium intybus*
Collard (smooth-leaved kale)	*Brassica oleracea,* acephala
Endive	*Chicorium endivia*
Escarole (broad-leaved endive)	*Chicorium endivia*
Kale	*Brassica oleracea,* acephala
Leek	*Allium ameloprasum*
Lettuce, head	*Latuca sativa*
Lettuce, leaf	*Latuca sativa*
Mustard	*Brassica campestris,* perviridis
Onions, green	*Allium cepa*
Parsley	*Petroselinum crispum*
Rhubarb	*Rheum* spp.
Spinach	*Spinacia oleracea*
Turnip greens	*Brassica campestris,* rapifera
Watercress	*Rorippa nasturtium-aquaticum*

Leafy vegetables not listed, but grown in temperate climates, can be assumed to have the same requirements as the above.

Recommended Conditions for Group

Temperature   Leafy vegetables should be promptly cooled as close to 0° C (32° F) as possible and held there throughout marketing. Wilting, diseases and disorders increase in severity as temperature increases.

Vacuum cooling is the most common method of precooling, although hydrocooling is used on some leafy crops, while others are packed in ice.

TABLE 6.1. RECOMMENDED TEMPERATURE AND RELATIVE HUMIDITY, APPROXIMATE STORAGE LIFE, WATER CONTENT, AND SPECIFIC HEAT OF VARIOUS VEGETABLES AND MELONS

Crop	Temperature (°C)	Temperature (°F)	Relative Humidity (%)	Storage[1] Life	Water Content[2] (%)	Specific Heat[2] (Btu per lb per °F)
Artichoke, globe	0	32	95+	2 weeks	84	.87
Artichoke, Jerusalem	-0.5-0	31-32	90-95	5 months	80	.84
Asparagus	0-2	32-36	95+	2-3 weeks	93	.94
Beans, lima					66	.73
in pod	4-7	40-45	95	3-5 days		
shelled	3	37	95	1 week	—	—
Beans, snap	3-6	38-42	95+	10 days	89	.91
Beets, bunched	0	32	95+	10-14 days	—	—
topped, fresh market	0	32	98-100	3-5 months	88	.90
topped, processing	0	32	98-100	8 months	—	—
Broccoli	0	32	95+	10-14 days	90	.92
Brussels sprouts	0	32	95+	3-5 weeks	85	.88
Cabbage, early	0	32	98	3-6 weeks	92	.94
late	-0.5-0	31-32	98	4-6 months	94	.94
Chinese	0	32	95+	1-2 months	96	.96
Carrot, immature, bunched	0	32	95+	3 weeks	88	—
immature, topped	0	32	98-100	1 month	88	.91
mature, topped	0	32	98-100	6-9 months		.91
Cauliflower	0	32	95+	1 month	92	.93
Celeriac	0	32	98-100	6-8 months	88	.91
Celery	0	32	95+	2-4 weeks	94	.95
Chard	0	32	95+	10-14 days	—	—
Chicory, witloof	0	32	95+	2-4 weeks		—
Collards	0	32	95+	10-14 days	87	.90
Cucumber	10-13	50-55	95	10-14 days	96	.97
Eggplant	10-13	50-55	95	10-14 days	93	.94
Endive and escarole	0	32	95+	2-3 weeks	93	.95
Garlic	-0.5-0	31-32	60	6-7 months	61	.69
Ginger	13	55	65	6 months	87	.90
Greens, various leafy	0	32	95+	10-14 days	—	—
Horseradish	-1.0	30-32	98-100	1 year	75	.80
Kale	0	32	95+	10-14 days	87	.89
Kohlrabi	0	32	95+	1 month	90	.92
Leek	0	32	95+	2-3 months	85	.88
Lettuce, head	0	32	95+	2-3 weeks	95	.96
leaf, semi-heading	0	32	95+	3-6 days	—	—

Commodity	Temperature (°C)	Temperature (°F)	Relative humidity (%)	Approximate length of storage period[1]	Water content (%)[2]	Specific heat[2]
Mushrooms	0	32	95	8-12 days	91	.93
Muskmelons					93	.94
Cantaloup, Hard ripe	3-5	38-41	95	10-14 days		
Eastern choice	3-5	38-41	95	7-10 days		
Western choice	3-5	38-41	95	4-6 days		
Western choice	1-3	34-37	95	5-7 days		
Casaba	7-10	45-50	85-95	3 weeks		
Crenshaw	7-10	45-50	85-95	2 weeks		
Honey Dew	7-10	45-50	85-95	2-3 weeks		
Persian	7-10	45-50	90-95	2 weeks		
Okra	7-10	45-50	95+	1 week	90	.92
Onions, dry	-0.5-0	31-32	65-70	see text	87	.90
green	0	32	95+	1 week	89	.91
Parsley	0	32	95+	1-2 months	85	.88
Parsnips	0	32	98+	4-5 months	79	.83
Peas, garden	0	32	95+	7-10 days	74	.79
edible podded	0	32	95+	3-5 days	—	—
Pepper, green	7-10	45-50	95	2 weeks	92	.94
ripe	5-7	41-45	95	1 week		
Potatoes, early		see text	90	see text	81	.85
late		see text	90	see text	78	.82
Pumpkins	10-15	50-60	60	see text	90	.92
Radish, spring, topped	0	32	95+	3-4 weeks	94	.96
winter	0	32	98	6 months	—	—
Rhubarb	0	32	98	2-3 weeks	95	.96
Rutabagas	0	32	98	2-4 months	89	.91
Salsify, topped	0	32	98	2-4 months	79	.83
Southern peas	3-5	38-42	95+	1 week	—	—
Spinach	0	32	95+	10-14 days	93	.94
Squash, summer	10	50	95	1 week	94	.95
winter	10-15	50-60	60	see text	85	.88
Sweet corn	0	32	95+	4-6 days	74	.79
Sweetpotatoes	13	55	90	4-6 months	68	.75
Tomatoes, unripe		see text	see text	see text	93	.94
ripe	2-7	35-45	90	3-5 days	94	.95
Turnip	0	32	95	2-4 months	91	.93
Turnip greens	0	32	95	10-14 days	90	.92
Water chestnuts	0	32	see text	10 months	—	—
Watercress	0	32	95+	4-7 days	93	.95
Watermelon	7-15	45-60	80-90	2 weeks	93	.94
Yam	16	61	60 or 100	see text	—	—

[1] Storage life given refers to quality rating of "good", and thus allows for a subsequent marketing period at somewhat higher temperature. This table is intended as a quick guide only; for details, consult text.

[2] From Lutz and Hardenburg, 1968. Water content rounded to nearest whole percent. Formula for specific heat above freezing: 0.008 (water content as %) + 0.20.

Efficient room cooling is adequate for crops adapted to prolonged storage, such as cabbage for processing.

Relative Humidity.   High humidity (at least 95%) is essential to prevent wilting. Even saturated atmospheres are not harmful at 0° to 1° C (32° to 34° F) (van den Berg and Lentz 1977), but they tend to encourage decay near 5° C (41° F).

Air Circulation   Rapid air movement accelerates water loss and thus should be avoided. Enough air must flow past each unit or package, however, to remove respiratory heat, which is high for many leafy vegetables.

Other requirements are given under individual crops.

QUALITY CRITERIA AND RECOMMENDED CONDITIONS FOR INDIVIDUAL CROPS

Brussels Sprouts

Quality Criteria.   High quality sprouts are about 2.5 cm (1 in.) in diameter, have green outer leaves, and are firm. Yellowing indicates advanced senescence.

In cross section, inner leaves are light yellow, fairly tightly arranged and without large air pockets in between.

Recommended Conditions   Vacuum cooling is effective. Dry sprouts can be cooled from about 10° to 2° C (50° to 36° F) and wet sprouts to 0° C (32° F) in 13 min (Stenvers 1971). However, bulk shipments usually are package-iced and top-iced.

CA storage retards yellowing. In California (Lyons and Rappaport 1962) and New York (Isenberg 1969) 5% CO_2 was found effective. In Canada (Eaves and Forsyth 1968) 7% CO_2 seemed beneficial. Higher concentrations are unnecessary and can be injurious. Low O_2 (2.5%) provides some added benefit, but 0% O_2 is injurious.

Packaging in vented bags or waxed, overwrapped cups is advantageous to reduce wilting.

Brussels sprouts keep in good condition 3 to 5 weeks at 0° C (32° F), but only half as long at 5° C (41° F). At 10° C (50° F) good quality is retained for 10 days at most. If losses of at least 20 to 30% are acceptable, sprouts can be stored 10 to 12 weeks at 0° to 1° C (32° to 34° F) and 98 to 100% RH.

Cabbage—Green, Red and Savoy

Quality Criteria   Cabbage should be green or dark purple (depending on cultivar), firm, and heavy for its size. When rubbed against each other, the heads should squeak, indicating crispness. Bloom on leaves is desirable.

Exposed inner, yellow leaves in green cultivars indicate extensive trimming has taken place.

Internally, the leaves should be yellow to light green or dark purple, depending on cultivar, and tightly packed. Presence of a seedstalk is undesirable.

Recommended Conditions   Cabbage is stored in mechanically refrigerated rooms or in ventilated common storage. In the latter, freezing must be avoided by use of insulation and the use of heaters during very cold weather. Slight freezing is harmless, but severe freezing damages quality. Further, solid heads are more susceptible to freezing injury than merely firm heads. European researchers recommend $-0.5°$ C $\pm 0.3°$ $(31°$ F $\pm 0.5°)$ for storage up to 6 months.

Cultivars of cabbage that have been developed for long-term storage can be kept 6 months or even longer with trim losses ranging from about 8 to 20% if sound, well-trimmed heads are held at $0°$ to $1°$ C $(32°$ to $34°$ F) in 97 to 100% RH and in 5 to 6% CO_2 with about 3% O_2. Under such conditions, the cabbage will still be firm and tender, have good color and flavor, and no (or only minimal) root growth. If CA storage is not feasible, quality will be slightly lower, but still acceptable as long as temperature is low and RH high. CA storage has no definite effect on vitamin C content (Bohling and Hansen 1977). A reduction in RH to 90 to 95% or an increase in temperature to $4°$ to $5°$ C $(39°$ to $41°$ F) can double or triple trim-losses during 4 to 6 months of storage. These conclusions are based on very similar results in various countries.

Cabbage keeps well for at least 8 weeks when held at $0°$ to $3°$ C $(32°$ to $38°$ F) in bins or crates lined with perforated polyethylene. There should be 1 hole 6 mm (¼ in.) in diameter per square foot of liner or bag (Parsons 1959).

When cabbage is stored more than a week or two, care must be taken that air circulation is adequate to remove respiratory heat. An air flow equivalent to about 20 air changes per hour through, not just around, bins or other containers appears to satisfy this requirement (Böttcher 1965).

Cabbage should never be stored with any product that emits substantial amounts of ethylene (see Table 1.3) because an accumulation of even 10 ppm can cause premature yellowing and abscission of leaves (Pendergrass *et al.* 1976).

When cabbage is held in CA, care must be taken that O_2 does not drop below 2.5% or else a sweet, although not unpleasant, flavor may develop. If CO_2 rises to about 10%, internal leaves may become seriously discolored.

Cabbage may be marketed naked or overwrapped with various types of perforated film. Red cabbage is more frequently wrapped than the white kind because its rate of turnover is slower, although white cabbage often would benefit from the practice.

The storage life of cabbage depends on cultivar and growing conditions. Rapidly growing types originating in warm areas can be stored only 3 to 6 weeks, whereas slow growing, large types can be stored 4 to 6 months.

Firm, but not excessively hard, heads that are relatively high in soluble solids and cellulose store best. Size of head does not seem to be related to storability within a given cultivar.

Savoy cabbage cannot be stored as long as the smooth-leaved types, but no precise information is at hand. Two to three months probably would be maximal in normal air.

Recommendations for CA storage of red or savoy cabbage closely resemble those for white cabbage. The former will keep about 7 months and the latter 5 to 6 months at 0° to 1° C (32° to 34° F) when CO_2 is 3 to 5% and O_2 is 2 to 3% (Stoll 1973).

Cabbage, Chinese

Quality Criteria   The heads should be firm and their outer leaves should be light green to yellowish green. Their odor should be slightly spicy but not too strongly so.

Recommended Conditions   The recommendations given for white cabbage should be followed except that Chinese cabbage should not be held below −0.6° C (31° F). However, prevention of wilting is even more critical because Chinese cabbage has more exposed leaves.

The usefulness of CA for long-term storage of Chinese cabbage is still in question, although the combination of 2% O_2 plus 2 or 5% CO_2 appears promising for periods of up to about 2.5 months. A discoloration similar to brown stain in lettuce is induced at 7.5% CO_2 (Weichman 1977).

The storage life in air is limited from 1 to at most 2 months. If a 20 to

30% wastage is acceptable, then the storage life is about 3 months at 0° C (32° F) and 98 to 100% RH (van den Berg and Lentz 1977).

Celery

Quality Criteria   Crispness is the essential quality attribute of celery. It also should be green, or creamy yellow if blanched, with straight petioles that are compactly arranged. Outer petioles are frequently tough or pithy and should be removed. The stem should be trimmed close to the outermost petioles. Celery of high quality does not have any seedstalk.

Recommended Conditions   Celery can be hydrocooled or vacuum cooled. The method is less important than the end-result, which should yield celery where the bulky parts are about 5° C (41° F) and the petioles 0° to 2° C (32° to 36° F). A poor job of hydrocooling is particularly dangerous because warm and wet celery decays rapidly. Thus, if ice is added to the crates or waxed boxes during packing, the amount in the containers and in the vehicle must be adequate to keep the celery near 0° C (32° F) during most of the marketing period. If celery is vacuum cooled, wetting it prior to cooling reduces weight loss during cooling and thus retards wilting. Such wetting is particularly advantageous when the stalks are above about 20° C (68° F) at harvest.

Since wilting is the chief defect of celery, packaging in ventilated wraps is advantageous. Box or crate liners should have about 12 holes per m² (1 hole per ft²) (Parsons 1960). Bags for individual stalks should have 4 to 6 holes, a relatively larger number, in case some holes are blocked during packing in master containers.

There is little advantage in holding celery under CA conditions during transit. Oxygen below 5% retards yellowing only slightly and CO_2 above about 2.5% may be damaging, although in some tests buildup to 9% over a period of 1 month seemed harmless (Parsons 1960). Nevertheless, all wraps should be perforated to avoid potentially dangerous accumulations of CO_2, or reductions in O_2 below 1%.

Butt discoloration has vexed the industry for many years, but there is still no effective and safe chemical to prevent it. The best preventative still is storage near 0° C (32° F). Further, packing the stalks butt-up seems to reduce discoloration somewhat, supposedly because it keeps "contaminated" water from running over the butts (Hall 1962). However, there is no proof that bacteria are involved in this discoloration.

The storage life of celery is 4 to 8 weeks at 0° to 1° C (32° to 34° F) and

98 to 100% RH, but it is only about half as long at 95% RH if storage losses cannot exceed 10 to 15% . If a 20 to 30% loss is acceptable, then 3 months of storage is feasible at the high RH. At 5° C (41° F) celery will keep only about 2 weeks at most.

Chard

Quality Criteria   The leaf blades should never be wilted nor the petioles be limp. High quality chard has dark green leaves and white or red petioles, depending on cultivar. Properly handled chard has few crushed or torn leaves.

Recommended Conditions   See Spinach.

Chicory (Witloof)

Witloof chicory that is offered in some markets in the United States mostly is imported from Belgium. Because of its relatively high perishability and high price, witloof almost invariably is shipped via air.

Quality Criteria   This delicate vegetable, which can be eaten either raw or cooked, should be creamy white to light yellow. The bullet-shaped heads should be firm and free of any brown discoloration. Browning of the margins is a common sign of aging and can lead to decay (Herregods 1971).

Recommended Conditions.   Chicory should be rapidly cooled to and held near 0° C (32° F) throughout marketing and in at least 95% RH to prevent wilting. Overwrapping with perforated film is beneficial.

Holding witloof in 3 to 4% O_2 with 4 to 5% CO_2 at 0° C (32° F) about doubles its useful life as compared to storage in air and delays greening of the tips of the leaves in light and opening of the heads.

The storage life of witloof, as terminated by the appearance of marginal browning, is rather variable, and presumably depends on initial quality. Marginal browning appeared after 2 to 4 weeks at 2° C (36° F), after 1 to 2 weeks at 5° C (41° F) and after 1 week at 15° C (59° F) in tests conducted in Belgium.

Chopped Salad Vegetables

Coleslaw, head lettuce, and other salad vegetables that are chopped in the production area or at distribution centers have become major items of supply for restaurants, institutions and even retail stores. Some of these items are vacuum packed in bulk after treatment with various preservatives and thus can no longer be considered fresh vegetables.

Quality Criteria   The chopped salad vegetables must be free of all discoloration, wilting, off-odors and off-flavors.

Recommended Conditions.- Vacuum cooling to near 0° C (32° F) and subsequent holding near 0° C are essential for maximum shelf-life. Cooling the vegetables before chopping reduces subsequent discoloration.

For chopped lettuce shipped fresh, Herner and Krahn (1973) found that quality was maintained best when all of the following conditions were met: lettuce is held continuously at 0° C (32° F); washing is done just before use, not before chopping; lettuce is packed in 0.05 mm (2 mil) thick polypropylene bags that then are heat sealed; CO_2 accumulation in the bags is allowed to reach 10 to 20% and O_2 levels are allowed to drop to 2 to 3%. These high CO_2 levels did not injure the chopped lettuce even though they would ruin entire heads. The quality of chopped lettuce remained "good" or better for 10 , 8, or 4 days, respectively, when storage was at 0°, 2° or 5° C (32°, 36°, 41° F). Researchers tried various chemicals but none were helpful in extending the useful life of chopped head lettuce. Very similar results were obtained by Priepke *et al.* (1976) with lettuce, carrots, celery, radishes, green onions, endive and a mixture of all of them. The results likely would be applicable to chopped cabbage, too.

For health reasons, marketing of chopped, raw salad vegetables demands the highest standards of sanitation and continuous refrigeration as close to 0° C (32° F) as feasible. Bacterial counts, including coliform bacteria, increased drastically at 4° to 5° C (39° to 41° F), a range commonly found in refrigerators (Libbey *et al.* 1972). Consequently, chopped salads should not be held longer than the time intervals given above for "good or better" lettuce.

Collards and Kale

Quality Criteria   The leaves should be uniformly green and not wilted.

Recommended Conditions   These greens should be rapidly cooled to 0° C (32° F) and held there throughout marketing. Hruschka (1971) recommends packing the leaves in boxes lined with polyethylene film and covering the leaves with ample crushed ice prior to shipment. During subsequent distribution the greens should be placed in perforated film bags and packed in master containers kept cool by packets of ice. Under such conditions kale remained in excellent condition for 3 weeks and was still considered salable after 4 to 5 weeks. At 5° C (41° F) the respective periods were 1 week and about 10 days and at 10° C (50° F) they were 3 and less than 5 days.

If kale or collards are washed before marketing, the leaves must be handled carefully, decayed leaves must be removed prior to washing, and fresh or at least chlorinated water must be used, or else storage life will be halved.

Endive and Escarole

Quality Criteria   These closely related greens must be crisp and free of discolored or decayed leaf margins. Particular attention must be paid to heart leaves to ascertain that they have no defects.

Recommended Conditions   These salad greens can be vacuum cooled or hydrocooled. If the latter, cooling to and storage at about 0° C (32° F) is essential if decay is to be minimized.

Wilting can be prevented by packaging or wetting. Since the appeal of endive and escarole depends on their fresh, green appearance, complete wrapping generally is avoided. Thus, both methods often are combined: the leafy heads are displayed in open-top plastic bags and are frequently sprinkled with chilled water.

The storage life of endive or escarole is at most 3 weeks at 0° C (32° F) and about half that at 5° C (41° F).

Leek

Quality Criteria   The base of leek stalks should be white for about 3 cm and the upper part of the leaves should be turgid and green, with a whitish bloom. The stem plate, where the leaves originate, must be present; if cut off, as all too often is the case, some of the best part has been removed and the cut ends discolor and are unsightly.

Leek must be free of any seedstalk. Its presence indicates a tough, overly strong-flavored stalk.

Recommended Conditions   Leek can be cooled by cold water, ice or vacuum. Whatever method is used, the final temperature should be as close to 0° C (32° F) as possible, for maximum quality retention.

High humidity is essential, or else leek will wilt. Overwrapping leek with perforated film seems highly advantageous to prevent wilting and physical abuse.

Long-term storage in atmospheres enriched with up to 10% CO_2 retards yellowing and decay, according to a Finnish report (Suhonen 1970). However, even with CA storage, losses ranged from 25 to 50% during 4 months at 1° to 2° C (34° to 36° F). Van den Berg and Lentz (1977) report similar losses for leek stored 3 months at 0° to 1° C (32° to 34° F) in air and at 98 to 100% RH, with even higher losses at 90 to 95% RH. However, Kurki (1971) obtained only minimal losses (8%) under the former conditions. Cultivar, storage and preharvest and harvest conditions, and degree of trimming prior to storage are as likely to influence the storage life of leek as well as of many other vegetables.

Even though CA storage of leek may be useful, caution is advisable since no information is available on the effect of CA on flavor of subsequently cooked leek.

Lettuce, Crisphead

Quality Criteria   Head lettuce of high quality as sold at retail should have crisp, green outer leaves that are free from any blemishes. Yellowish outer leaves indicate that the head was severely trimmed to remove damaged or decayed leaves, or that it is well into senescence.

The midribs should neither be crushed nor split crosswise. The former indicates physical abuse and the latter an excessively hard, burst head. The base of each midrib should be attached to the short stem, not cut off, as occurs when the butt is trimmed too closely.

Heads that are very heavy for their size are undesirable because they deteriorate more rapidly than less firm heads. A head that weighs about the same as leaf lettuce of equal size is too soft, and unless bought by weight, uneconomical. Heads of proper harvest maturity (firm) yield slightly when compressed from the top by moderate pressure within the palm of a hand, hard heads resist such pressure, and soft heads tend to cave in and feel spongy. Excessive variation of maturity in a given lot of lettuce is one of the chief complaints of receivers (Rij *et al.* 1976), but is a problem that may be solved once maturity is determined objectively by mechanical harvesters (U.S. Dept. Agr. 1974).

The color of the cut end of the butt is not necessarily a good indicator of quality. First, it might have been trimmed recently. Secondly, heads of lettuce held under identical conditions vary greatly in butt color, from light pink to reddish brown. Further, prevention of butt discoloration by holding lettuce in a low concentration of carbon monoxide during

Courtesy of United Fresh Fruit and Vegetable Assoc.

FIG. 6.1.   A FINE SPECIMEN OF HEAD LETTUCE

transit is temporary, normal discoloration occurring shortly after removal of the lettuce to air.

Internally, a head should be free of any discolorations. In cross section, the larger leaves should be folded so that layers of leaves are separated by thin layers of air. Lack of such air space indicates start of senescence, and excessively large air pockets indicate immaturity. However, leaves toward the heart (growing point) may be more closely packed than older leaves, without indicating inferior quality. Various degrees of maturity of head lettuce are illustrated in Fig. 6.2. Seedstalks in a head are objectionable because they are unattractive and unusable.

Recommended Condition   Lettuce should be precooled to $1° C \pm 1°$ $(34° F \pm 2°)$ in the leafy main portion of the head. Thorough precooling is essential because mechanically refrigerated vehicles are designed primarily for temperature maintenance, not reduction. Thus good precooling generally means good transit temperatures, while poor precooling likely means trouble on arrival, since lettuce deteriorates rapidly as temperature increases (Fig. 6.3). In lots where decay or russet spotting are potential problems, deterioration increases even more rapidly than indicated in Fig. 6.3. Under such conditions, lettuce cooled to and held at $1° C$ had significantly less decay, russet spotting, or pink rib than lettuce cooled to and held at 3° C (38° F) for 1 week (Lipton and Barger 1965). Some of the hazards of improper precooling are apparent at unloading (pink rib), whereas others (decay) show up primarily after the wholesale-retail period, during which refrigeration frequently is less thorough than desirable.

Details on how to achieve adequate cooling by vacuum are given in the section on *Precooling*. However, a few related points will be given here.

On dry days when lettuce is above about 25° C (77° F), it should be wetted before cooling, because the evaporation of the free moisture draws heat from the lettuce without removing a corresponding amount of water. Thus lettuce can be cooled by 28° C (50° F) and lose less than 1% of its original weight as compared to about 5% for dry heads (Barger 1961). Loss of 5% of the original weight may result in visible wilting.

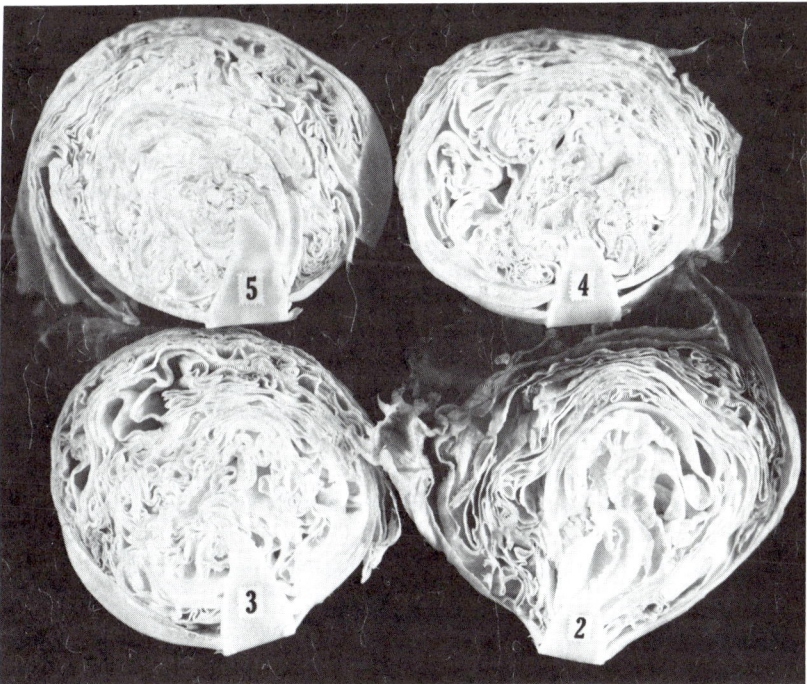

From Kader et al. (1973)

FIG. 6.2. FIRMNESS CLASSES FOR HEAD LETTUCE
Class 5—Overmature, may have cracked midribs. Class 4—Hard, near upper limit of desirable range. Class 3—Firm, most desirable maturity. Class 2—Fairly firm, near lower limit of desirable range. Class 1—(Not shown) Very soft, has excessive air spaces; not normally marketed.

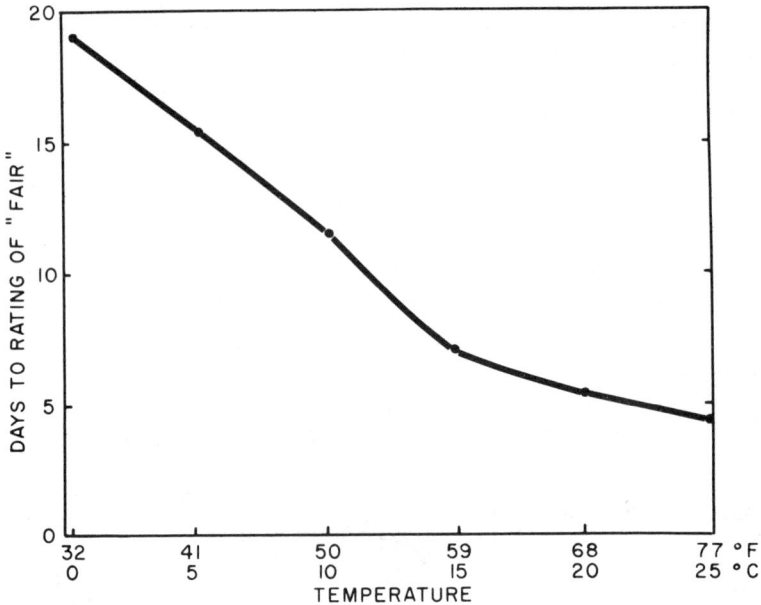

Adapted from Pratt et al. (1954)

FIG. 6.3.   DAYS REQUIRED FOR HEAD LETTUCE TO REACH FAIR QUALITY
AT VARIOUS CONSTANT TEMPERATURES

Many shippers avoid this risk by having the lettuce sprinkled with clean water just before the cartons are closed. This procedure incidentally also cleanses the cut ends.

Density of heads has no significant influence on the degree of cooling achieved, although firm heads cooled slightly more (1° C; 2° F) than hard heads under a given set of conditions.

When lettuce is packaged, the wraps or liners must be adequately perforated or sufficiently permeable to water vapor to permit evaporation under vacuum, or else proper cooling is impossible. Materials, such as polystyrene, commonly used for lettuce, permit adequate vapor transmission without perforation.

Hydrocooling of lettuce is also feasible. However, this method is not used on head lettuce in the United States because (1) packed lettuce would cool too slowly; (2) lettuce is generally field-packed in cartons that do not withstand wetting; and (3) wetting the lettuce would increase the likelihood of decay at temperatures even slightly above 0° to 1° C (32° to 34° F).

Lettuce must be held in high RH, 95% or higher. If RH is 100% (a saturated atmosphere), the danger of decay is greater than at 95 to 97%

RH, particularly as temperature rises above 2° C (36° F). Between 0° and 2° C (32° and 36° F) and during normal domestic marketing periods, 100% RH will cause problems only in inferior lettuce or in lots with active field infections of soft rot.

Lettuce is well adapted to packaging of individual heads in film wraps. This protects it physically and prevents wilting. Type of wrap is of little concern if it is sufficiently permeable or well enough ventilated to prevent accumulation of CO_2 above 1% and depletion of O_2 below 1% at temperatures normally encountered by lettuce, from 0° to about 20° C (32° to about 68° F). Further, lettuce requires wraps that permit ready passage of water vapor under vacuum to facilitate precooling.

Controlled atmosphere storage of lettuce in transit is justified for some lots of lettuce because it substantially reduces russet spotting in susceptible lots (Lipton 1967). This effect can be achieved by maintaining O_2 levels between 1% and about 8%. Since O_2 levels never should drop below 1% because of the danger of injury (see section on *Disorders*), and since the beneficial effect will decrease as O_2 approaches 10%, 3 to 5% O_2 is optimal. However, reduction in O_2 should not be accompanied by an increase in CO_2 because of the danger of injury, as noted below. Decay control at safe low O_2 levels is minimal during normal transit periods. However, during prolonged transit, as in export overseas, low O_2 can reduce decay incidence by about half, enough to warrant its use.

Butt discoloration is not reduced by O_2 concentrations that can be considered safe. Even in 0.5% O_2 the effect is minimal and transitory, since the butts discolor soon after exposure to normal air. Carbon monoxide (CO) at a concentration of about 1% effectively retards butt discoloration, but its effect also disappears after removal of the lettuce to air. Since butt color is not necessarily a good index of lettuce quality, the use of CA cannot be justified on an objective basis to control butt discoloration.

Carbon dioxide must be held below 2%, and preferably below 1%, during normal transit, because lettuce can be injured when exposed to 1 to 2% CO_2 for 1 week, as illustrated by Fig. 6.4 (also see section on *Disorders*). During 1 month's in-transit storage, however, the reduction in decay achieved by 2% CO_2 outweighs the danger of injury. Thus for storage of 1 month or longer, the optimum atmosphere is 2% CO_2 combined with 3% O_2. However, CO_2 never should exceed 3% because serious injury may follow.

Neither low O_2 nor high CO_2 is effective in materially inhibiting pink rib. In fact, low O_2 increases its intensity at moderate temperatures or during prolonged storage.

The storage life of lettuce under ideal conditions is at least 1 month, if we consider fair quality (major, but removable defects) the end of stor-

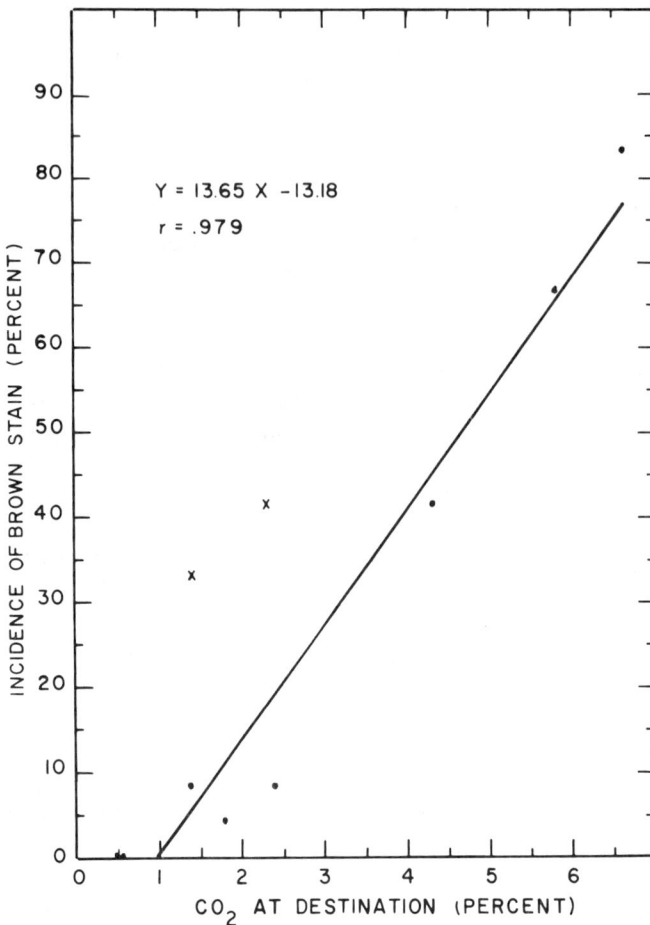

Y = 13.65 X − 13.18

r = .979

From Stewart et al. (1971)

FIG. 6.4. INCIDENCE OF OBJECTIONABLE BROWN STAIN IN RELATION TO CO_2 CONCENTRATION IN MECHANICALLY-REFRIGERATED RAIL CARS AFTER TRANSCONTINENTAL SHIPMENT

X denotes incidence in cars where O_2 averaged about 2% during transit. All other cars had near-normal O_2 concentrations.

age life. Under good commercial conditions the limit is about 3 weeks, and under commonly found conditions 2 weeks is realistic. If "good" lettuce (only minor defects) is expected, storage life is cut by at least half.

Storage life of head lettuce can be increased under any one set of environmental conditions by not harvesting overly dense heads and by removal of wrapper leaves at time of harvest. Separate studies in California (Morris *et al*. 1955) and in Arizona (Stewart and Burkhart 1956) have shown that hard lettuce deteriorates more rapidly than firm lettuce, the shortening ranging from 3 days to 2 weeks.

Removal of wrapper leaves at harvest can make the difference between salable and unsalable lettuce during prolonged storage, although during normal marketing the effect is minimal. Trimming of wrapper leaves is beneficial because their removal eliminates the oldest leaves, that often have incipient infections, and thus are most susceptible to decay. When lettuce is trimmed, film wrapping or near water-saturated atmospheres are essential if wilting is to be avoided.

Lettuce is extremely sensitive to injury from ethylene, which induces russet spotting, one of the serious disorders of head lettuce. Details on the disorder and on ethylene are given in the relevant sections. However, the precautions bear re-emphasis. Lettuce should never be stored or shipped together with commodities that emit appreciable ethylene, such as melons, apples or pears. Low O_2 and high CO_2 reduce the adverse effect of ethylene, but the former is not completely effective and the latter can injure the lettuce.

Lettuce intended for overseas shipment, which may have transit periods of two weeks or more, must meet more stringent requirements than lettuce that is in transit only about a week if the high investment in freight is to be justified. Freedom from decay, from internal rib necrosis and rusty brown discoloration, and precooling to 0° to 1° C (32° to 34° F) are essential. Further recommendations are detailed by Stewart *et al*. (1977), all of which imply that the best lettuce available on any given day is not necessarily good enough for export overseas.

Lettuce, Leaf, and Semi-heading

Quality Criteria   Attractive green leaves free of any wilting or discoloration are signs of freshness. The exact color of leaves ranges from pale yellowish green of some leaf lettuces via the deep green of bibb lettuce to the reddish brown of the outer leaves of some leaf lettuce.

Particular attention must be paid to the small inner leaves of the leafy types because they often show tipburn when it is not visible on older leaves.

Seedstalks are undesirable in any of these greens.

Recommended Conditions   These salad greens can be vacuum cooled or hydrocooled to near 0° C (32° F) and then packed in crushed ice. Hydrocooling can be used if done carefully. However, the more tender types, such as greenhouse grown leaf lettuce, are vacuum cooled. Those that are vacuum cooled should be prewetted before cooling if temperature of the lettuce is 24° C (75° F) or higher.

If hydrocooling is used, 100 to 200 ppm of active chlorine should be in the water to reduce the chance of soft rot infection.

These crops are packaged to advantage in individual open-topped polyethylene bags because they reduce moisture loss and physical abuse, and they permit wetting of the product at retail while still permitting its most advantageous display.

Modified atmospheres do not prolong the useful life of butter-type head lettuce (Tataru and Weichman 1974). However, Romaine appears to benefit from CO_2 levels up to about 5% combined with 2 to 10% O_2 when storage of 2 to 3 weeks in closed bags is involved (Aharoni and Ben-Yehoshua 1973). However, some of the benefits attributed to atmosphere modification may have been contributed by the high RH that existed in the closed but not in the open bags.

The storage life of these greens has not been determined in detail. However, it ranges from a few days for very tender types to 1 week or slightly longer for semi-heading types when held between 0° and 2° C (32° and 36° F). At higher temperatures, bacterial soft rot can be a serious problem.

Mustard Greens

Quality Criteria The quality attributes are essentially those for spinach, with one additional proviso. Flower stalks and flowers are not part of high-quality mustard. They indicate old plants that tend to be tough and overly strong in flavor.

Recommended Conditions See Spinach.

Onions, Green

Quality Criteria Green onions must be crisp, clean, and free of any discoloration. Roots should be trimmed close to the base, but the latter should not be injured or even cut off. Bunched onions should be tied only tightly enough to hold the stalks together, not so tightly as to break them, as all too often is the case.

Recommended Conditions Green onions are usually packed in ice to assure their crispness and to avoid decay. Vacuum cooling is feasible, but wilting must be guarded against, especially during warm weather.

If vacuum cooled, the onions should first be wetted and then packed in individual perforated bags or in master containers lined with perforated polyethylene film. Green onions packed in a polyethylene-lined box and top-iced had excellent appearance after 4 weeks of storage at 0° C (32° F); if they were not top-iced they still were considered at least "good." If held at 5° C (41° F) they remained in good condition only about a week (Hruschka 1974).

The combination of 1% O_2 and 5% CO_2 extended the storage life at 0° C another 2 to 4 weeks, depending on whether "excellent" or "good" appearance was required.

Parsley

Quality Criteria   Parsley must be green, turgid and clean, untainted by yellowish or limp sprigs or by soil adhering to the curly leaves.

Recommended Conditions   Parsley is generally package-iced to prevent wilting. Packaging in open-topped bags is advantageous during display.

Under ideal conditions (0° C, 32° F, high RH) parsley can be kept in good to excellent condition for about 2 months and in fair condition for 3 to 4 months (Apeland 1971). Under normal handling and display practices 1 to 2 weeks seems more realistic.

Judging by results at 5° C (41° F), CA storage (10% O_2 with 11% CO_2 or 2.5% O_2 without added CO_2) can add at least 1 to 2 weeks to the useful life of parsley.

Rhubarb

Quality Criteria   To be attractive, rhubarb stalks (petioles) must be crisp and straight. The bases of the stalks should be attached but their removal is not a major defect.

Recommended Conditions   Room-cooling seems to be adequate if 0° to 1° C (32° to 34° F) is reached within less than one day and if the stalks are well protected from wilting by ventilated box liners. Slow cooling increases the danger of wilting, because the stalks lose more moisture while they are warmer than the surroundings than when they are at the temperature of the cold-room. Hydrocooling to 0° to 2° C (32° to 35° F), followed by packing in waxed cartons lined with perforated film, should effectively stop wilting without enhancing decay, if the stalks are kept cold.

Storage life of rhubarb is about 4 weeks at 0° C (32° F), 2 weeks at 5° C (41° F), and 1 week at 10° C (50° F), if "acceptable" condition is used as criterion. For high quality, the times probably should be reduced by one-third or one-half.

Rhubarb should be marketed with the leaf blade removed because the inedible blade draws moisture from the stalk, readily decays, wastes space, and adds to transportation cost. Further, removal of the blade also prevents their accidental ingestion, which can be harmful because of their high oxalate content.

The blade should be cut just above its juncture with the petiole. If it is cut below, the petiole is more prone to splitting (Hruschka 1967).

Spinach

Quality Criteria   Spinach leaves should be uniformly green, fully turgid, clean and not physically damaged. If entire plants are bunched, the young inner leaves may be yellowish green.

Recommended Conditions   Spinach can be package-iced, hydrocooled, or vacuum cooled equally well. If hydrocooled, it should be centrifuged about 3 min to remove excess water to retard decay under higher than ideal temperatures. This procedure does not apply to commodities with the same general requirements as spinach, such as chard, collards, and kale or mustard and turnip greens. Spinach that is above 24° C (75° F) should be wetted before it is vacuum cooled.

Adding about 100 ppm chlorine to the water used for washing or cooling avoids buildup of bacteria in the water, but has little effect on decay of spinach, probably because most infections start in wounds made at harvest.

Most spinach is prepackaged in perforated plastic bags to avoid dehydration and physical abuse. If bunched, the ties should not be so tight as to break petioles and crush leaves. Further, once removed from ice, the bunches must be wetted frequently with iced water to avoid wilting.

Atmospheres enriched in CO_2 (10%) retard yellowing of spinach and maintain the product in "good quality" 3 weeks at 5° C (41° F) (Murata and Ueda 1967). Thus, CA prolongs the useful life of spinach by about 1 week at the temperature cited. The above researchers noticed no injuries in spinach held 3 weeks in 40% CO_2. Since, however, such a high level of CO_2 was no more beneficial than 10%, there is no point in risking injury from the higher concentration.

New Zealand spinach (*Tetragonia tetragonioides*), a leafy green that is used like the common spinach but which is not astringent, retains its quality better if held in an atmosphere that contains about 7% CO_2 than in air (McGill *et al.* 1966).

Spinach becomes unsalable after about 24 days at 2° C (35° F), 7 days at 10° C (50° F), or 2.5 days at 18° C (65° F) (Platenius 1939). However, these periods probably should be about halved for quality that meets current consumer standards.

Turnip Greens   See *Spinach.*

Watercress

Quality Criteria   Watercress should be deep green and fully turgid. A harmless purplish color of the leaves should not be mistaken for undesirable discoloration due to aging.

Recommended Conditions   This spicy, decorative green usually is packed by alternating a layer of cress with a layer of ice (Shear 1968). Hydrocooling also is effective, but must be followed by thorough refrigeration throughout marketing. Vacuum cooling has apparently not been tried, but probably would effectively cool the crop, particularly since it comes wet from the field.

Watercress is advantageously packed in containers lined with perforated film to minimize the chance of wilting. This practice would probably be essential if vacuum cooling were used.

Individual plastic bags should be open-topped to permit display of the cress. Consequently, water loss must be prevented by frequent wetting with chilled water.

High perishability limits the storage life of cress to 4 to 7 days at 0° to 2° C (32° to 36° F).

IMMATURE FLOWER HEADS

This group includes artichokes (*Cynara scolymus*), broccoli (*Brassica oleracea*, italica), and cauliflower (*Brassica oleracea*, botrytis). While the requirements of these commodities are similar, they differ sufficiently in detail to necessitate separate discussion for each.

Artichokes

Quality Criteria   These immature flower buds are most desirable when the outer bracts are free of any blemishes and when they are tightly closed. Partially or wide open buds indicate old age or wilting, or both. Turgid buds squeak when slightly compressed or when rubbed against each other.

Discoloration of outer bracts caused by freezing injury does not detract from culinary quality, although appearance is marred.

Size of buds does not determine their quality, only their utilization. However, small buds wilt more readily than large ones because of their larger surface-to-volume ratio.

Recommended Conditions   Artichokes must be precooled on the day of harvest for maximum quality retention. They either may be hydrocooled or room-cooled, but they should be below 5° C (41° F) within 24 hr. Subsequent holding as close to 0° C (32° F) as feasible is highly desirable for maximum quality retention, although 2 to 3° C (35° to 37° F) is satisfactory for normal marketing periods.

If artichokes are hydrocooled, subsequent water loss can be minimized by packing them in boxes lined with perforated film, in waxed cartons, or in various consumer packages. In the last case, hydrocooling must precede packing; in the other two, either sequence is satisfactory if handling is prompt.

If film liners are used, they must be perforated with about 60 5 mm (50 ¼ in.) holes per 1000 cm² (per ft²) to permit the water to drain and respiratory heat to be dissipated. For artichokes in film liners or consumer packs top ice is not needed if the storage temperature is near 0° C (32° F). For those packed in waxed cartons or wood crates, ice is advisable as coolant and source of moisture. Without it, wilting can be serious.

The rate of heat removal from artichokes during hydrocooling depends greatly on size of the buds. Large buds (36 size; about 90 mm [3.5 in.] long and across) cool from 21° to 5° C (70° to 41° F) in about 23 min, whereas small ones (72 size; slightly over 70 mm [3 in.] long and about 75 mm [2.75 in.] across) required only about 12 min if the cooling water is 1° C (34° F).

Artichokes room-cooled after being packed benefit from prior washing in cold water, because maintaining high RH in each package prevents wilting.

Holding artichokes in controlled atmospheres probably offers little advantage during usual marketing periods. However, if stored for about 1 month, at 1.5° C (35° F) artichokes keep better in an atmosphere containing about 3% CO_2 and 3% O_2 than in air. Reduction in browning of the bracts was given as the chief advantage of CA storage by Poma Treccani and Anoni (1969), although they did not specify whether the improvement was due to a reduction in decay or to a slowing of physiological aging.

Artichokes keep in good condition about 2 weeks at 0° to 3° C (32° to 37° F), about 10 days at 5° C (41° F) and only 5 days at 10° C (50° F). If fair quality is satisfactory, the storage life is at least doubled.

The length of useful storage life is clearly related to initial quality, as shown by Rappaport and Watada (1958). Buds with freezing injury and decay at harvest deteriorate about 1.5 times as rapidly as sound buds, especially if held at 5° C (41° F) or above. Research in Egypt suggests that there may be seasonal differences in keeping quality; buds harvested early kept better than those harvested late (Salama et al. 1962).

Addition of disinfectants to the water used for washing or cooling does not reduce decay. However, if water is recirculated, as in hydrocooling, 100 to 200 ppm chlorine will reduce buildup of organisms in the water.

Broccoli

Quality Criteria   Heads of broccoli must be entirely green and all flower buds must be completely closed to be desirable. A purplish cast to the surface is not at all objectionable. However, yellowing or any wilting is highly objectionable and indicates poor handling practices somewhere in market channels.

Generally, the large central heads are most desirable, but there is no evidence that side shoots are inferior except in attractiveness as a centerpiece.

Recommended Conditions   Broccoli, as one of the most perishable vegetables, must be promptly precooled to as near 0° C (32° F) as possible. This can be accomplished by hydrocooling or by packing the broccoli in ice. The best choice is the combination of the two procedures. Thus, quick cooling and continuous maximum refrigeration can be achieved. Broccoli can be hydrocooled from 21° to 2° C (70° to 35° F) in about 10 min if the water is held at 0° C (32° F).

Hydrocooling and package-icing will prevent wilting until the package is opened. Afterwards, the wilting can be prevented by sprinkling with chilled water or by prepackaging in ventilated film bags. Since high RH (95% or higher) is essential to avoid wilting, low temperature is essential to avoid mold growth. Further, 500 g (1 lb) bags should have about 20 5-mm (12 ¼-in.) holes to allow for adequate heat and gas exchange.

Broccoli benefits substantially from storage in low O_2, in high CO_2, or in a combination of the 2 adjustments when storage is above about 3° C (38° F) for at least a week (Lebermann et al. 1968A; Lipton and Harris 1974). Oxygen below 2% greatly retards yellowing but has little effect on decay or on the firmness of curds cooked after storage. Broccoli tolerates low O_2 very well and is permanently injured only at 0.25% O_2 or lower concentrations. Consequently, an O_2 concentration of 1% ± 0.5% would be optimal. In such an atmosphere broccoli remained green 3 weeks at 5° C (41° F) followed by 3 days at 10° C (50° F), whereas broccoli held equally long in air was completely yellow.

If broccoli should accidentally be held in nearly anaerobic conditions (0.1% O_2) for more than 2 weeks the stem and large branches may show a whitish-tan to tan discoloration or the smallest branches may appear pinched. These symptoms are evident only after broccoli is cooked. Such low O_2 concentrations also induce offensive off-odors and off-flavors.

CO_2 at 5 to 20% retards yellowing and toughening and 10% or more virtually prevents mold growth even during 3 weeks at 7.5° C (45° F). Since 15% CO_2 can induce persistent off-odors (Smith 1940) and since 10% CO_2 is effective, there is no need to risk the higher concentrations. The effectiveness of 10% CO_2 is equal to or slightly superior to 1% O_2 in retarding yellowing; in addition, 10% CO_2 not only retards toughening but renders broccoli more tender during subsequent cooking than it would have been if cooked soon after harvest. Slight off-odors that develop in raw broccoli stored with 10% CO_2 dissipate during cooking when storage is at 5° C (41° F) or below. However, when 10% CO_2 is combined with low O_2, the latter should not be below 1% because of the dangers of off-odors (Kasmire et al. 1974).

In summary, CA storage of broccoli for quality maintenance is advantageous only when it must be held longer than about 1 week above about 3° C (38° F). If preprocessing tenderization is desired, holding broccoli 2 or 3 days at 5° C (41° F) in 10% CO_2 likely would be optimal.

Initially high-quality broccoli can be held in excellent condition 2 weeks at 2.5° C (36° F) and 1 week at 5° C (41° F) when all aspects of quality are considered. Optimal CA conditions will approximately double the storage life and if "good" quality is satisfactory, another week can be added in air or CA storage. However broccoli is held, water loss must be minimized by use of ice or packaging in perforated plastic bags or box liners.

Cultivars of broccoli differ in their keepability, according to unpublished work from the University of California. However, such differences show up only after about 2 weeks at 5° C (41° F), and thus are of concern only for long transit periods. Under such conditions, Waltham 29 was superior to Puyallup Polycross or Early K and V.

Cauliflower

Quality Criteria   Snow white, compact curds surrounded by turgid green leaves describe a desirable head of cauliflower. A very slightly yellowish curd does not indicate improper postharvest conditions, but rather incomplete shading of the curd during maturation. Such curds have reduced eye-appeal but are acceptable, whereas dark cream to yellow ones tend to be overly strong flavored.

Since cauliflower stores rather well under proper conditions, spreading or dark-specked curds and yellowed, or even missing leaves, indicate gross mishandling or overlong storage. Ricy curds, those with protruding immature flower parts, also are objectionable. They are a sign of senescence that can be reached either before or after harvest.

Recommended Conditions   Cauliflower can be hydrocooled or vacuum cooled equally successfully. Final temperature should be below $7°$ C ($45°$ F), and preferably below $5°$ C ($41°$ F), followed by storage as close to $0°$ C ($32°$ F) as feasible.

Cauliflower can be hydrocooled from $21°$ C to $5°$ ($70°$ F to $41°$) in about 20 min if the water is $1°$ C ($34°$ F). Vacuum cooling requires about 30 min for equivalent cooling if the curds are wet; if dry, they cool to only slightly below $10°$ C ($50°$ F), which is higher than desirable (Stewart and Barger 1961). Since cauliflower is washed, wetting prior to vacuum cooling presents no problem.

When water is used to cool, film-wrapping follows cooling. Since cauliflower is grown in cool areas, no significant warming occurs during wrapping. However, to avoid waste of refrigeration, prompt removal to a refrigerated room or conveyance is advisable.

Cauliflower wilts readily unless held in at least 95% RH. This condition is now almost universally reached by wrapping each head in perforated film. Four to six 5 mm (¼ in.) holes provide adequate ventilation for any size head under normal conditions.

The importance of adequate ventilation cannot be over-stressed because cauliflower is severely injured by excessive CO_2 (Karch 1965; Lipton *et al.* 1967), and by low O_2.

Cauliflower can be injured by 5% CO_2; between 5 and 10% CO_2 injury usually develops; above 10% CO_2 injury is certain. This injury to cauliflower is unique, in that it is evident *only* after cooking. Then the curds are yellowish gray, excessively soft, and emit a strong off-odor. The injurious conditions can occur within 48 hr during normal marketing of cauliflower in nonperforated film wraps, where CO_2 can reach over 10%.

Interestingly, the CO_2 induced defects can be completely coun-

U.S. Dept. of Agriculture Photo

FIG. 6.5. DEGREES OF MATURITY OF CAULIFLOWER
A—Slightly overmature, still marketable. B—Optimum. C—Overmature, not marketable.

teracted by aeration for 6 hr or by cooking the cauliflower in acidified water (pH about 3.75). However, neither of these antidotes is practical in most cases, because raw cauliflower shows no adverse effects from high CO_2, and thus the user has no idea that aeration is needed. Cooking in acid (vinegar) is no help either, because it impairs the flavor of cauliflower.

The softening of cauliflower by CO_2 differs from that of asparagus, because the desirable tenderization in the latter is related to cellulose fibers which are absent in the immature florets of the former.

Cauliflower held about 6 days or longer at 2.5°, 5.0° or 7.5° C (36°, 41° or 45° F) with 2% or less O_2 developed a strong off-odor when cooked. This off-odor, unlike that induced by CO_2, does not disappear during aeration prior to cooking, but sometimes is even intensified by aeration (Lipton and Harris 1976).

The storage life of cauliflower extends at least 1 month, and possibly 6 weeks, under ideal conditions of initial quality, temperature and humidity (Hruschka and Kaufman 1949; Karch 1965). Usually, however, 2 weeks is the maximum for good final quality. At 5° C (41° F), the storage life is about 1 week to 10 days, at 10° C (50° F) it is about 5 days, and at 15° C (59° F) 3 days (Herregods 1964). Maximum storage life can be attained more readily with physiologically young, compact heads than with more mature ones, and by leaving on the wrapper leaves of heads that are not packed in film (Böttcher 1967).

Various plant growth regulators have been tested to retard yellowing and abscission of cauliflower leaves after harvest. Although several were found to be effective, none was or is used commercially. Apparently, not enough cauliflower is held more than two weeks to warrant the expense of obtaining government clearance for use of the chemicals.

REFERENCES

Commodity Requirements, General

LUTZ, J. M., and HARDENBURG, R. E. 1968. The commercial storage of fruits, vegetables, and florist and nursery stocks. U.S. Dept. Agr. Handbook 66.

MORRISON, W. W. 1961. Tips on selecting fruits and vegetables. U.S. Dept. Agr. Mktg Bull 13.

SMITH P. G., and WELCH, J. E. 1964. Nomenclature of vegetables and condiment herbs grown in the United States. Proc. Am. Soc. Hort. Sci 84, 535-548.

VAN DEN BERG, L., and LENTZ, C. P. 1977. Effect of relative humidity of (sic) storage life of vegetables. Acta Hort. No. 62, 197-208.

Brussels Sprouts

EAVES, C. A., and FORSYTH, F. R. 1968. The influence of light, modified atmospheres and benzimidazole on Brussels sprouts. J. Hort. Sci. *43*, 317-322.

ISENBERG, F. M. 1969. The use of controlled atmosphere on cole crops. *In* Controlled Atmospheres for the Storage and Transport of Horticultural Crops. D. H. Dewey, R. C. Herner, and D. R. Dilley (Editors). Mich. State Univ. Hort. Rept. *9*, 95-96.

LYONS, J. M., and RAPPAPORT, L. 1959. Effect of temperature on respiration and quality of Brussels sprouts during storage. Proc. Am. Soc. Hort. Sci. *73*, 361-366.

LYONS, J. M., and RAPPAPORT, L. 1962. Effect of controlled atmospheres on storage quality of Brussels sprouts. Proc. Am. Soc. Hort. Sci. *81*, 324-331.

RYGG, G. L., and McCOY, W. W. 1952. Pre-packaging Brussels sprouts. Western Grower and Shipper, *24*, No. 1, 46-49.

STENVERS, N. 1971. Preliminary experiments on vacuum cooling of vegetables and berries. Sprenger Inst. Rept. *1630* (Suppl.) (Dutch)

STEWART, J. K., and BARGER, W. R. 1963. Effects of cooling method, prepackaging and top-icing on the quality of Brussels sprouts. Proc. Am. Soc. Hort. Sci. *83*, 488-494.

Cabbage

BOHLING, H., and HANSEN, H. 1977. Storage of white cabbage (*Brassica oleracea* var. *capitata*) in controlled atmospheres. Acta Hort. No. 62, 49-54.

BÖTTCHER, H. 1965. Optimal storage conditions for vegetables and potatoes. Kälte *18*, 5-6, 8-10. (German)

GRÖSCHNER, P. 1962. Cold storage of late cabbage and onions. Deut. Gartenbau *9*, No. 2, 46-47. (German)

ISENBERG, F. M., and SAYLES, R. M. 1969. Modified atmosphere storage of Danish cabbage. J. Am. Soc. Hort. Sci. *94*, 447-449.

KURKI, L. 1971. Moisture in vegetable storage. Acta Hort. No. 20, 146-151.

MORRISON, W. W. 1962. Fresh cabbage. From grower to retailer. U.S. Dept. Agr. Mktg. Bull. *21*.

PARSONS, C. S. 1959. Effects of temperature and packaging on the quality of stored cabbage. Proc. Am. Soc. Hort. Sci. *74*, 616-621.

PARSONS, C. S., McCOLLOCH, L. P., and WRIGHT, R. C. 1960. Cabbage, celery, lettuce, and tomatoes. Laboratory tests of storage methods. U.S. Dept. Agr. Mktg. Res. Rept. *402*.

PENDERGRASS, A., and ISENBERG, F. M. R. 1974. The effect of relative humidity on the quality of stored cabbage. Hort. Science *9*, 226-227.

PENDERGRASS, A., ISENBERG, F. M. R., HOWELL, L. L., and CARROL, J. E. 1976. Ethylene-induced changes in appearance and hormone content of Florida-grown cabbage. Can. J. Plant Sci. *56*, 319-324.

STOLL, K. 1973. Tables on the storage of fruits and vegetables in controlled atmosphere. Mitteil. Eidg. Forschungsanst. Obst-, Wein-, and Gartenbau, Wädenswil. Flugschr. *78*. (German)

SUHONEN, I. 1969. On the storage life of white cabbage in refrigerated stores. Acta Agr. Scand. *19*, 18-32.

VAN DEN BERG, L., and LENTZ, C. P. 1966. Relative humidity and the refrigerated storage of carrots and cabbages. Food in Canada, July, 16-18.

VAN DEN BERG, L., and LENTZ, C. P. 1973. High humidity storage of carrots, parsnips, rutabagas, and cabbage. J. Am. Soc. Hort. Sci. *98*, 129-132.

YODER, O. C. 1977. Development of methods for long-term cabbage storage. Acta Hort. No. 62, 301-310.

Cabbage, Chinese

VAN DEN BERG, L., and LENTZ, C. P. 1977. Effect of relative humidity of (*sic*) storage life of vegetables. Acta Hort. No. 62, 197–208.

WEICHMAN, J. 1977. CA storage of Chinese cabbage *(Brassica pekinensis* (Lour.) Rupr.). Acta Hort. No. 62, 119–29.

Celery

GRIZZELL, W. G., and BENNETT, A. M. 1966. Hydrocooling stacked crates of celery and sweet corn. U.S. Dept. Agr. *ARS 52–12*.

HALL, C. B. 1962. Control of the darkening of the butts of pre-packaged celery. Proc. Am. Soc. Hort. Sci. *81*, 354–357.

KASMIRE, R. F. 1972. Windrowed top icing cools celery faster. Western Grower and Shipper *43*, No. 3, 29–30.

KURKI, L. 1971. Moisture in vegetable storage. Acta Hort. No. 20, 146–151.

PARSONS, C. S. 1960. Effects of temperature, packaging and sprinkling on the quality of stored celery. Proc. Am. Soc. Hort. Sci. *75*, 463–469.

PARSONS, C. S., McCOLLOCH, L. P., and WRIGHT, R. C. 1960. Cabbage, celery, lettuce, and tomatoes. Laboratory tests of storage methods. U.S Dept. Agr. Mktg. Res. Rept. *402*.

SCHOMER, H. A., SHOWALTER, R. K., HARDENBURG, R. E., and THOMPSON, B. D. 1955. Pre-packaging celery at production area in Florida. Florida Agr. Expt. Sta. Hort. Ser. *55–2*.

STENVERS, N. 1969. Storage of blanched celery. Groenten Fruit *24*, 1103. (Dutch)

STENVERS, N. 1971. Preliminary experiments on vacuum cooling of vegetables and berries. Sprenger Inst. Rept. *1630* (Suppl.) (Dutch)

STEWART, J. K., and BARGER, W. R. 1962. Effects of precooling method on the quality of crate-packed and pre-packaged celery. Proc. Am. Soc. Hort. Sci. *81*, 347–353.

U.S. DEPT. AGR. 1959. United States Standards for Celery. U.S. Department of Agriculture, Washington, D.C.

Lettuce, Crisphead

BARGER, W. R. 1961. Factors affecting temperature reduction and weight-loss in vacuum-cooled lettuce. U.S. Dept. Agr. Mktg. Res. Rept. *469*.

CALIF. DEPT. OF AGR. Various years. Regulations of the Department of Agriculture pertaining to fruit, nut, egg, and vegetable standardization. Sacramento, Calif.

CEPONIS, M. J., and KAUFMAN, J. 1968. Effect of relative humidity on moisture loss and decay of eastern lettuce pre-packaged in different films. U.S. Dept. Agr. *ARS 51*–18.

CHAPOGAS, P. G., and STOKES, D. R. 1964. Pre-packaging lettuce at shipping point. U.S. Dept. Agr. Mktg. Res. Rept. *670*.

HARVEY, J. M., *et al*. 1961. Field trimming of lettuce. Effects of package weight on market quality. U.S. Dept. Agr. Mktg. Res. Rept. *497*.

KADER, A. A., LIPTON, W. J., and MORRIS, L. L. 1973. Systems for scoring quality of harvested lettuce. HortScience *8*, 408-409.

KADER, A. A., MORRIS, L. L., and KLAUSTERMEYER, J. A. 1974. Postharvest handling and physiology of lettuce—an indexed reference list. Univ. Calif., Davis, Dept. Veg. Crops Ser. *161* and Suppl. , 1975.

LIPTON, W. J. 1967. Market quality and rate of respiration of head lettuce in low-oxygen atmospheres. U.S. Dept. Agr. Mktg. Res. Rept. *777*.

LIPTON, W. J. 1968. Low O_2 atmospheres. Benefits and dangers. *In* United Fresh Fruit and Vegetable Association Yearbook. pp 99–100, 103. United Fresh Fruit and Vegetable Assoc., Washington, D.C.

LIPTON, W. J. and BARGER, W. R. 1965. Market quality of head lettuce in relation to delays between harvest and precooling and temperature after cooling. U.S. Dept. Agr. *ARS 51-5*.

MORRIS, L. L., PRATT, H. K., and TUCKER, C. L. 1955. Lettuce handling and quality. Western Grower and Shipper. *26*, No. 5, 14–16, 18.

PARSONS, C. S., ATROPS, E. A., and STEWART, J. K. 1960. Effects of trimming and packaging methods on keeping quality of lettuce. U.S. Dept. Agr. *AMS 376*.

PARSONS, C. S., and WRIGHT, R. C. 1955. Effects of temperature, trimming, and packaging methods on lettuce deterioration. Proc. Am. Soc. Hort. Sci. *68*, 283–287.

PRATT, H. K., MORRIS, L. L., and TUCKER, C. L. 1954. Temperature and lettuce deterioration. Proc. Conf. Transport. Perishables. Univ. Calif., Davis. 77–83.

RIJ, R. E., HINDS, R. H., HINSCH, R. T., and HARRIS, C. M. 1976. Current practices and trends in marketing western iceberg lettuce in relation to other produce. U.S. Dept. Agr. Mktg. Res. Rept. *1052*.

STEWART, J. K. 1955. Arizona spring lettuce refrigeration requirements during marketing periods. Proc. Am. Soc. Hort. Sci. *65*, 387–392.

STEWART, J. K. *et al*. 1977. Guides to successful lettuce exporting. Western Grower and Shipper *48*, No. 1, 13–15.

STEWART, J. K., and BURKHART, L. 1956. Effects of temperature and maturity on lettuce in transit. Western Grower and Shipper *27*, No. 4, 19.

STEWART, J. K., CEPONIS, M. J., and BERAHA, L. 1970. Modified atmosphere effects on the market quality of lettuce shipped by rail. U.S. Dept. Agr. Mktg. Res. Rept. *863*.

STEWART, J. K., CEPONIS, M. J., and HARRIS, C. M. 1967. Market quality of film-wrapped and naked-packed head lettuce. U.S. Dept. Agr. *ARS 51-11*.

STEWART, J. K., HARVEY, J. M., CEPONIS, M. J., and WRIGHT, W. R. 1972. Carbon dioxide levels in rail cars and their effect on lettuce. U.S. Dept. Agr. Mktg. Res. Rept. *937*.

STEWART, J. K., and UOTA, M. 1976. Postharvest effect of modified levels of carbon monoxide, carbon dioxide, and oxygen on disorders and appearance of head lettuce. J. Am. Soc. Hort. Sci. *101*, 382–384.

U.S. DEPT. AGR. 1974. Harvesting lettuce electronically. Agr. Res. *22*, No. 7, 8–11.

U.S. DEPT. AGR. 1975. U.S. Standards for Grades of Lettuce. U.S. Department of Agriculture, Washington, D.C.

Miscellaneous Leafy and Chopped Vegetables

AHARONI, N., and BEN-YEHOSHUA, S. 1973. Delaying deterioration of Romaine lettuce by vacuum cooling and modified atmosphere produced in polyethylene packages. J. Am. Soc. Hort. Sci. *98*, 464–468.

APELAND, J. 1971. Factors affecting respiration and colour during storage of parsley. Acta Hort. No. 20, 43–52.

COOK, J. A. 1960. Quality deterioration of forced rhubarb during handling and marketing. Mich. Agr. Expt. Sta. Quart. Bull. *42*, 878–885.

FRANCIS, F. J. 1960. Discoloration and quality maintenance of cole slaw. Proc. Am. Soc. Hort. Sci. *75*, 449–455.

FRIEDMAN, B. A. 1951. Vacuum cooling of pre-packaged spinach, cole slaw and mixed salad. Proc. Am. Soc. Hort. Sci. *58*, 279–287.

HERNER, R. H., and KRAHN, T. R. 1973. Chopped lettuce should be kept dry and cold. Produce Mktg. Assoc. Yearbook 130, 132.

HERREGODS, M. 1971. The effect of some factors on witloof during storage. Acta Hort. No. 20, 36–42.

HRUSCHKA, H. W. 1967. Storage and shelf life of packaged rhubarb. U.S. Dept. Agr. Mktg. Res. Rept. *771*.

HRUSCHKA, H. W. 1971. Storage and shelf life of packaged kale. U.S. Dept. Agr. Mktg. Res. Rept. *923*.

HRUSCHKA, H. W. 1974. Storage and shelf life of packaged green onions. U.S. Dept. Agr. Mktg. Res. Rept. *1015*.

KAUFMAN, J., and LUTZ, J. M. 1954. Lengthening the shelf life of packaged cole slaw. Pre-Pack-Age *8*, No. 1, 23–26.

KURKI, L. 1971. Moisture in vegetable storage. Acta Hort. No. 20, 146–151.

LIBBEY, C. J., MARIANI, E. J., JR., and LITSKY, W. 1972. Chopping celery promotes organism growth. J. Environ. Health *35*, 43–44.

PRIEPKE, P. E., WEI, L. S., and NELSON, A. I. 1976. Refrigerated storage of prepacked salad vegetables. J. Food Sci. *41*, 379–382.

SHEAR, G. M. 1968. Commercial growing of watercress. U.S. Dept. Agr. Farmers Bull. *2233*.

STENVERS, N. 1971. Preliminary experiments on vacuum cooling of vegetables and berries. Sprenger Inst. Rept. No. *1630* (Suppl.) (Dutch)

SUHONEN, I. 1970. On the storage life of leek. Acta Agr. Scand. *20*, 25–32.

TATARU, D. P., and WEICHMANN, J. 1974. Storage of butter-type head lettuce in controlled atmospheres. Acta Hort. No. 38, Vol. *1*, 75–79.

VAN DEN BERG, L., and LENTZ, C.P. 1977. Effect of relative humidity of *(sic)* storage life of vegetables. Acta Hort. No. 62, 197–208.

Spinach

FRIEDMAN, B. A. 1951. Control of decay in pre-packaged spinach. Phytopathology *41*, 709–713.

McGILL, J. N., NELSON, A. I., and STEINBERG, M. P. 1966. Effects of modified storage atmospheres on ascorbic acid and other quality characteristics of spinach. J. Food Sci. *31*, 510-517. (Deals with New Zealand spinach.)

MURATA, T., and UEDA, Y. 1967. Studies on the CA storage of spinach. J. Jap. Soc. Hort. Sci. *36*, 449–454. (Japanese, English summary)

PLATENIUS, H. 1939. Effect of temperature on the rate of deterioration of fresh vegetables. J. Agr. Res. *59*, 41–58.

Artichokes, Globe

KASMIRE, R. 1958. Keep globe artichokes fresher, cleaner, and sell more!! Poster. Univ. Calif., Davis.

LIPTON, W. J., and HARVEY, J. M. 1960. Decay of artichoke bracts inoculated with spores of *Botrytis cinerea* Fr. at various constant temperatures. Plant Dis. Rptr. *44*, 837–839.

LIPTON, W. J., and STEWART, J. K. 1963. Effects of precooling on market quality of globe artichokes. U.S. Dept. Agr. Mktg. Res. Rept. *633*.

POMA TRECCANI, C., and ANONI, A. 1969. Controlled atmosphere, packaging in polyethylene and defoliation of the stalks in the cold storage of artichokes. Riv. Ortoflorofruttic. Ital. *53*, 203–215. (Italian)

RAPPAPORT, L., and WATADA, A. E. 1958. Effect of temperature on artichoke quality. Proc. Conf. Transport. Perishables. Univ. Calif., Davis. 142–146.

SALAMA, S. B., SAAD, M., and RAWHIA, I. 1962. Studies on artichoke storage. Agr. Res. Rev. (Cairo) *40*, No. 3, 56–70.

Broccoli

KASMIRE, R. F., KADER, A. A., and KLAUSTERMEYER, J. A. 1974. Influence of aeration rate and atmospheric composition during simulated transit on visual quality and off-odor production by broccoli. HortScience *9*, 228–229.

LEBERMAN, K. W., NELSON, A. I., and STEINBERG, M. P. 1968A. Postharvest changes of broccoli stored in modified atmospheres. 1. Respiration of shoots and color of flower heads. Food Technol. *22*, 143–146.

LEBERMAN, K. W., NELSON, A. I., and STEINBERG, M. P. 1968B. Post-harvest changes of broccoli stored in modified atmospheres. 2. Acidity and its influence on texture and chlorophyll retention of the stalks. Food Technol. *22*, 146–149.

LIPTON, W. J., and HARRIS, C. M., 1974. Controlled atmosphere effects on the market quality of stored broccoli (*Brassica oleracea* L., Italica group). J. Am. Soc. Hort. Sci. *99*, 200–205.

RYGG, G. L., and McCOY, W. W. 1952. Study shows broccoli good pre-packaging prospect. Western Grower and Shipper *23*, No. 6. 50–53.

SMITH, W. H. 1940. The storage of broccoli and cauliflower. J. Pomol. Hort. Sci. *18*, 287–293

Cauliflower

BÖTTCHER, H. 1967. On the storeability of cauliflower. Deut. Gartenbau *14*, 300–304. (German)

HARRIS, C. M., and LIPTON, W. J. 1964. Effect of atmosphere on cauliflower quality. Produce Mktg. *7*, No. 7. 35.

HERREGODS, H. 1961. Keeping of cauliflowers. Rev. Agr. (Bruxelles) *14*, 1433–1435. (French)

HERREGODS, M. 1964. The storage of cauliflower. Tuinbouwberichten. *28*, 486–487. (Flemish)

HRUSCHKA, H. W., and KAUFMAN, J. 1949. Storage tests with Long Island cauliflower to inhibit leaf abscission by using plant growth regulators. Proc. Am. Soc. Hort. Sci. *54*, 438–446.

KARCH, G. 1965. The practical use of polyethylene film during cold storage of cauliflower. Deut. Gartenbau *12*, 214–216. (German)

KAUFMAN, J., and RINGEL, S. M. 1961. Tests of growth regulators to retard yellowing and abscission of cauliflower. Proc. Am. Soc. Hort. Sci. *78*, 349–352.

LIPTON, W. J., and HARRIS, C. M. 1976. Response of stored cauliflower (*Brassica oleracea* L., *Botrytis* group) to low-O_2 atmospheres. J. Am. Soc. Hort. Sci. *101*, 208–211.

LIPTON, W. J., HARRIS, C. M., and COUEY, H. M. 1967. Culinary quality of cauliflower stored in CO_2-enriched atmospheres. Proc. Am. Soc. Hort. Sci. *91*, 852–859.

STEWART, J. K., and BARGER, W. R. 1961. Effects of cooling method on the quality of asparagus and cauliflower. Proc. Am. Soc . Hort. Sci. *78*, 295–301.

7

Commodity Requirements— Unripe Fruits and Miscellaneous Structures

UNRIPE FRUITS REQUIRING MODERATE TEMPERATURES

All crops in this category are subject to chilling injury. The group includes: lima beans *(Phaseolus lunatus)*; snap beans *(Phaseolus vulgaris)*; southern peas or edible cow peas *(Vigna unguiculata,* formerly *sinensis)*, which are really beans; cucumbers *(Cucumis sativus)*; eggplant *(Solanum melongena)*; okra *(Hibiscus esculentus)*; peppers— bell, sweet, or chili *(Capsicum annuum)*; and summer squash *(Cucurbita pepo)*. Even though these crops have certain requirements in common, they differ sufficiently to require individual discussion.

Beans, Snap

Quality Criteria   Snap beans, regardless of type—green or wax— should be free of any brown discoloration. Green beans should be deep to medium green, never yellowish, which is a sign of senescence. Individual seeds are best not noticeable at all, or at most should bulge the pod only very slightly; prominent bulges promise tough, stringy pods and tough seeds. Wilting, as shown by limpness of the pods, is highly objectionable; high quality snap beans literally must snap. While length of pod is not a good criterion of quality, exceptionally long pods in a given lot are likely to be the toughest ones.

Recommended Conditions   Snap beans are highly perishable, and thus must not be subjected to warm temperatures. However, since they are subject to chilling injury, they also must not be cooled to or held near

0° C (32° F). Consequently, their optimum storage range is narrow, and lies between about 3° and 6° C (38° and 42° F) (Watada and Morris 1966A), which is slightly lower than the 4.5° to 7° C (40° to 45° F) suggested by Smith et al. (1966). A rapid decline in quality can be expected if the deviation is more than 1° C (2° F) from this range in either direction (Fig. 7.1). This pattern of deterioration is typical for vegetables sensitive to chilling exposures, as seen earlier in Fig. 1.6.

The high perishability of beans necessitates rapid cooling after harvest, preferably to 4.5° C ± 1° (40° F ± 2°). Beans can be vacuum cooled, but hydrocooling is preferable because water not only cools more rapidly and more thoroughly, but the free moisture also retards wilting (Gorini et al. 1974). Beans packed in wirebound crates, bushel baskets, or waxed cartons most likely cool at about the same rate as green peas. Thus, beans starting between 25° and 30° C (77° and 86° F) should be 5° C (41° F) after being flooded 10 to 12 min with 2° C (35° F) water.

Beans must be held under high humidity. Even free moisture is harmless unless the beans have been chilled or exposed to unfavorably high temperatures. In general, the danger of wilting due to lack of moisture exceeds that of discoloration attributable to free moisture. However, when RH around the beans approaches saturation, as in consumer packages, temperature above 7° C (45° F) must be avoided, or decay is likely to be serious within a few days (Thompson 1964).

High quality beans frequently are packaged in pulp trays overwrapped with a perforated film. Such packaging retards moisture loss,

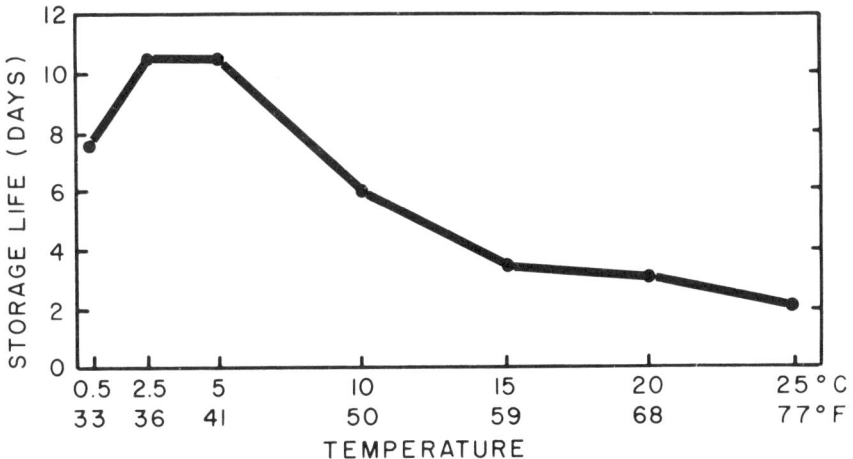

Adapted from Watada and Morris (1966)

FIG. 7.1. TIME REQUIRED FOR SNAP BEANS TO DETERIORATE FROM "FIELD FRESH" TO "GOOD" CONDITION AT VARIOUS CONSTANT TEMPERATURES

reduces physical abuse and can look very attractive. A 500 g (1 lb) package should have about 12 holes 3 mm (10 holes ⅛ in.) in diameter.

Snap beans do not benefit greatly from CA storage. The principal benefit that accrues from the combination of low O_2 (2 to 3%) and high CO_2 (5 to 10%) is a retardation of yellowing, which can be noticed after 4 to 5 days at 7° C (45° F) (Groeschel et al. 1966). According to these authors, CA did not affect texture, but this factor was checked only organoleptically. This does not exclude the possibility that 5 to 10% CO_2 reduces fiber formation. However, higher concentrations should not be used because they may result in off-flavored beans (Anandaswamy and Iyengar 1961). The storage life of beans is relatively brief—at most about 10 days (Fig. 7.1). At temperatures above 10° C (50° F), the storage life is even shorter than indicated in the graph, because seed content and toughness of the pods increase rapidly (Littman 1967), even more rapidly than visual deterioration, the criterion used by Watada and Morris (1966A).

The storage life can be lengthened by the proper choice of cultivar, provided it meets other quality characteristics (Table 1.4) (Gorini et al. 1974; Watada and Morris 1966B). If high fiber content is to be avoided, Tendergreen would be far superior to Bountiful or Black Valentine. Judging by the data of Watada and Morris (1966B) and Guyer and Kramer (1952), Tendergreen would be a good compromise for maximum storage life; it is neither highly sensitive to chilling nor undesirably fibrous. The fact that cultivars differ so greatly in susceptibility to chilling injury and in fiber content should be taken into consideration when beans are grown long distances from their markets.

Beans, Lima

Quality Criteria Fresh lima beans virtually are unknown on today's produce shelf. This sharp decline in popularity probably was caused largely by the poor quality of the product offered and the comparatively better quality of the frozen product. Pods of limas should be deep green, firm, and free of any blemishes. If marketed shelled, the seeds should be uniformly light green, shiny and dry, not slimy and sticky.

The skins of the seeds should be tender and easily pricked with a fingernail. Tough skins cover starchy, tasteless beans.

Recommended Conditions Limas, like snap beans, are chilling sensitive; however, the pods show the symptoms of injury more readily than the seeds. Unshelled beans should be held at 5° to 7° C (41° to

45° F), whereas about 3° C (37° F) is preferable for shelled beans. The suggestions given for precooling of snap beans also apply to limas.

Prepackaging of either entire or shelled limas is advantageous because it retards wilting, reduces physical injury, and allows good sanitary practices, an important consideration for shelled beans.

Holding *shelled* limas in high CO_2 seems highly advantageous because, according to Brooks and McColloch (1938), 25 to 35% CO_2 substantially reduces stickiness and spotting of the seeds by inhibiting fungal and bacterial growth. More recent tests on other crops and with fungi and bacteria suggest that 10 to 15% CO_2 will achieve the same effect. Such levels of CO_2 might also be advantageous if limas have to be held more than a day or two before being canned or frozen. The effect of low O_2 has not been tested, but concentrations down to 5% likely are safe. CA storage of limas in pods should be approached with caution, since there is inadequate information on the response of the pods.

The storage life of lima beans in the pod is less than one week even under the best conditions, and that of shelled beans is about a week if even reasonably good quality is expected. As temperature approaches 10° C (50° F), the storage life is about 3 days. Holding shelled limas in high CO_2 adds 1 or 2 days to their useful life.

Southern Peas

Little precise information is available on the proper storage condition for southern peas marketed fresh. However, following the suggestion for snap beans should give satisfactory results. Certainly, such practices will yield a more tender and generally more desirable product than mostly available to consumers. A storage life of 10 days is probably maximal under ideal conditions, with 6 to 8 days being more realistic.

Most of the commercial Southern pea crop is processed. A tender product of good flavor can be obtained only if the peas are cooled to presumably at least about 10° to 15° C (50° to 60° F) soon after harvest unless they are processed within 2 hr (Smittle and Kays 1976).

Cucumbers, Slicing

Quality Criteria   Dark green and firm slicing cucumbers are most desirable. They should neither be pitted, nor have wrinkled "pinched" ends. Good cucumbers can be elongated or fairly short and thick, as long as they are green. Yellowish, senescent cucumbers are undesirable, regardless of shape, although a small yellowish-green ground spot indicates only a negligible loss in quality.

Other cucumbers available, from the round, yellow lemon to the very long and ridged Armenian kind, differ from the most common type in color, but not in other major criteria.

Recommended Conditions   The susceptibility of cucumbers to chilling injury and to yellowing restricts desirable storage temperatures to a narrow range. If held at 10° C (50° F) or colder, they suffer chilling injury; if held at 15° C (59° F) or higher, they rapidly become yellow. Thus, the optimum is 12° to 13° C (54° to 55° F). However, for storage of 1 to 2 weeks, 10° C is preferable because chilling is minimal and yellowing is retarded, although Apeland (1966) claims that yellowing is slower at 13° C (55° F) than at higher or lower temperatures. The same author found that differences in chilling sensitivity among cultivars are minor. Thus, unless specific contrary information is available, high sensitivity must be assumed for all cultivars. Further, young (and thus small) cucumbers show chilling symptoms earlier and more severely than older fruit, but the specific relationship between size and symptom development depends on cultivar and season (Hirose 1971).

The susceptibility of cucumbers to chilling injury does not preclude their exposure to temperatures below 5° C (41° F) as long as they are utilized immediately after removal from cold storage, because symptoms develop rapidly only at higher temperatures. Thus, 2 days at 0° C (32° F), 4 days at 5° C (41° F), or 8 days at 7° F (45° F) are harmless under these conditions.

Cucumbers usually are not precooled, but are cooled after packing and loading into rail car or truck trailer. However, hydrocooling has been found useful for pickling cucumbers, and there is no obvious reason why it would not benefit slicing cucumbers harvested during hot weather. Cucumbers probably would cool at about the same rate as potatoes. Thus, 5° C (41° F) water would cool them from 24° to 13° C (75° to 55° F) in about 14 min or from 30° C (86° F) in about 17 min.

Cucumbers readily become flaccid unless they are held at high RH— about 95%. High RH not only retards this softening, but also delays pitting, which is a symptom of chilling injury. Water loss can be effectively guarded against by waxing of these fruits or by packaging in ventilated films (Okubo and Maezawa 1965; Wiebe 1969).

Yellowing of cucumbers can be retarded by holding them in about 5% CO_2 or 5% O_2, although a combination of the two seems most effective. If CA is used, care must be taken to avoid chilling temperatures, because high CO_2, and to a lesser degree, low O_2, aggravate chilling injury. Even at desirable temperatures CO_2 should not exceed 10% or O_2 fall below 2%.

Cucumbers can be expected to remain in good condition for 10 to 14 days at $10°$ C $(50°$ F). For fruits harvested relatively young, where yellowing is not an immediate problem, $13°$ C $(55°$ F) would be preferable and may extend the storage life 2 or 3 days, and proper CA conditions may add a further 4 to 6 days, for a total of about 3 weeks.

During any storage of cucumbers, be it in transit or in a cold room, ethylene must be scrupulously avoided, because according to Apeland (1961), even 1 ppm will cause noticeable yellowing in one day at $15°$ C $(59°$ F). Thus, melons, tomatoes, apples or pears should not be held together with cucumbers for more than a few hours at most. If a mixed load of cucumbers and tomatoes is unavoidable, reducing O_2 to 3% or increasing CO_2 to 5 or 10% would minimize the danger of yellowing and apparently even of decay because ethylene production and action would be limited (van Uffelen 1975). The other crops mentioned would not be shipped with cucumbers, because of different temperature requirements, but might inadvertently be held in the same cold room.

Cucumbers, Pickling

The general observations made for slicing cucumbers also apply to those intended for pickling. However, certain points deserve special note.

Fruit harvested by machine has a 6 to 20% higher rate of respiration than that harvested by hand (Weichman *et al.* 1975). Consequently, prompt precooling of such fruit is particularly important because respiratory heat can accumulate rapidly in bins. If pickling cucumbers are hydrocooled they should be stored no more than a few days prior to processing, because washing about halves their storage life. Thus, unwashed fruit retained "acceptable" quality 6 days at $4.5°$ C $(40°$ F) but washed fruit retained it for less than 4 days (Fellers and Pflug 1967). Cooling to and holding at $1°$ to $2°$ C $(34°$ to $36°$ F) likely would extend this period several days without development of chilling symptoms if removal from cold storage were immediately followed by processing.

Eggplant

Quality Criteria   There exist diverse colored cultivars of eggplant, but since the overwhelming proportion grown in the United States has purple skins, this is the only type we will consider.

The fruits of eggplant should be deep purple, glistening, and firm, and the calyx and stem should be a fresh green. A dull skin, particularly if slightly wrinkled, is a sign of excess water loss and aging. Pitting follows chilling injury, which may be accompanied by internal discoloration of the flesh.

Eggplants are best when their diameter does not exceed about 10 cm (4 in.), although those up to 15 cm (6 in.) usually are still tender and not overly strong-flavored. The small, elongated Japanese cultivars have exceptional quality when they are about 10 cm (4 in.) long and are only slightly less delicate up to 15 cm (6 in.).

Recommended Conditions   Little has been published on recommended procedures for ensuring maximum storage life of eggplant. However, following the recommendations given for cucumbers should be satisfactory. The only possible exception is the questionable usefulness of hydrocooling for large eggplants. Their low surface-to-volume ratio would result in slow cooling, and the water also might result in water-spotting of the fruits. If packaged to permit adequate passage of air between fruits, room-precooling eggplants should be satisfactory if their pulp temperature is between 13° and 15° C (55° and 59° F) within 24 hr of harvest. For transit or storage, McColloch (1966) has recommended 7 to 10° C (45° to 50° F), although he did not test slightly higher temperatures. Most likely, the optimum storage temperature is between 10° and 12° C (50° and 54° F). Eggplants never should be held in contact with ice.

Eggplants soon become spongy and wrinkled, unless held in about 95% RH. High RH is even more critical for the Japanese eggplants because their immature skin and high surface-to-volume ratio permits rapid water loss.

Single eggplants can be wrapped in shrink film that is perforated or incompletely sealed at one end. Perforated film bags would be satisfactory, but less attractive. Small eggplants benefit from packaging in ventilated bags (Viraktamath *et al.* 1963) or overwrapped trays to reduce water loss and physical injury. Eight to twelve 5 mm holes per 500 g (6 to 10 ¼ in. holes per lb) of eggplants provides adequate ventilation and keeps RH from levels that encourage decay, according to the report from India. Prepackaging also can delay the appearance of chilling-induced pitting by retarding drying of the injured tissue.

CA storage so far has not been shown to be beneficial in extending the storage life of eggplant. However, Viraktamath *et al.* (1963) found more than 7% CO_2 to be injurious.

Eggplant fruits can be held about 10 days at 10° C (50° F) or a week at 7 to 10° C (45° to 50° F) without development of objectionable symptoms of chilling injury when subsequently held 3 days at 21° C (70° F) (McColloch 1966). If continuously held at about 10° C and when prepackaged,

eggplants likely can be stored 2 to 3 weeks without serious deterioration, although the Indian researchers claim satisfactory quality even
after 1 month. However, the storage life at a given temperature also
depends on the temperature during development of the fruits. Independent and nearly simultaneous research in Israel and Japan (Warshavski *et al.* 1973; Abe *et al.* 1974) has shown that eggplant grown
during cool weather is relatively resistant to chilling injury. For example, fruit harvest in Japan in July was injured by 5 days of storage at
10° C (50° F), whereas that harvested in October showed no pitting or
decay even after 10 days at 6° C (43° F). Thus eggplant harvested in
summer should be held above 10° C, whereas that harvested during cool
weather can be held at 10° C or slightly lower.

Okra

Quality Criteria   Okra that appears bright green, firm, free of
blemishes, and is no longer than 8 cm (3 in.) likely will be enjoyable to
eat, but very young pods tend to taste "grassy" (Woodroof and Shelor
1958). Pods up to 13 cm (5 in.) can be satisfactory; however, they may be
more fibrous than desirable. Regardless of length, pods that are dull,
flaccid and yellowish are inferior, mainly because of their high fiber
content.

Height of ridges is not related to quality but is a genetic characteristic; however, the ridges should not be discolored.

Recommended Conditions   The high rates of deterioration and of
respiration dictate rapid cooling of harvested okra. Unless okra is cooled
to below 15° C (59° F) soon after being packed, the heat of respiration
will cause the temperature in the package to rise quickly and result in
rapid deterioration. In spite of this situation, hydrocooling generally is
not recommended, because of the fear that the water will cause spotting,
as prolonged contact with ice or with ice water does (Woodroof and
Shelor 1958). However, there is no experimental evidence that temporary contact with cold water in fact injures the okra. Thus, this efficient
method of cooling certainly should be tried on small lots. No data are
available on how fast okra can be cooled; however, the data for Brussels
sprouts should be fairly close. With the water at 5° C (41° F), 30° C
(86° F) pods packed in a container about 25 cm (9 in.) deep should cool to
10° C (50° F) in about 10 min.

Vacuum cooling of okra also may be feasible, although prewetting the
pods probably would be necessary to avoid excessive water loss.

Once okra is cooled, it should be held at 7° to 10° C (45° to 50° F). At higher temperatures toughening, yellowing and decay are rapid, whereas pitting, induced by chilling injury, can develop below 5° C (41° F).

Okra must be held at about 95% RH if wilting is to be avoided. Prepackaging in perforated film is a great aid not only in this respect, but also helps avoid physical injury of this tender vegetable. About 10 holes 5 mm in diameter should suffice for 500 g okra.

CA effects on okra have not been adequately evaluated. However, work on packaging (Anandaswamy *et al.* 1963) suggests that 5 to 10% CO_2 lengthens shelf-life at 11° to 13° C (52° to 55° F) by about a week. Higher concentrations of CO_2 caused off-odors that persisted through cooking. Definite recommendations on the potential benefits of CA storage for okra must await more systematic studies.

Under ideal conditions, okra can be held in air about 1 week without objectionable deterioration, or 10 days if lower quality is satisfactory.

Peppers, Bell

This section will deal primarily with green bell, or sweet peppers. However, any green peppers consumed fresh, whether hot or sweet, have the same quality criteria and storage requirements.

Quality Criteria   High quality bell peppers consumed green are dark green, shiny and firm. They spring back into shape when lightly compressed and their calyx and stem are green and turgid. Irregular shape does not detract from the edible quality, but reduces eye-appeal and may interfere with certain uses.

Red, ripe peppers should have the same general characteristics as green ones.

Recommended Conditions   Peppers, being susceptible to chilling injury, are held at 7° to 10° C (45° to 50° F), with the optimum being 8° to 9° C (46° to 48° F). At these temperatures chilling injury and ripening are minimal. Holding peppers at about 12° C (54° F), as found suitable in India and Romania (Habeebunnisia *et al.* 1963; Iordachescu *et al.* 1974), may result in some ripening if storage exceeds about 1 week. Fully ripe peppers likely can be held a week between 4° and 7° C (40° and 45° F) without injury.

Although peppers are hydrocooled, the practice cannot be recommended without reservation. Johnson (1964), working with peppers produced in the Rio Grande Valley of Texas, has clearly shown that

Courtesy of United Fresh Fruit and Vegetable Assoc.

FIG. 7.2.   BELL (SWEET) PEPPERS OF GOOD MARKET QUALITY

hydrocooling can increase the incidence of decay, even when the water is chlorinated. However, before deciding against hydrocooling, several factors must be considered. First, peppers grown in various areas are not equally susceptible to soft rot; consequently, hydrocooling may be safe in drier climates, such as in California. Second, unless an efficient method of air cooling, such as forced-air cooling, is available, more damage (decay and wilting) may result from slow cooling of warm peppers than from hydrocooling. Third, although wet stems are conducive to decay (Johnson 1968), a blast of cooled air directed at peppers after they leave the hydrocooler may dry them sufficiently to keep decay in check.

Although no specific information is available, on balance, peppers likely would remain in better condition if hydrocooled than if cooled slowly when the fruits are 25° C (77° F) or warmer, and if they cannot otherwise be cooled to below 13° C (55° F) in 3 or 4 hr.

Since hydrocooling may favor decay development in peppers, forced-air cooling appears to be an excellent alternative (Gaffney and Baird 1975). Peppers in a bulk bin (about 60 cm or 24 in. deep) had a half-cooling time of 1 hr (air inlet side) to 3 hr (air outlet side) when the air flow was about 3.3 m^3 min^{-1} m^{-2} (11 ft^3 min^{-1} ft^{-2} and 6 to 12 min, respectively, when air flow was about 122 m^3 min^{-1} m^{-2} (400 ft^3 min^{-1} ft^{-2}). For peppers in fiberboard boxes which had vents constituting about 5% of the area of the side panels, Kasmire (1976) obtained a half-cooling time of about 12 hr when pallet loads of boxes were placed in a room at 3° C (38° F). Thus, in 5° C (41° F) air, peppers starting at 25° C (77° F) would be 15° C (59° F) in 12 hr. The rate of cooling would, of course, be slower for boxes stacked tightly into a conveyance, so that non-precooled peppers would remain at undesirably high temperatures for at least the first day or two of transit. Prompt precooling to and transit at 7° to 10° C (45° to 50° F) would simultaneously minimize the danger of decay, ripening and chilling injury for any transit period. However, for transit periods of 5 days or less, 3° to 5° C (38° to 41° F) would probably be harmless, but such low temperatures must be avoided when transit exceeds 6 days (Lipton 1975).

Bell peppers are not generally prepackaged, although the practice certainly would retard wilting. Peppers with a large surface-to-volume ratio, such as the long or small types, are particularly susceptible to water loss and thus adapted to packaging, as has been shown by Anandaswamy et al. (1959). Ventilation of the packages should be adequate to avoid moisture condensation inside the packages.

Peppers must be held in high RH, (95 to 98%) or else they will rapidly become flabby (Iordachescu et al. 1974). Drying conditions also accentuate symptoms of chilling injury by accelerating dehydration of injured tissue and thus pitting. Wetting of peppers during 1 to 2 days of retail display is harmless at 4° to 7° C (40° to 45° F) but increases decay as temperatures approach or exceed 10° C (50° F).

The effects of CA on peppers have not been adequately tested to permit recommendations, but O_2 below 2% combined with 10% CO_2 can cause injury at 13° C (55° F).

The storage life of bell peppers under optimum conditions, as given earlier, is at most two weeks if ripening is objectionable. If some ripening is tolerable, initially sound peppers can be held three weeks with only minimal losses from decay.

If ripening of peppers is to be avoided during even brief holding, they must be protected from exposure to ethylene which is given off by tomatoes, melons and many other kinds of fruits, including peppers. However, ethylene production by peppers is low enough to pose no danger as long as the container, be it bag, box, rail car, or trailer, is reasonably well ventilated.

Peppers almost universally are waxed before shipment to reduce moisture loss and scuffing. However, in light of Johnson's work (1968), the procedure used should be carefully examined to avoid increasing decay by this treament. Strict sanitation on the packaging line and drying of surface moisture on the stem and calyx are essential steps in this direction.

Squashes, Summer

Quality Criteria   The three principal types of summer squash, yellow straight or crookneck, scallop, and zucchini, differ greatly in appearance, but share certain desirable characteristics. Their surface should be shiny, firm, and free of physical injury. Dullness is a sign of senescence and pitting is a sign of chilling injury. Dark green types should be entirely green; yellowish areas indicate senescence and poor flavor.

Size of the squashes is definitely related to quality: the smaller ones have a more tender flesh, their seeds are still soft, their skins are edible, and their flavor is mild and slightly sweet. While no definite limit separates desirable from undesirable sizes, long types less than 15 cm (6 in.) in length and round types less than 10 cm (4 in.) in diameter are preferable to those exceeding these dimensions by 2.5 cm (1 in.) or more, at least for the uses most common in the United States.

Recommended Conditions   The requirements are essentially those for cucumbers. However, squashes seem to be somewhat more resistant to chilling injury. One or two days below 5° C (41° F) does no discernible damage, but such exposure should be avoided, and holding at about 10° C (50° F) seems best.

Since squashes readily become soft, they should be held in about 95% RH. Free moisture does not seem to be harmful during a display of 1 to 3 days.

The storage life of summer squash is at most 1 week at 10° C (50° F) if only minor deterioration is tolerable, and 2 weeks at most for fair to good quality. Two to four days below 5° C (41° F) is permissible if the squashes are then immediately used.

UNRIPE FRUIT REQUIRING LOW TEMPERATURES

Peas, Garden Peas *(Pisum sativum)*

Quality Criteria   The pods (shells) of desirable peas are deep green, plump, but not overly swollen, relatively smooth and turgid. Even slight yellowing indicates that the enclosed peas (immature seeds) are starchy and tough. The seeds also must be grass green and well rounded.

Edible-podded, or Chinese, peas *(Pisum sativum,* macrocarpon) must meet the same criteria except that the seeds must be small, each one causing only a minor extension of the pod.

Recommended Conditions   Peas lose sweetness and tenderness very rapidly, and thus must be precooled to near 0° C (32° F) promptly after harvest and maintained there throughout marketing. Peas are cooled by ice water, crushed ice, or a combination of both.

Peas packed in baskets cool from 20° to 2° C (68° to 35° F) in about 12 min or to 5° C (41° F) in 4 min when the water is 0° C (32° F). Cooling to 5° C is adequate if the peas are then top-iced, or if package ice is added.

Peas readily wilt, but adequate use of ice provides the required high RH, 95 to 100%.

Peas can be vacuum cooled, but this process is less efficient than hydrocooling, even if the pods have previously been wetted (Stewart and Barger 1959). The adaptability of edible-podded peas to vacuum cooling has not been tested.

Fresh peas, a vanishing item on produce stands, usually are sold in bulk, although they would benefit from packaging. Ventilated film wraps would reduce wilting, and thus seem ideal, especially for the edible-podded type. Of course, the pea pod itself is a good package, and it has been shown repeatedly (Veda 1958; Wager 1964) that peas keep better in than out of the pod. However, fresh peas might regain favor if high quality shelled peas were sold packaged. This practice would help maintain quality and save effort by the consumer.

Five to 7% CO_2 maintains peas in much better edible condition during 20 days at 0° C (32° F) than air (Tomkins 1957). However, claims that similar conditions keep them in "good quality" for nine weeks (Wager 1964) must be regarded with skepticism. CO_2 concentrations higher than noted must be avoided because they cause off-odors and discoloration on cooking.

The storage life of peas cannot be accurately judged by visual criteria, because sugar loss and toughening proceed more rapidly than yellowing or decay. Thus, peas keep in "reasonably sound" condition for 20 days at 0° C (32° F) and 13 to 15 days at 4.5° C (40° F) (Tomkins 1957). For good quality, these periods must be at least halved, particularly if humidity is lower than recommended.

MISCELLANEOUS STRUCTURES REQUIRING LOW TEMPERATURES

In this group are vegetables that do not conveniently fit into any of the other categories of crops requiring low temperatures. They are asparagus (*Asparagus officinalis*), a shoot; kohlrabi (*Brassica oleracea, gongylodes*), a fleshy stem; mushrooms (*Agaricus bisporus*), a fungus; and sweet corn (*Zea mays*), a collection of many immature fruits.

Asparagus

Quality Criteria   In the United States, virtually all asparagus consumed fresh is entirely green, whereas in Europe white and green asparagus are marketed. The ensuing comments apply equally well to both, with the obvious exception of color.

Desirable spears are straight, green, possibly tinged with purple on the bracts and with tips tightly closed. Spears should not readily bend into a U-shape, but snap well before they reach a 90° angle. The more readily spears of a given diameter snap, the more turgid and tender they are. Spears always must be rounded and never ribby, because the latter indicates old age. Initially flattened or angular spears tend to be tough.

Excessive fibrousness distinguishes inferior from high quality asparagus. Minimal fiber content results when: (1) asparagus grows rapidly; (2) harvest is daily or at least on alternate days; (3) spears are at least 1.6 cm (⅝ in.) in diameter, 13 cm (5 in.) from the tip (because large spears have fewer fiber strands per area of cross section); (4) precooling promptly follows harvest; (5) refrigeration is continuous from precooling through use; (6) storage with crops that emit substantial ethylene is avoided; and (7) the atmosphere around the asparagus is enriched with CO_2 if holding exceeds a few days (Kaufman 1967; Haard *et al.* 1974; Clore *et al.* 1976).

Recommended Conditions   Asparagus must be cooled to below 5° C (41° F), preferably to near 0° C (32° F) as soon after harvest as possible, because the spears are highly perishable. As much quality is lost in 1 hr at 27° C (80° F) as in 14 hr at 2° C (36° F), and asparagus frequently is 27° C, or even warmer at harvest.

Asparagus almost universally is hydrocooled. Vacuum cooling is feasible (Stewart and Barger 1961), but less desirable, because cooling is less complete than during a good job of hydrocooling. With the former, asparagus cools from 21° C (70° F) to only 6° C (43° F) in 30 min, but with the latter in 3 to 4 min if the water is 1° C (34° F). A desirable 2° C (36° F) can be reached in 12 to 15 min by hydrocooling. Thorough precooling is essential because temperatures normally do not fall in transit, but may increase slightly, even in properly functioning rail cars or truck trailers.

Chlorine at 100 to 200 ppm added to the water used for cooling keeps bacterial population low. However, this precaution cannot be expected to eliminate the danger of decay, because bacteria that entered wounds made at harvest are not reached by the chlorine.

The requirement of asparagus for high humidity can be met two ways. Most commonly, the problem is avoided by setting the cut end of spears on pads of wet sphagnum moss or cardboard, from which the spears absorb moisture. Less common, but showing promise in tests from the United States and Europe, is prepackaging spears in perforated film bags. The use of non-perforated bags to conserve moisture and to simultaneously achieve CA conditions cannot be recommended, because the danger of uncontrolled buildup of CO_2 and depletion of O_2 outweighs any possible advantage.

If asparagus is packed in film bags or overwrapped, the unit must be sufficiently well ventilated to permit exchange of CO_2 and O_2 and the dissipation of respiratory heat. About 10 holes 5 mm in diameter should be adequate for 500 g of spears about 18 cm (7 in.) long; for shorter spears, with a higher rate of respiration, the number of holes should be doubled.

Controlled atmospheres are a useful adjunct to good refrigeration, even for relatively brief transit periods. CA is useful for asparagus because it retards decay and toughening, which occur rapidly after harvest, even at fairly low temperatures (Lipton 1958, 1960, 1965, 1968; Lougheed and Dewey 1966).

The main benefit of CA storage derives from CO_2. CO_2 concentrations above 5% effectively reduce the seriousness of bacterial soft rot during 1 week at 3° or 5.5° C (37° or 42° F), with the benefit being greater at the cut than at the tip end. This retardation of soft rot also has residual value, because spears held in CA at low temperature decay less rapidly after removal to air at a moderate temperature, 15° C (59° F).

Brief exposures (24 hr) to 20% CO_2 also reduce soft rot, but only at the butt end, during subsequent holding of the spears in air for 1 week at temperatures normally encountered by asparagus. Such a procedure might be useful for asparagus held for subsequent processing at canneries or freezers.

CO_2 at a concentration of about 10% not only retards toughening, but even seems to reduce fibrousness in harvested asparagus. The same CO_2 level also enhances the deep green of cooked asparagus. Some tasters object to the somewhat milder flavor of CO_2 treated spears, whereas others welcome it.

On balance, asparagus benefits from CO_2 concentrations of 7% ± 2% if decay reduction is the main objective and where temperature control is uncertain. If control of decay and of toughening are sought, 12% ± 2% CO_2 is permissible if the spears are held between 0° and 3° C (32° and 37° F).

Asparagus can be injured by 10% CO_2 if held 1 week above 5° C (41° F) or by 20% if held at 3° C (37° F). For 24 hr, 20% is not injurious even at 10° C (50° F).

Low O_2 concentrations, independent of elevated CO_2, have neither striking beneficial nor harmful effects, although levels below 10% should be and below 1% must be avoided.

The effectiveness of CO_2 in retarding toughening is enhanced by setting the cut end of spears in water, although water by itself also has a tenderizing effect. However, this practice cannot be used in commerce, if asparagus is sold by weight, because the resulting gain in weight, nearly 10% during 1 week in 15% CO_2, would be fraudulent.

Setting spears in water, as is often done at retail, is undesirable even if they are sold by the bunch, because the water makes an ideal medium for the propagation of bacteria. This is particularly true when the spears are not in refrigerated displays and if the water is not frequently changed. At room temperature bacteria reproduce at the rate of about one generation each 20 min. Further, setting spears in water causes them to elongate and give them an undesirable appearance. This effect is very pronounced after about a day at room temperature, or a week at 0.5° C (33° F). Consequently, the practice of setting spears in water, condemned 50 years ago by Krumbholz (1927), should be abandoned, especially since spears can be maintained turgid by prepacking or by being sprinkled with chilled water.

The storage life of asparagus is highly dependent on temperature (Fig. 7.3). Storage life decreases rapidly as 5° C (41° F) is exceeded, and for usual transit periods, the effect of chilling at 0° C (32° F) can be ignored. Fig. 7.3 indicates visual deterioration; however, less noticeable, but equally important processes of senescence occur simultaneously. Chief of these is an increase in toughness due to development of fibers, and a consequent reduction in the edible tender portion (Fig. 7.4). Besides this readily noted change, asparagus also loses sugar, vitamin C, and flavor.

Aside from the points detailed earlier, the storage life of asparagus can be lengthened by packing only spears with tightly closed tips. Spears with open, so-called "feathered" tips, not only look unattractive and are tough, but also decay more readily. After 1 week at 2° or 5° C (36° or 41° F) followed by 2 days at 15° C (59° F), nearly 3 times as many feathered tips as tight tips showed soft rot (16% vs. 6%) (Lipton 1968).

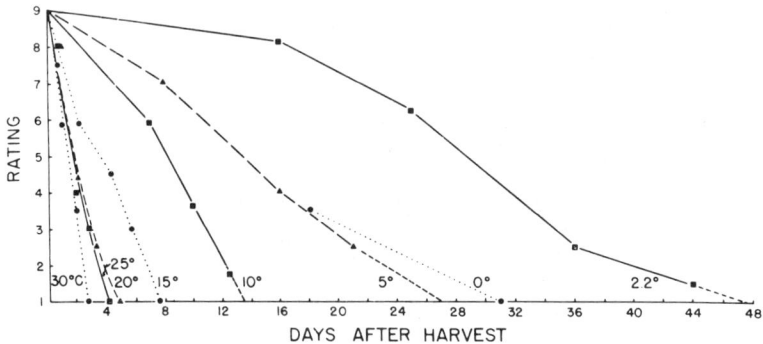

From Lipton (1958)

FIG. 7.3.   CHANGE IN VISUAL QUALITY RATINGS FOR ASPARAGUS SPEARS HELD AT VARIOUS CONSTANT TEMPERATURES
The curve at 0° C (32° F) is incomplete because of the unexpected occurrence of chilling injury.

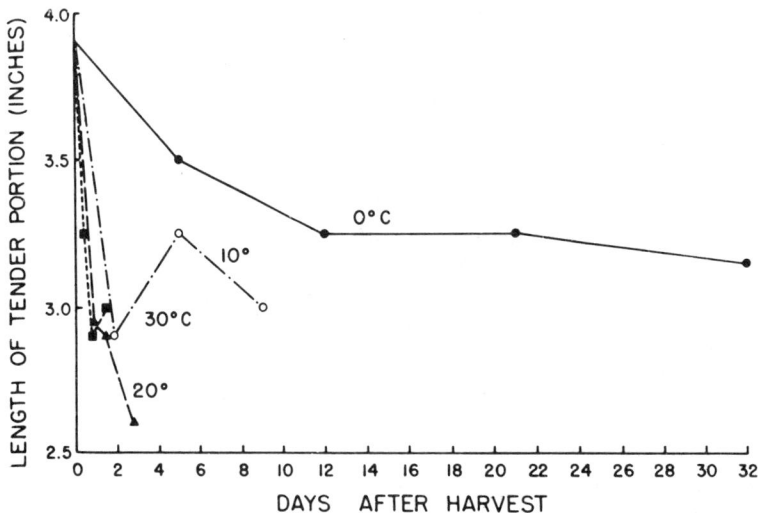

From Lipton (1958)

FIG. 7.4.   CHANGE IN LENGTH OF TENDER PORTION OF ASPARAGUS SPEARS DURING HOLDING AT VARIOUS CONSTANT TEMPERATURES

Kohlrabi

Quality Criteria   The most important quality factor, freedom from tough, fibrous cells, cannot be evaluated visually. However, if this bulbous stem appears fresh and green or purple, depending on cultivar, with healthy appearing leaves, and is 5 to 7 cm (2 to 3 in.) across, a good quality product is likely.

Recommended Conditions   Kohlrabi should be cooled to below 5° C (41° F) soon after harvest and held there during marketing. Humidity must be maintained at least at 95%, or else wilting and toughening are accelerated.

Topped kohlrabi can be packaged in perforated film to retard moisture loss. This practice would be particularly appropriate for this rather slow-selling vegetable.

No information on the effect of CA storage on kohlrabi is at hand. However, CO_2 effects should be tested, just in case this gas should have a tenderizing effect on kohlrabi as it does on asparagus.

Kohlrabi can be stored about 1 month if held near 0° C (32° F) under conditions that inhibit water loss.

Mushrooms

Quality Criteria   Fresh mushrooms are white or light buff, without dark marks on either cap (pileus) or stem (stipe). The veil is closed and the gills (lamellae) are not visible. The upper surface of the caps should be strongly convex and stems should be plump, rather than elongated. A relatively thin, long stem indicates that it has grown and toughened.

Whiteness categories for white mushrooms have been quantified by Gormley (1975) as based on Hunter L (lightness) values: (1) higher than 93, excellent (100 is the theoretical maximum); (2) 90–93, very good; (3) 86–89, good; (4) 80–85, reasonable; (5) 69–79, poor; (6) below 69, very poor. Mushrooms with values below 80 are considered unacceptable at wholesale and below 69 unacceptable at retail.

Recommended Conditions   Mushrooms should be cooled within 5 hr of harvest to as near 0° C (32° F) as feasible and held there throughout marketing (Tomkins 1966). Although mushrooms usually are room-cooled after being washed, hydrocooling would seem to be a logical way to clean and cool simultaneously. Vacuum cooling also can effectively reduce the temperature of the mushrooms with only little more weight loss than during room cooling (about 3 vs. 2.5%), while slowing deterioration more rapidly (Anon. 1969).

After being washed, the mushrooms must be dried because surface moisture causes a brown discoloration. Drying is accomplished within 3 to 5 min by capillary action on sponge belting. Strong air movement cannot be used because mushrooms readily wilt.

Mushrooms must be tightly packed without being forced, however. A loose pack leads to abrasion from movement and an excessively tight pack results in pressure bruises. Best results are obtained with packages that have rigid sides.

Overwrapping with moisture permeable film aids in retarding wilting without causing accumulation of free moisture on the film and undesirable condensation on the mushrooms. If condensation does occur, the mushrooms may become waterlogged and discolor internally.

Atmospheres containing 5 to 10% CO_2 tend to prolong the useful life of mushrooms by 2 to 3 days at 10° C (50° F) and by several weeks when held at 0° C (32° F). Low O_2 seems to be ineffective unless the concentration is only slightly (about 0.1%) above 0%. Lack of O_2 is highly detrimental. So far a systematic investigation of the effects of CA storage on mushrooms is lacking. Consequently, storage in air at 0° to 1° C (32° to 34° F) throughout marketing still is optimal.

The maximum storage life of mushrooms, as given by Tomkins (1966), is 17 to 20 days at 0° C (32° F), 10 to 15 days at 3° C (38° F), 7 to 10 days at 7° C (45° F), and 3 to 5 days at 12° C (54° F). However, for mushrooms that must meet all quality criteria noted earlier, the storage life is only two-thirds to one-half as long. If display will be above about 15° C (59° F) for 1 to 2 days, then the storage life is only about one-fourth that given. The storage life also is influenced by the initial quality of the mushrooms. Those relatively high in dry matter content appear to keep better than those high in moisture content (Gormley 1975).

Sweet Corn

Quality Criteria   Sweet corn that is enjoyable to eat cannot be recognized by looking at an unhusked ear. The leaves may be turgid and green, while the kernels are of low quality. In corn, as in peas, edible quality decreases much more rapidly than visual quality.

The best visual signs of high culinary quality in raw sweet corn are kernels that are pale creamy-yellow and plump but never indented. Yellow or indented kernels are a sign of senescence or improper handling. Ears with immature kernels at the tip half-inch more likely are sweet and tender than ears with full-size kernels to the tip. Selection based on these criteria will enhance, but not assure, the choice of high quality fresh sweet corn, because changes in chemical and physical composition that influence quality are more rapid than external changes.

Recommended Conditions   If a consumer several days from the production area is to get sweet corn of satisfactory or good quality, the ears must be cooled to as near 0° C (32° F) as soon after harvest as possible. Time is critical because sucrose, the compound primarily responsible for sweetness of sweet corn, changes rapidly to starch after harvest. This change occurs 6 times as rapidly at 10° C (50° F) as at 0° C, 10 times as rapidly at 21° C (70° F), and 20 times as rapidly at 32° C (90° F).

Satisfactory cooling can be achieved by vacuum cooling or hydrocooling. Both methods are equally effective if properly used. However, in large-scale operations, the likelihood of adequate precooling is greater when vacuum cooling is used. By this method, crated corn can be cooled from about 30° C (86° F) to a satisfactory 5° C (41° F) in a half hour, whereas nearly an hour is required to remove an equal quantity of heat from completely exposed ears held in a shower of ice water. Crated corn takes even longer (about 80 min). Since few, if any, operators are able to leave corn in the cooler for an hour or more, an inferior job of hydrocooling is almost inevitable.

If corn is vacuum cooled, it must be wetted beforehand, or else the husks will wilt and the kernels will become dented during marketing.

Regardless of method or thoroughness of precooling, sweet corn must be body-iced and top-iced during transit to remove respiratory heat, and ideally, to achieve further cooling.

Sweet corn also must be kept as close to 0° C (32° F) as feasible at wholesale and retail, or else all previous efforts can quickly be negated. Sweet corn should not be displayed on unrefrigerated counters unless a complete turnover requires less than about 8 hr. During this time corn loses about 10% of its sucrose content if held at 21° C (70° F) but only 1 to 2% if held just above freezing.

The husks of sweet corn make an excellent protective package for the kernel. However, this package keeps the corn in good condition only at low temperatures, below 5° C (41° F), and when ample water adheres to the husks. When either of these conditions is lacking, the husks withdraw moisture from the kernels via the shank, and dented, tough kernels result. Consequently, for maximum quality retention, the flag leaves must be removed and the shanks trimmed to 5–7 mm (¼ in.) prior to shipment. If this is not done, the kernels easily can lose 2% moisture and become dented.

Consumer packaging is confined to corn that is marketed partly or completely husked. Such corn must be film covered or the kernels will rapidly dry and become dented. The film must be perforated to permit proper precooling and dissipation of respiratory heat and gases. For proper quality maintenance, film-packed corn always must be kept well refrigerated; it never should be displayed on unrefrigerated counters, even briefly.

Corn derives little benefits from CA conditions, although 5 to 10% CO_2 slightly retards sugar loss. More than 10% injures corn; however, no precise description of benefits or injuries has been published.

The storage life of sweet corn is very limited, because sweetness and tenderness are lost so rapidly. Even under the best handling conditions—prompt cooling to a cob temperature of 5° C (41° F) followed by continued refrigeration near 0° C (32° F)—corn will have satisfactory culinary quality for a maximum of 6 to 8 days. At 5° C, the time is reduced to 3 to 5 days, and at 10° C (50° F) to about 2 days.

There is ample evidence (Guzman *et al.* 1967; Showalter *et al.* 1955, 1961; Winter *et al.* 1954) that the commodity requirements for sweet corn are not being fulfilled during marketing of much of this crop. Unless this practice is reversed, long-distance marketing of fresh sweet corn may well meet the fate of that for peas: virtual disappearance.

REFERENCES

Beans, Snap

ANANDASWAMY, B., and IYENGAR, N. V. R. 1961. Pre-packaging of fresh snap beans *(Phaseolus vulgaris)*. Food Sci. (Mysore) *10*, 279–283.

GORINI, F., BORINELLI, G., and MAGGIORE, T. 1974. Studies on precooling and storage of some varieties of snap beans. Acta Hort. No. 38, Vol. *2*, 507–529.

GROESCHEL, E. C., NELSON, A. I., and STEINBERG, M. P. 1966. Changes in color and other characteristics of green beans stored in controlled refrigerated atmospheres. J. Food Sci. *31*, 488–496.

GUYER, R. B., and KRAMER, A. 1952. Studies of factors affecting the quality of green and wax beans. Maryland Agr. Exp. Sta. Bull. *A68*.

LITTMAN, M. D. 1967. Effect of temperature on the post-harvest deterioration in quality of beans. Queensl. J. Agr. Anim. Sci. *24*, 271–278.

SISTRUNK, W. A. 1965. Effect of storage time and temperature of fresh snap beans on chemical composition of the canned product. Proc. Am. Soc. Hort Sci. *86*, 380–386.

SMITH, M. A., McCOLLOCH, L. P., and FRIEDMAN, B. A. 1966. Market diseases of asparagus, onions, beans, peas, carrots, celery, and related crops. U.S. Dept. Agr. Handbook *303*.

THOMPSON, B. D. 1964. Pre-packaging pole beans at grower level. Proc. Florida State Hort. Soc. 77, 131–137.

WATADA, A. E., and MORRIS, L. L. 1966A. Effect of chilling and nonchilling temperatures on snap bean fruits. Proc. Am. Soc. Hort. Sci. 89, 368–374.

WATADA, A. E., and MORRIS, L. L. 1966B. Post-harvest behavior of snap bean cultivars. Proc. Am. Soc. Hort. Sci. 89, 375–380.

Beans, Lima

BROOKS, C., and McCOLLOCH, L. 1938. Stickiness and spotting of shelled green lima beans, U.S. Dept. Agr. Tech. Bull. 625.

KAUFMAN, J., and CEPONIS, M. J. 1962. Extended shelf-life for green lima beans. Produce Mktg. 5, No. 7, 32–33.

McCOLLOCH, L. P., and VAUCHT, C. 1968. Refrigerated-storage tests with lima beans in the pod. U.S. Dept. Agr. ARS 51-23.

Cucumbers

APELAND, J. 1961. Factors affecting the keeping quality of cucumbers. Intern. Inst. Refr. Bull. Anex 1, 45–58.

APELAND, J. 1966. Factors affecting non-parasitic disorders of the harvested product of cucumber. Acta Hort. No. 4, 102–104.

FELLERS, P. J., and PFLUG, I. J. 1967. Storage of pickling cucumbers. Food Technol. 21, No. 1, 74–78.

HIROSE, T. 1971. Relations between degree of maturity of cucumber fruit and chilling injury during storage. Sci. Rept. Fac. Agr. Kobe. Univ. 9, No. 1/2, 38–42. (Japanese, English summary)

OKUBO, M., and MAEZAWA, T. 1965. Studies on the prolongation of the marketing life of fresh fruits and vegetables. I. Deterioration of cucumbers during storage at various temperatures. J. Jap. Soc. Hort. Sci. 34, 334–342. (Japanese; Hort. Abs. 36, Abs. 6571.)

VAN UFFELEN, J. A. M. 1975. Keeping quality of cucumbers. Landb. Tijdschr. 87, 295–299. (Dutch)

WEICHMAN, J., TATARU, D. P., and GARTE, L. 1975. Respiration of pickling cucumbers after different methods of harvesting. Gartenbauwissenschaft 40, 79–81. (German)

WIEBE, H. J. 1969. Storability of cucumbers packed in shrink film. Gemüse 24, 54–56. (German)

Eggplant

ABE, K., IWATA, T., and OGATA, K. 1974. Chilling injury in eggplant fruits. I General aspects of the injury and microscopic observations of pitting development. J. Japan. Soc. Hort. Sci. 42, 402–407. (Japanese, English summary)

McCOLLOCH, L. P. 1966. Chilling injury of eggplant fruits. U.S. Dept. Agr. Mktg. Res. Rept. *749*.

VIRAKTAMATH, C. S. *et al*. 1963. Pre-packaging studies on fresh produce—III. Brinjal-eggplant (*Solanum melongena*). Food Sci. (Mysore) *12*, 326–331.

WARSHAVSKI, S., TEMKIN-GORODEISKI, N., and SCHIFFMAN-NADEL, M. 1973. The storage of eggplant at various temperatures. 3. Cooling and ripening of fruits in relation to quality. Bull. Intl. Inst. Refrig. Suppl. 239–243. (French)

Okra

ANANDASWAMY, B. *et al*. 1963. Pre-packaging of fresh produce—IV. Okra (*Hibisus esculentus*). Food Sci. (Mysore) *12*, 332–335.

CULPEPPER, C. W., and MOON, H. H. 1941. The growth and composition of the fruit of okra in relation to its eating quality. U.S. Dept. Agr. Circ. *595*.

WOODROOF, J. G., and SHELOR, E. 1958. Okra for processing. Georgia Agr. Expt. Sta. Bull. New Ser. *56*.

Peppers

ANANDASWAMY, B., MURTHY, H. B. N., and IYENGAR, N. V. R. 1959. Pre-packaging studies on fresh produce: *Capsicum grossum* Sendt. and *Capsicum acuminatum* Fingh. J. Sci. Indust. Res. India. Sect. A. *18A*, 274–278.

GAFFNEY, J. J., and BAIRD, C. D. 1975. Forced-air cooling of bell peppers in bulk. Am. Soc. Agr. Eng. Winter Meet. Paper *75–6525*.

HABEEBUNNISA, PUSHPA, M. C., and SRIVASTAVA, H. C. 1963. Studies on the effect of protective coating on the refrigerated and common storage of bell peppers (*Capsicum frutescense*). Food Sci. (Mysore) *12*, 192–196.

IORDACHESCU, O., CERNAIANU, A., AMARIUTEI, A., and DOBREANU, M. 1974. Research on short-term storage of tomatoes and green peppers. Acta Hort. No. 38, Vol. 1, 217–226. (French)

JOHNSON, H. B. 1964. Effect of hot water treatments and hydrocooling on post-harvest bacterial soft rot in bell peppers. U.S. Dept. Agr. *AMS-517*.

JOHNSON, H. B. 1968. Heat and other treatments for cantaloups and pepper. *In* United Fresh Fruit and Vegetable Association Yearbook. pp. 9, 14, 51–52, 54, 56. United Fresh Fruit and Vegetable Assoc., Washington, D.C.

KASMIRE, R. F. 1976. Rapid forced air cooling recommended for peppers. Western Grower and Shipper *47*, No. 6, 33.

LIPTON, W. J. 1975. Temperature requirements for shipping California green peppers. Produce Mktg. Assoc. Yearbook, 208, 210, 212.

MCCOLLOCH, L. P. 1962. Chilling injury and Alternaria rot of bell peppers. U.S. Dept. Agr. Mktg. Res. Rept. *536*.

OGATA, K., KOZUKUE, N., and MURATA, T. 1968. Quality changes and the mechanism of chilling injury in pepper fruits stored at low-temperature (sic). J. Japan. Soc. Hort. Sci. *37*, 249–255. (Japanese, English summary)

Southern Peas

SMITTLE, D. A., and KAYS, S. J. 1976. Quality deterioration of Southern peas in commercial operations. HortScience *11*, 151–153.

Squash, Summer

LEWIS, W. E. 1958. Refrigeration and handling of two vegetables at retail. Green snap beans and southern yellow summer squashes. U.S. Dept. Agr. Mktg. Res. Rept. *276*.

MORRIS, L. L., and MANN, L. K. 1948. Storage of summer squash. Refrig. Res. Found. Fact File Sheet.

Peas

JAMISON, F. S. 1934. Studies of the effects of handling methods on the quality of market peas. Cornell Univ. Agr. Expt. Sta. Bull. *599*.

STEWART, J. K., and BARGER, W. R. 1959. Effects of cooling method and top-icing on the quality of peas and sweet corn. Proc. Am. Soc. Hort. Sci. *75*, 470–475.

TOMKINS, R. G. 1957. Peas kept for 20 days in gas store. Grower *48*, No. 5, 226–227.

VEDA, B. 1958. Prolonging the storage period of green peas. Sborn. Csl. Acad. Zemed. Ved, Rostl., Vyroba *31*, 893–908. (Czech. Hort. Abs. *29*, Abs. 1451).

WAGER, H. C. 1964. Physiological studies of the storage of green peas. J. Sci. Food Agr. *15*, 245–252.

Asparagus

CAROLUS, R. L., LIPTON, W. J., and APPLE, S. B. 1953. Effects of packaging on quality and market acceptability of asparagus. Mich. Agr. Expt. Sta. Quart. Bull. *35*, 330–342.

CLORE, W. J., CARTER, G. H., and DRAKE, S. R. 1976. Pre- and post-harvest factors affecting textural quality of fresh asparagus. J. Am. Soc. Hort. Sci. *101*, 576–578.

HAARD, N. F., SHARMA, S. C., WOLFE, R., and FRENKEL, C. 1974. Ethylene induced isoperoxidase changes during fiber formation in postharvest asparagus. J. Food Sci. *39*, 450, 453–456.

HERREGODS, M. 1961. The storage of asparagus. Tuinbouwberichten *25*, 48–50. (Dutch)

KAUFMAN, F. 1967. Influence of growth rate and duration on fibrousness of green asparagus spears. Arch. Gartenbau *15*, 89–100. (German)

KRUMBHOLZ, G. 1927. On the influence of watering on the quality of asparagus. Obst-und Gemüsebau *11*, 162–164. (German)

LIPTON, W. J. 1958. Effect of temperature on asparagus quality. Proc. Conf. Transport. Perishables. Univ. Calif., Davis. 147–151.

LIPTON, W. J. 1960. Effect of atmosphere composition on quality. In California asparagus: Effect of transit environments on market quality. U.S. Dept. Agr. Mktg. Res. Rept. 428, 17–25.

LIPTON, W. J. 1965. Post-harvest responses of asparagus spears to high carbon dioxide and low oxygen atmospheres. Proc. Am. Soc. Hort. Sci. 86, 347–356.

LIPTON, W. J. 1968. Market quality of asparagus—effects of maturity at harvest and of high carbon dioxide atmospheres during simulated transit. U.S. Dept. Agr. Mktg. Res. Rept. 817.

LOUGHEED, E. C., and DEWEY, D. H. 1966. Factors affecting the tenderizing effect of modified atmospheres on asparagus spears during storage. Proc. Am. Soc. Hort. Sci. 89, 336–345.

LOUGHEED, E. C., and FRANKLIN, E. W. 1965. Influence of carbon dioxide on the uptake of water by asparagus. Nature 207, 1313.

MORRIS, L. L., and WATADA, A. E. 1960. Elongation and bending of asparagus spears. Calif. Agr. 14, No. 11, 15.

PENTZER, W. T. et al. 1936. Precooling and shipping California asparagus. Univ. Calif. Agr. Expt. Sta. Bull. 600.

STEWART, J. K., and BARGER, W. R. 1961. Effects of cooling method on the quality of asparagus and cauliflower. Proc. Am. Soc. Hort. Sci. 78, 295–301.

WANG, S. S., HAARD, N. F., and DI MARCO, G. R. 1971. Chlorophyll degradation during controlled-atmosphere storage of asparagus. J. Food Sci. 36, 657–661.

Mushrooms

ANON. 1969. Mushroom cooling in commercial packs. Ann. Rept. East Malling Res. Sta. 30–31.

GORMLEY, R. 1975. Chill storage of mushrooms. J. Sci. Food Agr. 26, 401–411.

MURR, D. P., and MORRIS, L. L. 1974. Influence of O_2 and CO_2 on o-diphenol oxidase activity in mushrooms. J. Am. Soc. Hort. Sci. 99, 155–158.

MURR, D. P., and MORRIS., L. L. 1975A. Effect of storage temperature on postharvest changes in mushrooms. J. Am. Soc. Hort. Sci. 100, 16–19.

MURR, D. P., and MORRIS, L. L. 1975B. Effect of storage atmosphere on postharvest growth of mushrooms. J. Am. Soc. Hort. Sci. 100, 298–301.

NICHOLS, R., and HAMMOND, J. B. W. 1973. Storage of mushrooms in prepacks: The effect of changes in carbon dioxide and oxygen on quality. J. Sci. Food Agr. 24, 1371–1381.

SINGER, R. 1961. Mushrooms and Truffles. Interscience, New York.

SVEINE, E., KLOUGART, A., and RASMUSSEN, C. R. 1965. Ways of prolonging the shelf-life of fresh mushrooms. Mushroom Sci. 6, 463–474.

TOMKINS, R. C. 1966. Refrigerated stores for the storage of mushrooms. MGA Bull. 201, 477–478.

Sweet Corn

GRIZZELL, W. G., and BENNETT, R. H. 1966. Hydrocooling stacked crates of celery and sweet corn. U.S. Dept. Agr. *ARS 52-12*.

GUZMAN, V. L. *et al*. 1967. Sweet corn production on the organic and sandy soils of south Florida. Florida Agr. Expt. Sta. Bull. *714*.

KASMIRE, R. F., and VAN MAREN, A. F. 1959. Facts on hydrocooling sweet corn. Univ. Calif. Agr. Ext. Serv. Circ. (Unnumbered).

SHOWALTER, R. K. 1957. Effect of wetting and top-icing upon the quality of vacuum and hydrocooled sweet corn. Proc. Florida State Hort. Soc. *70*, 214—219.

SHOWALTER, R. K. 1967. Sweet corn shelf-life as affected by trimming and packaging. Proc. Am. Soc. Hort. Sci. *91*, 881–884.

SHOWALTER, R. K. *et al*. 1961. Long distance marketing of fresh sweet corn. Florida Agr. Expt. Sta. Bull. *638*.

SHOWALTER, R. K., GREIG, W. S., PARSONS, C. S., and DEMAREE, K. D. 1955. Quality of Florida sweet corn as affected by marketing practices. Proc. Florida State Hort. Soc. *68*, 182–185.

STEWART, J. K., and BARGER, W. R. 1959. Effects of cooling method and top-icing on the quality of peas and sweet corn. Proc. Am. Soc. Hort. Sci. *75*, 470–475.

WINTER, J. D., NYLUND, R. E., and COX, R. W. 1954. Marketing fresh sweet corn in the Midwest. Minn. Agr. Expt. Sta. Bull. *427*.

WINTER, J. D., NYLUND, R. E., and LEGUN, A. F. 1965. Relation of sugar content to flavor of sweet corn after harvest. Proc. Am. Soc. Hort. Sci. *65*, 393–395.

8

Commodity Requirements— Ripe Fruits

In this chapter the quality criteria and recommended conditions for the following crops will be considered:

Common Name	Botanical Name
Muskmelons	*Cucumis melo*
"Cantaloup"	*Cucumis melo, Reticulatus*
Persian	*Cucumis melo, Reticulatus*
Winter melons	*Cucumis melo, Inodorus*
Honey Dew	
Casaba	
Crenshaw	
Pumpkins and Winter Squashes	*Cucurbita maxima*
	Cucurbita mixta
	Cucurbita moschata
	Cucurbita pepo
Tomato	*Lycopersicon esculentum*
Watermelon	*Citrullus lunatus*

The popular terminology for pumpkins and squashes is so confused in relation to the botanical classification that we defer to Whitaker and Davis (1962) for details.

COMMODITIES

Muskmelons—Cantaloup

Quality Criteria   Picking out high quality cantaloups is not as difficult as many people believe, as long as the choice is based on several criteria rather than on only one. However, before the characteristics can be given, several terms need to be clarified. The "net" consists of the web of raised corky tissue that covers all or most of the surface. Areas sometimes not covered are the "ground spot," the part of the fruit in contact with the soil, and the "vein tracts," which are the longitudinal, shallow and smooth indentations on the surface of many cantaloups (Davis 1970). The "stem scar" is the round indentation that remains after a fruit has been pulled from the stem at the "full-slip" stage. If the fruit is not mature, only part of the stem pulls off, and leads to a "half-slip" fruit. Half-slip fruits always are green, but full-slip fruits range from entirely green to mostly yellowish-tan. The proportion of the two colors determines the commercial ripeness class: "hard ripe" cantaloups are entirely green to yellowish-green; "eastern choice" melons are greenish-yellow to light yellow; and "western choice" designates those entirely or almost entirely yellowish-tan. The two less ripe classes are hard at harvest, whereas the ripest one "gives" slightly at the blossom end when compressed with the thumb.

The size designation of cantaloups is based on the number of fruits that could be packed into a standard wood crate, thus the larger the size, the smaller the number. The most commonly shipped sizes are 45's, 36's and 27's, and occasionally 23's. The size designations and corresponding objective measurements are listed in Table 8.1. Since, however, precise size designations are not now officially required, a wide range in sizes often is packed in a given container. The advent of mechanical sizers will reduce this disparity in sizes.

Returning now to criteria of high quality, the degree of slip, condition of net, and color are the most obvious. Cantaloups always should be full slip when harvested, because almost half of the final concentration of sugars is accumulated during the last week of maturation, i.e., during the few days prior to the full-slip condition (Bianco and Pratt 1977). The

TABLE 8.1. RELATIONSHIP BETWEEN COMMON COMMERCIAL SIZES OF CANTALOUPS AND OBJECTIVE MEASUREMENTS

Commercial Size Designation	Diameter[1] (cm)	(in.)	Length[1] (cm)	(in.)	Volume[2] cm^3	(in.^{3})	Weight[2] (g)	(lb)
45	11.5	4½	11.5	4½	910	55.4	820	1.8
36	13.0	5⅛	14.0	5½	1130	68.9	1040	2.3
27	13.5	5¼	15.5	6⅛	1570	92.1	1360	3.0
23	—	—	—	—	1760	107.4	1590	3.5

[1]Source: Stewart and Lipton (1960).
[2]Source: Kasmire (1968).

net should be prominent and cover the entire melon, with the possible exception of the vein tracts. These may or may not be netted, depending on cultivar or even strain. Generally, wide unnetted vein tracts are considered a fault. Ideally, the net also covers the ground spot, although a weaker net in this area than over the remainder of the surface is common and is not an indicator of low quality.

Abrasion of the net is very common on cantaloups on the market. Fruits with more than minor abrasions should be avoided if the melons are not used within a day or two, because these areas tend to become depressed, due to water loss.

Desirable color, and by implication ripeness, depends on how soon the cantaloup is to be consumed. Light yellowish-tan is ideal for serving within 1 to 3 days, whereas greener melons are preferable for longer holding. Melons with tan to brown undercolor should be avoided because they are beyond their useful life and tend to be soft, and flat in flavor. Browning of the vein tracts also is a sign of aging, but traces of this defect do not indicate poor quality.

Cantaloups should never be flabby, but the precise degree of softness is a matter of personal preference. Since color changes and softening occur simultaneously, the former is a good guide to the latter.

The aroma of a cantaloup is an excellent guide to its quality: if the aroma is pleasant and the melon meets the other quality criteria noted, a high quality fruit is virtually assured. However, aroma is a good guide only if the fruits are at least eastern choice in ripeness and if they are near room temperature; less ripe or cold melons have little aroma, regardless of quality. Further, cantaloups develop their highest aroma a day or more after harvest, depending on degree of ripeness; even western choice fruits have little aroma when first picked.

There is no relation between quality and either size or shape of cantaloups in a given lot. However, growing conditions that produce globular rather than elongated fruits also tend to produce high quality fruits as measured by soluble solids concentration (Davis et al. 1964).

The concentration of soluble solids (SSC) in the juice of cantaloups has been taken as the single most reliable index to their quality. Since soluble solids are mostly sugars, melons with a high concentration are likely to be sweet, and since conditions that favor accumulation of sugars also seem to favor development of other desirable quality attributes, melons high in soluble solids are likely to be flavorful. However, SSC is not invariably a reliable guide to edible quality. Melons high in SSC (10 to 12%) may neither taste sweeter nor have better flavor than cantaloups with 3 or 4% lower SSC. So far there is no good explanation for this repeatedly observed lack of correlation between SSC and flavor (Aulenbach and Worthington 1974).

In recognition of the importance of concentration of soluble solids in quality determinations, cantaloups shipped from California must have a minimum concentration of 8%. This minimum is 2% lower than that considered desirable by Chace et al. (1924) over 50 years ago. While a 10% minimum concentration may be unrealistically high, a 9% minimum likely would serve the best longterm interests of growers, shippers and consumers.

When cantaloups and other melons are sampled for concentration of soluble solids, care must be exercised to obtain a representative sample of the flesh, because this constituent decreases by about 2% from the blossom to the stem end (Scott and MacGillivray 1940). These authors, therefore, recommend that the sample of juice be collected from a longitudinal segment, using care to remove a uniform percentage of the flesh. The latter injunction is important because soluble solids concentration increases about 2.5% from the rind toward the center. In contrast, the difference in soluble solids concentration between the half resting on the ground and the upper half of a melon is minor.

These internal gradients in the concentration of soluble solids are recognized in the California regulations for determining "maturity" of melons. Accordingly, two samples (plugs) must be taken from each fruit tested, one from the top center and the other from the bottom center.

Color of the flesh generally is a good index of eating quality. While the exact color depends on cultivar, the color should be strong rather than pale. The latter almost invariably signifies a bland flavor.

Finally, the popular belief that so-called "shakers" are inferior is not substantiated in fact. Whether or not the contents of the seed cavity can be heard sloshing about when a melon is shaken principally depends on ripeness, not on quality. A poor hard-ripe cantaloup will not be a shaker, but a good ripe melon will be. Physical abuse can accelerate loosening of the seeds and placental tissue, and thus result in shakers, but there usually would be external signs of damage.

In summary then, the ideal cantaloup fruit is "full slip," is covered by a dense (depending on cultivar) and prominent net, is firm, and has a desirable aroma when near room temperature. Internally, the concentration of soluble solids is at least 10% and the color of the flesh is deep rather than pale.

Recommended Conditions   Quality of cantaloups improves and deteriorates after harvest. The improvement, an increase in pleasant aroma, occurs naturally as the fruit ripens and thus requires no special attention. Deterioration also occurs naturally, but requires close attention if its rate is to be minimal during hot summer days.

Cantaloups harvested during the peak of the season frequently are about 30° C (86° F), and sometimes near 40° C (104° F), on arrival at the packing shed. At these high temperatures melons rapidly ripen and lose sugar and moisture. Consequently, cantaloups need to be precooled as soon after harvest as possible. However, while cooling to the recommended transit temperature of 3° to 5° C (38° to 41° F) within 2 or 3 hr would be desirable, it is not essential. It is essential, however, that cantaloups be cooled to between 10° and 15° C (50° and 59° F) as rapidly as possible, because cooling them by 17° to 22° C (30° to 40° F) reduces the rate of ripening and of sugar loss to about one-fourth of its rate at the higher temperature and thus brings them to a reasonable level. Once a moderate temperature has been reached, the rate of cooling can be slowed without noticeably affecting melon quality, as long as 3° to 5° C is reached within 24 hr of harvest.

Deterioration can be slowed immediately upon arrival of the cantaloups at the shed if the trucks or trailers are parked in a shaded area rather than under the open sky while waiting to be unloaded. If shaded, the melons in the top layer remain at or below air temperature in the shade; if left out in the sun they can heat by as much as 7° C (12° F) per hour. Thus, in 2 hr, an all too common period of exposure, they can reach near lethal temperatures when the air is about 38° C (100° F). Cantaloups that are heated to such an extent not only show more sunburn injury on the market, according to Kasmire et al. (1962), but also require more refrigeration for precooling than melons unloaded immediately or parked in the shade. Further, melons exposed to hot, dry air rapidly lose moisture, especially through areas where the net has been abraded. This moisture loss, added to that normally incurred during transit, can readily reach 3 to 4%. A weight loss of this magnitude results in a soft melon with shrivelling around the stem scars and unattractive depressions where the net was abraded (Kasmire and Parsons c. 1971).

Once unloaded, cantaloups can be successfully precooled either with cold water, cold air, or ice. Which method is chosen is less important than that it is properly used, the choice depending primarily on economic factors, type of container used for the melons, and on personal preference.

Hydrocooling is the most efficient method for rapidly cooling cantaloups. Cantaloups that are 35° C (95° F) can be cooled to 13° C (55° F) in about 22 min and those starting at 30° C (86° F) in about 18 min when the water is 0° to 1° C (32° to 34° F). In commercial practice, cantaloups rarely are hydrocooled below 10° to 15° C (50° to 59° F) because excessively expensive hydrocooling capacity would be needed. However, hydrocooling to at least 15° C (59° F) *at the center of the flesh* is highly desirable, because a warm, wet melon is ideal for the proliferation of fungi and bacteria. Following hydrocooling, the cantaloups should be rapidly packed if they have not been packed prior to cooling. Once packed, they should immediately be loaded into a refrigerated rail car or trailer, or moved to a cold room. If left outside, the melons will warm at a rate of about 4° C (7° F) per hour when the difference between melons and air is about 20° C (36° F) (Stewart and Lipton 1960). The rate will be slower at smaller differences and higher at greater differences.

Completion of cooling after hydrocooling normally is accomplished by refrigerated air, although ice can be used if the cantaloups are packed in water-resistant containers.

Cooling by freely circulating air is too slow, except when most of the field heat has already been removed by hydrocooling. With air cooling, containers in a cold room or conveyance must be stacked so that cold air can freely and directly reach each box or crate, or else "hot spots" will develop, because respiratory heat is produced faster than it can be dissipated.

If only cold air is used for precooling, it must be forced through the container and around each melon if adequate cooling is to be accomplished. Details of the procedure are presented in the general section on precooling. Here it suffices to note that melons packed in crates and held in a wind tunnel can be cooled from 32° C to 10° (90° F to 50°) in about 3 hr or to 15° C (59° F) in slightly over half that time if air at 5° C (41° F) is pushed past the melons.

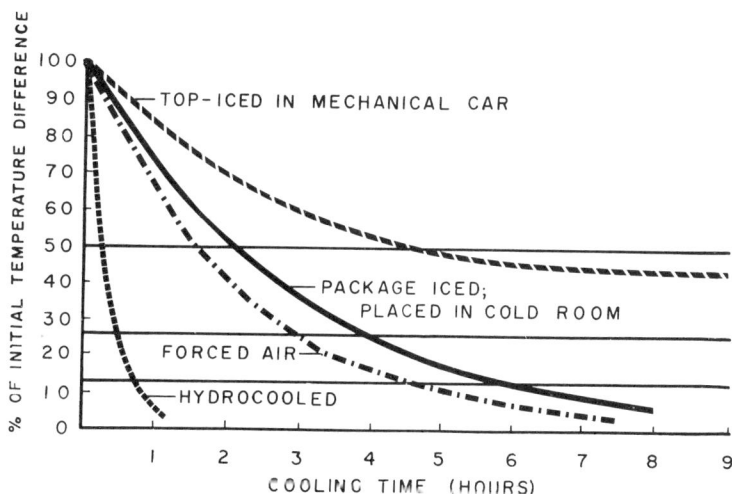

Redrawn from Kasmire and Parsons (1971)

FIG. 8.1. TEMPERATURE REDUCTION IN CANTALOUPS BY VARIOUS PRECOOLING METHODS
Horizontal lines, from top, indicate 1, 2 and 3 half-cooling periods respectively.

Generally the melons are left in the tunnel between 2 and 3 hr, after which cooling is completed in the rail car or truck trailer, as is the case following hydrocooling.

If melons are cooled with forced air, care should be taken to have a high RH, preferably at least 95%, because rapidly moving dry air would tend to remove moisture from the warm melons and deposit it as condensate on the cold refrigeration coils. Thus the difference between coil and air temperature should be minimal.

Crushed ice is still used to remove field heat from cantaloups. With ice blown in between rows of crates and over the load, cantaloups in a mechanically refrigerated car can be cooled from 35° to 13° C (95° to 55° F) in about 11 hr if the air is 5° C (41° F). If only 5 hr were available, the melons would still be about 21° C (70° F). Consequently, cooling is completed during transit by use of the refrigeration system of the rail car or trailer. The melons usually reach a desirable 3° to 5° C (38° to 41° F) within 1½ to 2 days. This rate of cooling is adequate to protect the quality of the melons, although, as noted earlier, cooling to 5° C within 24 hr would be preferable.

When top-icing is used, there is the danger that a thick, solid layer of ice will seal the surface and prevent air circulation through the load. Thus, cold air would circulate around the load and erroneously indicate to the thermostat that the load is cool when in fact the melons below the ice are still undesirably warm. Applying the ice in windrows, rather than in a uniformly thick layer, allows channels to form as the ice melts and thus permits cold air to reach the containers of melons. With this system the thermostat of the vehicle should be set at 2° C (36° F) and the following amounts of ice should be used (Anon. 1971):

Melon temperature at loading	°C	21	27	32	38
	(°F)	(70)	(80)	(90)	(100)
Ice per 100 crates, each	kg	590	750	860	1020
at 34 kg (75 lb) net weight	(lb)	(1300)	(1650)	(1900)	(2250)

Kasmire and Parsons (c. 1971) have suggested the use of package-icing for cantaloups shipped in moisture-proof boxes. This method of cooling is slower than hydrocooling or forced air cooling but faster than cooling by top-icing. Package-icing will cool 35° C (95° F) melons to 13° C (55° F) in about 3 hr or to 5° C (41° F) in about 6 hr, provided air is forced through the container at the rate of at least 9 cm³ per min per kg of melon (½ cfm per lb). If only natural convection prevails, a given amount of cooling will require about 60% more time, because, as the ice melts, a cavity is formed between melons and ice. This cavity slows heat transfer in the absence of forced air movement. In package-icing the amount of ice placed in each carton must be adjusted for the temperature of the melons. About 3 kg of ice must be supplied for 18 kg cantaloups (equivalent to a so-called ½ carton) for each 10° C cooling desired, with a suggested minimum of about 3.5 kg of ice per carton. In British units the equivalent values are 3.7 lb ice per 40 lb melons cooled 10° F. These recommendations assume a cooling efficiency of 70% and immediate transfer of the iced cartons into a refrigerated space.

The need for rapid and adequate hydrocooling, in contrast to the more leisurely cooling permitted when ice is used, is based on differences in packaging and loading methods. Hydrocooled cantaloups are usually packed in fiberboard boxes that are then tightly stacked in rail cars or truck trailers. In such loads, air circulation through the load is inadequate to remove a substantial amount of field and respiratory heat unless the cold air is forced through each box. Consequently the melons must be well precooled before loading. In more open, properly designed loads of crates, cold circulating air can readily remove field and respiratory heats after most of the ice has melted.

The previous paragraphs clearly illustrate that cantaloups, although chilling sensitive, are not injured by fairly extended contact with ice. In this they differ from all other muskmelons. Hard ripe or eastern choice melons can be held under ice for up to two weeks without apparent damage (Morris 1947). (Western choice melons are too ripe to be held two weeks.) Longer periods on ice should be avoided for hard ripe or eastern choice melons, because chilling injury may be induced, with resultant rapid decay and improper ripening at higher temperatures.

Cantaloups must be protected from drying, and thus should be held in about 95% RH when they are not in contact with ice, but still at a low temperature.

Controlled atmosphere storage of cantaloups has not been sufficiently tested to warrant recommendations.

The storage life of cantaloups is closely tied to their degree of ripeness. Hard-ripe melons can be held a maximum of 10 days to 2 weeks at 3° to 5° C (38° to 41° F), followed by 1 or 2 days of ripening at 15° C (59° F); for eastern choice melons the respective periods are between 7 and 10 days and 1 and 2 days. Western choice melons should be held no more than a total of 4 to 6 days at 3° to 5° C before use. Western choice melons can be held a week at 1° to 2° C (34° to 36° F), if followed by no more than 1 day near 15° C.

The storage periods given should be regarded as a general guide only, because cultivar (Ogle and Christopher 1957), date of harvest (Lipton and Stewart 1961), and other, less tangible factors, strongly affect the "carrying quality" of cantaloups. Generally, melons harvested late in the season keep less well than those harvested before or near the peak for a given area, and well netted melons are believed to "carry" better than those with a less well developed net.

The storage life of cantaloups can be extended by 1 to 3 days, depending on temperature, if the fruits are hydroheated before being packed or cooled. See section on diseases for details.

The soluble solids or sugar content changes little in harvested cantaloups (Rosa 1928). Since there are no starch reserves, there is no postharvest increase in sugars, and decreases are minor when storage is at recommended temperatures and does not exceed about two weeks.

The remainder of the muskmelons are not discussed according to their botanical classification, but rather in respect to their temperature requirements. While these differ slightly, this group has a common characteristic: none of those included form a natural abscission layer, or slip, that can be utilized for judging harvest maturity, as in cantaloups. Thus, they all are cut off the vine with about 2.5 cm (1 in.) of stem left on the fruit to reduce the chance of decay. Honey Dew melons are the most widely shipped in this group and will be discussed first.

Honey Dew Melons

Honey Dews can be the most disappointing or the most delightful of melons. Unfortunately, the former situation prevails all too often because the degree of maturity of Honey Dews is difficult to ascertain, especially under field conditions, because sorting is too rushed at packinghouses, and because requirements for ethylene treatment and transit temperatures often are not met.

Quality Criteria   As with cantaloups, we have to distinguish between characteristics that are desirable at harvest and those that are preferred at retail. A Honey Dew is ready for harvest when its background color is mostly white, but tinged with light green. Further, while a mature melon is well filled out, its surface still is covered by a fine fuzz of hairs. This is the earliest stage at which Honey Dews can be picked, if even satisfactory market quality is expected. However, such mature, but unripe, melons will not necessarily ripen properly within a normal marketing period, because Honey Dews that look alike at this stage may differ by two weeks in degree of ripeness. This peculiarity of the ripening process in Honey Dews is overcome, at least partly, by ethylene treatment, as noted in Chapter 1.

Internally, the melons must have a minimum soluble solids concentration (SSC) of 10% if they are to be shipped from California, although a higher concentration certainly is desirable. Honey Dews with 10 to 12%

SSC were considered only fair in eating quality, whereas those with 13 to 17% SSC were rated good to excellent.

Honey Dews that are ready to eat are white to creamy white, their surface feels waxy, their blossom-end is springy under moderate pressure and, above all, they emit the characteristic aroma when at or near room temperature. The flesh should be almost white, with a narrow rim of light green just under the rind. The flesh also should be soft, but not mushy, and the portion adjacent to the seed cavity should not be stringy.

The external indicators of various classes of commercially mature Honey Dews, given in the summary table which follows, as much else in this section, are adapted from Pratt *et al.* (1977).

Honey Dew Ripeness Classes   *(1) Unripe but Mature.*—Fruit rounded; background color white, tinged with light green; surface most likely covered with fine fuzz of hairs. Earliest stage of harvest maturity; ethylene gassing essential for proper ripening; some individual fruits may not ripen even with ethylene treatment.

(1-2) Fully Mature   Surface definitely white; very little wax; blossom-end hard to slightly springy; no aroma at room temperature; ideal commercial harvest maturity; ethylene treatment essential for uniform ripening.

(2) Ripening Initiated.   Background color mainly white; surface slightly waxy; small area of blossom-end springy; slight aroma at room temperature, mainly at blossom-end. Will completely ripen at proper temperature without added ethylene. Edible but too firm and too little aroma for best quality. Ethylene gassing will speed ripening.

(3) Ripe   Surface white to creamy white and waxy; entire blossom-end springy under moderate pressure; characteristic aroma emitted from all parts of melon at room temperature. Ideal dessert quality. Ethylene gassing superfluous.

(4) Overripe   Surface creamy white to pale yellow and very waxy; entire blossom-end soft; aroma strong at room temperature and evident even at normal refrigerator temperatures. Still enjoyable for eating when well chilled, but somewhat too soft, particularly around cavity.

(5) Senescent   Surface yellow; entire melon soft; aroma strong even at low temperatures. Texture mealy and stringy; flavor unpleasant; not normally edible.

Honey Dews, like cantaloups, do not possess their full aroma immediately after being harvested, even when they are in the early part of ripeness (class 3). However, one day at room temperature will usually bring such Honey Dews to optimum eating quality.

Some of the changes that accompany maturation and ripening of Honey Dew melons are depicted graphically in Fig. 8.2. Size of fruit obviously is not a good indicator of ripeness, since the melons are nearly full-grown well before they are harvest-mature. As for soluble solids content, the relevant curve indicates that the minimum legal concentration of 10% is lower than desirable, because fruits that merely meet the standard may not even have reached minimal commercial maturity (class 1). A minimum SSC of 11 or 12% would help to keep many inferior melons off the market and thus benefit everyone, from producer to consumer. Such a change also would tend to reduce the occurrence of chilling injury in Honey Dews shipped long distances at relatively low

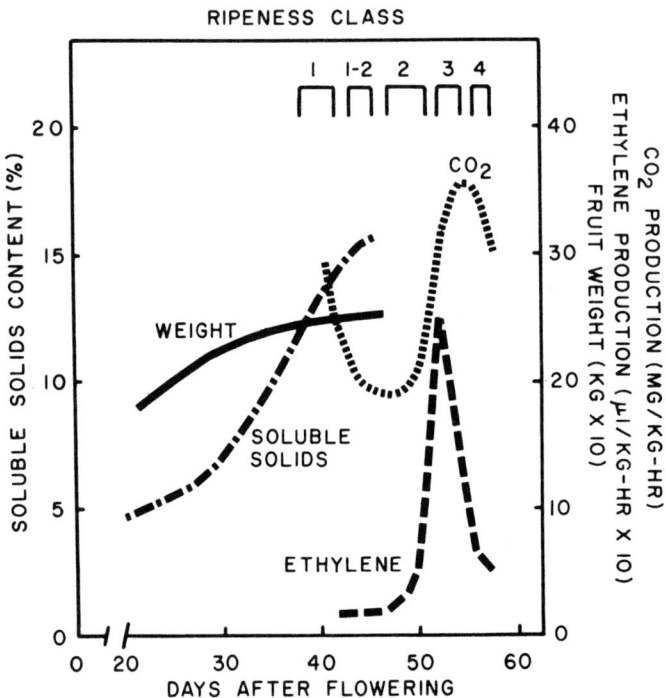

After Kasmire et al. (1970)

FIG. 8.2.   RIPENING OF HONEY DEW MELONS AS REFLECTED BY CHANGES IN FRUIT WEIGHT, SOLUBLE SOLIDS CONTENT, AND PRODUCTION OF CO_2 AND ETHYLENE AT 20° C (68° F)

temperatures, because fruits in maturity class 1, which are frequently low in SSC, also are more chilling sensitive than riper melons (Lipton 1978).

Neither production of CO_2 nor of ethylene can serve as commercially useful indicators of maturity or ripeness, but the pattern of the curve does illustrate how closely linked the two processes are and how their maximum rates coincide with the most obvious ripening changes that occur as the fruits pass through ripening classes 2 and 3.

The surface of Honey Dew melons sometimes shows areas with so-called "sugar cracks," actually ridges that resemble a rudimentary net. While no published support exists for the belief that such melons are particularly sweet, they certainly are not inferior in any respect, except possibly in appearance.

Recommended Conditions   Honey Dews do not need to be precooled unless they are to be in transit two weeks or longer, as to Asian markets. For these markets they should be cooled to 15° to 20° C (59° to 68° F) prior to shipment. Half-cooling times have not been determined, but they likely would be about twice those for cantaloups for size 5 or 6 (about 1700 to 2500 g) Honey Dews. Honey Dews harvested late in the season sometimes need to be warmed, because they properly respond to ethylene only when they are at least 21° C (70° F).

Details concerning the ethylene treatment will be found under *Vegetables as Living Products*. Once the ethylene treatment is completed, the melons should be cooled to about 15° C (59° F) within 2 to 2½ days and to 7° to 10° C (45° to 50° F) within 3 to 4 days. Honey Dews are chilling sensitive and thus never should be held below 5° C (41° F) or in direct contact with ice, except immediately before being served.

Honey Dews do not lose moisture as readily as cantaloups, but they still should be held between 90 and 95% RH to minimize this loss.

The storage life of Honey Dews, as normally shipped, extends over 2 to 3 weeks. They should not be kept longer even if there are no obvious signs of deterioration, because they may fail to ripen to acceptable quality.

Regardless of length of holding at low temperatures, ripening occurs most satisfactorily between 21° and 27° C (70° and 80° F).

Crenshaw Melons

Quality Criteria   Crenshaws are also superb melons when eaten at the proper stage of ripeness. Crenshaws are ready for harvest when the dark green of the rind gives way to yellow over a small area, other than the ground spot. At this time the blossom-end also becomes slightly springy. Entirely green melons may or may not be harvest-mature and thus should be avoided.

There is no precise indication of table-ripeness; however, for good dessert quality at least half the surface should be yellow, the blossom-end should be springy, and emit a pleasant aroma at room temperature.

Internally, the entire flesh, except for a narrow rim along the rind, should be salmon colored and have a melting texture.

Crenshaws that are entirely yellow externally and soft are senescent and are likely to have an unpleasant flavor.

Recommended Conditions   Crenshaws have the same temperature requirements as Honey Dews, but do not require any ethylene treatment if shipped mature. However, this does not mean that ethylene might not be beneficial, the point apparently just has not been investigated.

Crenshaws should not be held more than two weeks, because the delicate flavor and aroma are lost upon prolonged storage, even if other aspects of ripening proceed normally.

Persian Melons

Quality Criteria   Persians, which appear to be round, oversize cantaloups with a finer net, are ready for harvest when the background color of at least a small part of the surface has changed from dark green to a lighter green that appears speckled with light brown, and when the ground spot has a pink tone. This type of melon notoriously is picked before reaching maturity and thus cannot live up to its potentially high quality. Modern packaging techniques should be able to protect this tender melon from injury when mature.

Persians are table ripe when most of the melon is gray-green to brownish, slightly soft and springy, and when it gives off a slightly spicy aroma at room temperature. At this stage the flesh is deep salmon in color and has about the texture of a ripe peach.

These melons are no longer desirable when the entire surface is mostly brown with a tinge of red and when it feels soft.

Recommended Conditions   The recommendations for Honey Dews also apply, except that the ethylene gassing can be omitted. Persians also should not be held over two weeks, because flavor will be impaired. Further, their tender rind renders them more susceptible to injury and decay than either Honey Dews or Crenshaws at similar stages of ripeness.

Casaba Melons

Strictly speaking, the term Casaba applies to several cultivars, including Crenshaws, and what is popularly known as a Casaba is the cultivar Golden Beauty. However, in this discussion we will follow popular usage, and Casaba will refer only to the latter cultivar, which is characterized by a squat shape and a bright yellow rind when ripe.

Quality Criteria   Casabas should be harvested after about one-third of the fruit is yellow and when the blossom-end yields to firm pressure. If harvested earlier, the fruits will not attain their delicate flavor, but will taste more like ripe cucumbers, which, unfortunately, is the case for a large portion found on the market.

Softness at the blossom-end is the only reasonably reliable guide to their dessert quality. While they should be mostly yellow when ripe, yellowness alone is no guarantee of good flavor. Further, even excellent Casabas have only a barely detectable aroma at room temperature.

The flesh of ripe Casabas is soft and almost white, with possibly a slightly salmon cast around the seed cavity.

Recommended Conditions   Casabas again have the same temperature requirements as Honey Dews, but for prolonged holding, 10° C (50° F) is preferable to 7° C (45° F). These melons can be stored for 4 to 6 weeks because their rind is hard and resists decay. However, Casabas stored more than three weeks rarely have good dessert quality. Ethylene seems to be useful in ripening Casabas (Rosa 1928), although detailed information is lacking.

Miscellaneous Muskmelons

Numerous other melons also are marketed to a limited extent; among them are Honeyballs, Spanish Honey Dews, Pershaws and Santa Claus. The first resembles Honey Dews in appearance, flavor and storage requirements. Spanish Honey Dews are dark green externally and are inferior to Honey Dews in flavor, but can be held a month at 10° C (50° F). Pershaws, as their name implies, resemble the parent stock and have the same requirements. Santa Claus melons resemble Crenshaws in shape but in all other respects are more like Casabas.

Pumpkins and Winter Squashes

Quality Criteria   Pumpkins and winter squashes have few external indicators of flesh quality, although certain characteristics can give a clue. First, the rind must be hard, or else the fruit is immature and has a thin layer of tasteless, poorly colored flesh. However, hardness of flesh does not guarantee a high quality fruit. Table Queen (Acorn) squash may be hard but nevertheless insipid and pale yellow. This cultivar should show a slight amount of yellowish-orange on the dark green surface to assure full maturity. However, if more than about half is orange, stringiness is likely. Butternut squash also may have a hard rind without being fully mature. For proper table quality the rind should be entirely buff to light tan. A greenish undercolor indicates poorly-flavored squash.

The quality of banana squash is judged more readily than the others, at least at retail, because it usually is sold cut up and prepacked. The rind and flesh should be a deep orange and firm and free of obvious stringy material.

Pumpkins and winter squashes should be heavy for their size; light-weights tend to be dry and stringy.

Recommended Conditions   Pumpkins and winter squashes are chilling sensitive and thus require moderate storage temperatures. According to several reports, the most favorable conditions lie between 10° and 15° C (50° and 59° F), where chilling and ripening are minimal, although Guba (1950) favored 7° to 10° C (45° to 50° F).

Relative humidity of about 60% seems optimal if findings for butternut squash (Francis and Thomson 1965) are applicable to other cultivars. If RH exceeds 75%, decay ensues (Guba 1950), and if it gets too low, water loss is excessive and the texture suffers. In butternut, a weight loss exceeding 15%, and mostly due to transpiration, leads to hollow-neck, which is not evident externally but renders the fruit inedible.

Prepacking of winter squash or pumpkin so far is confined to fairly large pieces that are overwrapped. Prepeeled and cubed squash does not seem to have found a market, but the results obtained with that form by Francis and his group (1961A, B) are no doubt applicable to larger prepackaged pieces. Accordingly, the pieces should be smoothly cut with a knife to reduce the surface exposed to microbes and be overwrapped with perforated film to avoid anaerobic conditions from developing. Squash so prepared and held between 7° and 10° C (45° and 50° F) likely will have a shelf-life of about 6 to 12 days. Such great variation in shelf-life seems characteristic of winter squash (Francis et al. 1961B), although the cause for this variation remains unknown.

The storage life of intact pumpkins and winter squash also varies greatly, with some of the variation attributable to cultivar, as noted in the data below, which were compiled from various sources. We assumed a storage temperature of 10° to 15° C (50° to 59° F) and a RH of 60%.

Cultivar	Storage life, approximate
Table Queen (Acorn)	30 to 50 days
Butternut	50 days
Quality	80 days
Connecticut Field	60 to 90 days
Cushaw	60 to 90 days
Hubbard	180 days

Maximum storage life of all squashes and pumpkins can be attained only by careful handling to avoid injury. For prolonged storage, the fruits are best stored on slatted shelves, which provide for free air circulation and minimum contact between adjacent specimens. Further, disinfection of the storage rooms and shelves or boxes prior to storage avoids carrying disease organisms from one season to the next. Commonly used disinfectant washes or fumigants can be used for this purpose. Guba (1950) recommends 6 g of copper sulfate per liter of water (1 lb per 20 gal.). Alternatively, solutions of chlorine or formaldehyde or sulfur dioxide gas may be employed. The specific disinfectant used is less important than thorough coverage. Since all of these materials are toxic to man, strict adherence to directions given with the materials is essential.

Prolonged curing of winter squash or pumpkins at high temperature is not only unnecessary but actually harmful to some cultivars. Wound healing before storage probably can best be hastened by holding the fruits for a week between 15° and 21° C (59° and 70° F) before cooling them to below 15° C.

Extending the storage life of butternut squash by a 2-min dip in 54° to 60° C (130° to 140° F) water seemed promising to Francis and Thomson (1965). However, the effect was only noticeable if the storage period exceeded four months, which is at least twice the normal storage life of this cultivar. Since at this time about 30% of the fruits were decayed and many likely had hollow-neck, as judged by weight loss, hot-water treatment does not seem to be a promising way to extend the storage life of squash, unless other cultivars react very differently from butternut.

Tomatoes

All tomatoes normally used for food belong to the species *Lycopersicon esculentum*, even though the fruits range in size from that of small melons to that of cherries, and in color from nearly white via yellow, orange and pink to deep red. Their range in shape includes that of a globe, a pear, and even a small cucumber. In spite of this diversity in appearance, the red or pink, round-fruited cultivars that are 5 to 10 cm (2 to 4 in.) in diameter constitute the overwhelming bulk of tomatoes eaten fresh. We will confine our discussion to this group, with brief digressions for the increasingly popular cherry tomatoes. However, most comments, particularly those in respect to requirements for temperature and RH, apply to all cultivars.

Quality Criteria   Color is the single most important visual criterion of quality in tomatoes. However, because tomatoes change color as they ripen, this change is best discussed in conjunction with others that occur as tomatoes turn from green to red.

A tomato harvested at the mature-green or at a riper stage can be expected to develop satisfactory color if held at an appropriate temperature. However, visual differentiation between mature-green and immature-green tomatoes is difficult at best and completely successful visual separation is impossible, especially under commercial harvest and sorting procedures. Recently instruments have been developed that accurately separate tomatoes by color based on the light transmittance characteristics of the fruit at certain wavelengths. If these instruments are integrated into sorting lines, separation of tomatoes by color, and especially culling of immature-green fruit, will be feasible and rapid. Such instrumentation will help reduce losses incurred because immature-green fruit was shipped and will permit selecting and ordering fruit of a specific color for shipment at a specified temperature for arrival at a given and uniform degree of ripeness. Such changes would help maintain quality by eliminating the need for repeated sorting and thus save time, energy and money. However, the system will be useful only if all segments of the tomato industry cooperate by instituting strict temperature control throughout marketing. Unless this is done, the large investment required for high-speed electronic sorting for maturity will be wasted, because ripening schedules are based on degree of maturity and temperature (Worthington 1974; Worthington *et al*. 1977; Jahn 1975; Worthington 1976).

Mature-green tomatoes are well rounded rather than angular, and their color may range from medium to whitish-green, depending on cultivar. Their surface has a waxy gloss and the skin is not readily scraped off with a fingernail, as in an immature fruit. Internally, the seeds are imbedded in a jelly-like matrix and are shoved aside, rather than cut, as the tomato is halved with a sharp knife. Since neither the picking nor the sorting crew can do a perfect job of rejecting immature fruits, especially when a field is entered too early, immature fruits reach the market and cause customer dissatisfaction because they generally do not ripen properly, but remain yellowish to pale red, and are poorly flavored (Lutz 1944).

As tomatoes ripen they gradually become more and more red, and this change has been arbitrarily subdivided into six stages (stage 1 is "green") which are defined in the U.S. Standards for Grades of Fresh Tomatoes and summarized below:

(2) *Breakers*—not more than 10% of the surface is tannish-yellow, pink or red. (This color change first occurs on the blossom-end and is preceded internally by a pinkish coloration of the placenta.)

(3) *Turning*—the color change noted under (2) has occurred over 10 to 30% of the surface area.

(4) *Pink*—between 30 and 60% of the surface shows pink or red. (Note that tannish-yellow is no longer included.)

(5) *Light red*—more than 60% of the surface is pinkish-red or red, but no more than 90% is red.

(6) *Red*—more than 90% of the surface is red. (Note that pink is no longer included.)

These stages of ripeness are well illustrated in a color chart (U.S. Dept. Agr. 1975).

Aside from these official color designations, there also are those commonly used for tomatoes riper than stage 6. Table ripe fruits are entirely red and are ready for eating; those canning ripe are a deep red, but still firm and thus are ideal for eating; soft, ripe fruits, while still edible, are no longer suitable for slicing, because the "jelly" has become too watery.

The foregoing may suggest that all tomatoes color uniformly, which is not the case at all. Sometimes the shoulders ripen much more slowly than the rest of the fruit or they never turn completely red. Shoulders that are yellow or orange when the rest of the fruit is red, tend to be hard and may be green internally, and thus indicate undesirable fruits. There are various patterns and causes of irregular ripening, a subject dealt with in more detail under *Disorders*.

Firmness is another important criterion of quality. Desirable tomatoes remain firm until they are at their best ripe color. Some are soft while still green, because their locules are filled with air rather than cellular material. Such puffy fruits should be culled by flotation in specific gravity solutions because these relatively light fruits float on the top of the solution while normal fruits sink below the surface. Methods developed to separate ripe from green tomatoes by flotation (Kattan *et al.* 1968, 1969) likely could be adapted to separate puffy from normal fruits. Alternatively, separation by floating angle seems promising. Normal tomatoes float with the stem-end vertically above the blossom-end; puffy fruits float at a different angle, the difference from vertical being closely related to degree of puffiness (Chen and Studer 1976).

Fruits softened by physical injury are even less desirable than slightly puffy fruits, because they are watery internally and decay more readily than sound tomatoes.

Shape and size of tomato have no effect on edible quality as long as the fruit was harvested at least mature-green. Small fruits sometimes may be inferior because they have a greater chance of having been harvested immature than larger fruit. Such immature fruit will not ripen as readily as mature fruit and also is more susceptible to physical injuries (Kader and Morris 1976B). Angular tomatoes are undesirable because they frequently are immature, and if mature, they often prove to be puffy.

Tomatoes generally are preferable when free of blemishes, such as catfacing or cracking. However, if minor, such defects do not detract from the culinary quality of an otherwise desirable tomato.

Tartness and juiciness are considered desirable characteristics by most consumers of tomatoes, whereas flatness and mealiness, which often occur simultaneously, are considered objectionable.

Recommended Conditions *Temperature*   Tomatoes are harvested at a variety of stages of ripeness, from mature-green to light pink and some of the recommended conditions, particularly temperature, vary with the degree of ripeness of the fruits. Consequently, we will discuss the temperature requirements for mature-green and for riper fruits separately.

Mature-green Tomatoes   The need for precooling of mature-green fruits depends on their initial temperature and on the time-table for ripening. Unless the fruits are above 27° C (80° F) and ripening should be delayed, there is no need for rapid precooling. If rapid cooling is desirable, hydrocooling reduces the temperature of tomatoes from 32° C to 21° (90° F to 70°) in 8 to 10 min or to 15° C (59° F) in 13 to 15 min if the water is between 1° and 5° C (34° and 41° F). Cherry tomatoes will cool from 32° to 15° C (90° to 59° F) in 3 to 5 min in such water (Kasmire 1969). Although hydrocooling of tomatoes has not been extensively investigated, commercial use in the desert areas of California and limited tests by Kasmire have not uncovered any major problems. Splitting of the skin can occur if the fruits take up water. However, this should not be a problem if the fruits are showered in bulk, rather than when packed in boxes, where the fruits tend to be completely immersed in water. Further, the brief exposure to cold water does not cause any chilling injury, nor is there any discernible "shock" effect. Excessive increase in microbial population in the hydrocooling water should be guarded against by chlorination of the water at concentrations approved by regulatory authorities.

Where hydrocooling is not feasible, cooling mature-green tomatoes with air below 5° C (41° F) is not harmful when the fruits are exposed to such temperatures for no more than 1 day (Srivastava et al. 1962). In practice, of course, refrigeration would be wasted by cooling tomatoes to below 13° C (55° F), because they would just have to be re-warmed to avoid chilling injury. Unless prolonged holding in the mature-green stage is essential, tomatoes can be permitted to take 1½ to 2 days to drop from about 27° C (80° F) to the desired range of 13° to 18° C (55° to 65° F), without risking excessive ripening in transit (Johnson and Newsom 1957). Even with average transit temperatures between 13° and 15° C (55° and 59° F), fewer than 10% of the fruits likely will be table ripe after 10 days and only about half will be turning ripe. Transit temperatures between 10° and 13° C (50° and 55° F) are permissible if delay in ripening is desired, but if prolonged beyond a few days, such temperatures tend to adversely affect color and flavor in the ripened fruit. Temperatures below 10° C for more than a few days must be avoided, or else the various symptoms of chilling injury may seriously impair the market quality of the tomatoes. In this connection, it is essential to realize that transit and field chilling are additive, so that if field chilling is suspected, transit chilling must be scrupulously avoided.

The time required for mature-green tomatoes to ripen at various constant, nonchilling temperatures is shown in Fig. 8.3. Tomatoes in the "breaker" stage would require about 75% as much time, and those in the "turning" stage about 50% as much time, to reach a given degree of ripeness as those starting out mature-green (Kasmire et al. 1976). Since the data are from various authors, the origin, condition and evaluation of the fruits naturally also varied. Nevertheless, the graph gives a good general idea on how rapidly tomatoes can be expected to ripen at a given temperature. It also clearly demonstrates the magnitude of variation that can be expected between different lots of tomatoes.

Breakers   At this stage of ripeness the fruits are slightly less sensitive to chilling injury than when mature-green. Nevertheless, ripening has progressed so little that the recommendations for mature-green fruit are suitable.

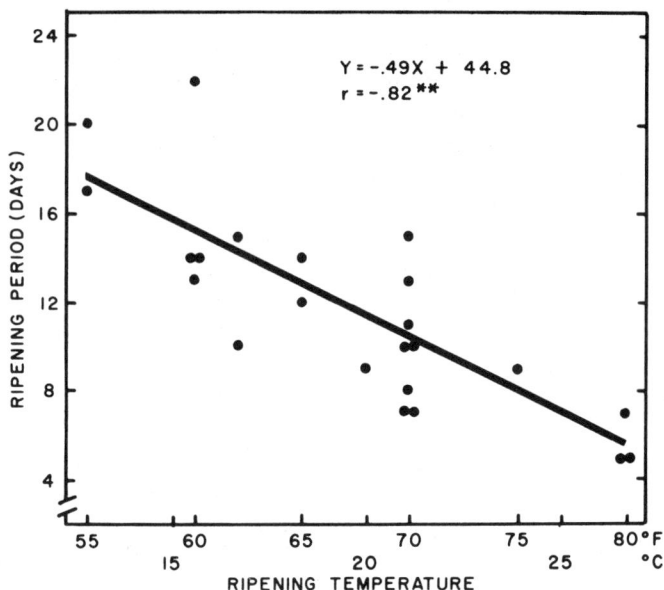

Data from various authors cited in text

FIG. 8.3. NUMBER OF DAYS REQUIRED FOR 75 TO 85% OF
MATURE-GREEN TOMATOES TO REACH FIRM-RIPE STAGE AT
VARIOUS CONSTANT, NONCHILLING TEMPERATURES
r significant at 99% probability level.

Turning or Riper Fruits   At these stages, ripening has progressed
sufficiently to render the fruits considerably less sensitive to chilling
injury than greener samples. Thus, turning fruits can be held at least 4
days, and probably 1 week, at 10° C to 13° (50° F to 55°) when ripening
must be slowed. Such an exposure does not impair their quality when
they later are ripened at a higher temperature. However, exposures of
more than 2 days to 5° to 7° C (41° to 45° F) likely will interfere with
ripening and increase decay (Hall 1965; McColloch *et al.* 1966).

Pink tomatoes are even less sensitive to chilling injury than turners,
and thus can be held at 5° C for 4 days without evident injury if a delay
in ripening is essential. If it is not, as would be the case in most
shipments, then 10° to 13° C is preferable.

If turning or pink fruits have been held 4 or 5 days between 13° and
15° C (55° and 59° F), nearly all of the fruits will be ripe within another 1
to 4 days at 21° C (70° F), but if held nearer 10° C (50° F), a week or even
longer may be required for equivalent ripening.

Red fruits (stage 6) are best fully ripened and then refrigerated
between 2° and 5° C (35° and 41° F) until ready for use. However, such

holding should be limited to a few days, because ripe tomatoes not only lose color and soften even at low temperature (Hall 1961), but also lose their characteristic aroma and flavor.

So far we have considered only the potentially detrimental effects of exposing unripe or partly ripe tomatoes to lower than desirable temperatures. Now we will consider the other end of the scale. If tomatoes are continuously exposed to temperatures above 30° C (86° F), most will be orange or yellow when "ripe," rather than red. Proper coloration is prevented because high temperatures inhibit synthesis of lycopene, the red pigment of tomatoes (Sayre et al. 1953). Consequently, the rate at which tomatoes can be properly ripened has an upper limit, which lies within a few degrees of 27° C (80° F). For best results, 24° C (75° F) should not be exceeded. If the temperature of the fruits exceeds 30° C (86° F), normal ripening can be restored by lowering their temperature to between 18° and 24° C (65° and 75° F), which simulates the diurnal pattern encountered by tomatoes ripening in the field during summer.

The general relationships between temperature and ripening hold for all commercially grown cultivars. However, specific cultivars differ in their susceptibility to defects induced by low or high temperatures (Segall and Hayslip 1966; Lipton 1970). While we cannot list the numerous cultivars grown in various geographic regions in respect to their specific responses to temperature, even if such information were available for all of them, such differences can influence the degree of success or failure under marginal conditions, and thus should be considered under such circumstances.

Relative Humidity   By general consensus tomatoes should be ripened or stored between about 85 to 90% RH. A few researchers have used or advocated drier conditions (Lockhart and Eaves 1967; Radspinner 1954; Tomkins 1963), whereas others, and even the same ones, have used more humid conditions (Lockhart et al. 1969; Hall 1964). However, none of these practices is based on results of experiments designed to carefully test the influence of RH on ripening or on the keeping quality of tomatoes. While there is no question that RH between 85 and 90% is suitable, there is no proof that this range is optimal. Generally, RH below 80% is avoided because water loss increases, and RH above 95% is avoided because of presumed danger of excessive decay, even though RH is likely to be at that level within shipping containers.

Light   Light is not required for normal postharvest ripening of tomatoes. However, exposure to white light reduced ripening time at 21° C (70° F) from mature-green to red by about 2 days and also accelerated softening (Jen 1974; Khudairi 1972). Tomatoes ripened in white light also had about twice the carotenoid content as fruit ripened in the dark (Paynter and Jen 1976). Nevertheless, ripening of harvested mature-green tomatoes in light is not commercially practical, because the procedure would require much space, substantial electricity, and extra handling of the fruit to expose it to the light.

Ethylene   Ethylene is used to more rapidly and uniformly ripen tomatoes harvested mature-green than would occur without an external source of the gas. Ripening time at 20° C (68° F) can be about halved by exposing the fruits to ethylene for 12 to 18 hr. Results with ethephon (2-chloroethyl-phosphonic acid), which is a chemical that releases ethylene upon application to fruits, would be similar. Ethylene application is useful only on mature-green fruit; riper fruit will not benefit from it because it produces sufficient ethylene for optimal ripening (Morris and Kader 1975; Kader and Morris 1975; Kasmire *et al.* 1976). Specific instructions for applying ethylene gas have been provided by Kasmire (1973) and more general information in Chapter 1.

Current evidence shows that mature-green tomatoes ripened with supplementary ethylene are equal to or very slightly higher in ascorbic acid than fruit ripened without ethylene and that there is no difference in beta carotene content between the two groups (Watada *et al.* 1976).

Controlled Atmosphere Storage   In contrast to attempts to speed ripening with ethylene are those that attempt to retard it by use of CA storage. Of the many atmospheres tested by various researchers, 4% ± 1% O_2 with the remainder N_2, has been found most effective. Effectiveness decreases as O_2 approaches 7% and disappears when O_2 reaches 10%. If tomatoes are held with less than 3% O_2, they may discolor, subsequent ripening will be uneven, and they develop off-flavors. Oxygen concentrations within the optimum range have no apparent effect on the major constituents of the fruits (Morris and Kader 1975; Mizuno 1971; Salunkhe and Wu 1973).

The effects of low pressure (hypobaric) storage are identical to those of CA storage at normal air pressure. The method is simply an alternate way of lowering the O_2 concentration.

Low O_2 extends the useful life of initially mature-green tomatoes held at 13° C (55° F) to about 6 weeks. If they are then ripened at about 20° C (68° F), they develop normal color, "acceptable" flavor and only minimal decay (Parsons *et al.* 1970). Extensions of useful life at 13° C to 3 months, as claimed by Wu *et al.* (1972), seems unrealistic, because decay likely would be excessive and flavor poor, although neither factor was measured. If tomatoes are held in low O_2 at about 20° C (68° F), ripening time from the mature-green to table ripe stage is stretched from 9 to about 26 days (Stenvers and Bruinsma 1975). Unless storage in low O_2 is excessively long, subsequent ripening (red coloration and softening) in air proceeds at a rate normal for a given temperature.

The addition of CO_2 to the storage atmosphere provides no advantage. CO_2 above 1% tends to increase decay and CO_2 above 5% leads to discoloration and development of off-flavors upon removal of the fruit to air (Kader and Morris 1974B).

The influence of CA storage on sensitivity of mature-green tomatoes to chilling injury is not completely clear. Kader and Morris (1974B) state that neither low O_2 nor high CO_2 increased the seriousness of chilling injury in tomatoes held 10 days at 0° C (32° F). However, there is no certainty that the results would be the same after a milder chilling exposure. Consequently, chilling temperatures must be avoided as rigorously in CA conditions as in air.

Packaging   Protection from physical injury is the chief benefit derived from properly packaging tomatoes for retail sale. Packaging also reduces water loss, but is of secondary importance, because tomatoes lose little water during the usual retail marketing period, particularly those that are waxed.

The most commonly used package is the so-called "tube," generally an elongated, plastic basket resembling latticework, which holds from 3 to 5 fruits and is overwrapped with a highly gas-permeable or perforated plastic film. Unfortunately, the edges of the latticework often are so keen that the tomatoes get permanently creased and thus bruised. Rounded edges on the basket, or baskets with solid sides, would prevent such needless injury. Since solid-sided baskets, unless transparent, restrict visibility of the fruits, the highest quality standards would have to be maintained to avoid disappointing the consumer.

Cherry tomatoes always are marketed prepacked, mostly in plastic strawberry baskets.

Storage Life   The storage life of tomatoes depends first on the stage of ripeness at which they are harvested, and second on the quality of fruit expected. Since ripening was discussed at length under *Temperature*, our concern here will be only with ripe fruit. Unquestionably, quality is highest immediately upon complete ripening, whether accomplished on or off the vine. Thus, if highest quality is expected, the storage life is limited to 2 to 4 days between 0° C and 5° (32° F and 40°). If the decorative effect of tomatoes suffices, firm ripe tomatoes can be held about 1 month at 0° C (32° F) or 2 to 3 weeks at about 10° C (50° F). The useful life of any one lot of tomatoes is, of course, strongly influenced by its initial quality, especially in respect to physical injury, and by cultivar (Iordachescu *et al.* 1974; Morris and Kader 1975; Hicks and Hayslip 1975; Parsons *et al.* 1960).

Parsons and co-workers emphasize that ripe tomatoes stored one month *must* be used *immediately* upon removal from cold storage, because they can completely deteriorate within 24 hr at room temperature. These authors also found that tomatoes ripened near optimum conditions will have a longer storage life when ripe than those ripened more slowly. If ripening is slow and storage is prolonged, the flesh becomes mushy and the fruits shrivel as moisture loss rises to between 5 and 10%.

In closing the discussion of recommended conditions, the relative merits of tomatoes ripened on or off the vine need examination. We purposely do not use the term "vine ripened," because it does not mean what it says. As used by the trade, the term designates a tomato that shows some pinkish or reddish color when it is picked, which means that most vine-ripes were not even half ripe at harvest (Manley and Godwin 1963). Thus, vine-ripe, as used in advertisements, is at least a misnomer. It leads to confusion and mistrust on the part of the consumer, who sometimes gets excellent and sometimes inferior vine-ripes. It seems that this term should be clearly defined in the U.S. Standards for Grades of Fresh Tomatoes. If this were done, vine-ripes would be just that, and any fruits harvested less ripe could be designated by their color, as given in the U.S. Standards.

During the last few years substantial evidence has accumulated from various parts of the world on the relative merits of tomatoes harvested mature-green and those harvested at more advanced stages of ripeness. Most of the researchers found that fruit ripened on the vine, or even those picked at the breaker stage, are higher in ascorbic acid than those harvested mature-green. The differences ranged from slight, but statistically significant, to a ratio of 2:1 in favor of fruit ripened on the plant. In no case was the difference in favor of mature-green fruit. Beta carotene content was only slightly influenced by stage of maturity at harvest; the differences, if any, were slightly in favor of tomatoes ripened on the vine. In respect to flavor, carefully controlled taste tests have shown that fruit ripened on the vine was rated significantly higher than that ripened off the vine. However, these differences are not equally great for all cultivars. Furthermore, the differences in ascorbic acid and carotene contents between fruit harvested at different stages of ripeness are overshadowed by differences among cultivars (Bisogni *et al.* 1976; Madamba *et al.* 1974; Matthews *et al.* 1974; Verma *et al.* 1970; Watada *et al.* 1976). All these results logically follow from the earlier findings of McCollum and Skok (1960) that organic materials move into the fruit until about the breaker stage, so that tomatoes harvested earlier would of necessity be lower in various important constituents.

Watermelons

Quality Criteria   To be enjoyable, the flesh of watermelons must be red, juicy, sweet and tender. However, picking out melons that have these characteristics, without sampling a piece or cutting the melon open, is reputedly difficult (Whitaker and Davis 1962). Nevertheless, high quality watermelons can be selected with reasonable assurance if the following criteria are observed: At harvest the tendril nearest the melon should be wilting and the ground spot should be pale yellow. If the tendril is turgid, the melon is immature; if it is withered the melon is overmature. Watermelons are most desirable if harvested about 45 days after bloom and when the soluble solids content is 12 to 13%. Watermelons harvested before 40 days are immature and those 50 days or older are overripe (Mizuno and Pratt 1973).

Choosing a watermelon that meets the external characteristics does not necessarily yield a good one, because there are large differences in quality between cultivars. For example, the difference in soluble solids content, a good measure of quality, can reach 3% between the best and poorest cultivar (Porter and Bisson 1934). Although these findings are outdated in respect to specific cultivars, they still are generally valid. High quality watermelons should have a soluble solids content of at least 10.5% in the flesh near the center of the melon. The location is important, because the flesh near the rind is about 3% lower in soluble solids than the center of the fruit, and the stem end is about 2% lower than the blossom-end (MacGillivray 1947).

Recommended Conditions   Watermelons, being chilling sensitive, must be held at moderate temperatures. Lutz and Hardenburg (1968) recommend 7° to 10° C (45° to 50° F) as acceptable, because neither chilling injury nor decay is serious in this range. However, there is clear evidence (Showalter *et al.* 1955; Showalter 1960) that the color and flavor of watermelons improve during storage at or above room temperature and that color fades at 10° C or below. Since properly handled watermelons do not decay readily, 13° to 15° C (55° to 59° F) may be preferable to lower or higher temperatures for marketing periods of 2 weeks or less. This temperature range seems safe, because watermelons no longer are shipped in box cars, but in refrigerated rail cars or truck trailers, where the fruit can be cooled to the desirable level within at most two days. If watermelons must be stored more than 2 weeks, 7° to

10° C might be safer, although optimum storage conditions for this melon apparently have not been determined.

The humidity requirements for watermelons are less exacting than for some other melons, because they do not readily lose moisture. Again, no optimum conditions have been determined, although 80 to 90% is usually satisfactory.

The storage life of watermelons is difficult to assess, because they remain edible for 2 to 3 months at moderate temperatures, even though their quality may be low by most standards. If substantial deterioration of taste and texture is to be avoided, watermelons should be held no longer than two weeks.

REFERENCES

Cantaloups

ANON. 1969. Faster cooling of cantaloupes. Western Grower and Shipper *40*, No. 5, 18, 41.

ANON. 1971. New top-icing method for melons solves problems. Western Grower and Shipper *42*, No. 8, 19, 27.

AULENBACH, B. B., and WORTHINGTON, J. T. 1974. Sensory evaluation of muskmelon: Is soluble solids content a good quality index? HortScience *9*, 136–137.

BIANCO, V. V., and PRATT, H. K. 1977. Compositional changes in muskmelons during development and in response to ethylene treatment. J. Am. Soc. Hort. Sci. *102*, 127–133.

CALIF. DEPT. AGR. Regulations of the Department of Agriculture pertaining to fruit, nut, egg, and vegetable standardization. Extracts, Title *3*, Agr. Calif. Administration Code. Sect. 1441.

CHACE, E. M., CHURCH, C. G., and DENNY, F. E. 1924. Relation between the composition of California cantaloupes and their commercial maturity. U.S. Dept. Agr. Bull. *1250*.

DAVIS, R. M., JR. 1965. Concerning flavor in cantaloupe. Univ. Calif. Veg. Crops Ser. *137*.

DAVIS, R. M., JR. 1970. Vein tracts, not sutures, in cantaloupe. HortScience *5*, 86.

DAVIS, R. M., JR., BAKER, G. A., and KASMIRE, R. F. 1964. Muskmelon quality characteristics—their variability and interrelationships. Hilgardia *35*, 479–489.

JOHNSON, H. B. 1968. Heat and other treatments for cantaloupes and peppers. *In* United Fresh Fruit and Vegetable Association Yearbook. pp. 9, 14, 51–52, 54, 56. United Fresh Fruit and Vegetable Assoc., Washington, D.C.

KASMIRE, R. F. 1968. Determining cantaloupe size by volume:weight relationships. Calif. Agr. *22*, No. 5, 13.

COMMODITY REQUIREMENTS—RIPE FRUITS   205

KASMIRE, R. F., and PARSONS, R. A. (c. 1971). Precooling cantaloups. A guide for shippers. Univ. Calif. Agr. Ext. Serv. (Unnumbered).
KASMIRE, R. F., SARQUIS, A. V., and WRIGHT, D. N. 1962. Midsummer cantaloupes. Market quality studies 1961. Univ. Calif. Agr. Ext. Serv. *AXT-50*.
LIPTON, W. J. 1976. Western-grown melons: Quality maintenance from field to consumer. 28th Ann. Intl. Conf. Handling Perishable Agr. Commod. Mich. State Univ. 99–107.
LIPTON, W. J., and STEWART, J. K. 1961. Effect of hydrocooling on market quality of cantaloupes. Proc. Am. Soc. Hort. Sci. *78*, 324–331.
MORRIS, L. L. 1947. The use of ice on cantaloupes and other melons. Univ. Calif. Truck Crops Mimeo. *38*.
OGLE, W. L., and CHRISTOPHER, E. P. 1957. The influence of maturity, temperature, and duration of storage on quality of cantaloupes. Proc. Am. Soc. Hort. Sci. *70*, 319–324.
ROSA, J. T. 1928. Changes in composition during ripening and storage of melons. Hilgardia *3*, 421–443.
SCOTT, G. W., and MacGILLIVRAY, J. H. 1940. Variation in solids of the juice from different regions in melon fruits. Hilgardia *13*, 69–79.
STEWART, J. K., and LIPTON, W. J. 1960. Factors influencing heat loss in cantaloupes during hydrocooling. U.S. Dept. Agr. Mktg. Res. Rept. *421*.
WEBSTER, B. D. 1975. Anatomical and histochemical modifications associated with abscission of *Cucumis* fruits. J. Am. Soc. Hort. Sci. *100*, 180–184.
WEBSTER, B. D., and CRAIG, M. E. 1976. Net morphogenesis and characteristics of the surface of muskmelon fruit. J. Am. Soc. Hort. Sci. *101*, 412–415.
WHITAKER, T. W. 1970. Muskmelon vs. cantaloupe. HortScience. *5*, 86.
WHITAKER, T. W., and DAVIS, G. N. 1962. Cucurbits. Interscience, New York.

Honey Dews

KASMIRE, R. F., PRATT, H. K., and CHACON, F. 1970. Honey Dew melon maturity and ripening guide. Univ. Calif. Agr. Ext. Serv. *MA-26*.
LIPTON, W. J. 1978. Chilling injury of "Honey Dew" muskmelons; symptoms and relation to degree of ripeness at harvest. HortScience *13*, 45–46.
PRATT, H. K., GOESCHL, J. D., and MARTIN, F. W. 1977. Fruit growth and development, ripening, and the role of ethylene in the "Honey Dew" muskmelon. J. Am. Soc. Hort. Sci. *102*, 203–210.

Pumpkins and Winter Squash

FRANCIS, F. J., JIMINEZ, M. A., and SANNA, E. M. 1961A. Alcohol content and atmospheric changes in pre-packaged squash. Proc. Am. Soc. Hort. Sci. *78*, 438–444.
FRANCIS, F. J., SANNA, E. M., and THOMSON, C. L. 1961B. Effect of some harvesting and preparation conditions on the shelf-life of prepeeled squash. Proc. Am. Soc. Hort. Sci. *78*, 431–437.

FRANCIS, F. J., and THOMSON, C. L. 1965. Optimum storage conditions for butternut squash. Proc. Am. Soc. Hort. Sci. *86*, 451–456.

GUBA, E. F. 1950. Spoilage of squash in storage. Mass. Agr. Expt. Sta. Bull. *457*.

MERROW, S. B., and HOPP, R. J. 1961. Associations between the sugar and starch content of and the degree of preference for winter squashes. J. Agr. Food Chem. *9*, 321–326.

SCHALES, F. D., and ISENBERG, F. M. 1963. The effect of curing and storage on chemical composition and taste acceptability of winter squash. Proc. Am. Soc. Hort. Sci. *83*, 667–674.

U.S. DEPT. AGR. 1963. Growing pumpkins and squashes. Farmers Bull. *2086*.

Tomatoes

BISOGNI, C. A., ARMBRUSTER, G., and BRECHT, P. E. 1976. Quality comparisons of room ripened and field ripened tomato fruits. J. Food Sci. *41*, 333–338.

CHEN, P., and STUDER, H. E. 1976. Detection of puffiness in tomatoes. Proc. 2nd Tomato Quality Workshop. Univ. Calif. Veg. Crops Ser. *178*, 16–18.

HABER, E. S. 1931. Acidity and color changes in tomatoes under various storage temperatures. Iowa State Coll. J. Sci. *5*, 171–184.

HALL, C. B. 1961. The effect of low storage temperatures on the color, carotenoid pigments, shelf-life and firmness of ripened tomatoes. Proc. Am. Soc. Hort. Sci. *78*, 480–487.

HALL, C. B. 1964. The ripening response of detached tomato fruits to daily exposures to high temperatures. Proc. Florida State Hort. Sci. *77*, 252–256.

HALL, C. B. 1965. Effect of holding just-turned tomato fruits at 40° F prior to ripening at 68° F. Proc. Florida State Hort. Soc. *78*, 241–244.

HICKS, J. R., and HAYSLIP, N. C. 1975. Fresh market tomatoes harvested red-ripe. HortScience *10*, 2.

IORDACHESCU, O., CERNAIANU, A., AMARIUTEI, A., and DOBREANU, M. 1974. Research on short-term storage of tomatoes and green peppers. Acta Hort. No. 38, Vol. *1*, 217–226. (French)

JAHN, O. L. 1975. Comparison of instrumental methods for measuring ripening changes in intact tomato fruit. J. Am. Soc. Hort. Sci. *100*, 688–691.

JEN, J. J. 1974. Spectral quality of light and the ripening characteristics of tomato fruit. HortScience *9*, 548–549.

JOHNSON, H. B., and NEWSOM, D. W. 1957. Transit refrigeration of mature-green tomatoes shipped by rail from the Lower Rio Grande Valley of Texas. U.S. Dept. Agr. *AMS-188*.

KADER, A. A., and MORRIS, L. L. 1974A. Postharvest handling and physiology of tomatoes. (An indexed reference list.) Univ. Calif., Davis. Veg. Crops Ser. *162*.

KADER, A. A., and MORRIS, L. L. 1974B. Consumer quality improvement foreseen with low oxygen atmosphere shipping. Western Grower and Shipper *45,* No. 7, 16–18.

KADER, A. A., and MORRIS, L. L. 1975. Further studies with ethephon. Univ. Calif. Dept. Veg. Crops Ser. *171*, 95–97.

KADER, A. A., and MORRIS, L. L. 1976A. Postharvest handling and physiology of tomatoes. (An indexed reference list.) Univ. Calif. Dept. Veg. Crops Ser. *177.*

KADER, A. A., and MORRIS, L. L. 1976B. Appearance factors other than color and their contribution to quality. Proc. 2nd Tomato Quality Workshop. Univ. Calif. Veg. Crops Ser. *178,* 8–12.

KASMIRE, R. F. 1969. Personal communication. Davis, Calif.

KASMIRE, R. F. 1973. Ripening market tomatoes with ethylene gas. Univ. Calif. Agr. Ext. Serv. *MA-71.*

KASMIRE, R. F., KADER, A. A., and MORRIS, L. L. 1976. Maturity, ripening, and transit temperatures. Calif. Tomatorama Info. Bull. *13.*

KATTAN, A. A. *et al.* 1968. Mass grading machine-harvested tomatoes. Ark. Farm Res. *17*, No. 1.

KATTAN, A. A., SHARP, C. Q., and MORRIS, J. R. 1969. A mechanical sorter for tomatoes. Ark. Farm Res. *18*, No. 1.

KHUDAIRI, A. K. 1972. The ripening of tomatoes—a molecular ecological approach to the physiology of fruit ripening. Am. Scientist *60*, 696–707.

KIM, B. D., and HALL, C. B. 1976. Firmness of tomato fruit subjected to low concentrations of oxygen. HortScience *11*, 466.

LIPTON, W. J. 1970. Growth of tomato plants and fruit production in high humidity and at high temperatures. J. Am. Soc. Hort. Sci. *95*, 674–680.

LOCKHART, C. L., and EAVES, C. A. 1967. The influence of low oxygen levels and relative humidity on storage of green tomatoes. J. Hort. Sci. *42*, 289–294.

LOCKHART, C. L., EAVES, C. A., and CHIPMAN, E. W. 1969. Suppression of rots on four varieties of mature-green tomatoes in controlled atmosphere storage. Can. J. Plant Sci. *49*, 265–269.

LUTZ, J. M. 1944. Maturity and handling of green-wrap tomatoes in Mississippi. U.S. Dept. Agr. Circ. *695.*

MADAMBA, L. S. P., MORALES, E. R., and VILLANUEVA, T. G. 1974. Some factors affecting the ascorbic acid contents of tomato fruits. Philippine J. Nutr. *27*, 7–12.

MANLEY, W. T., and GODWIN, M. R. 1963. Marketing Florida vine-ripened tomatoes. Florida Agr. Exp. Sta. Circ. *S-147.*

MATTHEWS, R. F., CRILL, P., and LOCASCIO, S. J. 1974. Carotene and ascorbic acid contents of tomatoes as affected by maturity. Proc. Florida State Hort. Soc. *87*, 214–216.

McCOLLOCH, L. P., and WORTHINGTON, J. T. 1954. Ways to prevent chilling mature-green tomatoes. Pre-Pack-Age 7, No. 6, 22–25.

McCOLLOCH, L. P., YEATMAN, J. N., and LOYD, P. 1966. Color changes and chilling injury of pink tomatoes held at various temperatures. U.S. Dept. Agr. Mktg. Res. Rept. *735.*

McCOLLUM, J. P., and SKOK, J. 1960. Radiocarbon studies on the transloca-
tion of organic constituents into ripening tomato fruits. Proc. Am. Soc. Hort.
Sci. 75, 611–616.

MIZUNO, S. 1971. Influence of CO_2 and O_2 on the ripening behavior of tomato
fruits at 20 degrees C. J. Japan. Soc. Hort. Sci. 40, 292–299. (Japanese,
English summary)

MORRIS, L. L., and KADER, A. A. 1975. Postharvest physiology of tomato
fruits. Univ. Calif. Dept. Veg. Crops Ser. 171, 36–48.

PARSONS, C. S., ANDERSON, R. E., and PENNEY, R. W. 1970. Storage of
mature-green tomatoes in controlled atmospheres. J. Am. Soc. Hort. Sci. 95,
791–794.

PARSONS, C. S., McCOLLOCH, L. P., and WRIGHT, R. C. 1960. Cabbage,
celery, lettuce, and tomatoes. Laboratory tests of storage methods. U.S. Dept.
Agr. Mktg. Res. Rept. 402.

PAYNTER, V. A., and JEN, J. J. 1976. Comparative effects of light and
ethephon on the ripening of detached tomatoes. J. Food Sci. 41, 1366–1369.

PLATENIUS, H., JAMISON, F. S., and THOMPSON, H. C. 1934. Studies on
cold storage of vegetables. Cornell Univ. Agr. Expt. Sta. Bull. 602.

RADSPINNER, W. A. 1954. Commercial aspects of ripening mature-green
tomatoes with ethylene gas. Pre-Pack-Age 8, No. 4, 17–18, 20–21.

ROBINSON, R. W., WILEZYNSKI, F. G., DENNIS, F. G., JR., and BRYAN,
H. H. 1968. Chemical promotion of tomato fruit ripening. Proc. Am. Soc. Hort.
Sci. 93, 823–830.

ROSA, J. T. 1926. Ripening and storage of tomatoes. Proc. Am. Soc. Hort. Sci. 23,
233–242.

SALUNKHE, D. K., and WU, M. T. 1973. Effects of low oxygen atmosphere
storage on ripening and associated biochemical changes of tomato fruits. J.
Am. Soc. Hort. Sci. 98, 12–14.

SAYRE, C. B., ROBINSON, W. B., and WISHNETSKY, T. 1953. Effect of
temperature on the color, lycopene, and carotene content of detached and of
vine-ripened tomatoes. Proc. Am. Soc. Hort. Sci. 61, 381–387.

SEGALL, R. H., and HAYSLIP, N. C. 1966. Susceptibility of Manapal and
Grothen's Globe tomatoes to Alternaria rot. Proc. Florida State Hort. Soc. 79,
227–229.

SHEWFELT, A. L., and HALPIN, J. E. 1967. The effect of light quality on the
rate of tomato color development. Proc. Am. Soc. Hort. Sci. 91, 561–565.

SRIVASTAVA, H. C., MOORTHY, N. V. N., and KAPUR, N. S. 1962. Refrigerated storage behavior of pre-cooled tomatoes (Lycopersicon esculentum (Mill)
(var. Marglobe). Food Sci. (Mysore) 11, 252–254.

STENVERS, N., and BRUINSMA, J. 1975. Ripening of tomato fruits at reduced
atmospheric and partial oxygen pressures. Nature 253, 532–533.

THOMPSON, B. D., GULL, D. D., and HALSEY, L. H. 1964. Ripening of three
varieties of tomatoes as influenced by age of fruit, preripening temperature
and position on the plant. Proc. Florida State Hort. Soc. 77, 156–162.

TOMKINS, R. G. 1963. The effects of temperature, extent of evaporation, and
restriction of ventilation on the storage life of tomatoes. J. Hort. Sci. 38,
335–347.

U.S. DEPT. AGR. 1961. United States Standards for Grades of Fresh Tomatoes.

U.S. DEPT. AGR. 1975. Color classification requirements in United States standards for grades of fresh tomatoes. U.S. Department Agriculture Visual Aid TM-L-1. (Sold by the John Henry Co., P.O. Box 1410, Lansing, Mich. 48904)

VERMA, A. N., SRIVASTAVA, D. C., MISHRA, H. R., and SHARMA, R. K. 1970. Quality determination of tomato (*Lycopersicon esculentum* Mill.) during natural and artificial ripening. Poona Agr. Coll. Mag. *60*, 72–74.

WATADA, A. E., AULENBACH, B. B., and WORTHINGTON, J. T. 1976. Vitamins A and C in ripe tomatoes as affected by stage of ripeness at harvest and by supplementary ethylene. J. Food Sci. *41*, 856–858.

WORTHINGTON, J. T. 1974. A light-transmittance technique for determining tomato ripening rate and quality. Acta Hort. 38, Vol. *1*, 193–215.

WORTHINGTON, J. T. 1976. Personal communication. Beltsville, MD.

WORTHINGTON, J. T., DAY, R., and AULENBACH, B. 1977. A rapid, accurate, pictorial technique for continual assessment of tomato ripening behavior in commercial volume. Acta Hort. No. 62, 351–361.

WORTHINGTON, J. T., PENNEY, R. W., and YEATMAN, J. N. 1969. Evaluation of light source and temperature on tomato color development during ripening. HortScience *4*, 64–65.

WRIGHT, R. C., and GORMAN, E. A., JR. 1940. The ripening and repacking of mature-green tomatoes. U.S. Dept. Agr. Circ. *566*.

WRIGHT, R. C., PENTZER, W. T., WHITEMAN, T. M., and ROSE, D. H. 1931. Effect of various temperatures on the storage and ripening of tomatoes. U.S. Dept. Agr. Bull. *268*.

WU, M. T., JADHAR, S. J., and SALUNKHE, D. K. 1972. Effects of sub-atmospheric pressure storage on ripening of tomato fruits. J. Food Sci. *37*, 952–956.

Watermelon

LUTZ, J. M., and HARDENBURG, R. E. 1968. The commercial storage of fruits, vegetables, and florist and nursery stocks. U.S. Dept. Agr. Handbook *66*.

MacGILLVRAY, J. M. 1947. Soluble solids content of different regions of watermelons. Plant Physiol. *22*, 637–640.

MIZUNO, S., and PRATT, H. K. 1973. Relations of respiration and ethylene production to maturity in the watermelon. J. Am. Soc. Hort. Sci. *98*, 614–617.

PORTER, D. R., and BISSON, C. S. 1934. Total soluble solids and sugars in watermelons. Proc. Am. Soc. Hort. Sci. *32*, 596–599.

SHOWALTER, R. K. 1960. Watermelon color as affected by maturity and storage. Proc. Florida State Hort. Soc. *73*, 289–293.

SHOWALTER, R. K. et al. 1955. Changes in Congo watermelons after harvest. Proc. Assoc. South. Agr. Workers *52*, 136–137.

WHITAKER, T. W., and DAVIS, G. N. 1962. Cucurbits. Interscience, New York.

9

Commodity Requirements— Underground Structures

This chapter deals with vegetables whose edible portion develops partly or entirely underground and includes bulbs, roots, tubers and other subterranean structures.

BULBS

Garlic

Quality Criteria   Garlic bulbs should be firm and heavy for their size. Light bulbs either have lost much moisture or may be decayed. Sprouting or root growth is undesirable.

Recommended Conditions   Garlic stores best at $-0.5°$ C to $0°$ ($31°$ F to $32°$) but $27°$ to $32°$ C ($80°$ to $90°$ F) is satisfactory for 1 month or less. Under either condition, RH should be below 70%. Temperatures between about $5°$ and $18°$ C ($41°$ and $65°$ F) are undesirable because they favor rapid sprouting, and high RH results in root and mold growth. Care must be taken that RH is below 70% around the bulbs, not just around the containers. Thus, air circulation through the container must be adequate to remove transpired water. Generally about 0.02 m^3 per sec per m^3 (1 cfm per cu ft) of garlic is adequate, judging by recommendations for mature onions (Comin 1955; Franklin *et al.* 1966). The high temperatures cannot be recommended for prolonged storage, because moisture loss would be excessive.

Fresh garlic can be prepackaged, but the bags must be well ventilated to maintain RH below 70%.

Garlic can be held at least 6 to 7 months in cold storage or 3 to 4 months in ventilated storage. However, regardless of which method is used, the bulbs must be thoroughly cured before storage. Incomplete curing results in excessive decay, particularly when the bulbs are held above 0° C (32° F).

Maleic hydrazide application before harvest or gamma-irradiation after harvest extended the storage life of garlic to 1 year at 0° C (32° F), with only about 10% weight loss. At uncontrolled temperatures (15° to 30° C; 59° to 86° F) the same treatments resulted in a similar loss after 4 months, and provided no advantage over storage of untreated garlic (El-Oksh *et al.* 1971).

Onions

Quality Criteria   Onion cultivars vary tremendously in color, size, shape and pungency; nevertheless, they share many quality characteristics. Bulbs should be well covered with dry scales, and the fleshy, edible scales should not be exposed. The bulbs should be firm, because soft bulbs either have been sunburned, bruised, have lost much moisture, or are affected by the translucent scale disorder. The neck should be dry and thin; a thick neck indicates improper curing, sprouting, or growth of a seedstalk. Root growth is also undesirable.

Color of the bulbs should be true to those of the cultivar—brown, reddish purple, yellow or white. The latter particularly should be free of any greening.

Recommended Conditions   Onions for fresh usage store best at a low temperature. In the United States 0° C (32° F) is generally recommended. In Europe, however, storage below the freezing point has been recommended for many years. When this method is used, the onions are quickly cooled to 0.5° to 1° C (33° to 34° F), and when the room is filled, the temperature is slowly lowered to −2° to −1° C (28° to 30° F). Before the onions are taken out of storage, they are thawed over a period of 1 to 2 weeks with the air about 5° C (41° F). Rapid thawing or any jarring of the bulbs when frozen will damage them. Sub-freezing storage is used mainly to retard sprouting, and may be a useful alternative when sprout inhibitors cannot be used. Further, storage below freezing is most suitable for onions high in soluble solids that are intended for processing, because the bulbs should be used shortly after thawing (Kessler 1960).

Onions also can be stored at high temperatures—from 30° to 35° C (86° to 95° F). While these temperatures yield satisfactory onions for the fresh market, their external color may be less attractive than that of bulbs from cold storage. However, onions stored at high temperatures are desirable for subsequent dehydration, because the dry flakes from such bulbs have better color retention than flakes made from onions stored cold (Yamaguchi *et al.* 1957). High temperature storage of bulbs for fresh use should be at RH levels just below where root growth occurs to avoid excessive water loss. Neither a report from India (Karmarkar and Joshi 1941) nor one from California cited above, indicates the proper humidity level, but about 75 to 85% RH probably would be satisfactory.

Most cultivars of onions cannot be stored for more than about a month between about 5° and 20° C (41° and 68° F), because sprouting and decay are most rapid in this range.

Relative humidity must be kept below the level where it encourages root growth. Generally, this level lies between 65 and 75% RH. If storage is below 0° C (32° F), RH is of minor importance (Platenius *et al.* 1934), but should probably not exceed 90%. If RH is too low, below about 50%, the bulbs become too dry and the dry outer scales shed, leaving the edible scales physically unprotected. Further, bulbs without dry scales or with cracked dry scales lose moisture much more rapidly than properly covered bulbs, the ratio being about 2.2:1.7:1 during 2 weeks at 5° C (41° F) and 75% RH (Apeland 1971). During long-term storage the disparity likely would be even greater in spite of a lower temperature (0° C or 32° F).

Air circulation must be sufficient to prevent heating of the onions and to remove moisture from within piles, bins or sacks. Near 0° C (32° F), about 0.12 m³ per min per m³ (1 cfm per cu ft) of onions is sufficient if forced through piles or bins (Comin 1955; Franklin *et al.* 1966). For onions in sacks, where air is not forced through the container, air movement must be rapid enough to maintain a sufficient gradient between the center of the sack and its periphery to cause moisture and heat to move outward and away from the onions.

For shipment of onions in mechanically refrigerated rail cars the thermostat should be set at about 3° C (37° F). Such conditions will be less favorable for decay development than higher temperatures. If substantial moisture condenses on the onions after unloading, the bulbs dry readily if the bags are stacked to permit free air circulation (Kasmire 1972).

If onions are packaged, the container must be well ventilated, or else humidity will be excessive and will induce root growth and decay. For this reason, mesh bags are preferable to plastic bags. If the latter are used, a 1.4 kg (3 lb) bag should be perforated with 30 to 40 holes each 5 mm (¼ in.) in diameter. The usefulness of CA storage for onions cannot definitely be evaluated on the basis of available data. In some tests the temperatures used were higher than generally recommended and in others the humidity was too high, as shown by root growth on the controls. On balance, 5% CO_2 plus 5% O_2 seems most promising in reducing losses from sprouting, root growth, and other defects during 8 months of storage. CO_2 at 10% induces a disorder that resembles the translucent scale defect (Adamicki and Kepka 1974). However, since properly cured and stored onions keep most of a year in air, the usefulness of CA storage is questionable.

The storage life of onions depends on many factors, but the most important is cultivar. Since cultivars change with time and since adaptability depends on location of production, no specific cultivars will be mentioned. However, certain characteristics tend to indicate superior storage quality, such as a high degree of pungency, high soluble and total solids contents, and globular shape.

Within a given cultivar, maximum storage life can be achieved by: (1) proper curing; (2) storing only well-matured onions; (3) treating them with a sprout inhibitor, such as maleic hydrazide, during maturation; and (4) bringing the onions rapidly to 0° C (32° F) once curing is completed, because delays in cold storage can lead to losses from the translucent scale disorder.

Finally, onions should never be stored with any other foods that conceivably might absorb the odor of onions.

ROOTS REQUIRING LOW TEMPERATURES

Members of Group

The vegetables considered in this section are classed as root crops, even though morphologically some are partly root and partly stem. Their common and botanical names are:

Common Name	Botanical Name
Beet, red	*Beta vulgaris*
Carrot	*Daucus carota*
Celeriac, celery root	*Apium graveolens,* rapaceum
Horseradish	*Armoracia rusticana*
Parsnips	*Pastinaca sativa*
Radish (spring, summer)	*Raphanus sativus*
Radish (winter)	*Raphanus sativus,* longipinnatus
Rutabaga, swedes	*Brassica napus,* napobrassica
Salsify, oyster plant	*Tragopogan porrifolius*
Turnip	*Brassica campestris,* rapifera

Close relatives of these crops, such as the various types of summer radishes, have the same requirements as those specifically noted.

Recommended Conditions for Group

Temperature   Storage near a constant 0° C (32° F) maximizes the storage life, or best preserves high quality during a given period in all crops of this group. Decay can cause substantial losses in root crops during even a week to ten days if they are held above 5° C (41° F).

Rapid precooling to storage temperature is not as critical in most of these crops as in leafy vegetables. However, roots should be brought into the desirable range the day of harvest during cool weather. If harvested when the soil or air is above 25° C (77° F), they should be cooled within 3 to 4 hr, because heating due to respiration can rapidly reduce quality as a load is hauled to or is waiting at a packing shed. Further, poorly precooled roots decay more readily during transit than those cooled to below 5° C (41° F).

All crops in this group can be hydrocooled, although packing in crushed ice also is effective. Horseradish, which is harvested late in autumn, does not normally require any precooling. None of these crops can be effectively vacuum cooled, because they lose insufficient moisture for adequate cooling.

If hydrocooling is used, loose carrots, for example, can be cooled from 25° C (77° F) to 5° C (41° F) in about 9 min if the water is 1° C (34° F); if in 23 kg (50 lb) mesh bags, the same degree of cooling requires about 11 min. The response of other roots in this group likely varies little from that of carrots, except celeriac and rutabagas, which have a smaller surface to volume ratio and thus cool more slowly.

Relative Humidity   A high relative humidity is essential for storage of cold-requiring roots if desiccation is to be avoided, particularly during prolonged storage. Older publications still recommend 90 to 95% RH because higher RH presumably increases the hazard of decay. However, evidence has been developed during the last few years that clearly establishes that root crops, such as carrots, remain in better condition if held at 98 to 100% RH during long-term storage (1½ months or longer) than at lower RH, as long as temperatures are between about 0° and 3° C (32° and 37° F). Apparently, the surface tissues retain their integrity better under very high RH than under even slightly lower RH and thus are better able to resist invasion by microorganisms (Apeland and Baugerod 1971, carrots; Hoyle 1956, horseradish; Kurki 1971, carrots, celeriac; Thorne 1972, carrots; van den Berg and Lentz 1977, carrots).

For relatively brief storage, as in transcontinental or overseas shipment of three weeks or less, RH level is less critical, but it should be high enough to avoid even slight wilting, i.e., at least 95%.

Packaging   All of these root crops lend themselves well to prepacking in ventilated film bags. However, so far, only carrots, parsnips and radishes are widely sold in this way. Adequate ventilation consists of about a dozen 5 mm holes per 1 kg bag (six ¼ in. holes per 1 lb bag). If these crops are prepackaged at origin, they must be precooled prior to packing, because heat is transferred very slowly through the bulk of tissue in a bag. Cooling these roots prior to packing presents no major problem because with modern machinery, handling is sufficiently rapid to prevent substantial warming during packing. Carrots, for example, warm only about 0.6° C (1° F) per min when the gradient between roots and air is 18° C (33° F).

Air Circulation   When root crops are stored several months in ventilated storages, in refrigerated warehouses, or more briefly in rail cars or truck trailers, air circulation must be adequate to remove respiratory heat, unless the vegetables are packed in ice. An air velocity of about 7 to 10 cm per sec (14 to 20 ft per min) is adequate for this purpose at low storage temperature (van den Berg and Lentz 1966). Under such air flow, carrots lost slightly less than 0.2% of their weight per month, a very small amount, when RH ranged from 98 to 100%. While this work refers to carrots, it undoubtedly is applicable to other crops.

Further recommendations are given under individual crops.

Beets

Quality Criteria   Loose or bunched beets should be deep red, firm and free of cracks, fibrous roots or corky tissue. They should be globular and 4 to 8 cm (1½ to 3 in.) across. Elongated roots indicate crowding during growth and toughness. Beets smaller or larger than indicated can be of excellent quality, but the chance of toughening increases at either end—on the small side due to crowding and on the large side due to senescence.

Tops of bunched beets must be turgid and healthy. Inferior tops suggest inferior roots as the former readily withdraw water from the latter.

Recommended Conditions   The recommendations for root crops presented above generally apply to beets. If beets are stored above the recommended temperatures, sprouting and root formation can be serious during prolonged storage, even if decay does not become a problem.

Effects of CA storage have not been adequately tested so far; however, preliminary results indicate that elevated CO_2 increases decay.

Topped beets store well for 3 to 5 months, but can be held as long as 8 months in cold storage if destined for processing (Chrimes 1967). Under most storage conditions relatively large roots keep better than small ones because the former shrivel more slowly. However, at 98% RH, this advantage of larger roots would be minimal.

Bunched roots have a short storage life because the tops are highly perishable. They can be held 10 days to 2 weeks at 0° C (32° F), and half as long at 5° C (41° F).

Carrots

Quality Criteria   Desirable carrots are crisp, sweet, and a deep yellow to orange. Limp or tough carrots are highly undesirable.

Recommended Conditions   Since the general recommendations given earlier largely are based on work done with carrots, they need not be repeated here. However, some topics referred to broadly will be given in greater detail.

Earlier the need for thorough precooling was stressed as an aid in keeping decay in check during transit. Barger and Radspinner (1956) showed that decay was minimal after more than a week near 5° C (41° F), but affected 2% of the roots shipped near 10° C (50° F). After an additional week at 21° C (70° F), those shipped at 10° C showed 13% decayed roots, whereas the lots shipped near 5° C showed only 3% decay after the same rather severe treatment. Thus, the benefits of thorough precooling may be more noticeable at retail than on arrival.

During prolonged storage of fully mature carrots held for fresh market or for processing, good temperature control is particularly critical if losses from decay, sprouting, and bitterness are to be held low. Even under the best conditions 10 to 20% of roots will show some decay after 7 months.

Low temperature greatly retards sprouting. It is minimal after 3 months below 5° C (41° F), but after 7 months it becomes objectionable. At 10° C (50° F) serious sprouting occurs after 3 months unless the plants are treated before harvest with a sprout inhibitor, such as maleic hydrazide.

Storage near 0° C (32° F) also reduces the chance of wastage due to development of bitterness in stored carrots. First, production of ethylene, which induces formation of the bitter compound (Carlton *et al.* 1961), is negligible near 0° C. Second, the low temperature reduces fungal infections which tend to accelerate ethylene production, and thus increase bitterness.

Relative humidity apparently cannot be too high for carrots when temperatures are low, as noted earlier. Even after 8 to 9 months, carrots were crisp if held in 97 to 100% RH at 0° to 1° C (32° to 34° F).

Weight loss of carrots is influenced by their size. Under conditions of fairly high moisture loss, roots that weighed 80 to 100 g (about 3 oz) lost about half as much weight in a given time as those that weighed 20 g ($\frac{2}{3}$ oz). However, per unit surface area, there was no difference in weight loss between large and small roots (Apeland and Baugerod 1971).

The usefulness of CA storage for carrots is questionable. So far there is no agreement on whether moderate levels of CO_2 (about 2 to 5%) are beneficial or detrimental; in respect to low O_2, the reports also are contradictory. The preponderance of the evidence suggests that O_2 below about 5% and CO_2 above about 5% tend to favor decay development (Apeland and Hoftun 1971; Baumann 1974; Phan 1974; Weichman 1971, 1973). Whatever the results, CA would be useless for carrots stored at 0° C (32° F) for 2 months or less, because losses likely would be minimal in normal air. For long-term storage CA may be useful because low O_2 reduces losses of sugars and carotene and high CO_2 may inhibit development of bitterness. However, definite recommendations must await results from comprehensive, carefully controlled tests.

The storage life of carrots depends on whether the tops are on or off, and whether the roots have "fully" developed, and, of course, on storage conditions.

Bunched carrots, now almost a historical item, keep only as long as their tops, which is about 3 weeks at 0° C (32° F), and about half as long at 5° C (41° F). Roots harvested before full maturation, the kind most generally marketed fresh, store well for at least 1 month if held near 0° C. Near 5° C, the storage life will only be 2 to 3 weeks at most. Since carrots differ in their susceptibility to decay, some lots may keep twice as long as others under the same conditions. Thus, if partly mature carrots are held longer than normal, they must be checked at weekly intervals to determine their condition.

Fully mature carrots have the longest storage life. As noted earlier, deterioration was minimal after 9 months near 0° C (32° F) and at high RH. Under commonly found conditions, i.e., between 0° and 5° C and 90 to 95% RH, 4 to 6 months is a more realistic expectation. Fully mature carrots also are less prone to oxidative browning of the surface than younger roots, and thus almost inevitable abrasions appear less prominent.

Bitterness can largely be avoided by low temperatures. However, carrots must still be stored separately from crops that emit ethylene, such as apples or pears.

Close trimming of tops also is essential for prolonged storage, because if any short stubs are left on, re-growth of sprouts will be more rapid than if the tops are trimmed almost flush with the roots.

Celeriac, Celery Root

Quality Criteria Celeriac should be firm, never spongy. Excessive branch roots should have been trimmed off, but without cutting off slices from the main root. The roots should be between 6 and 10 cm (2½ and 4 in.) across; larger ones are likely to have spongy centers and are tough, although smaller ones also may have these defects.

Recommended Conditions Recommendations given for roots in general apply, except that cooling is slower than for more elongated roots. Celeriac can easily be stored 3 to 4 months at 0° to 1° C (32° to 34° F) and with only minor losses for 8 months if RH is 97 to 99%. If storage is above 1° C, RH should be about 95%, or else decay will cause substantial losses (nearly 50%) during 6 months. At 4° to 5° C (40° to 41° F) the storage life is only 4 months if losses are to be held below 15% (Kurki 1971). Air circulation in the storage must be adequate to remove respiratory heat. Since dirt often adheres to celery roots, particular care must be taken not to stack them too tightly.

In cool climates celeriac can be held in common storage. Since freezing, heating, and drying all are more likely under such conditions, the storage life is more limited than under refrigerated storage. About 4 to 5 months is maximal if temperature in common storage does not exceed 3° C (38° F) (Wiersma 1973).

CA storage for celeriac is not advantageous. Low O_2 did not reduce losses but high CO_2 increased decay during storage lasting nearly 5 months (Weichman 1977).

Since this vegetable does not obviously show deterioration, proper care at retail often is neglected. Prepacking in perforated film would greatly retard quality loss during protracted display, because water loss is the main cause of deterioration.

Horseradish

Quality Criteria Roots of this unattractive but prized condiment should be firm and crisp; their surface should be fairly smooth with all side roots removed. "Sticks" should be at least 15 cm (6 in.) long and 3 cm (1¼ in.) across for fresh market use. For processing, smaller roots may also be acceptable.

Recommended Conditions   Unlike most other root crops requiring low temperatures, horseradish need not be precooled because it is harvested during cold weather. Some horseradish is stored in trenches outdoors or in cellars, although refrigerated storage also is used. Wherever it is held, $-1°$ to $0°$ C ($30°$ to $32°$ F) and an essentially water-saturated atmosphere slow deterioration most effectively. This beneficial effect of very high RH, stressed by Hoyle (1956), parallels that for carrots noted earlier, and suggests that all crops in this group may react similarly.

Storage of horseradish in containers lined with perforated film seems advantageous because it provides high RH around the roots while permitting adequate ventilation between containers to remove respiratory heat. Tightly sealed polyethylene wraps, as suggested by Hoyle for planting stock, cannot be recommended for roots to be used fresh, because off-flavors may develop, although this point has not been investigated.

Prepacking individual roots in perforated wraps would retard deterioration during display and might make horseradish a more commonly seen item on produce racks.

Horseradish can be stored a year under recommended conditions. There is, however, no precise information on the effect of various temperatures on storage life. In general, the smaller the roots, the greater the danger of losses, because small roots tend to pack tightly and thus are more likely to heat and rot. Further, light must be excluded in storage and minimized during display, or else the roots turn green and lose value.

Remarks by Hoyle suggest that somewhat limp roots can be rendered crisp again by placing them in ice water, as noted for carrots.

Parsnips

Quality Criteria   Desirable parsnips are buff, have a smooth surface, and are crisp, although they never are as crisp as carrots. The roots should be at least 4 cm (1½ in.) across at the top. Thin roots tend to be tough and stringy, while very large ones tend to have woody, inedible cores.

Recommended Conditions   Parsnips have to be stored near $0°$ C ($32°$ F) not only to retard deterioration, but also to improve their quality. Unless they pass through several freezes in the field or are held about 2 weeks near 0° C they lack desirable sweetness. In other respects parsnips have the same requirements as carrots, and can be stored 4 to 5 months near 0° C.

Radishes

Quality Criteria   Radishes, be they red and round or white and long, must be hard and crisp. Red ones should be bright red, not purplish, which indicates old age; white ones should be free of any dark blemishes.

Size of root is not always a good indicator of quality in the globe type, although generally, excessively large roots (more than 3 cm (1¼ in.) across) tend to be more pithy and tough than smaller ones. Globe type radishes that are elongated, most likely because of crowding in the field, also tend to be tougher than globular roots of the same diameter.

Internally, radishes should be free of pithy tissue, which is whiter than the rest and interspersed by many air spaces. Small, isolated masses of pithy tissue do not materially reduce the culinary quality of radishes, but large ones are highly objectionable. Very pithy roots can be recognized externally because they tend to be spongy and light for their size.

For bunched radishes, the tops must be turgid and green.

Recommended Conditions   The commonly used spring or summer radishes can be hydrocooled with even greater efficiency than carrots. Bunched and packed in cartons, 25° C (77° F) roots can be cooled to 5° C (41° F) in less than 4 min using 1° C (34° F) water. With this root crop, prompt cooling is important because radishes readily become spongy under warm, dry conditions. Thus, continued refrigeration and availability of free moisture are even more important with radishes than with other root crops. This need most commonly is met by package icing.

While radishes still are sold bunched, more and more are topped and then prepackaged in film bags. The bags should be ventilated, to permit adequate aeration. Shipping radishes in sealed bags, as commercially practiced, entails the risk of low-O_2 injury, especially during transit-marketing periods of two weeks or longer. While even 0.25% O_2 is harmless near 0° C (32° F), this concentration can lead to decay within about 10 days to 2 weeks when radishes are held at 5° C (41° F) or above. Since such temperatures can be encountered anywhere during marketing, respiratory depletion of O_2 is a potential hazard in unventilated film bags.

Where O_2 can be controlled, as in transit vehicles, $1\% \pm 0.5\%$ O_2 is beneficial because it reduces top and root growth and softening when temperatures are higher than desirable. If temperatures are continuously between $0°$ and $2°$ C ($32°$ and $36°$ F) there is no advantage in using low O_2, because topped radishes keep well for 2 to 3 weeks in this range (Lipton 1972).

The storage life of topped radishes is 3 to 4 weeks at $0°$ C ($32°$ F) and high RH, but at $10°$ C ($50°$ F) it is less than a week if decay is to be absent. The life of bunched radishes is limited by that of the tops; thus, they keep at most half as long as topped ones.

Radishes differ in their susceptibility to decay, but the addition of chlorine to the water used for cooling or washing (see section on *Diseases* for details) is always a good precaution to assure delivery of high quality roots.

Storage life also can be lengthened by removing the thin tail of the roots and by clipping the tops to within less than 1 mm of the roots. Such clipping is accomplished routinely with modern harvest machines.

Close trimming of the tops greatly retards re-growth of tops and both reduce decay. There is then no need for the use of growth regulators to inhibit top growth when radishes are held anywhere near recommended temperatures (Guzman 1970).

Winter radishes can be stored much longer than the others, and recommendations for topped mature carrots apply.

Rutabagas

Quality Criteria   Rutabagas should be firm and have a smooth surface; softness and wrinkles indicate excessive water loss. Size is not a good criterion of quality, although small roots shrivel faster than large ones.

Recommended Conditions   Rutabagas can be stored like carrots, except that the former almost invariably are waxed immediately before marketing to reduce moisture loss. While this process has been accepted for decades, storage at 98 to 100% RH might well make waxing unnecessary, particularly if followed by marketing in perforated film bags. Experiments on marketing of prepeeled rutabagas in film bags (Alexander and Francis 1964) suggest the feasibility of this approach if temperatures are kept below $2°$ C ($35°$ F). Knife-peeled rutabagas keep in good condition for 3 weeks at $1°$ C ($34°$ F), as compared to 2 to 4 months for unpeeled roots.

Salsify

Quality Criteria   Good quality salsify roots are smooth, slender, crisp and free of a tough core. If bunched, tops must be fresh, green and turgid.

Recommended Conditions   Recommendations for the group in general apply, but shrivelling is even more serious during long-term storage because the long, slender roots have a large surface to volume ratio. Thus, particular attention must be given to maintenance of a high RH. Losses from shrivelling could be reduced if salsify were marketed in perforated film bags, like most carrots.

The storage life of topped salsify approximates that of topped carrots, and that of bunched salsify approximates that of bunched carrots, although no precise information is available on salsify. The requirements of salsify can be met by storage in the ground in appropriate climates. However, they must be dug before sprouting starts, or else they will become tough.

Turnips

Quality Criteria   Turnips should be white, possibly with a purplish crown, depending on cultivar, and free of discolored, abraded tissue. The roots should be rounded, firm and heavy for their size, because size is not as good a criterion of quality as density. Light roots may be hollow or tough, the latter, because old roots contain a higher proportion of light-weight cellulose fibers.

Side roots should be trimmed for more attractive appearance and to reduce the incidence of decay (Haller 1947).

Recommended Conditions   Turnips, because of their propensity to shrivel, frequently are marketed waxed to reduce moisture loss. However, as with rutabagas, maintaining RH above 95% during storage followed by packaging in perforated bags might eliminate the need for waxing. Further, waxing must be done just before marketing and not before long-term storage (Franklin 1967).

Turnips can be prepeeled and then packaged in perforated film (Alexander and Francis 1964). Peeling, however, reduces their storage life at 1° C (34° F) from 2 to 4 months to 2 to 3 weeks.

CA storage of turnips may be worth testing, just in case concentrations of CO_2 that do no damage would retard the toughening.

Spraying turnips with maleic hydrazide before harvest virtually eliminates sprouting during normal storage.

ROOTS REQUIRING MODERATE TEMPERATURES

Sweetpotatoes *(Ipomoea batatas)*

This fleshy storage root belongs to the morning glory family. There are more than 400 species of Ipomoea, a majority of which are native to tropical America. Sweetpotatoes are an important crop in the central Atlantic and southeastern parts of the United States as well as in California. Limited production also occurs in most of the Midwest and Southwest. The sweetpotato is also grown as an important food crop in South America, Asia and Africa.

U. S. production of sweetpotatoes consists of two principal types. The so-called "dry-fleshed" type has a firm, dry, mealy texture after cooking and the flesh is usually pale to full yellow. The Porto Rico type, many cultivars of which are grown in the southern states, is soft and moist-fleshed after cooking and varies in flesh color from deep yellow to orange red. Cultivars of the Porto Rico type are commonly promoted and sold as "yams" by southern producers. However, this is a misnomer since the true yam belongs to the genus Dioscorea which is not even distantly related to the sweetpotato.

Quality Criteria   Sweetpotatoes should be firm, with smooth skin and slender, elongated to oval in shape. The roots should be free of growth cracks, insect and disease injury, and bruises or abrasions caused by rough handling. Unhealed cracks, cuts, bruises or abrasions are particularly objectionable because such areas are susceptible to invasion by decay-producing fungi, of which species of Rhizopus are the most common.

Skin color should be clean and of a color typical of the cultivar. The Jersey or "dry-flesh" roots usually have light yellowish-tan to medium-tan skin, while the Porto Rico or "moist-flesh" types vary from whitish-tan through brownish-red to dark purple.

While many sweetpotatoes are shipped to market immediately after harvest, in the so-called "green" stage, the finest quality roots are those that are cured before marketing. The curing process (see Chapter 11) heals damaged areas on the roots to reduce decay susceptibility, and increases dry matter and total sugar. The dry matter increase is closely related to loss of water during curing, but the increase in sugar is due primarily to increased hydrolysis of starch during the 4 to 8 day period at the elevated curing temperature (McCombs and Pope 1958).

Recommended Conditions   Sound, properly cured sweetpotatoes are adapted to storage for periods up to six months, the specific period depending upon type and cultivar. At harvest time the skin of the sweetpotato is thin and delicate. Such roots may lose noticeable amounts of skin during harvesting, hauling and handling. Primarily to heal such injuries, the roots should be cured at about 30° C (86° F) and 90% or higher RH for 4 to 8 days immediately after harvest (for details see Chapter 11). During the curing process enough ventilation should be provided to prevent accumulation of CO_2, depletion of O_2, or condensation of moisture. Under optimum curing conditions periderm begins to form in 2 days and is well developed in 5 to 6 days. At 13° C (55° F) or below, periderm does not form and above 35° C (95° F) very little develops. Such factors as excessive harvest damage, wet or cold soil before harvest, or chilling after harvest will reduce the effectiveness of curing and substantially reduce storage life of the roots.

After curing, sweetpotatoes should be held at 13° C to 15.5° (55° F to 60°) with 85 to 90% RH. Temperature control is critical for maintaining quality in stored sweetpotatoes. Chilling injury develops rapidly at temperatures of 10° C (50° F) or lower. The injury is expressed in many ways. The most common symptoms are internal breakdown, increased decay susceptibility, and impaired cooking quality. Chilling also causes loss of vitamin C, increases in chlorogenic acid, inability to synthesize carotene, accelerated respiratory activity, and a change in acidity of the tissue (for details on storage facilities and equipment, see Chapter 11).

Storage at temperatures above 15.5° C (60° F) increases the rate of growth of such decay-producing organisms as *Rhizopus* and *Fusarium*. Areas not completely healed during curing are particularly susceptible to decay, which can progress rapidly at temperatures above the optimum for storage. Exposures exceeding 3 hr to temperatures above 38° C (100° F) are harmful (Miller and Kimbrough 1948).

A virus disease of sweetpotatoes, known as internal cork, causes corky areas in the roots of susceptible cultivars. Some internal cork may be present at harvest, particularly during warm weather, but in storage the corky areas enlarge and develop if temperatures are 15.5° C (60° F) or above. The most susceptible cultivars are Porto Rico, Goldrush, Georgia Red, and Centennial. Many cultivars can carry the virus without development of internal cork symptoms.

While proper curing will reduce susceptibility of sweetpotatoes to chilling injury, the hazard of serious damage remains if the roots are exposed to temperatures below 10° C (50° F) during transport to market or at wholesale market. If they cannot be maintained at 13° to 15.5° C (55° to 60° F) during transport and at destination markets, a temperature above the optimum is preferable to a lower temperature.

Sweetpotatoes are usually sold at retail from bulk displays. Packaging in consumer-size bags or trays is developing slowly, primarily because of the susceptibility of the roots to decay when at the elevated RH often present in plastic film bags or overwrapped trays. However, treatment with a suspension of Botran 50 W (0.7 kg in 380 liters; 1½ lb in 100 gal. water) just before packaging is effective for decay control (Kushman 1967).

Information on the effects of CA storage on sweetpotatoes is limited. Mattus and Hassan (1968) reported that roots held in an atmosphere with 2 or 3% CO_2 and 7% O_2 suffered fewer losses during storage than comparable samples held in air. However, if CO_2 exceeded 10% or O_2 dropped below 7%, the roots developed unpleasant flavors. On the basis of this information, trials of CA storage of sweetpotatoes may be worthwhile, although gas concentrations must be carefully controlled and economic feasibility is by no means certain.

TUBERS

Jerusalem Artichoke, Girasole *(Helianthus tuberosus)*

Quality Criteria   The tubers should be buff to light tan, plump and firm.

Recommended Conditions   Jerusalem artichokes store best near freezing. Traub *et al.* (1929) found 0° to 2° C (32° to 35° F) to be satisfactory, but Lutz and Hardenburg (1968) recommend −0.5° to 0° C (31° to 32° F).

Relative humidity should be about 90%, or even somewhat higher, to avoid shrivelling.

Under the conditions of Traub *et al.* the tubers can be stored at least 5 months if a 20% loss due to shrivelling or decay is acceptable.

Potatoes *(Solanum tuberosum)*

This modified storage stem belongs to the nightshade family, of which there are many edible, widely cultivated vegetable members, as well as numerous native plants with poisonous fruits. Potatoes are a basic food crop in every temperate zone country and are grown in tropical areas where there is sufficient altitude to provide the required moderate temperatures.

Hundreds of cultivars are grown in various parts of the world, although each country generally has a few cultivars which are favored for commercial production because of regional adaptability, disease resistance, or consumer preference. Potatoes are produced in every state of the United States, in all provinces of Canada, and in the high plateau areas of Mexico, Central and South America. The countries of western Europe produce 4 to 5 times more potatoes than the United States, Canada and Mexico combined, and the Soviet Union produces somewhat more potatoes each year than the total production of 16 countries of western Europe.

Quality Criteria   The numerous cultivars of potatoes vary so much in shape, size, color and surface texture that only a general statement regarding these characters can be made. Shape varies from elongated to round, color from whitish yellow to dark brown, and surface from smooth to heavily russeted. Flesh color is usually white, although yellow-fleshed cultivars are grown and, in fact, are favored in certain western European countries.

Aside from shape and color of the tubers, market quality is determined largely by the absence of such external defects as sunburn, greening, growth cracks, air cracks, scab, rhizoctonia, insect damage,

Courtesy of Idaho Potato Commission

FIG. 9.1.   A GROUPING OF FINE QUALITY RUSSET BURBANK POTATOES

rot, or physical injury. Internal defects which affect quality include hollow heart, blackheart, internal browning, and freezing injury.

Since almost all potatoes are cooked in the home, or commercially processed before consumption, the quality of the cooked or processed product is of primary concern to consumers and manufacturers. Cooking and processing quality varies with cultivar, maturity, area of production, and postharvest treatment. However, certain cultivars are preferred for specific uses and this is generally a safe rule, e.g., Russet Burbank for baking, Irish Cobbler and Green Mountain for boiling, and Kennebec or Sebago for French fries and chips. However, when produced under optimum conditions, mature when harvested, and handled properly after harvest, most cultivars are suitable for any end use.

Potatoes for baking should produce a mealy, dry texture when cooked, whereas boiling potatoes should remain firm and intact after cooking and with no after-cooking darkening. Processors obtain better quality chips and French fries from tubers which are high in total solids and low in sugar. These qualities are eagerly sought by processors who now purchase about one-third of the total U.S. production.

Recommended Conditions Winter, spring, and early-summer crops of potatoes, as produced in the southern and western states, are often somewhat immature when harvested. When these are produced for table stock, they are usually marketed immediately, to take advantage of the early-crop prices. However, if such potatoes are free of serious bruising and are held at 15.5° to 21° C (60° to 70° F) for 4 or 5 days to heal harvest injuries, they can usually be stored successfully for several months at 4.5° C (40° F) and about 90% RH.

During recent years an increasing proportion of the early-crop potatoes has been used by chip manufacturers to supplement their supply of stored fall-crop tubers. Since these early-crop potatoes are particularly prone to sugar accumulation, even at intermediate holding temperatures, supplies held in storage require temperatures of 21° C (70° F) or above for maintenance of chipping quality. At such elevated temperatures decay may develop rapidly so extended storage is seldom advisable.

Late-crop potatoes, as produced in the northern United States, Canada and much of Europe are commonly stored for extended periods before marketing. Most of these are stored in nonrefrigerated (ventilated) commercial or farm warehouses (see Chapter 11 for storage facilities). A smaller part of the late crop is stored in refrigerated storages. If the tubers are held for sale as table stock, they should be cured at 7° to 15.5° C (45° to 60° F) for 10 to 14 days to permit healing of cuts and bruises through suberization and periderm growth. After curing, whether storage is under ventilation or refrigeration, the temperature should be lowered to 3.5° to 4.5° C (38° to 40° F) over a period of several days. Optimum conditions for prolonged storage of table stock potatoes are 3.5° to 4.5° C (38° to 40° F), about 90% RH, enough air movement to maintain uniform temperatures and prevent CO_2 accumulation, and as near complete darkness as possible. Under these conditions there is little or no sprout growth, shrinkage is low, decay is well controlled, and no greening develops during 5 to 7 months of storage.

Late-crop potatoes stored for manufacture into chips or French fries should be stored at 10° to 13° C (50° to 55° F) and 90% RH. At these temperatures, sugar does not accumulate to adversely affect the color of the processed product. Even fully mature fall-crop potatoes usually accumulate enough sugar when stored at 4.5° C (40° F) or below to make them unsuitable for immediate processing into chips, French fries, or granules. Often such tubers can be reconditioned by holding them at 21° C (70° F) until reducing sugars have been lowered and trial cooking tests indicate satisfactory processing quality. The length of the conditioning period depends upon the amount of reducing sugars present after cold storage, and since some lots never recondition satisfactorily after storage at 4.5° C (40° F), most processors now require higher temperature storage.

Storage below 3.5° C (38° F) is not desirable. All cultivars are susceptible to chilling injury in varying degrees, with many developing serious internal discoloration (mahogany browning) when stored 20 weeks or longer at 0° to 1° C (32° to 34° F). This disorder, together with freezing damage, is commonly found along the bin walls in poorly designed or operated ventilated storages.

Seed potatoes have the same storage requirements as table stock tubers. When seed stocks are removed from storage before the end of the tuber rest period, it is often desirable to warm them to 13° to 15.5° C (55° to 60° F) before shipping or during transit to stimulate rapid sprouting and emergence after planting. Seed stock from storage in northern areas is sometimes pre-cut before shipment for early planting in southern areas. It is particularly important to warm such seed before cutting and to keep it warm before and during shipment so that the cut surfaces will heal rapidly. Chilling of whole seed potatoes during storage and transit does not significantly affect emergence or subsequent yield (Hruschka et al. 1965).

Potatoes stored at moderate temperatures for manufacture usually develop sprouts 2 to 3 months after harvest. Such sprouting increases shrivel and adversely affects sales value. In recent years several growth regulating chemicals have been approved to control or reduce sprouting during storage. Maleic hydrazide is effective when sprayed on the plants in the field 2 to 4 weeks before harvest. CIPC (isopropyl N- (3-chlorophenyl) carbamate) can be applied as a vapor during storage or in a solution at removal from storage. Gamma irradiation, at 5 to 15 krad, is approved as a sprout inhibitor treatment in the United States and some other countries. Each of these treatments must be used at approved dosages and the chemical treatments must meet government tolerances for residues.

In some markets, particularly in eastern United States, potatoes are largely sold at retail in consumer packs of 2.2 or 4.5 kg (5 or 10 lb). These consumer units may be packed at origin, as is widely done in Maine and the Red River Valley of North Dakota and Minnesota, or they may be shipped in 45 kg (100 lb) bags in bulk to commercial or chain store repacking plants in destination markets.

Most of the consumer packages are bags, although a few fancy packs of sized baking potatoes are sold in overwrapped trays. Several types of bags made of Kraft paper, cotton, or paper mesh, or transparent plastic film are used for potato packaging. When paper or mesh bags are used the tubers will lose 3 to 4% weight in a week under retail display conditions. Plastic film bags of limited permeability will reduce moisture loss from the tubers, but unless properly ventilated, will maintain RH at a level high enough to stimulate tuber decay. Controlled tests have shown that films such as polyethylene should have 32 to 48 6.5 mm (¼ in.) ventilation holes for a bag containing 4.5 kg (10 lb) of potatoes. Greening is also a hazard when potatoes are held in clear plastic bags. Since exposure to light is directly responsible for greening, tubers in clear film bags should be protected from direct light as much as possible.

CA storage of potatoes destined for table use cannot be recommended. Oxygen concentrations of 5% or less inhibit periderm formation, and thus wound healing; 1% O_2 or less causes off-flavors and greatly increases decay, surface mold, and blackheart during 1 week at moderate temperatures 15° and 20° C (59° and 68° F). At low temperature (5° C; 41° F) these deleterious effects are less pronounced or absent (Lipton 1967).

High CO_2 (10% or more) increases the incidence of decay even at 4.5° C (40° F) and seems to aggravate the injurious effects of low O_2 at higher temperatures (Butchbaker et al. 1967; Nielsen 1968). Further, exposure of freshly harvested potatoes to at least 5% CO_2 for just 1 day increases their susceptibility to black spot, one of the most serious postharvest disorders of potatoes (Yamaguchi et al. 1964).

Accumulation of reducing sugars in potatoes stored at low temperatures and intended for processing can be retarded in 1% O_2. However, storage in air at moderate temperature seems more practical and safer.

Information in the literature on the effects of high CO_2 on sugar accumulation and subsequent chip color is contradictory, some reporting good, others poor results (Smith and Davis 1963, Butchbaker *et al.* 1967). On balance, potatoes destined for chipping are best held in air at moderate temperature.

CA conditions also can affect sprouting of potatoes. Oxygen at 10% or below increases sprouting in storage, but has no discernible effect on subsequent field performance of the seed potatoes (Burton 1958; Workman and Twomey 1967). The action of high CO_2 is more complex: concentrations between 1 and 5% stimulate sprouting, whereas higher concentrations are inhibitory. If CO_2 equals or exceeds 12% for 6 months, complete failure of seed potatoes results, whether storage is at 0° or 5° C (32° or 41° F). Most serious is the combination of high CO_2 (8% or more), low O_2 (5%), and low storage temperature 0° C (32° F) (Workman and Twomey 1969). This harmful combination likely is an example of chilling injury aggravated by CA conditions, as also observed on other crops.

Yams *(Diascorea spp.)*

The true yams are large tubers that are botanically distinct from the moist-type sweetpotato roots that in the United States are often called yams. Yams are a staple crop in tropical zones and are available to a limited extent in the continental United States and in Europe.

Quality Criteria   Yams should be firm and free of obvious defects. Since one type of rot converts the inside to a powdery mass without being visible externally, tubers that are light in weight for their size should be avoided.

Recommended Conditions   Yams are highly chilling sensitive. Researchers from various parts of the tropics have found that 16° ± 1° C (61° ± 2° F) is the lowest, safe and optimum storage temperature. If this temperature cannot be maintained, then 30° C (86° F) is preferable to intermediate temperatures (Coursey 1968; Martin 1976).

According to Adeniji (1970) RH should be at 100% or about 60%, because decay was lowest at 100%, intermediate at 60% and highest at other levels between 60 and 100%. However, others have successfully stored cured yams at 70 to 80% RH for at least 7 months (Gonzalez and Collazo de Rivera 1972; Been *et al.* 1977).

Curing is the critical factor in extending the storage life of yams at controlled or ambient temperatures. The yams are cured 7 to 8 days at 30° to 32° C (86° to 90° F) and 90 to 95% RH, although a 24 hr exposure to 40° C (104° F) appears to be equally effective. Such curing reduces weight loss and rotting. Its effect on sprouting is less decisive, but generally curing tends to reduce it, especially when storage temperature is optimal (Martin 1976; Been *et al*. 1977).

The normal storage life of yams without refrigeration is about 3 to 4 months. However, cultivar, physical damage, and depredations by rodents and insects result in wide variations in losses under otherwise similar conditions. In contrast, under refrigeration at about 16° C (60° F), visible deterioration can be absent even after 6 months.

MISCELLANEOUS UNDERGROUND STRUCTURES

Ginger *(Zingiber officinale)*

Quality Criteria   Fresh ginger of high quality is plump, firm, and buff to tan on the surface. Peeling of the skin, sprouting, shrivelling, softening and purplish discoloration of the surface are undesirable.

Recommended Conditions   Rhizomes of ginger must be protected from chilling injury and from sprouting during storage. Thus Akamine (1962), who developed most of the information presented here, recommends 13° C (55° F), where both dangers are avoided, even during 6 months' storage.

Ginger is susceptible to shrivelling and mold growth. Thus, RH must be at a level that minimizes both. Akamine suggests 65% RH as a compromise. After 6 months' storage, mold was absent and a weight loss of 16.5% did not result in "critical" shrivelling. Such shrinkage, although not critical in respect to quality, represents an economic loss to the producer, and therefore should be minimized. Various treatments tried by Akamine did not reduce mold growth at RH of 75% or higher. Hot water treatment as used on cantaloup seems worth trying, even though the exposures used by Akamine were ineffective.

RH higher than recommended now would not increase the undesirable purple discoloration of cut ends, because this defect develops only when free moisture is present during storage.

Packaging in vented polyethylene bags cannot be recommended unless a way is found to inhibit mold growth at fairly high RH.

The potential usefulness of CA storage cannot be evaluated on the basis of available data.

Ginger rhizomes can be stored 6 months at 13° C (55° F) and 65% RH, but only about 3 months at 35% RH if weight loss is to be limited to 16%. At room temperature, desiccation and sprouting limit storage to about 1 month, whether RH is 35 or 65%.

Waterchestnut *(Eleocharis dulcis)*

Quality Criteria   Waterchestnuts, which are used somewhat like potatoes, should be firm, crisp and sweet. Sweet corms can be separated from starchy ones by specific gravity solutions. Desirable corms should have a specific gravity of 1.05 to 1.08 (DeRigo and Winters 1964).

Recommended Conditions   Waterchestnuts can be stored at least 10 months at 0° C (32° F) and 8 months at 5° C (41° F) if they are submerged in aqueous sodium hypochlorite soon after harvest. The initial concentration of about 1000 ppm (0.1%) dwindles to essentially nothing within 3 to 5 days. However, concentration is not critical up to 5%. Under these storage conditions, flavor remained "acceptable," appearance "outstanding," and sugars decreased from an initial 12% to 10% during the 10 months. Anaerobiosis was not a problem with 23 kg (50 lb) lots stored in open containers that were about 60 cm (2 ft) deep. The standard method of storage, packing the waterchestnuts in moist sphagnum moss, limits storage to 1 to 2 months between 0° and 5° C if mold growth is to be essentially absent and to 2 to 4 months if a 50% mold incidence is acceptable (Kanes and Vines 1977; Vines 1976).

REFERENCES

Garlic

COMIN, D. 1955. New methods in onion handling and storage. Market Growers J. *84*, No. 4, 18–19, 32–33.
EL-OKSH, I. I., ABDEL-KADER, A. S., WALLY, Y. A., and EL-KHOLLY, A. F. 1971. Comparative effects of gamma irradiation and maleic hydrazide on storage of garlic. J. Am. Soc. Hort. Sci. *96*, 637–640.
FRANKLIN, D. F., WORKS, D. W., and WILLIAMS, L. G. 1966. Experiments in harvesting, curing and storing Yellow Sweet Spanish onions. Idaho Agr. Expt. Sta. Bull. *479*.
SIMS, W. L., and LITTLE, T. M. 1970. Growing garlic in California. Calif. Agr. Ext. Serv. *AXT-28*.

SMITH, H. P., ALSTATT, G. E., and BYROM, M. H. 1944. Harvesting and curing of garlic to prevent decay. Texas Agr. Expt. Sta. Bull. *651*.

Onions

ABDALLA, A. A., and MANN, L. K. 1963. Bulb development in the onion (*Allium cepa*, L.) and the effect of storage temperature on bulb rest. Hilgardia *35*, 85–112.

ADAMICKI, F., and KEPKA, A. K. 1974. Storage of onions in controlled atmospheres. Acta Hort. No. 38, Vol. *1*, 53–73.

APELAND, J. 1971. Effects of scale quality on physiological processes in onion. Acta Hort. No. 20, 72–79.

COMIN, D. 1955. New methods in onion handling and storage. Market Growers J. *84*, No. 4, 18–19, 32–33.

FRANKLIN, D. F., WORKS, D. W., and WILLIAMS, L. G. 1966. Experiments in harvesting, curing and storing Yellow Sweet Spanish onions. Idaho Agr. Expt. Sta. Bull. *479*.

GRÖSCHNER, P. 1962. Cold storage of late cabbage and onions. Deut. Gartenbau *9*, No. 2, 46–47. (German)

HANAOKA, T., and ITO, K. 1957. Studies on the keeping quality of onions. 1. Relation between the characters of bulbs and their sprouting during storage. J. Hort. Assoc. Japan *26*, 129–136. (Japanese, English summary)

HOYLE, B. J. 1947. Storage breakdown of onions as affected by stage of maturity and length of topping. Proc. Am. Soc. Hort. Sci. *50*, 353–360.

ISENBERG, F. M., and ANG, J. K. 1963. Northern-grown onions. Curing, storing, and inhibiting sprouting. Cornell Ext. Bull. *1116*.

JONES, H. A., and MANN, L. K. 1963. Onions and Their Allies. Interscience, New York.

KARMARKAR, D. V., and JOSHI, B. M. 1941. Investigations on the storage of onions. Indian J. Agr. Sci. *11*, 82–94.

KASMIRE, R. F. 1972. Low temperature settings best for shipping dry onions in mechanically refrigerated rail cars. Perishables Handling, Univ. Calif., Davis, No. *31*, 6.

KAUFMAN, J., HRUSCHKA, H. W., and HARDENBRUG, R. E. 1953. Onion pre-packaging tests. Pre-Pack-Age 7, No. 1, 9–13.

KESSLER, H. 1960. Fruits and vegetables. 2. Cold storage of various vegetables. *In* Handbuch der Kältetechnik, Vol. 10. H. Engerth (Editor). (German)

LIPTON, W. J., and HARRIS, C. M. 1965. Factors influencing the incidence of translucent scale of stored onion bulbs. Proc. Am. Soc. Hort. Sci. *87*, 341–354.

MAGRUDER, R. *et al.* 1941. Storage quality of the principal American varieties of onions. U.S. Dept. Agr. Circ. *618*.

PLATENIUS, H., JAMISON, F. S., and THOMPSON, H. C. 1934. Studies on cold storage of vegetables. Cornell Bull. *602*.

RASMUSSON, L. 1957. Metabolic disturbances of fruits and vegetables at low temperatures. Kältetechnik *9*, 293–294. (German)

WRIGHT, R. C., LAURITZEN, J. I., and WHITEMAN, T. M. 1935. Influence of storage temperature and humidity on keeping qualities of onions and onion sets. U.S. Dept. Agr. Tech. Bull. *475*.

YAMAGUCHI, M., PRATT, H. K., and MORRIS, L. L. 1957. Effect of storage temperatures on keeping quality and composition of onion bulbs and on subsequent darkening of dehydrated flakes. Proc. Am. Soc. Hort. Sci. *69*, 421–426.

Beets, Red

CHRIMES, J. R. 1967. Proper storage will extend the beet-root supply for processors. Com. Grower *3754*, 995–996.

Carrots

APELAND, J., and BAUGEROD, H. 1971. Factors affecting weight loss in carrots. Acta Hort. No. 20, 92–97.

APELAND, J., and HOFTUN, H. 1971. Physiological effects of oxygen on carrots in storage. Acta Hort. No. 20, 108–114.

APELAND, J., and HOFTUN, H. 1974. Effects of temperature-regimes on carrots during storage. Acta Hort. No. 38, Vol. *1*, 291–308.

BARGER, W. R., and RADSPINNER, W. A. 1956. Transit refrigeration studies with California pre-packaged carrots. U.S. Dept. Agr. *AMS-97*.

BAUMANN, H. 1974. Preservation of carrot quality under various storage conditions. Acta Hort. No. 38, Vol. *1*, 327–337.

CARLTON, B. C., PETERSON, C. E., and TOLBERT, N. E. 1961. Effects of ethylene and oxygen on production of a bitter compound by carrot roots. Plant Physiol. *36*, 550–552.

CHALUTZ, E., DEVAY, J. E., and MAXIE, E. C. 1969. Ethylene-induced isocoumarin formation in carrot root tissue. Plant Physiol. *44*, 235–241.

CHUBEY, B. B., and NYLUND, R. E. 1970. The effect of maturity and environment on phenolic compounds and oxidative browning in carrots. J. Am. Soc. Hort. Sci. *95*, 393–395.

HARDENBURG, R. E., LIEBERMAN, M., and SCHOMER, H. A. 1953. Prepackaging carrots in different types of consumer bags. Proc. Am. Soc. Hort. Sci. *61*, 404–412.

JOHNSON, H. B. 1956. Hydrocooling and shipping pre-packaged carrots from Texas. 10th Natl. Conf. Handling Perishable Agr. Commodities, Purdue Univ. Proc. 155–159.

KURKI, L. 1971. Moisture in vegetable storage. Acta Hort. No. 20, 146–151.

PHAN, C. T. 1974. Use of plastic films in the storage of carrots. Acta Hort No. 38, Vol. *1*, 345–350.

PLATENIUS, H. 1934. Physiological and chemical changes in carrots during growth and storage. Cornell Univ. Agr. Expt. Sta. Mem. *161*.

RYGG, G. L. 1949. Change in carotenoid content of harvested carrots. Proc. Am. Soc. Hort. Sci. *54*, 307–310.

THORNE, S. N. 1972. Studies of the behaviour of stored carrots with respect to their invasion by *Rhizopus stolonifer* Lind. J. Food Technol. 7, 139–151.

VAN DEN BERG, L., and LENTZ, C. P. 1966. High humidity storage of carrots and cabbage. Annex 1966-1, Intern. Inst. Refrig. 335–344.

VAN DEN BERG, L., and LENTZ, C. P. 1977. Effect of relative humidity of (sic) storage life of vegetables. Acta Hort. No. 62, 197–208.

WEICHMANN, J. 1971. Experiments concerning the CO_2—production and—storage of carrots in small store boxes. Acta Hort. No. 20, 98–107.

WEICHMANN, J. 1973. The influence of various partial pressures of oxygen on the gas exchange of carrots (*Daucus carota* L.). Gartenbauwissenschaft *38*, 253–262. (German)

WHITAKER, T. W. *et al*. 1970. Carrot production in the United States. U.S. Dept. Agr. Handbook *375*.

Celeriac

KURKI, L. 1971. Moisture in vegetable storage. Acta Hort. No. 20, 146–151.

WEICHMANN, J. 1977. CA storage of celeriac. Acta Hort. No. 62, 109–118.

WIERSMA, O. 1973. Storage of celeriac. Betrijfsoutwikkeling *4*, 79–80. (Dutch)

Horseradish

HOYLE, B. J. 1956. Storing horseradish stecklings. Calif. Agr. *10*, 6, 6, 14.

Parsnips

BOSWELL, V. R. 1923. Changes in quality and chemical composition of parsnips under various storage conditions. Maryland Agr. Expt. Sta. Bull. *258*.

Radishes

GUZMAN, V. L. 1970. Top regrowth inhibition of topped film-packaged radishes by growth retardants and mechanical means. Proc. Florida State Hort. Soc. *84*, 147–152.

LIPTON, W. J. 1972. Market quality of radishes stored in low-O_2 atmospheres. J. Am. Soc. Hort. Sci. *97*, 164–167.

LUTZ, J. M., KAUFMAN, J., and HRUSCHKA, H. W. 1954. Shelf-life of pre-packaged radishes in relation to: type of film, temperature, and amount of trimming. Pre-Pack-Age *8*, No. 4, 13–16.

Rutabagas

ALEXANDER, B., and FRANCIS, F. J. 1964. Packaging and storage of pre-peeled rutabagas. Proc. Am. Soc. Hort. Sci. *85*, 457–464.

Salsify

BEATTIE, W. R. 1946. Production of salsify, or vegetable-oyster. U.S. Dept. Agr. Leafl. *135*.
BECKX, A. 1960. Scorzonera and salsify. Courr. Hort. *22*, 148–150. (French)

Turnips

ALEXANDER, B., and FRANCIS, F. J. 1964. Packaging and storage of pre-peeled turnips. Proc. Am. Soc. Hort. Sci. *84*, 513–518.
FRANKLIN, E. W. 1967. The waxing of turnips for the retail market. Can. Dept. Agr. Publ. *1120*.
HALLER, M. H. 1947. Effect of root-trimming, washing, and waxing on the storage of turnips. Proc. Am. Soc. Hort. Sci. *50*, 325–329.

Sweetpotatoes

DEOBALD, H. J., HASLING, V. C., and CALALANO, E. A. 1971. Variability of increases in α-amylose and sugars during storage of Goldrush and Centennial sweetpotatoes. J. Food Sci. *36,* 413–415.
KUSHMAN, L. J. 1967. Preparing sweetpotatoes for market. U.S. Dept. Agr. Mktg. Bull. *38*.
KUSHMAN, L. J. 1969. Inhibition of sprouting in sweetpotatoes by treatment with CIPC. HortScience *4*, 61–63.
KUSHMAN, L. J., and DEONIER, M. T. 1957. Effects of storage temperature on Porto Rico, Allgold, and Goldrush sweetpotatoes. Proc. Am. Soc. Hort. Sci. *70*, 425–431.
KUSHMAN, L. J., and WRIGHT, F. S. 1965. Overhead ventilation of sweet-potato storage rooms. N. Carolina Agr. Expt. Sta. Tech. Bull. *166*.
KUSHMAN, L. J., and WRIGHT, F. S. 1968. A new system for storing sweet-potatoes. N. Carolina Agr. Expt. Sta. Tech. Bull. *187*.
KUSHMAN, L. J., and WRIGHT, F. S. 1969. Sweetpotato storage. U.S. Dept. Agr. Handbook *358*.
MATTUS, G. E., and HASSAN, F. M. 1968. Controlled atmosphere storage studies with sweetpotatoes. (Abstr.) HortScience *3*, 90.
McCOMBS, C. L., and POPE, D. T. 1958. The effect of length of cure and storage temperature upon certain quality factors of sweetpotatoes. Proc. Am. Soc. Hort. Sci. *72*, 426–434.
MILLER, C. A., and KIMBROUGH, W. D. 1948. Effect of length of exposure to sun on keeping of sweetpotatoes. Proc. Am. Soc. Hort. Sci. *52*, 322–324.

PATERSON, D. R., SPEIGHTS, D. E., and HORNE, C. W. 1967. Causes of handling injury and breakdown of sweetpotato roots. Texas Agr. Expt. Sta. Misc. Publ. *840*.

POOLE, W. D., and JONES, L. G. 1962. Controlled environment for sweet-potatoes in storage. Louisiana Agr. Expt. Sta. Circ. *72*.

SCOTT, L. E., and BOUWKAMP, J. C. 1975. Effect of chronological age on composition and firmness of raw and processed sweetpotatoes. HortScience *10*, 165–168.

TERESHKOVICH, G., and NEWSOM, D. W. 1964. The effect of storage and recuring on the development of periderm tissue in several sweetpotato varieties. Proc. Am. Soc. Hort. Sci. *85*, 434–440.

Potatoes—General

AGLE, W. M., and WOODBURY, G. W. 1968. Specific gravity-dry matter relationship and reducing sugar changes affected by potato variety, production area, and storage. Am. Potato J. *45*, 119–131.

BENNETT, A. H. 1961. An evaluation of methods for cooling potatoes in Long Island storages. U.S. Dept. Agr. Mktg. Res. Rept. *494*.

BENNETT, A. H., SAWYER, R. L., BOYD, L. L., and CETAS, R. C. 1960. Storage of fall-harvested potatoes in the Northeastern late summer crop area. U.S. Dept. Agr. Mktg. Res. Rept. *370*.

BUTCHBAKER, A. F., PROMERSBERGER, W. J., and NELSON, D. C. 1973. Weight loss of potatoes as affected by age, temperature, relative humidity and air velocity. Am. Potato J. *50*, 124–132.

CUNNINGHAM, H. H., ZAEHRINGER, M. V., and SPARKS, W. C. 1971. Storage temperatures for maintenance of internal quality in Idaho Russet Burbank potatoes. Am. Potato J. *48*, 320–328.

HEINZE, P. H., FINDLEN, H., and EWING, E. E. 1966. Storage and transportation of potatoes. Potato Handbook *11*, 5–6, 8–10, 12–14.

HRUSCHKA, H. W., AKELEY, R. V., and RALPH, E. H. 1961. Seed potato productivity after cooling, supercooling, or freezing. U.S. Dept. Agr. Mktg. Res. Rept. *507*.

HRUSCHKA, H. W., MARTH, P. C., and HEINZE, P. H. 1965. External sprout inhibition and internal sprouts in potatoes. Am. Potato J. *42*, 209–222.

HUNTER, J. H. 1961. Forced air ventilation systems for potato storage. Maine Agr. Expt. Sta. Misc. Rept. *98*.

LEACH, S. S., HUDSON, D. E., HUNTER, J. H., JOHNSTON, E. F., and WILSON, J. B. 1975. Precutting seed potatoes for higher quality seed and greater returns. U.S. Dept. Agr. Mktg. Res. Rept. *1035*.

SCHIPPERS, P. A. 1971. The relation between storage conditions and changes in weight and specific gravity of potatoes. Am. Potato J. *48*, 313, 319.

SINGH, R. P., HELDMAN, D. R., CARGILL, B. F., and BEDFORD, C. L. 1976. Weight loss and chip quality of potatoes during storage. Trans. Am. Soc. Agr. Eng. *18*, 1197–1200.

TOKO, H. V., and JOHNSTON, E. F. 1962. Effects of storage on post-harvest physiology of potatoes used for table stock and seed. Potato Handbook 7, 10–12, 14–17.

WILSON, J. B., and HUNTER, J. H. 1965. Airflow effect on distribution of isopropyl N-(3-chlorophenyl) carbamate applied to bulk bins of potatoes. Am. Potato J. *42*, 1–6.

Potatoes—Controlled Atmospheres

BURTON, W. G. 1958. The effect of the concentrations of carbon dioxide and oxygen in the storage atmosphere upon the sprouting of potatoes at 10° C. European Potato J. *1*, 47–57.

BURTON, W. G. 1974. The oxygen uptake, in air and in 5% O_2, and the CO_2 output of stored potato tubers. Potato Res. *17*, 113–137.

BUTCHBAKER, A. F., NELSON, D. C., and SHAW, R. 1967. Controlled atmosphere storage of potatoes. Trans. ASAE *10*, 534–538.

HARKETT, P. J. 1971. The effect of oxygen concentration on the sugar content of potato tubers stored at low temperatures. Potato Res. *14*, 305–311.

LIPTON, W. J. 1967. Some effects of low-oxygen atmospheres on potato tubers. Am. Potato J. *44*, 292–299.

NIELSEN, L. W. 1968. Accumulation of respiratory CO_2 around potato tubers in relation to bacterial soft rot. Am. Potato J. *45*, 174–181.

SMITH, O., and DAVIS, C. O. 1963. Controlled atmosphere storage of potatoes for chipping. Am. Potato J. *40*, 329. (Abstract)

WORKMAN, M. N., and TWOMEY, J. 1967. The influence of oxygen concentration during storage on seed potato respiratory metabolism and on field performance. Proc. Am. Soc. Hort. Sci. *90*, 268–274.

WORKMAN, M. N., and TWOMEY, J. 1969. The influence of storage atmosphere and temperature on the physiology and performance of "Russet Burbank" seed Potatoes. J. Am. Soc. Hort. Sci. *94*, 260–263.

YAMAGUCHI, M., FLOCKER, W. J., HOWARD, F. D., and TIMM, M. 1964. Changes in the CO_2 levels with moisture in fallow and cropped soils and susceptibility of potatoes to black spot. Proc. Am. Soc. Hort. Sci. *85*, 446–456.

Yams

ADENIJI, M. O. 1970. Influence of moisture and temperature on yam decay organisms. Phytopathology *60*, 1698–1699.

BEEN, B. O., PERKINS, C., and THOMPSON, A. K. 1977. Yam curing for storage. Acta Hort. No. 62, 311–316.

COURSEY, D. G. 1968. Low temperature injury in yams. J. Food Technol. *3*, 143–150.

GONZALEZ, M. A., and COLLAZO DE RIVERA, A. 1972. Storage of fresh yam (*Diascorea alata* L.) under controlled conditions. J. Agr. Univ. Puerto Rico *56*, 46–56.

MARTIN, F. W. 1976. Tropical yams and their potential. Part 3. *Diascorea alata*. U.S. Dept. Agr. Handbook *495*.

RIVERA, J. R., GONZALEZ, M. A., COLLAZO DE RIVERA, A., and CUEVAS-RIVERA, J. 1974. An improved method for storing yam (*Diascorea alata*). J. Agr. Univ. Puerto Rico *58*, 456–465.

Miscellaneous Underground Structures

AKAMINE, E. K. 1962. Storage of fresh ginger rhizomes. Hawaii Agr. Expt. Sta. Bull. *130*.

DeRIGO, H. T., and WINTERS, H. F. 1964. Effect of storage temperatures on physiological and chemical changes in Chinese waterchestnut corms. Proc. Am. Soc. Hort. Sci. *85*, 521–525.

KANES, C. A., and VINES, H. M. 1977. Storage conditions for Chinese waterchestnuts. *Eleocharis dulcis*. Acta Hort. No. 62, 151–160.

LUTZ, J. M., and HARDENBURG, R. E. 1968. The commercial storage of fruits, vegetables, and florist and nursery stocks. U.S. Dept. Agr. Handbook *66*.

TRAUB, H. P., THOR, C. J., WILLAMAN, J. J., and OLIVER, R. 1929. Storage of truck crops: the girasole, *Helianthus tuberosus*. Plant Physiol. *4*, 123–134.

VINES, H. M. 1976. Personal communication. Athens, Georgia.

10

Treatments Prior to Shipment or Storage

Vegetables and melons are subjected to various treatments prior to shipment to minimize deterioration during marketing. Precooling is by far the most important of these, with application of surface coating a distant second. Irradiation of produce with radioactive sources, now practiced only to a limited extent, is briefly discussed. Finally, fumigation is included because some commodities must be treated with toxic gases to avoid transportation of certain insect pests from area to area.

Treatment related to promotion or retardation of specific processes, such as ethylene for ripening, or hot water for disease control, are discussed in the relevant sections.

PRECOOLING

Definition

The term precooling, as used in the produce business, means the rapid removal of field heat from fresh vegetables or fruits during or after their preparation for market. Usually produce is precooled just before loading for transport to market, but for those products which are sometimes stored before shipment it may apply to rapid heat removal before storage.

Methods of Precooling

Several effective methods for rapid removal of heat from produce are in commercial use. The choice of method depends largely on the perishability and refrigeration requirement of the product, its adaptability to a specific method, and the availability of facilities.

Hydrocooling

Principles   Cooling with cold water is a rapid and effective method of precooling. Water is an excellent material for transferring heat from the surface of a substance to the cooling medium, which may be ice or refrigeration coils. Cooling is accomplished by flooding, spraying or immersion. The flood system showers water, through slots or holes in an overhead flood pan, over a product moving beneath on a moving conveyor. Water is recirculated past refrigeration coils or ice in a tank below the conveyor and back up to the flood pan by a high-volume pump. Spraying is done by pumping water through overhead or side nozzles and for immersion cooling the product is submerged in agitated chilled water. A properly designed flood system is more efficient than either the spray or

Courtesy of Western Grower and Shipper

FIG. 10.1.   HYDROCOOLING CANTALOUPS
Refrigerated water is pumped from a reservoir to a perforated flood pan to pour over the melons on a moving conveyor.

immersion system because it combines a great volume of water with rapid movement of the cooling medium over the product. When a film of cold water flows rapidly and uniformly over the surface of a warm substance, the temperature on the surface of the substance promptly becomes essentially equal to that of the water. Rate of internal cooling is limited by the rate of heat transfer from the interior tissues to the surface. This rate in turn is related to the volume of the product in relation to its surface area and the intrinsic thermal properties of the substance being cooled. The principal factors, other than size and nature of the product, which affect cooling rate are: (1) the difference in temperature between the water and the product; (2) the volume of water moving over the product; and (3) the exposure of the product to the water. Total cooling accomplished under optimum hydrocooling conditions is directly related to the period of exposure in the cooler.

Methods   -Hydrocooling may be accomplished by conveying loose products in a single layer or in multiple layers under a shower of water. More commonly the product is packed for shipment before it goes through the

Courtesy of Clarksville Machine Works

FIG. 10.2.   TUNNEL HYDROCOOLING OF PALLETIZED SWEET CORN

hydrocooler. If the container permits good contact between the water and product, this is a satisfactory method of cooling. However, obtaining the same heat removal will require more time for packed than for loose products, unless the loose products are piled very deeply on the conveyor.

Vegetables can also be hydrocooled in bulk bins by a combination of immersion and flood cooling. The bins pass through a tunnel on a slowly moving conveyor. The bottom part of this tunnel is a trough containing cold water through which the bottom part of the bin moves. Thus, the lower part of the product is submerged in cold water, whereas the upper part of the load is flooded from above with water pumped from the trough. Consequently, every item in the bin is rather thoroughly exposed to cold water.

From Grizzell and Bennett (1966)

FIG. 10.3.   ROOM HYDROCOOLING OF PALLETIZED SWEET CORN

Another hydrocooling innovation involves the cooling of palletized crates of packed vegetables in a room equipped with banks of nozzles through which cold water is sprayed over the stacks. This system is in limited use in Florida for celery and sweet corn. With a sufficient flow of cold water the system is as effective as cooling packed crates on a conveyor.

Efficiency in Hydrocooling Unfortunately the passage of vegetables through a flood or a bath of water, or the mark "hydrocooled" on the packed container, is no guarantee that sufficient cooling was accomplished to assure good market quality.

As indicated earlier, certain basic requirements must be met to assure that the cooling needs of a specific commodity have been met.

Studies with California cantaloups (Stewart and Lipton 1960) delineated several principles for obtaining satisfactory hydrocooling. Trials of many rates of water flow show that optimum flow rate is 0.49 m³/min/m² (12 gpm per sq ft) of cooler area. Cooling is not improved by increasing the flow rate above 0.49 m³/min (12 gpm).

Depth of loose cantaloups on the hydrocooler conveyor does not affect the cooling rate unless the pile is more than four fruits deep. Depth of piling is a factor, however, with products such as sweet corn which resist free water flow when piled.

Theoretically, the addition of a wetting agent to the hydrocooling water should improve contact betwen the cooling medium and the product by reducing the surface tension of the water. However, tests with 200 to 600 ppm of Triton W-30 in the water did not decrease half-cooling time of cantaloups, at two flow rates, as compared with plain water. It appears that contact between water and cantaloups is adequate without a wetting agent.

Hydraircooling Henry and Bennett (1973) studied a system for combining hydrocooling and air cooling. Pallet loads of celery or sweet corn are cooled by jets of chilled water applied above the pallet load, and forced air is circulated around and through the stack at the same time. Sweet corn in wirebound crates stacked 5 crates high was cooled from 32° C (90° F) to 1° C (34° F) in 1 hr with overhead flow from nozzles of 380 liters/min (100 gpm) in conjunction with air circulation of 78 m³/min (2760 cfm).

Warm-up after Hydrocooling After hydrocooling the precooled product should be promptly loaded into a refrigerated car or truck or placed in a refrigerated room. Hydrocooled melons, exposed to ambient summer temperatures, warm quite rapidly. A few hours of such exposure will result in loss of most of the refrigeration gained through hydrocooling.

Hydrocooled carrots, prepackaged in ventilated film bags and packed in multiwall paper bags, rewarm from below 4.5° C (40° F) to above 15.5° C (60° F) in about 30 min when exposed to 21° C (70° F) ambient. Part of the rewarming is due to heat transfer through the bags and part to heat of respiration.

Vacuum Cooling

Principles   Leafy vegetables are commonly cooled by reducing the atmospheric pressure in hermetically sealed chambers until the reduced vaporizing point of water, produced by low pressures in the cooling chambers, cools the product. The cooling is accomplished as follows: a pressure of 4.6 mm of mercury (normal air pressure is about 760 mm) reduces the boiling point of water from 100° C to 0° (212° F to 32°). The water thus rapidly boils off at 0° C (32° F). This evaporation requires energy (600 cal/g or about 1000 Btu per lb of water), which is taken from the lettuce. Eventually, evaporation, at a pressure of about 4.6 mm of mercury, will reduce the commodity to near 0° C (32° F) if continued for sufficient time at or below that pressure. The heat required to evaporate 1% of a quantity of water at room temperature is sufficient to reduce the temperature of the remaining water by 6.2° C (11° F). Controlled cooling studies with head lettuce (Barger 1961) show that the product cools an average of 5.6° C (10° F) for each 1% loss in weight. Since the loss consists almost entirely of water, the actual figure corresponds well with the calculated.

The outstanding advantages of vacuum cooling are the speed and uniformity of cooling of adapted commodities. Leafy vegetables, particularly lettuce, are difficult to cool with water or air, but they can be field-packed and then cooled quickly and uniformly by vacuum.

The rate of cooling and the final temperature attained by vacuum cooling are affected largely by the ratio of the surface area of the commodity to its mass, and the ease with which the product gives up water from its tissues. Commodities, such as tomatoes, with a small ratio of surface to mass and an epidermis which is resistant to water movement, are not adapted to vacuum cooling.

Lettuce is the vegetable most commonly vacuum cooled. Practically all commercial lettuce produced in the United States is now cooled this way. The numerous individual leaves of the lettuce head provide immense surface area in relation to mass and the product gives up water readily from all leaf surface. The fact that all tissues of the lettuce head

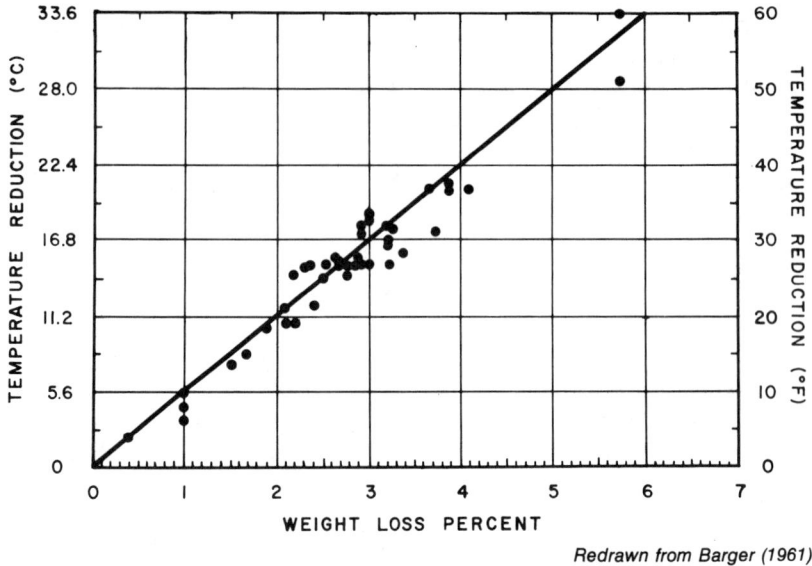

Redrawn from Barger (1961)

FIG. 10.4.   RELATION OF TEMPERATURE REDUCTION TO WEIGHT LOSS DURING
VACUUM COOLING OF LETTUCE
Minimum pressures 4.5 to 5.0 mm Hg; condenser 0° C (32° F); time in cooler 30 min.

lose water, instead of only the surface leaves, accounts for the lack of
wilting in surface leaves when loss of weight after cooling totals 4 or 5%.

Equipment   The vacuum cooling chamber must have walls which
will withstand external pressures of approximately 1034 g/cm² (14.7 lb
per sq in.). They must also be constructed so that they can be hermetically sealed. Most of the commercial chambers have a product capacity
of about ½ carload, or in the terms of lettuce, about 350 to 450 cartons.
Some of the portable chambers are ¼ carload capacity, and a few very
large fixed chambers exist which will hold a loaded rail car or highway
van.

Steam-jet System   There are two commercially used methods of producing the vacuum needed for cooling. The type used first produces the
necessary energy with a steam boiler. High pressure steam is expanded
through a bank of jets arranged in series, and is liquefied in barometric
condensers mounted below the jets. Cool water for condensing is produced in an induced draft cooling tower. Purging of the hermetically-
sealed chamber occurs as the pressure falls. When the boiling point of
water at low pressure is reached, vapor from the product to be cooled is
drawn through the ejector jets into the barometric condensers. A pres-

sure of 4.6 mm of mercury, corresponding to a 0° C (32° F) boiling point of water, can be obtained if the operation is continued for a sufficient time.

Vacuum-pump System   A more prevalent system for the newer equipment uses vacuum pumps, preferably of the rotary vane type. Vapor released from the product during cooling is condensed on direct expansion or secondary refrigerant coils, usually located in the vacuum line above the vacuum chamber, but sometimes in the chamber itself. Adequate condensing surface must be provided to handle the large amount of vapor removed from the produce in the few minutes of lowest pressure. Stored refrigeration in the form of cold brine or ice is advisable to take care of peak loads. A three-tube plant which at peak efficiency can cool three carloads of lettuce per hour will have a peak refrigeration load of at least 12,600 kcal (50,000 Btu) per min. This represents a refrigeration load of about 18 million kcal (250 tons).

Courtesy of Fudena Brothers Packing Co.

FIG. 10.5. VACUUM COOLING RETORTS BEING LOADED WITH CARTONS OF CAULIFLOWER

In those areas where lettuce production is limited to a few weeks each year, portable vacuum coolers are operating. These are moved from area to area as seasonal demand requires. Many of the mobile units use an ice condenser instead of the costly and heavy mechanically-refrigerated condenser.

Efficiency in Vacuum Cooling   Cooling head lettuce to internal temperatures below 4.5° C (40° F) requires 25 to 30 min in a commercial vacuum cooler. Delay in reaching the point at which pressure in the tank air drops below the vapor pressure in the leaves, largely a matter of pump capacity, increases cooling time. However, the speed of pressure reduction after this point has little effect on subsequent cooling. Lettuce in the cooling chamber cools more slowly than a wet-bulb thermometer in the tank, indicating that a wet-bulb reading is not a reliable guide to lettuce cooling. The solid center core in the base of the lettuce head cools more slowly than the leaves. After 12 min of vacuum cooling, the core temperature was about 3° C (5° F) warmer than the leaf temperature (Barger 1961), but after 30 min of vacuum, temperatures were uniform throughout the heads.

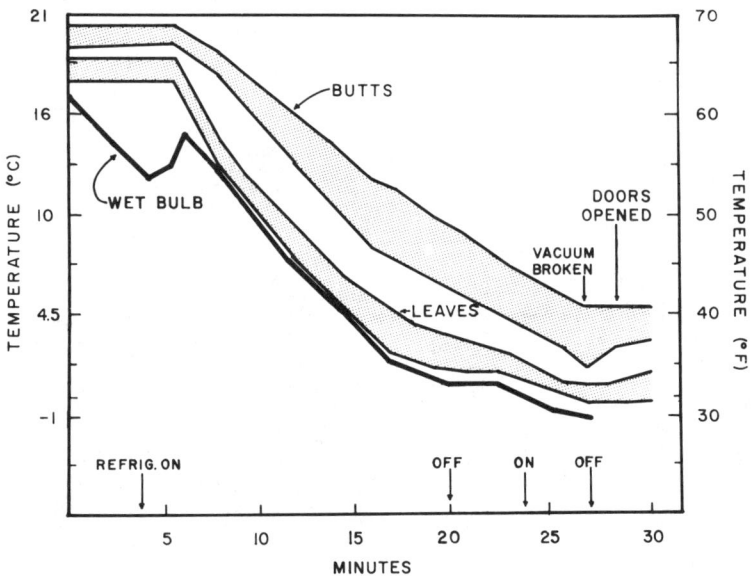

Redrawn from Barger (1962)

FIG. 10.6.   COMPARATIVE COOLING OF LEAF AND BUTT TISSUES DURING VACUUM COOLING OF LETTUCE

Packaging materials which interfere with free evaporation of moisture from the lettuce reduce cooling rate. At comparable cooling conditions naked-pack lettuce in cartons cools faster than lettuce heads individually packed in nonperforated polyethylene bags with folded tops. In the conventional naked pack, the heads in the corners of the cartons cool slightly more slowly than heads adjacent to top or bottom openings in the carton. Weight loss in the cooled lettuce is directly proportional to the temperature reduction. To illustrate the importance of ventilation to cooling, single heads of lettuce were heat-sealed in nonperforated polyethylene bags. This lettuce cooled only four degrees and lost only 0.4% moisture under conditions which cooled naked heads to below 4.5° C (40° F).

Adding free water to lettuce before cooling did not affect the final temperature after vacuum cooling, as compared with dry lettuce, but the wet lettuce cooled slightly faster than the dry and lost less moisture during cooling.

A series of tests in commercial vacuum cooling plants (Barger 1962A) show that a final vacuum chamber pressure of 3.8 mm of Hg is preferable to the commonly used 4.6 stopping point.

However, to avoid any hazard of freezing the product, pressure gauges more sensitive than those ordinarily used are required and close control of condenser temperatures in mechanical plants is necessary. A thermocouple should be used to measure surface temperatures at the inlet and outlet of the condenser. A minimum average coil temperature of −1.5° C (29° F) is safe and contributes to fast cooling.

Vegetables Adapted to Vacuum Cooling   As indicated earlier, adaptability to vacuum cooling is related to surface-volume ratio and the ease with which the product gives up moisture from its tissues. Generally speaking, the green and leafy vegetables can be cooled from field temperature to about 7° C (45° F) or below by the same treatment that cools lettuce to about 2° C (35° F). The list includes globe artichokes, asparagus, broccoli, Brussels sprouts, cabbage, celery, sweet corn and peas. Misting these vegetables with water before cooling improves cooling and reduces weight loss. However, evidence that such products can be cooled to 7° C (45° F) or lower does not mean that vacuum cooling is the indicated method of precooling. Cooling to 7° C (45° F) is not adequate for highly perishable products such as sweet corn or broccoli unless top ice is to be added to the load quickly. Also the amount of moisture lost may result in some damage, such as denting of kernels in sweet corn.

Vegetables which have a low surface-volume ratio, such as root crops,

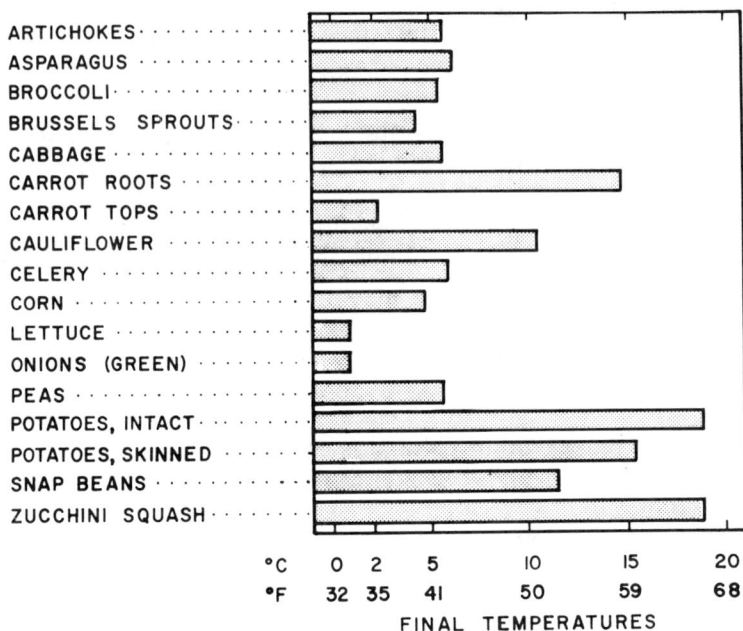

FIG. 10.7. SUITABILITY OF THE VACUUM PROCESS FOR COOLING VARIOUS VEGETABLES
Products initially at 20° to 22° C (68° to 72° F); minimum pressures 4.0 to 4.6 mm Hg; condenser −2° to 0° C (29° to 32° F); time in cooler, 25 or 30 min.

potatoes, tomatoes and cucumbers, can be cooled only a few degrees at pressures and time intervals which will cool lettuce −1° C (30° F).

Hydro Vac. A commercial cooler now in use in California (Anon. 1974) combines vacuum cooling and hydrocooling. Water pipes with nozzles are positioned below the ceiling of the vacuum chamber. After the vacuum is drawn, chilled water is showered over the load from above. After cooling, the product is drained for 30 min and is ready for loading. The retained water may be desirable for maintenance of high RH in transit. Rapid cooling was attained by this method, but no data are shown to compare Hydro Vac cooling rate with hydrocooling or vacuum cooling as separate procedures.

Vacuum versus Hydrocooling

As indicated previously, some vegetables can be cooled quickly and thoroughly by the vacuum treatment, while others which require rapid cooling are best adapted to hydrocooling. However, there are a few vegetables which can be cooled quite effectively by either method. The choice then depends upon the equipment available and comparative costs of the two methods.

A series of tests in California (Stewart and Barger 1960, 1962, 1963) compared the two rapid cooling methods for asparagus, Brussels sprouts, cauliflower, celery, garden peas and sweet corn.

Commodity Studies

Asparagus   Vacuum cooling asparagus (20 to 25 min at 3.5 to 5.0 mm of Hg) cooled the product from 20° C to 8° (68° F to 46°). Premoistening did not improve cooling by vacuum but did reduce weight loss from 1.4% to 0.5% based on weight before moistening.

Cooling to 6° C and 2° (43° F and 35°) was obtained during hydrocooling, depending upon the duration of cooling. Weight of the asparagus increased 2.1% during hydrocooling due principally to adhering moisture.

After holding for a simulated transit period of 8 days at 2.5° C (37° F), there were no differences in color, turgidity or feathering as a result of the precooling method used.

Brussels Sprouts   The amount of cooling is similar in sprouts whether subjected to good hydrocooling or vacuum cooling. Prewetting before vacuum cooling reduces weight loss and subsequent wilting. Temperature reduction from 15.5° C to 21° (60° F to 70°) to 2° C to 2.5° (36° F to 37°) is possible with either precooling method. Somewhat more wilting of outer leaves occurs during subsequent holding in vacuum-cooled than in hydrocooled sprouts, but this can be avoided by wetting the sprouts before the vacuum treatment or top-icing them soon after precooling.

Cauliflower   Premoistening trimmed cauliflower before vacuum cooling improved cooling from 9.5° C (49° F) for nonmoistened to 5.5° C (42° F) for premoistened from a starting temperature of 21° C (70° F). Nonmoistened heads lost 2.3% of their weight during cooling, whereas those moistened before cooling were heavier than initially because all of the added moisture was not evaporated.

Cauliflower was hydrocooled to both 9° C and 3.5° (48° F and 38°) with weight gains of 2.0 and 2.7%, respectively, due to adhering water.

After a simulated transit period of 8 days at 2.5° C (37° F), decay was negligible in all lots and no differences could be observed in conditions as a result of the cooling method used.

Celery   Cooling rates and subsequent market quality of freshly harvested celery and celery hearts show that both are satisfactorily precooled by either hydrocooling (flooding with 1.5° C (34° F) water for 18 to 20 min) or by vacuum cooling (30 min at a minimum of 4 mm of Hg and condenser at −1° to 0° C (30° to 32° F). There is no apparent advantage in wetting celery before vacuum cooling. The full size Green Pascal celery was cooled in standard wooden crates. The celery hearts were hydrocooled loose and then prepackaged, 2 to 5 hearts in each perforated polyethylene bag. The crated stalks and the prepackaged hearts were vacuum-cooled in their containers.

Hydrocooling, as used, resulted in somewhat lower celery temperatures than vacuum cooling, but after holding for simulated transit period with or without top ice, quality was good in all lots tested. Some celery is vacuum-cooled in California, but hydrocooling is the usual precooling method in most commercial celery areas.

Peas, Garden (English or Green)   Vacuum cooling has been used in a limited way for garden peas, but hydrocooling is the general and preferred method. Tests in California show that peas must be premoistened for successful vacuum cooling. Nonmoistened peas were cooled only 8.5° C (15° F) under the standard vacuum treatment used.

Hydrocooling in ice water maintained near 2° C (35° F) will reduce packed peas 11° to 14° C (20° to 25° F) in 20 to 30 min. The addition of crushed ice to peas after either precooling process is highly desirable for maintenance of freshness and turgidity during marketing.

Sweet Corn   Golden Cross Bantam corn, as it came from the field, cooled an average of 13° C (24° F) in the vacuum cooler and only 9° C (16° F) in a hydrocooling treatment similar to that used for peas. Wetting the corn before vacuum cooling does not increase cooling but is desirable for quality retention because the corn loses less of its original weight when prewetted. Studies in Florida (Showalter 1957) show essentially the same amount of cooling by vacuum as the California studies, and also indicate that kernel denting develops in corn that is not prewetted before vacuum cooling. The addition of crushed ice to corn after precooling is desirable, particularly if it is vacuum cooled, and is essential if more than five days elapse between harvest and consumption.

Contact Icing

Until the advent of vacuum cooling, many of the leafy vegetables were packed with crushed ice between layers of product and on top of the pack before lidding. The melting of this ice provides reasonably rapid reduction of product temperature to 0° C (32° F), the melting point of ice, and the water released keeps the products fresh and crisp. One kilogram (2.2 lb) of ice will cool 1.8 kg (4 lb) of product about 22° C (40° F). When package ice is combined with top or body ice, i.e., finely crushed ice distributed on or through the load during transportation to market, near optimum environments for these products results.

However, the method is limited to those products which will tolerate contact with ice and water. Furthermore, ice and the labor involved in its use are expensive. The size and weight of the package-iced containers, and the water dripping from them, make them unpopular in today's trend to smaller, more easily handled containers.

Package Icing

Because of their high respiratory rate, with resultant vital heat production, and the need to compact them in the shipping container to obtain practical shipping weights, spinach, kale and collards are the fresh vegetables that are commonly marketed with crushed ice in the shipping containers. Some sweet corn for local markets is now packed with crushed ice in wet-proof paper bags. This is done principally during the relatively brief sweet corn season in the Middle West.

Top-icing

When cantaloups were top-iced in ice-refrigerated rail cars, snow ice was blown over the top of the load immediately after loading was completed. This ice was then melted rapidly by operation of the built-in car fans or with portable auxiliary fans. The amount of ice added was based on a kcal (Btu) calculation of heat load. Ice-refrigerated cars are largely out of service in the 1970s, so top-ice precooling has been replaced by hydrocooling of the melons before loading. Some supplementary cooling is done in mechanically-refrigerated cars by limited use of top ice.

Top ice applied evenly over the load in a mechanically-refrigerated rail car or trailer interferes with the normal pattern of air circulation. If the air is blocked from passage through the load, heat removal from the product is slowed. A new method, "windrowed top-icing" (Anon. 1971; Kasmire 1972), provides air channels through the load by application of the crushed ice only over the lengthwise rows of melon crates. Spaces between rows of crates are left essentially ice-free for air movement. Recommended ice application as a supplement to mechanical precooling

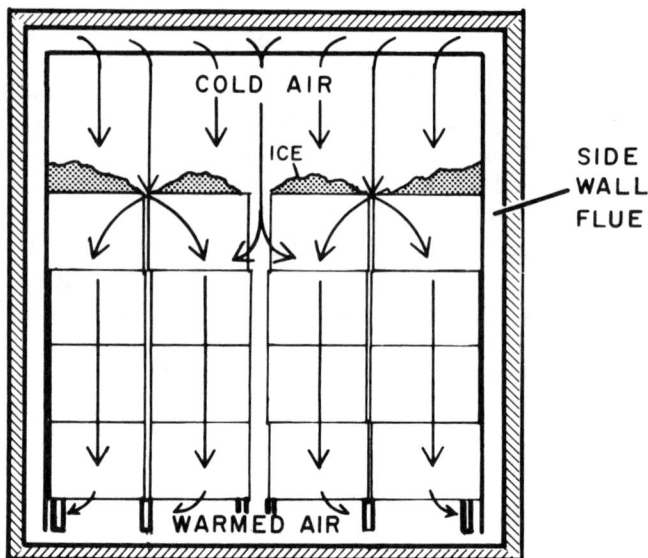

From Anon (1971)

FIG. 10.8.   WINDROWED TOP-ICING FOR MELONS AND
VEGETABLES TO HASTEN COOLING
Refrigerated air moves through the channels between lengthwise
rows of containers and returns under the floor racks.

varies from 613 kg (1350 lb) for melons loaded at 21° C (70° F) to 908 kg
(2000 lb) when initial melon temperature is 32° C (90° F).

About the only other vegetable commonly precooled with top ice is
cabbage. Since rapid precooling is not critical for most cabbage, it is
often loaded warm and top-iced immediately after loading. In mesh bags
or wirebound crates, loaded to provide some channels for ice between
rows, satisfactory cooling usually occurs during the first couple of days
in transit.

Air Precooling

The use of refrigerated air as a precooling medium is widely used for
precooling packed fruits, but the system is not widely used for vegetables. Precooling with air can be accomplished in a conventional cold
storage room, a special precooling room, a tunnel cooler, a forced-air
cooler (product containers baffled so that air must go through the containers instead of around them), or in refrigerated rail cars or vans.

Cooling with air requires a longer time than cooling with water or vacuum. Heat transfer from the product to air is less efficient than from product to water and the evaporative cooling obtained in the vacuum chamber is almost instantaneous once the pressure is at 4.6 mm of Hg or below. However, air precooling is an economical and satisfactory method for those commodities which do not require or tolerate rapid cooling to temperatures below 7° to 10° C (45° to 50° F).

Vegetables Adapted   When temperatures at harvest time are high, it may be desirable to remove excessive field heat even for those commodities which are not highly perishable, such as potatoes, or those subject to chilling injury, such as mature-green tomatoes. Most decay organisms grow most rapidly at temperatures near 27° C (80° F). Serious decay can develop in a few days if the products remain at elevated temperatures. In such cases, air cooling to 15.5° to 18.5° C (60° to 65° F) may be desirable before the product is shipped. Another hazard at high temperatures is excessive ripening of products such as mature-green tomatoes, cucumbers or peppers. Sometimes a few hours of air cooling can be justified just for removal of excess surface water, e.g., freshly washed potatoes.

Efficiency in Air Cooling   Rate of cooling with air, as with water, is governed largely by the temperature differential between the product and the cooling medium and the rate at which the coolant moves over the product. This is the reason that air volume and velocity are critical factors in heat removal and that adequate refrigeration capacity is essential to keep the cooling air well below the product temperature. Cooling is accomplished by sweeping heat from the surface of the product. The faster this is done, the greater the amount of heat that is transferred to the refrigerant, whether coils or ice.

Principles Applicable to All Methods

Regardless of the volume, velocity, or temperature of the cooling medium, the cooling rate will be unsatisfactory if the product to be cooled is not accessible to the coolant. This may involve access to the unit within a pile or a container or to the individual container in a stack. When sweet corn is hydrocooled loose, the depth of corn on the conveyor determines how much contact occurs between the water and the corn. When celery or sweet corn is hydrocooled in shipping containers, the type of container is an important factor in cooling rate. Generally, the more open the container the better the contact and the faster the cooling. Of course, the product in the container also affects accessibility.

Sweet corn packs very tightly, permitting little air or water flow through the container. On the other hand, packed cantaloups leave substantial open spaces in the container, permitting fairly free flow of the coolant. Forced-air cooling cannot be successful with products which pack so tightly that air cannot be forced through the container. Packaging materials, such as pads or liners, will also affect accessibility of the product to the coolant. While the effect is not as direct with vacuum cooling, it is essential that enough opening be provided in the container to permit rapid removal of water vapor.

When products are air cooled in a room or after loading for transport, the stacking must be arranged so that air can flow freely around each container. Spacing of about 5 to 7 cm (2 to 3 in.) between rows of containers is needed, particularly if air flow is downward through the load. Many loading tariffs require that nailed wood containers be loaded crosswise in the rail car to reduce breakage during transit. The ends of such boxes are normally of thicker wood than the sides. The crosswise load slows cooling somewhat because row spacing directs much of the air against the thick ends of the boxes, instead of the thinner side pieces which are exposed with a lengthwise load. When air movement is largely vertical, cooling of the crosswise load can be improved by using spacers between the crosswise stacks in the load so that some air can move down along the sides of the containers.

In refrigerated highway vans, the refrigerated air normally originates at the front of the van. To avoid short circuiting of the air, it should be, and usually is, ducted along the ceiling part or all of the way to the rear of the van. If space is left between the load and the rear doors, and longitudinal channels are provided through the load, excellent and uniform contact between the air and packed containers can be obtained. If the air can move only downward through the load, a diagonal pattern of air flow will usually result in delayed cooling in the rear of the van.

Mechanical refrigeration equipment, as now used for transit refrigeration in railroad refrigerator cars and most refrigerated highway vans, does not have sufficient refrigeration capacity for rapid precooling. Accordingly, those commodities which require rapid removal of field heat for good market quality should be thoroughly precooled, by one of the rapid cooling methods already described, before loading for shipment.

Half-cooling Time

Definition   The half-cooling time $(t_{1/2})$ is the interval, in any unit of time, during which the initial temperature difference between product and coolant (air, water, ice, etc.) is halved. For example, if cantaloups are at 33° C (92° F) and water is at 0° C (32° F), a difference of 33° C (60° F), the time required to cool the melons by 16.5° C (30° F), is t½.

Concept   The concept of half-cooling time lends itself admirably to calculations involving precooling, because $t_{1/2}$ theoretically is independent of initial temperature of the product and remains constant during cooling. Thus, once $t_{1/2}$ has been determined for a given crop and cooling condition, prediction of cooling accomplished in a certain interval is possible, regardless of the temperature of the product or coolant. Such prediction would not be possible if simple cooling rates were used, because they constantly change as the gradient between product and coolant changes. Thus, heat is removed very rapidly during first half-cooling period, while the difference between product and coolant is greatest. Heat removal then becomes progressively slower during subsequent half-cooling periods and eventually becomes nil as the temperature of the product and coolant converge. This condition approaches after the third period has elapsed (Fig. 10.9).

The theoretically valid conditions noted above do not always hold for rapid heat removal, such as occurs with hydrocooling, because heat conductivity and heat capacity of the product influence the rate of cooling. However, these difficulties were overcome by Couey who developed calcu-

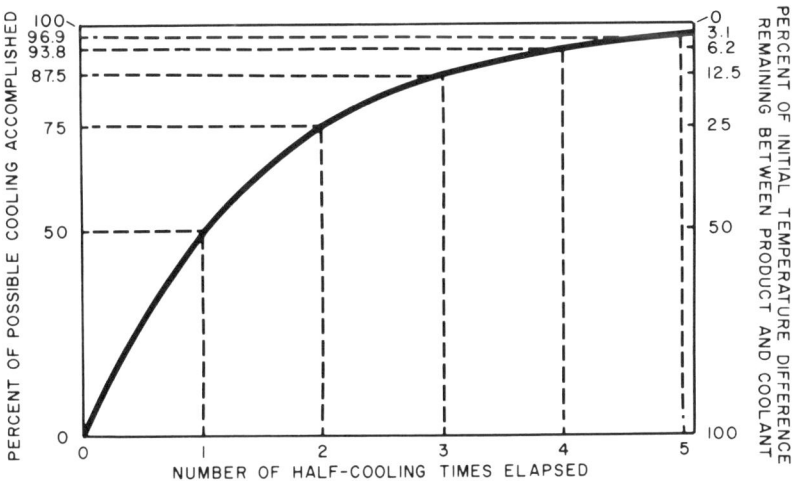

FIO. 10.9.   HEAT REMOVAL AO A FUNOTION OF HALF COOLING TIME IN TERMS OF COOLING ACCOMPLISHED (LEFT) AND IN TERMS OF TEMPERATURE DIFFERENCE REMAINING BETWEEN PRODUCT AND COOLANT (RIGHT)
Heat is removed most rapidly during the first half-cooling period when temperature differences are greatest.

lations that take into account these factors and yield reliable and highly practical data (Stewart and Couey 1963). These authors have determined $t_{1/2}$ for hydrocooling of many vegetables, while others have determined $t_{1/2}$ for different methods of cooling (Table 10.1).

Half-cooling times, however, cannot be applied to vacuum cooling. Here, heat removal does not depend on a coolant, such as air or water, but on evaporation of water from the tissue, a physical process that does not obey the same laws as heat removal from a surface.

The half-cooling times given in Table 10.1 primarily are for hydrocooling, where the extensive data of Stewart and Couey (1963) are available. For other methods of cooling, few half-cooling times have been published, and others could not be calculated, because coolant temperatures almost invariably were omitted from otherwise useful publications. Nevertheless, the array of half-cooling times demonstrates how much more rapidly cold water removes heat than even ice. This difference is particularly significant for peas, which need to be cooled as rapidly as possible after harvest. In contrast, cabbage, a bulky crop with many insulating layers of air between the leaves, cools very slowly under water. Cabbage, therefore, normally is precooled by vacuum or crushed ice rather than by water.

Application   The concept of half-cooling, developed primarily by Thévenot (1955) and Sainsbury (1955), was made a practical tool for anyone by Stewart and Couey (1963) through the development of nomographs that permit ready prediction of commodity temperature with a minimum of calculation.

Nomographs for crated asparagus, jumble-stacked cantaloups, and crated sweet corn are reproduced as Fig. 10.10, 10.11 and 10.12, respectively, and are used to explain the method in the following examples which were adapted from those of Stewart and Couey. (For metric example, see Fig. 10.13.)

Example 1   Determine how long crated asparagus at 90° F must remain in the hydrocooler if a final temperature of 40° F is desired and the water is maintained at 34° F.

Connect 90° F on the left and 34° on the right of the nomograph with a straight-edge. Answer: the sloped line intersects the horizontal line for 40° at slightly under 8 min.

Example 2   Cantaloups, jumble-stacked as on a conveyor belt (size 36) are 95° F as they enter the hydrocooler and the water is 35° F. Due to high volume, the melons can remain in the cooler only 10 min. How much cooling will have been accomplished?

ASPARAGUS , EXPOSED OR CRATED

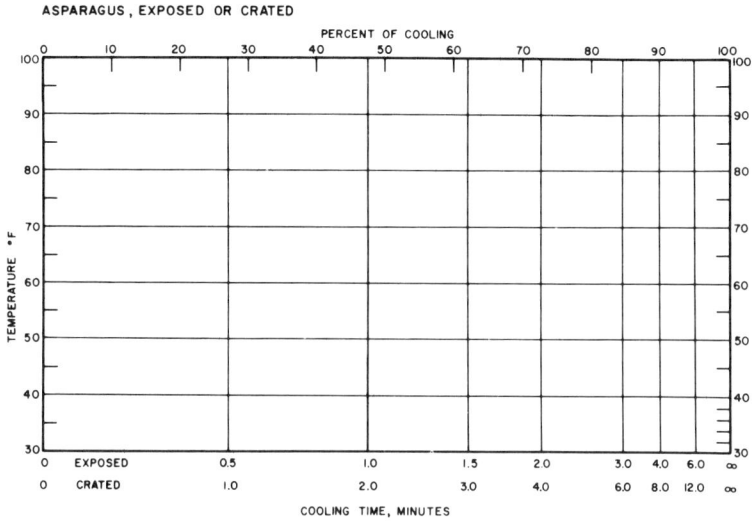

From Stewart and Couey (1963)

FIG. 10.10. NOMOGRAPH FOR HYDROCOOLING EXPOSED OR CRATED ASPARAGUS

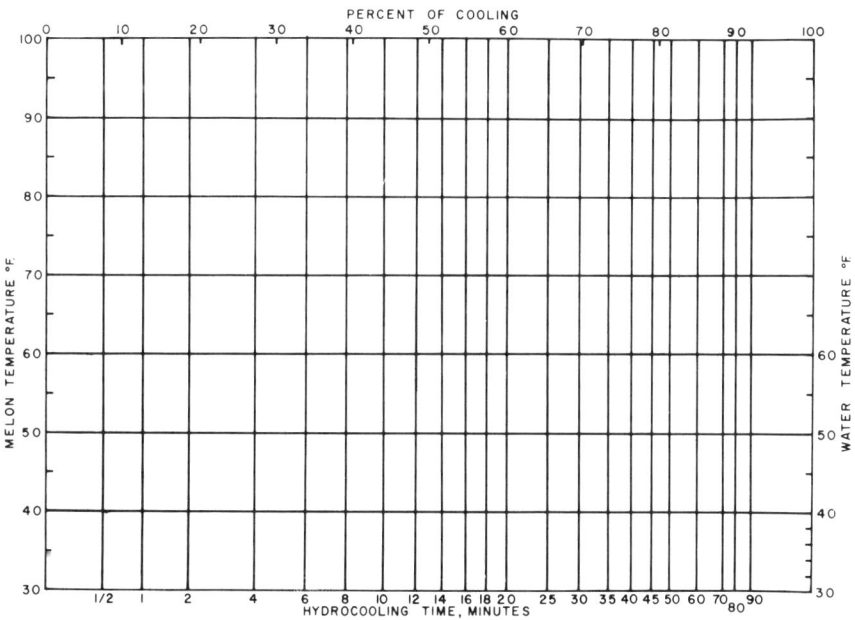

From Anon (1969)

FIG. 10.11. NOMOGRAPH FOR HYDROCOOLING JUMBLE-STACKED CANTALOUPS

TABLE 10.1. HALF-COOLING TIMES FOR SOME VEGETABLES AND MELONS[1]

Crop	Coolant[2]	Conditions During Cooling	Half-cooling Time[3]
Artichokes, globe	Water	Single buds, size 36	8 min
		In crate, uncovered	12 min
Asparagus	Water	Single spear	1.1 min
		In lidded pyramid crate	2.2 min
Broccoli	Water	Single head	2.1 min
		In crate with liner, ¾ filled with water, 4 layers deep	2.2 min
		In crate without liner, 4 layers deep	3.1 min
Brussels sprouts	Water	Single sprout	4.4 min
		In carton, 23 cm (9 in.) deep, filled with water	4.8 min
Cabbage	Water	Single head	1.1 hr
		In carton, 2 layers, lid open, filled with water	1.3 hr
Cantaloups	Water	Single fruit, size 36 or 27	13 min
	Air, ice	In crate, bunker ice, top ice, portable fans	3 hr
	Air	Tunnel cooler, air flow unknown, in crate	1.3 hr
Carrot	Water	Single root, 3.8 cm (1½ in.) diameter	3.2 min
		In 23 kg (50 lb) mesh bag, lying flat	4.4 min
Cauliflower	Water, forced	Single head, trimmed	7.2 min
	Air, forced	In single layer cartons, heads film wrapped	90 min
Celery	Water	Single stalk	5.8 min
	Air, forced	In sturdy crate, lidded, on edge, paper liner	9.1 min
	Air, forced	In wirebound crates, air movement side to side	35 min
		In ⅔ size cartons	60 min
Pea, garden	Water	Single pod	1.9 min
		In bushel basket, lid off	2.8 min

Commodity	Coolant	Description	Time
	Air, ice	In bushel baskets; bunker ice, top ice, car fans during precooling	2–3 hr
	Air, ice	As above, in transit, no precooling, car fans on when train moving	8–18 hr[4]
Potato	Water	Single tuber or stacked 23 cm (9 in.) deep	11 min
	Air	630 45 kg (100 lb) bags, mechanically refrigerated rail car	1 day
	Air	360 45 kg (100 lb) bags, ice car, ½ stage; protective floor pads	2–3 days
Radish, bunched	Water	Single bunch	1.1 min
	Water	In crate, 23 cm (9 in.) deep	1.9 min
	Water	In carton, 23 cm (9 in.) deep, filled with water	1.4 min
topped	Water	Stack 23 cm (9 in.) deep	2.2 min
Sweet corn	Water	Single ear, in husk	20 min
	Water	In wire-bound crates, 5 ears deep	28 min
Tomatoes	Water	Single fruit	10 min
	Water	Stack 5 fruits 25 cm (10 in.) deep	11 min
	Air	Forced air, pressure difference 0.25 cm (0.1 in.) water, carton	47 min

[1] Data were taken or calculated from various publications cited at end of chapter.
[2] In all cases where water is the coolant; the vegetables were flooded from above in a hydrocooler.
[3] Where the commodity is stacked several layers deep, the average for all layers is given.
[4] Wide range likely due to variations in placement of ice and movement of cars during first day in transit.

CORN , SWEET , CRATED

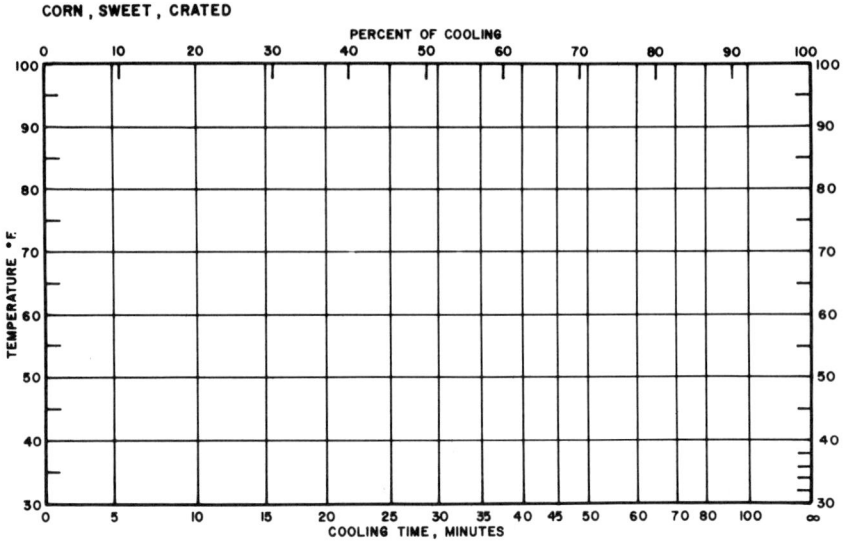

FIG. 10.12.   NOMOGRAPH FOR HYDROCOOLING CRATED SWEET CORN

Connect 95° F and 35° with a straight-edge. Answer: the line intersects the 10 min vertical line at about 68° F. Obviously, considerably more precooling will be required in the rail car or truck trailer if the melons are to carry satisfactorily. Incidentally, after 10 min, less than

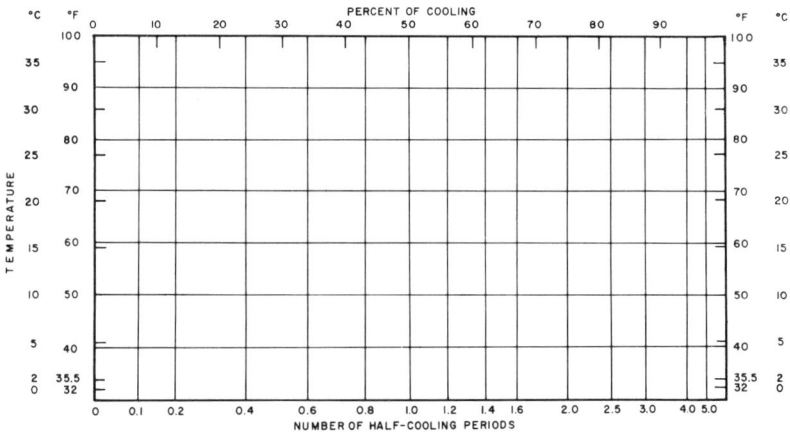

From Stewart and Couey (1963)

FIG. 10.13.   UNIVERSAL NOMOGRAPH FOR COOLING OR WARMING

50% (top horizontal line) of cooling will have been accomplished, since $t_{1/2}$ is 13 min.

Example 3   Sweet corn commonly is 85° F when harvested in Florida and is packed in wirebound crates before being cooled. Can such corn be adequately cooled in 20 min when the water is held at 32° F?

Connecting 85° F and 32° with a straight-edge, we find that the corn will be 65° F in 20 min, representative of an entirely unsatisfactory job of precooling. Hydrocooling should be followed by vacuum cooling and top-icing.

How long would corn, as described above, have to be cooled to reach 40° F? Answer: the line drawn previously intersects 40° F at 70 min.

Stewart and Couey also provided a universal nomograph that is applicable to any commodity or method of cooling (Fig. 10.13).

Example 4   Assume that potatoes packed in 100 lb bags and shipped in a rail car have a $t_{1/2}$ of 1½ days and that the air removing heat from the potatoes averages 5° C (41° F). How long would it take to cool the potatoes from 25° to 10° C (77° to 50° F)?

Connect 25° C and 5° C on the general nomograph with a straight-edge. The horizontal 10° C line is intersected at 2 half-cooling periods; now multiply the number of periods required (2) by $t_{1/2}$ of potatoes (1½ days). Answer: 3 days.

Example 5   Assume tomatoes packed in cartons are at 32° C (90° F) and cool to 15° C (59° F) by the end of the third day in transit when the air is 10° C (50° F). What is $t_{1/2}$ for tomatoes under these conditions?

Connect 32° C and 10° C with a straight-edge. The 15° C line is intersected at 2 half-cooling periods. Thus, 3 days is equivalent to 2 half-cooling periods and $t_{1/2}$ is 1½ days.

Note that $t_{1/2}$ can be determined only on the general nomograph; construction of the others required prior determination of $t_{1/2}$ for the specific commodity.

The general nomograph also can be used to solve problems such as those given for hydrocooling as long as $t_{1/2}$ is known. The same procedure as given in Example 4 applies.

Half-warming Time   The concept of half-cooling can be applied with equal facility to warming, except that the line drawn between product and coolant ascends rather than descends from left to right. Practical applications involve calculation of precooling that is wasted when cooled products wait in warm surroundings to be loaded into rail cars or truck trailers, or of heat that is gained during hot-water treatment for disease control.

Product Quality in Relation to Precooling

Rapid cooling of produce is occasionally accused of causing damage from "shock." There is no experimental evidence to substantiate this claim. On the contrary, such highly perishable products as head lettuce, asparagus, spinach, and sweet corn have all been shown to have better market quality and longer shelf-life when cooled just as rapidly as the most efficient vacuum cooling or hydrocooling system permits.

Cantaloups do not absorb water during hydrocooling, despite the prevalent notion that the surface netting acts as a sponge. Some leafy vegetables do gain some weight from absorbed or adhering water, but unless incipient decays are present at harvest the added moisture is beneficial rather than harmful.

Air cooling and vacuum cooling both remove some moisture from the product. However, vacuum cooling removes water uniformly from all tissues with the result that 3 to 4% water loss does not result in visible wilting. Air cooling removes the least water when refrigeration capacity and air velocity are high enough to remove heat rapidly. The longer the cooling period, the greater the water loss, because the vapor pressure differential between the product and the air is prolonged with extended cooling.

Decay can be increased by hydrocooling if the water becomes highly contaminated with decay organisms. Sound sanitation measures, such as prewashing, removal of any decayed products, daily cleanup, and disinfection of the hydrocooler, and sometimes the addition of a low concentration of chlorine to the hydrocooling water, will substantially reduce danger of contamination.

Products which are subject to chilling injury at temperatures below 7° or 10° C (45° or 50° F) seldom require precooling. However, there is no evidence that, when field heat is high, rapid cooling causes any injury, provided cooling does not extend below the chilling temperature. Such cooling is often desirable to slow ripening or senescence and reduce the growth of decay organisms.

FUMIGATION

Some vegetables imported from foreign countries or shipped across state lines must be fumigated to prevent the spread of various insects from infested to noninfested areas. Thus, fumigation permits commerce in potentially infested crops that otherwise would be barred from the United States or from some states. Since fumigants are poisonous to all living systems, the host as well as the insect can be injured. A successful treatment must kill the insect without damaging the crop. The treatments officially required for certain crops tread this narrow row. Strict adherence to prescribed procedures is essential for the treatment to be effective and nondamaging to the crop. Since the regulations dealing with fumigation are very detailed and have the force of law, we refer potential users to the specific "Quarantines" published by the Plant Quarantine Division of the U.S. Department of Agriculture, Beltsville, Md. We will confine ourselves to noting circumstances under which fumigation may be required, crops commonly fumigated, and types of treatments generally used.

Requirement for Fumigation

Fumigation may be required of all shipments of a certain crop from a given area, such as garlic from Portugal, unless the crop has been certified at origin to be free of the insect in question. For other crops, certification cannot be substituted for fumigation, because insect eggs may be present on the vegetable without being detectable. Tomatoes shipped from Hawaii to mainland United States fall into this category. Fumigation may be required throughout the year, regardless of destination within the United States, for the crops noted, or only seasonally and for some destinations. For example, okra from Mexico is subject to certain regulations when shipped to cotton-producing states east of the Colorado River, others when shipped to California, and these rules are further subdivided by season. This complex of rules is needed to prevent the importation of the pink boll worm of cotton, which also lives on okra, a relative of cotton. Domestically, potatoes fall into the same category—loads have to be fumigated if they move between certain states, but not between others. Here the determining factor is the presence of the potato tuber worm at origin.

Fumigation and Substitute Treatments

Chemicals used for various crops differ and old ones are phased out while new ones are introduced. Consequently, specific information must be obtained from the relevant authorities.

Generally, the vegetables are treated in specially constructed fumigation chambers, either at atmospheric pressure (e.g., tomatoes and okra) or under vacuum (garlic). In the former, surface treatment will reach the insects, whereas in the latter the gas must penetrate several layers of dry scales, which can be accomplished best under vacuum.

For certain crops a water vapor—heat treatment may be substituted for fumigation. With this procedure, the vegetables are exposed to saturated vapor at 43° C (110° F) that is mixed with a fine mist of water and air. Once the product reaches 43° C at its center, it must be held there 8¾ hr to assure death of the eggs and larvae of various fruit flies. The vegetables cannot be waxed prior to treatment because trapped flies or larvae might escape death. Once treatment is finished, the vegetables are cooled as rapidly as possible. This rather harsh treatment can injure some crops, such as eggplants. This fruit can be preconditioned for 6 to 8 hr at 43° C and 40% RH before the vapor-heat treatment, to minimize injury. The treatment turns the seeds of eggplants black, which detracts from internal appearance.

The vapor-heat treatment has the advantage of avoiding the use of highly toxic chemicals. However, the prolonged exposure to high temperature certainly tends to reduce the subsequent life of the crop, since the rate of deterioration approximately doubles for each 10° C (18° F) increase in temperature. Thus, 16 hr (preconditioning plus treatment) at 43° C (110° F) reduces shelf-life as much as 2½ to 3 days at 13° C (55° F), a desirable temperature for eggplants.

Quality also can be impaired by fumigation (Akamine and Shoji 1960). Tomatoes with either radial or concentric cracks or those with poorly healed stem scars will readily decay if fumigated with methyl bromide, a currently common fumigant. Thus only the highest quality fruits can be successfully fumigated. Mature-green tomatoes also should not be treated with MB because it substantially delays coloration and may lead to blotchy ripening. Cultivars also differ in their tolerance of fumigants, at least in tomatoes, and possibly in other crops.

Regardless of method of treatment, reinfestation of the product during subsequent handling must be prevented. To this end not only the treatment, but further handling, is under the supervision of Plant Quarantine inspectors.

An excellent source for detailed information on many aspects of fumigation is a manual prepared by Monro for the United Nations (1971).

IRRADIATION

Evaluation of Irradiation

Irradiation of fresh produce with gamma rays to extend storage life was thought by some to be the ultimate weapon in the fight against postharvest losses when the necessary equipment for application became available in the late 1950s, only to be unused and largely ignored by the late 1960s. The unrealistically high hopes for the process were often based on over-optimistic conclusions drawn from early and sketchy research. The chief fallacy was lack of recognition that fresh produce is alive, and not like a slab of bacon or a bandage. In living matter, such as fresh vegetables, any process that severely interferes with normal metabolism inevitably will cause damage to the organism, and radiation doses that are powerful enough to appreciably inhibit the growth of decay organisms are so high (200 to 400 krad) (Beraha *et al.* 1960) that they usually injure or kill the host before they effectively inhibit the pathogen.

Responses of Vegetables

The only vegetable, of many tested, to successfully undergo irradiation was mushrooms—a nonpathogenic fungus (Bramlage and Lipton 1965). Even with mushrooms the potential benefit is limited to mushrooms held at about 10° C (50° F), because changes are relatively slow near 0° C (32° F) and excessively rapid at higher temperatures regardless of irradiation (Skou *et al.* 1974). A dose (100 krad) that helped maintain their freshness severely injured other vegetables. In other vegetables, irradiation caused discoloration, excessive softening, uneven ripening, accentuation of chilling injury, or increased decay, depending upon the vegetables and the dose.

Even if irradiation would reduce decay without injuring the host, physiological aging of the vegetable would continue and thus limit the extension of its storage life.

While, so far, irradiation cannot be used to retard spoilage in most vegetables, it has been used successfully in retarding the sprouting of potatoes, sweetpotatoes and onions. Irradiation is useful as a growth inhibitor, because the low doses required (about 10 krad) prevent cell division in the growing points, without adversely affecting the rest of the structure (Dennison and Ahmed 1975). In onions, however, the growing point may darken unless storage is at 0° C (32° F) and subsequent marketing is prompt (Temkin-Gorodeiski *et al.* 1972).

Irradiation also is potentially useful for disinfestation of some tree fruits that harbor certain insects, such as fruit flies. (International Atomic Energy Agency 1971; Dennison and Ahmed 1975). However, the applicability of the procedure for quarantine treatment of vegetables is not at all certain.

Since Bramlage and Lipton (1965) reported their largely negative results, others (Maxie *et al.* 1971; Staden 1973) also have come to the conclusion that irradiation holds little promise for extending the useful life of vegetables or fruits, except possibly for sprout inhibition and insect control under special circumstances.

REFERENCES

Precooling

ANON. 1969. Faster cooling of cantaloups. Western Grower and Shipper 40, No. 5, 18, 41.
ANON. 1971. New top-icing method for melons solves problems. Western Grower and Shipper 42, No. 8, 19, 27.
ANON. 1974. Hydro Vac — another advance in cooling vegetables. Western Grower and Shipper 45, No. 4, 15.
BAIRD, C. D., GAFFNEY, J. J., and KINARD, D. T. 1975. Research facility for forced-air precooling of fruits and vegetables. Trans. Am. Soc. Agr. Eng. 18, 376–379.
BARGER, W. R. 1961. Factors affecting temperature reduction and weight loss in vacuum-cooled lettuce. U.S. Dept. Agr. Mktg. Res. Rept. 469.
BARGER, W. R. 1962A. Vacuum-cooling lettuce in commercial plants. U.S. Dept. Agr. AMS-469.
BARGER, W. R. 1962B. Vacuum-cooling of lettuce. Produce Mktg. 5, No. 5, 45.
BENNETT, A. H., HENRY, F. E., ADAMS, J. H., and TEELE, J. C. 1976. Precooling pallet loads of sweet corn packed in wirebound crates. U.S. Dept. Agr. ARS-S-99.
DEWEY, D. H. 1950. Air blast and vacuum cooling of lettuce—temperature and moisture changes. Proc. Am. Soc. Hort. Sci. 56, 320–326.
GIBBON, J. M. 1972. Some observations of temperature and cooling rates of vegetables in commercial cold stores. J. Agr. Eng. Res. 17, 332–337.
GRIZZELL, W. G., and BENNETT, A. H. 1966. Hydrocooling stacked crates of celery and sweet corn. U.S. Dept. Agr. ARS 52-12.
GRIZZELL, W. G., and HENRY, F. E. 1971. A central packing-precooling system for celery. U.S. Dept. Agr. Mktg. Res. Rept. 869.
HENRY, F. E., and BENNETT, A. H. 1973. "Hydraircooling" vegetable products in unit loads. Trans. Am. Soc. Agr. Eng. 16, 731–733, 739.
ISENBERG, F. M., and HARTMAN, J. 1958. Vacuum cooling vegetables. Cornell Ext. Bull. 1012.
KASMIRE, R. F. 1971. Forced-air cooling of cauliflower and celery. Fruits and Veg. Perishables Handling. Univ. Calif., Davis, No. 27.
KASMIRE, R. F. 1972. Windrowed top-icing proves best for cantaloupes. Western Grower and Shipper 43, No. 6, 32.
KASMIRE, R. F. 1975. Solid loads pose cooling problem. Western Grower and Shipper 46, No. 6, 16–17.
KASMIRE, R. F. 1976. A buyer's guide and responsibility in cooling. In United

Fresh Fruit and Vegetable Association Yearbook. pp. 245, 247–248, 251–252, 255–256, 258. United Fresh Fruit and Vegetable Assoc., Washington, D.C.

LINDSAY, R. T., NEALE, M. A., and MESSER, H. J. M. 1975. Cooling produce in large pallet-based boxes. J. Agr. Eng. Res. *20*, 235–243.

LIPTON, W. J., and BARGER, W. R. 1965. Market quality of head lettuce in relation to delays between harvest and precooling and temperature after cooling. U.S. Dept. Agr. *ARS 51–5*.

LIPTON, W. J., and STEWART, J. K. 1961. Effect of hydrocooling on the market quality of cantaloups. Proc. Am. Soc. Hort. Sci. *78*, 324–331.

LIPTON, W. J., and STEWART, J. K. 1963. Effects of precooling on the market quality of globe artichokes. U.S. Dept. Agr. Mktg. Res. Rept. *633*.

MITCHELL, F. G., GUILLOU, R., and PARSONS, R. A. 1972. Commercial cooling of fruits and vegetables. Calif. Agr. Expt. Sta. Manual *43*.

PENTZER, W. T., WIANT, J. S., and MacGILLIVRAY, J. H. 1940. Market quality and conditions of California cantaloups as influenced by maturity, handling, and precooling. U.S. Dept. Agr. Tech. Bull. *730*.

RAPPAPORT, L., and WATADA, A. E. 1958. Effect of temperature on artichoke quality. Proc. Conf. Transport. Perishables. Univ. Calif., Davis. 142–146.

RYALL, A. L. 1962A. The vacuum way. Am. Veg. Grower *10*, No. 5, 9, 35–36.

RYALL, A. L. 1962B. Cooling with water. Am. Veg. Grower *10*, No. 7, 7, 14.

SHOWALTER, R. K. 1957. Effect of wetting and top icing upon the quality of vacuum cooled and hydrocooled sweet corn. Proc. Florida State Hort. Soc. *70*, 214–216.

STEWART, J. K. 1962. Precooling methods for cantaloups. Produce Mktg. *5*, No. 7, 23–24, 32.

STEWART, J. K., and BARGER, W. R. 1960. Effects of cooling method and top-icing on the quality of peas and sweet corn. Proc. Am. Soc. Hort. Sci. *75*, 470–475.

STEWART, J. K., and BARGER, W. R. 1961. Effects of cooling method on the quality of asparagus and cauliflower. Proc. Am. Soc. Hort. Sci. *78*, 295–301.

STEWART, J. K., and BARGER, W. R. 1962. Effects of precooling method on the quality of crate-packed and pre-packaged celery. Proc. Am. Soc. Hort. Sci. *81*, 347–353.

STEWART, J. K., and BARGER, W. R. 1963. Effects of cooling method, pre-packaging and top-icing on the quality of Brussels sprouts. Proc. Am. Soc. Hort. Sci. *83*, 488–494.

STEWART, J. K., and COUEY, M. H. 1963. Hydrocooling vegetables, a practical guide to predicting final temperatures and cooling times. U.S. Dept. Agr. Mktg. Res. Rept. *637*.

STEWART, J. K., and KASMIRE, R. F. 1958. An evaluation of floor pads for transit protection of potatoes. Proc. Conf. Transport. Perishables. Univ. Calif., Davis. 182–188.

STEWART, J. K., and LIPTON, W. J. 1960. Factors influencing heat loss in cantaloups during hydrocooling. U.S. Dept. Agr. Mktg. Res. Rept. *421*.

THÉVENOT, R. 1955. Precooling. 9th Intern. Congr. Refrig. Proc. *0.10*, 0051–0071.

WANG, J. K., and GITLIN, H. M. 1964. Vacuum coolers: Principles and design criteria. Univ. Hawaii Coop. Ext. Ser. Bull. *69*.

Fumigation

AKAMINE, E. K., and SHOJI, K. 1960. Tolerance of tomatoes to methyl bromide fumigation. Hawaii Agr. Expt. Sta. Tech. Prog. Rept. *124*.
MONRO, H. A. U. 1971. Manual of Fumigation for Insect Control. U. N. Food Agr. Org., FAO, Rome.
U.S. DEPT. AGR. PLANT QUAR. DIV. 1968. Hawaiian fruits and vegetables quarantine. U.S. Department of Agriculture Plant Quarantine Division *13*, and amendments.
U.S. DEPT. AGR. PLANT QUAR. DIV. 1970. Fruits and vegetables quarantine. U.S. Department of Agriculture Plant Quarantine Division *56*, and amendments.

Irradiation

BERAHA, L., SMITH, M. A., and WRIGHT, W. R. 1960. Gamma radiation dose response of some decay pathogens. Phytopathology *50*, 474–476.
BRAMLAGE, W. J., and LIPTON, W. J. 1965. Gamma radiation of vegetables to extend market life. U.S. Dept. Agr. Mktg. Res. Rept. *703*.
DENNISON, R. A., and AHMED, E. M. 1975. Irradiation treatment of fruits and vegetables. *In* Postharvest Biology and Handling of Fruits and Vegetables. N. F. Haard and D. K. Salunkhe (Editors). AVI Publishing Co., Westport, Conn.
INTERNATIONAL ATOMIC ENERGY AGENCY. 1971. Disinfestation of Fruit by Irradiation. Intern. At. Energy Agency, Vienna.
MAXIE, E. C., SOMMER, N. F., and MITCHELL, F. G. 1971. Infeasibility of irradiating fresh fruits and vegetables. HortScience *6*, 202–204.
SKOU, J. P., BECH, K., and LUNDSTEN, K. 1974. Effects of ionizing irradiation on mushrooms as influenced by physiological and environmental conditions. Radiation Botany *14*, 287–299.
STADEN, O. L. 1973. A review of the potential of fruit and vegetable irradiation. Sci. Hort. *1*, 291–308.
TEMKIN-GORODEISKI, N., KAHAN, R. S., and PADOVA, R. 1972. Development and damage in the buds during storage of irradiated onions. Can. J. Plant Sci. *52*, 817–826.

11

Ventilated Storage

The marketable life of most fresh vegetables can be extended by prompt storage in an environment that will maintain product quality. These optimum environments vary considerably from product to product as described in Chapters 6, 7, 8 and 9. Optimum environment for a specific commodity is that which will permit the product to be stored as long as possible without appreciable loss of such quality factors as flavor, texture, and moisture content.

The period during which a given vegetable can be stored also varies widely, depending largely upon respiratory activity, susceptibility to moisture loss, and response to microorganisms which cause decay.

The desired environment may be obtained by providing facilities in which temperature, air circulation, relative humidity, and sometimes atmosphere composition, can be controlled. Temperature control is the most important factor for successful storage. Specifications for storage facilities must be based on the following factors: (1) quantity to be stored; (2) optimum temperature for product; (3) field heat to be removed; and (4) vital heat production during cooling and storage.

FACILITIES

A widely used type of storage is variously referred to as common storage, air storage, or ventilated storage. It involves considerably less capital investment and operating costs than refrigerated storage.

271

Principles

In temperate-zone areas ambient temperatures at night, after fall harvest, will usually produce favorable storage temperatures for such products as potatoes, dry onions, cabbage, and mature carrots, when applied under controlled ventilation in an insulated structure. Automatic control of louvers and fans to draw in outside air when ambient temperatures are favorable, and to circulate air inside the building when outside temperatures are higher or lower than wanted, will gradually cool the stored products and maintain the storage at desired temperature after field heat is removed.

Above-ground buildings are now favored over the older earthbank or below-grade air-cooled storages. Temperature control by ventilation is easier to attain in the above-ground structures because they do not have the input of ground heat during the early part of the storage season. The newer storages are also more accessible to trucks, which is important with the present emphasis on bulk storage.

Modern ventilated storages are usually of frame or cinder-block construction with 5 cm (2 in.) of rock wool or equivalent in the walls and 7.5 or 10 cm (3 or 4 in.) of insulation in the ceiling.

Exchange of Air

Equipment for automatic control of outside air intake and for mixing outside air with recirculated air is used. Maximum use can be made of cool night air during the fall cooling period, and in the winter months just enough outside air can be drawn in to maintain product temperature. Air can be circulated around the perimeters of the storage or through the product in the stacks or bins, depending on the design and application of the air system. A constant air flow rate of 0.023 m³ (0.8 cu ft) a min per 45 kg (100 lb) of stored product has been recommended for potatoes. Less air will permit vital heat to accumulate and stimulate decay organisms, while more air may cause excessive loss of moisture from the product.

Relative humidity requirements vary with the commodity. Optimum RH and methods for maintenance will be discussed under specific commodities.

POTATO STORAGE

Fall-harvested or late-crop potatoes, as grown in the northern part of the United States, in Canada, and in central and northern Europe, are usually stored for periods of 3 to 9 months before shipment to market. Most of these potatoes are stored in nonrefrigerated warehouses where temperatures are maintained by controlled ventilation with outside air. Much of the crop is stored in bulk bins at depths of from 2.5 to 5.5 m (8 to 18 ft).

Curing Before Storage

Potatoes, in common with most tubers and roots, are able to heal skinned areas, shallow cuts, and moderate bruises if an environment suitable for healing is provided. For this reason, it is important to provide a curing period of 10 to 14 days before cooling to storage temperature. Curing is accomplished by holding the tubers above 18.5° C (65° F) for a couple of days and then gradually cooling to 7.5° to 10° C (45° to 50° F) over a period of 10 to 12 days. High RH is essential to good healing so it should be at 90 to 95% to speed periderm growth and prevent shriveling during the curing period. Fortunately, ambient temperatures are such during fall harvest that tubers placed in ventilated storage are usually cooled slowly. However, it may be necessary to add moisture to the storage air to provide the desirably high RH. This can be done by vaporizing water into the ventilation ducts, or, less effectively, by frequent wetting of unoccupied floor space.

Schippers (1971) reported on Katahdin potatoes cured before storage for 2 weeks at 7.5° to 20° C (45° to 68° F) and 100% RH, as compared with similar tubers stored immediately after harvest. During storage at 5° C (41° F) and 85% RH the cured tubers lost 4.9 and 5.7% weight, respectively, in 2 seasons. The non-cured potatoes lost 6.8 and 7.5% under the same storage conditions.

Air Circulation in Storage

In the conventional type forced-air ventilation system, air is released from supply ducts placed on or near the floor (Fig. 11.1). The air travels up through the potato pile and returns above the pile. The area of floor available for ducts is limited, so air release at the ducts is often of high velocity. This results in excessive moisture loss from tubers near the ducts. Pressure bruising, which is known to be related to tuber desiccation, is increased in these areas.

A method for increasing the area through which air can be released at lower velocity appears to be desirable. One possibility is the cross-flow system studied by Hunter and Yaeger (1972). The method involves wall ducts with the air released from inner wall openings flowing through the pile to similar openings on the opposite wall. A positive pressure at

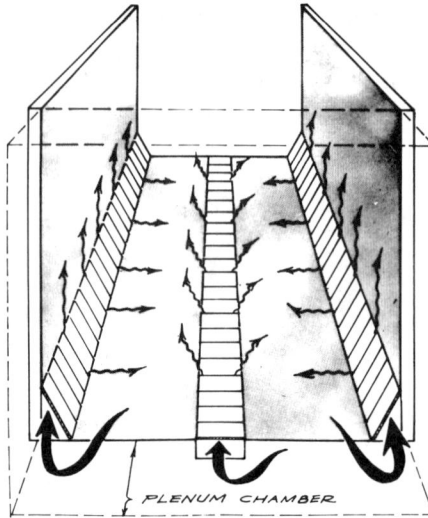

U.S. Dept. of Agriculture Photo

FIG. 11.1.   DIAGRAM FOR A METHOD
OF AIR CIRCULATION IN A
VENTILATED BIN STORAGE

one wall and a negative pressure at the other assures air movement without high velocity. The system can also be made reversible.

Limited comparisons of cross-flow and conventional systems have shown no particular advantage in weight loss or pressure bruising for the cross-flow system. However, modification of the wall duct system and limiting bin width to 4 to 5 m (12 to 15 ft) may make the cross-flow system a useful alternative to the vertical-flow system.

A detailed study of commercial potato storages in the Red River Valley (Schaper et al. 1976) indicates rather poor air distribution in the conventional multi-bin, vertical-flow system. Recommendations for improvement include a ratio of duct discharge area to duct cross-sectional area of about 1, and a ratio of total duct slot area to duct cross-sectional area of about 4.

Storage of Table Stock and Seed

After the curing process, potatoes for seed or table stock should be cooled as rapidly as possible to 3.5° to 4.5° C (38° to 40° F) and held at this temperature for the duration of storage. Relative humidity should be maintained at about 90% during storage. This is particularly important where black spot at pressure bruises is a troublesome storage disorder. Studies by Sawyer *et al.* (1965) show that air flow and RH are critical factors in moisture loss and black spot development.

When moisture was added to the ventilating air by means of centrifugal humidifiers attached to the incoming air duct, air volume of 0.025 m³ per 45 kg (0.83 cfm per cwt) caused considerably less shrinkage and black spot than similar air volume without added moisture. When the air volume was doubled, the added moisture did not control the detrimental effects of high air movement. When an effective sprout inhibitor was used in the Long Island tests, together with added moisture and 0.025 m³ (0.83 cfm) of air per 45 kg (cwt), storage at 10° C (50° F) gave better control of black spot, maintained firmness, and provided sprout control as good or better than 4.5° C (40° F) without added moisture, for 9 months. This is an important finding for potato producers in areas where mild fall climates make it impossible to rapidly cool potatoes to 4.5° C (40° F) after curing by ventilating the storage with outside air. When sprout inhibitors are not used, or cannot be used, as with seed potatoes, storage at 3.5° to 4.5° C (38° to 40° F) is essential if the tubers are to be held for more than 2 or 3 months. If late blight or frost damage is known to be present at harvest, it is usually desirable to forego a curing period and cool the tubers as rapidly as possible to 3.5° to 4.5° C (38° to 40° F). Lower RH and a higher rate of air circulation may also be desirable to prevent development and spread of decay. Such potatoes should be marketed as soon as possible before serious loss from decay occurs.

U.S. Dept. of Agriculture Photo

FIG. 11.2.   MODERN VENTILATED POTATO STORAGE
Includes six bulk rooms with sliding doors to permit truck entry for filling and emptying rooms. Note vents above doors.

Light should be excluded from potato storages because greening occurs as a result of chlorophyll production. This detracts from appearance and grade, and also produces a bitter compound (solanine) which also is somewhat toxic.

Cunningham *et al.* (1971) have recommended 7.5° C (45° F) for prolonged storage of Russet Burbank potatoes treated with a sprout inhibitor. Comparable tubers stored at 5.5° C (42° F) were less mealy, contained more sugar and had more yellow color than those stored at 7.5° C (45° F).

Rapid suberization and periderm formation are essential for precut seed potatoes. Ali *et al.* (1975) found that precut Red Pontiac tubers held at 27° C (80° F) and 85% RH showed suberin after 1 day and periderm after 3 days. At 15.5° C (60° F) suberin was first observed after 3 days holding and periderm growth required 5 days.

Storage for Processing

Potatoes intended for manufacture into chips or French fries are stored at somewhat higher temperatures than potatoes for the fresh market or for seed. Processing potatoes are usually stored at 10° C (50° F), but recommendations for storage temperatures vary from 9° to 15° C (48° to 60° F). The principal reason for the elevated storage temperature is the tendency of potatoes to accumulate sugar at lower temperatures. This accumulated sugar causes potatoes to fry dark. This is particularly undesirable for potato chips in which light color is an important quality factor. Sugar content of the tubers is not as critical for French frying as for chip manufacture. However, excessive sugar content is undesirable for either product. Storage at 7.5° to 10° C (45° to 50° F) is usually satisfactory for potatoes intended for French frying.

Potatoes vary substantially in their tendency to accumulate sugar. Such factors as season of harvest, tuber maturity, cultivar, area of production, planting date, and soil moisture at harvest have been shown to affect sugar content, tendency to accumulate sugar in storage, and ease or difficulty of reconditioning at 21° C (70° F) to reduce sugar content to levels satisfactory for chip manufacture. Some potatoes for processing are stored at 4.5° C (40° F), but such tubers usually require reconditioning for 1 to 4 weeks at 21° C (70° F) before processing into chips, and occasionally even prolonged reconditioning will not reduce sugar to satisfactory levels for chip manufacture.

Potatoes intended for dehydration to flakes or granules can usually be stored at 4.5° to 10° C (40° to 50° F) but may need some reconditioning before use. Apparently sugar content is not critical to the eating quality of dehydrated potatoes, but too much does adversely affect their shelf-life.

Sprout Inhibitors

Sprouting of potatoes during storage is related directly to storage temperature. At 3.5° to 4.5° C (38° to 40° F), as recommended for table stock and seed, sprouting is seldom a problem unless the tubers are stored for more than 8 months. However, at the higher temperatures at which processing potatoes are held, sprouting usually becomes a problem in 2 or 3 months. Although limited sprouting does not affect the food value of potatoes, it does affect appearance, and badly sprouted potatoes are shriveled and difficult to grade or process. The potato processing industry, and particularly the chip manufacturers, are demanding quality products. This means high total solids, low reducing sugar, and wanted textures and sizes. Thus, the producer who seeks this market must grow, handle and store his potatoes to meet the requirements.

Inhibitor Materials   At elevated storage temperatures and even for prolonged storage at 3.5° to 4.5° C (38° to 40° F), inhibition of sprouting is essential for good marketability. Certain sprout inhibiting chemicals (growth regulators) have been approved by the U.S. Food and Drug Administration and regulatory authorities in other potato producing countries for control or reduction of postharvest sprouting in potatoes. Those which have been approved in the United States include isopropyl N-(3-chlorophenyl) carbamate (CIPC), maleic hydrazide (MH), and tetrachloronitrobenzene (TCNB). Low dosage gamma irradiation (10 to 15 krad) has also been approved for sprout inhibition but has had little commercial use. These treatments act by inhibiting or killing the meristematic tissue in the "eyes" of the tuber. Other materials which have been successfully tested and are approved for use in some countries include the methyl ester of naphthalene acetic acid (MENA) and nonyl alcohol.

All of these materials, except MH, are applied after harvest, during storage, or, if sprouting has not occurred during storage, as they are prepared for market.

Maleic Hydrazide   This material is applied to the vines in the field, 2 weeks after full bloom, or 2 to 4 weeks before harvest. It is applied at the rate of 2.6 liters (6½ pints) of MH (amine form) in 100 to 140 liters (80 to 120 gal.) of water per hectare (2½ acres). This is a very effective sprout inhibitor treatment, but the user must know, before use of this chemical, that the treated potatoes are to be used only for table stock or processing. It is obvious that application of a sprout inhibitor is undesirable for seed potatoes.

CIPC. This sprout inhibitor is applied as a vapor or aerosol after the potatoes have been in storage for at least a curing period. One application after the potatoes have been in storage for several months, but before sprouting has started, usually is sufficient. Special fog-producing applicators are available through the suppliers of CIPC. Rate of application is usually 0.26 liter per 10 m³ (1 quart per 1000 bu) of potatoes. It is essential that sufficient air volume 3370 to 6740 cm³ per sec per m³ (¼ to ½ cfm per bu) be provided for distribution of the inhibitor and that it be directed in such a way that uniform coverage is obtained.

In the extended storage of potatoes for processing, a sprout inhibitor is essential because sprouts are initiated early in storage at the higher temperatures used. The inhibitor most commonly applied is CIPC. When application is uniform and at sufficient concentration to completely control sprouting, the results are excellent. When external sprouts are only partially suppressed, with production of rosette sprouts, internal growth of sprouts may occur. Such sprouts grow inward into the flesh of the sprouting tuber or into one in close contact. The growth of internal sprouts renders the affected tubers unsuitable for chip or French fry manufacture. There is some evidence that potatoes stored in a room previously treated with CIPC or in the close proximity to treated tubers, will develop internal sprouting from the minute amount of volatile CIPC present (Hruschka et al. 1965). Concentrations of CIPC vapor or aerosol sufficient to inhibit all bud growth eliminates both external and internal sprouting. A dip in 0.5% suspension of CIPC, as sometimes used when table stock potatoes are removed from storage, prevents development of both external and internal sprouts.

Irradiation   Research on gamma irradiation of potatoes shows that at low dosage (5 to 15 krad) sprouting can be effectively inhibited. Low level irradiation for sprout inhibition in potatoes for food was approved in Canada in 1960 and more recently in the United States. However, even this low dosage interferes with the meristematic activity necessary for wound healing. Irradiation cannot safely be applied before the potatoes have been in storage long enough to be thoroughly healed. Studies by Sparks and Iritani (1964) show that irradiation before 70 days storage at either 10° or 21° C (50° or 70° F) resulted in increased wastage. Since the treatment cannot be applied to the potatoes in storage, the extra handling involved in removal from storage for treatment appears to limit its usefulness. A number of limited scale commercial trials of potato irradiation have been made with rather variable results. It appears that there will be no large-scale application of irradiation for storage potatoes in the United States in the foreseeable future.

Nonyl Alcohol   This is material which is used in the United Kingdom and in some other European countries as a sprout inhibitor. It is effective when applied as a vapor in the ventilation system at a concentration of 1 g per m^3 (1 oz per 1000 cu ft) at an air flow rate of 2360 cm^3 per sec (5 cfm) per long ton of potatoes. However, the effect is temporary, so the stored potatoes must be retreated every few weeks during the sprout initiation period.

ONION STORAGE

Most onions grown for dry onions in north temperate areas are stored in ventilated storage for winter and spring sale. Spring and summer crops of onions, as produced principally in the southwestern states, are either marketed directly after harvest or held in refrigerated storage. Onions of the Bermuda type are seldom stored and, because of relatively poor storage quality, should be stored under optimum conditions for not more than 1 or 2 months. Globe type onions, as commonly grown in New York State, Michigan and Wisconsin, will usually remain in marketable condition until March in a well-operated ventilated storage. If the onions are treated in the field with maleic hydrazide to prevent sprout growth, they can often be stored into May. Spanish type onions usually have a somewhat shorter storage life, but when held consistently at 0° C (32° F) in refrigerated storage they can be held for 3 to 5 months.

Curing in Storage

Curing of onions in the field and in the packinghouse is discussed in Chapter 3. Further curing for storage onions is usually accomplished in ventilated storages during the first week or two of storage. This is accomplished by forced ventilation at a higher rate than is used for later storage. Outside air may be used, or the air may be artificially heated to 24° to 29.5° C (75° to 85° F) if outside air is too cool or humid. For this added curing period about 25,000 cm^3 per sec (1½ cfm) of air per m^3 (cu ft) of onions is usually adequate. During this forced ventilation the bulbs should lose 3 to 5% of their prestorage weight and the necks should become dry and the outer scales brittle.

Overcuring will cause excessive loss of outer scales, and excessive humidity or temperature during curing may cause staining of the outer scales. Condensation on the onions should be avoided. This can happen if humid air is brought into contact with onions at a temperature below the dewpoint of the outside air.

Storage Facilities

Ventilated storages for onions are designed and operated much the same as those for potatoes. The buildings are usually of frame or cinderblock construction with insulated walls and ceiling. The principal difference in operation involves the lower temperature and relative humidity requirements for dry onions as compared with potatoes. Optimum for onions after the curing period is 0° C (32° F) with RH of 65 to 70% and just enough air movement to pick up respired heat and maintain uniform temperature throughout the stacks or bins.

Onions stored under ventilation are usually in deep bins with actual bulb depths of 3 to 4.6 m (10 to 15 ft). Depths greater than 3 m (10 ft) will cause some distortion of soft bulbs in the bottom of the pile. Slatted floors with air ducts beneath allow air to flow through the pile. They may also be stored in bags, hand-stacked or on pallets, or in slatted crates or pallet bins. Less air circulation through the product is obtained with piled sacks or pallet bins, so open stacking arrangements must be provided to avoid heating and excessive decay. Storage in row-spaced slatted crates provides for good air circulation. Open mesh bags are also good storage containers, provided the stacking arrangement permits free air access.

Temperature and Relative Humidity   ·Since control of temperature and RH of the storage air are essential to success in onion storage, these conditions must be known. Accurate thermometers and psychrometers should be an integral part of the storage equipment and they should be read regularly. Fan capacities and static pressures against which they operate should also be known and the knowledge applied to sound ventilation practice.

The optimum RH for onions in ventilated storage is not always easy to attain at temperatures near 0° C (32° F), especially in areas where outside RH is high. The relative humidity of the inside air can be lowered by bringing in outside air if (1) RH of the air outside is lower than that inside and both are at the same temperature; (2) RH of the air outside is the same as that inside, but the temperature outside is lower than inside, so its RH will be lower when warmed to storage temperature. Humidity inside will be increased if (1) air of higher RH and at the same temperature is introduced, or (2) if warmer air at the same RH is introduced. For detailed discussion of RH, see Chapter 1. Under extreme conditions of high outside air moisture, artificial dehumidification of the storage air may be necessary.

Onion Sets

The small dry onions, which are used as planting stock for production of early green onions, require the same storage environment as large onions. They are usually held in ventilated storage in shallow slatted trays, rather than bags or crates. Because of their small size they tend to pack tightly if piled deeply. This limits air circulation through the sets and increases root and top growth and decay. Neither respiratory heat nor transpired moisture can be adequately dissipated in deep piles.

SWEETPOTATO STORAGE

Most commercial sweetpotato production in the United States is in the southeastern and southwestern states. Fall and winter temperatures are moderate to warm and the growing season is long. If low temperature storage were required for sweetpotatoes, the ambient temperatures in these production areas would not be suitable. Fortunately, sweetpotatoes do not require low temperature storage and, in fact, most cultivars are injured by exposure to temperatures below 13° C (55° F) for more than a day or two. Consequently, 60 to 65% of the

From Kushman and Wright (1968)

FIG. 11.3. MODERN VENTILATED SWEETPOTATO STORAGE
The small roof vents are over curing rooms and the large vents over storage rooms.

commercial sweetpotato crop is held in ventilated storage for 1 to 6 months. Approximately 25% of the crop is sold in the fresh market directly after harvest, and only part of the additional 25%, which is processed, is cured and stored before manufacture.

Root Handling

Sweetpotatoes are subject to postharvest decay by several pathogens. When disease infections are present at harvest, or if injuries are incurred during harvest, decay development can be serious at the elevated storage temperature necessary for prevention of chilling injury. For this reason special effort must be devoted to avoidance of physical injury to the roots during harvest, and to removal of any roots showing preharvest infections. Curing and storage rooms must be clean and if storage containers are reused they should be steam-heated to 50° C (122°) for 6 hr before use to reduce black rot and scurf contamination.

Sweetpotatoes which have been exposed to excessively wet or cold soils near harvest are not good prospects for storage. Carbon dioxide accumulates in the roots in saturated soils and this is accompanied by depletion of oxygen in the root tissues. Warm and wet soil damages roots more rapidly than cool wet soils, because of the higher respiration rate in the warm soils. However, even in the absence of excessive moisture, chilling injury often occurs in cold soils. If harvest is not completed soon after the first vine-killing frost, chilling will reduce storability of the roots.

Curing the Roots

Freshly harvested sweetpotatoes have a thin, delicate skin which is easy to slip or remove. The most careful harvesting procedures, and the gentlest handling from the field, produce some skinning and other physical injury. The primary purpose of curing is the healing of these harvesting and handling injuries, so that the roots will resist invasion by rot-producing organisms during storage and marketing.

The Healing Process   Healing, primarily the production of wound cork cells, takes place rapidly at 29.5° C (85° F) in the presence of high RH. Recommendations for RH during curing usually call for 85 to 90%, but recent studies indicate that higher RH (95 to 97%) results in faster healing. When the roots are held at optimum curing environment, wound cork begins to form in 2 days and is well developed in 5 or 6 days.

Excessive temperature must be avoided, for very little healing occurs at 35° C (95° F) or above. Development of wound cork is much slower at lower temperatures and stops entirely at 13° C (55° F) or below. Healing which occurs in 4 to 7 days at 29.5° C (85° F) would require 15 to 20 days at 24° C (75° F). Slow formation of wound cork permits decay-producing organisms to gain entrance before the protective layer is well formed.

Kushman (1975) reported that weight loss during curing of Centennial sweetpotatoes at 26° C (79° F) was reduced by increasing RH in the curing room from 80 to 90% and from 90 to 97%. However, weight loss was not reduced by increasing the RH from 97 to 100%. The study further showed that weight loss during 7 days of curing was positively correlated to decay development during 5 months of storage at 15° C (59° F). When weight loss during curing was less than 4%, decay during storage was about 1%. When weight loss was as high as 10% during curing, decay averaged about 25% during storage.

Some compositional changes also occur in the roots during curing and subsequent storage. The eating quality of cooked sweetpotatoes is better if the roots have been cured for a few days after harvest than when cooked immediately after harvest. The quality change involves mainly conversion of starch to sugar and dextrins. Although the change is relatively small in the raw roots during curing, the conversion of starch to sugars and dextrins during cooking is greater in cured than in freshly harvested roots.

Curing Facilities   Until rather recently, curing of sweetpotatoes was done either in a large one-room storage, or in a multiroom storage in which each room was used for both curing and storage. The one-room facility does not provide a good curing environment because the optimum temperature and RH cannot be maintained in an area where freshly harvested roots are being added each day and outside doors are open for extended periods. The storage with several rooms, each of which could be filled for curing and subsequent storage in the same room, is an improvement over the one-room storage. However, for such a storage to provide optimum conditions for curing, each room must have more heating, humidification, and air circulation equipment than is needed for storage after the roots are cured. This involves a sizeable investment for facilities needed for only a few weeks each year.

The principal reason for the multi-purpose curing and storage rooms is the labor involved in manual handling of small storage containers. When individual crates or baskets of sweetpotatoes are hand-stacked, the required labor, and the possibility of physical damage to the roots and containers in rehandling, discourages moving the containers after they are placed in a room. Thus, the strong tendency is to store in the same room in which they are cured.

Most of the newer sweetpotato storages have ground-level concrete floors, and aisle and door widths adaptable to the operation of forklift trucks. This enables palletization of the harvest containers, and allows mechanized handling from the field through curing, storage, and into the packing room. This addition of rapid, convenient, and damage-free movement of the filled crates, makes the use of separate curing rooms practical and economical.

From Kushman and Wright (1969)

FIG. 11.4. HANDLING OF PALLETIZED CRATES OF SWEET-POTATOES IN STORAGE

Separate Curing Rooms   The provision of separate curing rooms reduces investment in construction and equipment because only the special curing room or rooms require the added equipment for this relatively brief process. Storage rooms are then used only for storage and can be continuously operated at optimum temperature and humidity for this purpose. Experience in North Carolina (Kushman and Wright 1969) indicates that about $1/6$ to $1/4$ of the total storage capacity should be curing space. If sweetpotatoes are removed from the curing room on a seven-day schedule, the curing room can be used for six batches during a six-week harvest season. At the end of each seven-day curing period the palletized containers are moved gently and with small labor expenditure to the storage rooms. The system also enables relatively simple segregation in storage of lots by grower, cultivar, or date of harvest.

Added heat is almost always required in the curing room. This can be provided by oil- or gas-burning furnaces or by electric resistance elements located in heating trenches in the floor. Successful application of heat from either source can be accomplished by forced air circulation through floor trenches with wooden covers that are sufficiently separated to permit heat to flow up through the palletized crates. Usually trenches around the periphery of the room with one through the center of the room are sufficient. Air circulation is obtained by directing air from a blower into the ducts. An auxiliary fan near the ceiling is sometimes needed to return air directly to the blower-heater unit. The amount of heat and air required can be calculated on the basis of room

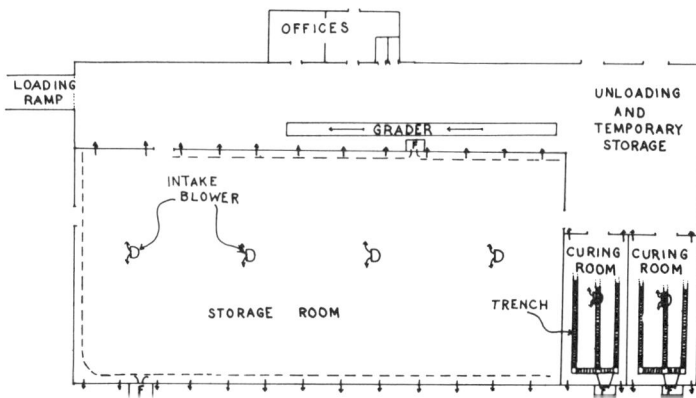

U.S. Dept. of Agriculture Photo

FIG. 11.5. DIAGRAM OF MODERN SWEETPOTATO STORAGE DESIGNED FOR SEPARATE CURING AND PALLETIZED HANDLING

size, anticipated outside temperatures, heat leakage, and vital heat production by the roots.

The high RH necessary for effective curing can be obtained by adding live steam, mist from a mechanical humidifier, or by adding water to the floor trenches if they are used to circulate heated air.

Storage Facilities

After sweetpotatoes are cured they should be cooled to 13° to 15.5° C (55° to 60° F) as quickly as possible and held in this temperature range for the duration of storage. Relative humidity for storage needs to be in the range of 85 to 90%. A small amount of ventilation is required to prevent atmosphere modification in a tight storage. However, in ventilated storage the air exchange needed for temperature maintenance is sufficient.

Ventilated storages may be constructed of poured concrete, cinder or concrete blocks, or of wood frame with asbestos-cement, galvanized steel, or aluminum sheathing. Insulation, as poured mineral or plastic granules, between-the-stud batts of fiberglass or mineral fiber, or inside insulation board, is essential to keep the storage cool in fall and warm for frost protection in the winter. A vapor barrier, usually sealed 2- to 6-mil polyethylene sheets, should be placed on the warm side of the wall, which (in the case of sweetpotato storages) is the inside wall during most of the storage season. As long as moisture can move out of the inside wall faster than it moves in from the inside, the insulation will remain reasonably dry.

Air Movement   Air exchange and air circulation in ventilated storages are usually attained by one of the two following methods: (1) warm air is exhausted from the top of the storage through vents at the ceiling or near the top of the walls and cool air is introduced through open doors or special vents near the floor; or (2) cool air is introduced to the top of the storage through baffled ceiling vents with thermostatically controlled fans, moved across the top of the stacked containers, and is exhausted through vents along the top of the walls. The latter system is favored by Kushman and Wright (1965) and is being successfully applied in the newer storages in North Carolina.

Supplementary Refrigeration   Some of the larger sweetpotato storages have one or more rooms equipped for cooling with mechanical refrigeration. This permits maintaining optimum temperatures into the spring months when ambient temperatures are too high to achieve optimum storage conditions by ventilation. Such rooms may be air cooled during the winter months and converted to mechanical refrigeration for late-marketed roots. Blower-coil units mounted on the ceiling provide refrigeration and air circulation. As a rule of thumb for refrigeration requirements, 1 ton (72.576 kcal or 288,000 Btu per 24 hr) is needed for each 1000 boxes (25 kg or 55 lb each) stored in rooms insulated sufficiently to maintain the recommended curing temperature with an outside air temperature of $-1°$ C ($30°$ F) or lower.

High Ceilings   Economical utilization of space in a palletized operation requires ceiling heights of 5.6 to 6 m (18 to 20 ft). Such height is necessary because field containers, usually wirebound crates holding 25 to 27 kg (55 to 60 lb), are stacked 5-high on the pallets, and the pallets in turn are stacked 3-high in curing and storage rooms. Sufficient aisle space must be maintained in each room to permit forklift operation and access to all pallet stacks.

Sprout Inhibition

At the relatively high storage temperature necessary to avoid chilling injury, sprouting often becomes objectionable during prolonged storage. Studies with several preharvest and postharvest applications of growth regulators have shown commercial possibilities only with CIPC. Aerosol application to the stored roots at a rate of 194 g per m^3 (0.015 lb per bu) CIPC significantly reduced sprouting at $13°$ to $18.5°$ C ($55°$ to $65°$ F) (Kushman 1969). While in-storage application of CIPC is widely used for sprout control in stored potatoes, use of this material for sprout control in sweetpotatoes is not presently approved by federal authorities.

CARROT STORAGE

Carrots matured in the field until the tops have begun to die are suitable for storage. Well-matured roots will usually keep well for 4 or 5 months if temperature is maintained near the optimum of $0°$ C ($32°$ F) and RH is maintained at 90 to 95%. Longer storage has been attained by maintaining RH at 98 to 100% (van den Berg and Lentz 1974).

Most stored carrots are intended for processing. The relatively low price of the product seldom justifies the use of refrigerated storage, but in northern United States and in Canada ventilated storage provides the desired extension of the processing season.

Carrots are usually stored in pallet bins or slatted crates, but if directed, forced-air circulation is provided, bulk bins, with roots piled as deep as 10 ft, are satisfactory.

Low concentrations of ethylene in the storage air are known to cause bitterness in stored carrots. For this reason, products which produce ethylene, such as apples or pears, should not be stored with or near carrots.

Even well-matured carrots are quite subject to moisture loss with subsequent wilting. They should be moved into storage promptly after harvest and topped to avoid moisture loss in the field. During storage high RH is essential and air movement should be limited to maintenance of uniform temperature.

CABBAGE STORAGE

Fall cabbage, as grown in northern areas of the temperate zone, has a storage life of 3 or 4 months when held at or near 0° C (32° F) with high RH. Although an increasing amount of cabbage is held in refrigerated storage, the vast bulk of late cabbage is stored under ventilation.

Before storage, the tap root should be trimmed fairly close to the base of the head and loose leaves should be removed. Several tight wrapper leaves should be left on the head for protection, although these will probably be removed when the cabbage is marketed.

Facilities for ventilated storage are similar to those provided for carrots. Relative humidity should be maintained at above 95% to prevent wilting and enough air circulation should be provided to maintain uniform temperatures.

Cabbage is usually stored in pallet bins or in shallow layers on slatted shelves. However, it may be piled to a depth not exceeding 1.5 m (5 ft) if forced-air circulation through the bin is provided. Protection from freezing is necessary. This can usually be assured by insulation of the storage building, but in severe winter weather heat may be necessary.

PUMPKIN AND SQUASH STORAGE

All squashes and pumpkins are subject to chilling injury. While critical temperature varies somewhat between cultivars, storage at 10° C (50° F) or above is advisable for all winter squash and pumpkins. Relative humidity of 50 to 70% is recommended. Higher RH increases decay and very low humidity causes excessive weight loss. Storage at temperatures above 15.5° C (60° F), particularly with low (20 to 40%)

RH causes hollow neck in Butternut squash, which in severe form renders them unsalable (Francis and Thomson 1965). Moisture loss during storage should not exceed 15% in any of the hard squashes.

Cultivar Adaptability

Well-matured Hubbard squash will store for 6 months or longer at 10° to 13° C (50° to 55° F) with RH in the medium range. Pumpkins have a shorter storage life, usually a maximum of 2 or 3 months under optimum conditions and Butternut usually a month longer. All should be clean and sound when stored and have stems completely removed to avoid physical damage to the product during handling.

Pre-storage Treatment

A curing period of 10 to 20 days at 21° to 26.5° C (70° to 80° F) has often been suggested for pumpkins and squashes as a means of drying injuries and hardening the shells. However, recent studies have not confirmed the usefulness of this treatment (Schales and Isenberg 1963). Curing of Hubbard and Butternut squashes was not beneficial to storage life, and was distinctly detrimental to the external color and eating quality of Table Queen. Present recommendations tend toward storage immediately after harvest at a moderate temperature (10° to 15.5° C; 50° to 60° F) and with RH in a range low enough to reduce infection by microorganisms but high enough to prevent excessive weight loss.

Facilities for Storage

Buildings similar to those used for sweetpotato storage are excellent for squash storage. However, any space which can be kept cool and dry in the fall and warm enough to avoid chilling injury in the winter is suitable. Heated basement or insulated sheds are commonly used. Storage can be in pallet bins, in shallow piles on the floor or in crates. Probably the best arrangement for prolonged storage is single-layer, spaced-placement on slatted shelves.

REFERENCES

AGLE, W. M., and WOODBURY, G. W. 1968. Specific gravity-dry matter relationship and reducing sugar changes affected by potato variety, production area, and storage. Am. Potato J. 45, 119–131.

ALI, S. A., NELSON, D. C., and FREEMAN, T. P. 1975. Suberization and periderm development in Norchief and Red Pontiac potatoes. Am. Potato J. *52*, 201–209.

BENNETT, A. H. 1961. An evaluation of methods for cooling potatoes in Long Island storages. U.S. Dept. Agr. Mktg. Res. Rept. *494*.

BENNETT, A. H., SAWYER, R. L., BOYD, L. L., and CETAS, R. C. 1960. Storage of fall-harvested potatoes in the Northeastern late summer crop area. U.S. Dept. Agr. Mktg. Res. Rept. *370*.

COTTER, D. J., and SAWYER, R. L. 1961. The effect of gamma irradiation on the incidence of black spot, and ascorbic acid, glutathione and tyrosinase content of potato tubers. Am. Potato J. *38*, 58–65.

CUNNINGHAM, H. H., ZAEHRINGER, M. V., and SPARKS, W. C. 1971. Storage temperature for maintenance of internal quality in Idaho Russet Burbank potatoes. Am. Potato J. *48*, 320–328.

EWING, E. E., LAYER, J. W., BOHN, J. C., and LISK, D. J. 1968. Effects of chemical sprout inhibitors and storage conditions on internal sprouting in potatoes. Am. Potato J. *45*, 56–71.

FINDLEN, H. 1962. Storage of potatoes in pallet boxes for chip manufacture. U.S. Dept. Agr. Mktg. Res. Rept. *535*.

FLUCK, R. C., and KUSHMAN, L. J. 1965. Pallet boxes and palletized containers for handling and storing sweetpotatoes. U.S. Dept. Agr. *ARS 52-2*.

FRANCIS, F. J., and THOMSON, C. L. 1965. Optimum storage conditions for Butternut squash. Proc. Am. Soc. Hort. Sci. *86*, 451–456.

HEINZE, P. H., FINDLEN, H., and EWING, E. E. 1966. Storage and transportation of potatoes. Potato Handbook *11*, 5–6, 8–10, 12–14.

HRUSCHKA, H. W., MARTH, P. C., and HEINZE, P. H. 1965. External sprout inhibition and internal sprouts in potatoes. Am. Potato J. *42*, 209–222.

HUNTER, J. H. 1961. Forced air ventilation and circulation systems for potato storage. Maine Agr. Expt. Sta. Misc. Rept. *98*.

HUNTER, J. H., and YAEGER, E. C. 1972. Evaluation of cross-flow circulation systems for potato storages. Am. Soc. Agr. Eng. Annual Meet. North Atlantic Region, College Park, Maryland. Paper No. *NA 72-410*.

JOHNSTON, E. F., TOKO, H. V., and WILSON, J. B. 1965. Pallet boxes vs. deep bins—a comparison of potato quality control. Maine Agr. Expt. Sta. Bull. *636*.

KUSHMAN, L. J. 1969. Inhibition of sprouting in sweetpotatoes by treatment with CIPC. HortScience *4*, 61–63.

KUSHMAN, L. J. 1975. Effect of injury and relative humidity during curing on weight and volume loss of sweetpotatoes during curing and storage. HortScience *10*, 275–277.

KUSHMAN, L. J., and DEONIER, M. T. 1957. Effects of storage temperatures on Porto Rico, Allgold, and Goldrush sweetpotatoes. Proc. Am. Soc. Hort. Sci. *70*, 425–431.

KUSHMAN, L. J., DEONIER, M. T., LUTZ, J. M., and WALTERS, B. 1954. Effects of temperature and soil moisture at harvest and of delay in curing on keeping quality of Porto Rico sweetpotatoes. Proc. Am. Soc. Hort. Sci. *63*, 415–419.

KUSHMAN, L. J., and WRIGHT, F. S. 1965. Overhead ventilation of sweet-potato storage rooms. N. Carolina Agr. Expt. Sta. Tech. Bull. *166*.

KUSHMAN, L. J., and WRIGHT, F. S. 1968. A new system for storing sweet-potatoes. N. Carolina Agr. Expt. Sta. Tech. Bull. *187*.

KUSHMAN, L. J., and WRIGHT, F. S. 1969. Sweetpotato storage. U.S. Dept. Agr. Handbook *358*.

LUTZ, J. M., and FINDLEN, H. 1954. Storage behavior of field-sprouted potatoes. Am. Potato J. *31*, 218–221.

McCOMBS, C. L., and POPE, D. T. 1958. The effect of length of cure and storage temperature upon certain quality factors of sweetpotatoes. Proc. Am. Soc. Hort. Sci. *72*, 426–434.

OGATA, K., IWATA, T., and CHACHIN, K. 1959. The effect of gamma radiation on sprout prevention and its physiological mechanism in the potato tuber and onion bulb. Bull. Inst. Chem. Res., Kyoto Univ. *37*, No. 5 & 6, 425–436.

POOLE, W. D., and JONES, L. G. 1962. Controlled environment for sweet-potatoes in storage. Louisiana Agr. Expt. Sta. Circ. *72*.

SAWYER, R. L., BOYD, L. L., CETAS, R. C., and BENNETT, A. H. 1965. Potato storage research on Long Island with forced-air ventilation systems. N.Y. Agr. Expt. Sta. Bull. *1002*.

SCHALES, F. D., and ISENBERG, F. M. 1963. The effect of curing and storage on chemical composition and taste acceptability of winter squash. Proc. Am. Soc. Hort. Sci. *83*, 667–674.

SCHAPER, L. A., CLOUD, H., and LUNDSTROM, D. 1976. An engineering evaluation of potato storage ventilation system performance. Trans. Am. Soc. Agr. Eng. *19*, 584–590.

SCHIPPERS, P. A. 1971. The influence of curing conditions on weight loss of potatoes during storage. Am. Potato J. *48*, 320–328.

SINGH, R. P., HELDMAN, D. R., CARGILL, B. F., and BEDFORD, C. L. 1975. Weight loss and chip quality of potatoes during storage. Trans. Am. Soc. Agr. Eng. *18*, 1197–1200.

SMITH, W. L., JR., and SMART, H. F. 1959. Suberin and wound periderm formation and decay of potato slices as affected by duration of tuber storage at 40° F. Am. Potato J. *36*, 64–69.

SPARKS, W. C. 1973. Influence of ventilation and humidity during storage on weight and quality changes in Russet Burbank potatoes. Potato Res. *16*, 213–223.

SPARKS, W. C., and IRITANI, W. M. 1964. The effect of gamma rays from fission product wastes on storage losses of Russet Burbank potatoes. Idaho Agr. Expt. Sta. Res. Bull. *60*.

SPARKS, W. C., and SUMMERS, L. V. 1974. Potato weight losses, quality changes and cost relationships during storage. Idaho Agr. Expt. Sta. Bull. *535*.

TERESHKOVICH, G., and NEWSOM, D. W. 1964. The effect of storage and recuring on the development of periderm tissue in several sweetpotato varieties. Proc. Am. Soc. Hort. Sci. *85*, 434–440.

TOKO, H. V., and JOHNSTON, E. F. 1962. Effects of storage on post-harvest physiology of potatoes used for table stock and seed. Potato Handbook 7, 10–12, 14–17.

VAN DEN BERG, L., and LENTZ, C. P. 1966. Effect of temperature, relative humidity, and atmospheric composition on changes in quality of carrots during storage. Food Technol. 20, 104–107.

VAN DEN BERG, L., and LENTZ, C. P. 1974. Effect of relative humidity on decay and other quality factors during long-term storage of fresh vegetables. ASHRAE Symp. Semi-annual Meet. Chicago 1973. 12–18.

WILLSON, G. B. 1968. Lateral pressures on walls of potato storage bins. U.S. Dept. Agr. ARS 52-32.

WILSON, J. B., and HUNTER, J. H. 1965. Airflow effect on distribution of isopropyl N-(3-chlorophenyl) carbamate applied to bulk bins of potatoes. Am. Potato J. 42, 1–6.

WORKMAN, M., and TWOMEY, J. 1970. The influence of storage on the physiology and productivity of Kennebec seed potatoes. Am. Potato J. 47, 372–378.

12

Refrigerated Storage

Commodities which require prompt cooling after harvest, and storage at a controlled, constant temperature, must be held in refrigerated storage. A relatively few vegetables can be stored for six months or more when held in environments optimum for the commodity. Many more are not adapted to prolonged cold storage. For such commodities storage is usually at the wholesale level, with the purpose of avoiding oversupply in the retail market during periods when unloadings of certain commodities, or a single item, exceed customer demand.

Both long-term and short-term storage are essential tools in the marketing of fresh vegetables and melons. The extended period of product supply provided by storage is responsible for the orderly marketing and ready availability of the many kinds of produce found in today's food stores.

PRINCIPLES OF REFRIGERATION

Refrigeration is produced mechanically by the evaporation of a compressed, liquefied gas in a closed system. The heat required to change the refrigerant from a liquid to a vapor is taken from the space in which this change occurs. When heat is removed from a space or a commodity in that space, refrigeration is being applied. Ammonia has been widely used as a refrigerant for many years, and retains first rank for large industrial units. Some of the halide compounds (such as Freon 12 and 22) have replaced ammonia in the smaller mechanical units and, in some cases, are displacing ammonia in large commercial installations.

REFRIGERATION EQUIPMENT

The basic equipment for mechanical refrigeration consists of compressor, condenser, expansion valve and evaporator. The refrigerant is compressed, cooled by passage through an air- or water-cooled condenser, and then expanded, through an expansion orifice of some type, into the evaporator coils. During this evaporation and expansion phase, heat is absorbed from the area or product to be cooled. The absorbed heat is returned through the cycle to eventual elimination in the condenser. (See Fig. 12.1.)

Refrigeration may be applied in a storage room from baffled, wall-mounted coils, from blower-coil units mounted along the ceiling, from a centrally located coil room with air ducted to the storage rooms, or from ceiling-mounted expansion or brine coils. The last-named system is not installed in new storages because it provides only convection circulation of air. This is inadequate for rapid cooling or maintenance of uniform temperature. All modern room refrigeration systems provide forced-air

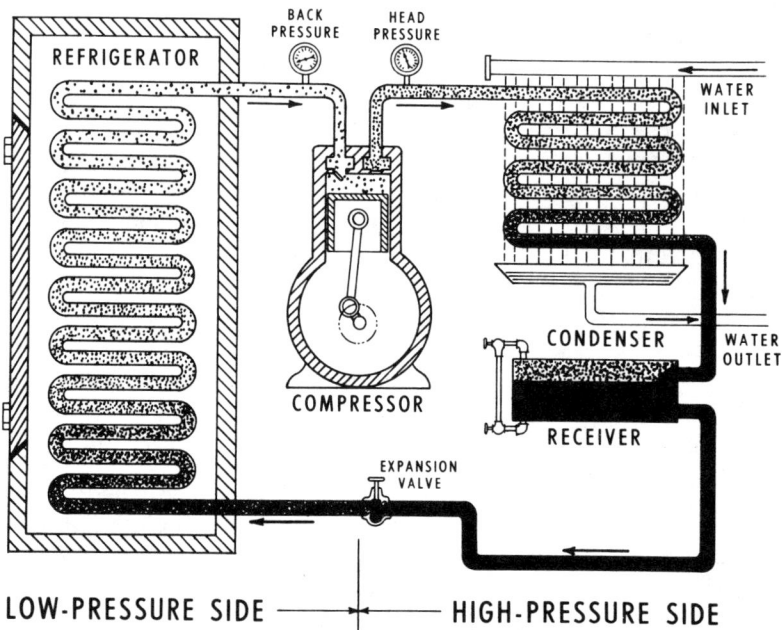

From Patchen (1971)

FIG. 12.1. ESSENTIAL COMPONENTS OF A COMPRESSION-EXPANSION REFRIGERATION SYSTEM

circulation. The favored system uses prefabricated units containing both evaporator coils and blowers for air circulation. When these are of sufficient refrigeration capacity, and mounted to produce uniform air velocities throughout the storage space, they provide excellent storage environments. If substantial heat must be removed from the product in storage, it is apparent that greater refrigeration capacity and air volumes must be available. Since both are expensive, a common procedure is to provide separate precooling facilities (see Chapter 10) where much of the product heat can be removed before it is placed in storage. Methods for calculation of refrigeration requirements and sample exercises are in the Appendix.

STORAGE CONSTRUCTION

Reinforced concrete or cinder block are commonly used materials for construction of refrigerated storages. Prefabricated insulated panels are now available from several manufacturers. These are laminates of plywood, metal, or vitreous porcelain-on-steel exteriors with cores of fiberglass or expandable plastic for insulation. The panels are commonly 1.2 m (4 ft) wide and 7.4 m (24 ft) long. They include vapor seals and built-in locking devices for sealing panels together. They are freestanding, load-bearing, and easily and rapidly assembled. Several thicknesses of insulation are available to meet various needs. Conventional cold storages generally require 10 to 15 cm (4 to 6 in.) for efficient operation.

Single-story buildings are now favored, largely as a result of the mechanized handling of palletized products. Often a refrigerated corridor is provided for loading and unloading refrigerated vehicles. Such a room maintained at 7° C (45° F) or lower reduces warmup and condensation during the handling involved in moving products into or out of the holding rooms. Further refinements involve cushioned gaskets at outside doors to prevent heat gain when loading or unloading refrigerated trailers, and telescopic tunnels to connect to refrigerated rail cars.

Insulating materials used in conventional construction include cork, fiberglass, fibrous or cellular mineral products, and foamed plastics such as polystyrene and polyurethane. When properly applied and protected from moisture, each of these has good thermal properties, but vary in such important characteristics as moisture resistance, and susceptibility to rot, fire, and invasion by insects or rodents.

Vapor barriers prevent moisture movement from the warm side into insulated walls or ceilings. They are essential for maintenance of heat-resistant property in insulation. Such materials as rigid metal sheets, metal foil, plastic film, or hot mastics will provide adequate vapor seals if properly applied.

ENVIRONMENT CONTROL

In conventional refrigerated storage rooms the three factors which must be controlled are temperature, relative humidity and air movement.

Temperature

Temperature control is based largely on tight, well-insulated structure, sufficient refrigeration capacity for maximum demand, and control of refrigerant flow through the system by means of thermostats and/or pressure-controlled expansion valves. The amount and nature of the evaporator coil surface, its freedom from ice or other heat transfer impedances, and the rate of air flowing over the coil are all factors in temperature control and efficiency of operation.

Moisture

Relative humidity is stated in numerical terms as the percentage of saturation of air with water vapor at a given temperature. As the temperature of air increases so does its water-holding capacity. Accordingly, air with 90% RH at 21° C (70° F) contains much more water by weight than air of the same RH at 4.5° or 0° C (40° or 32° F). As the RH of air decreases so does its vapor pressure (VP) and as VP decreases, the capacity of the air for removing water from moist sources increases. Thus, it is important to maintain a high VP, and as small a VP differential between the stored product and the storage air as possible, if drying is to be avoided. Effective ways of accomplishing this are rapid equalization of product and air temperatures, maintenance of as high RH in the storage room air as the product will tolerate, and no more air movement than required for even temperature distribution.

In a study of RH as related to the storage of fresh produce, Lentz and van den Berg (1973) found that commodities with a high coefficient of transpiration were affected little by initial RH of the incoming air, except at the point of entry of the air. There, air with low RH had a severe effect on moisture loss. They also reported that heat of product respiration strongly affects temperature gradient in the storage and increases moisture loss from the product.

Although the vaporization of water in a storage room will raise RH temporarily, the only permanent solution to maintenance of high RH in a mechanically refrigerated storage is accurate control of refrigerant temperature. If the temperature of the refrigerating surface (coil or spray) is below the dew point of air at a given temperature and RH, then moisture will condense on its surface and the air circulating over the surface will lose the amount of moisture condensed. The greater the difference between air and refrigerating surface, the more rapidly the air will lose moisture and the RH will drop. The critical factor is the total amount of refrigerating surface, since with limited surface a low coil temperature must be maintained to obtain the necessary heat transfer. When high RH (95% or higher) is required, the solution is provision of sufficient coil or spray surface so that adequate refrigeration can be supplied with a split of only 1° or 1.5° C (2° or 3° F) between the refrigerating surface and the air moving over it.

Jacketed Rooms   An effective system for maintenance of high RH involves a modification in construction of the storage room. The jacketed storage is built so that the cooling air circulates around the room in a sealed envelope, instead of through the room as in the conventional system (Fig. 12.2). The walls and ceiling of the room provide the cooling surface. These are, in turn, cooled by the air which moves over evaporating coils, located in or near the jacket, and then through the envelope. With the entire wall and ceiling as cooling surface, a small differential between wall surface and room air can be maintained. This greatly reduces the possibility of moisture loss through condensation on the cooling surface. Also, the lack of forced air movement in the room reduces loss of moisture from product to air (Jorgensen 1974).

Relative humidity approaching 100% can be maintained in these rooms and condensation of water in the insulation, which is outside the jacket, is prevented. However, such rooms are suitable only for precooled products or those not requiring rapid cooling, because lack of positive air movement slows the rate of cooling. Furthermore, construction and operating costs are somewhat higher than those for conventional storages.

Van den Berg and Lentz (1974) studied the effects of essentially saturated air (98 to 100% RH) on six vegetables during long-term storage at several temperatures. Carrots, cabbage, celery and parsnips held in jacketed, refrigerated storages at 98 to 100% RH lost less weight and developed less decay than comparable products held in conventional cold storage at 90 to 95% RH. Decay in onions increased in the high RH at 4.5° to 5.0° C (39° to 41° F), but was less in high RH at 0° to

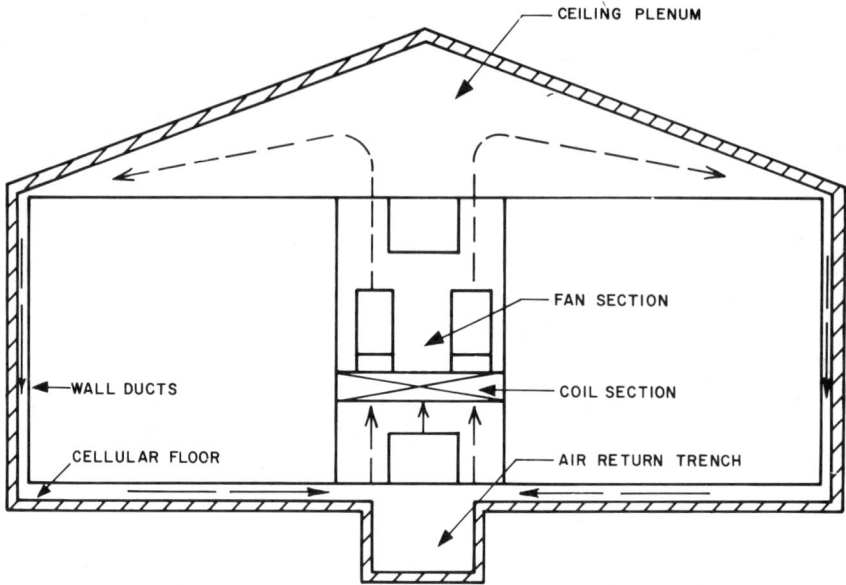

From Jorgensen (1974)

FIG. 12.2.   SCHEMATIC SECTION THROUGH JACKETED STORAGE BUILDING

1° C (32° to 34° F) than in lower RH at 4.5° to 5° C (39° to 41° F). High RH at 9.5° to 10.5° C (49° to 51° F) increased decay in potatoes, but at lower temperatures 4.5° to 5° C (39° to 41° F) and 7° to 8° C (44° to 46° F), 98 to 100% RH had little effect on decay as compared with 85 to 90% RH.

Air-Water Counterflow System   In conventional cooling systems heat is removed from air by passing it over cold metal surfaces, or through sprays of brine or water. Since the cooling surfaces always are cooler than the air, moisture (derived mainly from the stored product) is condensed out. This problem has been reduced by a new, patented system based on the so-called "Filacell." A Filacell consists of a thin plastic filament wound on a water-resistant wood frame that also provides for small spaces between adjacent strands. During cooling, chilled water or a solution with a somewhat lower freezing point is sprayed downward through the cells, and air is forced upward through the fine spray. This counterflow mixing of air and water provides for good heat exchange and yields essentially water-saturated cool air (Meredith 1974).

During precooling the high RH reduces water loss from the warm product, and during storage the possibility of condensation on products is reduced because fluctuations in air temperature are minimal. Finally, control of temperature and RH in this system are excellent, because both variables are controlled by simple adjustments in the rate of counter air flow and the water temperature.

Air Movement

Air movement must be in sufficient volume to remove respiratory heat and heat entering the room through exterior surfaces and doorways. It is also essential that it be directed in such a way that all parts of the room are subjected to uniform flow of air. This is attained in well-designed storages by proper placement of blowers or ducts and by arrangement of stacked containers to permit free air flow in designated directions.

COMMODITIES STORED

Low Temperature

Storage a few degrees above their freezing point is desirable for all of the commonly grown leaf, stem, and bud vegetables, and for most root vegetables. Notable exception among roots is the sweetpotato.

Storage life of most of the leafy vegetables is only a few weeks, even in optimum environments. Usually these products are moved directly from the packinghouse to the wholesale warehouse, where they may be held for short periods in cold storage for market advantage.

Those root crops, including carrots, parsnips, turnips, beets and horseradish, which are adapted to storage for several months, are commonly held in ventilated storage. However, refrigerated storage is used each year for a part of each of these crops, that either are to be stored for prolonged periods or are held in areas where outside temperatures are not favorable for ventilation.

Other products, which for reasons of economy are usually stored under ventilation, may be placed in refrigerated storage during the later holding period for marketing beyond the season feasible from ventilated storage. These products include potatoes, carrots, sweet potatoes, turnips, dry onions and cabbage. Some smaller part of each of these crops is held continuously in refrigerated storage, particularly in the southern and western states.

Intermediate Temperature

It is a general rule that fruits or vegetables which were native to subtropical or tropical areas are not adapted to low temperatures, either in the field or in storage. Vegetables in this category include cucumbers, eggplant, green beans, okra, sweetpotatoes, squash and tomatoes. The larger muskmelons such as Honey Dew, Casaba and Persian are also included.

Such commodities are sensitive to low temperatures in various degrees, but all are seriously damaged by prolonged exposure to temperatures below the recommended minimum.

For detailed recommendations on storage environments, see Chapters 6, 7, 8 and 9.

CONTROLLED ATMOSPHERE STORAGE

Terminology and Background

Controlled atmosphere (CA) storage is a system for holding produce in an atmosphere that differs substantially from air in respect to the proportion of nitrogen (N_2), oxygen (O_2), or carbon dioxide (CO_2). The concern is only with the physiologically active O_2 and CO_2, because N_2 is merely an inert "filler." The concentrations of O_2 and CO_2 usually are controlled within ± 1%. Occasionally other gases, such as carbon monoxide (CO), are added in low concentrations to keep cut surfaces from darkening, but this practice is not a standard part of CA storage.

Modified atmosphere (MA) storage does not differ in principle from CA storage. The term merely refers to a system of storage under which control of O_2 or CO_2 concentration is less precise or is even lacking; respiratory CO_2 or CO_2 derived from dry ice is allowed to accumulate and O_2 is allowed to decrease. The term "gas storage" is inappropriate because air is a mixture of gases, just like any artificial combination.

The historical development of CA and MA storage from its scientific beginnings in England by Kidd and West in the 1920s and in the United States by Smock in the 1940s has been traced by Dalrymple (1967). Since its beginnings, the literature on CA storage has grown enormously, so that Morris et al. (1971) could list over 2300 references in their bibliography and Murr et al. could add almost 400 more by 1974. In spite of this wealth of information, long-term CA storage is largely confined to apples, a relatively small quantity of pears, and a minor but growing supply of cabbage for processing. Consideration of the purpose of CA storage will shed light on this apparent incongruity.

Purpose of CA Storage

CA conditions must be able to influence the physiology or pathology of the vegetable in such a way as to slow ripening, undesirable color changes, toughening, and the development of disorders or growth of pathogens. These conditions would be met by crops that complete ripening after harvest or that deteriorate relatively rapidly even at optimal storage temperatures.

Among vegetables that normally are stored several months, such as potatoes or carrots, proper attention to temperature control and use of sprout inhibitors, where appropriate, permits their successful storage in air. In fact, CA conditions tend to accelerate rather than delay deterioration in these crops. In contrast, CA storage of cabbage will probably increase, because the major causes of loss, yellowing of leaves and decay, are retarded by appropriate CA conditions (see Chapter 6). Another factor that has prevented a substantial increase in CA storage of vegetables is an efficient transport system that can bring in out-of-season items from production areas in other parts of the continent or the globe. Thus, most vegetables are stored only relatively briefly prior to being processed or during transit.

Asparagus and broccoli are crops that would benefit from CA if storage prior to processing is necessary, because elevated CO_2 retards their yellowing and toughening. Tomatoes and lettuce can benefit from in-transit CA because, in their case, low O_2 retards ripening and development of certain disorders, respectively, when they are shipped to distant markets.

For a given vegetable, CA storage is most effective when one or both of the two main variables of storage, time and temperature, are unfavorable. If a vegetable, such as lettuce, remains in good condition for 7 days when held at 0° to 2° C (32° to 36° F), money spent on CA storage would be wasted. If, however, the lettuce is in transit 30 days, CA storage may well be justified even at optimum temperatures. Should it be impossible to reduce the temperature below 5° to 7° C (41° to 45° F), CA may prove beneficial even during 7 days of storage. Here, however, a warning is due: a combination of gases that may be beneficial during 30 days at 0° to 2° C may damage the product during seven days at 5° to 7° C.

Precautions

The previous warning is only one of several that must be observed in relation to CA storage of any product. Most importantly, the product to be stored must be of first-class quality. CA conditions can only maintain quality; they cannot improve initially inferior products. The crop to be stored must have been harvested at the correct stage of maturity. It must be free of disease and should have only minimal physical damage due to harvest and handling procedures. Further, experience has taught that no one mixture of gases is suitable under all circumstances: storage temperature, storage period, and the commodity to be stored are interdependent factors, each influencing the decision on which gas mixture to use. Of these three factors, the most critical one is the commodity, because of the wide range in response among them, even when all other factors are held constant. Even members of the same botanical species differ greatly in their tolerance to low O_2 or high CO_2. For example, cauliflower (*Brassica oleracea*, botrytis) is injured during 1 week at 5° C (41° F) in 10% CO_2, whereas broccoli (*Brassica oleracea*, italica) remains in excellent condition in that atmosphere.

Obviously, no one atmosphere is best for all vegetables, or even closely related ones. Specific recommendations and cautions must be determined for each crop over a wide range of storage temperatures and periods. Such specific recommendations have been included in the chapters on *Commodity Requirements*.

When the use of in-transit CA first was heavily promoted in the early 1960s, its advocates claimed that CA reduced the need for close attention to temperature. This claim was based on the mistaken premise that CA would greatly delay undesirable physiological changes and growth of pathogens. While under the proper circumstances CA does retard some physiological changes, such as yellowing in broccoli, or the spread of decay in asparagus, it can have the opposite effect. CA can induce off-flavors or lead to increased decay when the atmosphere is more injurious to the host than to the pathogen; in potatoes this occurs in concentrations of 1% O_2 or less at 15° C (59° F). However, decay can be extensive in CA even when it has no adverse effect on the vegetable. This can occur when temperatures are high enough to permit growth of an organism that is not inhibited by the atmosphere used. For example, lettuce held 1 week in 5% O_2 at 5° to 10° C (41° to 50° F) would likely have more decay than a similar lot held at 2° C (36° F) in air or CA. Consequently, maintenance of proper temperatures is essential for successful use of CA.

A second assumption made by some advocates of CA storage held that the approximately 30% reduction in the rate of respiration (Toledo *et al.* 1969) that usually accompanies CA storage would induce a commensurate reduction in the rate of deterioration. This assumption was based on the fallacious idea that respiration is a chief cause of deterioration. While respiration and deterioration often follow a parallel course, respiration causes deterioration only through its use of substrate, which is a very minor aspect of deterioration. Consequently, even a major reduction in the rate of respiration in CA would not necessarily signify a similar reduction in the rate of deterioration.

Briefly then, CA storage for vegetables can be useful, but it is no panacea that can effortlessly cure the ills connected with the storage of vegetables. Once adopted, however, the atmosphere chosen must harmonize with the commodity and the other storage conditions, or else potential gain can turn into real loss.

Methods for Achieving CA Conditions

The composition of the atmosphere in a closed space may be altered by adding individual gases while reducing the proportion of others, by scrubbing the atmosphere of CO_2 or O_2, by restricting venting, and, if only O_2 is lowered, by continuous evacuation of the storage space (low pressure or hypobaric storage).

Individual gases are added from pressurized cylinders by boiling off the gas from its liquid form stored in an insulated tank, or by catalytic burners that scrub O_2 from the storage space and replace it with CO_2 and N_2. These methods rapidly change the atmosphere and are used mainly during initial establishment of the desired levels of O_2 and CO_2.

Scrubbers, other than catalytic burners, serve to remove respiratory CO_2 from the storage atmosphere by adsorption or by absorption in solid or liquid CO_2 traps.

Details on methods for adding individual gases and on use of scrubbers can be found in Fidler and Mann (1972), Stoll (1971), Ryall and Pentzer (1974).

Venting usually results in only moderately precise control of O_2 and CO_2 levels because control depends on manipulation of louvers to admit air and release CO_2, but CO_2 scrubbers also are used in such systems. Restricting air exchange from plastic box-liners or film bags also can achieve changes in O_2 and CO_2 levels. Here, lack of control tends to yield MA rather than CA conditions and the levels of O_2 and CO_2 cannot be adjusted independently.

A more controllable and elaborate system of venting has been developed by Marcellin (1974), who employs "diffusion windows" made of a silicone rubber set into heavy polyethylene bags. The size of the windows regulates the passage of O_2 and CO_2 into and out of these bags. These bags are large enough so that many packed boxes can be stored in them.

Low pressure storage (LPS) refers to holding products in a partial vacuum. With this system O_2 levels are controlled by a continuously applied vacuum and they are predictable, because a given reduction in pressure yields an equivalent reduction in O_2 concentration. Thus, if pressure is reduced from 760 mm Hg (air at sea level) to 76 mm, the O_2

level in the container is lowered from 21 to 2.1%. Since air pressure can be controlled very precisely, O_2 levels can be maintained to within less than $\pm\, 0.1\%$. However, such precise control is not normally necessary for CA storage. Concomitant with continuous but controlled bleeding of air into the system, volatiles such as CO_2, ethylene, aldehydes and alcohols, and other organic compounds produced by the stored product are removed. It is the continuous and efficient removal of the organic volatiles from the atmosphere and from within the tissue that is the chief benefit claimed by the advocates of the system and that distinguishes it from conventional CA storage. In normal CA storage, the diffusion of potentially damaging volatiles depends on the concentration gradient of the volatile between the tissue and the surrounding air and on the rate at which the volatile diffuses through the tissue and surface layer. Under LPS, however, this gradient is inversely proportional to air pressure so that if the pressure is $^1/_{10}$ normal (76 mm Hg) then the volatiles are removed ten times as rapidly as at normal pressure (760 mm Hg). Thus, their concentrations in the tissue remain low.

With LPS, water vapor must be supplied as air is bled into the system or else the continuous removal of water vapor from the plant tissue would result in excessive water loss and wilting. This need can be turned to advantage if addition of volatile decay inhibitors or insecticides is needed, as in quarantine procedures.

Today, LPS is still largely experimental although prototype vans are available. Two major barriers to commercial application are the high cost of equipment and the so far limited experimental evidence that LPS has substantial advantages over well-administered conventional stationary or in-transit CA storage. The equipment is expensive (about twice that of conventional storages or vans) because its walls must be strong enough to withstand the pressure exerted on a partially evacuated body. The evidence is not yet convincing because some comparisons favorable to the LPS system were only with storage in air rather than with CA storage at normal air pressure. However, LP storage or transit may well become feasible for expensive crops shipped to distant markets, such as overseas. Greater detail on LPS can be found in articles by Bangerth (1973) and by Burg (1975), the inventor of the system.

REFERENCES

Conventional Storage

ASHRAE. 1971. Thermal insulation and water vapor barriers. ASHRAE Handbook of Fundamentals *17*, 291–318.
ASHRAE. 1974. Refrigerated warehouse design. ASHRAE Handbook and Product Directory, Applications *41*, 41.1–41.14.

BUILDING RESEARCH ADVISORY BOARD. 1963. Cold-storage facilities: a guide to design and construction. National Research Council, Washington, D.C., Publ. *1098*.

CHALUTZ, E., and FELSENSTEIN, G. 1973. Considerations in the design of experimental cold storage plants for perishable commodities. HortScience *8*, 169–170.

CHALUTZ, E., FELSENSTEIN, G., and WAKS, J. 1973. A simple method for controlled introduction of fresh air into experimental cold storage rooms. HortScience *8*, 96–97.

GIBBON, J. M. 1972. Some observations of temperature and cooling rates of vegetables in commercial cold stores. J. Agr. Eng. Res. *17*, 332–337.

GINSBURG, L. 1965. Recommended storage temperatures, percentage relative humidities and storage life for fruits and vegetables. Decid. Fruit Grower (South Africa) *15*, No. 3, 80–86.

JORGENSEN, E. G. 1974. Jacketed fruit and vegetable storages in Canada— design and operating experience. Symposium, ASHRAE Semi-annual Meet. Chicago 1973. 35–39.

LENTZ, C. P., and VAN DEN BERG, L. 1973. Factors affecting temperature, relative humidity and moisture loss in fresh fruit and vegetable storage. ASHRAE J. *15*, No. 8, 55–60.

LUTZ, J. M., and HARDENBURG, R. E. 1968. The commercial storage of fruits, vegetables, and florist and nursery stocks. U.S. Dept. Agr. Handbook *66*.

MEREDITH, D. 1974. The humi-fresh system-design and operating experience. ASHRAE Symp. Semi-annual Meet. Chicago 1973. 29–34.

PARSONS, C. S., McCOLLOCH, L. P., and WRIGHT, R. C. 1960. Cabbage, celery, lettuce, and tomatoes—laboratory tests of storage methods. U.S. Dept. Agr. Mktg. Res. Rept. *402*.

PATCHEN, G. O. 1971. Storage for apples and pears. U.S. Dept. Agr. Mktg. Res. Rept. *924*.

PENTZER, W. T. 1966. The giant job of refrigeration. *In* Protecting Our Food, U.S. Dept. Agr. Yearbook, 123–138.

PHILLIPS, W. R., and ARMSTRONG, J. G. 1967. Handbook on the storage of fruits and vegetables for farm and commercial use. Can. Dept. Agr. Publ. *1260*.

RYALL, A. L. 1964. The storage of farm crops. *In* Farmers World, U.S. Dept. Agr. Yearbook, 303–308.

VAN DEN BERG, L., and LENTZ, C. P. 1972. Respiratory heat production of vegetables during refrigerated storage. J. Am. Soc. Hort. Sci. *97*, 431–432.

VAN DEN BERG, L., and LENTZ, C. P. 1974. Effect of relative humidity on decay and other quality factors during long-term storage of fresh vegetables. ASHRAE Symp. Semi-annual Meet. Chicago 1973. 12–18.

Controlled Atmosphere Storage

BANGERTH, F. 1973. On the effect of reduced pressure on the physiology, quality, and storability of fruits, vegetables, and flowers. Gartenbauwissenschaft *38*, 479–508. (German)

BLANPIED, G. D., and SMOCK, R. M. 1968. Handbook for controlled atmosphere rooms. Cornell Univ. Bull. *S-504*. (Review).

BURG, S. P. 1975. Hypobaric storage and transportation of fresh fruits and vegetables. *In* Postharvest Biology and Handling of Fruits and Vegetables. N. F. Haard and D. K. Salunkhe (Editors). AVI Publishing Co., Westport, Conn.

BURTON, W. G. 1974. Some biophysical principles underlying the controlled atmosphere storage of plant material. Ann. Appl. Biol. *78*, 149–168.

DALRYMPLE, D. G. 1967. The development of controlled atmosphere storage of fruit. U.S. Dept. Agr. Fed. Ext. Serv., Washington, D.C.

FIDLER, J. C., and MANN, G. 1972. Refrigerated storage of apples and pears—a practical guide. Commonwealth Agr. Bu. Hort. Rev. No. *2*.

GRIERSON, W. 1969. Some random thoughts on CA research. *In* Controlled atmospheres for the storage and transport of horticultural crops. D. H. Dewey, R. C. Herner, and D. R. Dilley (Editors). Mich. State Univ. Hort. Rept. *9*, 77–79.

LIPTON, W. J. 1975. Controlled atmospheres for fresh vegetables and fruits—why and when. *In* Postharvest Biology and Handling of Fruits and Vegetables. N. F. Haard and D. K. Salunkhe (Editors). AVI Publishing Co., Westport, Conn.

MARCELLIN, P. 1974. Storage of vegetables under controlled atmosphere in polyethylene bags with elastomeric silicone windows. Acta Hort. No. 38, Vol. *1*, 33–45. (French)

MORRIS, L. L., CLAYPOOL, L. L., and MURR, D. P. 1971. Modified atmospheres. An indexed reference list through 1969, with emphasis on horticultural commodities. Univ. Calif. Div. Agr. Sci.

MURR, D. P., KADER, A. A., and MORRIS, L. L. 1974. Modified atmospheres. An indexed reference list with emphasis on horticultural commodities. Univ. Calif. Veg. Crops. Ser. *168*.

RYALL, A. L., and PENTZER, W. T. 1974. Handling, Transportation, and Storage of Fruits and Vegetables, Vol. 2. AVI Publishing Co., Westport, Conn.

STOLL, K. 1971. Storage of fruits and vegetables in controlled atmosphere. Schweiz. Z. Obst-Weinbau. *107*, 572–578, 614–623, 648–652, 711–714, 741–745. (German)

TOLEDO, R., STEINBERG, M. P., and NELSON, A. I. 1969. Heat of respiration of fresh produce as affected by controlled atmosphere. J. Food Sci. *34*, 261–264.

13

Transportation by Rail
and Highway

The domestic and international distribution of fresh vegetables and melons would be impossible without the rapid and controlled-environment transport now available to every major production area. The production of many crops is now concentrated in areas that have favorable climatic and soil conditions, and that can provide an adequate and uniform water supply. For example, in 1973, 84% of the head lettuce in the United States and 85% of the Honey Dew melons were produced in California and Arizona (U.S. Dept. Agr. 1975). In the same year more than 90% of U.S. celery was produced in two states, California and Florida. Approximately 70% of U.S. sweetpotatoes are currently produced in four southeastern states.

Major markets for the above crops, and others with production in limited areas, are in population centers in the Northeast, Middle West and Pacific Coast. Modern storage and transportation facilities provide fresh vegetables and melons from the United States to markets, not only in the United States, but also to Canada, western Europe and the Orient. Many of the more perishable vegetables, such as tomatoes, cucumbers, sweet peppers, and the leafy products, would be scarce in the winter months if it were not for production of these crops in Florida, Texas, Arizona, California, Mexico and some of the Caribbean islands, and modern transportation to deliver them to market.

Providing transit protection for vegetables and melons is a complex problem. It involves meeting the specific environmental requirement for each commodity under the numerous and varied seasonal and regional weather conditions which the load encounters on the way to market. In North America, outside temperatures vary from the 38° C (100° F) plus of the southwestern deserts to the subzero extremes of winter in the great plains of the United States and Canada. To meet these requirements, the transport vehicle must be well insulated to slow inside response to extreme ambients, and must be equipped with adequate refrigeration and heating capacity to maintain a near optimum environment for the product in the cargo compartment.

COMMODITY LOSSES IN TRANSIT

The fact that transportation equipment and services have not yet reached the ideal for moving fresh produce from production areas to market is clear from the millions of dollars that U.S. railroads pay in claims to shippers and receivers each year. It is true that some of the transit losses are due to container failure, careless loading and bracing by the shipper, and unpredictable vagaries of nature. However, there are sufficient justifiable claims based on equipment or personnel failure, heavy impacts in transit, and significant delays in market delivery to indicate that additional improvement in equipment and services is needed.

Claim costs, due to loss and damage in potatoes and vegetables during transport on Class 1 U.S. rail lines, amounted to more than $16,000,000 in 1974 (Assoc. of American Railroads 1974). During that year 163,412 carlots of fresh vegetables and potatoes were originated, of which a little more than one-third were potatoes. Average loss and damage per load was $22.69 for potatoes and $104.67 for all other fresh vegetables.

Between 1969 and 1974 railroad claim costs per car rose consistently from $13.30 per carload of potatoes in 1969 to $39.05 in 1974. The average gain in per-carload fresh vegetable losses was more pronounced—from $36.64 in 1969 to almost $130 in 1974. Much of this increase can probably be attributed to heavier loads and larger refrigerator cars. The trend to heavier loading of all rail cars, and the increasing use of 50- and 60-ft mechanically-refrigerated cars has substantially increased the number of packed containers per carload. Thus with more shipping containers per car, the loss and damage per load would logically be greater.

TRANSPORTATION BY RAIL CAR

Background

The railroad industry of the United States, through development of the specialized refrigerator car, pioneered the interstate movement of perishable commodities. The initial development of this service dates back about 100 years, but the early cars were little more than box cars with ice on some areas of the floor. The beginnings of effective transit protection dates back to about 1880 when insulation and special ice compartments were added to create a genuine railway refrigerator car. By 1890, carloads of produce were moving transcontinentally from California.

Rail Equipment in United States

By January 1, 1977, the railroads and associated car lines of the United States had 31,416 refrigerator cars in service for fruits and vegetables. Of these only 7067 were ice bunker (RS) cars. As recently as 1971 there were 31,083 ice bunker cars in service. Total refrigerator cars for fresh produce have declined steadily for more than 20 years. This is due in part to the larger capacity of the cars now in service, but an even greater factor is the increased use by produce shippers of refrigerated trailers-on-flatcar (TOFC), containers, and highway trucks and trailers.

Rail Transport in Europe

European railways have provided some refrigerated service for perishable commodities for many years, almost entirely in ice-refrigerated equipment. However, until the organization of Interfrigo in 1949, movement of equipment between countries of Europe was complicated by national ownership of railway equipment. The organization of the cooperative company known as Interfrigo by six Western European countries permitted joint ownership of refrigerated rail cars and greatly facilitated intercountry movement of perishables.

Additional European countries have since joined Interfrigo. As of 1973, 21 countries are members, and activities cover most of the European continent, including the Mediterranean area. About 18,500 refrigerated railcars belonging to various members were operated by Interfrigo in 1974. Additionally, the organization managed 8000 of its own ice- or mechanically-refrigerated cars.

Two general types of refrigerated rail equipment are used for transporting perishable products in Europe: (1) water-ice refrigerated cars; (2) mechanically-refrigerated cars, and van container cars. Most of the ice-refrigerated cars are smaller than the RS cars in the United States. However, some of the newer mechanically refrigerated are some 17.7 m (58 ft) inside length and 2.5 m (8 ft 4 in.) inside width. This is comparable to the largest produce cars operated in the United States.

Equipment and Services

RS-type Rail Cars   In the classification system of the Association of American Railroads the RS car is fully insulated and equipped either with a bunker at each end or with a full-length bunker above the load. The end-bunker car predominates in the RS series. Three general types of services are available for the end-bunker RS car: (1) refrigeration with ice in the bunkers; (2) ventilation, accomplished by manipulation of the hatch covers; and (3) heater service with the addition of heaters in the bunkers.

The RS car served the produce industry well for about 70 years. Such refinements as floor racks, basket type bunkers, air-circulating fans, and thermostatically-controlled alcohol heaters were added over the years. The flexibility of the equipment was important to produce shippers. They could order several different icing services to meet the needs of different products, and at substantial savings when minimum refrigeration was needed. During moderate outside temperature periods several types of ventilated service were available, and in the winter months, northern shipments could be protected by installing heaters in the empty bunkers.

From Hinds and Bongers (1976)

FIG. 13.1.   A LARGE MECHANICALLY-REFRIGERATED RAIL CAR USED IN EUROPE
Refrigeration unit at end of car, and two access doors to load compartment.

However, the relentless wheels of progress moved to designate the mechanically-refrigerated car more efficient than the RS car. As a result the number of RS cars was reduced from a peak of about 100,000 in 1955 to a few over 7000 as of January 1, 1977. The remaining RS cars are operated primarily by carriers serving areas of major potato production. Origin loads in these areas are frequently hauled under ventilation or heater service for which the RS car is useful at minimum protective service cost.

Specialized Winter Equipment   Some special rail cars are in service in northeastern United States and Canada for the winter movement of potatoes. These are essentially insulated box cars used for protection against product freezing. Heat is supplied to these cars by circulating a heated solution through bare-pipe coils on the car floor under the floor racks. The heater is mounted underneath the car near one of the car doors. The modern units are fired with methanol and thermostatically controlled. The Canadian Railways operate more than 2000 of these cars and limited numbers are available in the United States.

Mechanically-refrigerated Rail Cars

The increase in mechanically-refrigerated equipment for transporting fresh produce was a phenomenon of the decade 1960 to 1970. From less than 4000 cars in 1960, the fleet of mechanically-refrigerated rail cars increased to almost 24,000 by 1971. Although the number of mechanically-refrigerated cars has remained essentially stable since 1971, these cars now represent about 77.5% of the total refrigerator cars in freight service for fruits and vegetables in the United States.

Most of the mechanically-refrigerated (RP) rail cars have a 15.2 m (50 ft) load compartment as compared with 12.1 m (40 ft) load space for the RS-type car. The RP car also has a higher ceiling. The resultant increase in load capacity, from about 56.5 to 85 m³ (2000 to 3000 cu ft), with potential for railroad economies and rate benefits, is a major factor in the move to mechanical refrigeration. The trend in mechanical cars is toward capacities of 113 m³ (4000 or more cu ft) with a load-carrying ability of 58 to 68 thousand kg (130 to 150 thousand lb). Additional advantages are thermostatic control of temperature in the load compartment, built-in load-restraining devices, better riding qualities, and fewer delays in transit. The new equipment is quite generally acclaimed by the produce industry, despite less flexible and often more costly protective services.

Mechanical Equipment The mechanical refrigerator car differs from the modern box car mainly in such supplementary equipment as high speed trucks with snubbing devices; improved draft gears for shock reduction; cushion under-frames; a single sliding 2.4 or 3 m (8 or 10 ft) door that permits forklift operation; movable steel load dividers; 10 to 20 cm (4 to 8 in.) of insulation in walls and roof; and a diesel engine to drive an electric generator for operating refrigeration, heating and air circulating equipment. Most of the newer mechanical cars have a 20 kw generator connected directly to a 34 hp, 2-cycle diesel engine.

The engines are equipped with automatic shut-down devices for protection against overheating or loss of oil pressure. Many of the newer units have a two-speed engine. When refrigeration demand is great, as during some initial cooling, the engine operates at full speed. After the car temperature is within a few degrees of the thermostat setting, low speed is used.

Most of the refrigeration systems use Freon 12. Compressors may be two-cylinder, or multi-cylinder open or hermetic types. Many compressors are equipped with unloaders on all or part of the cylinders for unloaded starts and for refrigerant capacity control. Condensers are cooled by air drawn through louvers in the side of the car and discharged out the other side of the car. Condenser fans are usually mounted directly on the motor shaft and operated to deliver 226.5 m³

Courtesy of Pacific Fruit Express Co.

FIG. 13.2. MODERN MECHANICALLY-REFRIGERATED RAIL CAR

per min (8000 cfm) of air. Evaporator defrosting is automatic and is controlled either by an electric timer or a switch activated by pressure drop across the evaporator coils when a predetermined amount of frost has formed.

Air Circulation – It has long been recognized that forced-air circulation in the load compartment is essential for effective removal of residual field heat or vital heat from the load, and infiltrated heat from exterior surfaces. Floor racks to permit air circulation beneath the load are standard equipment in all types of refrigerator cars and side- and end-wall flues or vertical corrugations are used in most of the newer RS cars and in most RP cars. The flues permit air to move freely around the load and prevent direct contact between product containers and very cold or warm car walls.

There are three principal types of air circulation systems in mechanical refrigerator cars. One type is an open design in which all the cooled or warmed air is discharged directly over the load from a grill at the evaporator end of the car or through openings in a ceiling duct. The air passes downward through openings in the load and the side- and end-wall flues. It then returns to the evaporator and blower through the space under the floor racks.

Another system includes a plenum chamber in the car ceiling through which air is discharged downward with a modified jet action from a perforated false ceiling. As in the open system, the air moves through the load and floor racks and returns to the unit through the spaces between the floor stringers or through floor channels. Good air distribution is obtained by maintaining a positive pressure in the plenum for end-to-end uniformity of air discharge.

A third system is the complete envelope in which air circulates around the load rather than through it. The air is discharged into a ceiling duct and circulated completely around the load by passing downward through side- and end-wall ducts and returning to the unit through a floor duct. The air completely surrounds the load, but no air enters the load space. As in the case of the jacketed cold storage room, the system maintains uniform temperatures and high RH. However, the lack of forced-air circulation within the load compartment reduces its effectiveness for heat removal when temperature reduction of the load is needed. This equipment is best adapted for transport of frozen foods.

Temperature Controls and Indicators   The sensing element for activating the temperature control thermostat is usually located in the duct through which air is returned to the evaporator coil. In this

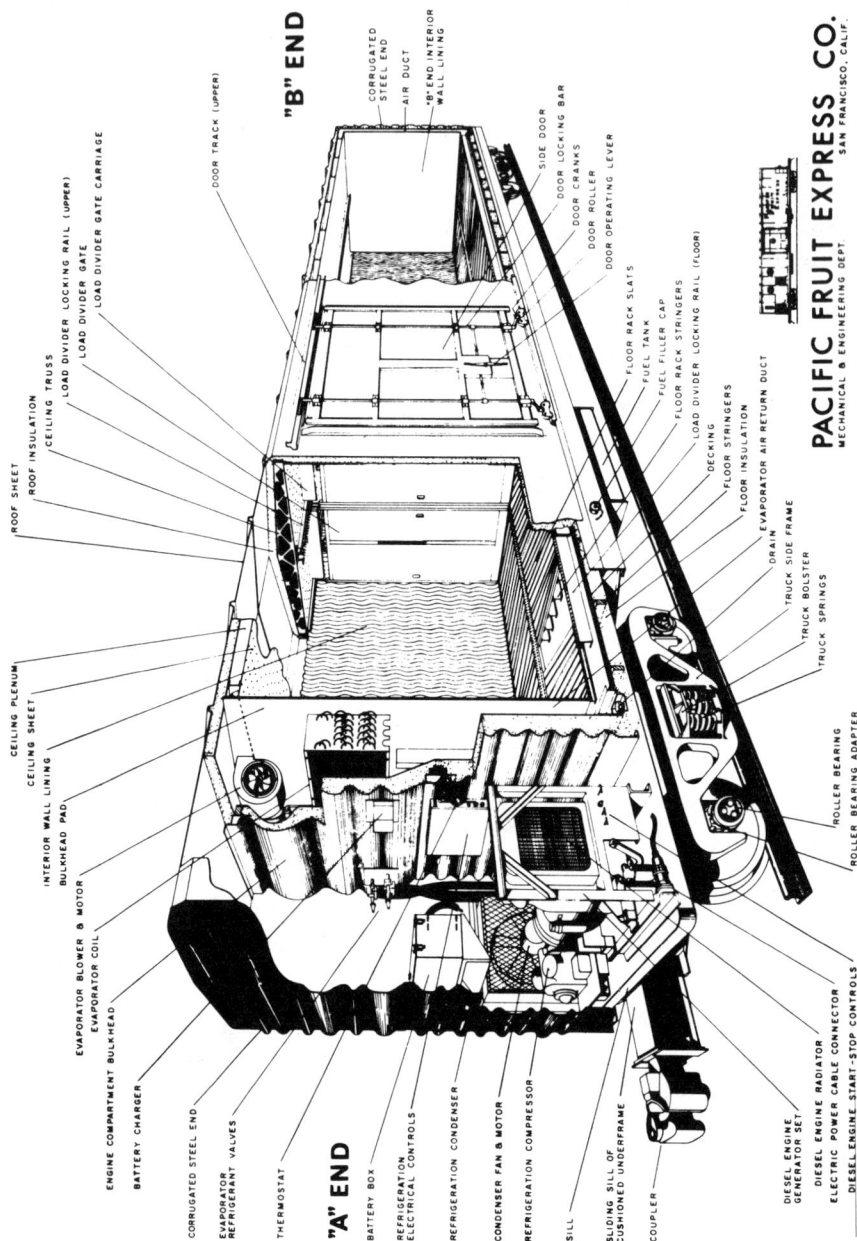

"B" END

CORRUGATED STEEL END
AIR DUCT
"B" END INTERIOR WALL LINING
DOOR TRACK (UPPER)
LOAD DIVIDER LOCKING RAIL (UPPER)
LOAD DIVIDER GATE
LOAD DIVIDER GATE CARRIAGE
SIDE DOOR
DOOR LOCKING BAR
DOOR CRANKS
DOOR ROLLER
DOOR OPERATING LEVER
ROOF INSULATION
CEILING TRUSS
FLOOR RACK SLATS
FUEL TANK
FUEL FILLER CAP
FLOOR RACK STRINGERS
DECKING
LOAD DIVIDER LOCKING RAIL (FLOOR)
FLOOR STRINGERS
FLOOR INSULATION
EVAPORATOR AIR RETURN DUCT
DRAIN
TRUCK SIDE FRAME
TRUCK BOLSTER
TRUCK SPRINGS
ROLLER BEARING
ROLLER BEARING ADAPTER

ROOF SHEET
CEILING PLENUM
INTERIOR WALL LINING
CEILING SHEET
BULKHEAD PAD
EVAPORATOR BLOWER & MOTOR
EVAPORATOR COIL
ENGINE COMPARTMENT BULKHEAD
BATTERY CHARGER
CORRUGATED STEEL END
EVAPORATOR REFRIGERANT VALVES
THERMOSTAT

"A" END

BATTERY BOX
REFRIGERATION ELECTRICAL CONTROLS
REFRIGERATION CONDENSER
CONDENSER FAN & MOTOR
REFRIGERATION COMPRESSOR
SILL
SLIDING SILL OF CUSHIONED UNDERFRAME
COUPLER

DIESEL ENGINE GENERATOR SET
DIESEL ENGINE RADIATOR
ELECTRIC POWER CABLE CONNECTOR
DIESEL ENGINE START-STOP CONTROLS

PACIFIC FRUIT EXPRESS CO.
SAN FRANCISCO, CALIF.
MECHANICAL & ENGINEERING DEPT.

Courtesy of Pacific Fruit Express Co.

FIG. ... CUTAWAY DIAGRAM OF MECHANICALLY-REFRIGERATED RAIL CAR

position it senses the average temperature of the load compartment, provided that the air has circulated through a major part of the load before returning to the evaporator.

Most of the thermostats have multiple switches which act in sequence during temperature reduction to unload the compressor, reduce speed in multi-speed systems, or to stop the compressor. If commodity temperatures drop below the thermostat setting, the heating system will be activated. Thermostats are either of the electric resistance bulb and bridge system or mechanical with activation by a mercury-filled system.

Temperature indicators, to give outside readings of inside air temperatures, may use mercury in a pressure tube to move a dial pointer, or toluene under pressure with three brass bellows to actuate the dial pointer, in which case two of the bellows perform compensating functions for temperature changes in the tubing and case. The Canadian railroads use the bellows type indicator with one dial for top-air temperatures and another to indicate bottom-air temperature.

Temperature Records   Shippers or receivers of produce sometimes want to have their own record of temperature in the car during its journey to market. Such records can be obtained with instruments which can be purchased by the user or rented by the trip or month. Several instruments are available, some showing only maximum and minimum temperatures attained while in use, and others providing a continuous temperature record on a tape. At least two recording instruments, the Ryan Recorder (Fig. 13.4) and the Therma-Gard, are available to the produce industry. Both are small, compact units which, properly maintained and operated, provide dependable records of transit temperatures.

Location of the instrument in the loaded car is important, particularly since only one instrument per car is ordinarily used. Placing the instrument in one of the produce containers is preferable to attachment on a side wall because the air delivery temperature above the load is often substantially lower than commodity temperature in the load. However, there can never be certainty that one air or commodity record within the car reflects average commodity temperatures.

Heating Equipment   When outside temperatures are low, as in winter shipments, a source of heat is essential for maintenance of the desired load temperature. Most of the mechanical refrigerator cars have electric heaters with a total heating capacity of about 9000 watts. These are used both for heating the load when necessary and for

Courtesy of Ryan Instruments, Inc.

FIG. 13.4. COMPACT RECORDING THERMOMETER FOR OBTAIN-
ING TRANSIT TEMPERATURES

defrosting the evaporator coils. The reverse cycle system, which di-
verts hot refrigerant gas directly from the compressor to the
evaporator during the defrost period, is used in a few mechanical cars.

Protective Services   Most of the fresh vegetables and melons
shipped in mechanically-refrigerated cars come under one of three
tariff rules. The commonest of these is comparable to "Standard Refrigeration" in the RS-type car and charges per carload are comparable. The shipper specifies the optimum temperature desired in transit
and whether or not the shipment was precooled before loading. The
carrier then assumes responsibility for operation of the mechanical
unit and maintenance of the desired temperature during transit. A
second service corresponds roughly to "Modified Refrigeration" in the
RS car. The shipper may specify the points enroute during which the
mechanical unit is to be operated. The protective service charge is

based on the point from which service is initiated to destination, or from origin to point at which service is terminated. A third service, often used for cantaloups and leafy vegetables, is body icing in conjunction with mechanical protective service. For those mechanical cars which are equipped with open floor racks and floor drains, crushed ice may be placed in the body of the car after loading. If all the ice is not melted before the car is accepted for transport, an extra charge is made for transporting the ice.

Top Ice in Mechanical Cars   The use of crushed ice over and through the load is general practice for such highly perishable products as celery, broccoli and sweet corn. The presence of crushed ice in the load presents no special problem in the ice bunker (RS) car, but with the advent of mechanical refrigeration systems in rail cars, snow ice in the lading is responsible for some poor performance.

In the ice bunker car the circulating air is normally above the freezing point of water, but in the mechanically-refrigerated cars air delivered from the cooling unit can be below $0°$ C ($32°$ F), even with a thermostat setting of $1.5°$ C ($34°$ F). Sub-freezing air moving over the top of the load will prevent the crushed ice from melting. The congealed ice not only interferes with normal air circulation through the lading, but by failing to melt, it defeats the purpose of providing additional refrigeration and supplying moisture to the commodity.

The same problem occurs when top ice is applied completely over the load for precooling. A modified top icing system called "windrowed" top icing has largely resolved the problem of blocked air circulation by applying the crushed ice in such a way that openings are left between lengthwise rows of containers (see *Precooling*, Chap. 10).

Carbon Dioxide Accumulation   Some of the newer mechanically-refrigerated cars are so well sealed that atmosphere modification may occur when products with relatively high respiration rates are transported to market. Increased CO_2 levels in carlots of head lettuce have been related to a disorder known as brown stain (Stewart *et al*. 1972). Later studies (Stewart *et al*. 1973) determined that propping open one of the two water drains at each end of the car prevented the accumulation of damaging levels of CO_2 during transit.

Liquified and Solidified Gas Refrigerant in Transit   Over the years many attempts have been made to use the direct refrigeration, obtainable from the evaporation of liquid N_2 or the sublimation of solid CO_2, for the transit protection of fresh and frozen produce (Harvey 1967). Relatively few cars so equipped are now in service. Many systems have been tried, some of which have expanded the refrigerant directly into the load compartment through nozzles mounted on a pipe header on the car ceiling. A serious problem with this system is that velocity from the ceiling nozzles is not sufficient to provide good air circulation through the load, especially when space between stacks or rows are minimal. When the ceiling nozzles are augmented by forced-air circulation, particularly with the addition of some heat-exchanger coils in the side walls or under the floor racks, temperature distribution is much improved. When N_2 or CO_2 gas is released into the load compartment, a modification of the car atmosphere occurs. The extent of this modification depends upon refrigeration demand and the tightness of the car structure. Such modification may be desirable or undesirable, depending upon the tolerance of the commodity carried and the potential of the equipment to control the atmosphere within desirable limits.

Liquid N_2 and solid CO_2 can also be expanded within a closed system, with the heat transfer from finned coils or sealed ducts, or they may be expanded to cool a secondary refrigerant (such as ethylene glycol), which is then circulated through heat exchangers.

Expendable or closed liquid- or solid-gas systems have the advantage of simplicity of design and operation and great cooling capacity. However, the cost per ton of refrigeration is consistently higher with either liquid N_2 or solid CO_2 than with ice or mechanical refrigeration. Additionally, supplies of these materials are not always available where and when needed. When atmospheres are modified by released gases, there is some hazard to personnel entering the load compartment before normal atmospheres are restored.

CARGO UNITIZATION

Palletization

The increasing cost of labor in producing areas and terminal markets has heightened interest in handling, shipping and receiving fresh fruits and vegetables in palletized loads. Produce associations have been studying pallet-shipping container compatability through special committees for several years, and have encouraged research on the subject by industry and government.

The principal problems in converting to palletized loading and handling of fresh vegetables have been: (1) Most of the shipping containers in general use do not make maximum use of the preferred 48 × 40 in. pallet (comparable to the 120 × 100 cm pallet favored in Europe). (2)

Many produce shippers favor a 110×90 cm (42×35 in.) pallet, but most receivers are equipped to handle 120×100 cm pallets. (3) The larger pallet does not use the space in a rail car as economically as the smaller pallet, but loads on the larger pallet have been found to shift less in truck transport than those on the smaller pallets.

Despite problems of container and pallet dimensions the move toward palletized loads in the western produce areas has increased tremendously in the past few years (Fig. 13.5). During 1975 more than 50% of all fresh fruits and vegetables shipped from California were on pallets (Anon. 1976).

Continuing problems with palletization are: the cost of the pallets; the space occupied in the transport vehicles by the pallets; and the problems of returning permanent pallets to the originating shippers. Various types of pallets, both permanent (wood and molded plastic) and expendable (fiberboard and expanded foam plastic), have been used experimentally. Anthony *et al.* (1975) studied 8 types of pallets for transport of 22.5 kg (50 lb) bags of potatoes. Three permanent pallets were completely satisfactory for maintaining load alignment, but none of the expendable were rated as satisfactory. One California lettuce shipper has satisfac-

Courtesy of Bud Antle, Inc.

FIG. 13.5.   CONTAINERS OF HEAD LETTUCE, PALLETIZED IN THE FIELD, BEING LOADED FOR TRANSPORT IN A REFRIGERATED TRAILER

torily resolved the pallet puzzle by changing the carton size to fit the 120 × 100 cm (48 × 40 in.) pallet, and using permanent, returnable pallets which are sold to the customer. If the pallet is returned it is repurchased at ⅔ of the original price.

Pallet loads often require some type of stabilization, particularly if the containers are bulged or spaced for air circulation. Both metal and plastic strapping with suitable fasteners are available for this purpose. The strapping can be applied manually with hand tools, or with a totally automatic mechanical system.

Slip Sheets

Sheets of fiberboard, corrugated paperboard or plastic have been used for many years for the mechanized handling of stacked cases of processed foods. The produce industry has recently begun experimenting with this method of handling for fresh fruits and vegetables. Slip sheets are cheaper than wooden pallets, which eases the disposal or return problem that has slowed conventional palletization.

The principal problem in conversion from wooden pallets to slip sheets is in the special equipment needed to handle loads on slip sheets. The standard forklift will not pick up these loads. Special lift units, or adapting attachments, for handling slip-sheet loads are expensive. Additionally both shipper and receiver must be equipped to handle slip sheets. A shipper who wants to convert to slip-sheet loading may find that his customers cannot handle them.

In view of the apparent advantages in material cost and space economy of slip sheets, as compared with wooden pallets, it seems that they will be used to a greater extent in the years ahead.

Pallet Bins

Another approach to the handling and transport of fresh vegetables is the pallet-based bin. Nailed wood, wirebound veneer and fiberboard bins have been tested for such diverse crops as watermelons, tomatoes, lettuce, cantaloups, Honey Dew melons and consumer-bagged potatoes and onions. Potential economies exist in mechanized handling of large units—a common bin size is 120 × 100 × 91 cm deep (48 × 40 × 36 in.)—from the origin shipper directly to the terminal repacker, or even to the retail store.

The problems which have prevented widespread use of pallet bins are: (1) cost of the bins and the difficulty of returning them to origin; (2) potential cooling problems with a large mass of product in a single

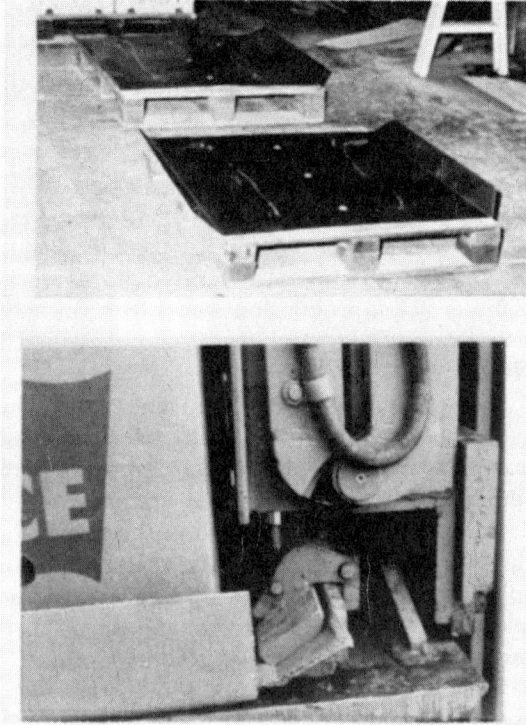

U.S. Dept. of Agriculture Photo

FIG. 13.6.   UPPER: SLIP SHEETS ON PALLETS
Note raised tab on ends of slip sheets.
LOWER: CLAMP ON PUSH-PULL ATTACHMENT OF
FORKLIFT TRUCK HOLDS TAB
Stack of boxes on slip sheet has been pulled from pallets onto
tines of forklift truck for loading.

container; and (3) acceptability by retailers as a display vehicle for fresh
produce. Some progress has been made in developing light-weight and
collapsible bins with minimum space occupancy for return shipment.

There appears to be practical application of pallet-based bins for
produce shipments to terminal repackers, and for wholesale-retail distribution of 2.3 and 4.6 kg (5 and 10 lb) bags of potatoes and of large
items such as watermelons, winter squash and Honey Dew melons.
Research is underway in Maine with a combination shipping
container-retail display unit for consumer packs of potatoes. Designed
to fit the standard pallet 120 × 100 cm (48 × 40 in.) it consists of
reinforced corrugated fiberboard containers 61 × 100 × 64 cm (24 × 40

× 25 in.). These are stacked 2 wide and 2 high on the pallet and strapped for stability. Instructions are included in each container for utilization as a retail display (Hallee and Sides 1976).

Bulk Car Transport

Background   The changing market for potatoes has stimulated interest in newer and more economical methods of transport. As recently as 1966, 59% of the potatoes sold in the United States were used as table stock. By 1972 53% of U.S. production was sold for processing to chips, French fries, dehydrated flakes and granules and canned potatoes (U.S. Dept. Agr. 1975).

The processors, particularly the chip manufacturers whose plants are usually in major cities, are naturally interested in obtaining their raw material as cheaply as possible. Most of the chippers handle potatoes in bulk, often in pallet bins in the plant. They are not interested in paying for shipping containers and prefer to avoid the cost of handling individual containers during unloading and in the warehouse.

This situation has led directly to an interest in and development of equipment and services for the bulk transportation of potatoes from producers to processing plants (Hudson 1970).

The principal justifications for a bulk transport system for potatoes and other adapted perishable commodities are: (1) economies of operation through mechanized loading and unloading; (2) elimination of costly shipping containers that also interfere with heat transfer during transit; and (3) improved transit environment for the product by circulating air directly to each unit of the product instead of around the containers.

Modified RS Cars   During a period when many RS-type cars are being replaced by mechanically-refrigerated equipment, there is incentive for the railroads to find other uses for these older cars. At least one railroad has accomplished this by modification of some RS cars for bulk transport of potatoes.

The Burlington Northern Railroad had in service, in 1970, 840 RS cars converted for bulk transport, primarily of processing potatoes (Hudgens 1970). Some potatoes for repacking at market are also hauled in these cars. The conversion to bulk transport is accomplished by the addition of rod-chain conveyors on the floor for unloading purposes and slope boards on the side walls. A lengthwise conveyor extends from the bunker wall in each end of the car to the doorway area. In the doorway a crosswise conveyor removes the potatoes to portable conveying equipment outside of the car for loading into trucks, pallet bins, or directly onto the processing line. Slope boards extending from the edge of the longitudinal conveyor to a few feet up the side walls assure a flow of tubers onto the conveyor belt (Fig. 13.7). The bunkers are retained in these cars so that ice or heaters can be placed in them, as required by the season. Loading of the cars is accomplished through the doorway with portable conveyors which are somewhat similar to the bin fillers used in potato storages. Loading equipment must be supplied by the shipper since it is not built into the car.

Modified Insulated Box Cars   As mentioned earlier, a few insulated box cars with underslung heaters are in use by railroads of the United States for winter transport of potatoes. Similar equipment is widely used by the Canadian railroads. About 75 of these cars have been converted for bulk transport by the Bangor and Aroostook Railroad in Maine. Conveyors are permanently installed in these cars for both loading and unloading. Potatoes are loaded through the doorway by two independently operated belt conveyors, one extending into each end of the car from the doorway. Cables suspend these conveyors from the

Courtesy of Burlington Northern Railroad

FIG. 13.7.   INTERIOR OF ICE-REFRIGERATED RAIL CAR MODIFIED FOR BULK TRANSPORT OF POTATOES
Slope sheets to direct product to conveyors in floor.

ceiling, permitting them to be raised as loading progresses. A movable, padded diverter is mounted on each loading conveyor to discharge the potatoes where needed for uniform distribution. Unloading is accomplished by the operation of fixed rod-chain conveyors on the car floor, cross conveyors at the doorway, and slope sheets at the side walls, essentially the same system as used in converted RS cars. These bunkerless cars are used only for winter service. When heat is required, it can be provided under the floor from a heater beneath the car.

Converted Mechanical Refrigerator Cars　A car line serving important fall-crop potato areas has converted one hundred 15.5 m (50 ft) mechanically-refrigerated cars to multi-use for hauling potatoes in bulk, bags or boxes. The conversion was accomplished by installing longitudinal chain conveyors down the center of the car. These converge at the doorway, where a transverse conveyor carries the tubers from the car to a conveyor installed by the receiver for unloading. The receiver also supplies the loading conveyors and the power for conveyor operation.

Removable boards cover the conveyors during loading and are removed as the bulk potatoes are unloaded. Floor boards are sloped from the sides of the car when bulk potatoes are loaded, so that the tubers will flow to the center conveyor during unloading. When bags or boxes of potatoes, or other perishables, are loaded the cover boards are flat on the floor. Advantages are the multi-use feature and the thermostatically controlled temperature (Anon. 1972).

Modified Covered Hopper Cars　The "Conditionaire" car is an externally-insulated modification of the "Center Flow" covered hopper car. Equipment has been added for air circulation, refrigeration and heating. A diesel-generator power unit is located at one end of the car, and a unitized refrigeration and heating package at the other end. The funnel shape of each of the three hoppers provides space at each end of the car for the power and temperature control units, and space between hoppers is sufficient for the fuel tank. Urethane foam is sprayed on all exterior surfaces of the car for insulation. Two large railways in the United States now operate 161 of these special cars (Anon. 1973B).

Air circulation through the hoppers is provided by a 5 hp blower which moves air through hollow sills along each side of the car near the bottom of the hoppers. The refrigerated or heated air is discharged into openings on each side of each hopper and moves up through the commodity before returning across the top of the loads to the temperature control unit and blower. Excellent commodity temperatures can be maintained because air moves uniformly through the load and the absence of shipping containers enables intimate contact between air and product.

Each hopper is loaded through a top hatch opening and unloaded by gravity flow through a sliding gate at the bottom of the hopper.

The car was originally designed primarily for movement of potatoes for processing or repacking in consumer packages at market. However, a number of shipments, in cooperation with commercial repackers and processors, have shown that packaged and bulk carrots, and dry onions can be economically transported in the Conditionaire car (Ryall 1970).

Courtesy of ACF Industries, Inc.

FIG. 13.8.   MECHANICALLY-REFRIGERATED HOPPER CAR FOR BULK TRANSPORT OF PRODUCE

Courtesy of ACF Industries, Inc.

FIG. 13.9.   LOADING BULK HOPPER CAR THROUGH TOP
HATCH OPENINGS

REFRIGERATED TRUCKS AND TRAILERS

Background

Three general types of equipment, with numerous variations within types, are used for over-the-road transport of fresh vegetables and melons (Ashby 1970). These include trucks with a refrigerated load compartment carried on a conventional truck chassis; refrigerated trailers, usually 12 to 14 m (40 to 45 ft) long and hauled by separate power units, the tractors; and refrigerated containers from 6 to 12 m (20 to 40 ft) long which can be attached to a truck or trailer chassis, carried on a rail flatcar, a ship's deck or hold, or even in the cargo compartment of large aircraft.

Definite figures on total refrigerated vehicles of these types are not available, but probably more than 200,000 units are used in the United States for the transport of fresh and frozen foods.

Ice Refrigeration

Some trucks and trailers hauling fresh produce are refrigerated with water ice, but the number of such units is rapidly declining. Ice bunkers are located in the front end, usually with a fan driven by a separate engine to move air through the ice and into the load compartment. Uncertainty of ice supplies, delays for icing, and lack of adequate temperature control have contributed to the decline in this equipment. These same trucks and trailers are commonly used for top ice service when products such as leafy vegetables are carried. Keeping such products wet is usually an advantage and the presence of an adequate supply of crushed ice assures low temperatures for vegetables in the upper layers of the load. However, the bottom layers of the load often do not receive adequate refrigeration, particularly if the truck bodies are not well insulated.

Such equipment may also be used under ventilation during seasons when ambient temperatures are at or below desired product temperatures. Ventilation is commonly done by opening small doors at the front and rear of the vehicle so that the air current caused by the forward movement of the unit will force air through the load compartment. Since the driver must operate the ventilation doors, the success of this system depends largely on his judgment and interest.

Mechanical Refrigeration

Most of the refrigerated trucks, trailers, and containers now in service for hauling perishable products have thermostatically controlled temperature, provided by mechanical refrigeration equipment and a heating unit.

Such equipment is usually driven by its own engine, often with an auxiliary electric motor for standby operation on plug-in power. Some units are mounted on the nose of the trailer. Others extend over the roof of the tractor and some are mounted beneath the trailer. The power source and condensing unit are on the outside of the insulated body, while the evaporator is on the inside. The two sections are separated by an insulated plug which is attached to the vehicle wall and which supports the various parts of the cooling unit.

Units for trailers weigh from 360 to 690 kg (800 to 1500 lb), and have a refrigeration capacity ranging from 5000 to 8750 kcal (20,000 to 35,000 Btu) per hr at a load compartment temperature of 2° C (35° F) in an ambient temperature of 38° C (100° F). Truck units of similar type weigh from 180 to 360 kg (400 to 800 lb) with somewhat less refrigeration capacity than those used in the larger trailers. As is true with most mechanical refrigeration equipment for transport vehicles, refrigeration capacity is inadequate for rapid precooling of warm loads. The more perishable products, which require continuous temperatures near 0° C (32° F) for satisfactory delivery, must be precooled before loading (McKee 1966).

Insulation   Some of the older produce trucks and trailers had granular fill material as insulation in the side walls. As this material settled, areas were left with no insulation. More recently, fiberglass batts or sheets of expanded polystyrene have been widely used. The use of foamed-in-place plastics, principally polyurethane, is rapidly increasing. A thorough job of foaming in such material will more completely fill all wall and ceiling areas than any other system of insulation. Additionally, thinner wall construction is possible because when high molecular weight gas is used in the foam, k factors of 0.18 or lower are possible.

Refrigerated trucks and trailers are commonly designed for transporting both fresh and frozen foods. Specifications for such equipment commonly require 6 in. of an insulating material with a k factor of lower than 0.3 (Cal per hr per 900 cm² per 2.5 cm) (Btu per hr per sq ft per in. of insulation thickness). If the vehicles are to be used only for maintaining temperatures of 0° C (32° F) or above, 5 to 10 cm (2 to 4 in.) of approved insulating material are sufficient.

Insulation in the floor of over-the-road vehicles is particularly important. Actual road tests have shown that engine waste heat and radiation from hot road surfaces in the summer months will raise the under-floor surface temperature as much as 11.5° C (20° F) above ambient air. Either wood or metal floors must be sealed against water penetration. Satisfactory insulating materials for floors are corkboard, or expanded polystyrene or rubber. When used in a floor, these materials must be sealed with hydrolene or emulsified asphalt.

Interior walls of trucks or trailers may be of plywood, metal, or glass-reinforced plastics. Vertically corrugated materials may be used on interior walls to provide channels for air movement.

Air leakage into the truck or trailer body can be a critical source of heat gain. Road tests of 10.5 m (35 ft) commercial trailers have shown air leakage rates as high as 42.5 m³ (1500 cu ft) per hr at 80 km per hr (50 mph). Much of this is caused from ram or static pressure caused by the motion of the vehicle. To minimize this problem, all exterior surfaces of an insulated body must be made as nearly air and water vapor tight as possible. The foamed-in-place plastic insulation is probably the most effective sealing method. Two other methods can be used for sealing the metal skin of trailers and insulated containers. One is addition of a nonpermeable vapor barrier to the inside of the exterior wall. Aluminum foil or Mylar film with sealed joints and a plastic binder are satisfactory. A second method involves coating the inside of the exterior wall with a vapor-sealing compound, such as neoprene. It is particularly important that the vapor seal not be broken where wiring, piping, or frames penetrate the exterior surface.

The inner wall of a refrigerated vehicle need not be vapor tight, but it must be water resistant to facilitate cleaning. Any water vapor entering through the outer wall will remain in the insulation unless it can pass through the inner wall and condense on the evaporating coils. A practical combination of outer and inner walls is one in which the small amount of water vapor entering from outside is balanced with the rate of transfer from the interior of the wall of the evaporator. Water accumulating in the insulation will not only increase heat transfer through the wall, but will also add to the tare weight of the vehicle.

Air Circulation   Forced-air circulation in the body of a refrigerated vehicle is essential for maintenance of desired commodity temperatures. Fresh vegetables and melons are producing some vital heat, even when thoroughly precooled before shipment. This heat must be picked up by moving refrigerated air through all parts of the load and, as nearly as possible, past at least two surfaces of each shipping container. The only way this can be done is to have the containers spaced for free air access, to have a sufficient volume and velocity of air to reach all containers, and to have the air directed in such a way that it will not bypass some parts of the load.

Almost all refrigerated trucks, trailers and containers have the evaporator coils and the air blower located in the front end of the load chamber. Air released directly from the blower has a tendency to short circuit, returning to the cooling unit instead of moving to the far end of the load compartment. Thus the front end of the load is well refrigerated, while products near the rear receive little air. In order to overcome this deficiency, most of the newer refrigerated units have air ducts attached to the ceiling. Air is moved from the blower through the ducts toward the rear of the load compartment, from whence most of the air must return to the evaporator through or around the entire load.

In addition to vital heat from fresh produce, there is always some heat leakage through the floor, walls and ceiling of the load compartment whenever outside ambient temperatures are above those in the interior. Air channels along the side walls and under the load will permit much of this leaked heat to be carried directly to the refrigerating surface rather than raising the commodity temperature. Side wall flues or vertically corrugated walls will take care of the side wall problem. Many vehicles are equipped with formed metal floors which provide limited channels for air movement along the length of the vehicle. Most of these do not provide sufficient space for a free air flow. Some vehicles, particularly those used for transporting frozen foods, have an air flue located between a false floor and the permanent floor, a system that would probably be desirable for all refrigerated trucks and trailers.

Since air always flows in the path of least resistance, it is important that channels be provided where air flow is needed. Longitudinal air channels through the load are highly desirable for fresh products. Load patterns have been designed to meet this need (Hinds and Robertson 1965). When lengthwise load channels are provided, a space must be left inside the back door for air to enter the channels. This can be accomplished by placing a false bulkhead with vertical stringers against the rear stack of the load to hold it away from the rear doors.

If sufficient space is provided between the stacks or rows of containers in the load, air can move vertically and diagonally through the load and provision for longitudinal air channels within the load is unnecessary. Wooden shipping containers can be spaced with nailed cross strips or preformed wood spacers of several types. Stack- and row-spacing of fiberboard containers is not satisfactory with presently available materials.

Trailer on Flatcar   The TOFC service, commonly referred to as "piggy-back," is a rather recent development. Based on surveys by the Association of American Railways, about 3000 mechanically-refrigerated trailer-on-flatcar units were in service in 1963. A rather precipitous increase occurred in the late 1960s, but leveled off later. An AAR count of TOFC units transporting fresh and frozen produce on U.S. railroads as of January 1, 1977 showed 2583 owned by railroads and car lines, with 1573 more owned by users, for a total of 4156. The advantages of TOFC units are convenience, flexibility, economy of moving the units on long hauls by rail and door to door service. Produce can be loaded at a packing or precooling facility, whether located on a rail siding or not, hauled to a loading ramp, loaded onto a flatcar, moved to destination via rail, rolled off the flatcar by ramp and moved over the road directly to the wholesale or chain store distribution warehouse.

Construction, insulation, and refrigeration equipment are essentially similar to that already described for over-the-road trailers. Differences, where they exist, largely involve structural strength to resist the longitudinal shocks sometimes encountered in rail hauls, and extra size fuel tanks to keep the diesel engine operating on transcontinental trips.

Rates for this service tend to be somewhat lower than in railway refrigerator cars. This is particularly true when one shipper can load two TOFC units on a flatcar to take advantage of the flatcar rate. Under this tariff the produce shipper pays a fixed freight and protective service charge for the two trailer loads, regardless of the quantity of product carried. The obvious hazard of this rate system, or any per-van or per-car rate, is the strong temptation it presents to overload, resulting

Courtesy of Pacific Fruit Express Co.

FIG. 13.10.   MODERN REFRIGERATED VAN
Air delivery ducts are on ceiling, floor ducts for lengthwise or crosswise air movement, and corrugations on side walls for vertical air movement.

in interference with air circulation, and the possibility of increased physical damage to the product.

Refrigerated Containers   The refrigerated cargo container for perishable commodities is essentially an insulated box equipped with refrigeration and heating equipment for maintenance of a preset cargo temperature (ASHRAE 1974). The container differs from TOFC unit mainly in the built-in arrangement for rapid and convenient detachment from the trailer chassis on which it moves over the road. The container is equipped with corner fittings for attachment of lifting devices. When loaded onto a flatcar, ship's deck, or the hold of a specially-designed container ship, it is lifted from the chassis by crane for placement on the container carrier. Containers do not have front and rear ventilation hatches as do most refrigerated trailers.

Courtesy of Pacific Fruit Express Co.

FIG. 13.11.   REFRIGERATED TRAILER-ON-FLATCAR
Refrigeration unit is beneath trailer body.

From Hinds and Bongers (1976)

FIG. 13.12.   MECHANICALLY-REFRIGERATED HIGHWAY VEHICLE USED IN EUROPE

The refrigerated container may be equipped with its own source of power, usually a diesel engine, or it may operate entirely on power provided by the conveyance on which it is carried. A common arrangement provides an engine to power the temperature-control equipment while the containers are carried on a trailer chassis or a flatcar, and a plug-in electric power system for operation on shipboard.

This type of protection for fresh produce is now widely used, particularly where a combination of land and sea transport is required. The principal advantages of containerization are: (1) less physical damage to the products and reduced pilferage, as a result of continuous transport in one unit; (2) better maintenance of product temperature because exposures during multiple loadings and unloadings are avoided; and (3) more economical use of highway chassis because they are not attached to the containers on rail or sea transit.

Containers are usually built in standard lengths of 6, 9 or 12 m (20, 30 or 40 ft) in the United States. International size and performance standards are needed (Guilfoy 1970), but the refrigerated containers now in use are handled in most world markets without problems.

Transit Environments

The optimum postharvest temperature and RH for holding each type of vegetable and melon are given in Chapters 6, 7, 8 and 9. For prolonged storage of the less perishable products, or for brief holding of highly perishable items, close adherence to these recommended environments is essential for maintenance of quality.

However, there are situations, such as brief transit periods, when strict adherence to optimums can be relaxed a little. This is particularly true of the less perishable items which are shipped to market soon after harvest and which will move quickly through the markets to consumption. Such items as potatoes, dry onions, sweetpotatoes and tomatoes will often carry well under ventilation service, or if transported under refrigeration, with modified icing services or with thermostat settings above those recommended for storage of the commodity.

On the other hand, such highly perishable commodities as green and leafy vegetables should be maintained as closely as possible to optimum conditions even when the transit period is brief and movement to retail sale is rapid. Limiting factors in the maintenance of optimum environments for these products are the suitability of the transport vehicle for maintaining uniform temperature in the desired range, and the accuracy of the thermostat in mechanically refrigerated rail or highway equipment. Suggested temperatures to specify for shipments of a number of vegetables and melons are shown in Table 13.1.

TABLE 13.1. SUGGESTED TEMPERATURE SPECIFICATIONS AND THERMOSTAT SETTINGS FOR PRODUCE SHIPMENTS MOVING UNDER MECHANICAL REFRIGERATION OR LIQUID-FUEL HEAT

Commodity	Mechanically-refrigerated Equipment (°C)	(°F)	Liquid-fuel Heaters (°C)	(°F)
Artichokes, globe	0.5	33		—
Asparagus	2.0	35		—
Beans, snap	7.0	45		—
Broccoli	1.5	34		—
Brussels sprouts	1.5	34		—
Cabbage	1.5	34		—
Cantaloup	2.0	36		—
Carrots	0.5	33		—
Celery	1.5	34	2.0	35
Corn, sweet	1.5	34		—
Cucumbers	7.0	45		—
Honey Dew melon	7.0	45		—
Lettuce	1.5	34		—
Peppers, sweet	7.5	46	7.0	45
Potatoes				
early crop	10.0	50		—
late crop	4.5	40	4.5–7.0	40–45
late crop for chipping	10–15.5	50–60	15.5	60
Sweetpotatoes	13	55		—
Tomatoes				
mature—green	13	55	10	50
pink	7.0–10	45–50	10	49

Source: Redit (1969).

Lack of Air Circulation in Solid Loads

Interference with air circulation, from excessively heavy or solid loads, is particularly serious with nonprecooled loads in mechanically refrigerated cars or vans. A test with a solid load of warm Texas tomatoes in wirebound crates (Johnson 1963) illustrates the slow and uneven cooling obtained when air flow is restricted. With the trailer thermostat set at 15.5° C (60° F), the coolest position in the load (top layer) was only 16° C (61° F) after 72 hr in transit. The warmest position at this time (middle layer) was 21° C (70° F). In a second test, similar containers of tomatoes were loaded so that lengthwise channels were provided between all rows in the first 3 layers. After 72 hr in transit, this load had cooled to 13° C (56° F) in the top layer and 17° C (63° F) in the middle or warmest layer. Similar results have been obtained with produce in fiberboard containers. Spaced loads do not permit loading as many containers as the solid load, so with any per-car rate the cost per unit of product is greater in the spaced load; thus, the continuing tendency to heavy, solid loads with inadequate air circulation. As a general rule, tomatoes and other chilling-susceptible crops should be precooled to about 15.5° C (60° F) if product temperatures are above

From Ashby (1970)

FIG. 13.13. STACKING PATTERN FOR BAGGED ONIONS TO PERMIT UNIFORM AIR DISTRIBUTION IN HIGHWAY VAN

26.5° C (80° F) at packing. Precooling before loading is necessary if a solid load is to be placed in mechanically-refrigerated equipment.

Commodity Compatibility

As stated in previous chapters, the quality of some vegetables is maintained best at temperatures a few degrees above their freezing point. Others are seriously damaged by relatively brief exposure to temperatures below 10° C (50° F). Some are tolerant of prolonged contact with crushed ice, while others are injured by brief exposure. Leafy and most root vegetables need RH near saturation to prevent wilting, but others keep best at RH of 75% or less.

Knowledge of these different requirements and tolerances is essential to the successful shipment of mixed loads of vegetables. Additionally, produce shippers must be aware that all fruits are not compatible with vegetable shipments. Lipton and Harvey (1977) have published lists of compatible fruits and vegetables with recommended holding conditions for each group. Table 13.2 gives the recommendations for most of the fresh vegetables. When these commodities are to be in transit for more than 2 or 3 days, vegetables from one group should not be loaded with those from another.

TABLE 13.2. GROUPING OF COMPATIBLE VEGETABLES FOR TRANSPORT IN MIXED LOADS

Temperature 0° to 1.5° C (32° to 34° F) RH 95–100%		Temperature 4.5° to 7.5° C (40° to 45° F) RH 90–95%	Temperature 10° to 13° C (50° to 55° F) RH 85–90%	Temperature 13° to 18° C (55° to 65° F) RH 85–90%
Artichokes	Asparagus[1]	Snap beans[3]	Cucumbers	Potatoes, early crop
Beets	Broccoli	Okra	Eggplant	Sweetpotatoes
Brussels sprouts		Sweet peppers	Potatoes, late crop	Tomatoes, green
Cabbage	Carrots	Squash, summer	Pumpkins	Casaba melons
Cauliflower	Celeriac	Tomatoes, pink	Squash, winter	Crenshaw melons
Celery	Endive	Watermelons		Honey Dew melons
Escarole	Horseradish	Cantaloups[3]		Persian melons
Kohlrabi	Leeks			
Lettuce	Mushrooms[1]			
Onions, green[2]	Parsley			
Parsnips	Peas			
Radishes	Rhubarb			
Rutabagas	Salsify			
Spinach	Sweet corn			
Turnips	Watercress			

Source: Lipton and Harvey (1977).
[1]All except asparagus and mushrooms in Group 1 can be top iced.
[2]Green onions should not be loaded with rhubarb, mushrooms or sweet corn.
[3]Lower part of range preferable for snap beans and cantaloups.

TESTING AND RATING TRANSPORT EQUIPMENT

Railway Refrigerator Cars

Active testing of equipment for the transportation of perishable foods has been underway in the U.S. Department of Agriculture since 1905. Research with ice-refrigerated equipment during the development stage of railroad refrigerator cars was concerned largely with basic improvements in ice bunkers, floor racks, and car insulation. Later studies developed modified and half-stage icing services, newer and more effective types of insulation, and air-circulating fans.

In 1944 the United Fresh Fruit and Vegetable Association, through its Refrigerator Car Committee, fostered cooperative research with the U.S. Department of Agriculture, the railroads, and some refrigerator car lines. These studies culminated in the adoption for freight refrigerator cars of easy-riding undercarriages, steel framing, improved draft gears, practical forced-air systems, and thermostatically controlled alcohol heaters.

With the rapid development of the mechanical refrigerator car during the 1960s, the tests continued as a cooperative effort of the U.S. Department of Agriculture, the railroads, and the produce industry. These studies have largely involved refrigeration capacity, air circulation systems, and thermostatic temperature control.

While the extensive research with railway equipment has resulted in substantial advances in the transportation of perishable commodities by rail, no formal industry or government standards for such equipment exist in the United States, and except for performance tests by individual car lines, no ratings are available as a basis for the produce shippers' guidance.

Performance tests on refrigerated vehicles have been underway in western Europe for at least 20 years. Pioneer development of test procedures was done in Italy by the Italian State Railways. As early as 1951, test results were reported from Italy, Germany, and also from Australia. These dealt primarily with overall heat transfer and resulted in some generally accepted k factors for both refrigerator cars and trucks.

Trucks and Trailers

The Vehicle Testing Laboratory at Antony, France, had a truck and trailer testing program underway by about 1955. Some form of international standards has been in force since about 1950, and in 1970 a set of standards was adopted by the United Nations at Geneva. In most of the

European nations, including Poland and Czechoslovakia, performance regulations have the force of law to the extent that equipment which does not meet the national or international standards is required to be taken out of service.

A joint study by the National Bureau of Standards and the U.S. Department of Agriculture was initiated in 1957 to develop a method for measuring the cooling capacity of refrigerated trailers. The study included both laboratory testing under controlled external and internal environments and actual road tests to correlate with results under controlled conditions in the test facility. These tests resulted in publication of a rating method for refrigerated trailer bodies (Phillips *et al.* 1960).

A later study by the same organizations (Phillips and Penney 1967) developed a method and the necessary facilities for testing refrigerated truck bodies. The methods are essentially like those used for refrigerated trailers, including heat transmission and air and moisture infiltration under rather extreme controlled environments. The principal difference is in greater emphasis on solar radiation for trucks because many are used for local delivery service and are stationary a larger proportion of operating time than highway trailers.

There is no legal requirement in the United States for trucks or trailers to meet the performance standards recommended by these studies. However, most of the larger buyers of refrigerated trucks and trailers specify that the equipment be rated before purchase. If after operation of the equipment the buyer is not satisfied, he can have units retested to establish whether they are meeting the certification.

MODIFIED ATMOSPHERES IN TRANSIT

The excellent results obtained with controlled atmospheres (CA; decreased O_2 and increased CO_2 at controlled concentrations) in apple storages have greatly stimulated research and commercial interest in CA applications for other crops. Despite this wide interest and ongoing research in almost every state and country that has a postharvest research program on fruits and vegetables, practically no commercial use of CA in storage has developed for products other than apples and pears.

Interest in atmosphere modification during transportation of fresh fruits and vegetables arose originally as a by-product of trials with liquefied or solidified gases as refrigerants. Many attempts have been made to use solid CO_2 or liquid N_2 as a refrigeration source for the transit protection of perishable commodities. The sublimation of solid CO_2 or the evaporation of liquid N_2 requires heat. This process provides refrigeration by removal of heat from the exposed product. If the CO_2 or N_2 released in the refrigeration process remains in the load compartment, the concentration of O_2 is reduced and that of the released gas is increased. Modified atmospheres (MA) increase CO_2 or N_2 and decrease O_2, but not at controlled concentrations.

The effects of MA in transit on a number of fresh vegetables have been studied both in the laboratory, under simulated transit environments and periods, and in actual shipping tests (Harvey 1967; Stewart et al. 1966, 1968; Lipton 1968 A, B).

The initial hope, particularly of several producers of inert gases, was that atmosphere modification would eliminate or reduce the need for refrigeration in transit. This notion was quickly dispelled by controlled tests and by a few disastrous commercial experiences. It is now widely accepted that modified atmospheres in transit are not a satisfactory substitute for adequate precooling and optimum transit temperatures. Low O_2 or high CO_2 atmospheres, for those commodities tolerant to either or both, are only supplements to refrigeration.

Temperature Effects in MA

The degree of atmosphere modification which any vegetable will tolerate is directly related to temperature. At temperatures near the freezing point, oxygen requirement for normal respiration is low, but as temperature of the product increases, the oxygen requirement doubles, or even triples, with each 10° C (18° F) of increase. Thus, an atmosphere containing 0.5% O_2 can be beneficial to head lettuce at 0° C (32° F) during prolonged holding, but disastrous at 10° C (50° F) or higher, even for brief periods. Regardless of temperature, the complete absence of O_2 in the atmosphere will cause anaerobic respiration in fresh vegetables, with resultant fermented or obnoxious odors and flavors.

Research has shown that each kind of vegetable and melon, and sometimes even each different cultivar within a type, has its own tolerance to atmosphere modification, and its own optimum atmosphere and temperature for potentially beneficial effects. Some products are so intolerant of atmosphere modification, or so little benefited by optimum modifications, as to eliminate them from commercial application. Others, particularly highly perishable items such as asparagus, lettuce and Brussels sprouts, can derive sufficient benefits from atmosphere modification during refrigerated transit to justify the added cost. Because of the specific commodity requirements the tendency for atmosphere modification in transit is toward closer control of O_2 and CO_2, rather than simply additions of inert gases.

Commercial Use of MA in Transit

Several atmosphere modification systems for use in fresh produce transport have been developed, used in a limited way, and then largely abandoned. A system using liquid nitrogen for refrigeration and atmosphere modification never fulfilled its expectations. Refrigeration was provided by thermostatically controlled release of N_2 in the load compartment. When refrigeration demand was great the N_2 release displaced too much oxygen. When little refrigeration was needed, atmosphere modification was minimal. Undesirably wide ranges of product temperature also occurred in monitored shipments (Stewart $et\ al.$ 1966).

Another system, with limited commercial use, combined standard mechanical refrigeration and vaporization of nitrogen. The N_2 was used only for atmosphere modification. Release of N_2 was controlled by an oxygen sensor located in the air return area. A controller which responded to sensor signals could be set to maintain O_2 within a 2 to 5% concentration. These units were reasonably successful, particularly for protection of vegetable shipments in TOFC and shipboard containers to export markets.

The TransFresh Corporation has operated a commercially successful system of atmosphere modification since 1963. Initially the system was used primarily for export shipments of lettuce and strawberries. As of 1977 some 5000 mechanically-refrigerated rail car shipments are treated annually with TECTROL. Additionally, refrigerated trailer units used in roll-on/roll-off service to Hawaii, Puerto Rico and Alaska are serviced. A fairly recent development in atmosphere modification involves palletized units sealed in plastic film bags.

A prepared atmosphere is added to the refrigerator car or trailer by displacing the air with a specified mixture of N_2, CO_2, O_2 and CO (Fig. 13.14). Composition of the mixture is tailored to meet the requirements and tolerances of the product treated.

Transport vehicles used must meet air-tightness standards established by TransFresh. Additional sealing around doors is done by the company, and an overhead plastic bag in each car or trailer load is added to compensate for atmospheric pressure changes.

The atmosphere modification involves only the initial charge. No additional modification occurs in transit except that caused by respiration of the product and leakage. For products which are injured by relatively low concentrations of CO_2, bags of hydrated lime are included with the load to absorb evolved CO_2.

Courtesy of TransFresh Corp.

FIG. 13.14. MODIFIED ATMOSPHERE APPLICATION TO MECHANICALLY-REFRIGERATED RAIL CAR

Mobile equipment provides predetermined gas mixture to replace air in load compartment.

REFERENCES

Rail Transport

ANON. 1972. WFE reefers tailored to handle bulk potatoes. Ry. Age *173*, No. 10, 29.

ANON. 1973A. Bulk car saves money. The Packer *80*, No. 24, 5A.

ANON. 1973B. Perishables: bulk shipping pays off. Ry. Age *174*, No. 8, 51–52.

ASHRAE. 1974. Railway refrigerator cars. ASHRAE Handbook Product Direct., Applications. *46*, 46.1–46.12.

ASSOC. OF AMERICAN RAILROADS. 1974. Freight loss and damage. Freight Claim Div., Chicago. *FCD-2347*.

BARGER, W. R., HARVEY, J. M., and RINGEL, S. M. 1959. Transit temperatures of California mature-green tomatoes shipped by rail. U.S. Dept. Agr. Mktg. Res. Rept. *349*.

BARGER, W. R., HARVEY, J. M., STEWART, J. K., CEPONIS, M. J., and LIPTON, W. J. 1960. California asparagus—effect of transit environments on market quality. U.S. Dept. Agr. Mktg. Res. Rept. *428*.

BARGER, W. R., and McKILLOP, A. A. 1957. A railway transportation test with California early potatoes. U.S. Dept. Agr. *AMS-160*.

BARGER, W. R., and RADSPINNER, W. A. 1956. Transit refrigeration studies with California prepackaged carrots. U.S. Dept. Agr. *AMS-97*.

BARGER, W. R., STEWART, J. K., HARVEY, J. M., CEPONIS, M. J., MORRIS, L. L., and KASMIRE, R. F. 1958. Transit temperatures of California lettuce. U.S. Dept. Agr. Mktg. Res. Rept. *285*.

BREAKIRON, P. L., NICHOLAS, C. J., STEWART, J. K., and KURTENACK-ER, R. S. 1967. Reducing transport damage in top-iced shipments of fresh vegetables in bushel baskets. (A study of rail shipments of fresh peas). U.S. Dept. Agr. Mktg. Res. Rept. *772*.

HARVEY, J. M. 1967. Modified atmospheres in transit. *In* United Fresh Fruit and Vegetable Association Yearbook. pp. 193–194, 196, 199. United Fresh Fruit and Vegetable Assoc., Washington, D.C.

HINDS, R. H., JR., and BONGERS, A. J. 1976. Highway and railroad equipment for transporting perishables in Europe. U.S. Dept. Agr. Mktg. Res. Rept. *1061*.

HRUSCHKA, H. W. 1959. Protecting Maine potatoes from freezing, overheating, and bruising during rail transport. Maine Agr. Expt. Sta. Misc. Rept. *89*.

HUDGENS, H. H., JR. 1970. Burlington Northern Co., St. Paul, Minn. Personal Communication.

HUDSON, D. E. 1970. Maintaining the quality of bulk potatoes shipped by rail from the Red River Valley in winter. U.S. Dept. Agr. *ARS 51-40*.

KASMIRE, R. F. 1975. Solid loads pose cooling problem. Western Grower and Shipper. *46*, No. 6, 16–17.

LIPTON, W. J. 1968A. Low O₂ atmospheres, benefits and dangers. *In* United Fresh Fruit and Vegetable Association Yearbook. pp. 99–100, 103. United Fresh Fruit and Vegetable Assoc., Washington, D.C.

LIPTON, W. J. 1968B. Market quality of asparagus—effects of maturity at harvest, and of high carbon dioxide atmospheres during simulated transit. U.S. Dept. Agr. Mktg. Res. Rept. *817*.

McKEE, R. F. 1966. Handling of fresh fruits, melons, and vegetables in mechanically refrigerated equipment. Proc. Intern. Conf. on Handling Perishable Agr. Commod. Purdue Univ., Lafayette, Ind., 59–62.

McKEE, R. F. 1971. Personal communication. San Francisco, Calif.

PALMIERI, D. 1955. Measurement of k transfer coefficient, methods and comparison. Proc. Ninth Intern. Cong. Refrig. *2*, Sec. 7, 106.

PENNEY, R. W., and GUILFOY, R. F. 1959. Laboratory tests of refrigerator cars for perishable foods. U.S. Dept. Agr. Mktg. Res. Rept. *365*.

PRATT, H. K., MORRIS, L. L., RYALL, A. L., and FRIEDMAN, B. A. 1957. Tests of modified protective services in the transportation of Honey Dew melons from California to New York City. Calif. Agr. Expt. Sta. Veg. Crops Ser. *90*.

REDIT, W. H. 1969. Protection of rail shipments of fruits and vegetables. U.S. Dept. Agr. Handbook *195*.

RIES, R. A., and TOKO, H. V. 1965. Bulk handling and quality evaluation of potatoes shipped in conveyorized railroad cars. U.S. Dept. Agr. *ARS 52-8*.

RYALL, A. L. 1953. Refrigeration of California early potatoes. Kern County Potato Growers Assn. Yearbook *9*, 1–5.

RYALL, A. L. 1970. Bulk transport in the marketing of fresh vegetables. Western Grower and Shipper *41*, No. 4, 24–26.

SCHLEY, L. D. 1967. Developments in rail transportation of perishables. Proc. Fruit and Veg. Perishables Handling Conf., Univ. Calif., Davis. 51–55.

STEWART, J. K., and CEPONIS, M. J. 1962. Transit temperatures and quality of cantaloups—effect of load size and icing service on rail shipments. U.S. Dept. Agr. Mktg. Res. Rept. *554*.

STEWART, J. K., CEPONIS, M. J., and BERAHA, L. 1970. Modified-atmosphere effects on the market quality of lettuce shipped by rail. U.S. Dept. Agr. Mktg. Res. Rept. *863*.

STEWART, J. K., CEPONIS, M. J., and BILLETER, B. A. 1973. Ventilation of mechanical refrigerator cars to prevent carbon dioxide accumulation and brown stain in lettuce loads. U.S. Dept. Agr. Mktg. Res. Rept. *978*.

STEWART, J. K., and HARVEY, J. M. 1967. Temperatures, relative humidity, and atmosphere composition in a mechanically refrigerated car and a trailer loaded with lettuce. U.S. Dept. Agr. *ARS 51-13*.

STEWART, J. K., HARVEY, J. M., CEPONIS, M. J., and WRIGHT, W. R. 1972. Carbon dioxide levels in railcars and their effect on lettuce. U.S. Dept. Agr. Mktg. Res. Rept. *937*.

STEWART, J. K., KAUFMAN, J., and BURTON, C. L. 1968. Temperatures, relative humidity and market quality of early potatoes shipped in ice-bunker and mechanically refrigerated rail cars. Potato Growers Assoc. of Calif. Yearbook, 55, 57, 59, 61, 63.

Highway Transport

ASHBY, B. H. 1970. Protecting perishable foods during transport by motor truck. U.S. Dept. Agr. Handbook *105*.

ASHRAE. 1974. Trucks, trailers and containers. ASHRAE Handbook Product Direct. Applications. *45*, 45.1–45.14.

BIALES, A., and MOFFITT, T. 1970. A bonded-block loading pattern for refrigerated van container shipments of radishes. U.S. Dept. Agr. *ARS 52-50*.

BLACK, W. R. 1968. Loading patterns for ventilated rail and truck shipments of dry onions. U.S. Dept. Agr *ARS 52-30*.

BLEVINS, M.W. 1973. Trucks offer speed and flexibility. The Packer *90*, No. 22, 7.

BREAKIRON, P. L. 1974. A definitive approach to engineering-improved refrigerated trailer vans and containers. Trans. Am. Soc. Agr. Eng. *17*, 38–41, 45.

CAMPBELL, P. 1972. Strong move to transport by truck. The Packer 79, No. 17, 13, 17.

CHIASSON, A. E. 1964. Perishables riding piggyback. Proc. Fruit and Veg. Perishables Handling Conf., Univ. Calif., Davis. 88–92.

DARLOT, A., and PERRIN, J. 1955. Measurement of the k factor of a refrigerated vehicle by two methods, influence of the water content of the insulation. Proc. 9th Intern. Congr. Refrig. 2, Sec. 7, 122.

FRANC, K. 1969. Liquid nitrogen refrigeration—economy and profitability of refrigerating systems. Intern. Inst. Refrig. Bull. (Vienna) Annex 1965-3, 63–68.

GUILFOY, R. F. 1970. Impending European standard for vehicles used to transport perishable foods. U.S. Dept. Agr. ARS 52-59.

HARVEY, J. M. 1967. Modified atmospheres in transit. In United Fresh Fruit and Vegetable Association Yearbook. pp. 193–194, 196, 199. United Fresh Fruit and Vegetable Assoc., Washington, D.C.

HARVEY, J. M., and STEWART, J. K. 1964. Research on transit temperatures in piggyback trailers. Proc. Fruit and Veg. Perishables Handling Conf., Univ. Calif., Davis. 92–96.

HINDS, R. H., JR., and ROBERTSON, J. K. 1965. Airflow loading patterns for truck shipments of early potatoes. U.S. Dept. Agr. Mktg. Res. Rept. 689.

JOHNSON, H. B. 1963. Truck-rail and sea-land shipping tests with Texas fruits and vegetables. U.S. Dept. Agr. Mktg. Res. Rept. 589.

LIPTON, W. J., and HARVEY, J. M. 1977. Compatibility of fruits and vegetables during transport in mixed loads. U.S. Dept. Agr. Mktg. Res. Rept. 1070.

McKEE, R. F. 1966. Handling of fresh fruits, melons, and vegetables in mechanically refrigerated equipment. Proc. Intern. Conf. on Handling Perishable Agr. Commod. Purdue Univ., Lafayette, Ind. 59–62.

MEFFERT, H. F. T., and van VLIET, P. 1971. Experimental methods for evaluation of air circulation in containers. Proc. 13th Intern. Cong. Refrig. (Washington, D.C.) 4, 501–506.

MELBY, E. 1967. Developments in truck transportation of perishables. Proc. Fruit and Veg. Perishables Handling Conf., Univ. Calif., Davis. 55–60.

PHILLIPS, C. W., GODDARD, W. F., ACHENBACH, P. R., JOHNSON, H. D., and PENNEY, R. W. 1960. A rating method for refrigerated trailer bodies hauling perishable foods. U.S. Dept. Agr. Mktg. Res. Rept. 433.

PHILLIPS, C. W., and PENNEY, R. W. 1967. Development of a method for testing and rating refrigerated truck bodies. U.S. Dept. Agr. Tech. Bull. 1376.

STEWART, J. K., and CEPONIS, M. J. 1968. Effects of transit temperatures and modified atmospheres on market quality of lettuce shipped in nitrogen-refrigerated and mechanically-refrigerated trailers. U.S. Dept. Agr. Mktg. Res. Rept. 832.

STEWART, J. K., HARVEY, J. M., CEPONIS, M. J., and WRIGHT, W. R. 1966. Nitrogen—its effect on transit temperatures and market quality of western lettuce shipped in piggyback trailers. U.S. Dept. Agr. Mktg. Res. Rept. 759.

STEWART, J. K., KAUFMAN, J., and BURTON, C. L. 1968. Temperatures, relative humidity and market quality of early potatoes shipped in ice-bunker and mechanically refrigerated rail cars. Potato Growers Assoc. of Calif. Yearbook. 55, 57, 59, 61, 63.

Cargo Unitization

ANON. 1973. Unitization for the industry: challenges and solutions. *In* United Fresh Fruit and Vegetable Association Yearbook. pp. 123–124. United Fresh Fruit and Vegetable Assoc., Washington, D.C.

ANON. 1976. Palletized loads winning the West. The Packer, Annual Review and Outlook Issue—Focus 76–77. 81.

ANTHONY, J. P., JR., VOLZ, M. D., and MONGELLI, R. C. 1975. Palletization for potatoes. *In* United Fresh Fruit and Vegetable Association Yearbook. pp. 105–106, 108, 110, 113–114. United Fresh Fruit and Vegetable Assoc., Washington, D.C.

BIALES, A., ANTHONY, J. P., JR., and MOFFITT, T. 1971. Problems in palletized transport of Florida fresh vegetables. U.S. Dept. Agr. *ARS 52-51*.

CHAPOGAS, P. G., and ANTHONY, J. P., JR. 1971. Unitized shipment of selected fresh fruits and vegetables on 48 × 40-inch pallets. *In* United Fresh Fruit and Vegetable Association Yearbook. pp. 67–68, 70, 72, 74, 78, 80. United Fresh Fruit and Vegetable Assoc., Washington, D.C.

DANIELSON, L. 1976. Spud industry using more slip sheets. The Packer, Annual Review and Outlook Issue—Focus 76–77. 98.

GOLOMB, J. D. 1976. Palletization—smoothing out the bumps. The Packer, Annual Review and Outlook Issue—Focus 76–77. 99.

HALLEE, N. D., and SIDES, S. E. 1976. Retail shipping—display unit for Maine Potatoes. Am. Soc. Agr. Eng., Dec. Meet., Chicago, Paper No. *76-6508*.

JOHNSTON, P. 1973. Palletization comes of age. The Packer *80*, No. 1, 6A–7A.

MARTIN, B. 1976. Slip sheets—an answer to the pallet dilemma? The Packer, Annual Review and Outlook Issue—Focus 76–77. 84, 86.

O'NEILL, B. 1976. Bulk bin explorations continue. The Packer, Annual Review and Outlook Issue—Focus 76–77. 83, 87.

STOKES, D. R. 1972. Standardized pallets, containers. The Packer *79*, No. 52, 11A.

U.S. DEPT. AGR. 1975. Agricultural statistics. U.S. Dept. of Agriculture, Washington, D.C.

14

Transportation by Air and Sea

Two phenomena of the 1960s had a profound effect on the domestic and international movement of fresh produce. The first is the development and rapid acceptance of the refrigerated container, which can be transported on a truck chassis over the highway, or carried off wheels on railway flatcars, or on ships or barges on the ocean or inland waterway. The second is the rapidly increasing quantity and variety of fresh fruits and vegetables transported on aircraft. In relation to the total of perishable products transported, shipments in containers and aircraft are modest. However, the totals are destined to continue significant growth through the 1970s and beyond.

TRANSPORTATION IN AIRCRAFT

Background

A measure of the rapidity with which aircraft and air transport services are developing is found in reports made by airline representatives at research conferences. In 1958 California produce people were told the advantage of the DC6A as a cargo carrier over the older DC4. Cargo compartment had been increased from 139 to 185 m³ (3570 to 5000 cu ft) and payload from 8.3 to 13.7 metric tons (9.2 to 15.1 tons) (Stark 1958). At the same conference another speaker told of a proposed turbo-prop aircraft which, in the cargo version, would carry a payload of about 32 metric tons (35 tons) at an estimated cost of 3.8 ¢ per ton-mile as compared with 7.5 ¢ in the DC-6A (Edwards 1958). At a similar conference 9 years later the Boeing 707, with a payload of 40.2 metric tons (45 tons), was only a basis for comparison with the coming Boeing 747, which as a cargo carrier can transport a payload of more than 90 metric tons (100 tons) (Stark 1967). Based on estimates from the commercial airlines, each increase in size and payload, from the DC-3 with 2.5 metric tons (2-3/4 tons) net load to the Boeing 747 with about 40 times as much capacity, reduces the ton-mile cost of transporting air freight.

Air freight, both perishable and nonperishable, is carried by airlines which carry only freight, and by regularly scheduled airlines which carry both passengers and freight. In the early stages of produce transport by air, practically all of it was carried in the cargo compartments of passenger aircraft. Now, both the freight and passenger lines have all-cargo flights which maintain published schedules. Special charter flights are also available from air freight terminals.

Air Shipment of Vegetables

California originates most of the U.S. air shipments of fresh produce. Figures from Federal-State Market News Service reports show that in 1965 air shipments of asparagus, lettuce and tomatoes totaled about 454,000 kg (1 million lb), and in the same year miscellaneous vegetables added slightly more than that amount.

Table 14.1 compares total air shipments of vegetables from California for 1965, 1970, and 1975. From less than 1 million kg (2,143,300 lb) of only 4 commodities in 1965, totals had increased to more than 4 million kg (about 9 million lb) by 1970. Also, by 1970 the number of vegetable crops included had increased from 4 to 19. A few more commodities are included in the 1975 total of almost 5.5 million kg (11.8 million lb). Shipments of individual commodities vary from year to year depending on supply and price, but there is a consistent increase in the total. Fruit shipments by air far surpass vegetable and melon movement, e.g., in 1975 strawberry shipments constituted about 40% of the total air shipments from California.

Shipments of California vegetables to Hawaii and foreign markets are increasing gradually, but do not compare with the vast quantities of mainland U.S. fruits going to these markets. Almost 94 thousand kg (about 207 thousand lb) of vegetables moved by air to Hawaii, and more than 50,000 kg (115,550 lb) were air carried to foreign markets (Table 14.1).

In addition to California shipments, the Pacific Northwest shipped about 810,000 kg (1,785,000 lb) of mushrooms by air; Pennsylvania air-shipped about 295,000 kg (649,000 lb) of mushrooms; and Hawaii fowarded some 132,000 kg (291,000 lb) of Chinese cabbage to the U.S.

TABLE 14.1.   AIR SHIPMENTS OF CALIFORNIA VEGETABLES AND MELONS

| Commodity | Total to All Markets | | | To Hawaii | To Other Markets |
| | 1965 | 1970 | 1975 | 1975 | 1975 |
	Net Product Weight (kg)[1]				
Artichokes, globe	—	162,668	988,207	—	23,978
Asparagus	80,199	444,783	255,134	1,362	12,309
Beans, snap	—	3,632	4,699	1,025	—
Broccoli	—	72,231	10,113	5,578	—
Brussels sprouts	—	—	218,251	—	2,180
Cabbage	—	1,066	813	—	—
Carrots	—	96,293	—	—	—
Cauliflower	—	54,616	851,847	—	—
Celery	—	64,513	2,282	1,362	—
Cucumbers	—	—	3,874	2,815	—
Honey Dew melons	—	12,803	13,343	14,301	—
Lettuce	163,054	1,196,245	1,934,120	18,698	8,804
Melons (miscellaneous)	—	22,087	1,271	—	1,362
Oriental vegetables	515,880	1,465,421	943,548	4,086	3,772
Onions, green	—	2,565	1,051	—	—
Parsley	—	126	2,589	—	—
Peas, sugar	—	—	13,493	5,651	—
Peppers	—	11,532	589	628	—
Potatoes, new	—	—	6,405	4,899	—
Radishes	—	1,861	1,028	—	—
Spinach	—	4,812	636	—	—
Tomatoes	213,924	406,739	73,329	33,349	—
Watercress	—	772	20,998	—	—
Totals	973,057	4,024,765	5,347,620	93,754	52,405

Source: Anon. (1965, 1975).
[1]Multiply by 2.205 to determine pounds.

mainland by air. Minor air shipments of fresh vegetables originated in Arizona, Florida, Illinois and Missouri.

Air shipment is, and probably always will be, more costly per ton-mile than any form of surface transportation. However, when certain vegetables or melons are in short supply, or so perishable that other modes of transport cause excessive deterioration, the cost of air transport can be justified on the basis of price received. Out-of-season and specialty crops are particularly suited for air transport since the luxury markets handling these products expect to pay and receive premium prices.

Product Protection

When air transport of fresh produce was seriously undertaken, after the end of World War II, the concept of most airline people was that speed of movement alone was sufficient for delivery of quality produce. Little attention was paid to providing a transit environment consistent with the needs of the commodity.

It soon became apparent to everyone involved that fast transport itself was not enough to guarantee sound arrival of highly perishable products such as asparagus, lettuce and celery. As originally handled, the produce was not only exposed to unfavorable environments during flight, but even more seriously, it was exposed to variable and uncontrolled temperatures during transport to the air terminal, while awaiting loading on the aircraft, and again during unloading and transport to market. Somewhat reluctantly, users recognized that some form of refrigeration must be provided before, during, and after air transport.

Environment Control   Permanent attachment of a mechanical refrigeration system on aircraft does not presently appear to be practical. The weight of such a unit reduces salable payload and usable cargo compartment volume. Additionally, the heat from the condensing unit must be disposed of, which presents problems in a sealed, pressurized compartment. The problem of temperature reduction in an entire cargo compartment is also complicated by the frequency of mixed cargos, some of which would be injured or even destroyed (e.g., baby chicks) by low temperatures. Thus, emphasis for product protection during air trans-

Courtesy of American Air Lines

FIG. 14.1. LOADING AIR FREIGHTER WITH CARGO IN IGLOO CONTAINERS

port has been directed to precooling, insulated containers, and individual container cooling with liquid N_2 or solid CO_2.

Precooling Before Shipment   This method of product protection is the simplest and the most widely used. Lettuce is always vacuum cooled soon after packing. For air shipment it can be transported to the air terminal in a refrigerated vehicle, and when loaded into an insulated cargo container will remain at a reasonably good temperature for the relatively brief flight times on modern aircraft. Most of the other more perishable vegetables can readily be hydrocooled 4.5° C (40° F) or below. With some protection during transport to terminals and in flight, this will maintain reasonably safe temperatures for domestic flight times. Less perishable products such as tomatoes and Honey Dew melons need little or no refrigeration during the 24 to 36 hr period from field to wholesale market.

Containerization   Most of the cargo containers for presently used aircraft are shaped to fit the interior contour of the plane. These so-called igloos are loaded on the ground and moved into the cargo aircraft by forklift and roller conveyor equipment (Fig. 14.2). Containers for the new super-jets will not be shaped to make maximum use of the interior volume of the airplane. Most of the shipping containers in use for vegetables are rectangular so loading into a straight-sided container is

less wasteful of container space. Additionally, rectangular containers are better adapted to intermodal transport, with ease of transfer from motor truck to aircraft and from aircraft to truck. These containers will be sealed reusable units, too large for manual handling, and with or without a self-contained refrigeration source. The containers may be loaded either at the shipper's facility or at the air freight terminal.

Containers for the superjets will probably be standardized at about 2.4 × 2.4 × 3 m (8 × 8 × 10 ft) and insulated with high efficiency, rigid, plastic foam. In the absence of built-in mechanical refrigeration, the containers would have provision for an attachable refrigeration duct for original pull down of the product temperature when necessary and for standby operation on the ground when exposed to high ambient temperatures.

Smaller insulated units with capacities of 0.3 to 5.6 m³ (12 to 200 cu ft) are available. Many of these are of fabricated sandwich construction (insulation between two bearing walls) with closed-cell, plastic foam insulation. The smaller units are designed to fit conventional pallets and all are suitable for materials handling systems at airline freight terminals.

Cooling at High Altitudes   At altitudes of 9000 to 12,000 m (30 to 40 thousand ft), as flown by modern jet aircraft, outside temperatures are well below −19° C (0° F). Theoretically, this natural refrigeration could be used for the protection of perishable products, but the extremes of such ambients, the very low RH at such altitudes, and the varying tolerances and needs of cargo carried, make use of this source impractical. Furthermore, the cargo compartment would have to be unpressurized to cool effectively with outside air. However, at jet plane speed the skin temperature in flight is 25° to 28° C (45° to 50° F) above ambient. This provides a moderating influence on cargo compartment temperatures, enabling the basic aircraft air conditioning system to maintain cargo compartment temperatures as low as 5° C at 9000 m (40° F at 30,000 ft) or −0.5° C at 12,000 m (30° F at 40,000 ft) when such temperatures are needed for cargo protection.

Expendable Refrigerants   Solid CO_2 (dry ice) and liquid N_2 are both used to a limited extent for refrigeration of produce in rail cars and highway trailers. Atmosphere modification is possible as a supplement to refrigeration for those commodities benefited by increased CO_2 or reduced O_2 in the atmosphere.

The low equipment cost, compared with mechanical refrigeration, encourages the use of expendable gases for produce containers. However, when used as primary refrigerants within the container, atmosphere modification from uncontrolled release of CO_2 or N_2 is hazardous to the product carried. Only a few vegetables are tolerant of high concentrations of CO_2, even at low temperature, and O_2 concentrations below 5% are harmful to some commodities. On the other hand, controlled release of CO_2 or N_2 to stabilize container atmospheres at optimum levels of CO_2 and O_2 for specific commodities would be desirable. Release of the primary refrigerant within the produce container also creates a freezing hazard. Produce close to the dry ice or near the N_2 outlet may be cooled excessively.

Secondary Refrigerants   The use of a secondary refrigerant cooled by dry ice or liquid N_2 is a possible solution to refrigeration in containers for air cargo. With thermostatic control of the refrigerant flow, products could be cooled to a desired temperature or maintained at a temperature attained before loading.

A refrigerated air freight container using dry ice as a primary refrigerant is described by Tyree (1971). Dry ice (solid CO_2) in pellet form is added to a bunker in a produce container with a volume of 3.5 m³ (125 cu ft). A secondary refrigerant, cooled by the dry ice, flows through a fluorocarbon thermosyphon loop. Refrigerant flow through the loop is controlled by an adjustable, temperature-sensitive, vapor-pressure-operated valve. Air temperature within the container can be controlled to protect either frozen or fresh commodities.

Container refrigeration systems which use liquid nitrogen, either directly vaporized into the load or expanded in sealed coils or plates, are also in limited use. The release of CO_2 or N_2 within the container could produce desirable atmosphere modification for some fresh vegetables, but would be disastrous for others. Research is continuing on temperature and atmosphere controlling systems for small cargo containers. A serious problem is disposition of CO_2 or N_2 needed for refrigeration, but not usable within the container. Release of either of these gases into the cargo compartment of the plane is potentially dangerous unless ventilation of the cargo compartment is provided. This is particularly true of passenger carrying aircraft with produce in the cargo compartment. Under these circumstances limitations are now set on the amount of dry ice which can be carried in each type of aircraft. Similar restrictions could well be coming for the release of N_2 in load compartments.

Protection on the Ground   The advantage of rapid transport by air can readily be lost by slow or careless handling of perishable cargo on the ground. Fortunately, with the completion of specialized air freight terminals and the improvement of cargo handling and loading equipment, the sight of unprotected pallet loads of highly perishable cherry tomatoes or fresh asparagus exposed to hot sun on an airport ramp is now rare. Some air freight terminals even have refrigerated rooms where produce can be placed if loadings are delayed. However, produce loadings at some of the smaller air terminals often are far from efficient.

Destination handling of fresh produce must also be prompt. Receivers, or contract carriers employed by them, generally transport produce from the destination air terminal to the wholesale market or chain store warehouse. Refrigerated vehicles are essential, unless loads in insulated containers can be moved from the packinghouse to the market as a unit. If prompt pick-up at the terminal is not available, the more perishable items should be moved into refrigerated rooms for temporary holding. In times of peak movement, refrigerated vans can be used as temporary holding rooms when receiver pick-up is delayed.

Recommended Environments

As early as 1951 the produce industry recognized the need for some guidelines for desirable temperature and RH for produce shipped by air. To meet this need, scientists in California prepared a publication listing temperature and RH requirements for most of the fresh horticultural crops likely to be shipped by air (Claypool et al. 1958). Included also is a discussion of perishability of the products and some of the problems involved in marketing perishables. Flight times have been shortened and air terminal handling has been much improved since the 1958 revision of the publication. However, their recommendations are as applicable to today's need as when written.

During any holding or transit period for fresh produce, maintenance at the recommended optimum storage temperature and RH (see Table 6.1) is the ideal. However, when the total transit and market delivery time is only 24 to 36 hr, some relaxation from the optimum is possible. This is indicated in the data assembled in Table 14.2.

TRANSPORTATION IN SHIPS

Background

The rather prolonged transit period involved in marine transport of perishable commodities requires environments close to optimum for successful deliveries. Usually the produce is moved by rail or highway to the port facilities, and in some cases has been in storage before the initial transport. Accordingly, relaxation during any step of the total marketing process will result in quality loss.

Until rather recently, all products requiring refrigeration in marine

TABLE 14.2. TEMPERATURE AND HUMIDITY REQUIREMENTS FOR VEGETABLES IN AIR TRANSPORT (COMMODITIES COMMONLY AIR-SHIPPED FROM CALIFORNIA)

Commodity	Recommended Storage Temperature[1] (°C)	(°F)	Recommended RH for Storage[1] (%)	Permissible Temperature Range for 48 hr Period[2] (°C)	(°F)	Precool Before Shipment	Perishability
Artichoke, globe	0	32	95+	0 to 10	32 to 50	desirable	moderate
Asparagus	0 to 2	32 to 36	95+	0 to 4.5	32 to 40	essential	very high
Beans, snap	3 to 5.5	38 to 42	95+	0 to 10	32 to 50	desirable	high
Broccoli, sprouting	0	32	95+	0 to 4.5	32 to 40	essential	very high
Brussels sprouts	0	32	95+	0 to 10	32 to 50	essential	high
Carrots, immature	0	32	98 to 100	0 to 10	32 to 50	desirable	moderate
Cauliflower	0	32	95+	0 to 10	32 to 50	essential	high
Celery	0	32	95+	0 to 4.5	32 to 40	essential	high
Endive, escarole	0	32	95+	0 to 4.5	32 to 40	essential	moderate
Lettuce	0	32	95	0 to 10	32 to 50	desirable	moderate
Cantaloups	3 to 4.5	38 to 40	85 to 95	0 to 10	32 to 50	no	high
Honey Dews	7 to 10	45 to 50	95+	0 to 24	32 to 75	essential	moderate
Onions, green	0	32	95+	0 to 4.5	32 to 40	desirable	high
Parsley	0	32	95	0 to 4.5	32 to 40	no	moderate
Peppers, sweet	7 to 10	45 to 50	95+	0 to 15.5	32 to 60	desirable	moderate
Radishes	0	32	95+	0 to 4.5	32 to 40	no	very high
Tomatoes, cherry	7 to 10	45 to 50	90	10 to 15.5	50 to 60	no	high

[1]From Table 10, Chapter 6.
[2]From Claypool et al. (1958).

transport were carried in refrigerated holds. This required unloading of the shipping containers from rail or highway vehicles at the pier, and reloading the product into the ship's hold, the so-called breakbulk system. At destination the process was reversed—removing the cargo from the hold to the pier and reloading it in rail cars or vans for delivery to the market. Since about 1960, the use of refrigerated holds is often supplemented, and in many cases replaced, by refrigerated containers in which the entire load of produce moves from producer to the port, onto and off the ship, and to the market as a unit. The individual shipping containers are handled only at origin and final destination instead of receiving the numerous handlings of the breakbulk system. Both systems are discussed in the following sections, as well as possible modifications of the latter.

Refrigerated Ship's Holds

Refrigerated holds are built-in refrigerated compartments, equipped and operated much the same as land-based cold storage rooms. Ships providing refrigeration service may have only a few cooled holds, with the remaining space for dry cargo, or the ship may be designed and operated entirely for refrigeration service.

Principles   Ships which have only a part of the loading space refrigerated are usually arranged so that these compartments are located under the topmost deck. This arrangement permits perishable cargo to be loaded and unloaded without interference from loads of dry cargo. Since perishables should be the last cargo loaded and the first unloaded, this is a desirable arrangement. The refrigerated compartments are generally placed forward of mid-length or grouped near the middle section of the vessel because these holds will often be empty during some parts of the voyage. Perishables usually weigh less than dry cargo, so the ship's trim is less affected by mid-section placement of the refrigerated compartments.

Equipment   For efficiency of space utilization, the ideal arrangement for an all-refrigerated ship would be one large hold, with only the main structural boundaries insulated. The volume occupied by insulated partitions, cooling apparatus, and access areas substantially reduces loading space when many subdivisions are included in refrigerated compartments. However, the single large compartment has too many disadvantages to be practical. Maintaining uniform temperatures in a large compartment is difficult, particularly when the hatch is open for extended periods for loading and unloading. It is also recognized that individual produce items have different temperature requirements and tolerances. The modern refrigerated cargo ship must provide near optimum environments for frozen foods at zero or below, for fresh fruits and vegetables requiring temperatures near 0° C (32° F), and for chilling sensitive products (such as tomatoes) at 10° C (50° F) or higher.

Insulation Insulation requirements of refrigerated ships' holds are much the same as for land-based cold storages. However, insulation in ships must meet conditions of vibration, mechanical damage, and intermittent refrigeration which are more demanding than those of shore-side installations. The insulation for ships' chambers must be light in weight, impervious to moisture, fire resistant, odorless, flexible enough to accommodate ships' stresses, resistant to heat flow, and rat proof.

Moisture-vapor barriers and water resistance of the insulating materials are critical in ship compartments. In addition to vapor seals on the warm side (outside), the refrigerated compartment on a vessel requires vapor proofing on the cold side (inside). This is necessary because after refrigerated cargo is discharged, there are extended periods when the cargo compartment becomes much warmer than the insulated walls. Without a good vapor seal on the inside, moisture moves into the insulation to adversely affect its heat shield properties. In the absence of a vapor barrier, this absorbed moisture will migrate out of the insulation when the compartment is again refrigerated. Removal of the moisture will gradually renew the insulation properties, but it adds to the frosting of refrigerating surfaces.

Refrigeration Equipment Compressors, condensers and refrigerants for ship refrigeration are essentially the same as those used in shore-side cold storages. Refrigerant-12 is generally used for reciprocating compressors instead of ammonia, largely because ammonia is toxic to personnel and products, and there is always the possibility of leakage. Shipboard condensers are commonly cooled by sea water, so resistance to corrosion must be considered in selection of the condenser materials.

Heat Transfer Systems The individual refrigerated chambers may be cooled by direct expansion coils, by circulation of chilled brine, or by ducted air circulated to the chambers from a central bank of evaporators or brine coils. Direct expansion coils in the chambers are troublesome when the refrigerated space is located far from the refrigeration machinery because the capacity of the compressor cylinders is reduced by the rarified gas return through long lines that also require large charges of refrigerants.

The distribution of refrigeration by circulation of chilled brine has several advantages over direct expansion in each chamber. The brine cooler is in the refrigeration machinery room, so the primary refrigerant has short piping runs and small total pressure drops as compared with the long piping runs necessary to get the primary refrigerant to the individual rooms.

Since brine has only sensible heat capacity, temperature control with brine is much less sensitive than with the direct-expansion, latent heat system. Excellent results can be obtained with manual control of return brine flow, whereas automatic control of direct expansion systems is necessary for close temperature control.

Air Movement   As in land-based refrigerated storages air must be circulated through the load compartment to pick up vital heat from the product, and heat from air infiltration and wall conductance. A substantial volume of air is needed to transport heat from these sources to the heat-absorbing surfaces.

Positive air movement in ships' holds is obtained by essentially the same methods as in land-based storages (See Chapter 12). The most common method is air flow across the hold, with a delivery duct on one side wall and a return duct on the opposite wall. With properly stacked cargo this cross-flow method provides good temperature control.

Cargo Arrangement

Breakbulk System   The method of stacking cargo in the hold is critical to maintenance of specified cargo temperatures. Spaces must be provided between rows, stacks or layers, so that the circulating air can reach one or more surfaces of each shipping container. Such spacing can be provided by placing wood strips (dunnage) vertically between rows or stacks as the cargo is loaded. Sometimes it is necessary to place dunnage between layers, but this is not desirable when the product is packed in corrugated shipping containers. These containers tend to sag or crease as they absorb moisture. This may close the air channels between layers or damage the containers and product (Hinds 1970).

Stacking in refrigerated holds with high ceilings presents special problems. For efficient use of space, the maximum amount of cargo must be loaded. Manual stacking of shipping containers in such holds is practical to only about 1.6 m (6 ft) from the floor. Stacking to heights of 3 or 3.5 m (10 or 12 ft) requires planks or plywood sheets on the lower layers of the load to allow workmen to reach upper layers. The cargo is often walked on during this operation, which together with the weight of the overhead containers frequently causes damage in the lower layers.

Unitized Handling   Among the numerous disadvantages of manual handling of individual shipping containers are high labor costs, product and container damage from numerous handlings, and pilferage of product. Pilferage alone has been found to be as high as 10% of the product's value in individual shipments (Hinds 1970). Handling produce as units of 24 to 60 containers on pallets substantially reduces the labor requirement and handling damage. Palletization, begun at the packinghouse and continued through transport to shipside, in and out of the ship's hold, and to the wholesale market permits almost complete mechanization of handling and transfer of the product by forklift from origin to destination.

Palletization has distinct possibilities, but also many problems. Present obstacles to its use for ship's cargo are similar to those encountered in rail and highway shipments (See Chapter 13). A unique difficulty in using pallets in a ship's hold relates to the odd shape of many holds as a result of curved hold walls. Produce containers stacked and strapped on pallets cannot make economical use of space in these holds. The use of pallet bins for bulk or packaged produce in refrigerated holds presents even greater problems than palletized loads. However, limited use has been made of palletized bins for marine transport of bulk winter vegetables from Carribbean areas to Florida, where the products are packed and distributed to mainland markets.

Ventilated Ship's Holds

Winter shipments of produce to western Europe can sometimes be adequately protected in holds of ships by judicious use of cool outside air (Hatton and Winston 1958). This service is generally limited to vessels using the North Atlantic route during the months December through March. The service is not suitable for such highly perishable items as leafy vegetables, but properly operated, should provide adequate protection for potatoes, most melons, peppers and tomatoes. The ventilation equipment and operating principles are similar to those for ventilated storages as described in Chapter 11.

Intermodal Refrigerated Containers

The increasing use of refrigerated containers for domestic transport by rail and highway is discussed in Chapter 13. The advantages of continuous product refrigeration from origin to destination, and reduced handling damage to product and containers, are magnified when marine transport is added to the land haul needed to move the products to shipside. The advantages of one handling of the product at origin and one handling at destination are readily apparent when compared with the multiple handlings involved in loading at origin, unloading at the pier, reloading into the ship's hold, unloading from the ship at destination port, reloading into van or rail car, and final unloading at the market. Each handling in the conventional breakbulk system requires much manual labor, increases product damage, and interrupts refrigeration.

The refrigerated containers for marine transport are of two types. The first is the trailer-on-flatcar (TOFC) in which the chassis is an integral part of the unit. It is used on the highway, transported on rail flatcars and secured on ship's decks for overseas transport. It moves on wheels from one carrier to another, but must be hoisted from pier to ship's deck. These TOFCs on ship's decks carried the first fresh produce outside of the ship's holds. The second, and more widely used, is simply an insulated box with a built-in refrigeration system. It is completely independent from a chassis, but when transported over the highway is carried on a removable truck chassis.

The most significant development in produce transport by water is the refrigerated intermodal container, and the specialized ships which carry them. Clark (1973) estimated that U.S. marine carriers handled some 15,000 refrigerated containers in 1973, and that more than 30,000 were handled by all carriers.

Container Construction   Refrigerated containers for marine transport have essentially the same construction, insulation, and temperature control systems as those for use exclusively on truck chassis and rail flatcars. The principal additional requirement for shipboard containers is sufficient structural strength to permit stacking six units high. The marine container is usually equipped with a nose-mounted refrigeration unit. This is recessed into the front of the container to permit on-deck stowage compatible with dry cargo containers. Many of the refrigeration units operate with a diesel engine during highway or rail travel and then are plugged in on shipboard to operate on an electric motor.

Intermodal transfers will require eventual standardization of container dimensions, fastenings, and fittings for lifting on and off truck chassis, rail flatcars, and ship's holds or decks. Uniformity of dimensions is particularly important in international movement of containers. Highway regulations, bridge capacities, underpass heights, and street widths vary greatly in different countries. If containers are not designed to meet these varying conditions, true intermodal transportation on an international basis is impossible. Standard overall dimensions are now considered to be 2.4 m wide, 2.4 m high (8 ft wide, 8 ft high), and from 3 to 12 m (10 to 40 ft) long in multiples of 3 m (10 ft). Standards have been established in the United States but can only be enforced in marine transport by specifying that container ships subsidized by the government must accommodate containers of standard size. Provisional standards have now been devised for international use (Guilfoy 1970). However, there are commercial container systems established before standards were developed which do not conform to the provisional standards.

Air movement of sufficient volume, velocity and direction to maintain uniform product temperatures in refrigerated containers is the first essential in successful operation. Mayrsohn (1973) has stressed the need for stacking patterns which permit uniform air circulation, and several studies (Stewart et al. 1976, 1977) have evaluated load patterns designed to improve air movement. In the standard container air is directed over the load from front to back. Depending on load pattern the air moves either vertically through the load or horizontally in returning to the evaporator. The most effective method, particularly for products with high vital heat production, appears to involve lengthwise channels through the load and maintenance of a vertical space at the back of the container to permit air to move to the lengthwise channels.

An observed and instrumented series of product shipments from the United States to Europe (Hinds 1970) clearly shows that shipment in refrigerated containers is no guarantee of good product deliveries. The arrival condition of fresh fruits and vegetables in the test shipments ranged from excellent to very bad. When inadequate equipment and poor cooling and loading practices were used, the produce did not receive adequate protection in transit. The study revealed that sound arrival of fresh produce in refrigerated containers depends upon: (1) adequate cooling of the product before loading; (2) protective packaging; (3) proper stacking and bracing of the shipping containers; (4) maintenance of suitable temperature and RH in transit; and (5) scheduling to avoid lay-overs in transit.

Experimental Container   Development of a multi-purpose container has been underway in the U.S. Department of Agriculture for several years, and is described by Breakiron (1970). A van, based on this study, is now being tested for thermal efficiency and air circulation patterns. The distinguishing feature of this van is the lateral air circulation system. Instead of having the evaporator located at one or each end of the van, the evaporator coils are mounted on the surface of the ceiling in two rows, extending the length of the van body. A false ceiling provides a duct for air movement. Air is moved down side wall plenums by centrifugal blowers. When fresh produce is the load, the air returns through the cargo to openings in the false ceiling. When frozen foods are carried, air is circulated peripherally around the load by operating blowers on only one side of the van. Other features under study are rehumidification of the circulating air by evaporation of condensate from coil defrosting, and compartmenting of the interior with insulated removable partitions. The coil location, the lateral air circulation, and the removable partitions allow the possibility of carrying products at different temperatures in each of the 3.0 m (10 ft) compartments.

Stewart (1976) conducted two shipping tests to compare solid loads in the USDA experimental unit with spaced loads in commercial containers. Fresh carrots, cabbage, celery and lettuce, mostly in cartons, were included in the tests. The important finding in these accompanied tests is that solidly stacked products in the experimental containers were held at acceptable temperatures, despite rather indifferent precooling. Spaced loads in the commercial containers provided comparable product protection, but previous experience has shown that the front to back air circulation in commercial units is not adequate for solid loads. Solid loads provide advantages in ease of loading, space economy and maintenance of load alignment during transport as compared with spaced loads.

Container-carrying Ships   The initial use of cargo containers in marine transport involved placement of a few containers on the deck of conventional ships. This practice is still followed by several ship lines, but the trend is to specialized ships which carry cargo only in containers. These container ships are constructed so that containers can be stacked in the holds and above deck. They carry both dry cargo and perishable products, but all in containers. Temperature-controlled containers are carried above deck in most specialized ships, with dry cargo below.

Sea-Land Service, Inc. provided the first regularly scheduled container ship service for the United States. In the mid-1950s the company carried 60 trailers on each voyage between Newark, New Jersey and Houston, Texas. In 1977 Sea-Land operated more than 50 container ships, serving 137 ports in 51 countries (Fig. 14.3). "Feeder vessels" also transport containers from small tonnage ports to larger ports serviced by transatlantic or transpacific vessels. The larger container ships are designed to carry more than 1000 10.5 to 12 m (35 to 40 ft) containers. They are designed for a service speed of more than 30 knots. Several thousand refrigerated containers are in service along with more than 50,000 units for nonrefrigerated cargo.

Several other American flag carriers operate ships which are partially or exclusively containerized (Fig. 14.4). Many foreign flag lines also offer container service, and the service continues to grow. Most of these specialized ships require movable dock-side cranes to load and unload containers. Not all ports have these facilities and this delays the use of containers. However, some container ships have ship-based gantry cranes for lifting containers from the land-based truck chassis to the ships hold or vise versa. Saving in port time by rapid loading and unloading of containers, as compared with breakbulk handling, is an important advantage of the container ship.

Barge-carrying Ships   A development more recent than the container-carrying ships is the LASH (lighter aboard ship). This

Courtesy of Sea-Land Service, Inc.

FIG. 14.3.   REFRIGERATED CARGO CONTAINER BEING LOADED ONTO CONTAINER SHIP FROM PIER
Note recessed refrigeration unit on container.

Courtesy of Sea-Land Service, Inc.

FIG. 14.4.   LOADED CONTAINER SHIP AT PIER

specialized ship is designed to carry lighters (barges), each of which holds several cargo containers.

The principal advantage of the system is the ability to load and unload barges offshore. Tugs bring barges to the ship and pick up barges from the ship. The system is particularly adapted to serving shallow-water ports where large cargo ships cannot dock. It even permits delivery of barge loads of containers to inland waterways.

The system evolved in Italy in the early 1960s, primarily to serve Italy's shallow-water ports. The first U.S. built LASH was placed in Mediterranean service in 1971 by Prudential-Grace Lines. This 250 m (820 ft) vessel carries 63 lighters, each 18.5 m (61 ft) long. It is equipped with a 450 metric ton (500 ton) capacity crane for hoisting lighters from the water and stowing them in open holds.

REFERENCES

Air Transport

ANON. 1965 and 1975. Air shipments of California fruits and vegetables. Federal-State Market News Service, San Francisco, Calif.

ASHRAE. 1974. Air transport. ASHRAE Handbook and Product Direct. Applications, *48*, 48.1–48.6.

BREAKIRON, P. L. 1970. Putting wings on your food. *In* Contours of Change, U.S. Dept. Agr. Yearbook. 333–337.

CLAYPOOL, L. L., MORRIS, L. L., PENTZER, W. T., and BARGER, W. R. 1958. Air transportation of fruits, vegetables and cut flowers: temperature and humidity requirements and perishable nature. U.S. Dept. Agr. *AMS-280*.

EDWARDS, J. B. 1958. What's ahead in air freight equipment. Proc. Conf. Transp. Perishables, Univ. Calif., Davis. 217–227.

HARVEY, J. M. 1961. Time and temperature effects on perishables shipped by air. Proc. Conf. Transport. Perishables, Univ. Calif., Davis. 56–64.

HUNTER, J. H. 1964. Shipping farm products abroad in the jet age. U.S. Dept. Agr., Foreign Agr. *2*, No. 13, 3–5.

STARK, D. U. 1958. Present capabilities of airline transportation. Proc. Conf. Transport. Perishables, Univ. Calif., Davis. 211–217.

STARK, D. U. 1967. Developments in air transportation of perishables. Proc. Fruit and Veg. Perishables Handling Conf., Univ. Calif., Davis. 60–64.

TYREE, L., JR. 1971. Refrigerated containerized transport for jumbo jets. Proc. 13th Intern. Cong. Refrig. (Washington, D.C.) *4*, 515–525.

Sea Transport

ANDERSON, D. M. 1970. United effort for unitization. *In* United Fresh Fruit and Vegetable Association Yearbook. pp. 161–162. United Fresh Fruit and Vegetable Assoc., Washington, D.C.

ANTHONY, J. P., JR. 1969. Development of stacking patterns for handling and transporting unitized shipments of Florida citrus. U.S. Dept. Agr. *ARS 52-42*.

ANTHONY, J. P., JR., and REBENTISCH, J. A., JR. 1970. An evaluation of various types of disposable pallets for handling and transporting Florida citrus. U.S. Dept. Agr. *ARS 52-43*.

ASHRAE. 1974. Marine refrigeration. ASHRAE Handbook and Product Direct. Applications, *47*, 47.1–47.20.

BREAKIRON, P. L. 1961. Pallet containers for transportation of agricultural perishables—progress and problems. Proc. Natl. Conf. Handling Perishable Agr. Commod., Purdue Univ., Lafayette, Ind. 50–57.

BREAKIRON, P. L. 1970. A definitive approach to engineering improved refrigerated trailer vans and containers. Winter Meet. Am. Soc. Agr. Engr., Chicago. Paper No. *70-894*.

CLARK, J. L. 1973. Refrigerated containers: a carrier describes problems. U.S. Dept. Agr., Foreign Agr. *11,* No. 20, 9–10.

DANAGHER, J. H. 1971. Automatic supervision and recording of temperatures and pressures in refrigerated container ships. Proc. 13th Intern. Cong. Refrig. (Washington, D.C.) *4,* 653–659.

GUILFOY, R. F., JR. 1970. Impending European standards for vehicles used to transport perishable foods. U.S. Dept. Agr. *ARS 52-59.*

HATTON, T. T., JR., and WINSTON, J. R. 1958. Overseas ventilated shipping tests with Florida oranges and grapefruit. U.S. Dept. Agr. Mktg. Res. Rept. *274.*

HINDS, R. H., JR. 1970. Transporting fresh fruits and vegetables overseas. U.S. Dept. Agr. *ARS 52-39.*

JOHNSON, H. B. 1967. Containerized overseas shipping test with red grapefruit, carrots and other vegetables. Texas Citrus Veg. Growers and Shippers Yearbook. 113–114, 116–117.

MAYRSOHN, B. 1973. Refrigerated containers: a shipper outlines experience. U.S. Dept. Agr., Foreign Agr. *11,* No. 20, 7–8.

STEWART, J. K. 1976. Transit temperatures and quality of fresh vegetables shipped in an experimental and a commercial van container to the Far East. U.S. Dept. Agr. Mktg. Res. Rept. *1054.*

STEWART, J. K. *et al.* 1977. Guide to successful lettuce exporting. Western Grower and Shipper *48,* No. 1, 13–15.

STEWART, J. K., BONGERS, A., and HINDS, R. H. 1976. Spaced load patterns for improved temperature control in export shipments of lettuce. U.S. Dept. Agr. Mktg. Res. Rept. *1051.*

WESTLING, L. L. 1973. A challenge to developments in refrigerated transport. ASHRAE J. *15,* No. 12, 54–56.

15

Market Disorders, Physical Injuries and Diseases

GENERAL DISCUSSION

Definition of Terms

We apply the term *Disorder* to symptoms of disturbances in the normal metabolism of vegetables or melons. Under *Physical Injuries* we include symptoms of damage imposed by mechanical forces, chemicals, freezing, or solar radiation. *Disease* refers to symptoms of infections by bacteria, fungi, viruses or related entities.

The terms disorder and disease often are used interchangeably and plant pathologists refer to all disturbances as diseases. Nevertheless, use of the two terms is advantageous, because disorders and diseases differ in cause, in prevention, and cure (when there is one) and, once defined, the words need no modifiers such as "physiological," "parasitic" or "nonparasitic."

A given trouble may be changed from one classification to the other as research elucidates its true cause, as when black spot of radishes, long thought to be a disorder, was found to be caused by a bacterium. Further, a given symptom may be a sign of a disorder or of a disease, just as an elevated temperature in human beings is a symptom of heat stroke and of virus infection; for example, blotchy ripening of tomatoes may be symptomatic of chilling injury or of a virus infection.

Interrelationships Among Disturbances

We realize that the distinction between disorders and physical injuries is somewhat arbitrary in some cases. The crux of the distinction lies in the immediacy and severity of the injury. Consequently, we

366

regard freezing as a physical injury, but chilling as a disorder. Similarly, solar injury, which can be induced within at most a few hours, is among physical injuries, whereas greening of potatoes, which tends to require days to develop, is considered a disorder.

The causes of disorders are diverse. They can result from internal changes, such as normal senescence, from exposure to unfavorably low, but nonfreezing temperatures, or from the effects of physiologically active, but not inherently phytotoxic volatiles, such as ethylene or CO_2.

Physical injuries are the result of strictly external factors: a blow, a toxic chemical, radiant energy or freezing temperatures.

The distinction between disorders and physical injuries has important practical implications: disorders often are impossible or at least difficult to control, although their rate of progress may be slowed. In contrast, physical injuries can be completely prevented or at least substantially reduced from levels commonly encountered. Ironically, the latter result in much greater losses during marketing of produce than disorders. In onions, for instance, translucent scale causes only a fraction of the losses attributable to bruising or freezing. In tomatoes, waste due to senescence is nil, whereas that due to rough handling is enormous.

Some of the organisms that incite the symptoms characteristic of a given disease can invade a presumably healthy host and become established. Species of *Phytophthora* that cause a rot of watermelons are examples of such virulent organisms. Other organisms can become established only if their host has first suffered some physiological or physical injury, such as chilling injury or a bruise, respectively. Thus, the "weak" bacterium or fungus is the immediate cause of the disease, but the injury is a necessary precondition.

Since origins and symptoms of disorders and diseases are intimately related to the characteristics of the affected vegetables, their general discussion would be fruitless. Some physical injuries, however, share origins, symptoms and cure, and can be discussed as a group, although certain specifics also depend on the crop.

CAUSES OF MECHANICAL INJURIES

Physical Handling

General Aspects   Improper physical handling can result in injuries caused by impact, compression, abrasion, puncturing, tearing, or by two or more actions combined. Any vegetable is susceptible to physical damage from one or more of these abuses, and *there are no so-called* *"hardware" items* on any produce man's list. Certainly, some vegetables are more easily injured than others, and some show objectionable symptoms more readily, but none is immune to damage. Once damaged, the items lose value because they become discolored, unsightly, and prone to invasion by decay organisms.

Impact   Impact damage occurs when a specimen hits a surface with sufficient force to damage or even separate its cells, the external symptom being a bruise or crack. Vegetables may sustain impact injury when they are dropped from a harvesting machine into a box, bin or truck, or as they are dumped on a conveyor belt or sorting table. Sizing via gravity drops also may cause injury unless the receiving surface is adequately cushioned and the vegetables are prevented from hitting each other. Such mutual impact also can be serious on inclined sorting tables as used for cantaloups.

Impact also can bruise or shatter the contents after packing, as when a box of lettuce is dropped accidentally, or carelessly, on a conveyor or on a concrete floor.

The danger of impact injury also extends into a trailer or rail car, where sudden stops can convert containers into missiles that hit the walls or each other with sufficient force to damage their contents.

Finally, careless dumping of produce from containers onto the retail display can largely negate the benefits of prior careful handling.

Compression   Compression, like impact, causes bruising or cracking, but occurs primarily during or after packing as a result of forcing too much product into too little container. While vegetables and melons should be packed firmly enough to avoid chafing, they should not be stuffed in so tightly that their curved surfaces become flat, as all too often is the case with lettuce. Further, with overstuffed containers, the contents rather than the box must bear any overhead load, which further aggravates the injury.

Packing more produce in a container than its design allows is misplaced generosity, because the recipient, be it retailer or consumer, will not only lose salable or edible produce, but confidence in the supplier as well.

Containers stacked higher than their design allows causes them to yield and thus shift the load to the contents in the lower layers. The resulting compression damage suggests that weak containers can be expensive bargains.

Abrasion   Abrasion can occur during harvest when roots or tubers are dug and conveyed at excessive speed, during packing, when tomatoes roll on dirty belts, or during transit of slackly packed containers which permits the individual units to rub against each other or against the container surfaces.

Punctures   Puncturing is not a serious problem with most vegetables because the main contributor to puncture, the stem or pedicel, is detached during harvest. However, punctures are sometimes sustained by cucumbers, eggplants, and some packs of tomatoes because their pedicels accidentally or intentionally remain attached.

Tears   Tears are sustained by leafy vegetables and, because of the tissue exposed, contribute to rapid dehydration, discoloration, or decay of the affected leaf.

Freezing Injury

Symptoms   Freezing injures vegetables and melons by destruction of cells after the formation of ice crystals. The damaged or dead cells lose their resistance to dehydration and to microbial infections. Further, freeze-damaged tissue loses its normal rigidity and becomes mushy upon thawing, leading to the water-soaked appearance commonly associated with thawed vegetables.

Freezing also may lead to development of strong off-odors upon cooking the damaged vegetable. Broccoli is a serious offender in this respect, because almost unnoticeable freezing injury of the florets yields a very objectionable odor.

Susceptibility to Freezing Injury   Unfortunately, type of vegetable does not necessarily yield a clue to its susceptibility to freezing injury. Among leafy vegetables, lettuce is very readily injured at freezing temperatures, whereas cabbage and some of its relatives are not; among roots, sweetpotatoes are ruined by freezing, while parsnips are improved by slight freezing; among fruits, green beans are damaged more severely than green peas. Table 15.1 lists some vegetables according to their relative susceptibility and also gives their highest determined freezing point.

This table does suggest that crops that are readily chilled also are readily injured by freezing, although chilling sensitivity is not a prerequisite.

Preharvest vs. Postharvest Freezing   Disputes sometimes arise upon arrival of shipments on the origin of freezing injury. Analysis of the distribution of the frozen items in a rail car or trailer frequently can

TABLE 15.1. SUSCEPTIBILITY OF SOME VEGETABLES[1] TO FREEZING INJURY AND THEIR HIGHEST MEASURED FREEZING POINT[2]

Vegetable[3]	Susceptibility Class[4-5]	Freezing Point (°C)	Freezing Point (°F)
Artichoke, globe	1	−1.7	29.9
Asparagus	1	−0.6	30.9
Beet, red, root	3	−1.1	30.1
tops	1	−0.4	31.3
Broccoli, buds	1	−1.7	29.9
stalks	—	−0.6	30.9
Brussels sprouts	3	−0.8	30.5
Cabbage, early	2	−0.9	30.4
late	3	—	—
red	2	−0.2	31.7
Carrot	2	−1.4	29.5
Cauliflower, curd	2	−0.8	30.6
Celeriac	3	−0.9	30.3
Celery, outer stalk	1 to 2	−0.5	31.1
heart	1	−0.2	31.6
Chives	2	−0.9	30.4
Collards	3	−0.8	30.6
Corn, sweet	1	−0.6	30.9
Dandelion	—	−0.3	31.4
Dill	—	−0.7	30.7
Endive	2	−0.3	31.4
Escarole	2	−0.1	31.9
Garlic	—	−0.8	30.5
Horseradish	3	−1.8	28.7
Kale	3	−0.5	31.1
Kohlrabi	3	−1.0	30.2
Leek, green leaves	2	−0.7	30.7
white base	2	−0.9	30.3
Lettuce, Bibb	1	−0.2	31.7
Big Boston	1	−0.2	31.7
head, (Iceberg)	1	−0.4	31.3
Romaine	1	−0.2	31.7
Mushroom	—	−0.9	30.4
Mustard greens	—	−0.3	31.4
Onion, green, base	—	−0.9	30.4
bulb	2 to 3	−0.8	30.6
Parsley	2	−1.1	30.0
Parsnips	3	−0.9	30.4
Peas, shelled	2	−1.2	29.9
pod	2	−0.6	30.9
Radish, red, roots	2	−0.8	30.5
leaves	—	−0.5	31.1
white, roots	2	−0.7	30.7
leaves	—	−0.6	31.0
Rhubarb	—	−0.9	30.3
Rutabagas (swedes)	3	−1.1	30.1
Salsify, roots	3	−1.1	30.0
tops	—	−0.9	30.4
Shallot, green leaves	—	−0.2	31.7
white base	—	−0.2	31.6
dry bulb	—	−1.1	30.0
Spinach	2	−0.3	31.5
Turnip, root	3	−1.1	30.1
top	—	−0.9	30.4
Watercress	—	−0.3	31.4

[1]Chilling-sensitive crops are omitted from this table because they should never be held near their freezing point; further, all are highly susceptible to freezing injury.
[2]Freezing points from Whiteman (1957).
[3]Edible portion, unless otherwise indicated.
[4]Susceptibility classes mostly from Lutz and Hardenburg (1968); dashes indicate no information available.
[5]Class 1—highly susceptible. Slight freezing likely will substantially reduce quality of product. Sometimes not noticeable until time of cooking, e.g. broccoli.
Class 2—moderately susceptible. One slight freezing will reduce quality only slightly.
Class 3—fairly resistant to freezing. Repeated slight freezing will reduce quality only slightly, or not at all.

resolve the question. If the frozen specimens are rather evenly distributed throughout the load, freezing likely occurred prior to harvest, or at least before loading. If freezing mainly is concentrated in certain locations, such as in the top layers in mechanically refrigerated vehicles, or near bunkers, doors, or walls in ice-cooled units, then the damage most likely occurred in transit. If freezing occurred during vacuum cooling, as may happen with lettuce, the injured lots likely would be concentrated in one part of the load. However, unlike in-transit freezing, the affected contents would tend to be evenly distributed from top to bottom and from side to side of the car or trailer, and the most severe injury would be in heads adjacent to the vents of the cartons.

Salvage of Frozen Vegetables   If a vegetable is accidentally exposed to freezing temperatures, damage may be avoided if the endangered lot remains completely undisturbed until it has warmed up. Absence of movement can prevent crystallization even if the temperature drops several degrees below the freezing point, a situation known as supercooling. However, even slight vibrations cause immediate crystal formation and consequent danger of injury. Warming should be done at about 5° C (41° F) (Lutz 1936; Parsons and Day 1970); lower temperatures prolong freezing while higher ones can result in dangerously rapid thawing.

Successful salvage should be followed by immediate utilization of the vegetable to avoid decay of specimens with undetected injury.

Supercooling is confined to stationary storage. Shipments frozen in transit almost invariably are worthless on arrival. Even crops not readily damaged by freezing, such as parsnips, may be injured if frozen in transit because frozen vegetables are highly susceptible to mechanical injury.

Solar Injury; Heat Injury

Definition of Terms   Heat injury refers to damage sustained when a vegetable, or a part thereof, becomes substantially hotter than the surrounding air. Since the high temperature was a consequence of exposure to the sun or of contact with a surface (usually soil) that was heated by the sun, "solar heating" seems a fitting term for the cause of heat injury. However, not all so-called heat injury is caused by high temperatures; some of the symptoms appear to be induced by ultraviolet (UV) radiation (Lipton 1977). Consequently, solar injury is an appropriate term when heat and UV are involved and when their separate effects are not distinguished.

Consequences of Solar Injury   Although specific consequences of solar injury vary with crops, softening, discoloration, collapse and eventual drying of affected tissue are common to many. These lesions are not only unsightly and inedible, but also offer avenues of entry for decay organisms. Losses from decay are particularly serious if the injury escapes detection at origin and the affected specimens decay in transit or after arrival. These infections can spread decay throughout the entire lot.

Conditions for Solar Injury and Their Avoidance   Solar injury may follow after the surface or shallow interior of a vegetable has been at 40° to 50° C (104° to 122° F) from a few minutes to an hour or more, depending upon the particular crop. Solar radiation may damage crops before or during harvest, during transportation from field to packing shed, or during the wait before unloading.

Before harvest, melons, tomatoes, potatoes, or lettuce, and others may be sufficiently exposed to direct solar radiation to suffer permanent damage, commonly called sun scald. Sun scald can be minimized in some crops by maintaining good foliage cover over the fruits, or when foliage becomes sparse, by a cover of nontoxic whitewash that is a water suspension of a proprietary material mainly consisting of aluminum silicate and of a spreader-sticker (Lipton 1975). While this procedure has been used extensively on ripe or nearly ripe tomatoes in the arid West, its use on other crops was still limited in 1977.

During harvest, injury may follow contact with the ground. The soil surface may reach 55° to 65° C (130° to 150° F) by early afternoon. This danger of heat injury can be avoided by limiting harvesting to the relatively cool first half of the day, particularly with heat sensitive crops, such as potatoes, where contact with the soil surface may be unavoidable. Further, delay between harvest and pick-up should be kept below 15 min any time the soil surface exceeds 38° C (100° F). Alternatively, exposure never should exceed a half hour when air temperature is 32° C (90° F) or higher (Jensen 1929).

After harvest, solar injury is a constant danger when crops are transported from field to shed in open trucks or trailers, and while they are awaiting unloading. Melons left sitting in the sun can exceed 50° C (122° F) within 2 hr, with permanent damage the result (Kasmire *et al.* 1962). Such damage can be avoided by shading the load during transit to and after arrival at the packing shed. Canvas serves well during transit, but should be opened sufficiently after arrival to permit dissipation of respiratory heat unless the entire load is below about 20° C (68° F). Even a canvas-covered load should be parked in the shade, which is an essential practice for open loads during sunny weather. Excessive respiratory heating can occur under the cover as the load warms.

Injuries Induced by Chemicals

Ethylene and ammonia are the only chemicals likely to damage vegetables after harvest. Since ethylene is a product of the normal metabolism of plants, the specific problems it causes are discussed among disorders of affected crops, and, in more general terms, in Chapter 1.

Ammonia, in contrast, is a toxic gas used as a refrigerant in mechanical refrigeration systems. If a leak develops and ammonia concentration in the room exceeds 0.5%, the stored vegetables may be seriously injured in an hour or less (Ramsey and Butler 1928).

Ammonia injury manifests itself as a brown to black discoloration, particularly in peripheral tissue that is naturally red, yellow or brown. Normally, white tissue, such as in white onions, turns greenish yellow. After severe injury, deeper tissue may be affected and become mushy.

Injury from ammonia is best avoided by proper maintenance of refrigeration equipment and by daily inspection of each storage room. Since ammonia irritates eyes and nasal passages at much lower concentration (about 0.01%) than it causes injury to vegetables, monitoring by odor is effective (Anon. 1961).

For CA storage rooms, or others where daily entry is impossible, a nontoxic refrigerant, an automatic alarm system, or an indirect cooling system is advisable.

If an ammonia leak is detected, prompt and thorough aeration is essential if injury is to be minimized. Prolonged exposure will render any vegetable useless. Since the gas is readily soluble in water, a fogging system or water spray can aid in removing ammonia, unless free water or high RH permanently harms the vegetable.

ASPECTS OF DISEASE PREVENTION

General Comments

The old adage "An ounce of prevention is worth a pound of cure" is doubly appropriate in respect to diseases of vegetables and melons. First, relatively few dollars invested in prevention can literally save thousands in losses. Second, prevention generally is the only choice, because once started, postharvest diseases of vegetables cannot be cured but only slowed.

Careful physical handling throughout marketing and diligent concern for maintaining vegetables and melons at near optimum temperature and relative humidity can help tremendously in reducing losses from diseases, because many organisms that affect stored produce are weak pathogens.

The incidence of some diseases can be reduced by bactericides or fungicides. However, the array of these chemicals, their legal status, and their tolerances constantly change. Therefore, we will discuss only a few of particular interest. We defer to local authorities with current information for details on other compounds, rate of application, and necessary precautions.

Chemical Decay Inhibitors

Chlorine   The most commonly used chlorine compound is hypochlorous acid, which is formed when either hypochlorite tablets or gaseous chlorine is dissolved in water.

Chlorine compounds are useful because they prevent a buildup of bacteria or fungi in recirculated water that is used to wash or cool vegetables. They generally are useless in combatting established infections, because the chlorine is inactivated by contact with organic matter. This loss of efficacy also occurs by contact with organic matter that is suspended in wash water. This instability of Cl can be reduced by maintaining the solution in a pH range of 8.0 to 8.3. If this is not done the usual, effective concentration of 100 to 200 ppm of active Cl will rapidly become lower and thus the treatment will be useless. Consequently, chlorine concentration and pH must be checked several times each day, if soil adheres to the vegetable. Suppliers of chlorine have simple test kits for Cl and pH determinations.

Antibiotics   In the late 1950s, antibiotics seemed like the long sought miracle cure for many diseases of plants, including such serious postharvest diseases as bacterial soft rot (U.S. Dept. Agr. 1956). None is currently used to control diseases on fresh vegetables, principally for two reasons. First, the high cost of the compounds prevented their widespread use; second, none are officially approved because their use on vegetables which are eaten raw may endanger the medicinal effectiveness of the antibiotics.

Ozone   Ozone, one of the major deleterious components of smog, repeatedly has been promoted for decay control. However, concentrations of the gas that inhibit infections by or growth of fungi also seriously injure vegetables and cause discomfort and possible hazard to workers exposed to the gas (Spalding 1966, 1968; Mallison and Spalding 1966). Thus, there no longer is any justification for the use of ozone for decay control on any fresh vegetable or melon.

Hot Water   Incongruous as it may sound at first, hot water baths substantially reduce decay in some vegetables and melons. Although the method has been used for many years on some fruits, its application to vegetables is relatively new, and was pioneered by Johnson (1968).

The treatment is based on the fortunate fact that hot water of a specified temperature and applied for a certain time is more harmful to the microorganism than to the product treated. Generally, the water is between 49° and 60° C (120° and 140° F) and the vegetables mostly are exposed for ½ to 1½ min. Specific recommendations are given for the crops of concern, mainly peppers and cantaloups.

Hot water has certain specific advantages over chemical control agents and one primary disadvantage. First, hot water leaves no potentially dangerous residue. Second, hot water penetrates more deeply than chemicals, and thus inactivates organisms that already have grown below the surface. The chief disadvantage of hot water is its lack of residual protection. However, if combined with proper subsequent handling, this need not be a major problem.

If residual protection is essential, hot water can be combined with a fungicide that is dissolved or suspended in the water. This combination permits substantial reduction in the amount of fungicide normally used, and thus reduces the danger of excessive residue. Hot water with a fungicide is highly effective in controlling decay of cantaloups (Stewart and Wells 1970).

Lastly, a word of caution: directions must be scrupulously followed. If the water temperature is too low or the exposure time too short, the treatment will be useless. If the water is too hot or the exposure too long, the commodity can be seriously injured. However, accurate thermostats and positive, controlled flow of fruits through the water bath make decay control via hot water commercially practical.

Diseases of Specific Crops

The sections on specific crops include diseases that are likely to be found on vegetables or melons on the market. However, we have not attempted encyclopedic coverage. Diseases we selected actually or potentially cause serious losses to shippers, transportation companies, receivers or consumers. Further, the incidence of many of these diseases can be reduced or even eliminated by proper handling, shipping and storage practices.

We relied heavily on the comprehensive presentation contained in the series of U.S. Department of Agriculture Handbooks on market diseases of various vegetables. For primary sources not cited by us, we refer you to this series, the titles of which are listed in the references. Other sources cited were consulted in the original publication.

REFERENCES

ANON. 1961. Matheson Gas Data Book. Matheson Co., East Rutherford, N.J.

ECKERT, J. W. 1975. Postharvest diseases of fresh fruits and vegetables—etiology and control. In Postharvest Biology and Handling of Fruits and Vegetables. N. F. Haard and D. K. Salunkhe (Editors). AVI Publishing Co., Westport, Conn.

JENSEN, H. 1929. Heat injury to early potatoes at harvest time. Proc. Am. Soc. Hort. Sci. 26, 27–28.

JOHNSON, H. B. 1968. Heat and other treatments for cantaloupes and peppers. In United Fresh Fruit and Vegetable Association Yearbook. pp. 9, 14, 51–52, 54, 56. United Fresh Fruit and Vegetable Assoc., Washington, D.C.

KASMIRE, R.F., SARQUIS, A. V., and WRIGHT, D. N. 1962. Midsummer cantaloups. Market quality studies 1961. Univ. Calif. Agr. Ext. Serv. AXT-50.

LIPTON, W. J. 1975. Whitewashing Crenshaw and cantaloup melons to reduce solar injury. U.S. Dept. Agr. Mktg. Res. Rept. 1045.

LIPTON, W. J. 1977. Ultraviolet radiation as a factor in solar injury and vein tract browning of cantaloups. J. Am. Soc. Hort. Sci. 102, 32–36.

LUTZ, J. M. 1936. The influences of rate of thawing on freezing injury of apples, potatoes, and onions. Proc. Am. Soc. Hort. Sci. 33, 227–233.

LUTZ, J. M., and HARDENBURG, R. E. 1968. The commercial storage of fruits, vegetables, and florist and nursery stocks. U.S. Dept. Agr. Handbook 66.

MALLISON, E. D., and SPALDING, D. H. 1966. Use of ozone in tomato ripening rooms. U.S. Dept. Agr. ARS 52-17.

McCOLLOCH, L. P., COOK, H. T., and WRIGHT, W. R. 1968. Market diseases of tomatoes, peppers, and eggplants. U.S. Dept. Agr. Handbook 28.

PARSONS, C. S., and DAY, R. H. 1970. Freezing injury of root crops: beets, carrots, parsnips, radishes, and turnips. U.S. Dept. Agr. Mktg. Res. Rept. 866.

RAMSEY, G. B., and BUTLER, L. F. 1928. Injury to onions and fruits caused by exposure to ammonia. J. Agr. Res. 37, 339–348.

RAMSEY, G. B., FRIEDMAN, B. A., and SMITH, M. A. 1959. Market diseases of beets, chicory, endive, escarole, globe artichokes, lettuce, rhubarb, spinach, and sweetpotatoes. U.S. Dept. Agr. Handbook 155.

RAMSEY, G. B., and SMITH, M.A. 1961. Market diseases of cabbage, cauliflower, turnips, cucumbers, melons, and related crops. U.S. Dept. Agr. Handbook 184.

SMITH, M. A., McCOLLOCH, L. P., and FRIEDMAN, B. A. 1966. Market diseases of asparagus, onions, beans, peas, carrots, celery, and related vegetables. U.S. Dept. Agr. Handbook 303.

SPALDING, D. H. 1966. Appearance and decay of strawberries, peaches, and lettuce treated with ozone. U.S. Dept. Agr. Mktg. Res. Rept. 756.

SPALDING, D. H. 1968. Effects of ozone atmospheres on spoilage of fruits and vegetables after harvest. U.S. Dept. Agr. Mktg. Res. Rept. 801.

STEWART, J. K., and WELLS, J. M. 1970. Heat and fungicide treatments to control decay of cantaloupes. J. Am. Soc. Hort. Sci. 95, 226–229.

U.S. DEPARTMENT OF AGRICULTURE. 1956. Antibiotics for the control of vegetable crop diseases. U.S. Dept. Agr. ARS 22-33.

WHITEMAN, T. M. 1957. Freezing points of fruits, vegetables, and florist stocks. U.S. Dept. Agr. Mktg. Res. Rept. 196.

16

Physical Injuries, Market Disorders and Diseases of Leafy Vegetables and Immature Flower Heads

ARTICHOKES, GLOBE

Physical Injury

Freezing *Description* When freezing is slight the epidermis becomes detached and forms blisters, whose color ranges from whitish to light tan. When the blisters are broken the underlying tissue turns brown. Light freezing detracts from the appearance of the buds but has no adverse effect on culinary quality. However, severe freezing turns the buds black and unsalable and is first detectable internally near the juncture of stem and bud.

Cause Artichoke bracts freeze at −1.4° to −1.1° C (29.5° to 30° F), temperatures that are readily reached on clear nights in winter when radiation cooling below air temperature is likely. Nothing is published on freezing points of internal tissue of the fleshy receptacle.

Prevention While freezing injury cannot be prevented, its impact can be reduced by careful handling and prompt cooling of buds that were only slightly frozen. The first step minimizes opening the blisters and the second reduces darkening of exposed tissue.

When more than superficial freezing is suspected, longitudinal sections through the fleshy base reveal the injury after thawing. Extensive freezing damage precludes shipment of the crop. Permissible tolerances are defined by state regulations in California.

Mechanical *Description, Development, and Cause* Scuffed and split bracts are the common symptoms of mechanical abuse. Scuffing removes the epidermis, whether normal or frozen, and causes the under-lying tissue to turn dark brown or even black. Rubbing of buds against each other and against containers during harvest and packing are the chief causes of scuffing (Kasmire *et al.* 1958).

Split bracts result from any excessive force that has a tendency to bend or fold the bracts, particularly at the tips. However, some splits are present at harvest. The splits themselves are not objectionable, but the exposed tissue is prone to gray mold rot.

Prevention   Careful handling at each step during marketing can reduce scuffing and splitting of bracts. Prompt cooling to and shipment at or below 5° C (41° F) reduces darkening and decay that follow the injuries.

Similar Discoloration   Gray mold causes an identical darkening and may be indistinguishable from nonpathogenic darkening. How-ever, gray mold tends to spread rapidly at room temperature, whereas scuffed areas do not enlarge.

Disorder

Wilting   *Description*   Wilted buds are soft and pliable rather than crisp, and, unlike turgid buds, do not squeak when rubbed against each other. Prolonged wilting causes the bracts to fold inward. Wilted buds are unattractive and are a sign of serious mishandling.

Prevention   Wilting can readily be prevented by hydrocooling or by washing the buds in cool water, followed by immediate cold storage (Lipton and Stewart 1963). Ventilated bags or overwraps also reduce moisture loss. However, wet buds must be kept cold or else gray mold rot will become rampant.

Disease

Gray Mold Rot   *Pathogen Involved*   *Botrytis cinerea.*

Description   The lesions, which are light brown to almost black, can be found on any part of affected buds. The discolored areas are dry in normal air and moist in high humidity. In the latter case, the typical gray mold that produces grayish-brown spores covers the lesion.

Internally, decayed tissue is brown and firm in the bracts and stem, but somewhat spongy in the less fibrous, fleshy, edible base.

Development   The fungus can penetrate uninjured tissue, but it spreads much more rapidly when the spores land on a crack or abrasion. Most, possibly all, natural infections start at wounds either before or after harvest. The most frequent sites are the tips of bracts and the cut end of the stem, although abraded or frost-blistered surfaces also serve as sites of infection.

Botrytis grows at all temperatures normally encountered in growing or marketing of artichokes. However, its rate of growth at 5° C (41° F) is only about half that at 10° C (50° F), and at 0° C (32° F) it is insignificant. However, if an infection is present, removal to intermediate or higher temperatures results in rapid decay, particularly under high humidity.

Prevention   Holding artichokes below 5° C (41° F) minimizes the seriousness of this disease even during one month's storage of injured buds. However, gentle handling is still imperative, because ideal temperatures cannot always be maintained during marketing, and because injuries can accelerate decay as much as a 10° C (18° F) rise in temperature (Lipton and Harvey 1960). Prepackaged artichokes particularly must be kept cold because moisture commonly condenses in the package, thus creating ideal conditions for decay.

Similar Disorders   Scuff marks also turn brown but are superficial and do not enlarge.

BEETS (TOPS) AND CHARD (SWISS CHARD)

These closely related vegetables are considered together because they are subject to the same diseases.

Diseases

Bacterial Soft Rot   *Pathogens Involved*   *Erwinia carotovora* and other bacteria.

Description   Soft rot primarily is a problem on the tops of beets and the leaf blades and petioles of chard. Affected leaves appear gray-green, water-soaked, and they are slimy in advanced cases. Petioles of affected chard also are slimy, but brown.

Development and Prevention   Wounded tissue and mild temperatures combined with high relative humidity favor bacterial soft rot.

Thus, careful handling and prompt and continuous refrigeration near 0° C (32° F) help retard bacterial soft rot.

Cercospora Leaf Spot *Pathogen Involved* *Cercospora beticola.*

Description Affected leaves of beets and chard show spots that are light gray to tan. Their margins are reddish brown to purple and sharply defined.

Development and Prevention Infection occurs in the field and cannot be prevented after harvest. Storage near 0° C (32° F) will retard bacterial soft rot as a secondary disease.

BROCCOLI

Physical Injury

Freezing *Description and Development* The youngest florets at the center of the curd are most sensitive to freezing and turn brown on thawing. The dead tissue is a likely site for decay. Further, broccoli that has been frozen has an unpleasantly strong odor.

Cause The freezing points of buds and stalks are nearly the same, a few tenths of a degree above or below −1.1° C (30° F).

Prevention Broccoli is not as well protected by leaves as cauliflower, so that mild freezing can cause substantial damage. If freezing is suspected, the heads should be carefully examined after a day or two, and if damaged, should not be shipped.

Disorders

Boron Deficiency *Description* Leaves of boron-deficient broccoli are deformed and discolored, petioles are cracked and have corky growth, and the immature florets are brown.

Development, Cause, and Prevention. See *Cauliflower.*

Hollow Stem *Description* Hollow stem derives its name from the cavity that occupies the center of the stalk from just below the curd to varying distances along the stalk. The hole sometimes can be seen at the cut stem when broccoli is displayed and it may become discolored during marketing (Hipp 1974).

Cause and Prevention   Hollow stem can be induced by any factor that results in rapid growth of the plants and thus can be counteracted by measures that result in moderate growth rates. While hollow stem may interfere with acceptability of broccoli, no postharvest factors are involved in its development.

Yellowing   Yellowing of florets is the most common disorder of broccoli and is a sign of senescence. Holding for prolonged periods or at temperatures that are too high leads to yellowing. Exposure to ethylene also accelerates yellowing, particularly at temperatures above 5° C (41° F).

Yellowish-green broccoli tends to be poor in flavor and tough. It should be removed from display because appearance and eating quality have deteriorated too much.

Diseases   See *Crucifers, leafy*

BRUSSELS SPROUTS

Disorders

Tipburn and Brown Heart   Tipburn of Brussels sprouts discolors the margins of relatively mature leaves and closely resembles tipburn symptoms in cabbage. Brown heart takes its name form a discoloration of the heart leaves. No definite causes have been established for either disorder, although unfavorable water-relations and inadequate calcium availability have been implicated (Nieuwhof 1971; Maynard 1972). Production of resistant cultivars and assurance of adequate calcium during growth should minimize the problems.

Black Leaf Speck   Black speck on Brussels sprouts resembles that on cabbage sufficiently to assume that it is caused by the same factor or factors. Lacking contrary information, all other comments made for cabbage also apply.

Yellowing   All too frequently Brussels sprouts at retail are yellow and wilted instead of green and crisp. These defects are signs of senescence and betray unsatisfactory holding environments.

Diseases   See *Crucifers, leafy*

CABBAGE

Physical Injuries

Freezing *Description*   Thawed leaves of cabbage first are water-soaked, translucent, and limp; then they either dry out or become centers of decay, depending on the relative humidity of the surroundings. Water-soaked, green outer leaves are a dull tan-green. Outer leaves are less likely to be permanently injured than head leaves and heavy ribs and veins freeze more slowly than thin blades.

Development and Cause   The freezing point of cabbage ranges from slightly below −1.1° C (30° F) to only slightly below 0° C (32° F), but, paradoxically, cabbage is fairly resistant to permanent freezing injury. Slight and brief freezing may actually improve the flavor of cabbage, although some of the outer leaves may wilt slightly and become tough.
Solid heads are more susceptible to freezing injury than merely firm heads.

Prevention   Since the extent of damage may not be apparent while cabbage is frozen, decisions on its marketability should be delayed until after thawing. For further precautions, see Chapter 15.

Solar Injury   Intense sunlight causes the epidermis of an outer leaf or two to blister, and eventually it leads to the bleached papery appearance typical of solar injury (sunscald, heat injury).
The desiccated leaves always should be removed before marketing because they are unsightly and subject to decay.

Thrips Pustules   Thrips feeding on cabbage puncture the surface, which causes the puncture sites to dry up when on outer leaves and to swell when on inner leaves. Thus, feeding areas appear speckled brown with irregular outlines or slightly warty.

Similar Disorder   Black leaf speck resembles thrips damage, but usually is more widespread in a head and not accompanied by pustules.

Disorders

Black Leaf Speck   *Description*   The brown to black specks are sunken and occur anywhere in the head, in a few or on almost all leaves (Fig. 16.1).

Development and Cause   No definite cause for black leaf speck has been determined, although inability of cabbage to adequately utilize oxygen near 0° C (32° F), involvement of cabbage mosaic virus, and exudates from the leaves themselves have been implicated (Nelson 1926; Natti 1958; Strandberg *et al.* 1969). Conceivably, several factors simultaneously or separately contribute to the development of this disorder before or after harvest. Severe symptoms can occur after 1 or 2 weeks of storage at low temperature.

Prevention   The causes are too uncertain to permit suggestion of a cure, although use of resistant cultivars appears promising.

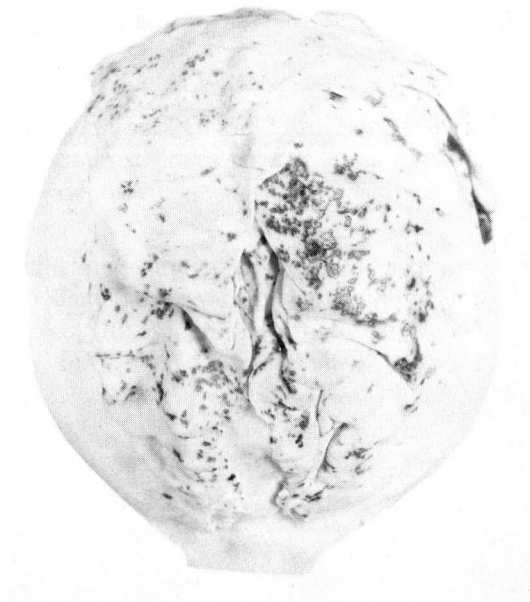

U.S. Dept. of Agriculture Photo

FIG. 16.1.   BLACK LEAF SPECK OF CABBAGE

Similar Defects   The specks resemble early stages of Alternaria spot which, however, is more common on outer leaves.

Boron Deficiency *Description*   A hollow stem is the only symptom of boron deficiency in mature cabbage. Consequently, the disorder is of concern only in kraut manufacture where the stems also are shredded. When thus used, affected cabbage should be rejected or trimmed if discolored pieces are to be avoided (Walker *et al*. 1940).

For further comments, see *Cauliflower*.

Tipburn *Description*   The margins or larger portions of head leaves are light tan to dark brown. Outer leaves occasionally are affected, whereas those near the growing point appear immune to tipburn.

Tipburn often is noticeable only upon cutting a head, when it appears as a semicircular brown band parallel to the surface.

Development and Cause   Circumstances leading to tipburn are complex, but the disorder is more common late in the season and in large heads. Further, some cultivars are much more susceptible to tipburn than others. Rapid growth and poor soil aeration also seem to contribute to tipburn (Nieuwhof 1961; Nieuwhof *et al*. 1960; Walker *et al*. 1961).

Prevention   Until the precise cause or causes of tipburn have been determined, the only preventative is production of resistant cultivars.

Diseases See *Crucifers, leafy*

CAULIFLOWER

Physical Injury

Freezing *Description*   Freezing injury is readily detectable only after the injured curd has turned brown. Frozen cauliflower also has a strong, disagreeable odor when cooked.

Development and Cause   Curds of cauliflower freeze between about $-1.1°$ and $-0.8°$ C ($30°$ and $30.5°$ F). Since the curds generally are protected by leaves during development, air temperature can drop to $-2.2°$ to $-2.8°$ C ($27°$ to $28°$ F) before the curds are frozen. However, leaves protect mainly during radiative cooling that lasts only a few hours, not during prolonged freezes.

Prevention   Keeping curds well covered by leaves retards freezing, but once frozen, cauliflower should not be shipped or marketed, because the product is unsightly, subject to decay, and unpalatable.

Solar Browning   *Description*   Any part of curds not covered by leaves shows a superficial discoloration that ranges from yellow to brown to black, depending upon length of exposure.

Development and Cause   Browning is caused by exposure of curds to ultraviolet light and an exposure of only 3 hr elicits discoloration within 2 days. Browning is induced whether the curd is exposed to the sun before or after harvest (Brouwer 1955).

Prevention   Solar browning is prevented by keeping curds well shaded by leaves during growth and by avoiding their exposure to sun during or after harvest.

Disorders

Boron Deficiency   *Description and Cause*   A brownish discoloration of the curd and of the pith of stems, and blisters and cracks on midribs are signs of boron deficiency. In severe cases, the pith shrinks and the stem thus becomes hollow. Boron-deficient cauliflower tastes bitter raw or cooked (Dearborn and Raleigh 1936).

Prevention   Proper fertilization is the only cure. Affected curds never should be marketed because a discolored curd is highly unappetizing.

Riciness   *Description*   In ricy cauliflower the curds are loose instead of compact. The rudimentary florets are separated instead of being tightly packed together. Ricy curds are unattractive and tend to have an excessively strong flavor.

Development and Cause   Riciness can be induced when cauliflower plants are exposed to high growing temperatures (above 20° C; 68° F) before curd initiation and to low temperatures (7° C; 45° F) thereafter (Wiebe and Krug 1974). Riciness is also a sign of senescence that appears on curds that have been cut too mature or that have been held at too high a temperature after harvest.

Prevention   Since weather determines field temperature there is no recourse against riciness induced by growing conditions. However, timely harvest and holding cauliflower near 0° C (32° F) will avoid development of riciness after harvest.

CELERY

Physical Injury

Freezing *Description*   Freezing causes leaves and petioles to appear wilted and water-soaked upon thawing. Milder freezing causes depressions in the parenchyma tissue between the ridges on the convex side of the stalks. Further, the epidermis tends to separate, loosen and sometimes rupture. On the concave side the frozen areas are circular and the epidermis is loose but entire, thus giving a bubble effect. Both types of lesions turn brown with age (White-Stevens 1936).

Development and Cause   Celery freezes at about $-0.5°$ C $\pm$ 0.3° (31° F $\pm$ 0.5°), depending on the tissue involved. Petioles freeze more readily than leaves.

Disorders

Blackheart *Description*   Water-soaked or dry, brown heart leaves give the disorder its name. Entire leaves or only their tips may be dead.

Development and Cause   Blackheart develops during growth in response to a deficiency of calcium in the soil. However, affected tissue may darken after harvest and readily becomes a center for soft rot infection.

Prevention   Various sprays of calcium salts during growth have been effective (Geraldson 1954). Celery with blackheart should never be shipped because it is unsightly and the danger of decay is substantial.

Cracked Stem and Brown Checking (Boron Deficiency)   Cracked stem and brown checking are symptoms of boron deficiency and are, therefore, discussed together. However, both symptoms do not necessarily appear simultaneously

Description   Cracked stem is characterized by many brown isolated cracks across or tears in the ribs of the outer (abaxial) surface of the petioles, although the inner surface also may be affected. Brown checking only affects the inner surface of petioles along the longitudinal axis. The injured area appears corrugated and ranges from greenish-tan through dark brown. Horizontal cracks open in the lesions in severe cases (Spurr 1952; Yamaguchi *et al.* 1953).

Development and Cause   Deficiency symptoms can develop on any age plant when boron is deficient in the soil.

Prevention   Cracked stem only can be prevented by proper fertilization. Harvest of visibly affected plants is a waste of money because such stalks are unmarketable.

Pithiness   *Description*   Pithiness is invisible externally but affected petioles are soft and collapse when squeezed. The central part of such petioles is hollow and some or most of the tissue is white, spongy and appears dry. Since pithiness refers to a disorder of the petioles, the term hollow stem is a misnomer.

Development and Cause   Pithiness seen on the market is a sign of senescence that may appear before or after harvest. Outer, old petioles become pithy before young ones and often only the two outermost whorls are affected. Pithiness of field origin may be induced by cultural practices that interfere with normal growth or simply by excessive delay of harvest. When celery is stored at 0° C (32° F), slight pithiness in outer petioles becomes noticeable after 60 days and definitely objectionable symptoms can appear within 90 days (White-Stevens 1938; Coyne 1962).

Prevention   Proper cultural practices and timely harvest minimize the incidence of preharvest pithiness. Postharvest pithiness is avoided by limiting storage to less than 60 days. Further, with a year-round supply of fresh celery available, little storage-induced pithiness should reach terminal markets. The cultivars Utah and Utah Pascal are somewhat resistant to pithiness.

Diseases

Bacterial Soft Rot   *Pathogen Involved*   *Erwinia carotovora.*

Description   Small, soft and water-soaked spots are the early signs on petioles and leaflets. As the lesions enlarge, the entire structure becomes watery and the color changes from green to brown. Decayed tissue readily sloughs, and leaflets may entirely disappear.

Development Soft rot bacteria enter any wound and often invade lesions caused by other pathogens. Warm, wet conditions are particularly conducive to spreading of the disease.

Prevention Celery must be rapidly cooled below 2° C (36° F) after harvest and held there throughout marketing, particularly during tropical weather. Sanitation during harvest and packing is equally important. Any recycled water should be chlorinated to about 70 to 100 ppm and frequently checked for concentration, because organic matter inactivates the chlorine.

If hydrocooling is practiced, the water must be kept well chilled and the petioles cooled to 0° to 2° C (32° to 36° F), because warm and wet celery decays very rapidly.

Similar Diseases Several fungi also cause soft rots, but generally they produce some mycelium, which is absent in bacterial rots.

Brown Spot *Pathogen Involved* *Cephalosporium apii.*

Description Lesions are irregularly shaped, tan to brown, and up to about 2 cm (¾ in.) across. They can occur on either side of a petiole, may enlarge by coalescing, and in serious cases can cause distortion of mature petioles.

Development and Control The disease originates in the field, but incipient infections can spread after harvest unless the temperature is near 0° C (32° F).

Gray Mold Rot *Pathogen Involved* *Botrytis cinerea.*

Description Lesions are water-soaked but firm initially. In older lesions the skin slips off readily, the tissue is grayish-buff, and may be covered with a dense mass of grayish-brown spores.

Development and Prevention Gray mold primarily causes losses in celery stored a month or longer, but may also affect a freshly harvested crop during and after cool, moist weather.

For immediate marketing, a transit temperature between 0° and 2° C (32° and 36° F) is adequate, but for prolonged storage 0° C is essential if substantial losses are to be avoided.

Late Blight   *Pathogen Involved*   *Septoria apiicola.*

Description   Blighted spots are yellowish when small but change to brown, grayish, or even black with advancing age. The spots may be isolated or coalesced into large decayed areas. Shiny black fruiting bodies grow on dead and adjacent normal-appearing tissue (Fig. 16.2).

Development   Late blight infections originate before harvest, but undetected incipient lesions will enlarge during transit or storage.

Prevention   After harvest, spread of the disease can be prevented only by prompt cooling to and holding at 0° C (32° F). Suspected lots should be marketed immediately.

Watery Soft Rot (Pink Rot)   *Pathogen Involved*   Various species of *Sclerotinia.*

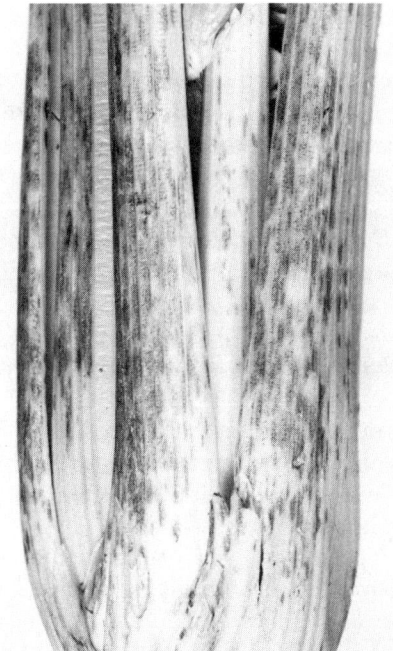

U.S. Dept. of Agriculture Photo

FIG. 16.2.   LATE BLIGHT OF CELERY

Description.—As the name suggests, affected tissue is water-soaked and soft, and the light-brown lesions have a pinkish-brown border. White fungal growth may adhere to older lesions, which also may show fruiting bodies that are white when young and black when mature.

Development and Prevention   The pathogen may enter with or without prior wounding, but much more readily in the former case. Infection can occur at temperatures normally encountered by celery, but the disease is slowed at 0° C (32° F). If field infections are suspected, prolonged storage, even at 0° C, could be disastrous.

CHARD (SWISS CHARD)

Physical Injury

Mechanical   *Description*   Abrasion of the petioles and crushing of the leaves are the most common and objectionable evidence of physical injury.
Abraded white petioles turn tan to brown and thus are unsightly. The discoloration is less noticeable on red cultivars, but they nevertheless indicate poor handling practices.

Development and Cause   Abrasion of petioles and crushing of leaves probably occur mainly during harvest and packing, when the bunches are packed too tightly into their containers.

Prevention   Chard must be handled carefully and not be over-packed. Prompt cooling to and shipping at 0° C (32° F) retards discoloration of abraded and crushed areas. Rapid turnover at retail is also essential.

Disorder

Wilting   See *Spinach.*

Diseases   See *Beets (Tops)*

CRUCIFERS, LEAFY

Diseases

Diseases of leafy and similar crucifers (broccoli, Brussels sprouts, cabbage, Chinese cabbage, cauliflower, collards, kale, mustard, watercress) are arranged by organism or common name, rather than by crop, because the same organisms attack several crops in this group. Further, they often cause similar symptoms. The name of the disease will be followed by a listing of affected crops.

Alternaria Leaf Spot   *Pathogen Involved*   *Alternaria brassicae, Alternaria oleracea.*

Crops Affected   All leafy crucifers.

Description   Initially, the grayish-brown to black spots are small, but they may enlarge to a diameter of 25 mm (1 in.) or more as they age.

Spots caused by *A. brassicae* may have concentric light and dark zones and the growth of the mold may be obvious in high relative humidity.

Development   Alternaria leaf spot starts in the field, particularly in wet seasons, but spreads during storage or transit, particularly above about 10° C (50° F).

Prevention   Storage near 0° C (32° F) greatly retards the spread of *Alternaria.* Low humidity has the same effect, but cannot be used because it causes wilting of the stored vegetables.

Bacterial Leaf Spot   *Pathogen Involved*   *Pseudomonas maculicola.*

Crops Affected   Broccoli and cauliflower mainly.

Description   Broccoli: purplish gray to black lesions ranging from pinpoint size to circular or oblong spots about 1 mm ($^{1}/_{32}$ in.) in diameter mar florets, petioles, stems and leaves. Coalescing can increase the size of the lesions.

Cauliflower: small, water-soaked spots with dark specks at the center are found on leaves. On curds the spots are gray, brown or black and may be superficial or deeper. Diseased tissue is firm unless softened by secondary organisms.

Development and Prevention   The fungus enters through the pores (stomata) of leaves. Symptoms are most abundant on the lower (abaxial) surface. The disease develops most rapidly at moderate temperatures; thus storage near 0° C (32° F) is most appropriate.

Similar Disease   Brown rot on cauliflower curds.

Bacterial Soft Rot   *Pathogens Involved*   *Erwinia carotovora* mainly, but also other species.

Crops Affected   All leafy crucifers.

Description   This occasionally serious disease starts out as small water-soaked spots on leaves or curds but can convert a specimen into a slimy mass when humidity is high and temperature is above about 10° C (50° F). Severe soft rot is accompanied by a nauseating odor.

Development and Prevention   Soft rot bacteria are ever present, but only invade tissue that has been injured in some way—mechanically, physiologically, or by a primary organism. During harvest, knives often carry the bacteria into the open wound.

Bacterial soft rot can be minimized by careful handling, avoiding freezing, trimming diseased tissue before shipment, and above all, by keeping vegetables near 0° C (32° F).

High CO_2 reduces soft rot in broccoli but is injurious to cauliflower and the effect of CO_2 for decay control on other crucifers has not been adequately tested.

Bacterial Zonate Spot   *Pathogen Involved*   *Pseudomonas cichorii*.

Crops Affected   Cabbage primarily.

Description   The spots are round to irregular, about 2 to 15 mm ($1/16$ to ½ in.) in diameter, initially buff and eventually dark brown. The lesions are target-like, with a dark center surrounded by a lighter area that, in turn, has a darker rim. Infected areas soften little and remain dry.

Development   The bacterium enters the leaf through wounds and spreads most rapidly at room temperature.

Prevention   Avoidance of wounding and holding cabbage below 5° C (41° F) presumably minimizes the disorder.

Black Rot   *Pathogen Involved*   *Xanthomonas campestris*.

Crops Affected   All leafy crucifers.

Description   Cabbage: This serious disease spreads via the vascular system to all parts of a head. Thus, veins appear black, and the midrib has a dark, central line that is diffuse because the dead tissue is covered by normal cells. Cutting across the stem often reveals a circle of black conducting elements in the white tissue.

The earliest conspicuous symptoms often are yellow to light-brown spots or areas along the leaf margins.

Unless invaded by secondary organisms, the black tissue remains firm.

Cauliflower: Symptoms generally resemble those in cabbage, but during wet weather black veins may be absent, but leaves wilt and eventually dry.

Chinese cabbage: Black discoloration of veins may be accompanied by numerous brown spots on the leaf blade.

Development   Black rot is favored by wet, warm days and cool nights. It does not become more severe after harvest, although associated soft rot may give the opposite impression.

Prevention. -Mildly affected heads of cabbage can be trimmed, but severely affected ones must be discarded. Cauliflower with sound curds can be marketed with a minimum of leaves, or the curds can be used for processing. If stored, 0° C (32° F) is advisable.

Brown Rot *Pathogen Involved*   *Alternaria brassicae.*
This is the same organism that causes leaf spot. Since, however, this serious disease commonly is known as brown rot when it occurs on curds of cauliflower, this separate section is included.

Crops Affected   Cauliflower (curd).

Description   Lesions on curds change from light brown to greenish black with age. Mycelial growth may be evident at high humidity. The lesions may be isolated and small or large, dry and firm, or wet and soft.

Development and Prevention   Shallow lesions may form within a week at humidities above about 75% even at 2° C (36° F). Thus, low temperature is the best, but not a complete preventative.

Similar Diseases   Bacterial leaf spot on curds.

Downy Mildew   *Pathogen Involved*   *Peronospora parasitica.*

Crops Affected   All leafy crucifers, but mainly cabbage and cauliflower.

Description   On leaves, the typical white, downy patches are preceded by small, pale, greenish-yellow and angular spots. Old spots are yellowish brown.

The fungus also invades the stem, which then turns grayish-black internally. During prolonged storage of such cabbage, the leaves around the growing point also may get infected. In cauliflower, the branches of the curd as well as leaves can become mildewed.

Development   Downy mildew readily attacks crucifers during mild, moist growing weather, and infections become visible within 3 days at 21° C (70° F). The disease also spreads rapidly in storage after field infection and at warm storage temperatures, but more slowly at 5° C (41° F).

Prevention   Any leaf with mildew should be trimmed before packing, and affected curds discarded. Storage near 0° C (32° F) is the only useful retardant when an infection is present.

Gray Mold Rot   *Pathogen Involved*   *Botrytis cinerea.*

Crops Affected   Broccoli, Brussels sprouts, cabbage and cauliflower.

Description   Lesions are greenish-brown and water-soaked on leaves, but may be topped by a fine white cushion of mold. As lesions age, they become grayish brown, as do the mounds of mold when spores are formed.

In fleshy tissue of cauliflower or broccoli, the diseased portions are gray to light brown and moist, but not wet like soft rots.

Development and Control   Gray mold rot spreads even at 0° C (32° F), although more slowly than at even slightly higher temperatures. The fungus incites decay only if debris or wounds are present to provide nutrients. Consequently, for long-term storage of cabbage, careful handling and removal of injured, wilted or other defective leaves prior to storage will retard this, the most destructive, decay of cabbage. RH of 98 to 100% and CA conditions (about 3% O_2 plus 5% CO_2) also help to slow spread of this rot (Yoder 1977).

Rhizoctonia Head Rot   *Pathogen Involved*   *Rhizoctonia solani.*

Crops Affected   Cabbage mainly.

Description   Somewhat coarse, cream to brown surface mycelium and chocolate brown, hard masses of dry, resting mycelium (sclerotia) typify this disease. In head rot, the lesions are dark brown and sunken.

Development   Since this fungus is found in soils wherever vegetables are grown, it cannot be avoided. However, high humidity favors and dry conditions hinder infection.

When any evidence of this rot is present, storage near 0° C (32° F) is essential for storage periods of one month or more.

Rhizopus Soft Rot   *Pathogen Involved*   *Rhizopus stolonifer.*

Crops Affected   Brussels sprouts, cabbage, cauliflower.

Description   This fungus, as the descriptive name implies, almost literally dissolves the infected tissue, rendering it mushy. The dead, light brown tissue is often covered by coarse, stringy mycelium that may bear masses of white to black clusters of spores (sporangia).

Development and Prevention   Rhizopus rot almost inevitably will be serious if susceptible crops are held under moist conditions and above about 13° C (55° F) for just a few days. Further, wounded tissue is particularly susceptible.

Development is slow between 7° and 13° C (45° and 55° F), and nil below 5° C (41° F).

Similar Diseases   The dark fungal growth distinguishes Rhizopus rot from watery soft rot and lack of strong odor from bacterial soft rot.

Ring Spot   *Pathogen Involved*   *Mycosphaerella brassicicola.*

Crops Affected   Mainly cauliflower from California or Oregon; occasionally on Brussels sprouts, cabbage and kale.

Description   Young spots are small, circular, and their dark centers are surrounded by greenish-yellow, water-soaked borders. In older, larger spots, the centers are surrounded by narrow olive-green or olive-gray borders. Further, black fruiting bodies may be found in the central area.

Development and Prevention   Moist, cool conditions encourage the disease, but 0° C (32° F) virtually stops its spread.

Watery Soft Rot (Sclerotinia Rot, Cottony Rot)   *Pathogen Involved.* —*Sclerotinia sclerotiorum.*

Crop Affected   Cabbage mainly.

Description   The two popular terms describe this decay: the mushy or actually leaking tissue is often covered by a white cushion of mold growth.
The color of initial lesions is not consistent, but they appear water-soaked.

Development   Initial infestation with this soil-borne fungus occurs in the field, but spreads from infected plants to adjacent healthy ones. The disease spreads most rapidly at about 24° C (75° F) and at high relative humidity. But even low temperatures do not stop its growth.

Prevention   Storage near 0° C (32° F) substantially retards the spread of the disorder.

Similar Diseases   Bacterial soft rot: this disease produces a putrid odor and lacks the cottony mycelium.

LEEK

Physical Injury

Mechanical   *Description and Cause*   Stalks of leek at retail frequently have lower ends that have been butchered rather than trimmed. Instead of only roots and possibly a sliver of the bulbous base being cut off, a half inch or more is removed. This sloppy practice results in an unsightly stalk that readily discolors and is difficult to sell.

Prevention   Simple care in trimming would eliminate this waste.

Disorder

Seedstalks   *Description and Cause*   The center of stalks sometimes is occupied by a solid, round seedstalk instead of by young leaves.

This situation is particularly common in leek harvested after high temperatures in the field have initiated bolting.

Leek with a seedstalk tends to be tough and the seedstalk itself is inedible.

Prevention   After bolting has started, leek should be carefully inspected at packing and all "seedy" plants should be rigidly culled. Harvest should be discontinued when culling becomes uneconomical.

LETTUCE, HEAD

Physical Injuries

Freezing   *Description*   Separation of the epidermis from underlying tissue, also called blistering, is the most common sign of freezing in lettuce. The dead cells of the separated epidermis are tan when on outer leaves, but are white when on those more protected from drying. The blisters may involve a few mm^2 of area or they may encompass most of the leaf, depending upon the severity of the freezing exposure.

Severely frozen lettuce has a water-soaked appearance once the tissue has been thawed.

Development and Cause   Lettuce freezes at $-0.6°$ C $\pm$ $0.2°$ ($31°$ F $\pm$ $0.3°$), a temperature encountered in the field in winter production areas or in other areas late in the season. Freezing also may occur in transit due to improperly adjusted or malfunctioning refrigeration, or extremely low ambient temperatures.

Transit freezing usually can be distinguished from field freezing; the former tends to be confined to or is more severe in the periphery of a carton, and also is more common in cartons on the periphery of a load. In contrast, field freezing is randomly distributed through the load.

Freezing also may occur during vacuum cooling, but only rarely, particularly when compared to the frequency of inadequate precooling.

Prevention   The frequency of transit freezing can be minimized by careful calibration, adjustment, and maintenance of thermostats and of refrigeration equipment, and periodic inspection of the equipment and temperature indicators during transit.

Damage to deep tissue from field freezing can be avoided by delaying harvest until frozen lettuce has completely thawed. Similarly, lettuce frozen in transit should be thawed at about $5°$ C ($41°$ F) before being unloaded, because frozen tissue is exceptionally sensitive to mechanical injury.

Mechanical Injury   *Description*   Mechanical injury is readily recognized by the crushed, bruised or torn tissue. Usually 1 or 2 midribs are bruised or crushed, but sometimes the forces are so great that the entire head tends to be cubical rather than spherical. In contrast, slight bruising may be mainly noticeable because of the pink discoloration of the injured cells.

Abrasion or chafing, recognized by the flattened, brown parts of exterior leaves, frequently occurs in heads adjacent to walls of cartons.

Tearing usually is confined to wrapper leaves, which are discarded by the retailer, and thus is not serious unless conditions favor decay of the wounded tissue.

Separation of head leaves from the stem is another symptom of physical damage and results in an unsightly, discolored lower portion of the head.

Causes   Mechanical injury is principally caused by careless or rough handling during all stages of marketing—from field to kitchen. However, the most serious injury usually occurs at harvest, when too much lettuce is forced into too little container. Although the advent of the flat-pack carton has reduced this problem, many heads still are damaged during filling and closure of the boxes. Further injury is done if a carton is accidentally dropped to the ground during loading.

After arrival at the cooling plant, cartons all too often drop off the pallets as they are moved from truck to concrete slab or from slab to vacuum retort. Instead of being lifted back onto the load, the cartons are often thrown back.

Once cooled, cartons may drop on the concrete floor as they are transferred to the conveyor belt that carries them to a rail car or truck trailer. During loading further damage may result from tossed, dropped or kicked cartons.

During transit, the lower layers of cartons are sometimes depressed several inches because the overhead weight is too great for the carton. Thus the weight rests on the lettuce. Further, sudden stops or impacts during transit can dislodge cartons and damage the contents.

Unloading and transshipment to warehouses or stores provide further opportunity for mishandling. And finally, at retail, leaves are often cut as butts are trimmed, resulting in an insightly head.

Prevention   Methods of prevention are implicit in the causes of mechanical damage. They include: (1) the use of containers that are large enough for their load and strong enough to protect, not just envelope, it; (2) handling methods and machinery that minimize the chance of rough treatment; and (3) sufficient and properly trained supervision. Finally, bulk handling of wrapped lettuce in bins should reduce mechanical injury because the heads are not forced into boxes and because individual boxes no longer can be mishandled.

Similar Disorders   Pink discoloration of bruised tissue resembles pink rib, although close examination will reveal physical injury, when present.

Solar Injury   *Description*   Thin, papery or bronzed areas frequently characterize solar injury on leaves exposed to direct rays of the sun. The cap leaf or an adjacent one most frequently shows severe symptoms, whereas the next underlying leaf may have only a small yellowish-tan spot on the outer (abaxial) surface.

Alternate symptoms are a band of tan discolored tissue along veins of green leaves and discrete light tan spots or small areas in exposed, pale head leaves.

Development and Cause   Solar injury can develop in heads of lettuce that mature during clear weather when air temperatures are about 24° C (75° F) or higher, because leaves facing south or southwest may then exceed 38° C (100° F). The time and temperature combinations that are lethal to lettuce have not been determined, but repeated heating to between about 40° and 43° C (104° and 110° F) is probably injurious. However, the symptoms suggest that ultraviolet radiation, not only infrared radiation, may contribute to the damage.

Prevention   Solar injury cannot normally be prevented and is of little concern on the market unless the necrosis becomes a focus for decay.

Disorders

Some disorders of lettuce are difficult to distinguish from each other because cells of lettuce often die in groups, turn some shade of red or brown and collapse, no matter what the cause. Consequently, the shape, exact color, and distribution of the lesions in the head are essential knowledge for their identification. Furthermore, information on the background of the lettuce from field to market can greatly aid in identification. The task of identification has been aided by the publication of a guide that illustrates some of the disorders in color (Lipton *et al*. 1972).

The occurrence of some of the defects of head lettuce (Fig. 16.3) is highly seasonal and is influenced by climatic conditions and cultivar (Beraha and Kwolek 1975).

Carbon Dioxide Excess   *Description*   Brown stain (BNS) is the most characteristic symptom of high CO_2 injury and is expressed as oval to irregular lesions that range from yellow to brown and usually have darker margins than centers. However, some CO_2 induced lesions simply are reddish-brown spots or streaks. In serious cases the lesions coalesce and form larger, depressed, nearly uniformly colored patches. Regardless of severity, the necrosis is confined to the epidermis and a few additional cell layers. BNS develops on any head leaf and usually affects the midribs before the thin blades (Lipton *et al.* 1972).

A yellowish to reddish-brown discoloration of midribs and adjacent tissue is further evidence of CO_2 injury. The dead areas lack distinct

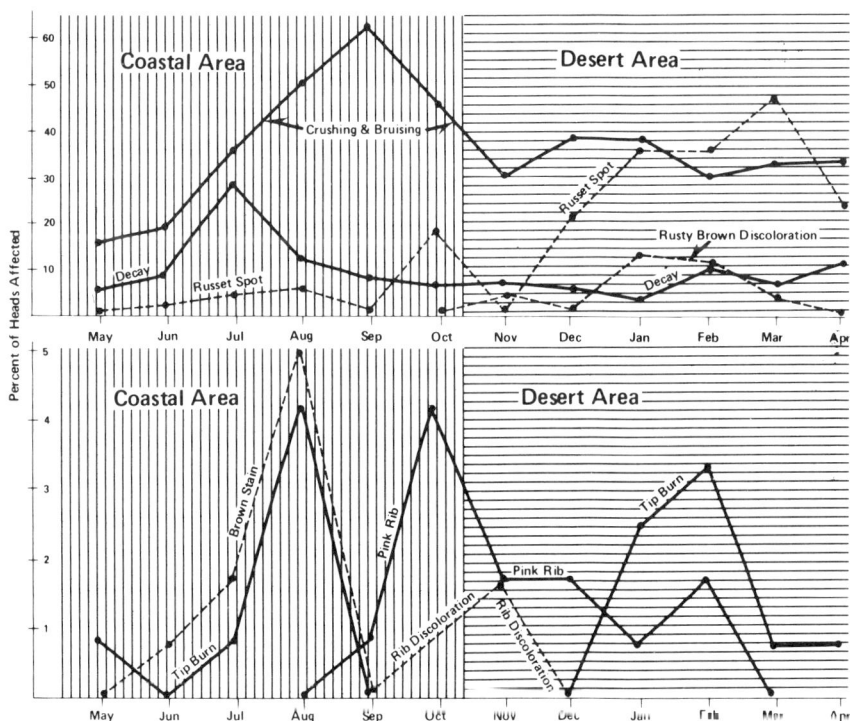

From Beraha and Kwolek (1977)

FIG. 16.3.   INCIDENCE OF EIGHT DEFECTS OF WESTERN-GROWTH HEAD LETTUCE IN RETAIL MARKETS IN CHICAGO DURING 1973–74
Note that scales on upper and lower graph differ by a factor of about 15.

margins and tend to extend along the main curvature of midribs, which lends them a corrugated appearance. Unless other evidence exists, this discoloration cannot be used as positive identification for CO_2 injury (Lipton 1971).

Death of leaflets clustered about the growing point sometimes is the first and only symptom of CO_2 injury. The reddish discoloration starts along the margins of such leaflets, progresses inward and, when severe, may discolor all heart leaves. This type of injury, unlike most disorders, is more extensive in soft than in firm or hard heads. Further, in soft heads the margins of inner green leaves are more commonly discolored than those of firm heads. In such leaves the necrotic areas are grayish rather than red (Lipton 1971).

Water-soaked lesions and exudation of droplets result from exposure to at least 20% CO_2, conditions that normally are not encountered during marketing of lettuce.

Development and Cause   Lettuce can be slightly injured by CO_2 concentration above about 1%, depending upon temperature and duration of exposure. One week's storage in 1 to 2% CO_2 at 3°C (38°F) can cause objectionable BNS, but 1 month's storage under those conditions likely will cause serious incidence of all symptoms. When CO_2 ranges from 4 to 10%, injury is likely even after 1 week, and almost certain after 1 month. In the range of 0° to 20°C (32° to 68°F) the severity of BNS decreases as temperature increases, at least during storage lasting about 1 week. Under such conditions the incidence was negligible at 10°C (50°F) or higher. Consequently, storage at otherwise desirable temperatures does not inhibit development of BNS. Once the injury has been induced, maximum expression of symptoms occurs during about 3 subsequent days at 10°C in air (Brecht *et al.* 1973A, B).

Some lots of lettuce are highly resistant to CO_2 injury and do not show signs of injury under any of the conditions just noted. Apparently cultivar and area of production greatly affect the susceptibility of lettuce to BNS.

Since new cultivars are introduced every year and old ones are abandoned, giving details here would be useless. However, in general, lettuce produced in the coastal valleys of California is more susceptible to BNS than lettuce grown either in the desert areas of California or Arizona or in the San Joaquin Valley of California. While these results are clear (Stewart and Matoba 1972; Brecht *et al.* 1973C), they do not explain why these differences exist.

Prevention   Lettuce should be held only where gas exchange with the outside is sufficient to maintain respiratory CO_2 below 1%. In transit vehicles this can be accomplished by opening one drain at each end (Stewart *et al.* 1973). If gas exchange must be restricted, as in certain CA transit systems, some respiratory CO_2 can be absorbed by hydrated lime ($Ca(OH)_2$). For 1000 boxes of lettuce at 22.7 kg (50 lb) each, held at 5°C (41°F), about 18 kg (40 lb) hydrated lime would be needed per day if efficiency were 100%.

When lettuce is held with less than 10% O_2, BNS is aggravated, so that particular care must then be exercised to prevent accumulation of CO_2. Carbon monoxide alone, and especially when combined with low O_2, also aggravates BNS (Stewart and Uota 1972; Kader *et al.* 1973). This finding further argues against use of CO simply to retard butt discoloration.

Similar Disorders   For comparison with russet spotting, see the relevant section.

Heart leaves are injured by high CO_2 and low O_2, but in the latter case the discoloration is more brown than red. Further, low O_2 injury likely is accompanied by a flat sweet flavor, whereas high CO_2 has no effect on flavor.

Rusty-brown discoloration resembles the broad discolored areas along the midribs; however, the former spreads along veins into the leaf blades, whereas CO_2 injury does not follow veins.

Marginal Browning   *Description*   Marginal browning (MB) is confined to wrapper and outer head leaves and the dead, brown edges may be curled.

Development and Causes   Conditions leading to MB have not been clearly identified. MB can be aggravated by long transit periods or by undesirably high transit temperatures.

Prevention   MB, once present, can be avoided only by removal of affected wrapper leaves before lettuce is packed. However, if the disorder is widespread, the field should be carefully checked to ascertain that the lettuce is neither too hard nor affected by tipburn.

Similar Disorders   Tipburn resembles MB but is not necessarily confined to outer leaves.

Oxygen Deficiency   *Description*   Severe O_2 deficiency results in shiny to water-soaked, grey, dead patches on outer and cap leaves, in reddish-brown spots on the inner (adaxial) surface of midribs of young head leaves, and in reddish-brown heart leaves. The injury on the midribs commonly only affects the inner surface (Lipton 1967).

A flat, sweet flavor, completely unlike that of normal lettuce, accompanies visible low-O_2 injury, but disappears almost completely within 3 or 4 days in air.

Development and Cause   The first and sometimes only sign of low-O_2 injury is discoloration of heart leaves, which can occur at 0.4% O_2 at 10° C (50° F). Other injuries appear only when O_2 drops to 0.25% or less. Whatever the visible injury, its severity increases as temperature rises and the symptoms become more intense upon exposure of the lettuce to air.

All head lettuce seems to be susceptible to low-O_2 injury, which contrasts with high-CO_2 injury, at least for CO_2 concentrations of 10% or lower.

Prevention   Oxygen deficiency is prevented by careful monitoring of the O_2 concentration during establishment of low-O_2 conditions and by careful maintenance of control equipment. When the atmosphere is only initially adjusted, the O_2 reservoir in the free space of the loading compartment and leakage from outside must be adequate to maintain the O_2 concentration at 1% or higher.

Pink Rib   *Description*   Pink rib (PR) refers to a pink discoloration of midribs and, in severe instances, of smaller veins.

Three types of pink rib can be distinguished (Lipton 1961): (1) diffuse, which centers about air spaces (lacunae) often found in large midribs; (2) laticiferous, which involves the tubules (laticifers) that contain the normally milky white latex; and (3) xylar, which affects the water-conducting tissue (vessel members in xylem). Diffuse PR can occur by itself, but always accompanies either of the other types.

Diffuse PR usually is confined to the thick broad basal part of midribs in large head leaves and appears more intense on the inner (adaxial) side of the rib. Pinkness mostly is associated with walls of disorganized parenchyma cells around the lacunae and with those walls of entire cells adjacent to the injured ones. However, pink walls also occur in groups of parenchyma cells distant from lacunae.

Laticiferous PR is the result of discoloration of latex that has escaped from a laticifer, of the ruptured wall, and of some or all walls of adjacent parenchyma cells.

In xylar PR only the walls of some conducting elements are pink, and the affected elements may be scattered singly or in groups among normal ones. Sometimes plugs of orange-yellow material are present in pink xylem elements.

Development   Diffuse PR develops as a consequence of the cellular disruptions that accompany formation of air spaces in midribs. However, not all torn cells turn pink nor are all pink cells torn.

Laticiferous PR develops around escaped latex, probably in response to a toxic substance that is diffusible, as judged by its effect on cells not in contact with latex.

The development of xylar pink rib has not been investigated.

Cause   No specific cause of PR has been identified, although some factors influence its incidence and severity.

Rapid growth is one suspected cause because diffuse PR frequently is associated with disrupted cells. Senescence also seems involved since hard heads are more susceptible to PR than firm heads, and since high storage temperatures encourage PR.

Pink rib, unlike russet spotting, is not aggravated by ethylene nor is it reduced by low O_2. In fact, PR has been increased substantially by low O_2 (about 2%) during 1 week at 10° C (50° F) or 1 month at 2.5° or 5° C (36° or 41° F) (Lipton 1967, 1971).

Prevention   The disorder can be minimized by (1) avoiding harvest of hard heads, (2) precooling to and shipment at 2.5° C (36° F) or below, and (3) cultural practices that discourage excessively rapid growth and thus hollow midribs.

Similar Disorders   Pink discoloration due to physical mishandling. A pink discoloration of veins associated with infection by a bacterium resembles xylar pink rib (Hall *et al.* 1971).

Rib Discoloration   *Description*   Rib discoloration (RD) manifests itself as yellow to black lesions on the inner surface of the midrib of cap leaves and in one or more of the next 4 or 5 younger leaves. Older and younger leaves occasionally may be affected. The discoloration frequently is located at the maximum curvature of the midrib and below the surface, although the epidermis can become involved. A cavity may be associated with the disorder.

Development   RD originates before harvest, and the number and size of lesions do not change noticeably during storage at 3° or 8° C (37°

or 47° F). The lesions do darken during storage and affected heads are more likely to show decay several weeks after harvest than normal ones (Marlatt *et al.* 1957).

Causes   No definite cause of RD has been identified, although RD is more common in lettuce grown when day temperatures exceed about 27° C (80° F) or when night temperatures are between 13° and 18° C (55° and 65° F) than in lettuce grown during cooler periods (Sharples *et al.* 1963). While these temperature limits are not precise, they suggest that conditions favoring rapid growth also favor RD. As with some other disorders of lettuce, senescent heads are most frequently affected.

Prevention   Since RD originates before harvest, cultural practices that provide for steady but not excessively rapid growth likely would be advantageous. Misting lettuce during hot days almost eliminated RD, presumably because water cooled the lettuce directly and indirectly via evaporative cooling (Jenkins 1959). Finally, restricting harvest to heads of desirable maturity leaves those most susceptible in the field.

After harvest, darkening of the lesions and danger of decay can be reduced by low temperatures.

Similar Disorders   Pink rib superficially resembles mild RD, but cross sections of the former are decidedly pink, whereas those of RD are yellowish to tan. Internal rib necrosis greatly resembles old lesions of RD in color, but is located near the base of the midrib rather than along the major curvature.

Russet Spotting   *Description*   Russet spotting (RS) is characterized by small tan, brown, or olive spots randomly distributed over the affected leaf (Rood 1956; Lipton 1961). When severe, the spots may coalesce and form irregularly shaped discolored areas. On the midrib, spots are usually longitudinal and pit-like, while those on the blade appear shallow, rounder and more diffuse (Fig. 16.4). On the blade spots may be on the vein, between them, or both.

Most spots are depressions of the surface, but some are subsurface and appear as diffuse dark areas through the outer healthy layers. Such internal spots have been observed only on midribs and large veins.

Development   RS is strictly a postharvest disorder in lettuce of normal harvest maturity, although lesions may occur before harvest in hard, senescent heads.

Frequently, but not necessarily, spots first appear on the lower (outer,

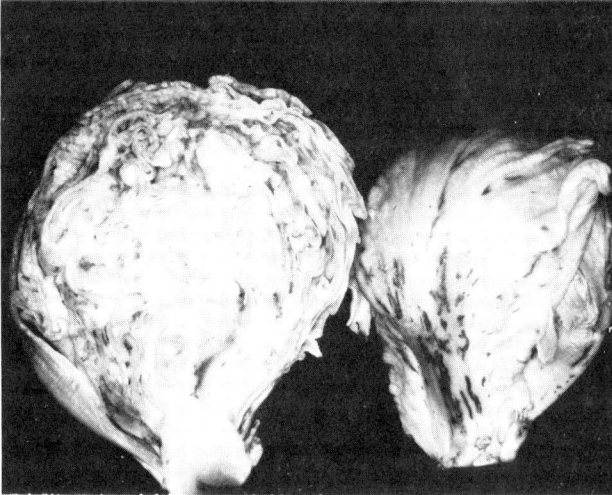

U.S. Dept. of Agriculture Photo

FIG. 16.4.   RUSSET SPOTTING OF LETTUCE

abaxial) side of midribs of outer head leaves, where they also tend to be most severe. However, the upper (inner, adaxial) surface also can be severely affected. Leaf blades show spots only in advanced stages, with those on veins preceding those on interveinal tissue. Even though russeting may follow veins, vascular bundles remain unaffected.

RS usually progresses inward, but absence of spots on outer head leaves does not necessarily indicate absence on inner leaves. Wrapper leaves seem to escape the disorder.

Causes   RS is induced or aggravated by several factors, one of which is ethylene. This gas induces RS at concentrations down to about 0.5 ppm, with rate and severity of development increasing as concentration increases up to about 10 ppm (Klaustermeyer and Morris 1975). Ethylene damage is most severe at about 5° C (41° F) and minimal or even absent at 0° C (32° F), even when ethylene concentration exceeds 20 ppm.

Lettuce can show RS even when no ethylene is introduced into the atmosphere. While the cause of RS is, then, uncertain, some of the following conditions favor development of RS: (1) heads well into senescence; (2) storage at 3° C (38° F) or higher; and (3) prolonged storage, i.e., longer than 10 days. These three conditions, however, are not always sufficient to cause RS; some predisposing factor seems to be involved.

Thus, when temperatures 9 to 14 days before harvest exceed 30° C (86° F) on 2 or more consecutive days, lettuce is more susceptible to RS than when cooler weather prevails (Lipton *et al.* 1972).

No matter which factors are responsible for a given outbreak of RS, they share one aspect: all accelerate aging or are signs of aging in lettuce. Thus RS is a symptom of aging.

Prevention   RS can be curtailed or even prevented by one or more of the following: (1) avoid shipping hard lettuce; (2) never store or ship lettuce with a commodity that produces much ethylene, such as strawberries, melons, apples or pears; (3) precool to and ship lettuce at 0° to 2.5° C (32° to 36° F); (4) ship lettuce that may have been exposed to high temperature 1 to 2 weeks before harvest, or lettuce that will be in transit several weeks in a low-oxygen atmosphere (Lipton 1967). Concentrations of O_2 between about 2 and 6% effectively reduce the incidence of RS. However, O_2 never should be below 1% or above 8%; danger of low-O_2 injury is acute below 1% and effectiveness decreases above 8%. Addition of 1% CO to the atmosphere also reduces RS in the presence of ethylene, but is superfluous when lettuce is shipped with low O_2.

Similar Disorders and Diseases   Some symptoms of excess CO_2 resemble RS lesions, but can be distinguished from RS by one or more of the following differences: (1) RS never affects heart leaves; (2) RS lesions are either surface or subsurface, while CO_2 affects only the outer few cell layers; (3) RS frequently induces some olive lesions and CO_2 injury does not; and (4) unlike CO_2 injury, RS would be rare after CA transit, because low O_2 inhibits RS.

Lesions of spotted wilt virus seem to be indistinguishable from those of RS. However, heads with spotted wilt sometimes are asymmetrical, whereas those with RS are not. Further, since spotted wilt is now uncommon, at least in the western United States, RS should be suspected unless definite proof of spotted wilt is available.

Initial lesions of bacterial soft rot should not be confused with RS in spite of their similarity because soft rot lesions tend to appear moist and almost invariably can be traced to a decayed leaf that was in contact with the leaf in question.

Tipburn. *Description*   Light tan to dark brown margins of leaves are characteristic of tipburn (TB). The dead margins may be a few millimeters wide or extend inward 3 cm or more in severe cases (Fig. 16.5). TB may affect any age leaf although the youngest ones usually escape.

Development   Tipburn is initiated before harvest by the rupture of latex ducts and the consequent spreading of latex among other cells (Tibbitts *et al.* 1965; Olson *et al.* 1967). Initially the lesions appear as individual whitish-tan spots that gradually turn darker, coalesce, and eventually give rise to the commonly recognized symptoms. This sequence of events is reminiscent of laticiferous pink rib, where rupture of latex ducts leads to pink discoloration. The difference in color may simply be due to a difference in the tissue involved—pink, where chlorophyll is lacking; tan to brown, where it is present.

Causes   Rupture of laticifers is encouraged when ample accumulation of carbohydrates is followed by substantial water uptake. Such conditions exist when warm, bright days are followed by cool nights and when soil moisture is ample (Tibbitts and Read 1976).

Prevention   The entry of lettuce with tipburn into markets is regulated by various agricultural codes because affected lettuce is unsightly and prone to decay under warm or moist conditions. The best guarantee against excessive TB on arrival is clean or nearly clean lettuce at harvest. However, even lots that are legally satisfactory at harvest may fail inspection on arrival for two principal reasons. First, initially

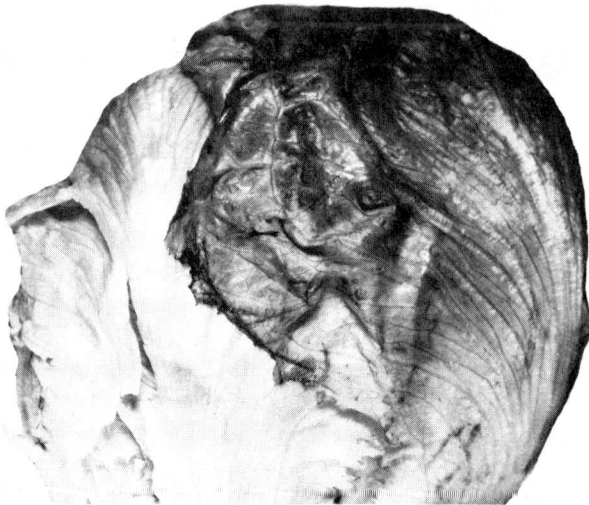

U.S. Dept. of Agriculture Photo

FIG. 16.5.   TIPBURN OF HEAD LETTUCE
Note darkened areas at margin of leaves.

barely noticeable specks may darken during transit. Secondly, variations in incidence within fields and necessarily limited sampling may qualify a load from one part of the field but not from a different part.

Since the presence of any amount of tipburn includes a potential for aggravation during transit, low temperatures are essential to retard darkening of lesions and to reduce the chance of decay should conditions favor it (Lipton 1963).

Similar Disorders   Marginal browning resembles TB, but is not found in inner head leaves.

Diseases

Bacterial Soft Rot   *Pathogen Involved*   Various species of bacteria.

Description   Slime, the popular synonym for this disease, aptly describes the symptom. Even initial infections along leaf margins feel slimy when rubbed between the fingers, although the tan discolored tissue has not completely disintegrated.

When the rot starts at or near the midrib, the first signs are small, yellowish-tan to rusty colored flecks or spots that then enlarge and coalesce. Subsequently, the veins turn reddish-brown, even well ahead of the lesions. As the disease spreads further, the entire head may become a slippery brown mass.

Infections on the outer leaves may be arrested under drying conditions and result in brown, papery leaf margins or segments.

Sometimes the only sign of soft rot is a softening, sinking, and tan discoloration at the center of the cut end of the stem (butt).

Development   Bacterial soft rot may start at leaf margins, along the midribs of wrapper or outer head leaves, or in the pith of the short stem. Tipburn or other injuries may provide an entry for the bacteria, although readily noticeable injuries are not essential for soft rot infection. Further, soft rot often follows fungal diseases as a secondary invader.

Infection may occur in the field or after harvest, and expansion of the decayed area is favored by above-normal temperatures during growth or by storage above about 2° C (36° F). However, even 0° C (32° F) does not completely stop soft rot from spreading once it has started.

Prevention   Lettuce from fields of harvest-mature lettuce infected with soft rot must be checked carefully before packing to avoid shipment of diseased heads. For storage of about one month, removal of wrapper leaves before packing and storing lettuce in an atmosphere with 2% CO_2 and 3% O_2 reduces the incidence and severity of soft rot (Lipton 1971). Even though such an atmosphere may cause some CO_2 injury, this damage likely will be less serious than the degree of soft rot that otherwise would develop during one month.

Prepacking of trimmed heads in individual wraps reduces the spread of soft rot, but heads that become infected decay readily when temperature is above about 1° C (34° F).

Overall, holding lettuce as close to 0° C (32° F) as possible is the best preventative, regardless of length of storage period.

Big Vein   *Pathogen Involved*   *Olipidium brassicae,* a soil-inhabiting fungus as a carrier of what appears to be a virus or closely related entity (Campbell and Fry 1966).

Description   Big vein succinctly describes the networks of prominent translucent veins of affected heads. Individual leaves appear puckered and are thicker and tougher than normal leaves; affected heads are small and coarse.

Heads with big veins are undesirable, but they store at least as well as normal heads (Morris *et al.* 1955).

Development   Big vein develops before harvest and symptoms are evident primarily at air temperatures from 5.5° to 15.5° C (42° to 60° F), when almost entire fields may become affected (Grogan *et al.* 1955). The disease is not aggravated during storage.

Prevention   So far there is no practical way to reduce the incidence of big vein. Development of cultivars resistant to the disease seems to be the best hope.

Downy Mildew   *Pathogen Involved*   *Bremia lactucae.*

Description and Development   Initially lesions tend to be small and confined to the upper (adaxial) surface of wrapper leaves. The lesions may be covered with fuzzy whitish-gray mycelium when humidity is high. As the decayed areas enlarge, they turn from light green or yellowish to brown and become soft, because secondary organisms invade the tissue. The decay can spread to head leaves at undesirably high temperatures or during prolonged storage.

Prevention   Lettuce from fields with downy mildew should be trimmed closely so that infected wrapper leaves are not included in the cartons. With affected lots, prompt cooling and transport at recommended temperatures are particularly important, because the fungus grows rapidly above 5° C (41° F).

Gray Mold Rot   *Pathogen Involved*   *Botrytis cinerea.*

Description   Botrytis causes water-soaked, grayish-green or brown lesions. The tissue becomes soft, slimy, and covered with the characteristic gray mycelium and gray spore masses.

Development   Gray mold generally is not serious during normal transcontinental shipping periods, but can affect many heads after prolonged storage, such as are encountered in overseas shipments.

Prevention   Trimming off old wrapper leaves, prompt precooling, and low transit temperature greatly reduce the chance of losses due to gray mold rot.

Internal Rib Necrosis   *Description*   Internal rib necrosis (IRN) appears dark brown to black and extends 2.5 to 5 cm (1 to 2 in.) along the midrib, starting at or near the junction with the stem. The cap leaf and 3 or 4 outer head leaves also may show lesions. The lesions are mostly subsurface, which gives them a diffuse appearance, but they may reach the surface in severe cases. Parenchyma tissue always is affected, but laticifers also may be involved. They and adjacent cells are dark brown.

Development   Symptoms of IRN may be present at harvest, but the incidence and severity of the discoloration increase during storage at temperatures normally encountered by lettuce. A darker discoloration develops at 10° C (50° F) than at 0° C (32° F).

IRN is confined to the cultivar Climax, which is one of the principal cultivars grown in the desert areas of California and Arizona.

Cause   The discoloration is a response to infection by the lettuce mosaic virus (Coakley *et al.* 1973).

Prevention   Control of sources of infection by use of disease-free seed or abandonment of the cultivar Climax are presently available alternatives for elimination of the disease.

Similar Discoloration   IRN resembles old lesions of rib discoloration, but the latter mostly are near the middle of the midrib, rather than near its base.

Rusty-brown Discoloration   *Description*   Midribs of leaves or entire leaves may show the characteristic discoloration. The defect tends to follow veins but is not confined to them. In some heads the veins may be normal and the interveinal tissue discolored. In most cases only leaves in the outer half of a head are discolored, although in severe cases the entire head may be affected (Lipton *et al*. 1972).

Dead cells mostly are confined to the epidermis and a few adjacent layers of cells.

Development and Cause   Rusty-brown discoloration (RBD) originates before harvest but can subsequently become much worse, especially at temperatures recommended for lettuce. RBD, like internal rib necrosis, is confined to the cultivar Climax and it is aggravated by infection of the lettuce with lettuce mosaic virus (Kader 1977). The incidence of RBD is increased in CO_2-enriched atmospheres (Stewart and Uota 1976).

Prevention   RBD can be prevented by growing resistant cultivars or by planting disease-free seed. Storage of lettuce at low temperature will not retard its spread within affected heads.

Watery Soft Rot   *Pathogens Involved*   *Sclerotinia sclerotiorum* or *S. minor*.

Description   This rot mostly occurs on the lower part of heads but may be found on any part. Diseased tissue is water-soaked and light or pinkish-brown.

A white, cottony mold spreads over the decayed tissue, and the head eventually becomes a watery mass. Finally, black fungal resting bodies grow in the decayed mass.

Development and Prevention   Watery soft rot starts in the field under humid conditions and most readily between 21° and 27° C (70° and 80° F).

Removal of diseased wrapper leaves, and following recommended procedures for precooling and transit, reduce the likelihood of development or spread of the disease after harvest.

LETTUCE—LEAF AND SEMI-HEADING, LEAF LETTUCE, ENDIVE, ESCAROLE, AND CHICORY

Disorders

These salad greens are subject to some of the same disorders as head lettuce, except for blackheart which seems to be confined to escarole and chicory.

Blackheart   *Description, Development and Causes*   In plants with blackheart (brownheart) the margins of young leaves at the center of the plant turn brown or black, and eventually entire leaves die. In some cases most of the leaves may be affected. Blackheart is a symptom of a calcium deficiency and is most serious when the plants are growing rapidly (Westgate and Forbes 1959; Maynard *et al*. 1962).

Prevention   Sprays of calcium salts completely prevent the disorder. Even slightly affected heads should not be shipped to distant markets, because the injured tissue readily becomes a focus for soft rot.

Marginal Browning   This disorder seems to be caused by the same factors as in head lettuce. However, it is more serious in these greens because their outer leaves are eaten or used for decoration.

Tipburn   Some of the more tender relatives of head lettuce readily become tipburned and affected specimens readily decay, unless they are held near 0° C (32° F).

Diseases

Leaf lettuce and the semi-heading types, as well as chicory, endive and escarole, mostly are affected by the same diseases as head lettuce, except for big vein. Since the factors noted for head lettuce also apply to these salad greens, reference to the relevant sections under head lettuce is suggested.

RHUBARB

Disorder

Wilting.   *Development and Causes*   Rhubarb wilts rapidly: it is unacceptable after 3 days at 0° C (32° F) or after 1 day at 21° C (70° F) when relative humidity is between 85 and 95%. Wilting becomes objectionable when weight loss exceeds about 5%.

The broad leaves of rhubarb rapidly lose moisture and thus aggravate wilting.

Prevention   Wilting can readily be prevented by packing rhubarb without leaf blades in perforated wraps and holding it between 0° and 5° C (32° and 41° F).

Setting the stalks in water prevents wilting, but can cause growth and splitting of the petioles, particularly at room temperature (Hruschka 1967).

Diseases

Anthracnose   *Pathogen Involved   Colletotrichum erumpens.*

Description   Lesions are watery, translucent, soft, oval spots along petioles. Numerous black specks, which are fruiting bodies, likely cover spots once they reach about 15 mm (½ in.) in diameter.

Development and Prevention   Infection occurs in the field, but the disease may spread from stalk to stalk by contact, even in the absence of wounds. Humid, warm weather favors the disease.

Postharvest spread of the disease can be minimized by prompt cooling of the petioles to near 0° C (32° F) and by keeping them cold during marketing.

Gray Mold Rot   *Pathogen Involved*   Various species of *Botrytis.*

Description   On the stalk young lesions are small red spots, but at the base or on other injured tissue they are brown. Large lesions, which are brown, generally are covered by grayish-brown mycelium that produces masses of spores of about the same color.

Development and Prevention   Wounds are the most likely sites for infection, but do not seem to be necessary. Holding or shipping rhubarb at 0° C (32° F) will substantially retard, but not stop, the spread of the serious disease.

SPINACH

Disorder

Wilting   Wilting is the one major disorder of spinach. While spinach readily wilts, the occurrence of this defect can be minimized by the following procedures: (1) harvest spinach only during the cool part of a day, because spinach loses water more rapidly when warm than when cool, even at high humidity; (2) precool soon after harvest, the sooner the better because spinach loaded in bins or harvest trailers heats from respiration and thus wilting is aggravated; (3) after cooling, the product must be kept cold and prevented from drying, which can be accomplished by prepacking in perforated plastic bags or by top-icing; and (4) at retail, prepacked spinach must be kept cold, and loose spinach cold and wet.

Diseases

Bacterial Soft Rot   *Pathogen Involved*   *Erwinia carotovora* and other species of bacteria.

Description   Infected leaves are gray-green, appear water-soaked, and feel mushy.

Development   The causative bacteria almost invariably enter through wounds, even minute ones, or via fungal lesions. The decay progresses rapidly above about 7° C (45° F) and at high humidity.

Prevention   Harvested spinach should be handled as carefully as possible because every nick in a leaf is a potential site for bacterial soft rot. Prompt cooling to near 0° C (32° F) and continuous refrigeration are essential to avoid this most serious postharvest disease of spinach. Removal of free water from the surface of washed leaves by centrifugation and subsequent vacuum cooling also help reduce the incidence of soft rot (Friedman 1951).

Downy Mildew   *Pathogen Involved*   *Peronospora effusa (farinosa).*

Description   Pale-yellow, irregularly shaped areas without distinct margins are the first signs of the disease. At high humidity, whitish-gray mycelium grows on either surface, although first on the lower (abaxial) one, and may precede discoloration of the leaf. In older lesions, purplish-gray fruiting bodies cover the mycelium.
Under low humidity, mycelium usually is absent.

Development   Infection primarily occurs in the field, but the disease can become more prominent after harvest. Temperatures between

0° and 5° C (41° and 77° F) and relative humidity above 85% favor infection.

Prevention   Spinach affected by mildew should not be shipped, and all spinach should be held near 0° C (32° F). Resistant cultivars, some of which are available, are the best long-range choice.

REFERENCES

Artichokes, Globe

KASMIRE, R. F., GREATHEAD, A. S., and SNYDER, M. J. (c. 1958). A demonstration of the effect of careful handling and rapid precooling on the market quality of California globe artichokes. Univ. Calif., Davis. Unnumbered Mimeo.
LIPTON, W. J., and HARVEY, J. M. 1960. Decay of artichoke bracts inoculated with spores of *Botrytis cinerea* Fr. at various constant temperatures. Plant Disease Reptr. *44,* 837–839.
LIPTON, W. J., and STEWART, J. K. 1963. Effects of precooling on the market quality of globe artichokes. U.S. Dept. Agr. Mktg. Res. Rept. *633.*

Celery

COYNE, D. P. 1962. Chemical and physiological changes in celery in relation to pithiness. Proc. Am. Soc. Hort. Sci. *81,* 341–346.
GERALDSON, C. M. 1954. The control of blackheart of celery. Proc. Am. Soc. Hort. Sci. *63,* 353–358.
SPURR, A. R. 1952. Fluorescence in ultraviolet light in the study of boron deficiency in celery. Science *116,* 421–423.
WHITE-STEVENS, R. H. 1936. Some cellular changes in celery during freezing and frost hardening. Proc. Am. Soc. Hort. Sci. *34,* 570–576.
WHITE-STEVENS, R. H. 1938. Carbohydrate and cellular changes in relation to pithiness in celery in cold storage. Proc. Am. Soc. Hort. Sci. *35,* 649–653.
YAMAGUCHI, M., ZINK, F. W., and SPURR, A. R. 1953. Cracked stem of celery. Calif. Agr. 7, No. 5, 12.

Crucifers

DEARBORN, C. H., and RALEIGH, G. J. 1936. A preliminary note on the control of internal browning of cauliflower by the use of boron. Proc. Am. Soc. Hort. Sci. *33,* 622–623.

DeBROUWER, W. M. T. J. 1955. Brown-colouring of cauliflower after cutting. Proc. 14th Intern. Hort. Cong. Sect. 1c. *14*, 556–559.

HIPP, B. W. 1974. Influence of nitrogen and maturity rate on hollow stem in broccoli. HortScience *9*, 68–69.

LIPTON, W. J., and HARRIS, C. M. 1976. Response of stored cauliflower (*Brassica oleracea* L.,*Botrytis* group) to low O₂ atmospheres. J. Am. Soc. Hort. Sci. *101*, 208–211.

MAYNARD, D. N. 1972. Internal browning of Brussels sprouts: A calcium deficiency disorder. HortScience *7*, 350. (Abstr.)

NATTI, J. J. 1958. Cabbage mosaic and leaf spotting in storage. Farm Res. June. 13.

NELSON, R. 1926. Storage and transportational diseases of vegetables due to suboxidation. Mich. Agr. Expt. Sta. Tech. Bull. *81*.

NIEUWHOF, M. 1961. Internal tipburn of white cabbage. I. Variety trials. Euphytica *9*, 203–208.

NIEUWHOF, M. 1971. Factors affecting the incidence of internal deviations in Brussels sprouts (*Brassica oleracea* L. var. *gemifera* DC.) Euphytica *20*, 527–535.

NIEUWHOF, M., GARRETSEN, F., and WIERING, D. 1960. Internal tipburn in white cabbage. II. The effect of some environmental factors. Euphytica *9*, 275–280.

STEWART, J. K., and BARGER, W. R. 1963. Effects of cooling method, prepackaging and top-icing on the quality of Brussels sprouts. Proc. Am. Soc. Hort. Sci. *83*, 488–494.

STRANDBERG, J. O., DARBY, J. F., WALKER, J. C., and WILLIAMS, P. H. 1969. Black speck, a nonparasitic disease of cabbage. Phytopathology *59*, 1879–1883.

SUHONEN, I. 1969. On the storage life of white cabbage in refrigerated stores. Acta Agr. Scand. *19*, 18–32.

WALKER, J. C., EDGINGTON, L. V., and NAYUDU, M. V. 1961. Tipburn of cabbage. Nature and control. Univ. Wisconsin Res. Bull. *230*.

WALKER, J. C., MCLEAN, J. G., and JOLIVETTE, J. P. 1940. The boron deficiency disease in cabbage. J. Agr. Res. *62*, 573–587.

WIEBE, H. J., and KRUG, H. 1974. Effect of temperature on quality and duration of harvest of cauliflower. Gemüse *15*, No. 2, 34–37. (German)

YODER, O. C. 1977. Development of methods for long-term cabbage storage. Acta Hort. No. 62, 301–310.

NOTE: *See also Chapter 15.*

Lettuce and Other Salad Greens

BARDIN, R. E. 1971. Diseases of lettuce in the Salinas-Watsonville area of California. Monterey Co. Dept. Agr., Salinas.

BERAHA, L., and KWOLEK, W. F. 1975. Prevalence and extent of eight market disorders of western-grown head lettuce during 1973 and 1974 in the greater Chicago, Illinois, area. Plant Disease Reptr. *59*, 1001–1004.

BRECHT, P. E., KADER, A. A., and MORRIS, L. L. 1973A. Influence of post-harvest temperature on brown stain of lettuce. J. Am. Soc. Hort. Sci. *98*, 399–402.

BRECHT, P. E., KADER, A. A., and MORRIS, L. L. 1973B. The effect of composition of the atmosphere and duration of exposure on brown stain of lettuce. J. Am. Soc. Hort. Sci. *98*, 536–538.

BRECHT, P., MORRIS, L. L., CHANEY, C., and JANECKE, D. 1973C. Brown stain susceptibility of selected lettuce cultivars under controlled atmospheres and temperatures. J. Am. Soc. Hort. Sci. *98*, 261–264.

CAMPBELL, R. N., and FRY, P. R. 1966. The nature of the associations between *Olpidium brassicae* and lettuce big-vein and tobacco necrosis viruses. Virology *29*, 222–233.

COAKLEY, S. M., CAMPBELL, R. N., and KIMBLE, K. A. 1973. Internal rib necrosis and rusty brown discoloration of Climax lettuce induced by lettuce mosaic virus. Phytopathology *63*, 1191–1197.

GROGAN, R. G., SNYDER, W. C., and BARDIN, R. 1955. Diseases of lettuce. Calif. Agr. Expt. Sta. Circ. *448*.

HALL, C. B., STALL, R. E., and BURDINE, H. W. 1971. Association of *Pseudomonas marginalis* with pink rib of lettuce. Proc. Florida State Hort. Soc. *84*, 163–165.

JENKINS, J. M., JR. 1959. Brown rib of lettuce. Proc. Am. Soc. Hort. Sci. *74*, 587–590.

KADER, A. A., BRECHT, P. E., WOODRUFF, R., and MORRIS, L. L. 1973. Influence of carbon monoxide, carbon dioxide, and oxygen levels on brown stain, respiration rate, and visual quality of lettuce. J. Am. Soc. Hort. Sci. *98*, 485–488.

KADER, A. A. 1977. Personal communication. Davis, Calif.

KLAUSTERMEYER, J. A., and MORRIS, L. L. 1975. The effects of ethylene and carbon monoxide on the induction of russet spotting on crisphead lettuce. Plant Physiol. Suppl. *56*, No. 2, 62. (Abstr.).

LIPTON, W. J. 1961. Anatomical observations on russet spotting and pink rib of lettuce. Proc. Am. Soc. Hort. Sci. *78*, 367–374.

LIPTON, W. J. 1963. Post-harvest changes in amount of tipburn of head lettuce and the effect of tipburn on incidence of decay. Plant Disease Reptr. *47*, 875–879.

LIPTON, W. J. 1967. Market quality and rate of respiration of head lettuce held in low-oxygen atmospheres. U.S. Dept. Agr. Mktg. Res. Rept. 777.

LIPTON, W. J. 1971. Controlled atmosphere effects on lettuce quality in simulated export shipments. U.S. Dept. Agr. *ARS 51-45*.

LIPTON, W. J., STEWART, J. K., and WHITAKER, T. W. 1972. An illustrated guide to the identification of some market disorders of head lettuce. U.S. Dept. Agr. Mktg. Res. Rept. *950*.

MARLATT, R. B. 1974. Nonpathogenic diseases of lettuce. Their identification and control. Florida Agr. Expt. Sta. Tech. Bull. *721*.

MARLATT, R. B., STEWART, J. K., and BERKENKAMP, B. B. 1957. Storage of lettuce with rib discoloration. Phytopathology *47*, 231–232.

MAYNARD, D. N., GERSTEN, B., and VERNELL, H. F. 1962. The cause and control of brown-heart of escarole. Proc. Am. Soc. Hort. Sci. *81*, 371–375.

MORRIS, L. L., PRATT, H. K., and TUCKER, C. L. 1955. Lettuce handling and quality. Western Grower and Shipper *26*, No. 5, 14–16, 18.

OLSON, K. C., TIBBITTS, T. W., and STRUCKMEYER, B. E. 1967. Morphology and significance of laticifer rupture in lettuce tip burn. Proc. Am. Soc. Hort. Sci. *91*, 377–385.

ROOD, P. 1956. Relation of ethylene and post-harvest temperature to brown spot of head lettuce. Proc. Am. Soc. Hort. Sci. *68*, 296–303.

SHARPLES, G. C., FAZIO, S., and BESSEY, P. M. 1963. Oxidase activity and rib discoloration in Great Lakes lettuce in relation to seasonal temperature. Proc. Am. Soc. Hort. Sci. *82*, 391–396.

STEWART, J. K., CEPONIS, M. J., and BILLETER, B. A. 1973. Ventilation of mechanical refrigerator cars to prevent carbon dioxide accumulation and brown stain in lettuce loads. U.S. Dept. Agr. Mktg. Res. Rept. *978*.

STEWART, J. K., CEPONIS, M. J., and HARRIS, C. M. 1967. Market quality of film wrapped and naked-packed head lettuce. U.S. Dept. Agr. *ARS 51-11*.

STEWART, J. K., and MATOBA, F. 1972. Some factors influencing susceptibility of lettuce to CO_2 injury. Plant Disease Reptr. *56*, 1051–1054.

STEWART, J. K., and UOTA, M. 1972. Carbon dioxide injury to lettuce as influenced by carbon monoxide and oxygen levels. HortScience 7, 189–190.

STEWART, J. K., and UOTA, M. 1976. Postharvest effect of modified levels of carbon monoxide, carbon dioxide, and oxygen on disorders and appearance of head lettuce. J. Am. Soc. Hort. Sci. *101*, 382–384.

TIBBITTS, T. W., and READ, M. 1976. Rate of metabolite accumulation into latex of lettuce and proposed association with tipburn injury. J. Am. Soc. Hort. Sci. *101*, 406–409.

TIBBITTS, T. W., STRUCKMEYER, B. E., and RAO, R. R. 1965. Tipburn of lettuce as related to release of latex. Proc. Am. Soc. Hort. Sci. *86*, 462–467.

WESTGATE, P. J., and FORBES, R. B. 1959. Blackheart of chicory. Soil and Crop. Sci. Soc. Florida, Proc. *19*, 389–393.

Rhubarb

HRUSCHKA, H. W. 1967. Storage and shelf life of packaged rhubarb. U.S. Dept. Agr. Mktg. Res. Rept. *771*.

Spinach

FRIEDMAN, B. A. 1951. Control of decay in prepackaged spinach. Phytopathology *41*, 709–713.

17

Physical Injuries, Market Disorders and Diseases of Unripe Fruits and Miscellaneous Structures

BEANS, LIMA

Disorder

Chilling Injury *Description*   Rusty brown specks, spots or areas, and eventually decay follow chilling exposures.

Development and Cause   Injury is certain after 7 days' exposure to temperatures between 0° and 7° C (32° and 45° F), although shorter exposures probably would reduce storage life, particularly at subsequent nonchilling temperatures (McColloch and Vaught 1968).

Prevention   See *Beans, snap.*
  No other serious disorders of lima beans have been described, but they may be subject to the same ones as snap beans. However, since the shells are not eaten, their discoloration is of less concern than those of snap beans.

BEANS, SNAP

Physical Injuries

Mechanical Injury. *Description*   Scattered tan to dull brown spots or areas of irregular outline characterize some types of physical injury, whereas in others the damaged area appears chafed, although both may occur simultaneously.

Development and Cause   Physical injury can be inflicted by blowing sand, by pods rubbing against each other during growth, by machine harvest, or by rubbing of pods against rough containers. The injuries caused by these objects are difficult or impossible to distinguish.

Prevention   Injuries due to blowing sand cannot readily be prevented, unless sprinkler irrigation is feasible. Damage incurred during harvest or packing can be minimized by proper adjustment of machinery and by using smooth-sided containers, respectively.

Similar Disorders   See *Chilling Injury.*

Solar Injury *Description*   Solar injury (sunscald, light injury) first is indicated by minute brown or reddish spots on one side of the pod only. The spots may enlarge into short streaks that run across the injured side, eventually coalesce, and become water-soaked and slightly sunken.

Development and Cause   Solar injury may be induced in pods exposed to direct solar radiation and appears to be primarily an effect of shortwave radiation. The injury, however, has been described only for pods of dry-type beans grown in Colorado (MacMillan 1923).

Prevention   No practical preventative has been developed. If snap beans are affected, they must be culled at origin. This not only removes the defective beans but also helps avoid disputes when chilling injury is found at destination.

Similar Disorders   See *Chilling Injury.*

Disorders

Chilling Injury (Russeting)   The term russeting has long been associated with a disorder that eventually was identified as chilling injury. Since the cause is now known and more detailed symptoms have been identified, we shall use the more precise term.

Description   Symptoms of chilling injury depend on the temperature of exposure. Temperatures between 0.5 and 3° C (33° and 37° F) cause surface pitting, diagonal brown streaks, a dullness of the normal surface, and heightened susceptibility to decay. Exposure to 5° C (41° F) leads to these symptoms in addition to those associated with normal aging: leathery, slightly depressed surface, a fading of the normal green, darkening of tip and calyx and collapse of the fleshy tissue of the pod (Watada and Morris 1966A, B).

Development and Cause   Chilling injury is induced within 2 days at 5° C (41° F). However, the symptoms become noticeable primarily after the beans subsequently have been held at a nonchilling temperature (13° C; 55° F or higher) for about 24 hr.

Cultivars differ greatly in their susceptibility to chilling injury, some decreasing to a "fair" quality rating within 15 days, others after only about 2 months (Table 1.4).

Prevention   Chilling injury can be minimized by holding beans between about 7° and 10° C (45° and 50° F) after harvest, although general deterioration will be slower near 5° C (41° F). At higher temperatures the danger of decay becomes acute.

Similar Disorders   Chilling injury is readily confused with solar injury, sand scarring, and lesions of powdery mildew. Sunscald, however, always is unilateral, and severely affected tissue appears water-soaked and then sunken. Sand scarring is relatively rare, would likely be noted at origin, and the lesions are dull rather than slightly shiny. If powdery mildew has caused the lesions, the typical white fungus usually can be found somewhere in a container or shipment; if not, holding a small sample of beans in a ventilated polyethylene bag for about one day likely will induce visible fungal growth if mildew is present.

Wilting   The often serious wilting associated with excessive water loss can be prevented, or at least substantially delayed, by prepacking the beans either in perforated bags or by overwrapping them on trays.

Diseases

Anthracnose   *Pathogen Involved*   *Colletotrichum lindemuthianum.*
This disease occurs wherever beans are grown in areas of high rainfall and RH.

Description   Oval or circular greenish-brown specks on bean pods are the first symptom. These spots enlarge as the organism grows, and become reddish-brown to black. Individual spots may reach 12 mm (1/2 in.) in diameter, and as they enlarge their centers sink. In the presence of moisture the centers of the spots become covered with coral-colored spots of spores. When the beans are dry, the spore clumps are reduced to a dark-colored, granular surface.

Control The fungus is seed-borne so the disease can be prevented by planting disease-free seed. Such seed is now generally available from arid production areas of the western United States.

Cottony Leak *Pathogen Involved* *Pythium butleri.*
This disease occurs wherever beans are grown. Initiation occurs in the field whenever temperatures are high and rainfall is heavy.

Description The infections usually start where the abrasive action of soil has damaged the cuticle of the pods. Early stages of the rot show a water-soaked condition which may appear on injured areas or on apparently normal tissues. At elevated temperatures, 24° to 32° C (75° to 90° F), white cottony mycelium develops freely on the pod surfaces. The symptoms are somewhat similar to those of watery soft rot, but the mycelial pad of cottony leak is pure white and fluffy, whereas that of watery soft rot is coarser, slightly grayish, and soon produces dark sclerotia.

Control When the disease is visible on pods at harvest, losses from decay during marketing are almost certain, even when all possible precautions are taken. Careful removal of all pods showing water-soaked areas will reduce the decay potential. The beans should be rapidly precooled to 10° C (50° F) and maintained continuously at 7° to 10° C (45° to 50° F) during marketing. Even brief periods of warm-up will allow incipient infections to develop and from these the disease can be spread to other pods. Beans from fields with known infections should be disposed of rapidly in local markets.

Soil Rot *Pathogen Involved* *Rhizoctonia solani.*
This is a soil-borne fungus which is widespread in all bean-producing areas. Decay during marketing develops from incipient infections present at harvest or active lesions that were overlooked during sorting.

Description The small, rusty-brown lesions occur anywhere on the pod. They may be few or numerous. The infected areas are irregular in shape and without definite margins, but as the infections grow the affected tissues either become soft and brown, or dry out and turn to a chocolate brown. Under moist conditions the surface mycelium spreads over infected and healthy pods to produce a nest of decay.

Control   Beans from infected fields must be dry when packed and thoroughly sorted to remove all pods with visible infections. Prompt cooling to 7° to 10° C (45° to 50° F) and maintenance in this range during marketing will reduce development and spread of the disease.

Watery Soft Rot *-Pathogen Involved   Sclerotinia* spp.
These are widely distributed soil fungi which can cause serious losses in snap beans in seasons when cool, moist weather precedes harvest. Incipient infections occurring in the field develop into active decay at temperatures favorable to growth.

Description   Lesions are at first water-soaked, and of various sizes and shapes. Above 20° C (68° F) the decay develops rapidly, accompanied by mycelium, either cottony or somewhat appressed. Sclerotia, which are at first white, but later turn black, are the best diagnostic feature of the decay in advanced form.

Control   Visibly diseased beans must be sorted out at harvest. Aside from thorough sorting, prompt precooling to 7° to 10° C (45° to 50° F) will slow development of the disease. Such beans should be moved through the marketing channels without delay, preferably within five days. Exposure to high temperature, even for short periods, can be disastrous.

CUCUMBERS

Disorders

Chilling Injury *Description*   Rather shallow surface pits of various sizes are the first sign of chilling injury; prolonged chilling causes small droplets to come to the surface, and both are followed by decay, commonly Fusarium rot. All symptoms develop much more rapidly at a subsequent nonchilling temperature, and the injured fruits even may appear normal while held at low temperature (Eaks and Morris 1957).

Development and Cause   Cucumbers are slightly chilled after 4 days at 0° C (32° F) to 2° C (36° F) and severely after 8 to 16 days at 0° to 5° C (32° to 41° F). Obvious symptoms of chilling, such as pitting, are lacking after storage between 7° and 10° C (44° and 50° F), but the rate of deterioration is more rapid than at 13° C (55° F), indicating that some chilling occurs in this range. Cucumbers grown in greenhouses may show obvious injury even after 1 week at 10° C (50° F) (Wiebe 1969).

FIG. 17.1. CHILLING INJURY OF CUCUMBER

U.S. Dept. of Agriculture Photo

Pitting is aggravated by low relative humidity (55 to 70%), and may be nearly prevented in saturated air, which however, does not indicate that chilling injury is absent.

Chilling temperatures also render cucumbers more sensitive to injury from high CO_2 in the atmosphere. The fruits are injured by 3% CO_2 at 5° C (41° F) but only by 39% at 15° C (59° F) (Eaks 1956).

Prevention   The maximum storage life of cucumbers is at about 13° C (55° F). However, to prevent yellowing, 10° C (50° F) is preferable for shipping periods of 1 to 2 weeks. Storage a few days below 5° C (41° F) is permissible if the cucumbers are utilized *immediately* after storage.

Water Loss   *Description and Development*   Cucumbers at retail all too frequently have shrivelled and pinched blossom ends and are soft. This shrivelling results from dehydration that occurred somewhere during marketing. If the fruits are green, water loss occurred during prolonged holding at or below recommended temperatures; if they are yellowish they lost moisture during a briefer period at a warm temperature. Shrivelling indicates poor handling or storage practices, or slow turnover of stock.

Prevention   Waxing effectively retards water loss of cucumbers and is widely used for this reason. However, cautions noted under *Application of Surface Coatings* should be observed. Prepacking in film bags or overwrapping with ventilated films also provides protection against excessive water loss.

Yellowing   *Description and Development*   Yellow or yellowish-green cucumbers are unattractive, unless they are lemon cucumbers. The best fruits are entirely green, although slight yellowing at the ground spot is not a serious defect.

Yellowing is a sign of senescence. It is accelerated by warm temperatures and the presence of ethylene in the air (Morris and Mann 1946).

Prevention   Cucumbers held between 7° and 10° C (45° and 50° F) yellow only slowly. This fruit should not be stored with commodities that produce much ethylene, such as melons or apples.

Diseases

Anthracnose   *Pathogen Involved*   *Colletotrichum lagenarium.*

Description   Approximately round, sunken, and water-soaked lesions eventually become covered with slimy, orange-pink spore masses. Old lesions are black and may have white centers topped by black dots, which are fruiting bodies. The flesh is dry and may be cracked.

Development   Anthracnose develops on cucumbers grown in fields or greenhouses, and becomes aggravated as storage time lengthens. The fungus does not depend on injuries for entry and grows best between about 21° and 27° C (70° and 80° F). Since symptoms do not appear until about 5 days after infection, fruit shipped presumably clean may show the disease on arrival.

Prevention   Spread of the disease can be retarded at recommended temperatures, about 10° C (50° F), but fruits with even minimal symptoms should be discarded whenever found.

Bacterial Soft Rot   This disease can be destructive of cucumbers, but occurs more frequently in Honey Dew melons (See section for details.)

Bacterial Spot   *Pathogen Involved*   *Pseudomonas lachrymans.*

Description   Minute, circular, water-soaked spots become conspicuous when the centers sink, dry and become chalky white.
Gummy sap often is exuded from the lesions before they dry. In older

infections, brown lesions develop in the flesh and along the vascular strands.

Development   Fruits grown in humid or semihumid areas are infected in fields or packing sheds. However, spots may appear in the market only, because six days are required for symptom expression.

Prevention   Refrigeration at about 10° C (50° F) slows down the disease.

Black Rot   *Pathogen Involved   Mycosphaerella citrullina.*

Description   Initially white, cottony mycelium that grows on water-soaked spots eventually darkens and develops black fruiting bodies.

Development   See *Watermelon.*

Cottony Leak   *Pathogen Involved   Pythium aphinidermatum.*

Description   Dark green, soft, water-soaked lesions precede the growth of the typical cottony fungus that may cover much or all of an affected fruit. During this stage, watery sap leaks from the lesions.

Development and Prevention   The fungus mainly affects pickling cucumbers before harvest, but infections can spread rapidly after harvest at 20° C (68° F) or above. The fruits should be hydrocooled to below 15° C (59° F) immediately after harvest, transported at about 10° C (50° F), and kept cool until processed (McCombs and Winstead 1963).

Mosaic   *Description*   Only mildly affected fruits, as shown by mottled coloration, usually reach the markets. However, even such fruits should not be shipped because they are unattractive, and they seem to senesce more rapidly than healthy fruits.

Rhizopus Rot   See *Muskmelons.*

Scab   *Pathogen Involved   Cladosporuim cucumerinum.*

Description   Small, grayish, slightly sunken spots characterize early lesions that later turn dark and emit a gummy exudate. Eventually, a dark, olive-green layer of mycelium and spores covers the decayed tissue.

Development   Scab is serious mainly on cucumbers grown in greenhouses or for pickling, particularly at about 21° C (70° F) and high RH.

Prevention   Fruits with lesions must be culled at origin to prevent decay in transit, but resistant cultivars are the best defense.

EGGPLANT

Disorders

Chilling Injury   *Description*   Pitting and so-called scald are definite external symptoms of chilling injury (McColloch 1966). Scald refers to brown spots or areas that are first flush with the surface but may become sunken with time. Scald, however, is an obvious misnomer, and we suggest the more descriptive "pocking" instead. Discoloration and death of the calyx are further, but not certain, signs of chilling exposures because they also are symptoms of normal aging.

Browning of the flesh due to death of the cells is the conspicuous internal symptom of chilling injury.

Decay (Alternaria rot) almost invariably follows chilling injury.

Development and Cause   Signs of chilling injury become noticeable primarily after the fruits subsequently have been at nonchilling temperatures for 1 or 2 days, and not all symptoms are induced equally rapidly. Pitting following breaks in the skin is induced during 4 days or even fewer at 0° C (32° F) and within 10 days at any temperature between 0° and 10° C (32° and 50° F).

Pocking, Alternaria rot, and death of the flesh are clearly evident at room temperature after prior exposures to 0° to 5° C (32° to 41° F) for 6 days or to 7° C (45° F) for 10 days. These symptoms are absent or minimal after 10 days' exposure to 10° C (50° F), which approaches the upper limit of the chilling range. However, symptoms will develop more rapidly in eggplant grown during warm than during cool weather (Abe *et al*. 1974).

Prevention   If eggplants are held at 10° C (50° F), chilling injury is minimized and other defects do not develop as rapidly as at higher temperature. However, eggplants that mature during very warm weather likely would keep better at 12° to 13° C (53° to 55° F). These fruits should never be iced.

Water Loss *Description* Shrivelled skin and a general softening indicate that water loss has been excessive, a condition often found in retail displays.

Prevention Eggplants lose water readily and, therefore, stock should be replenished frequently. Prepacking in ventilated wraps is advantageous in this respect, and waxing also may retard shriveling, although too impermeable a layer could be injurious (see *Application of Surface Coatings*).

Diseases

Alternaria Rot *Pathogen Involved* *Alternaria tenuis.*

Description Numerous brown, sunken, circular spots, 3 to 13 mm (1/8 to 1/2 in.) in diameter, are the initial sign of Alternaria rot. The spots, which occur anywhere on the surface, including the calyx, have definite margins when small or after they coalesce to form irregularly shaped areas. Surface mold grows on old lesions and is dark gray, but may appear velvety and olive-green if covered with spores.

The lesions may penetrate the flesh, where the affected tissue turns tan to grayish-tan and spongy.

Development and Prevention Alternaria rot develops in response to chilling injury; thus, the decay can be controlled by holding eggplants at about 10° C (50° F). They should never be iced, either in transit or during retail display.

Bacterial Soft Rot *Pathogen Involved* *Erwinia carotovora.*

Description Lesions are grayish brown, the skin is wrinkled and readily punctured, and the underlying tissue is watery. No strong off-odor is associated with this decay on eggplants.

Development and Control The bacteria enter through any puncture of the skin and grow very rapidly during warm rainy weather.

Very careful handling and rapid cooling to 10° C (50° F) retard this decay even after weather favoring this disease.

Similar Diseases Rhizopus rot is less watery and the lesions are penetrated by fungal growth.

Phomopsis Rot   *Pathogen Involved*   *Phomopsis vexans.*

Description   The lesions have circular and well-defined margins, are tan to light brown, and are slightly sunken. The infection frequently originates under the calyx, but may occur anywhere on the surface of the fruit. Older lesions are darker brown at the center with a wide lighter colored margin, and a few may completely cover the fruits.

Older lesions are pimpled with masses of fruiting bodies that lie just below the surface, but emerge when they break.

Internally, much of the tissue may be affected as shown by its light brown discoloration and spongy texture.

Development and Prevention   This common and destructive disease of eggplants originates before harvest, particularly during warm wet weather. The fungus grows best at about 27° to 30° C (80° to 86° F). Thus, prompt cooling to 10° C (50° F) will substantially reduce this decay, even if fruits with undetected infections are shipped.

PEAS, GARDEN

Diseases

Gray Mold Rot   *Pathogen Involved*   *Botrytis cinerea.*
The cool, moist climates favorable to production of garden peas are highly favorable for the development of the *Botrytis* fungus which causes this rot. Peas from most commercial areas are apt to carry spores of the disease.

Description   The rot starts as small, water-soaked spots on the pods. These gradually enlarge and become grayish-buff. Under warm, moist conditions a pale gray mycelium develops on the surface, later becoming brown and covered with clusters of spores.

Control   Prompt cooling of the peas and maintenance of 0° C (32° F) during transport and distribution will usually reduce loss from gray mold. However, if the growing season is favorable for development of the fungus, the peas should be speedily marketed.

Watery Soft Rot   See *Beans, Snap.*

PEPPERS, BELL

Physical Injuries

Freezing *Description* Water-soaking of tissue and extreme softening upon thawing are the primary symptoms of freezing injury. The shoulders appear to be most sensitive to freezing injury and show softening after only 1/2 hour at −7° C (20° F). Pitting of the surface and shrivelling follow thawing as the injured peppers lose moisture. Darkening and water-soaking of the stem and calyx are symptoms that appear only after severe freezing, and they are more prominent once the peppers have been thawed for a day. Freezing does not enhance the incidence of decay substantially unless the peppers are subsequently held for at least a week above 5° C (41° F) (Parsons and Day 1971).

Cause Peppers freeze at about −0.8° C (30.5° F).

Similar Disorder Sheet pitting, a symptom of chilling injury, tends to appear as shallow depressions whereas pits caused by freezing are deep for their size.

Solar Injury *Description, Development, and Cause* Sunscald, where affected tissue is dry and papery, is not of concern here, because such fruits would be discarded at harvest. Milder forms of solar injury induce a unilateral yellowing and sometimes a slight wilting.

Solar injury of peppers has been attributed to the effect of heating of the tissue to at least about 50° C (122° F). Fruit in the lower portion of the plants is more readily injured, because heat reflected from unshaded soil is added to that imposed by direct exposure of the pods to the sun (Szirmai 1938).

Prevention Good foliage is the best preventative.

Disorders

Blossom-end Rot. See *Tomatoes, Blossom-end Rot.*

Chilling Injury *Description* Numerous minute to fairly large shallow, roundish depressions that may be distributed over most of a mature-green pepper are the chief symptom. This has been termed sheet pitting by McColloch (1962). Chilling-induced pits at surface wounds also may be present, but are irregular in shape and not evenly distributed.

Browning of the seeds (Ogata *et al.* 1968), discoloration, and death of the calyx and a grayish-brown, dull surface of the pod instead of the normal glossy one are further symptoms (McColloch 1962). The latter symptom has been misnamed scald, a term that should not be used for an injury induced by low temperature.

Finally, Alternaria rot follows severe chilling injury.

Development and Cause   Symptoms develop more rapidly at non-chilling temperatures following chilling exposures than at continuously low temperatures. Chilling injury incurred during 9 days at 5° C (41° F) became evident after 4 days at 18° C (65° F), whereas such symptoms showed only after 15 continuous days at 5° C (41° F). Deterioration of the calyx and sheet pitting generally precede dull browning and Alternaria rot.

Generally, chilling injury can be expected within 2 to 4 days at 0° C (32° F), within 7 days at 1° C (34° F), within 9 days at 5° C (41° F), and within 14 to 15 days at 6° to 7° C (42° to 45° F). However, symptoms may be absent until after several subsequent days at 18° C (65° F), a non-chilling temperature.

Chilling-induced pitting is aggravated by drying conditions and can be delayed, but not prevented, by high relative humidity (above 96%). Further, ripe (red) peppers are immune to sheet pitting.

Prevention   Storage at 10° C (50° F) prevents chilling injury within normal marketing periods. Since, however, some ripening occurs at 10° C, 8° to 9° C (46° to 48° F) is preferable.

Sheet pitting at 0° C (32° F) can be prevented by prior storage of the pods at 10° C (50° F) for 5 to 10 days. However, such conditioning apparently does not retard other symptoms of chilling.

Ripening   *Description and Development*   Change of the normal dark green to a brownish-red and eventually to red, starting at or near the blossom end, is a sign of ripening.

Cause and Prevention   Ripening is accelerated as temperatures increase and can become a problem at 10° C (50° F) or above. Thus storage at 8 to 9° C (46° to 48° F) would be preferable if ripening is to be avoided.

Wilting   Peppers readily become soft and flabby when held a few days below 90% RH, in spite of their natural waxy surface. Consequently peppers are commonly waxed to reduce moisture loss. Nevertheless, low humidity and temperatures above 10° C (50° F) should be avoided.

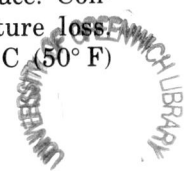

Diseases

Alternaria Rot *Pathogen Involved* *Alternaria tenuis.*

Description Small lesions are circular with a distinct margin, grayish-green, water-soaked, and level with the surface or slightly sunken. The lesions may appear on any part of the fruit, including the calyx. As they enlarge they become tannish-brown to muddy brown or even black. At this stage the lesions are clearly sunken and partly or completely covered with gray mycelium. When humidity has been high, an olive-green velvety mass of spores may cover the lesion.

Development Alternaria rot can infect peppers through intact skin, but only affects tissue that has been physiologically injured by too much sun or too low temperature, with the latter by far the most important contributing factor. Chilling injury before or after harvest is equally harmful.

Prevention Holding peppers at 7° to 10° C (45° to 50° F) effectively inhibits Alternaria rot if the storage period is 2 weeks or less.

Bacterial Soft Rot *Pathogen Involved* *Erwinia carotovora.*

Description Liquefaction of the tissue is the end product of this rot. The skin over the rot is sunken and wrinkled but usually only slightly discolored, and it remains intact even over large lesions.
The penetrating odor often associated with bacterial soft rot is absent in peppers.

Development The bacteria enter via wounds, either before or after harvest. High humidity and a temperature between about 25° and 30° C (77° and 86° F) results in complete decay of a pod within a few days.

Prevention Reducing physical injury reduces the incidence of soft rot. Since some wounding, such as cutting the stem, is inevitable, further measures are needed. Immersing the peppers for 1-1/2 min in 52.5° to 53.5° C (126° to 128° F) water substantially reduces soft rot without injuring otherwise sound pods. The time and temperature are critical: too short an exposure or too low a temperature has no value, whereas excessive treatment can seriously injure the pods. After heating, the peppers should be air-cooled to 7° to 10° C (45° to 50° F) as rapidly as feasible. Hydrocooling, even with 300 ppm chlorine in the water, completely negates the benefit of the heat treatment. Heat treatment of peppers, introduced by Johnson (1964), has been commercially used in Texas.

Similar Diseases   See *Rhizopus rot.*

Bacterial Spot   *Pathogen Involved*   *Xanthomonas vesicatoria.*

Description   Affected peppers are flecked by numerous small, brown pustules. Larger lesions are slightly sunken with the pustules at the center of the concavity.

Development and Prevention   See *Tomatoes, Bacterial spot.*

Cladosporium Rot   *Pathogen Involved*   *Cladosporium herbarum.*

Description   Lesions are slightly depressed, whether they are tiny spots or 6 mm (1/4 in.) across. Initially they are light tan, but they become dark brown or black as they enlarge. The depressed margins remain green or turn light tan to brown. When humidity is high, a dense, velvety, olive-green mass of spores covers old lesions.
Internally, decayed tissue is spongy and grayish-brown.

Development and Prevention   Cladosporium rot develops mainly in response to chilling injury, and thus can be prevented by shipping peppers between 7° and 10° C (45° and 50° F) and by ceasing harvest after field chilling has occurred.

Gray Mold Rot (Botrytis rot)   *Pathogen Involved*   *Botrytis cinerea.*

Description   Small, cream-colored, irregularly shaped, almost lacy spots are the first sign of gray mold rot. As the spots enlarge and coalesce, they darken, become slightly sunken and smoother in outline. Under moist conditions the lesions are covered by brownish-gray mycelium that often is topped by spores of the same color (Fig. 17.2).

Development   *Botrytis* attacks peppers that have wounds or those that have been chilled either before or after harvest. Even 7° C (45° F) is low enough to induce sufficient chilling in 2 weeks to cause gray mold rot.

Prevention   Prevention of injury and chilling injury will minimize this disorder. Since chilling injury is induced within about 2 weeks at 7° C (45° F), and since undesirable ripening occurs about 10° C (50° F),

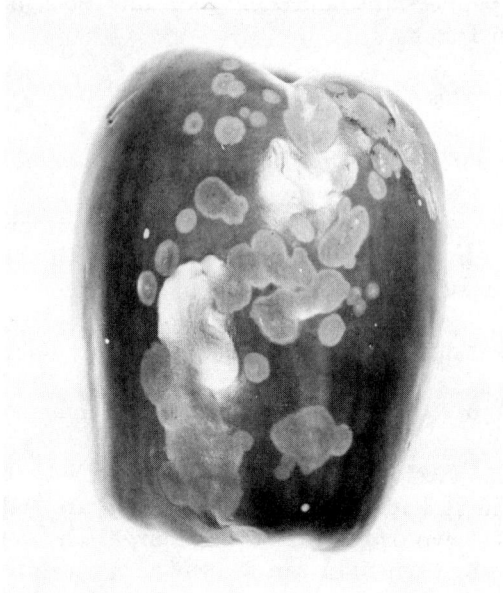

U.S. Dept. of Agriculture Photo

FIG. 17.2.   BOTRYTIS ROT OF BELL PEPPER

temperature must be carefully controlled and prolonged storage avoided.

Similar Diseases   See *Rhizopus rot.*

Rhizopus Rot   *Pathogen Involved*   *Rhizopus stolonifer.*

Description   The skin appears to be stretched over the mushy lesions, and thus tends to be flat rather than rounded like the normal contour of a pepper. White mycelium grows out of any break in the skin and then forms numerous fruiting bodies. Since not all spores mature simultaneously, the surface appears dotted white and black, the most typical symptoms of this disorder.

Development   Rhizopus enters mainly through wounds but spreads readily from infected to healthy peppers where the two touch. The decay spreads most rapidly between 24° and 27° C (75° and 80° F) and is virtually stopped below 10° C (50° F).

Prevention   Careful handling and rapid cooling of peppers to below 10° C (50° F) minimizes the danger of Rhizopus rot.

Similar Diseases   Tissue rotted by gray mold remains firmer than that affected by Rhizopus rot, and its surface conforms to the natural shape of the pepper. Further, if chilling is suspected, gray mold rather than Rhizopus is the likely pathogen. Bacterial soft rot results in the softest tissue and is not accompanied by any mycelial growth.

Virus Mottling   Peppers severely discolored or distorted by virus infections rarely are shipped. However, yellowish streaks or splotches sometimes are found on peppers on display. Such fruits are edible but unattractive.

SQUASH, SUMMER

Physical Injury

Mechanical Injury   All types of summer squash are extremely tender and are injured by the slightest scratch, bruise or scuff.

The yellow and scalloped squash show scuffing clearly because the ensuing darkening is very obvious on a light background.

All summer squash should be handled gently through marketing, and sorters and packers should wear cotton gloves to prevent cuts from fingernails.

Disorders

Chilling Injury *Description*   Chilled summer squash shows surface pitting and decays rapidly at nonchilling temperatures, although damage may be absent while the squash is refrigerated.

Development, Cause, and Prevention   Summer squash is slightly chilled during 4 days at 0° to 7° C (32° to 45° F) and definitely injured during 8 days (Morris and Mann 1948). Storage at about 10° C (50° F) minimizes chilling and normal deterioration. Summer squash should never be held on or under ice.

Wilting   Wilting of summer squash is very common at retail and can be minimized by moving stock rapidly or by prepacking. Ice should never be used because of the danger of chilling injury.

Diseases

Summer squashes are attacked by some of the same diseases as cucumbers, muskmelons and watermelons, and the symptoms are sufficiently similar so that no separate description is necessary.

MISCELLANEOUS STRUCTURES

ASPARAGUS

Physical Injuries

Freezing   *Description*   Limpness and darkening are a sign of freezing in tips, and water-soaking is symptomatic of the rest of the spear. Thawed spears are mushy and unacceptable for use.

Development and Cause   The tender tips freeze readily when they are cooled to their freezing point of $-0.8°$ C $±0.3°$ (30.5° F $±0.5°$). They are not only the most exposed portion in a packed crate but also are relatively low in soluble solids.

Prevention   See *Market Disorders   Freezing Injury.*

Similar Disorders   Thawed tips resemble those affected by chilling, but the latter does not engender water-soaking.

Mechanical Injury   *Symptoms*   Broken tips and crushed spears are the most common signs of physical abuse.

Causes   Tips may be broken anywhere from harvest through the retail store. However, most of them are lost during sorting and packing and during bunching at retail.
    Crushing often accompanies closure of bulging crates, as a result of over-packing the container.

Prevention   Breakage of fragile tips can be reduced only by careful handling during all operations. Bunching at the source or some other means of prepackaging reduces breakage not only because each spear is physically protected but also because it is handled less often.
    Crushing can be prevented by abandoning the big bulge on the standard pyramid crate in favor of a firm, but not forced, pack.

Any method of machine harvest must be carefully evaluated for its impact on mechanical damage.

Disorders

Carbon Dioxide Excess   *Description, Development, and Cause* Small round pits are formed in the zone of elongation (just below the tips) of spears held 1 week in 5% CO_2 at 6° C (43° F). If the concentration is 10% or higher, the pits become longer and deeper and extend further down the spear. Round to oblong areas with corrugated surface are another sign of CO_2 injury, below the tip at 6° C (43° F) and nearer the base at 2° C (35° F). However, at 2° C injury is unlikely unless CO_2 concentration exceeds 15% (Lipton 1965).

Prevention   See *Oxygen Deficiency.*

Chilling Injury   *Description*   Tips of spears that have been chilled are dull, gray-green and limp, as if wilted. A few millimeters at the very tip or the entire tip may show the symptoms.

Development and Cause   Spears are chilled during storage for 3 to 4 weeks at 0° to 3° C (32° to 37° F). Symptoms develop about equally rapidly in this range, but the incidence at 0° C is about twice that at 3° C after a given storage period (Lipton 1958).

Prevention   Since asparagus usually is held less than two weeks, chilling injury rarely is commercially important. If chilling temperatures are combined with CO_2 concentrations of 20% or more, chilling injury may be noted after only 1 week (Lipton 1965).
For prolonged storage, 2° C (36° F) would likely result in the least deterioration, considering the dangers of chilling injury near 0° C (32° F) and of decay near 5° C (41° F).

Similar Disorders   Chilling injury resembles soft rot, but whereas tips with the former are soft and dry, those with the latter are soft and wet, particularly when slight pressure is applied.
Chilling injury also resembles freezing and O_2-deficiency, as noted in the relevant sections.

Elongation and Bending   *Description*   Bending is obvious and needs no elaboration. Elongation results in longitudinal separation of bracts above the zone of elongation and results in an unsightly spear.

Development and Cause   Bending can originate before or after harvest, but only the latter concerns us here. Asparagus bends upward, a negative geotrophic response, when it lies horizontally for a day or more at above optimum temperatures. Bending also occurs after packing when tips grow to the lid and are deflected.

Spears elongate after harvest only if their cut ends are in contact with free moisture, such as in a pan of water or on wet pads. Growth is negligible below 5° C (41° F) but rapid above 10° C (50° F) (Morris and Watada 1960).

Prevention   Bending and elongation are prevented by holding asparagus between 0° and 2° C (32° and 36° F), whether free water is available or not. At retail, stock set in water should be renewed several times daily, especially in poorly refrigerated displays.

Feathering   *Symptoms and Development*   Feathered tips are no longer compact with bracts tightly against the spear, but their bracts are partly unfolded due to growth of the underlying axillary buds.

Cause   Feathering is a sign of senescence and indicates that the spear either was senescent when harvested or that it was exposed to an unfavorably high temperature after harvest. Postharvest feathering is aggravated by low relative humidity.

Prevention   Spears feathered at harvest should be culled out during sorting and all others held at low temperatures.

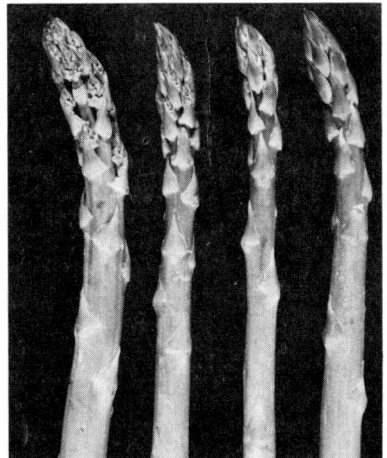

FIG. 17.3.   FEATHERING OF ASPARAGUS SPEARS
Decreasing severity in tips from left to right.

U.S. Dept. of Agriculture Photo

Oxygen Deficiency   *Description, Development, and Cause*   Large, depressed greenish-tan or greenish-white areas are characteristic of injury sustained in 1 to 10% O_2. These discolorations mostly are below the zone of elongation. Absence of O_2 leads to dark green, water-soaked tissue in the zone of elongation, which turns brown shortly after removal of the spears to normal air. Anaerobic conditions also can cause an amber exudate or white specks to form on the surface. All symptoms of low-O_2 injury occur about equally between 2° and 6° C (35° and 43° F) Lipton (1965).

Similar Disorders   Darkening below the tip is reminiscent of chilling injury, but the browning in air serves as a distinguishing mark.

Prevention   High-CO_2 and O_2-deficiency are unlikely to occur in normal handling of asparagus. However, if asparagus is prepackaged, the film must be properly ventilated. Respiration rate is high and atmosphere modification is rapid in a sealed container.

Diseases

Bacterial Soft Rot   *Pathogen Involved*   *Erwinia carotovora.*

Description   This most destructive of all market diseases that attack asparagus causes the tips to become dull-gray-green and watery soft. The softening is particularly noticeable when the tips are squeezed between thumb and finger.
   At the butt, or cut end, bacterial growth is first noticeable as small drops of exudate on the cut surface. Soon the entire cut surface is covered by the milky exudate and eventually the entire lower portion of the spear is a water-soaked, soupy mass. At this stage, the affected portion collapses, with the fiber bundles standing out as ridges.
   Bacterial soft rot is invariably accompanied by a nauseating odor that can be detected even in the early stages of decay.

Development   The bacteria enter any wound; thus the butt-end invariably is affected before the tips. However, soft rot at the tip-end may not always be a consequence of wounding. Possibly, aging may weaken the tissue enough to permit an infection to become established. This is suggested by the more rapid rate of decay of feathered as compared to tightly closed tips.
   Tough, woody, white cut ends resist soft rot longer than less tough green surfaces. However, cut surfaces a few millimeters below the tip decay more slowly than those nearer the base of all-green spears.

Soft rot develops on asparagus at all commonly encountered temperatures. However, its development is negligible below 2° C (36° F) and very rapid above 10° C (50° F).

Prevention   Bacterial soft rot can be minimized by holding asparagus at 2° C (36° F) or lower (see *Chilling Injury* under *Disorders* for caution), by culling any spears with feathered tips and those bruised or cut anywhere along the side (Lipton 1968).

Bacterial soft rot at the butt end, and to a lesser extent at the tips, can be retarded by holding asparagus in about 7% CO_2 ±2%. Below 5% the effect is absent and injury may occur at 10% CO_2. A brief (24 hr) exposure to 20% CO_2 at 2° to 10° C (36° to 50° F) also reduces soft rot during subsequent holding of the spears in air, without causing injury (Lipton 1965, 1968).

Similar Disorder   Chilling injury also causes dull-gray-green tips, but they are only limp, not watery, and have no foul odor.

Fusarium Rot   *Pathogen Involved*   Various species of *Fusarium.*

Description   This white, fluffy mold most commonly grows on bracts and tips, but may be found on any part of a spear. The tissue at the lesions is soft and water-soaked and changes from dark green to yellow or brown with age.

Development and Prevention   *Fusarium* mainly grows on asparagus weakened by prolonged storage: a few days at 21° C (70° F) or a month at 2° C (36° F). Holding asparagus between 0° and 2° C (32° and 36° F) controls the disease during a usual marketing period.

Phytophthora Rot   *Pathogen Involved*   Various species of *Phytophthora.*

Description   Lesions occur along the spear between the base of the tip and the butt end, appear water-soaked, and range from green to light brown. Surface mycelium is rare, but when present, is grayish-white and adheres closely to the spear.

Development and Prevention   Phytophthora occurs mostly during wet springs, particularly in California.

Proper refrigeration provides the best control.

MUSHROOMS

The principal postharvest disorders of cultivated mushrooms are discussed as a unit because they all result from the same causes and can be prevented by the same measures.

Development

Brown discoloration of cap and stem, opening and darkening of the gills, and wilting of the entire structure follow handling that is too slow or proceeds at too high a temperature.

Excessively high RH causes unattractive elongation of the stem and a slimy surface unless temperature is low.

Prevention

Mushrooms should be washed (see details under *Commodity Requirements*) soon after harvest, surface dried, and then held as close to 0° C (32° F) as possible during marketing (Hughes 1959). High RH, achieved by overwrapping containers with vented polyethylene, reduces wilting.

Exposing mushrooms to 100 krad of gamma irradiation also effectively reduces discoloration, opening of veils, and elongation of stalks (Bramlage and Lipton 1965). However, at this time the process is not economically feasible, nor is it approved by the U.S. Food and Drug Administration.

Physical Injury

Finger marks, cuts and bruises readily discolor, even at low temperature. Thus, mushrooms must be handled gently from grower to consumer if losses are to be avoided.

REFERENCES

UNRIPE FRUITS

Beans

MacMILLAN, H. G. 1923. Cause of sunscald of beans. Phytopathology *23*, 376–380.

McCOLLOCH, L. P., and VAUGHT, C. 1968. Refrigerated-storage tests with lima beans in pod. U.S. Dept. Agr. *ARS 51-23*.

SMITH, M. A., McCOLLOCH, L. P., and FRIEDMAN, B. A. 1966. Market diseases of asparagus, onions, beans, peas, carrots, celery, and related vegetables. U.S. Dept. Agr. Handbook *303*.

WATADA, A. E., and MORRIS, L. L. 1966A. Effect of chilling and nonchilling temperatures on snap bean fruits. Proc. Am. Soc. Hort. Sci. *89,* 368–374.

WATADA, A. E., and MORRIS, L. L. 1966B. Post-harvest behavior of snap bean cultivars. Proc. Am. Soc. Hort. Sci. *89,* 375–380.

ZAUMEYER, W. J., and THOMAS, H. R. 1957. A monographic study of bean diseases and methods for their control. U.S. Dept. Agr. Tech. Bull. *868*.

Cucumbers

EAKS, I. L. 1956. Effect of modified atmospheres on cucumbers at chilling and nonchilling temperatures. Proc. Am. Soc. Hort. Sci. *67,* 473–478.

EAKS, I. L., and MORRIS, L. L. 1957. Deterioration of cucumbers at chilling and nonchilling temperatures. Proc. Am. Soc. Hort. Sci. *69,* 388–399.

McCOMBS, C. L., and WINSTEAD, N. N. 1963. Control of cucumber cottony leak in transit. Proc. Am. Soc. Hort. Sci. *83,* 538–546.

MORRIS, L. L., and MANN, L. K. 1946. Effect of a volatile from honey dew melons on the storage behavior of certain vegetables. Proc. Am. Soc. Hort. Sci. *47,* 368–374.

WIEBE, H. J. 1969. Keeping quality of cucumbers wrapped in shrink film. Gemüse *24,* 54–56. (German)

Eggplants

ABE, K., IWATA, T., and OGATA, K. 1974. Chilling injury of eggplant fruits. I. General aspects of the injury and microscopic observations of pitting development. J. Japan. Soc. Hort. Sci. *42,* 402–407.

McCOLLOCH, L. P. 1966. Chilling injury of eggplant fruits. U.S. Dept. Agr. Mktg. Res. Rept. *749*.

Peppers, Bell

JOHNSON, H. B. 1964. Effect of hot water treatments and hydrocooling on postharvest bacterial soft rot in bell peppers. U.S. Dept. Agr. *AMS-517*.

JOHNSON, H. B. 1966. Bacterial soft rot in bell peppers. Cause and commercial control. U.S. Dept. Agr. Mktg. Res. Rept. *738*.

McCOLLOCH, L. P. 1962. Chilling injury and Alternaria rot of bell peppers. U.S. Dept. Agr. Mktg. Res. Rept. *536*.

OGATA, K., KOZUKUE, N., and MARATA, T. 1968. Quality changes and the mechanism of chilling injury in pepper fruits stored at low-temperature. I.

(sic.) J. Japan. Soc. Hort. Sci. *37*, 249–255. (Japanese, English Summary)

PARSONS, C. S., and DAY, R. H. 1971. Freezing injury to bell peppers. U.S. Dept. Agr. Mktg. Res. Rept. *895*.

SZIRMAI, J. 1938. Heat injury of peppers. Phytopathol. Z. *2*, 1–13. (German)

Squash, Summer

FRANCIS, F. J., and THOMSON, C. L. 1965. Optimum storage conditions for butternut squash. Proc. Am. Soc. Hort. Sci. *86*, 451–456.

GUBA, E. F. 1950. Spoilage of squash in storage. Mass. Agr. Expt. Sta. Bull. *457*.

McCOLLOCH, L. P. 1962. Alternaria rot following chilling injury of acorn squashes. U.S. Dept. Agr. Mktg. Res. Rept. *518*.

MORRIS, L. L., and MANN, L. K. 1948. Storage of summer squash. Refrig. Res. Found. Fact File Sheet. Mimeo.

SCHALES, F. D., and ISENBERG, F. M. 1963. The effect of curing and storage on chemical composition and taste acceptability of winter squash. Proc. Am. Soc. Hort. Sci. *83*, 667–674.

MISCELLANEOUS STRUCTURES

Asparagus

LIPTON, W. J. 1958. Effect of temperature on asparagus quality. Proc. Conf. Transport. Perishables. Univ. Calif., Davis. 147–151.

LIPTON, W. J. 1965. Post-harvest responses of asparagus spears to high carbon dioxide and low oxygen atmospheres. Proc. Am. Soc. Hort. Sci. *86*, 347–356.

LIPTON, W. J. 1968. Market quality of asparagus—effects of maturity at harvest and of high carbon dioxide atmospheres during simulated transit. U.S. Dept. Agr. Mktg. Res. Rept. *817*.

MORRIS, L. L., and WATADA, A. E. 1960. Elongation and bending of asparagus spears. Calif. Agr. *14*, No. 11, 15.

Mushrooms

BRAMLAGE, W. J., and LIPTON, W. J. 1965. Gamma radiation of vegetables to extend market life. U.S. Dept. Agr. Mktg. Res. Rept. *703*.

HUGHES, D. H. 1959. Mushroom discoloration research at the University of Delaware. Mushroom Sci. *4*, 447–449.

Physical Injuries, Market Disorders and Diseases of Ripe Fruits

MUSKMELONS

CANTALOUPS

Physical Injuries

Mechanical Injury *Description* Bruising and scuffing are common indications of mechanical injury. Bruised areas are soft, possibly flattened, and in severe cases the flesh appears water-soaked. Scuffing removes the net of the melons partially or completely on spots or over areas 5 to 8 cm (2 to 3 in.) in diameter, thus giving them a sandpapered look.

Development and Cause Much of the mechanical damage is inflicted before the melons are shipped, mainly at harvest, by rough handling at packing sheds, and during packing and closing of crates. Damage done at origin is often compounded by in-transit damage and further rough handling at destination.

As with other disorders, damage often is not evident on arrival but becomes obvious only at retail, where the loss is then incurred either by the retailer or the consumer.

Prevention Cantaloups should never be dropped more than a few centimeters on any surface unless it is well padded, when drops of 60 cm (2 ft) are acceptable. Neither should melons be allowed to strike each other with force, such as occurs on inclined sorting tables. A drop of 1 m (3 ft) spread over 3 m (10 ft) can be as harmful as an equal vertical drop.

Crates of adequate size or properly designed cartons will reduce bruising and chafing, much of which is incurred when cantaloups are overpacked in containers that bulge substantially after being lidded. For example, if 34 kg (75 lb) of 27-size cantaloups were packed in a crate, on average, one melon showed moderate to severe damage at destination. However, for weights of 36 or 38 kg (79 or 84 lb) the average number of damaged fruit increased to nearly 3 and 6 respectively (Kasmire and Baird 1970).

Solar Injury   *Description*   Severely injured melons, those with dry, sunken, and white to light tan areas, are invariably culled before shipment. However, fruits with milder forms, where the ground color is a spotty brown instead of buff and where the net is darker than normal over the same area, often reach markets.

Development and Cause   Sunburn may literally be sunscald, i.e., caused by heat alone, although shortwave solar radiation also is involved. Cantaloups may be injured either during maturation if foliage is sparse or while they wait in trucks exposed to the sun until unloaded. Under such conditions melons can reach an injurious 49° C (120° F) within 2 hr when air temperature is about 38° C (100° F) (Kasmire *et al*. 1962).

Prevention   See Chapter 15.

Disorders

Chilling Injury   *Description*   Decay is the chief sign of chilling injury in cantaloups, although softening of the tissue also is evident. These symptoms are usually noticeable after injured melons have been one or more days at room temperature.

Development and Cause   Cantaloups suffer chilling injury when held 1 to 2 weeks at 0° to 1° C (32° to 34° F). Fully ripe melons are less sensitive to chilling than "hard ripe" or "eastern choice" fruits and can be held under ice for one week without noticeable injury (Morris 1947).

Prevention   Cantaloups are best shipped at about 3° to 5° C (38° to 41° F), which is high enough to avoid chilling injury and low enough to prevent objectionable ripening during transit periods up to 2 weeks. They are not suitable for prolonged low-temperature storage.

Vein Tract Browning *Description* The unnetted strips that are characteristic of some cultivars of cantaloups are reddish-brown to dark brown instead of their normal buff or greenish-tan (Fig. 18.1). In completely netted fruits the discoloration also may be present, but it is less noticeable. The discolored tissue is just a few cells deep.

Development and Cause VTB appears to be a symptom of aging, the development of which is accelerated by exposure of cantaloups to substantial solar ultraviolet radiation during maturation. Such exposure occurs when the fruits are not adequately shaded by vines. VTB is aggravated by undesirably high holding temperatures (Lipton 1977).

Prevention VTB is minimized by maintaining the vines in good condition throughout the harvest period. After harvest, prompt cooling to and holding of the fruit at about 3° to 5° C (38° to 41° F) will delay VTB.

HONEY DEW MELONS

Physical Injuries

Mechanical *Description* Honey Dew melons frequently are bruised or cut. Bruised areas are soft and sometimes somewhat flat-

U.S. Dept. of Agriculture Photo

FIG. 18.1. VEIN TRACT BROWNING OF CANTALOUP
Normal—left. Affected—right.

tened, whereas the cuts may range from minor indentations to cuts into the flesh.

Development and Cause   Bruises may be due to impact or pressure. Impact bruises can occur before packing, by rough handling in field or shed, or during impacts in transit. Pressure bruises are incurred when the melons are forced into their container and gradually "give" as they soften.

Melons are cut when they are forced against the edges of rigid containers.

Prevention   Honey Dews should never be thrown and should never be allowed to hit each other as hard as often occurs during unloading onto sorting tables. Strong fiberboard containers or resilient liners in wood crates, with the melons firmly but not tightly packed, would prevent much of the cutting.

Solar Injury   *Description*   Excessive exposure of Honey Dews can result in tan to brown discolored areas (brown blotch) or in bleached to gray wrinkled or sunken areas. The darkening and death of epidermal cells appears to be caused by ultraviolet radiation (Campbell 1962), whereas the other symptoms most likely are caused by excessive heating of the tissue. Such heating can lead to off-flavors in adjacent flesh.

Pale to bright yellow surface patches also derive from exposure to the sun but are harmless.

Prevention   Good foliage cover is the best preventative. Whitewashing exposed with certain materials may offer some protection (See Chapter 15).

Disorders

Chilling Injury   *Description and Development*   Failure to ripen to satisfactory dessert quality is the most common symptom of slight but economically significant chilling injury (CI). An early visible sign of CI is a reddish-tan discoloration that appears as if it were just under the surface. The discoloration may be in patches or may affect the entire melon. In severe cases the discolored areas may become slightly sunken (Lipton 1978). Water-soaking of the rind and exudation of juice are extreme symptoms that apparently develop only after a prolonged chilling exposure of partly mature Honey Dews. Alternaria and/or Cladosporium rots commonly follow chilling injury.

The reddish-tan discoloration may disappear during subsequent holding of Honey Dews at about room temperature (20° C; 68° F) if the affected melons were harvested at maturity class 1–2 (see Chapter 8) but likely will intensify if the melons were in class 1. All other symptoms tend to become more prominent after removal of the melons from chilling to higher temperatures.

Cause and Prevention   Honey Dews are chilled by being held below about 5° C (41° F) for about 10 days or longer. Shipping only Honey Dews that are maturity class 1–2 or riper reduces the chance of development of visible chilling injury.

Mature melons properly treated with ethylene should be shipped between 7° and 10° C (45° and 50° F). This range avoids chilling and excessive ripening in transit. Ripe Honey Dews can be stored without ill effects up to 2 weeks at about 5° C (41° F), but they should never be held on or under ice.

Similar Disorder   A light to dark tan discoloration at or near the ground spot can develop without exposure of the melons to chilling conditions.

Warts   *Description*   Warts are small, tan, corky growths on the surface of the fruits. In immature melons the sites of the warts are dark green.

Development and Cause   Incomplete evidence suggests that the warts grow in response to injuries to the hairs (trichomes) that cover young Honey Dews (Masuda and Hayashi 1958).

Prevention   Present knowledge offers no suggestions for avoidance of warts. Severely warty fruit should be culled, even though their flavor is normal and decay susceptibility is not increased.

MISCELLANEOUS MUSKMELONS

Crenshaw and Persian melons are subject to the same disorders as cantaloups and particularly share their degree of sensitivity to chilling injury. However, both of these melons are more sensitive to mechanical injury because their flesh is more buttery than that of cantaloups. They also seem to be more susceptible to solar injury.

Preventative measures for the various physical injuries and disorders also parallel those for cantaloups.

Diseases

Muskmelons, including cantaloups, Honey Dews, Persians, Crenshaws, Casabas, and various derivations or hybrids of these, are discussed as a group because most diseases are common to several, or all, of them.

Alternaria Rot   *Pathogen Involved*   *Alternaria tenuis.*

Crops Affected   All muskmelons.

Description   *Cantaloups:* Infected stem scars initially are crisscrossed by wisps of dark mycelial strands, but eventually are completely covered by black mycelium. On the netted surface the lesions also are covered by black mycelium and spores but have diffuse margins because the surface is not sunken. The mycelium usually is not cushiony, but adheres closely to the surface, thus permitting the netting to be seen. When *Alternaria* invades the flesh, the diseased and healthy tissue are clearly delineated, and plugs of decayed tissue can be lifted out.
The symptoms presumably are the same on Persian melons.
Honey Dews: The dark brown to black lesions contrast sharply with the creamy color of the surface. Some of the lesions have alternating light and dark concentric rings. These eventually turn black and are covered by a grayish-olive mat of fungus or by sparse mycelium covered by a velvety cushion of spores.
Internal symptoms are those of cantaloups.

Development   *Alternaria* is a weak pathogen and thus infects melons primarily following solar injury, chilling injury or wounding, such as at the stem scar. The decay does not show up at low temperature but develops rapidly above 15° C (59° F).

Prevention   Culling of all injured melons and avoiding chilling injury, particularly with Honey Dews, will eliminate most Alternaria rot. With cantaloups, the incidence can be reduced by dipping them in or passing them through 54° C (130° F) water for 30 sec before they are precooled. Addition of certain approved fungicides renders the treatment even more effective (Johnson 1968; Stewart 1973). Judging from experience with bell peppers, hydroheating should not be followed by hydrocooling. Cooling with cold air would be preferable.

Similar Diseases   Late stages of Cladosporium rot can be distinguished from Alternaria rot only by microscopic examination.

Bacterial Soft Rot   *Pathogen Involved*   Species of *Erwinia.*

Crop Affected   Honey Dews, mainly.

Description   Infected areas become water-soaked and soft and eventually the fruit becomes a hollow shell full of liquified tissue with a nauseating odor.

Development and Prevention   Soft rot enters via injuries and spreads rapidly at summer temperatures. While refrigeration at 7° to 10° C (45° to 50° F) almost stops the disease in Honey Dews, the best preventative is careful handling.

Bacterial Spot   *Pathogen Involved*   *Pseudomonas lachrymans.*

Crop Affected   Honey Dews, mainly.

Description   Lesions are greenish-tan, slightly sunken, circular to oblong, and water-soaked. The lesions may coalesce to form large brown or black areas.

Development and Prevention   Unlike bacterial spot of cucumbers, which also is caused by *P. lachrymans,* that on Honey Dews can originate in arid growing areas. For further comments, see *Cucumbers.*

Blue Mold Rot   *Pathogen Involved*   Species of *Penicillium.*

Crops Affected   Cantaloups and Honey Dews, mainly.

Description   The typical blue to blue-green spore masses are seen externally only on well established lesions, or internally in cavities of diseased tissue. Earlier, the organism causes clearly outlined lesions that are darker than the rind, slightly depressed, and 1 to 5 cm (1/2 to 2 in.) in diameter. Diseased and normal tissues are sharply delineated. Affected melons have a musty odor and flavor.

Development and Prevention   *Penicillium* primarily attacks melons that have been stored too long. Thus, prompt handling at recommended temperatures avoids the disease.

Cladosporium Rot. (Green Mold Rot)   *Pathogen Involved*   *Cladosporium cucumerinum.*

Crops Affected   Cantaloups and Honey Dews, most frequently.

Description   *Cantaloups:* The stem scar is the most common site for this disease, although any part of the surface may be covered by the initially olive-green and later black mold. The stem scar may be completely hidden by mycelium, whereas other parts of the surface usually are more thinly covered, giving it a dirty appearance.

When the fungus penetrates below the surface, the rind remains firm but the flesh becomes soft and spongy. The diseased portion readily separates from normal flesh.

Honey Dews: Tiny to large circular to rounded black spots or areas are a typical symptom. The spots may be partly or completely ringed by a buff-colored band. The lesions are smooth and shiny unless humidity is high, when olive to black surface mycelium becomes abundant.

Lesions are shallow and may dry up when humidity is low.

Development   Cladosporium rot develops more readily at the stem scar of cantaloups than on their netted surface. At the scar, mycelium may be objectionable after 1 week at 5° C, whereas surface growth becomes objectionable only after about 2 weeks at 5° C or after 2 to 3 days at 15° C (59° F) subsequent to a week or more at the lower temperature.

In Honey Dews, Cladosporium rot often follows chilling injury.

Prevention   Cantaloups shipped or stored at 3° to 5° C (38° to 41° F) and Honey Dews shipped between 7° and 10° C (45° and 50° F) are unlikely to become seriously infected by *Cladosporium,* unless the marketing period exceeds 2 weeks for cantaloups and 3 or 4 weeks for Honey Dews.

Similar Disease   See *Alternaria Rot.*

Fusarium Rot   *Pathogen Involved*   Various species of *Fusarium.*

Crops Affected   All muskmelons.

Description   Tufts of white or pinkish-white mycelium are the typical early symptom of the disease. The tufts may coalesce and eventually cover any part of the diseased melon. The lesions may be shallow or deep and affected tissue may be normally colored or pink. Some species of *Fusarium* cause a red to purple rather than a pink discoloration. Diseased flesh may be extremely bitter, taste like raw mushrooms, or be nearly normal, depending on the species of *Fusarium* involved.

Development and Prevention   Fusarium rot develops mainly when temperatures are above those recommended for the several types of melons. Since wounds, however small, seem to be essential for infection to occur, careful handling will greatly reduce the incidence of this disease.

Hot water treatment, as described under Alternaria rot, proved to be an effective control on cantaloups but has not been tested on other muskmelons.

Rhizopus Soft Rot   *Pathogen Involved*   *Rhizopus stolonifer,* mainly.

Crops Affected   All muskmelons.

Description   Softening and water-soaking of the flesh are signs of Rhizopus rot. However, the tissue, though very soft, does not completely disintegrate. Mycelium is not always visible, but when present, it is white and wispy.

In cantaloups the lesions are barely noticeable until they are fairly large, and often are discovered when a finger or thumb suddenly plunges into the softened flesh. In Honey Dews, however, the lesions are readily noticeable and have distinct, although not sharp margins.

Development and Prevention   Rhizopus rot develops only slowly on melons held at 10° C (50° F) or below, but very rapidly above 21° C (70° F). Recommended storage temperatures readily control this disease, but hot water treatment, as noted under Alternaria rot, is a useful adjunct.

Similar Disease   Bacterial soft rot also causes softening of tissue, but brings almost complete dissolution of tissue. Further, mycelium is absent in bacterial diseases.

PUMPKINS AND WINTER SQUASHES

Disorders

Chilling Injury   *Description*   Rot, mostly due to *Alternaria*, is the only visible sign of chilling injury. Alternaria rot first appears as islands of a root-like network that eventually coalesce. Older infections are gray or olive-green if spores are abundant (McColloch 1962).

Decay is not visible during one month's storage at chilling temperatures but spreads rapidly after transfer of the fruits to higher temperatures.

Development and Cause   Table Queen (Acorn) squash and probably other members of this group are chilled during 15 days or more at 0° C (32° F), during 25 to 30 days at 5° C (41° F), or during 60 days at 7° C (45° F). The exact chilling exposure required for injury to develop varies from year to year and with the type and cultivar stored. Butternut is highly chilling-sensitive. Table Queen and Hubbard are somewhat resistant, and Quality is intermediate (Schales and Isenberg 1963).

Prevention   Table Queen squash, stored about 1 month, should be held at 7° C (45° F), where chilling and yellowing are minimized or absent. For longer periods this and other squashes and pumpkins must be held between 10° and 15° C (50° and 59° F) to avoid chilling injury.

Hollow-neck *Description*   The solid portion, the "neck," of Butternut squash becomes hollow and the remaining flesh stringy (Francis and Thomson 1965). So far the disorder, or a similar one, has not been reported for other cultivars.

Development and Cause   The disorder develops when Butternut squash loses about 15% or more of its original weight during storage. This loss is mainly due to transpiration, and usually shows up only after prolonged storage (about 100 days) at recommended RH (about 60%) or more rapidly at lower RH.

Prevention   Butternut squash should be held in about 60% RH for no longer than about 50 days.

Diseases

Alternaria Rot *Pathogen Involved*   *Alternaria tenuis.*

Description   Superficial, circular, cream-colored or bleached areas with ill-defined margins are early signs of Alternaria rot. Eventually, individual spots coalesce until most of the fruit is covered. Surface mycelium is gray, or olive-green if spore-bearing.
Internally, the decay first renders the flesh soft, mealy, and slightly bleached, but later causes it to turn firm and black.

Development and Prevention   Alternaria rot attacks only squashes that have been weakened, principally via chilling injury. Thus, the disease can readily be avoided by storing squashes at nonchilling temperatures (Fig. 18.2).

Courtesy L. P. McColloch

FIG. 18.2. EFFECT OF STORAGE TEMPERATURE ON ALTERNARIA ROT OF SQUASH AFTER STORAGE
Storage temperatures from left: 10° C (50° F); 7° C (45° F); 4.5° C (40° F); 0° C (32° F). Stored for 35 days at indicated temperature, then 6 days at 13° C (55° F).

Bacterial Soft Rot   See *Muskmelons*.

Bacterial Spot   See *Cucumbers*.

Black Rot   Pathogen Involved   *Mycosphaerella citrullina*.

Description   In Acorn squash, the lesions first are water-soaked and greenish-brown, but turn firm and black when fruiting bodies are formed.

Development   See *Watermelon*.

Cottony Leak   See *Cucumbers*.

Fusarium Rot   See *Muskmelons*.

Rhizopus Soft Rot   See *Muskmelons*.

Scab   See *Cucumbers*.

TOMATOES

Physical Injuries

Freezing   Description and Development   Some signs of freezing are evident immediately after thawing, whereas others are delayed for one to several days.

Severely frozen tomatoes are water-soaked and soft as soon as thawed. In partially frozen fruits the margin between healthy and dead tissue is distinct, particularly in green fruits. If freezing is less severe, the tissue may not be completely killed, but the injured cells dry out, and the surface becomes rough, sunken, and slightly bleached. If only small, isolated groups of cells are frozen, they collapse and leave a depression surrounded by normal tissue.

A characteristic yellow, usually unilateral, discoloration of mildly frozen tissue is evident 1 to 2 days after exposure to sunlight.

Internal evidence of freezing is a drying of the gelatinous substance about the seeds. This symptom is not necessarily accompanied by external signs of freezing.

Cause   Tomatoes freeze at about $-0.8°$ C ($30.5°$ F). Freezing occurs either in the field or in transit, but the symptoms are identical, except that tissue frozen in the field dries more rapidly due to exposure to sun and wind.

Prevention   Freezing injury cannot be prevented once ice has formed, but its impact on market quality can be minimized by certain precautions (McColloch 1960).

When field freezing is certain or suspected, harvest should be delayed until all fruits have thawed so that obviously injured fruits remain in the field. If harvest still seems profitable, the crop should be held at origin 1 to 3 days to allow culling of fruits with delayed symptom expression, because such fruit is highly susceptible to decay. Further, if even a light freeze was preceded by several days of temperatures well within the chilling range (below $10°$ C; $50°$ F), the potential for decay would make harvest inadvisable. This caution particularly applies to mature-green fruit, which is more sensitive to chilling injury than riper fruit.

Mechanical Injury   Mechanical damage accounts for more defects of tomatoes at shipping point and on the market than all other defects combined. Among tomatoes commercially harvested mature-green, 55% showed some mechanical defect at shipping point. After ripening, nearly 80% of this fruit showed such defects, because injuries that are not evident in green tomatoes are prominent in ripe fruit (MacLeod *et al.* 1970).

Description   Cuts, punctures, bruises, scars, scuff marks and discolored areas, all are evidence of mechanical injury. Of these, bruises are the most common and serious and account for about half of all mechanical damage.

Bruised tomatoes may be flattened or indented and soft; the locules either are dry, or if gelatinous tissue is present, it may be thick and stringy from continuous pressure, or watery from severe impacts.

Scuffing and scarring are followed by pitting and browning, because the injured tissue dries out.

Development and Cause   Tomatoes may be bruised any time between field and kitchen by being (1) thrown into picking box or bin; (2) pressed out of shape in a bin loaded too deeply; (3) dumped too vigorously from box or bin to sorting belt or dropped too far from sorting belt to shipping container; (4) squashed during stacking, loading, or in transit; (5) handled roughly during sorting in the ripening room or during prepacking; (6) dumped into bulk retail display; (7) squeezed in the hand of the customer or between harder items in the grocery bag.

External bruising mainly occurs before the fruit is packed, which allows removal of most of them during sorting at origin. Internal bruising, however, occurs mainly during or after packing.

The riper the fruit, the more readily it bruises. However, degree of bruising under given conditions is not related to size, weight, or mass of fruit of any one cultivar, although the latter do differ in their susceptibility to bruising.

Extensive studies by McColloch (1962) have shown that a mature-green fruit bruises less readily than riper fruits, but that injuries that seem minor before ripening are serious once the fruit is ripe. He further found that green fruits sorted repeatedly during ripening showed 2 to 4 times as much objectionable bruising when ripe as fruits that were marketable after the first sorting.

Tomatoes are scuffed and scarred when they rub against rough sur-

TABLE 18.1.   MAJOR CAUSES OF CULLAGE OF TOMATOES AT PACKINGHOUSES IN CALIFORNIA, 1972 AND 1973

Cause of Cullage	Average Incidence	
	Mature-green (%)	Partly Ripe (%)
Under-sized	25	8
Physical damage	21	25
Catfacing, scars	10	14
Solar injury	10	16
Insect damage	7	5
Over-ripe	5	20

Source: Abstracted from Kader and Morris (1976).

faces, such as boxes or dirty sorting belts, or even against each other, particularly when dirty. Tomatoes below 15° C (about 60° F) scuff more readily than warm fruit.

Prevention   Mechanical injury can be prevented, or at least reduced, only by careful analysis of each step during handling and by devising ways to minimize throwing, dropping or squeezing the fruits. Where drops are unavoidable, padding with 3 cm (1 in.) thick foam rubber substantially reduces injury. Drops of 15 cm (6 in.) or more should be avoided, whether the fruits hit a solid object or each other. Dumping fruit into water instead of directly onto a belt also would help reduce bruising.

Scuffing and scarring can be minimized by keeping boxes, bins, or belts clean and by packing fruit firmly, but not too tightly. A loose pack allows fruits to rotate and rub against each other in transit, which leads to scuffing injury.

Disorders

Blossom-end Rot   *Symptoms*   Brown to nearly black discoloration of the surface and flesh at the stylar (blossom) end is typical of severe blossom-end rot (BER) (Fig. 18.3). The disorder initially may be only below the surface and appear as a shadow-like area through the green wall. Mild BER is typified by a small, irregularly shaped dark area around the stylar end.

Development and Cause   BER can develop during prematuration or maturation and is the end-result of the collapse and death of affected cells. Death, in turn, is caused by adverse water supply and lack of available calcium in the soil.

Prevention   Severely affected fruits never reach markets because they are not packed, and mostly not harvested. Careful sorting will detect most fruits with subsurface BER, and mild cases are not objectionable.

Prevention in the field is the only cure, a topic discussed in manuals on tomato production.

Carbon Dioxide Excess   Retarded and blotchy ripening, abnormally rapid softening, a brown discoloration, increased decay and development of off-flavors are consequences of storing tomatoes about 1 week in

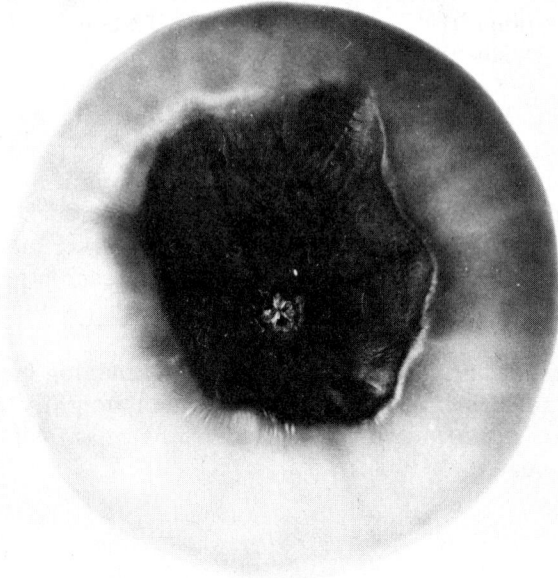

From Barksdale et al. (1972)

FIG. 18.3.   BLOSSOM-END ROT OF TOMATO

5% CO_2, whether O_2 is at normal or reduced levels (Parsons *et al.* 1970; Kader and Morris 1974).

Chilling Injury   *Symptoms*   The most obvious symptoms of chilling injury are delayed and blotchy coloration and great susceptibility to decay, principally Alternaria rot. Pitting, shrivelling, and a greater softening than suggested by the color of the affected fruits are further signs. Uniformly dark or brown seeds also indicate that chilling has occurred.

Development and Cause   Induction of chilling injury is governed by temperature, duration of the chilling exposure, and degree of ripeness of fruits so exposed. Further, if chilling is induced in green fruit, obvious symptoms are delayed until the onset of ripening.

The less ripe a tomato, the more susceptible it is to chilling injury.

For mature-green fruit the critical exposures are 1 day at 0° C (32° F), 3 days at 5° C (41° F), 5 days at 7.5° C (45° F), or 8 days at 10° C (50° F).

For light pink fruits the respective critical periods are 2, 5, 8 and 12 days (Morris and Kader 1974). Ripe fruit would not be obviously harmed by 1 week at 0° C, although the upper limit of the chilling range is about 13° C (55° F). Just how strikingly chilling can increase decay during subsequent ripening is illustrated in Fig. 18.4. Without chilling, 4 to 5% of the fruits were lost, but if chilled 6 days, a common transit period, losses were more than doubled. Finally, if tomatoes were exposed to one week each of chilling in the field and in transit, the incidence of decay would be about ten-fold that at recommended temperatures.

Tomatoes most commonly are chilled either before harvest or during transit. Preharvest chilling is of concern principally for mature-green fruits harvested in fall or winter in California and in Florida, respectively. According to Morris (1954), if such fruits are exposed 95 to 115 hr to temperatures below 15.5° C (60° F) their yield of salable ripe fruit likely will be below that of nonchilled fruit. For exposures between 115 and 135 hr substantial losses are almost certain, and if 135 hr were below 15.5° C, harvest would be an economic waste.

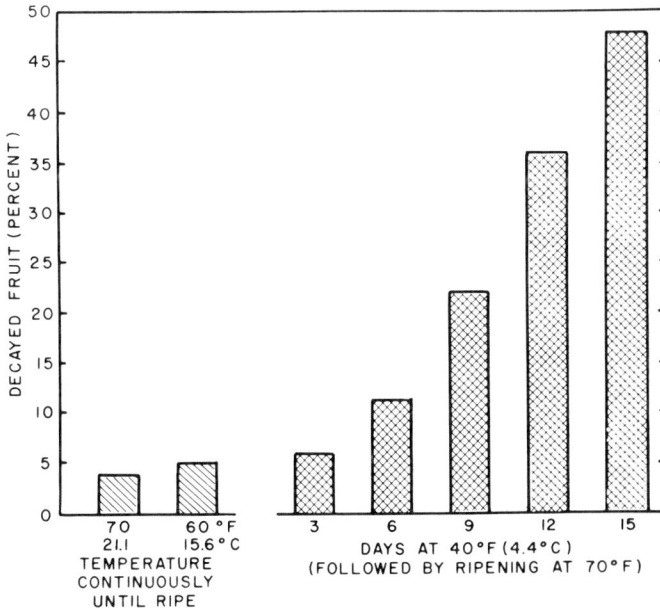

From McColloch and Worthington (1952)

FIG. 18.4.   EFFECT OF VARIOUS CHILLING EXPOSURES AT 4.5° C (40° F) ON INCIDENCE OF DECAY OF INITIALLY MATURE-GREEN TOMATOES WHEN RIPENED AT 21° C (70° F)
Control lots were held continuously at 21° or 15.5° C (70° or 60° F).

Transit chilling can occur any time of year. Temperatures below 13° C (55° F) should be brief, and those below 10° C (50° F) must be avoided for mature-green fruits. If the transit period is less than 4 days, 10° to 13° C probably is harmless for mature-green fruits and 5° C (41° F) for pink fruits, although such conditions are not recommended. Cooling below 13° C should be avoided, particularly in fall, because chilling exposures are cumulative. Thus, while neither field nor transit exposure may itself be harmful, when added, they may be decidedly injurious.

Prevention   Low temperatures in the field cannot be prevented, but their duration can be recorded. Weather bureau records may be adequate when the station is similarly located as the field in respect to elevation and remoteness from large buildings. In other situations, weatherproof temperature recorders may be advisable. Alternatively, conscientious reading of an accurate thermometer placed next to a tomato vine or comparable shaded location will yield a satisfactory record.

Transit chilling is avoided by shipment at recommended temperatures.

Similar Disorders   Blotchy ripening is also caused by several other factors, but the presence of Alternaria rot is an almost certain sign of chilling injury.

Cracking   *Description*   Cracks may radiate from the stem scar (radial cracking) or generally follow the circumference of the fruit (concentric cracking).

Development and Cause   Cracks develop as fruits approach maturity and appear to be caused by rapid changes in their rate of expansion. Cultivars differ greatly in their susceptibility to cracking, which suggests that toughness of skin also may be involved.

Prevention   No cracked fruits should be shipped to market because they are unsightly and the cracks are likely sites for decay.

Fruit Tumor   Fruit tumor formation could properly be included among physical injuries, but is treated separately because of its unique symptoms.

Description   Fruit tumors, formerly called waxy blisters, are blister-like growths on the surface of mature-green tomatoes (Treshow

1955). However, unlike a hollow blister, a tumor consists of numerous enlarged cells. The tumors may occur singly or in groups and usually are less than 12 mm (½ in.) in diameter, but sometimes may cover half a fruit. The tumors collapse and turn light brown as fruits ripen.

Development and Cause   The tumors grow in response to the rubbing of tomatoes against each other or against rough surfaces. Breaking of the skin does not induce growths.

Tumor growth is absent when fruits are held below 21° C (70° F) or above 33° C (91° F), but within this range, the rate of tumor growth increases with temperature: at 33° C tumors form within 30 hr but at 21° C only after 60 hr.

Susceptibility to this response to physical injury decreases as tomatoes ripen, and pink or riper fruits are not so affected. Thus shoulders, which ripen last, remain susceptible longest.

Prevention   Mature-green tomatoes must not be permitted to rub against each other or against rough surfaces during any phase of handling. This injunction is particularly relevant if the fruits are to be rapidly ripened, that is, between 21° and 24° C (70° and 75° F).

Irregular Ripening   *Description*   Irregular, blotchy or mottled ripening refers to coloration that does not proceed uniformly over the entire fruit, but leaves green, yellow or orange areas among the normal red or pink ones. The abnormal color may be in patches that are large or small, and on shoulders or sides, reticulated like netting on a cantaloup, or in ray-like streaks converging at the blossom end.

Development and Cause   Irregular ripening has many causes and may be related to storage temperature, preharvest environmental effects, cultural practices, or virus infections. Here, our concern will be with all but the last.

Irregular ripening of tomatoes shipped mature-green most commonly is attributable to chilling injury sustained before harvest or during transit, a topic discussed separately.

Unilateral heating of fruit during clear, warm days can result in "solar yellowing," also known as sunburn. The lack of red pigment seems to be the combined effect of high temperature and exposure to shortwave radiation. Fruit temperatures above about 27° C (80° F) interfere with the synthesis of lycopene, the chief coloring matter of tomatoes. The action of shortwave radiation is not certain but may be related to the functioning of ethylene in ripening. Since not only infrared or heat waves, but also shorter solar wavelengths are involved, solar yellowing seems a more appropriate term than sunburn (Lipton 1970). Further, the distinction between this disorder and sunscald becomes clearer because the words "burn" and "scald" are essentially synonyms, though the symptoms are not. Sunscald, in which the affected tissue appears bleached and becomes sunken and hard, is not discussed here in detail because affected fruits would be discarded at harvest.

Cultural practices, such as excessive or inadequate supplies of a nutrient element, or excess soil moisture may interfere with normal ripening. Such disorders are more common in tomatoes grown in greenhouses than outdoors; however, a discussion of their etiology is not within the scope of this book.

Prevention   Elimination of irregular ripening due to field or transit chilling is discussed under *Chilling Injury*.

Most fruits with solar yellowing are culled before packing. However, injury mild enough to escape detection in mature-green fruit may still be severe enough to lower the value of such fruits when ripe. This, and perhaps more serious solar yellowing, can be reduced by spraying the fruits in the field with a nontoxic whitewash after they are no longer protected by foliage. Such material, which washes off readily, has been successfully used for canning tomatoes and may be adaptable to market tomatoes.

Advice on prevention of irregular ripening rooted in cultural practices can be found in publications on production of tomatoes.

Oxygen Deficiency   *Description, Development, and Cause.*— Irregularly shaped, superficial to slightly sunken, brown discolorations develop when mature-green tomatoes are stored about 1½ weeks in 1.5% O_2 or less or 6 weeks in 2.5% O_2. However, not all fruits show this symptom. Those that do ripen color very unevenly, with large, sharply delineated, dull, yellowish-pink patches of irregular outline alternating with normal areas. Injured areas on shoulders may be brownish and slightly sunken.

Prevention   See general discussion of *CA storage*.

Similar Disorders   Uneven ripening due to other causes generally has diffuse margins, and the discolored areas have a normal shine and are not sunken.

Puffiness   *Description*   Puffy tomatoes feel excessively soft for their stage of ripeness, light for their size, and on cutting have large hollow spaces where the gel normally is found. One or more locules may be hollow.

Development and Cause   Puffiness develops in response to improper fertilization and seed development caused by high or low temperatures during flowering or in response to growth regulators that improve fruit set.

Prevention   Prevention strictly is via cultural practices. However, puffy fruits should be culled because they are worthless for slicing, and because they bruise even more readily than normal tomatoes. Separation of puffy fruits by flotation in water might be feasible, since normal fruits barely float whereas puffy ones float fairly high.

Separation by floatation angle also seems feasible (Chen and Studer 1976).

Thin-wall   *Description*   The terms thin-wall and gray-wall have been used interchangeably by McColloch *et al.* (1968) to describe a disorder referred to as gray-wall or thin-wall by Lorenz and Knott (1942), and to distinguish it from internal browning. However, more recently, others have applied gray-wall to a defect that seems synonymous with internal browning. Consequently, to avoid further confusion of these defects, we will apply the term thin-wall to the disorder described by Lorenz and Knott and reserve gray-wall (internal browning) for a defect that now is known to be a disease.

The thin walls of this disorder are confined to one side of the fruit and often are grayish-green in mature-green fruit but turn white or yellow during ripening.

Development and Cause   Thin walls apparently result from unilateral heating of fruits, which results in smaller cells on the exposed than on the shaded side. The associated discoloration is probably a form of solar yellowing, which is discussed separately.

Prevention   Thin-wall can probably be prevented or reduced by the methods cited under *Irregular Ripening*. Thin-walled fruits should be removed during sorting if the defect is obvious, because such fruits readily bruise.

Similar Disorders   The discoloration associated with thin-wall may be synonymous with solar yellowing.

Diseases

Alternaria Rot   *Pathogen Involved*   *Alternaria tenuis.*

Description   The appearance of Alternaria rot is influenced by the factors that contribute to its occurrence.

The lesions are about level with the surface when the fungus attacks at cracks, abnormal blossom ends, after sunburn or physical injuries. Following chilling injury, the lesions are usually sunken because the fungus is secondary to pitting induced by chilling exposures. The lesions tend to be dark brown to black in ripe fruit, tan to medium brown in partially ripe ("turning") fruit, and dark brown in green fruit.

Generally the lesions are firm, and the rot causes the flesh to turn dark and dry. Gray mycelium often is present in the rotted tissue, and under high humidity also on the surface. Velvety-appearing, olive-green to black spore masses may cover the fungal growth.

Development   Alternaria rot attacks only tomato fruits that have been injured in some way: by excessively high or low temperatures, by improper physical handling, or by growing conditions that result in cracks or blossom-end rot.

Alternaria grows at any temperature tomatoes likely encounter during marketing, although the rate of growth decreases as temperature decreases.

Prevention   Avoid injuries of any type, particularly chilling injury. Prompt ripening of tomatoes between 18° and 21° C (65° and 70° F) greatly reduces the chance of serious losses from Alternaria rot.

Similar Diseases   When Alternaria rot develops at the stem scar, it is initially indistinguishable from Phoma or Pleospora rot. Later, however, the other rots show white or black fruiting bodies, whereas Alternaria rot does not.

Bacterial Soft Rot   *Pathogens Involved*   *Erwinia carotovora* and other bacteria.

Description   Initially small, water-soaked spots rapidly enlarge and decompose underlying tissue into a watery mass. The color of the lesions may be that of the fruit or it may be light tan. When the surface cracks, a yellowish mixture of decomposed cells and bacteria oozes to the surface.

A nauseating odor usually accompanies soft rot.

Development   Bacteria can enter through any wound or other weakened tissue during any phase of preparation of the fruits for market. Particularly damaging is the practice of washing tomatoes in water that is neither frequently nor continuously renewed, nor sanitized with an approved disinfectant. In such wash water bacterial counts become extremely high after only a few hours of operation and any injury likely will be invaded by bacteria. Chilling injury also aggravates this type of rot.

Bacterial soft rot also may spread from fruit to fruit in containers or in ripening rooms.

Prevention   Good sanitation is the primary requirement for minimizing losses from bacterial soft rot. This can be accomplished by chlorination (100 ppm) of the water in the dump-tank into which pallet-bins are emptied and of any subsequent recirculated wash water. Chlorination of either one alone is ineffective (Segall and Dow 1976). Avoidance of physical and of chilling injury also are important in controlling this disease. Ripe or nearly ripe tomatoes are less susceptible to bacterial soft rot than mature-green or even pink fruit (Parsons and Spalding 1972). Ripe fruit also can be held at about 7° C (45° F) where soft rot development is nil.

Similar Diseases   Soft tissue rotted by *Rhizopus* initially is mushy rather than watery; thus even the decayed tissue holds together. Further, threads of the fungus are usually present in the tissue.

Sour rot also appears water-soaked, but has a sour rather than putrid odor.

Bacterial Spot   *Pathogen Involved*   *Xanthomonas vesicatoria.*

Description   On mature-green tomatoes, brown to black collections of pustules 3 to 6 mm (1/8 to 1/4 in.) across disfigure the fruits. However, lesions initiated long before harvest are sunken at harvest and gray or bleached, because the skin is dried and torn.

Development and Prevention   Tomatoes are infected in the field, mainly in warm humid areas of production. Immature fruits are readily infected, whereas ripe ones are not.

Careful culling of affected fruits would eliminate the disease at terminal markets, because the disease does not develop or spread during transit.

Similar Disorder   Nailhead spot lesions are flat or sunken, have definite brown margins, and enlarge after harvest.

Buckeye Rot   *Pathogen Involved*   Various species of *Phytophthora.*

Description   The rotted area on green fruits first is brown to grayish-green and hard, but the advancing margin becomes water-soaked. The lesions most commonly consist of broad, irregular zones alternating between brown and grayish-brown, but occasionally may appear water-soaked. The smooth surface of the lesion remains unbroken.

In ripe fruit the water-soaked appearance predominates, but little other discoloration is present.

Under high humidity, mycelium that is white and fluffy when dry, but matted and tough when wet, grows on the surface.

Development   Buckeye rot is favored only by warm, wet conditions before harvest. Thus, though it appears sporadically, it can cause serious losses.

Infection of green or ripe fruits occurs before harvest but can develop and spread rapidly during marketing, particularly above about 15° C (59° F).

Prevention   As a field disease, buckeye rot cannot be prevented after harvest. However, its postharvest incidence can be limited by careful culling of affected fruit. If infection is suspected but not certain, holding the fruits 24 hr at about 21° C (70° F) brings out incipient infections, and thus permits closer culling before shipment.

Holding tomatoes at 13° C (55° F) slows the advance of the disease, but offers little help, because ripening has to be done at a higher temperature.

Similar Disease   See *Soil Rot.*

Cladosporium Rot   *Pathogen Involved*   *Cladosporium herbarum.*

Description   This disease most commonly is seen on mature-green or partly ripe fruits. The lesions start out as small, light-tan spots that become slightly sunken as they enlarge. Then they have dark brown to black centers with lighter margins. When humidity is high, a fine, granular, dark-green mold grows on the surface. The lesions readily separate from healthy tissue.

Development and Prevention   Cladosporium rot usually develops only in response to chilling injury, and thus can be readily prevented by avoiding such injury.

Gray Mold Rot, Ghost Spot   *Pathogen Involved   Botrytis cinerea.*

Description   Gray mold lesions most commonly start on the shoulders as small, conspicuous spots. Larger lesions are typically grayish-green on unripe fruit and grayish-tan on ripe fruit. They also appear water-soaked, have distinct margins and the skin is wrinkled.

When *Botrytis* infects green tomatoes, the symptoms usually show as small, whitish rings with a distinct outer but diffuse inner margin, thus the name ghost spot. Occasionally the white area is solid rather than ring-shaped.

The decay rapidly rots fruits, that then are soft and watery.

Gray mycelium may emerge from lesions, and in humid air, likely will be covered by a dense mass of gray to light brown spores.

Development   *Botrytis* develops only during cool, moist growing conditions, but once started, spreads most rapidly near 27° C (80° F). The spores usually enter via cuts or cracks, such as at the stem scar. Infection usually occurs before harvest, but the decay can spread during packing, transit or ripening.

Chilling injury favors gray mold rot although to a lesser extent than Alternaria or Cladosporium rots.

Prevention   Shipping tomatoes near 13° C (55° F) and ripening them promptly upon arrival reduces the chance of serious *Botrytis* infections.

Late Blight Rot   *Pathogen Involved   Phytophthora infestans.*

Description   Late blight frequently starts as water-soaked or greasy appearing areas at or near the stem scar. Diseased tissue may completely encircle the stem scar and reach over the shoulders as the lesions age. Then they may appear smooth or roughened. When smooth, their margins are greenish on unripe fruit, slightly rough, water-soaked, and rusty-tan. The center is brown. Roughened lesions are composed of many small sunken areas that vary in color but tend to be rusty to dark brown.

Development   Late blight is most serious when the preharvest and harvest periods are wet, have nights between 10° and 15° C (50° and

59° F) and days between 15° and 21° C (59° and 70° F). Thus, the disease is most common from fall through early spring.

This disease does not spread appreciably from fruit to fruit after harvest, but large losses sometimes are sustained because fruits with invisible field infections are shipped.

Prevention - Late blight must be controlled before harvest. Thereafter, control is impossible because the fungus grows well at temperatures used for ripening tomatoes.

If suspected fruit is picked green, it can be held 4 to 7 days at 21° C (70° F), during which time infected fruit will decay. The remainder can then be marketed as "pinks."

Pleospora Rot.- *Pathogen Involved   Pleospora lycopersici.*

Description   Small, brown, oval spots at the stem scar or at sites of physical injury are the initial sign of this rot. Larger lesions may show some gray or grayish-brown mycelium, often interspersed with black, pimply fruiting bodies.

Development   Pleospora rot so far has been confined to tomatoes grown in California or Mexico in winter, when temperatures are moderate and when rain or fog keeps plants and fruits moist for several hours.

Infection occurs in the field or during harvesting or packing and is minimal thereafter. The decay advances slowly in mature-green fruit, but rapidly during ripening.

Prevention   The incidence of Pleospora rot can be minimized by shipping only high quality fruit and ripening it promptly.

Similar Disease   See *Alternaria Rot.*

Rhizopus Rot   *Pathogen Involved   Rhizopus stolonifer* mainly.

Description   In severe cases of Rhizopus rot, and there seem to be no mild ones, the fruit resembles a red, water-filled balloon. Eventually the fruit collapses and the liquid leaks out. Gray, coarse mycelium may be present at either stage, but mainly the latter. The mycelium generally is dotted with white and black spore masses, a characteristic symptom. Decayed fruits emit a slightly fermented odor.

Development   *Rhizopus* starts at physical injuries or in growth cracks. The latter often are initial sites because fruit flies spread the spores as they lay eggs into the cracks. The disease spreads readily from fruit to fruit via contact and grows most rapidly at 24° to 27° C (75° to 80° F).

Prevention   Rapid cooling of warm tomatoes to 13° to 18° C (55° to 65° F) and careful handling will reduce the incidence of this rot. For high value fruit, molded trays that minimize contact between fruits may be useful.

Similar Disease   See *Bacterial Soft Rot.*

Soil Rot   *Pathogen Involved*   *Rhizoctonia solani.*

Description   Initially brown, small, round spots on the blossom-end half of tomatoes show definite concentric rings when the spots are about 5 mm (¼ in.) across or larger. These rings may disappear as the lesion further enlarges and the fruit ripens.

The decayed tissue of ripe fruits is reddish brown and firm, except for the margin, which appears water-soaked and clearly defined. The skin over the lesions frequently is cracked.

Development   As the name implies, the causative fungus inhabits the soil and attacks tomatoes in contact with wet soil or splattered with soil during rains. Injuries are not necessary for the organism to invade the fruits.

The disease develops most rapidly at about 24° C (75° F) and is inhibited below 10° C (50° F).

Prevention   Staking tomatoes is the only effective method for avoiding soil rot. Shipments should be suspended for five days for nonstaked fruits following wet weather. Then all incipient infections have developed and thus can be culled.

Similar Disease   The well-defined margin, flattened surface, narrow concentric rings, and cracked skin distinguish soil rot from buckeye rot.

Sour Rot (Watery Rot, Oospora Rot)   *Pathogen Involved* *Geotrichum candidum.*

Description   *Mature-green fruit*: The lesions are a light greenish gray and may extend wedge-like from stem-scar to blossom-end or encompass the entire fruit. The affected tissue remains fairly firm until much of the fruit is decayed. When cut, it emits a sour odor. The skin remains smooth. A white, scum-like mycelium may emerge from the stem scar or from wounds.

Ripe fruit: Affected tissue is soft and appears water-soaked. A cheesy-white or scum-like mycelium may grow from cracks in the wrinkled skin. Bacteria likely follow sour rot and change the odor from sour to putrid.

Development   The fungus enters only via wounds or cracks, either in the field or thereafter. Fruit flies are a principal disseminator of the fungus. Chilling injury also predisposes tomatoes to sour rot. The fungus is infectious from below 4° to about 38° C (40° to about 100° F).

Prevention   Careful handling, adequate precooling, and avoidance of chilling injury help retard sour rot.

WATERMELONS

Physical Injury

Mechanical   *Description*   Bruising at the thin blossom-end is the most common form of mechanical injury. Sometimes bruising is so severe that this end is concave rather than convex. Other parts of watermelons also can be bruised, although cuts and abrasions are more common on the sides.

Severe impacts during handling or transport can crack the flesh internally or even split the melons open and render them worthless.

Development   Mechanical injury can occur during any part of marketing: when the melons are handled roughly during harvest, handling or loading into trailers or railcars; when the floors of vehicles are not adequately padded; as a result of impacts during transit, or during rough handling at destination.

Loading patterns also affect injury, at least for some cultivars. Serious injury of Congo watermelons was reduced by about two-thirds when they were loaded crosswise rather than lengthwise, which is the conventional way. However, for the more tender Klondike melons, bruising was about equal in both types of loads.

Prevention   The importance of careful handling of watermelons cannot be overemphasized. Their weight may give the erroneous impression that they are tough.

Injuries can be reduced during harvest by delay until the fruits have warmed up. The melons are more subject to injury when cool and turgid than when warm.

Adequate bedding, limiting load height to 3 to 5 melons, depending upon cultivar, and avoiding of sitting or walking on a load will reduce injury. Watermelons should be loaded crosswise because it usually reduces damage. Packing watermelons in cartons with fiberboard dividers also helps alleviate this serious problem (Close *et al.* 1971).

Disorder

Internal Rind Spot, Rind Necrosis   *Description*   Tan to brown discolored masses of cells lying between the surface and the flesh characterize this disorder. The unsightly patches may be small or they may nearly encircle the fruits when seen in cross section. Affected tissue remains firm and does not extend into the edible portion.

Development and Prevention   Definitive information on the cause of the disorder is not available, although bacteria may be involved (Kontaxis and Kurupas 1975). No preventive measures are known.

Diseases

Anthracnose   *Pathogen Involved*   *Colletotrichum lagenarium.*

Description   Circular or elongated welts that are initially dark green disfigure the surface of affected fruits (Fig. 18.5). As the welts enlarge, their centers turn brown and become sunken. Under high humidity, pink fruiting bodies that include pink spores cover the welts.

The tissue eventually may crack at the lesions and expose decayed tissue or a cavity.

Development   The disease is initiated before harvest, but since the fungus may remain dormant in the rind, and thus undetected, melons that seem free of anthracnose at shipping point may be severely affected on arrival at the market, particularly if they were inadequately cooled and exposed to high relative humidity.

Prevention   Principal control of anthracnose must occur before harvest. However, shipping melons between 5° and 10° C (41° and 50° F) will retard breaking dormancy of the fungus if it is present.

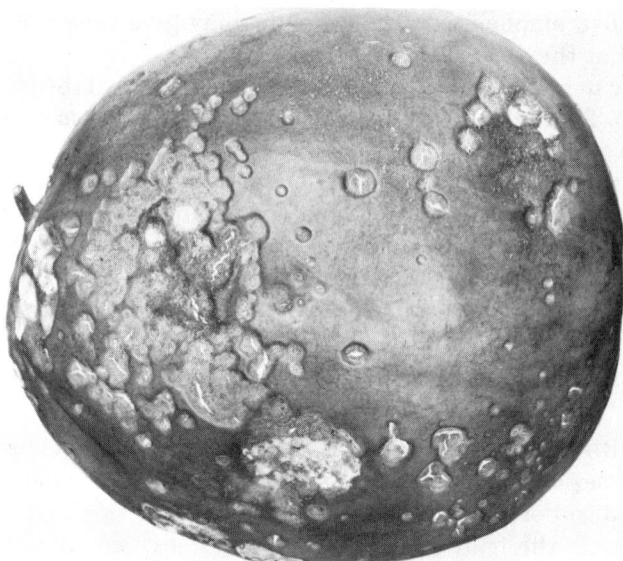

U.S. Dept. of Agriculture Photo

FIG. 18.5.   ANTHRACNOSE ROT OF WATERMELON

Black Rot   *Pathogen Involved*   *Mycosphaerella citrullina.*

Description   This disease initially is characterized by greenish-tan to black, water-soaked spots with distinct margins. The lesions, which are 2.5 to 5 cm (1 to 2 in.) across, have brown, depressed centers that may be covered with black fruiting bodies under humid conditions. Later, the lesions show fluffy white mycelium and they may have cracks radiating from their center. The rind is brown to black and the underlying tissue softens as the disease progresses.

Development and Prevention   Black rot is most common on watermelons grown during warm, humid weather. Infection may occur via the small injuries in the field but escape notice at harvest.

Careful handling at all stages, and shipping watermelons between 5° and 10° C (41° and 50° F) tend to prevent or retard black rot.

Phytophthora Rot   *Pathogen Involved*   Various species of *Phytophthora*, but mainly *P. capsici.*

Description   Small, irregular-shaped, water-soaked spots are the first sign of the disease. In deep green melons the lesions are grayish-green, but in light green melons they usually are brown. The rind remains fairly firm and becomes sunken only when much of a fruit is diseased. White to gray, cottony mycelium covers the lesions in a humid environment.

Internally the tissue becomes water-soaked and bleached.

Development and Control   Phytophthora rot develops rapidly at moderate to warm temperatures. The fungus can invade a fruit with or without prior injury, and thus it can spread rapidly from fruit to fruit in a load.

Shipping melons between 5° and 10° C (41° and 50° F) retards the spread of the fungus.

Stem-end Rot   *Pathogen Involved*   *Diplodia natalensis.*

Description   *Diplodia* causes a softening and water-soaking of infected tissue, that ultimately turns brown and shrivels. Then, dark gray mycelium covers the lesions and black fruiting bodies also may be present.

Development   This rot, as its name implies, most frequently starts at the wound created at the stem end during harvest. However, the fungus also may enter at any other open wound or at bruises, although its growth is inhibited when humidity is low and temperature high.

Prevention   In moist and warm areas, stems should be cut as long as possible at harvest and recut to about 2.5 cm (1 in.) during loading. At this time the wound should be treated with a paste of copper sulfate.

REFERENCES

Muskmelons

CAMPBELL, R. N. 1962. Ultraviolet radiation as a probable cause of brown blotch of honey dew melons. Phytopathology *52*, 360. (Abstract).

JOHNSON, H. B. 1968. Heat and other treatments for cantaloupes and peppers. *In* United Fresh Fruit and Vegetable Association Yearbook. pp. 9, 14, 51–52, 54, 56. United Fresh Fruit and Vegetable Assoc., Washington, D.C.

KASMIRE, R. F., and BAIRD, W. S. 1970. Automatic sizing of cantaloupes. Univ. Calif. Agr. Ext. Serv. (Unnumbered).

KASMIRE, R. F., SARQUIS, A. V., and WRIGHT, D. N. 1962. Market quality studies 1961. Midsummer cantaloupes. Univ. Calif. Agr. Ext. Serv. *AXT-50.*

LIPTON, W. J. 1975. Whitewashing Crenshaw and cantaloup melons to reduce solar injury. U.S. Dept. Agr. Mktg. Res. Rept. *1045.*

LIPTON, W. J. 1978. Chilling injury of 'Honey Dew' muskmelons: Symptoms and relation to degree of ripeness at harvest. HortScience *13*, 45–46.

LIPTON, W. J. 1977. Ultraviolet radiation as a factor in solar injury and vein tract browning of cantaloupes. J. Am. Soc. Hort. Sci. *102*, 32–36.

MASUDA, T., and HAYASHI, K. 1958. Verruca on the fruit of melon. 1. The formation of verruca due to artificial treatment and its anatomical observation. Sci. Rept. Fac. Agr. Okayama Univ. *11*, 79–86. (Japanese, English summary)

MORRIS, L. L. 1947. The use of ice on cantaloupes and other melons. Univ. Calif. Truck Crops Mimeo *38.*

STEWART, J. K. 1973. Hot water and fungicides for control of mold on cantaloups. U.S. Dept. Agr. Mktg. Res. Rept. *986.*

WIANT, J. S. 1937. Investigations of the market diseases of cantaloups and honey dew and honey ball melons. U.S. Dept. Agr. Tech. Bull. *573.*

WIANT, J. S. 1938. Market-storage studies of honey dew melons and cantaloups. U.S. Dept. Agr. Tech. Bull. *613.*

Pumpkins and Squashes

FRANCIS, F. J., and THOMSON, C. L. 1965. Optimum storage conditions for butternut squash. Proc. Am. Soc. Hort. Sci. *86*, 451–456.

GUBA, E. F. 1950. Spoilage of squash in storage. Mass. Agr. Expt. Sta. Bull. *457.*

McCOLLOCH, L. P. 1962. Alternaria rot following chilling injury of acorn squashes. U.S. Dept. Agr. Mktg. Res. Rept. *518.*

MORRIS, L. L., and MANN, L. K. 1948. Storage of summer squash. Refrig. Res. Found. Fact File Sheet. Mimeo.

SCHALES, F. D., and ISENBERG, F. M. 1963. The effect of curing and storage on chemical composition and taste acceptability of winter squash. Proc. Am. Soc. Hort. Sci. *83*, 667–674.

Tomatoes

BARKSDALE, T. H., GOOD, J. M., and DANIELSON, L. L. 1972. Tomato diseases and their control. U.S. Dept. Agr. Handbook *203.*

CHEN, P., and STUDER, H. E. 1976. Detection of puffiness in tomatoes. Proc. 2nd Tomato Quality Workshop. Univ. Calif., Davis. 16–17.

COOPER, A. J. 1956. Blotchy ripening and allied disorders of the tomato: a critical review of the literature. Ann. Rept. Glasshouse Crop Res. Inst., 39–47.

HATTON, T. T., JR., and REEDER, W. F. 1963. Effect of field and packing-house handling on bruising of Florida tomatoes. Proc. Florida State Hort. Soc. *76*, 301–304.

KADER, A. A., and MORRIS, L. L. 1974. Consumer quality improvement foreseen with low oxygen atmosphere shipping. Western Grower and Shipper *45*, No. 7, 16–18.

KADER, A. A., and MORRIS, L. L. 1976. Appearance factors other than color and their contribution to quality. Proc. 2nd Tomato Quality Workshop. Univ. Calif. Veg. Crops Ser. *178*, 8–15.

LIPTON, W. J. 1970. Effects of high humidity and solar radiation on temperature and color of tomato fruits. J. Am. Soc. Hort. Sci. *95*, 680–684.

LORENZ, O. A., and KNOTT, J. E. 1942. Studies of gray-wall of tomato. Proc. Am. Soc. Hort. Sci. *40*, 445–454.

MacLEOD, R. F., KADER, A. A., and MORRIS, L. L. 1976. Damage to fresh tomatoes can be reduced. Calif. Agr. *30*, No. 12, 10–12.

McCOLLOCH, L. P. 1960. Salvaging tomatoes from frozen vines. U.S. Dept. Agr. Mktg. Res. Rept. *423*.

McCOLLOCH, L. P. 1962. Bruising injury of tomatoes. U.S. Dept. Agr. Mktg. Res. Rept. *513*.

McCOLLOCH, L. P., COOK, H. T., and WRIGHT, W. R. 1968. Market diseases of tomatoes, peppers, and eggplants. U.S. Dept. Agr. Handbook *28*.

McCOLLOCH, L. P., and WORTHINGTON, J. T. 1952. Low temperature as a factor in the susceptibility of mature-green tomatoes to Alternaria rot. Phytopathology *42*, 425–427.

McCOLLOCH, L. P., YEATMAN, J. N., and LOYD, P. 1966. Color changes and chilling injury of pink tomatoes held at various temperatures. U.S. Dept. Agr. Mktg. Res. Rept. *735*.

MORRIS, L. L. 1954. Field and transit chilling of fall-grown tomatoes. Proc. Conf. Transport. Perishables. Univ. Calif., Davis. 101–105.

MORRIS, L. L., and KADER, A. A. 1974. Postharvest physiology of tomato fruits. Fresh Market Tomato Res. 1974. Univ. Calif. Vegetable Crops Ser. *171*, 36–48.

PARSONS, C. S., ANDERSON, R. E., and PENNEY, R. W. 1970. Storage of mature-green tomatoes in controlled atmospheres. J. Am. Soc. Hort. Sci. *95*, 791–794.

PARSONS, C. S., and SPALDING, D. H. 1972. Influence of a controlled atmosphere, temperature, and ripeness on bacterial soft rot of tomatoes. J. Am. Soc. Hort. Sci. *97*, 297–299.

SADIK, S., and MINGES, P. A. 1966. Symptoms and histology of tomato fruits affected by blotchy ripening. Proc. Am. Soc. Hort. Sci. *88*, 532–543.

SEGALL, R. H., and DOW, A. 1976. Soft rot of tomatoes resulting from dump-tank and wash-water contamination and its control by chlorination. Proc. Florida State Hort. Soc. *89*, 204–205.

TRESHOW, M. 1955. The etiology, development, and control of tomato fruit tumor. Phytopathology *45*, 132–137.

WEDDING, R. T., HALL, B. R., GARBER, M. G., and TAKATORI, F. M. 1959. Abnormalities in tomato fruits. Calif. Agr. *13*, No. 1, 5, 14.

Watermelons

BORDER, A. 1956. Method of loading and breakage of watermelons. Proc. Conf. Transport. Perishables. Univ. Calif., Davis. 4–5.

BREAKIRON, P. L., WINSTON, J. R., KAUFMAN, J., and EARLE, C. B. 1956. Crosswise loading of long-type watermelons. U.S. Dept. Agr. Mktg. Res. Rept. *133*.

CLOSE, E. G., VARICK, J., and RISSE, L. A. 1971. Comparative methods of handling watermelons—bulk and cartons. Florida Dept. Agr. and Consumer Serv. Mkt. Anal. Ser. *MAI-71*.

IVANOFF, S. S. 1957. Powdery mildew pimples on watermelon fruits. Phytopathology *47*, 599–602.

KONTAXIS, D. G., and KURUPAS, T. 1975. Watermelon rind necrosis in Imperial Valley. Calif. Agr. *29*, No. 9, 14–15.

LUEPSCHEN, N. S., and SMITH, M. A. 1962. Watermelon diseases on the Chicago market 1960–1961. Plant Disease Reptr. *46*, 41–42.

RAMSEY, G. B., SMITH, M. A., WRIGHT, W. R., and BERAHA, L. 1960. Phytophthora rot of watermelons on the market. Plant Disease Reptr. *44*, 692–694.

SCHENCK, N. C. 1962. Mycosphaerella fruit rot of watermelon. Phytopathology *52*, 635–638.

WHITAKER, T. W., and DAVIS, G. N. 1962. Cucurbits. Interscience, New York.

19

Physical Injuries, Market Disorders and Diseases of Underground Structures

BULBS

GARLIC

Physical Injury

Freezing *Symptoms and Development* Thawed garlic cloves appear water-soaked and grayish-yellow, just like onions, but their freezing point is lower. Garlic freezes between about $-3.3°$ C ($26°$ F) and somewhat over $-1.1°$ C ($30°$ F), depending on its soluble solids content.

Prevention See *Onions*.

Disorder

Waxy Breakdown *Symptoms and Development* Slightly sunken, light yellow areas in the fleshy cloves are an early sign of waxy breakdown. With increasing severity the entire clove becomes amber, slightly translucent, and waxy to the touch, but still firm.

Cause No cause has yet been identified, but a certain similarity to translucent scale of onions suggests a similar etiology: high temperature during growth and/or after harvest, leading to early senescence.

Prevention If the suggested cause is the correct one, then the measures advocated for prevention of translucent scale of onions should be effective.

Diseases

Blue Mold Rot   *Pathogen Involved*   Various species of *Penicillium.*

Description and Development   Light yellow lesions on the outer cloves precede the formation of blue to bluish-green spore masses. However, these symptoms are not visible unless the dry scales are first removed. The disease almost literally "eats up" the fleshy scales, thus rendering the bulbs feather-light.

The disease primarily affects garlic that is harvested immature or that has not been properly cured.

Prevention   Harvest of mature bulbs, thorough curing, and storage at 0° C (32° F) and 60 to 70% RH minimizes losses from blue mold.

Fusarium Rot   See *Onions.*

Gray Mold Rot   See *Onions—Neck Rot.*

ONIONS, DRY

Physical Injuries

Ammonia Injury   *Symptoms*   The natural pigments in onion skins change color when exposed to ammonia (Ramsey and Butler 1928). White onions turn yellowish to greenish-yellow, yellow bulbs change to greenish-yellow and eventually to dark brown, and red bulbs first become yellowish-green and then greenish-black. The dark colors often have a metallic sheen.

Ammonia turns the edible scales greenish-yellow when not protected by dry scales, and severe exposure renders them watery.

Development and Cause   Slight damage is detectable after less than 10 min in 0.8% ammonia, whereas the same concentration causes serious injury within 24 hr. Discoloration is first noticeable on broken edges of dry scales, then on patches of skin, and eventually over the entire bulb.

Temperatures in the range from near freezing to 21° C (70° F) have little influence on the rate or intensity of discoloration. However, high humidity—about 85% or higher—accelerates and enhances the reaction.

Prevention   See Chapter 15.

Freezing Injury   *Symptoms*   Thawed onions are soft and appear grayish-yellow and water-soaked in cross section, although a freshly cut surface tends to appear dry. Translucence does not necessarily affect an entire thawed scale, but may be interspersed with opaque areas. Freezing causes separation of the epidermis, and the peeled concave (adaxial) surface appears grainy and rough (Lipton and Harris 1965).

Development   Onion tissue freezes at about $-1.1°$ C $\pm$ $0.3°$ ($30°$ F $\pm$ $0.5°$), depending on cultivar and soluble solids content. Freezing injury invariably progresses from surface to center within the bulbs and containers.

Slight freezing may not damage some bulbs at all, especially if they remain undisturbed while frozen and are thawed at about $5°$ C ($41°$ F). In fact, in Europe, onions are successfully stored at or slightly below their freezing point to retard sprouting, as noted in Chapter 9.

Prevention   While freezing can be prevented by proper temperature control during storage and transit, the injury, once present, can only be minimized. For specific suggestions, see Chapter 15.

Similar Disorders   Freezing injury and translucent scale resemble each other, but can be distinguished by criteria listed under the latter disorder. Consequences of freezing also resemble those of sunburn and a form of mechanical injury, as noted under the relevant sections.

Mechanical Injury   *Symptoms*   Bruising is the most common mechanical injury suffered by onions, although cuts also are common. Bruising results in undesirable softening of damaged tissue and to watery scales. Affected scales appear translucent and are particularly soft. The damage that inflicts bruises and cuts also tends to remove the protective dry scales and thus exposes the bulb to increased danger of decay and moisture loss.

Causes   Bruising and cutting can occur during any stage of handling, but machine harvest, rough floors in truck trailers or rail cars, and bouncing during transit are the most common causes.

Prevention   Successful avoidance of injury is suggested by the causes: careful handling throughout marketing and use of protective pads on floors of conveyances, unless onions are packed in cartons. The watery scale symptom of bruising quite readily recedes or even disappears within 2 to 4 days after the onions have arrived on the market. Room temperature (20° to 25° C; 68° to 77° F) is more conducive to this reversal than low temperatures (Wright and Billeter 1975).

Similar Disorders   Freezing injury and translucent scale resemble watery scale. In case of question, holding a sample of affected onions a few days likely will help resolve the confusion, because neither freezing damage (unless very mild) nor translucent scale will disappear. Also, freezing tends to discolor the stem, but bruising does not. In translucent scale, venation is distinct in the affected area and it occurs only in onions stored several months.

Sunburn   *Symptoms*   Sunburned scales are wrinkled, and this symptom can extend from the dry outer scales to 1 or 2 fleshy scales. The latter, if injured, are soft and sometimes watery. Injured tissue also may be bleached, depending on the color of the bulb.

Sunburn occurs most frequently at or near the shoulder of bulbs, although any of the exposed portion may be sunburned.

Severe sunburn may lead to bacterial soft rot in storage or transit, particularly in incompletely cured bulbs.

Development and Cause   Direct insolation during growth causes most sunburn. However, curing of bulbs without protection from direct sunlight can also cause it. In either case, the outer layers of onions can reach the lethal temperature of about 50° C (120° F), even if the air is at only 38° C (100° F) 1.8 m (6 ft) above the soil surface (Lipton and Harris 1965).

Prevention   Sunburn can be prevented by keeping bulbs under 2.5 to 5 cm (1 to 2 in.) of soil once they would have emerged above the soil surface. However, this method has only been tested on organic soil in the dry western United States.

The danger of sunburn during field curing can be eliminated by windrowing onions so that all bulbs are covered by a layer of tops, except at the end of a row where soil is used as a shade.

Prompt storage is advisable after curing because burlap bags do not effectively shade their contents.

Similar Disorders   Taken singly, a fleshy scale with sunburn resembles one that was frozen or one with translucent scale. However, in entire bulbs confusion seems remote, because only scales with sunburn are wrinkled.

Disorders

Greening   *Symptoms*   Outer fleshy scales are light to dark green and may have an undesirable flavor.

Development and Cause   Exposure of onions to bright light for a few days or to mild light for a week or two results in greening, particularly in white onions. Specific light levels that induce greening in onions have not been determined.

Prevention   Greening readily is prevented or minimized by storing onions in the dark or under dim light as soon as they are field cured. Artificial curing avoids any postharvest greening in the field.
At retail, only a few days' supply of onions should be displayed and the stock should be properly rotated.

Root Growth   *Symptoms and Development*   Roots emerge from the base of the shortened stem and can grow several centimeters long during storage. Roots render the bulbs unsightly and may become a focus for decay.

Cause   Root growth is confined to onions held in high relative humidity, generally above about 85%, conditions that occur in insufficiently ventilated plastic bags. When humid conditions and high temperatures exist, roots will grow within a few days (Kaufman *et al.* 1953).

Prevention   Root growth can be prevented by keeping onions under fairly dry conditions, always below 85% RH, and preferably between 65 and 70%.

Sprouting   *Symptoms*   Emergence of a sprout is only the external indication that growth has occurred, and is preceded by the gradual elongation of the sprout within the bulb. Such internal sprouts are not objectionable while small, but as they enlarge they separate the center of the bulb from the periphery, thus leaving a hole in the middle of bulbs sliced transversely.

Development and Cause   Onions vary greatly in their tendency to sprout   pungent cultivars are least likely to sprout under given storage conditions, whereas mild ones sprout most readily.
Sprouting is a result of normal physiological changes in stored bulbs, which, as biennials, develop a reproductive shoot in their second year.

Thus, storage conditions cannot cause sprouting, but only affect its rate.

Prevention   Low temperature, 0° C (32° F) or slightly below, effectively retards sprouting, but does not prevent it in most onions if they are stored 6 months or longer. High temperatures (about 30° C; 86° F) also tend to inhibit sprouting but likely can result in substantial weight loss (Stow 1975).

Relative humidity has a negligible effect on sprouting (Wright *et al.* 1935).

Sprouting also can be inhibited by preharvest application of various growth regulators, chiefly maleic hydrazide (Isenberg and Ang 1963). Postharvest irradiation with low doses of gamma rays also retards or even prevents sprouting, but may lead to death of the growing point and a consequent undesirable discoloration. Further, irradiation is not now a permitted method of sprout control.

Translucent Scale   *Symptoms*   Translucent scale, once called physiological, internal or storage breakdown, renders scales partly transparent, which contrasts with the opaqueness of normal tissue. Translucence makes venation very distinct, particularly in light transmitted through the scale. In severe cases the epidermis sloughs readily, the entire bulb softens, and a slight off-odor may develop.

When viewed microscopically, walls of parenchyma cells are disintegrated and the cell contents completely disorganized.

Development   The disorder appears after onions have been in cold storage at least 3 to 4 months, and its incidence is much higher in large (diameter over 7.6 cm or 3 in.) than in small bulbs.

Translucence commonly starts on the most curved portion of scales and most frequently affects the second/third fleshy scales.

Sunburn frequently accompanies translucent scale, but is not a prerequisite for its development.

Prevention   The incidence of translucent scale can be substantially lowered by prompt cold storage (0° C; 32° F) of onions immediately after curing, and it can be eliminated if this practice is preceded by covering bulbs with 2.5 to 5 cm (1 to 2 in.) of soil once they have swelled above the soil surface.

Similar Disorders   Watery scale resulting from bruising may be confused with translucent scale as noted under *Physical Injury*. Freezing injury also resembles translucent scale, but can be distinguished by observing certain criteria:

Criterion	Freezing	Translucent Scale
Cut Surface	Dry	Wet
Location	Follows heat transfer pattern	No specific pattern; stem plate never affected
Epidermis	Separated from scale	Separated only in severe cases
Concave surface with epidermis removed	Grainy, rough	Smooth, slick

Clear distinction between these disorders is valuable in avoiding or settling disputes where freezing injury is suspected, but not certain.

Diseases

Bacterial Soft Rot   *Pathogen Involved   Erwinia carotovora.*

Description   Individual fleshy scales or the entire onion is water-soaked and pale yellow to light brown. Affected scales are soft and filled with putrid smelling liquid that may ooze out at the neck when the upper part of an affected bulb is squeezed.

Development and Prevention   Bacteria can enter at the neck before or after harvest, or through any wounded, bruised, frozen or sunburned tissue. Before harvest, the bacteria enter via wounds made by the feeding of onion maggots. The disease progresses rapidly under warm, humid conditions. Onions with properly dried tops, without injury and stored at 0° C (32° F) and moderately low relative humidity (65 to 70%) should escape infection by bacterial soft rot.

Black Mold Rot   *Pathogen Involved   Aspergillus niger.*

Description   Black powdery spore masses adhere to the outer scale or are lodged between the two outer scales. In the latter case, the spore masses follow the veins. Lesions are not always associated with this fungus, but when present, they are sunken, discolored and shrivelled.

Development   Infection usually occurs in the field, but the disease readily spreads from bulb to bulb after harvest, particularly when the bulbs are moist.

Prevention   The surface of bulbs must be dry at and after harvest to avoid infection. Storage at 0° C (32° F) and moderate relative humidity arrests the spread of this disease.

Fusarium Bulb Rot   *Pathogen Involved*   **Various species of** *Fusarium.*

Description   The base of a bulb is the usual first site of infection. There the surface is covered by white to pink mycelium that usually renders affected tissue watery. After prolonged storage, entire bulbs may be rotted.

Development   High field temperatures favor the disease, although some decay occurs even below 10° C (50° F).

Prevention   Storage at 0° C (32° F) and moderate relative humidity keep the disease from spreading, but control in the field through crop rotation is the best preventative.

Neck Rot (Botrytis Neck Rot, Gray Mold)   *Pathogen Involved* Various species of *Botrytis.*

Description and Development   The descriptive names indicate the first and most common infection site of this highly destructive decay, the color of the mycelium, and that of the decayed tissue. In severe cases the surface of the neck and the space between the scales is overgrown with the mycelium and the characteristic grayish-brown spore masses.

Internally, the rot advances from top to base of scales, and diseased and healthy tissue are clearly defined.

One species of *Botrytis (B. squamosa)* is confined on the market to white onions, and usually affects only the base of the neck. In this species, small, black fruiting bodies appear early in the decay, rather than late as in the others, and the decayed tissue is brown rather than gray (Fig. 19.1).

Botrytis cinerea can induce a superficial discoloration of the dry scales of onions termed "brown stain." Affected portions commonly are brown with dark brown to black margins but may be solid brown to black (Clark and Lorbeer 1973A, B).

Prevention   Neck rot can be slowed after harvest, but not stopped, by storage at 0° C (32° F) and between 65 and 70% RH. However, its incidence can be held low by avoiding bruising of bulbs and by proper drying of the tops before storage. This can be accomplished by field curing in arid areas, and in humid areas by artificial curing with heated, forced air.

Recommendations for such curing range from 13 to 15 hr at 45° to 48° C (113° to 118° F), via 5 days at 38° C (100° F) to 14 days at 34° to 35° C (93° to 95° F), in the Soviet Union, New Zealand and United States, respectively. All agree that curing should follow harvest as quickly as possible; if delayed a week or more, the treatment will only be partially effective, at best. During curing, air flow should be 2 to 3 m³ per min per m³ (2 to 3 ft³ per min per ft³) of onions. Prompt high temperature curing, followed by rapid (within 2 to 3 days) cooling to the storage temperature of 0° C (32° F) virtually eliminates the danger of neck rot (Diatchenko 1974; Harrow and Harris 1969; Gunkel *et al.* 1971).

Similar Disorder   Mild neck rot slightly resembles severe translucent scale in color, but the disease starts at the neck, whereas the disorder rarely affects that portion.

Smudge   *Pathogen Involved*   *Colletotrichum circinans.*

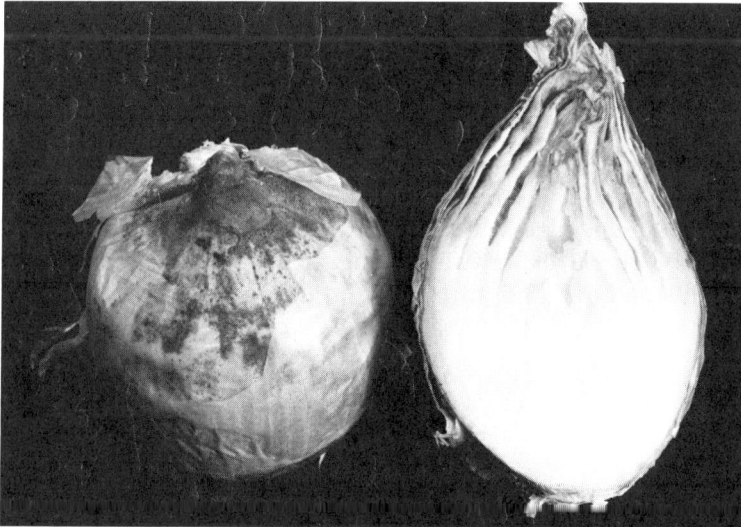

U.S. Dept. of Agriculture Photo

FIG. 19.1.   BOTRYTIS NECK ROT OF ONION

Description   This disease principally affects white onions where it discolors the outer scales with small, dark green to black dots. These dots may form blotches or concentric rings. Thickened scales are destroyed only when onions are wet.

Development and Prevention   Initial infection occurs before harvest and spreads rapidly during warm and moist weather. Thus protection from rain after harvest, thorough curing, and low storage temperature will check the spread of this disease.

ROOTS, TUBERS AND OTHER STRUCTURES

BEETS

Physical Injury

Freezing   *Description*   Beets that have been slightly frozen may show only blackened remnants of the petioles. When seen in cross section, the root tissue may be slightly water-soaked and have interspersed patches of white tissue.

Severe freezing causes external and internal water-soaking and sometimes blackening of the ring and rays of conducting tissue. Such beets also become soft and susceptible to decay.

Cause   Beets freeze between −1.7° and −1.1° C (29° and 30° F).

Prevention   Beets should never be held where they may cool below their freezing point for more than a few hours.

Slightly frozen beets can be salvaged if they are thawed slowly and then used within a day or two. During such delays they must be held at between 0° and 5° C (32° and 41° F), or else they may decay.

Disorder

Internal Black Spot   *Description*   Internal black spot (IBS) is a discoloration of the interior of beets. The necrotic areas are hard, but not dry, and cavities are absent. The disorder may occur in discrete areas as seen in cross section or may be scattered throughout the root. Symptoms occasionally reach the surface (Walker 1939).

Development and Cause   IBS develops in response to a deficiency in boron during growth, and is more common in old roots than in the young ones which usually are marketed bunched.

Prevention   The disease can be prevented only by proper fertilization. However, affected beets can be avoided by harvesting beets young, particularly when symptoms on leaves (twisted, bent, uneven development on both sides of midrib) are present.

Diseases

Black Rot   *Pathogen Involved*   *Phoma betae.*

Description   Black rot is usually confined to topped beets out of storage. Initially the lesions are brown and water-soaked, but later become black, dry, spongy, and sharply delineated from normal tissue. The tip of the roots is most commonly affected, but the crown or other wounded areas also may show black rot.

Grayish-white mycelium covers the surface under humid conditions and also may line cavities within the diseased tissue.

Development and Prevention   The disease develops slowly in cold storage in beets infected before harvest. Close clipping of tops, good air circulation about the beets, and storage at 0° C (32° F) retard development of black rot.

CARROTS

Physical Injury

Freezing   The average freezing point of carrots is about −1.7° C (29° F). Undisturbed roots will undercool several degrees below the freezing point without formation of ice crystals, but when moved at low temperature ice crystals will form at or near the freezing point.

Description   While the carrots are still frozen, the ice crystals just below the surface will often give the roots a blistered appearance. When severely frozen, jagged, lengthwise cracks may appear before thawing occurs.

After the frozen roots thaw, a dark brown or black discoloration develops on the surface. This may show only on the carrot tip, or cover the entire surface of severely frozen roots. Carrots subjected to severe freezing show a water-soaked, darkened interior after thawing. Liquid is easily squeezed from such tissues. Frozen carrots which have completely thawed show internal cracks near the periphery, caused by expansion from ice crystals.

Development   Most of the damage from freezing is due to rupture of cells from ice crystal formation. Moisture loss follows this cell rupture with weight loss as high as 12% in one day after thawing.

Severely frozen roots discolor when thawed at any temperature, but slightly frozen carrots discolor less when thawed at low temperature than at room temperature.

Carrots which have been subjected to freezing temperatures should not be moved until they are warmed to well above the freezing point. Unless the roots have been exposed to −6.7° C (20° F) or below for ½ hr or more, there may be no ice crystal formation and hence no damage if thawed before movement.

Even slight freezing injury greatly increases susceptibility to decay. Accordingly, roots which are still marketable after slight freezing injury should be moved quickly through the market.

Disorder

Scab Spot Complex   This disorder appears to be related to climatic, nutritional and genetic factors. It has caused considerable market losses in carrots produced in southwestern United States.

Description   Lesions most frequently occur at or near lateral rootlets. In early stages the lesions are brown to maroon and may be raised, but in later stages they may crack and become sunken. The lesions are usually elongated laterally and appear black and scablike. Sharp constrictions, encircling the root at point of damage, may also occur.

Development and Cause   The disorder was originally attributed to a bacterium and called bacterial blight. However, it is now known to be physiological, although several species of bacteria may be found in the lesions as a result of invasion after the injury occurs. Cultivars of carrots with abnormally high oil content are particularly susceptible and the disorder is affected by weather and nutrition.

Diseases

Bacterial Soft Rot   *Pathogen Involved   Erwinia carotovora.*

Now that most freshly harvested young carrots are topped and packaged, this disease is rarely found in the market. Mature carrots sometimes develop the disease during storage, particularly if temperatures during storage are above 5° C (41° F) for prolonged periods.

Description   Lesions may develop anywhere on the root, usually at injuries. Infection often occurs at the crown and spreads down the core. Lesions are soft, watery, and gray to brown. Advanced infections are slimy, and as other organisms become involved, they have a putrid odor.

Control   Avoidance of injury, sanitation in handling, and maintenance of temperatures at 2° C (36° F) or below will control soft rot in carrots.

Black Rot   *Pathogen Involved*   ***Stemphylium radicinum.***
This disease sometimes affects growing plants, but most of the losses occur in storage. It often causes large losses in ventilated storages in northern United States.

Description   Infections at the crown usually penetrate into the core. They may show black mold on the surface, particularly under humid conditions. Infections on the sides of the roots are circular to irregular, usually slightly depressed, and have dry, mealy, dark-colored tissues. Under high storage humidity, the affected tissues are soft and wet.

Development   The causal fungus is seed-borne, or it may over-winter in the soil. Most carrots have spores on their surface at harvest, and may have actual infections if conditions have been favorable to the organism in the field. Infections after harvest usually occur through broken roots tips, dying rootlets, or wounds.

Prevention   Care during harvesting and handling, and removal of visibly infected roots before storage are the only effective preventatives. The organisms will grow slowly at low temperatures so control cannot be attained by cold storage. However, maintenance of temperatures near 0° C (32° F) will delay development.

Gray Mold Rot   *Pathogen Involved*   ***Botrytis cinerea.***
This is a disease of stored carrots. It is not a problem with freshly harvested topped and packaged carrots.

Description   Lesions usually occur at injuries. Affected tissues are water-soaked, spongy, and light brown. Gray to brown mold and spore masses develop on the lesions. The rot spreads from infected to sound carrots, forming nests of decay.

Control   Storage at 0° C (32° F), with prompt cooling, will reduce losses from the disease. Careful handling of the roots is essential and maintenance of RH of at least 95% is desirable.

Rhizopus Soft Rot   *Pathogens Involved*   *Rhizopus tritici, R. stolonifer,* and *R. oryzae.*

Description   The decayed tissues are soft and watery. They are distinguished from lesions of bacterial soft rot by the presence of mycelial threads through the affected tissues. In well-developed infections, the surface of lesions is covered with coarse, white mycelium.

Control   The fungus will not grow at temperatures below 5° C (41° F). Prompt storage at 0° C (32° F) provides excellent control. Maintenance of high RH also should reduce the incidence of this disease, because, at least *R. stolonifer* invades carrots only after they have lost about 8% of their original fresh weight (Thorne 1972).

Watery Soft Rot   *Pathogen Involved*   *Sclerotinia sclerotiorum.*
Infections after harvest are largely due to infections which occurred in the field before harvest. Cool and rainy weather at harvest is favorable to development of the fungus.

Description   Water-soaking and softening of affected tissues together with white, fluffy mycelium are typical symptoms of the disease. In later stages, sclerotia of the fungus, which are at first white, then bluish, and finally black, may be formed in the mold growth (Fig. 19.2).

Control   The principal effort should be devoted to careful sorting of the roots before storage to remove all visibly infected carrots. Carrots from fields known to be infected should not be stored for more than 30 days. Storage at 0° C (32° F) and at least 95% RH is desirable.

GINGER

Disorders

Chilling Injury   *Description*   Ginger that has been chilled softens, shrivels readily, and oozes moisture from the surface, particularly from cut ends. These symptoms are followed by extensive mold growth over the surface.

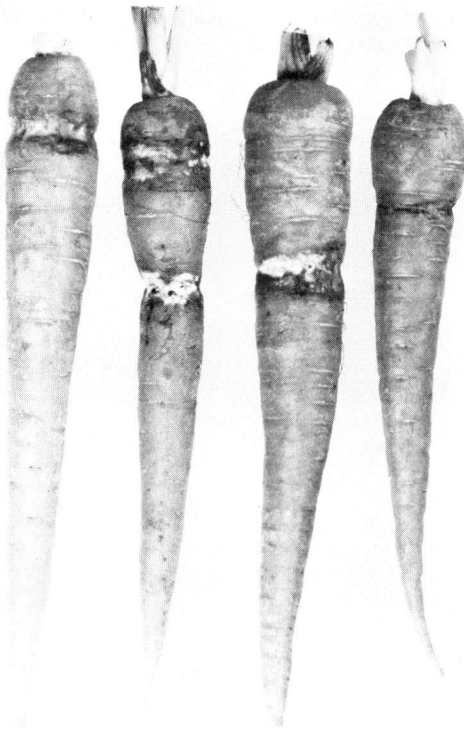

U.S. Dept. of Agriculture Photo

FIG. 19.2.   WATERY SOFT ROT OF CARROT

Development and Cause   No information is available on just how rapidly chilling injury develops in ginger. However, the data of Akamine (1962) suggest that 2 to 3 weeks at 7° C (45° F) or lower seriously damages the rhizomes.

Prevention   The optimum and probably lowest safe storage temperature for ginger is 13° C (55° F).

Discoloration   *Description*   A purple discoloration may be faintly visible below the skin and readily on cut surfaces.

Development and Cause   Purple pigmentation is a natural accompaniment to sprouting, although free moisture seems to be required for development of the color. When free moisture is available, purpling occurs in the absence of sprouting.

Prevention   Storage at recommended temperature and RH (13° C or 55° F, 65%) prevents the discoloration during usual storage periods.

Purpling must be prevented in Hawaii-grown ginger because discolored rhizomes cannot be exported (Akamine 1962).

Shrivelling   Shrivelling due to moisture loss can be minimized by storage at 65% RH for no more than 6 months.

HORSERADISH

Diseases

Bacterial Root Rots   *Pathogens Involved*   Various bacteria.

Description   Numerous bacteria can cause soft rot or dry rot in horseradish. The various types in each group are difficult to distinguish, but their lack of mycelium avoids confusion with fungus diseases.

Penicillium Root Rot   *Pathogen Involved*   *Penicillium hirsutum.*
Diseased roots are covered by a greenish-blue mass of spores. Storage of horseradish in pits rather than in cold storage seems to favor development of the disease.

Rhizoctonia Root Rot   *Pathogen Involved*   *Rhizoctonia solani.*
This common rot of horseradish renders the roots light yellow to grayish-tan. The surface mold is creamy white and may be dotted with brownish-black resting bodies (sclerotia). Infected tissue separates readily from normal tissue.

Prevention   Temperatures between −1° and 0° C (30° and 32° F) most readily retard any of the rots noted.

PARSNIPS

Diseases

Bacterial Soft Rot   See *Carrots.*

Gray Mold Rot   See *Carrots.*

Parsnip Canker   *Pathogen Involved*   *Itersonilia perplexans.*
The fungus occurs in the field in soils, crops and weeds. It enters

through wounds or insect injuries, and may infect roots from airborne spores when harvested roots are exposed in the field.

Description   The slightly depressed lesions are at first rust-colored, but later turn black. Many small lesions may ultimately enlarge to cover most of the root surface. Sometimes dark brown to black ring-like areas occur on the roots. The disease occurs principally in storage, but may develop in plastic-bagged roots at retail display.

Control   All roots harvested during rainy seasons should be marketed promptly. Careful handling and prompt storage at 0° C (32° F) are the best control measures.

POTATOES

Physical Injuries

Freezing   The freezing point of potatoes varies from $-2°$ to $-0.5°$ C (28.2° to 30.9° F), depending primarily on total solids content. Some cultivars are consistently higher in total solids than others, so this is responsible for some of the variation, as are maturity and area of production.

The extent of injury from exposure to subfreezing temperatures is directly related to the severity of the temperature and the period of time during which the tubers are exposed to it.

Description   Tubers that are exposed to prolonged freezing, or very low temperatures, collapse quickly upon thawing, becoming soft and watery. Such solidly frozen tubers are often referred to as "leakers" when thawed. Shorter exposures to temperatures just at the freezing point or brief exposures to temperatures much below the freezing point usually result in damage to only the most susceptible tissues. External symptoms may not be evident, but when such tubers are cut, freezing injury shows as gray or bluish-gray patches beneath the skin, or sometimes as a dark discoloration of the xylem and phloem strands in and adacent to the vascular ring. Affected tissues may be slightly dry, and in one type of freezing injury dark blue-gray to black blotches are present in the vascular ring and surrounding tissues.

Freezing injury in the field, before or during harvest, is usually manifested by bluish-gray blotches beneath the skin, or flabby, watery areas on one side of the tuber. If the freezing occurs in storage or in transit, any or all of the previously described symptoms may be present. Location of the injured tubers is the best clue as to where and when the damage was done. If the affected tubers are well scattered throughout the room or transit vehicle, it is good evidence that freezing occurred before the potatoes were stored or loaded. On the other hand, if freezing injury is limited to areas along outside walls or near air inlets, it indicates that the tubers were frozen in place.

Prevention.   The obvious way to prevent freezing injury is to avoid exposing potatoes to temperatures below the tuber freezing point. This means that in northern storage areas provision must be made for the application and uniform distribution of heat during periods of extreme winter weather. Also, loads of potatoes in transit through areas of low ambient temperatures must be protected with adequate heating devices.

Heat Injury   This injury is often referred to as "scald," but since it results directly from excessive temperatures on the surface of the tubers the term "heat injury" is more accurate. The injury is caused by exposure in the field after digging, exposure on the truck during hauling, or while standing at the packing shed. It is usually associated with radiated heat from direct sunlight, but any source of heat which raises surface tissues to 49° C (120° F) or higher will cause injury. This disorder most frequently occurs in potatoes harvested on hot days from late spring through mid-summer.

Development and Cause   Heat injury may show as watery and blistered areas on the tuber surface soon after exposure to high surface temperatures. When heat exposure is less severe the symptoms may not appear for several hours. The most serious effects of heat injury are those which follow the initial symptoms. Under moist conditions the injured tissues are almost invariably invaded by soft rot bacteria, often with disastrous results. Under dry conditions the tubers which are not already infected with soft rot will lose moisture rapidly. Injured areas become sunken and leathery, and tissue under the surface rapidly turns dark brown to black when exposed to air.

Prevention   During harvest, in areas of high ambient temperatures or bright sunlight, it is essential that the tubers be picked up quickly after digging: in less than 30 min if air temperatures are above 32° C (90° F). Tubers exposed to bright sunlight will often attain surface temperatures 11° to 16° C (20° to 30° F) higher than air temperature. Mechanical harvesting of potatoes greatly reduces the hazard of heat injury in the field, but the danger of heat injury to the tubers still exists during loading of the bulk trucks in the field, in transit to the packing shed, and while waiting to unload at the shed. Canvas covers over bulk loads are essential during high ambient temperatures and bright sunlight periods and desirable even under less severe conditions for protection from drying winds. When delays are necessary for unloading at the packinghouse, shade should be provided for the loaded trucks.

Greening   When potato tubers are exposed to light, either before or after harvest, chlorophyll develops in the surface layers. The amount of this green pigment which develops depends upon the intensity and quality of the light, the duration of exposure, and the maturity of the tubers. The number and intensity of fluorescent lights in the modern supermarket have increased the problem of greening in potatoes during marketing.

Greening is a serious defect of potatoes because it not only adversely affects the appearance and grade of potatoes, but the development of chlorophyll is often related to formation of solanin, a bitter and potentially toxic compound. Chlorophyll itself is harmless and tasteless and its appearance on tubers is not always indicative of increased solanin content (Isenberg and Gull 1959). Only chemical analysis will determine the presence and amount of solanin, so the development of green pigment can be considered only a visual defect unless solanin is definitely identified.

Description   In white-skinned cultivars of potatoes, and particularly in immature tubers, greening develops rapidly on exposure to light. It develops through a series of stages from a yellowish cast to a definite green. As the intensity of green color increases on the surface, the depth to which it extends increases. It is often necessary to cut greened tubers to determine the extent of the defect. Flavor may or may not be affected, depending on severity of the greening and whether the tubers are peeled before cooking (Gull and Isenberg 1960).

Development and Cause   Tubers growing near the soil surface may show greening at harvest, but most of the greening that causes trouble in the market develops after harvest. The greening effect of light is cumulative. Tubers which receive light during storage may show some greening at removal. Additional light exposure occurs during grading, packing, and in the terminal market. Such potatoes will usually green rapidly when exposed to the bright lights of a modern supermarket, particularly when displayed in open piles or in transparent plastic bags.

Prevention   The simplest way to prevent tuber greening is to avoid exposure to the duration and intensity of light which induces it. Exclusion of light from potato storages, protection from light during terminal and wholesale handling, bulk retail display of quantities which will be sold rapidly, consumer packaging in light-resistant materials such as opaque paper, or colored plastic (frowned on in some states), and reduced intensity or modified wavelength of display lights all reduce the possibility of chlorophyll development (Hardenburg 1964).

Other methods of control have been explored, including: breeding cultivars for resistance to postharvest greening (Akeley *et al.* 1962); holding in a high CO_2 atmosphere (Forsyth and Eaves 1968); exposure to low dosage gamma irradiation (Schwimmer and Weston 1958); and applying a light coating of vegetable or mineral oil to the tubers before exposure to light (Wu and Salunkhe 1972). Of these suggested remedies, the most hopeful for long-term results appears to be development of resistant cultivars. Meanwhile, avoidance of exposure to excessive light in every step of the marketing process is the best preventative of tuber greening.

Mechanical Injury   Probably the greatest single cause of loss in commercial potatoes is mechanical injury in the form of cuts, punctures and bruises. Certainly the most frequent concern of potato consumers involves trim waste caused primarily by mechanical damage. Studies in Idaho indicate that 15 to 20% of Russet Burbank potatoes are reduced from U.S. No. 1 grade because of injuries incurred in harvesting and handling prior to grading (Sparks 1977). The same study showed that digger cuts and severe bruises caused the greatest total loss during storage, and were responsible for much of the decay in storage. Tuber temperature is one critical factor in handling injury. Tubers dug or handled at 5° to 7° C (41° to 45° F) developed 25 to 30% bruise damage compared with less than 5% damage for tubers handled at 16° to 21° C (60° to 70° F).

The movement of potatoes from harvest equipment to storage also causes damage. Commercial harvest and bin filling operations in a mid-west production area had on average 47% of the tubers injured. Critical factors in bulk scoop operations were type of bucket, condition of the storage pile and operating speed of the equipment. Cultivars varied in susceptibility to damage, with Viking showing the most and Norchip the least damage. Tuber damage increased with each handling step from field truck to bin piling through storage (Hudson and Orr 1977).

There is evidence that, in addition to handling practices, the structure of the tuber influences mechanical damage. Hudson (1975) found that low specific gravity, large cell size and above average intercellular space, characters affected by soil moisture, fertilizer and temperature during growth, increase bruise susceptibility.

Disorders

Black Spot, Internal   This disorder is responsible for substantial grade-outs and market losses. Both freshly harvested and stored potatoes are affected but with somewhat different causes and symptoms. The disorder has been observed for many years, particularly in western Europe where it was first described (Horne 1912). It has been studied extensively in England and Holland, and more recently in the United States.

Description   The principal symptom of the disorder is a blackening of small areas of cortex tissue, although occasionally deeper tissues are affected (Fig. 19.3). In the early stages, the discoloration does not extend to the surface. However, in severe cases of black spot the symptoms may become strikingly evident. The external symptoms develop from drying out of the affected internal tissue with subsequent depression of the tuber surface over the areas. Freshly affected internal tissues are of nearly normal texture, but with time they dry out and become granular. Symptoms may appear within 24 hr of harvest in the more susceptible cultivars, or may develop only when potatoes are handled after prolonged storage.

Development and Cause   Extensive tests in Holland have linked black spot incidence to low potassium (K) levels during growth. California studies (Lorenz *et al*. 1957) confirmed that high rates of K during growth reduced, but did not control the disorder. It appears likely that the low tyrosine content of tubers, that have been heavily fertilized with K, reduces the intensity of black spot by controlling the intracellular concentration of melanin, a dark oxidation product of tyrosine.

The disorder is directly related to cell damage, whether occurring directly after harvest as a result of bumps received during harvesting and grading, or as pressure bruises which develop in deep bin storages. In freshly harvested potatoes, the spots are invariably at or near the stem end of the tuber. In potatoes from storage, the spots are not confined to the stem end, but are almost always associated with visible pressure bruises.

A potato sequence analysis conducted in Kern County, California (Harvey *et al*. 1970) clearly shows an increase in black spot of White

U.S. Dept. of Agriculture Photo

FIG. 19.3.   INTERNAL BLACK SPOT OF POTATO
CAUSED BY IMPACTS DURING HANDLING
This type usually occurs at or near the stem end of
the tuber.

Rose potatoes with each step of mechanical harvesting. Tubers removed from the blade of the digger developed an average of 2% tubers with black spot, whereas after passage over the draper, boom, and into the truck, 14% of the tubers developed the disorder. By contrast, only 0.3% of the tubers that were hand dug and carefully handled showed black spot after reaching the packinghouse.

Studies with Kennebec and Katahdin potatoes on Long Island (Sawyer *et al.* 1965) showed that black spot susceptibility of tubers during prolonged bin storage was related to moisture loss during storage. The addition of moisture to maintain RH of ventilating air at about 85%, and a moderate air flow (0.05 m³ per min per 100 kg) (0.83 cfm per cwt) decreased black spot as compared with a greater flow of drier air.

High CO_2 concentration in tubers harvested from wet or compacted soils has been shown to increase susceptibility to black spot (Howard *et al.* 1962) Exposure of bruised tubers to a continuous flow of 3 or 5% CO_2 at 20° C (68° F) increased black spot development, but exposure to ethylene as high as 10 ppm for 11 days did not increase the disorder (Timm *et al.* 1976). Elevated temperatures also hasten the symptoms of black spot following bruising. Tubers held at 10° C (50° F) after bruising took 48 hr for maximum black spot development, but at 40° C (104° F) severe symptoms developed in 6 hr (Dwelle and Stallknecht 1976).

Prevention   Careful handling of the tubers at all stages of marketing, from harvesting through grading, transport, and destination handling, is the best protection against losses from black spot. This is true whether the tubers are freshly harvested or have been stored in deep bins with development of some pressure bruises (Fig 19.4). While the factors which increase susceptibility to black spot are not completely understood, there is abundant evidence that impacts to susceptible tubers cause visible symptoms within 24 hr. Precautions, such as a few days' delay in grading potatoes from wet or compacted soils, avoidance of excessive wilting in stored tubers, and careful management of soil fertility during tuber growth should be observed. However, all such practices are largely negated by rough handling of the tubers at any point in the postharvest period.

Blackheart   This is primarily a storage and market disorder of potatoes, but it occurs occasionally in tubers harvested from waterlogged fields during periods of high temperatures. The disorder causes

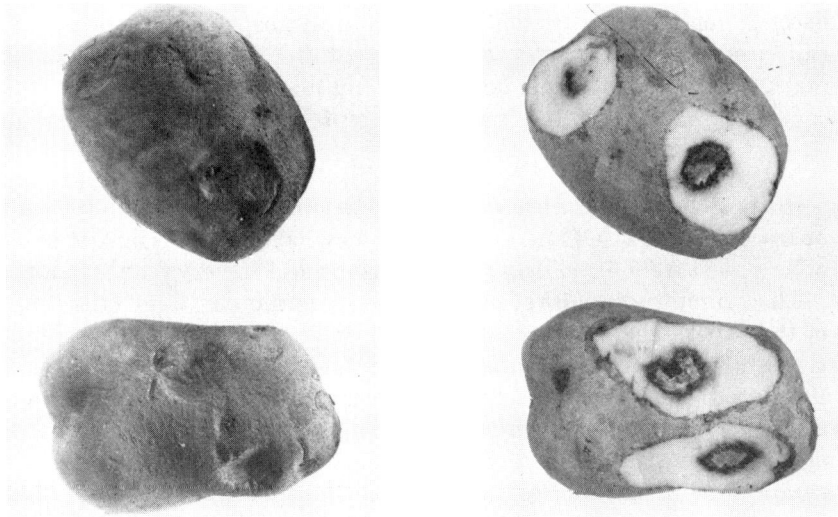

U.S. Dept. of Agriculture Photo

FIG. 19.4.   EXTERNAL AND INTERNAL SYMPTOMS OF POTATO BLACK SPOT RESULTING FROM PRESSURE BRUISES
Such bruises are usually caused by prolonged storage in deep piles.

some market losses, but improved storage ventilation and transit environments have decreased incidence of blackheart in recent years.

Description   Internal symptoms are dark-gray to purplish or black discolorations. Freshly cut tissues may not show discoloration, but after brief exposure to air the typical symptoms appear. The affected tissues are usually in the central part of the tuber and sharply differentiated from healthy areas. In advanced stages the affected tissues may dry out and separate to form cavities. External symptoms are not evident in the early stages, but advanced blackheart may show moist, discolored areas on the tuber surface.

Development and Cause   The direct cause of blackheart is a deficiency of O_2 which results in death of cells in inner tissues. The deficiency of O_2 may be due to inadequate aeration, particularly in large bin piles, or solidly loaded, heated vehicles. Oxygen deficiency may occur at any temperature, but damage is most likely to occur at temperatures 30° C (86° F) or above, when respiratory activity is high and O_2 demand great.

Prevention   The most important step in avoidance of blackheart is adequate ventilation. It is particularly important to aerate the center of large piles in bin storage where heat accumulates and O_2 tends to become depleted. Excessive heating and atmosphere modification in rail cars and vans must also be avoided during winter shipment to market. Modern storage ventilation methods and thermostatically controlled alcohol heaters for transit protection provide the basis for further reductions in blackheart losses.

Hollow Heart   This is a growth-related disorder caused by too rapid or irregular growth. Cultivars vary somewhat in susceptibility, and it occurs most frequently during wet seasons and in very fertile fields.

The symptoms consist of more or less irregular cavities in the center of the tuber. The cavities are usually lined with light to dark brown tissue. The disorder is sometimes confused with blackheart, but is unrelated. The symptoms do not increase during storage or transit, and decay does not follow it except when tubers are cracked to the surface. Detection of hollow heart is often a problem in otherwise sound tubers. A nondestructive method based on an X-ray radiographic image of submerged tubers shows promise (Finney and Norris 1973).

Mahogany Browning   Potatoes are subject to chilling injury. Cultivars vary in susceptibility, but under sufficient exposure to chilling temperatures (0° to 1° C) (32° to 34° F), most will develop some degree of mahogany browning. Of the commonly grown commercial cultivars, Katahdin is the most susceptible to this disorder.

Two cultivars of potatoes stored at 0° C (32° F) showed typical mahogany browning after 11 weeks. Some surface scald and surface mold growth appeared later. Comparable tubers held at 5° C (41° F) had no chilling symptoms after 19 weeks storage, except some slight skin browning (Hruschka *et al*. 1967).

Description   Reddish-brown areas or blotches in the flesh of affected tubers are distinctive symptoms of chilling injury. They occur in irregular patches anywhere in the flesh. The margins are not definite, and no sharp lines exist between discolored and normal tissue. The color of affected tissue varies in intensity from light to reddish brown. The affected tissues are of normal texture, but cooking quality is adversely affected.

Prevention   As with chilling injury of any susceptible product, the avoidance of exposure to chilling temperatures is a sure preventative for the disorder. Rather prolonged exposure to temperatures below 2° C (36° F) is usually necessary to produce the symptoms. Accordingly, it usually occurs in potatoes stored for 20 weeks or longer. In poorly insulated or inadequately ventilated storages, it commonly occurs in tubers near outside walls or near air inlets.

Intermittent warming of tubers held inadvertently or purposely at 0° C (32° F) has been found to essentially eliminate chilling injury. Tubers moved to 15.5° C (60° F) for 1 week after every third week at 0° C eliminated mahogany browning during prolonged storage. Comparable tubers held continuously at 0° C developed typical chilling symptoms. Holding tubers for 1 to 4 weeks at 15.5° C before storage at 0° C did not reduce chilling injury (Hruschka *et al*. 1969).

Translucent End   This is primarily a production problem, but the symptoms develop during storage. Iritani and Weller (1973) report that moisture stress sometimes reverses the normal pattern of dry matter in Russet Burbank potatoes. When dry matter concentrates in the apical end rather than the basal, translucent end develops during storage. This presents a problem for processors, due to sugar-induced darkening of chips and French fries.

Diseases

Bacterial Soft Rot   *Pathogens Involved*   *Erwinia carotovora* and *Pseudomonas marginalis*.

Both of these organisms cause a slimy soft rot in many vegetables. *Erwinia* probably causes more loss in the spring- and summer-harvested potatoes than all other diseases combined. It may be the primary decay organism, as when gaining entrance through unhealed cuts, bruises, heat injury, or enlarged lenticels, or it may occur as a secondary rot following field infections of late blight or Fusarium tuber rot.

Description   Soft rot of tubers, entering at bruised or heat-injured areas, is first light colored but with time and exposure to air it becomes dark brown to black. The boundary between infected and sound tissue is well-defined and the inner tissue often disintegrates, while the outer parts of the tuber remain intact. Invasion by secondary organisms often produces slimy tissue with foul odor (Fig. 19.5).

Soft rot infections at lenticels are indicated by swollen and water-soaked tissue in areas up to 6 mm (¼ in.) in diameter around each infected lenticel. If such early infections are exposed to dry air for several days, the infection will usually dry up, but a sunken area will remain. However, under humid, warm conditions the lenticel infections will usually develop into active and destructive soft rot.

Development and Control   The three essential conditions for development of bacterial soft rot are entry points such as unhealed bruises or heat injury; high RH or free moisture on the tuber surface and tuber temperatures from 21° to 33° C (70° to 90° F). Growth of

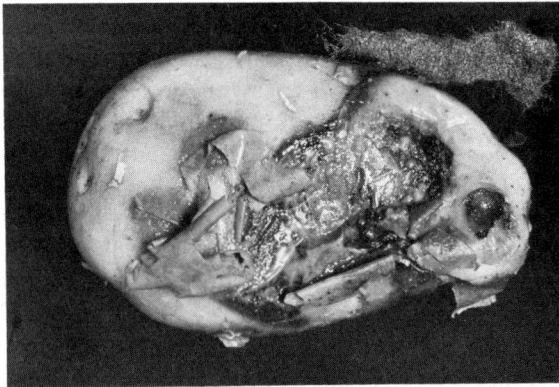

U.S. Dept. of Agriculture Photo

FIG. 19.5.   BACTERIAL SOFT ROT OF POTATO

Erwinia carotovora will occur as low as 10° C (50° F), but development is slow and little rot actually occurs at temperatures below 21° C (70° F). Infection rarely occurs even at skin breaks, when the tubers are dry and RH is low. Potatoes dug from wet fields often have greatly enlarged lenticels. The bacteria are abundant in all soils, so contamination of the tubers before and during digging is inevitable. Soak tanks and washers for soil removal are heavily inoculated with the organism and are often a source of infection. It has been demonstrated that submerging tubers to depths of several feet in soak tanks will increase soft rot infections from hydrostatic pressure which forces bacteria into lenticels (Dewey and Barger 1948).

During the period 1965–1969 soft rot decay was the principal cause for rejection of carlots of Washington State potatoes in the market. A survey (Cromarty and Easton 1973) showed that 63% of rejections resulted from serious amounts of bacterial soft rot in the shipments. As in other observations, free moisture and elevated temperatures were associated with the rejected shipments.

The proper curing of potatoes, before or during storage or shipment, is probably the best insurance against soft rot decay. Studies with freshly cut tuber slices (Smith and Smart 1955) showed that under optimum healing environments 21.0° to 26.5° C (70° to 80° F in moist chamber), suberin and periderm formation developed rapidly enough in 2 or 3 days to prevent most infections when the slices were subsequently inoculated with active *Erwinia atroseptica*. Slices held at 5° C (41° F) in moist chambers developed no periderm and very little suberin in 4 days and were readily infected when later inoculated with bacteria and held at 21.0 to 26.5° C.

Prevention   While many soft rot infections do occur after harvest, the control of this disease must start in the field. Such field diseases as late blight, brown rot, and blackleg produce lesions through which soft rot infections often occur. Avoidance of waterlogging the soils near harvest time is also important, for open or enlarged lenticels are common sites of infection. Prompt pickup of tubers during harvest and protection of loads on the way to and at the packing shed are essential for prevention of heat and wind injury with subsequent soft rot infection.

Frost- or heat-injured tubers must be removed before storage as these can be sources of infection for other tubers in the pile. When damaged tubers are not sorted out before storage, a temporary increase in air flow through the bin piles is desirable. Air flow rates of more than 0.12 cu m per min per 100 kg (2 cfm per cwt) will dry up many of these potential infections (Hunter and Toko 1965), but are not desirable for prolonged use because of increased moisture loss from sound tubers.

Kendrick *et al.* (1959) have proposed a temperature-relative humidity index which appears useful for predicting the incidence of bacterial soft rot in potatoes. The formula: $x = 2.5$ (hours above 90% RH) + (degree hours above 5° C). A high reading gave a positive and significant correlation to the incidence of bacterial soft rot in White Rose potatoes.

Fusarium Tuber Rots *Pathogens Involved* Various species of *Fusarium*.

Numerous species of *Fusarium* are found in cultivated soils. Several of the species appear to be present in all potato-growing regions, but in a given soil or locality one species often predominates. The rots caused by *Fusarium* occur in potatoes from all areas, with the greatest loss from these organisms occurring during storage and transit.

Description The symptoms of Fusarium tuber rots depend largely upon the species of *Fusarium* causing the infection. Affected tissues are usually brown to dark brown and as the decay progresses the tissues become sunken and wrinkled. Later, tufts of mycelium become visible at

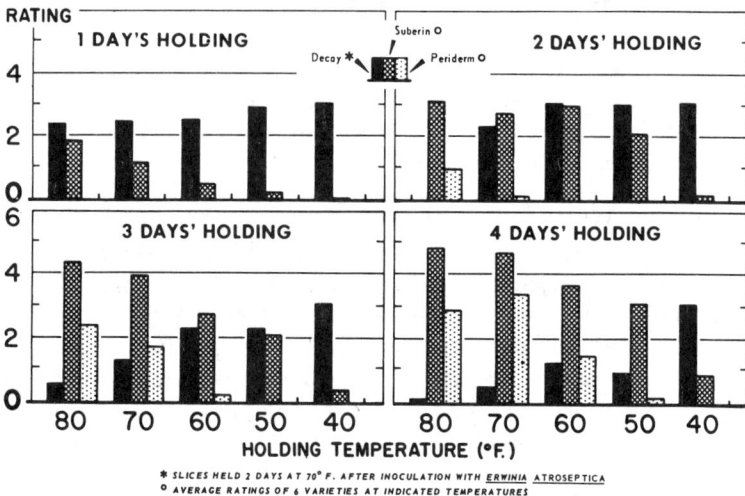

From Smith and Smart (1959)

FIG. 19.6. POTATO WOUND BARRIER FORMATION AND DECAY RATINGS BY HOLDING PERIODS AND TEMPERATURES
Metric equivalents for holding temperatures: 26.5°, 21°, 15.5°, 10°, 4.5° C.

infection sites. These tufts of mold may be white, yellow, or from pink to bluish-purple, depending upon the species infecting the tuber. At low temperatures they are often wet and soft (Fig. 19.7).

Development and Control   At least four species of *Fusarium* attack growing potato plants in the field and infect the growing tubers. However, most of the species of *Fusarium* are wound parasites which infect tubers after harvest. Mycelium and spores of *Fusarium* abound in soils, on the tubers, on field implements, in used bags, and even on the floors and walls of storage bins. Digger cuts and injuries caused by rough handling during harvesting and sorting are prime sites of infection. Whether or not decay follows inoculation depends on the degree of healing which has occurred and the temperature and moisture conditions around the tuber.

Most of the tuber-rotting species of *Fusarium* are high temperature organisms. They grow best between 26° and 30° C (78° and 86° F) and

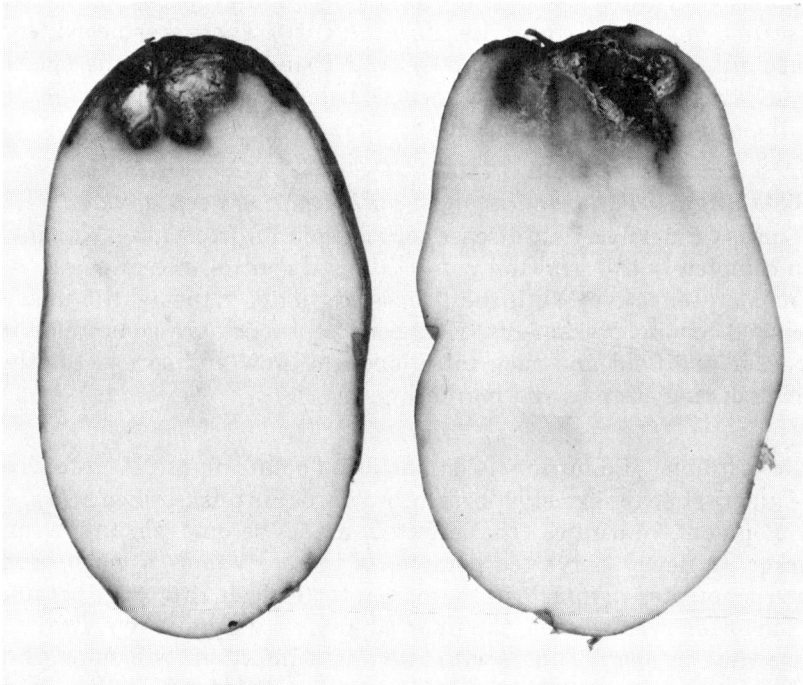

U.S. Dept. of Agriculture Photo

FIG. 19.7.   FUSARIUM ROT OF POTATO

slowly below 10° C (78° and 86° F). Under the most favorable conditions, infections at wounds will be visible within 4 or 5 days, and serious decay of the tuber will occur within 2 weeks. When potatoes are cooled rapidly to below 15.5° C (60° F) after harvest, healing of injuries does not progress fast enough to prevent infection. Even though the *Fusarium* spp. grow slowly at 5° C (41° F), infections can occur at this temperature. Such infections will progress little at 4° to 5° C (38° to 41° F), but when infected tubers are removed from storage and warmed up, decay will develop.

Prevention   Sanitation, careful handling, and a curing period before storage or shipment are the surest means of reducing losses from Fusarium tuber rot. The most important of these steps is prevention of cuts and bruises during harvest, hauling, and packinghouse handling. Such bruised, cut, diseased or frozen potatoes as are present after harvest should be carefully sorted out before storage or shipment. After curing at moderate temperature and high RH for several days after harvest, the tubers should be stored at 4° to 5° C (38° to 41° F). Gamma irradiation of tubers at dosages as high as 456 krad did not control *Fusarium* on tuber surfaces (Beraha *et al.* 1959). There is some evidence that chilling tubers (10 weeks at 0° C) (32° F) increases later susceptibility to *Fusarium* infections, as compared to holding tubers at 5° C (41° F) for the same period (Griffin 1964).

Late Blight   *Pathogen Involved*   ***Phytophthora infestans*.**
This is primarily a field disease of potato plants. In cool, wet seasons it can completely kill growing potato vines if control measures are not prompt and effective. While the disease originates in the field, it must be included among market diseases, because tubers are sometimes infected in the field and such infections can grow and spread to other tubers during storage and marketing.

Description   Following field infection of potato plants, symptoms on the tubers appear as reddish-brown, brown, or purplish-brown areas. As development continues, the affected areas become shrunken and darker. In newly harvested potatoes of the early crop, a moist decay often penetrates 12 mm (½ in.) or more into the flesh. In storage potatoes of the fall-harvested crop, the infected areas are usually dry, firm and somewhat leathery. Tubers with late blight infections will show white tufts of mycelium at eyes and lenticels when held under moist conditions. Invasion by bacteria and other fungi often occur at late blight lesions.

Development and Cause   The primary source of field infections of late blight is diseased tubers. When tubers containing the mycelium are planted, the disease grows up the sprouts and infects the emerging stalks. Under moist conditions the fungus produces spores on the stalks and lower leaves. These are carried by rain and wind to nearby healthy plants, and during extended periods of wet, cool weather, entire fields may be completely infected. Another source of field infections is cull potatoes which are discarded near packinghouses or on dumps near potato fields. In weather favorable to late blight, the fungus grows and sporulates on the surface of the tubers and in the volunteer plants from the cull tubers. Great numbers of these spores can be carried by winds to potato fields.

Spores from diseased vines fall or are washed to the ground and will readily infect tubers growing within a few centimeters of the soil surface. Tubers can also be well-inoculated with spores if the crop is dug while infected tops are still green and succulent. However, the presence of spores on tubers does not always mean infections. Under dry conditions or at temperatures below 5° C (40° F) the spores will not germinate.

The principal postharvest hazard, in tubers from late-blight-infected fields, is from minute infections that may occur before or during harvest but are not visible when the potatoes are stored or shipped. Under favorable conditions these infections may develop into serious decay at some point in the marketing process.

Prevention   The critical factor in control of late blight tuber rot is elimination of the disease in the field. This can be accomplished by the use of disease-free seed, care in disposal of cull potatoes, and the use of effective fungicides in the field at the first sign of disease in the vines. Several fungicides which effectively control late blight in the field are now available. Specific recommendations for control should be obtained from local authorities.

When potatoes are harvested from a field in which late blight has occurred, digging must not begin until the tops have been killed by frost, a chemical vine killer, or natural maturity. Tubers from such fields should be carefully sorted before storage or shipment to remove all tubers with any evidence of decay.

Leak   Pathogen Involved   Various species of *Pythium*.

Several species, including *Pythium debaryanum*, *Pythium ultimum*, and others, are known to be involved in the disease referred to as "leak." All of the species are soil-inhabiting. They are primary causes of damping-off in plant seedlings, and rots in a number of vegetables.

Description   The first evidence of infection by *Pythium* is usually at or near the stolon attachment. The skin appears somewhat water-soaked and may be discolored and somewhat depressed. The margins of lesions are often sharply defined both internally and externally. The most characteristic symptom of advanced infections is the watery nature of affected tissues. When pressure is applied to such tissues, the skin is broken and a yellowish or brownish liquid is released, justifying the name leak. Under some conditions the entire interior of the tuber may be liquified even when only small external lesions are visible.

Development and Control   The various species of *Pythium* are particularly destructive under unusually wet conditions. The fungi may infect stolons in the field and from there enter the tubers at the stem end. However, infection of tubers usually takes place through cuts and other wounds. When infection has occurred, decay progresses very rapidly in the range of 21° to 30° C (70° to 85° F). Entire tubers may be rotted in a few days under warm, moist conditions. Development of the organism is slow between 5° and 10° C (41° and 50° F). The disease does not appear to spread from decaying to sound potatoes during storage or transit.

Prevention   Careful handling to avoid any skin breaks is the best insurance against *Pythium* infection. When leak threatens, every effort should be made to keep the tubers cool and dry during harvest and in the packinghouse, as well as during storage and transit.

Ring Rot   *Pathogen Involved   Corynebacterium sepedonicum.*
This is potentially one of the most important diseases of potatoes because of the ease and rapidity with which it can increase during a single growing season. However, the wide use of certified seed, disinfectants and precautions during seed cutting have greatly reduced the incidence in commercial potato-growing areas.

Description   The principal initial symptom of ring rot in tubers is an odorless decay in the vicinity of the vascular ring. The decayed tissues are soft and of a cheesy consistency. When the tuber is squeezed or pressed with a hard object, the decay tissues are forced out of the ring. As the infection develops further, the diseased tissue can be readily pushed aside, leaving a cavity part or all the way around the cut tuber. The infection may eventually reach the surface in the vicinity of the eyes, resulting in characteristic cracks that extend into the vascular ring. Secondary rots may then enter and mask the primary infection.

Potato plants are infected in the field from ring-rot-infected seed. Symptoms in the plant usually do not appear until late in the growing season, but all tubers produced by infected plants will develop the disease by infection through the stolon attachment.

The extent of the disease in tubers is difficult to determine because the tubers must be cut before detection is possible. Undetected ring rot in table stock potatoes is sometimes responsible for important market losses.

Prevention   The causal bacteria survive from one season to the next in infected tubers. When such tubers are planted, the bacteria move through channels of the vascular ring to all parts of the growing plant. Control involves planting only ring-rot-free seed, precautions against contamination during seed cutting and planting, and sanitation of storage bins, bags, crates and tuber-handling equipment.

RADISHES

Physical Injury

Freezing   *Description*   Freezing, followed by thawing, causes the injured tissue to appear translucent. However, when freezing is severe enough to destroy cells, thawed roots soften, rapidly lose moisture, and shrivel. In red radishes the pigment oozes out of the roots with the moisture and leaves them yellowish and bleached (Parsons and Day 1970).

Cause   Radishes freeze between -1.1 and $-0.8°$ C ($30°$ and $30.5°$ F).

Prevention   Radishes cannot withstand even brief freezing without major loss in quality after thawing. Thus, if they are packed in ice, care must be taken that the ice is not below their freezing point.

Disorders

Pithiness   *Description*   Pithy radishes show textured white spots, streaks, or a network that contrasts with the even white of normal tissue when viewed in cross section. Pithiness occurs anywhere in the roots, but large air spaces develop more frequently near the center than near the periphery.

Severely pithy radishes are relatively light for their size and feel spongy when squeezed. They also are unpleasantly tough and dry.

Radishes any size may be pithy, but large air spaces are more common in large than in small roots.

Development and Cause   Pithiness results from the separation of cells from each other. This creates numerous minute air spaces and the textured white appearance. Eventually the air spaces coalesce to form large ones.

Pithiness can develop before or after harvest. During growth, pithiness seems to be induced by conditions that permit overly rapid thickening of the roots and concomitant premature senescence (Takano 1967). After harvest, pithiness is aggravated by undesirably high holding temperatures.

Prevention   Pithiness can be minimized by growing radishes under conditions that permit steady, but not too rapid, enlargement of the roots. Thus, radishes grown during cool periods are less likely to be pithy than those grown during hot weather.

Pithy radishes have a lower specific gravity than normal roots (Takano 1966B). Thus, the two groups likely could be separated by means of specific gravity solutions. Their composition remains to be determined, however, and may depend on cultivar and area of production. Further, the method could be applied only to topped roots.

Finally, holding radishes below 5° C (41° F) slows the increase in pithiness during marketing (Lipton 1972).

Translucence   *Description*   Translucent areas, as seen in cross section, contrast sharply with normal tissue, are irregular in outline, and may be small or encompass the entire root. Takano (1966A) found these areas, at least in their initial stages, to be associated with the conductive tissue.

Translucent and normal tissue have about the same firmness and texture.

Development and Cause   Translucence can develop before or after harvest. According to Takano (1966A), translucence precedes pithiness, and thus may be another sign of premature aging. However, translucence and pithiness can occur independently (Lipton 1972).

Prevention   Information on this disorder is insufficient to suggest preventive measures.

Diseases

Bacterial Black Spot *Pathogen Involved* *Xanthomonas vesicatoria.*

Description   The bacterial lesions initially are brown and range from about 1 to 3 mm ($^1/_{25}$ to $^1/_{10}$ in.) in diameter. They turn black 1 or 2 days later and may coalesce to cover a large part of a radish.

Development   Injuries sustained by radishes during harvest and subsequent handling predispose them to infection (Segall and Smoot 1962). Temperatures above 10° C (50° F) greatly accelerate the spread of the disease, particularly when accompanied by high humidity, as in plastic bags.
So far the disease has been of concern only in Florida. However, the reason may not be geographical, or even climatic, but related to the high proportion of Florida-grown radishes that are prepackaged.

Prevention   Bacterial black spot can best be prevented by holding and shipping radishes between 0° and 2° C (32° and 36° F), assuming that some injury is inevitable. Washing radishes in chlorinated water (100 to 200 ppm) reduces the incidence of the disease but not as effectively as low temperature. A chlorine wash nevertheless is useful, because radishes often warm above 2° C (36° F) during marketing.

Downy Mildew *Pathogen Involved* *Peronospora parasitica.*

Description   Initial lesions on red radishes are purplish-red to brown, and from them later emerges a thread-like white mycelium strung with white spore masses. When magnified these resemble a loose bud of cauliflower. In advanced lesions the surface is rough or even cracked. Internally, the normally white tissue is grayish brown to black.

Development and Prevention   See *Crucifers—Leafy.*

Rhizoctonia Root Rot   See *Turnips.*

RUTABAGAS

Disorder

Boron Deficiency   See *Turnips.*

Diseases See *Turnips.*

SWEETPOTATOES

Physical Injury

Freezing   The range in average freezing points of ten cultivars of sweetpotatoes is reported as $-1.9°$ to $-1.2°$ C ($28.7°$ to $29.4°$ F) (Whiteman 1957). Soluble solids content of the roots was not consistently related to freezing point. The highest freezing point of Porto Rico roots was $-1.1°$ C ($30.1°$ F).

Description   Roots that have been slightly frozen show a yellowish-brown discoloration in the vascular ring and a yellowish-green, water-soaked appearance of the other tissues. Severe freezing, with ice formation in the tissues, is characterized by immediate softening of the roots as the injured cells collapse on thawing. Badly frozen roots are often invaded by rot-producing fungi before they dry up.

Prevention   Freezing of sweetpotatoes seldom occurs in storage since avoidance of chilling injury requires maintenance of temperatures well above freezing. However, freeze damage does sometimes occur during winter transport to northern markets and during delivery to retail markets in severe weather. Heated vehicles for transport and market delivery during cold weather are essential for protection against both chilling and freezing injury.

Disorders

Chilling Injury   Harmful physiological changes occur in sweetpotatoes that are held at temperatures below $13°$ C ($55°$ F). Cultivars vary in response to low temperature, but usually 10 days at $10°$ C ($50°$ F) or shorter periods at lower temperatures will cause injury.

Description   Internal discoloration ranging from brown to almost black is the principal symptom of chilling injury. The discolored areas are somewhat scattered but are usually associated with the vascular ring and the vascular elements in the central part of the root. Cooking quality of chilled roots is also adversely affected.

Development and Cause   The direct cause is exposure to temperatures below $13°$ C ($55°$ F). The duration of such exposure and the number of degrees below the critical temperature determine the extent and severity of the injury. In addition of tissue discoloration chilling injury occurs in the form of "hardcore" areas in cooked sweetpotatoes. Exposure to 1° C (33° F) for as little as 3 days before curing at 27° C (80° F) caused significant amounts of hardcore after boiling. Sweetpotato roots cured before any chilling exposure did not develop hardcore when cooked (Daines *et al.* 1974). Buescher *et al.* (1976) found that reduced levels of alpha-amylase activity occurred in chilled roots, and propose that this is associated with increased levels of starch and pectic substances after processing.

Symptoms of chilling injury are also found in sweetpotatoes exposed to cold, wet soils before harvest, even though no chilling occurs after harvest. Reductions in titratable acidity, typical of postharvest chilling injury, resulted also from unfavorable preharvest exposure. The data do not indicate whether wet soil, cold soil or a combination of both cause the damage (Kushman and Pope 1970).

Properly cured sweetpotatoes are more resistant to chilling injury than noncured roots. Chilling injury after harvest can be completely prevented by avoidance of exposure to temperatures below 13° C (55° F) at any time during storage, transport and marketing.

Internal Breakdown   This disorder sometimes develops in storage. It is related to storage environment, cultivar, and intercellular space of the roots at harvest.

Description   Internal tissues of affected roots are pithy or dry and spongy. In advanced cases the roots are light in weight and compress easily. Cavities may form in the roots as the tissues separate, and the spongy tissues are sometimes white or light yellow (Fig. 19.8).

Development and Cause   Pithiness, with subsequent internal breakdown has been shown to result from excessive intercellular space in certain roots (Kushman and Pope 1969). This characteristic varies with cultivar and growing conditions. Intercellular space also increases during storage and is most prevalent when roots are stored at temperatures above those recommended or at low RH.

Curing sweetpotatoes for more than 1 week at 30° C (85° F) increased the development of intercellular space, as did storage above the 13° to 15° C (55° to 59° F) recommended range. Cultivars vary in susceptibility to internal breakdown. The disorder is least prevalent in cultivars with high dry matter content, low intercellular space, low water loss rate and low respiration rate at harvest (Kushman and Pope 1972).

FIG. 19.8.   INTERNAL
BREAKDOWN OF SWEETPOTATO
This is a common symptom of chilling
injury to the roots.

U.S. Dept. of Agriculture Photo

Prevention   Measurement of intercellular space at harvest time provides a useful index of susceptibility to internal breakdown. A relatively simple method for this determination is available (Kushman and Pope 1968). Since the pithiness and breakdown occur during storage, those lots of roots with a high proportion of intercellular space at harvest time should be marketed soon after harvest. Aside from avoidance of the disorder by forecasting incidence in certain lots, accurate control of storage temperature, RH, and air flow will reduce severity of the disorder.

Diseases

Black Rot   *Pathogen Involved   Ceratocystis fimbriata.*
This is a serious and widespread disease of sweetpotatoes. It affects plants in the seedbed and field, but most of the damage occurs in the form of root decay during storage and marketing.

Description   The early symptoms of black rot are round, slightly sunken spots about 6 mm (¼ in.) in diameter. As the infections grow, the spots enlarge to 12 to 50 mm (½ to 2 in.) and become black to greenish-black. Small black fruiting bodies are often present at this stage. These appear to the naked eye as small black bristles. The rot is usually shallow and firm. Affected internal tissues are dark colored and have a bitter taste which affects the entire root when cooked (Fig. 19.9).

Development   Infections with black rot occur in the field through wounds, dead rootlets, or even apparently uninjured tissues. The fungus persists from season to season in sweetpotato fields in roots, plant debris, and soil. Infection of roots is favored by wet soil and warm temperatures. Growth of the fungus occurs over a wide range of temperatures, but is most rapid at 24° to 26.5° C (75° to 80° F).

Many black rot infections are so small at harvest that removal of infected roots is impossible. These minute infections develop within 4 to 6 weeks in storage and are often responsible for substantial decay losses in stocks thought to be free of the disease. The disease can also be spread by washing sound sweetpotatoes in water with roots infected with black rot.

Prevention   Discard of all visibly infected roots before storage and storage isolation and early marketing of sweetpotatoes from soils known to be infected are essential procedures in reduction of losses from black rot. Special high-temperature curing 35° C (95° F for 4 days)

U.S. Dept. of Agriculture Photo

FIG. 19.9.   BLACK ROT OF SWEETPOTATO

reduces black rot development in storage (Kushman 1959). A more severe heat treatment 40.5° to 43° C (105° to 110° F for 24 hr) will prevent the development of black rot, but sometimes adversely affects root quality (Kushman and Cooley 1949). Chemical treatments are not consistently effective.

Charcoal Rot   *Pathogen Involved   Macrophomina phaseoli.* Sweetpotatoes grown in the South show the greatest losses from charcoal rot, but the disease causes some loss in storage wherever sweetpotatoes are grown.

Description   Decay usually starts at the upper end of the sweetpotato and then progresses the length of the root. Early infections show as variously sized and shaped, light brown discolorations of the surface, that are sharply delineated from healthy tissues. The diseased areas remain firm and become dark brown until water loss causes shrivel. The cut surface of a decaying sweetpotato shows three color zones. The advancing edge of the decay is light brown and slightly spongy, the intermediate zone is reddish-brown and firm, and the oldest part of the decayed area is dark gray to black and firm with some small, black sclerotia within the tissue.

Development and Control   Charcoal rot develops rapidly in uncured sweetpotatoes marketed soon after harvest. Slight infections at broken ends of the roots will develop in transit and result in substantial loss in the market. Optimum temperature for growth of this organism is 31.5° C (88° F), but it will grow even at 42° C (108° F). Infections which have occurred in the field or before curing will grow very slowly at recommended storage temperatures, but development speeds up when the roots are removed to higher temperatures.

Prevention.   Roots with the slightest sign of decay at broken or injured ends should all be removed before shipment or storage. Roots free from infection before curing are protected from charcoal rot by the wound-cork development which curing favors.

Dry Rots   *Pathogens Involved   Diaporthe batatatis* and several species of *Fusarium.* These fungi cause dry rots of sweetpotato roots. The rots usually enter through broken ends but can infect through wounds or previous infections at other locations.

Description   Even in the early stages, decay caused by these fungi is firm and dry. The affected area loses water rapidly and soon becomes dark and hard. In the central Atlantic states, *Diaporthe* alone, or in conjunction with *Fusarium*, causes a serious end rot in commercial sweetpotatoes.

Prevention   The only known control for these dry rot losses is prompt curing to prevent infection of wounds made during harvest and handling.

Internal Cork   *Pathogen Involved*   A virus.
Slight symptoms may be visible at harvest time, but these increase substantially after harvest, particularly at storage temperatures above optimum.

Description   Often the symptoms do not show externally, but sometimes a surface depression indicates that a corky area is present just below the skin. When the root is sliced through, the hard, corky spots are sharply outlined and the unaffected tissue remains normal. The corky areas remain hard and gritty after cooking, but flavor and texture of the surrounding flesh is normal. Cultivars vary in susceptibility and symptoms. The Porto Rico is more severely affected than other common cultivars.

Prevention   High temperatures favor development of internal cork, so roots suspected of infection with this virus should be held continuously close to 13° C (55° F) after curing. Sweetpotatoes known to be infected with internal cork should be marketed soon after harvest.

Java Black Rot   *Pathogen Involved*   *Diplodia tubericola.*
This disease affects sweetpotatoes during storage and marketing and often causes heavy losses. It is present to some extent in most sweetpotato storages, but losses from the disease are usually more severe in southern and tropical areas than in the more northern growing areas.

Description   In the early stages, about ten days after infection, the decay is brown and moderately firm. As the decay progresses, all the tissues become involved. The interior tissues are then light brown and the skin and tissues just beneath change from dark brown to black as fruiting bodies form and push up through the skin. The fruiting bodies form in such great numbers in 3 or 4 weeks that they create domelike elevations on the surface of the root. Eventually the root becomes a hard, black mummy.

Development and Control   This *Diplodia* occurs in soils and in plant debris. The fungus may be on the roots as they go into storage or it may be carried over in the storage rooms. It is essentially a high temperature organism with most rapid growth at 29° to 31° C (84° to 88° F). Most infections are at wounds and can occur over a wide range of temperatures.

Prevention   As with most decay organisms affecting sweetpotatoes, the best control measures are careful handling to reduce wounds, prompt curing under optimum conditions, and storage at 13.0° to 15.5° C (55° to 60° F) immediately after curing.

Rhizopus Soft Rot   *Pathogens Involved*   *Rhizopus nigricans* and *Rhizopus tritici*.

Decay caused by these organisms is the principal cause of loss in sweetpotatoes during storage and marketing. In fact, in most markets, it causes more wastage than all other sweetpotato diseases combined. All cultivars of sweetpotato are susceptible to the disease and it occurs in roots from all production areas.

Description   Affected tissues are at first soft and watery, but change little in color. Later, such areas darken to light or dark brown. Freshly decayed areas will yield a yellowish-brown liquid when broken, but as water is lost from decayed tissues the areas become withered and firm. Surface mold growth under moist conditions shows as coarse, white mycelium with numerous black spore balls throughout. External molds usually are conspicuous at the ends of the roots and at breaks in the skin. When the roots decay under dry conditions, surface mold may not develop.

Development and Control   Infection by *Rhizopus* occurs at broken ends of the roots or at any unhealed wound. At moderate temperatures the rot develops more rapidly than that caused by other organisms. Decay may become evident within 24 hr of infection, and at favorable temperatures a root can be completely destroyed within 4 to 6 days (Fig. 19.10).

Kushman (1975) reported that loss of weight during curing at 26° C (78° F), was positively correlated to decay development after 5 months of storage at 15° C (59° F). Weight loss was reduced by increasing RH from 80–90% to 90–97% for curing, but not by a further increase to

U.S. Dept. of Agriculture Photo

FIG. 19.10.   RHIZOPUS SOFT ROT OF SWEETPOTATOES

97–100%. When weight loss was less than 4% during curing only 1% decay developed in storage. When curing resulted in weight loss of about 10%, due to injuries and low RH, decay was as much as 25% after 5 months of storage.

Many species of *Rhizopus* are present in cultivated soils. All sweetpotatoes are contaminated with one or more species of *Rhizopus* during and after harvest. The extent of decay from this inoculum depends upon moisture and temperature conditions and whether or not fresh wounds are present on the roots. Surface moisture and unhealed wounds offer favorable conditions for infection. Temperatures between 18.0° and 29.5° C (65° and 85° F) are favorable for growth of both species of *Rhizopus* responsible for most soft rot decay.

Prevention   Careful handling of the roots during harvest and hauling, together with prompt curing at optimum temperature and humidity, are of the greatest importance in preventing Rhizopus soft rot during storage. When the roots are washed, sorted and packed after storage, additional wounding may occur. Several fungicidal treatments have been developed which will reduce infections at new wounds when applied during preparation of the roots for market (Kushman 1967). Recuring the roots for 2 days at 29.5° C (85° F) after packing for market has also been reported as reducing decay (McClure 1959).

TURNIPS

Physical Injury

Freezing   *Description*   Small, water-soaked spots on the surface are symptomatic of light freezing. The spots may coalesce and encompass the entire root upon severe freezing. The extent of internal translucent tissue also depends on the severity of freezing injury. Once thawing is completed, the roots rapidly lose moisture and soften. Injured tissue appears tan or gray and gives off an objectionable, fermented odor. Less severely frozen tissue may show only pithiness upon thawing.

Surface pitting is another symptom of freezing injury, but may be obscured by shrivelling and decay (Parsons and Day 1970).

Cause   The freezing point of turnips is slightly above $-1.1°$ C (30° F).

Prevention   Turnips must be well protected from freezing when they are stored outside in pits or in other unheated spaces. If slight freezing has occurred, slow thawing will permit use of the turnips for one or two subsequent days.

Disorder

Boron Deficiency   *Description*   The interior of affected roots is water-soaked and may have brown spots and cracks. Leaves of affected plants are dwarfed and curled.

Prevention   See *Cauliflower.*

Diseases

Alternaria Root Rot   *Pathogen Involved*   *Alternaria herculea.*

Description   Concentric rings of light and dark brown areas form typical circular lesions. Under high humidity a gray to grayish-brown growth covers the surface. Internally, the dead tissue remains firm.

Development   Infection occurs in the field or storage, via the crown or by contact with spores or mycelium. Injured roots are more readily infected than sound ones.

Control　See *Crucifers—Leafy, Alternaria Leaf Spot.*

Black Rot　*Pathogen Involved*　*Xanthomonas campestris.*

Description　This disease blackens the vascular strands, giving cross sections a speckled appearance. External symptoms usually are absent.

Development and Prevention　See *Crucifers—Leafy.*

Downy Mildew　*Pathogen Involved*　*Peronospora parasitica.*

Description and Development　When leaves are severely mildewed, the fungus sometimes invades the root via the crown. First, brown mottling or streaks extend from crown to root, and eventually most of the center of the root will be black. External symptoms are missing on these roots.

Prevention　See *Crucifers—Leafy.*

Similar Disorder　Boron deficiency, which, however, is not as black, but more watery.

Gray Mold Rot　See *Crucifers—Leafy.*

Rhizoctonia Root Rot　*Pathogen Involved.—Rhizoctonia solani.*

Description　Surface lesions are round and light brown at first, but dark and slightly sunken as more tissue is affected. Internally, the rotted tissue becomes spongy. In turnips, the lesions frequently consist of concentric light and dark brown rings. Brown mycelium, growing or in resting bodies, may be present or absent.

Prevention　See *Crucifers—Leafy.*

Watery Soft Rot　See *Crucifers—Leafy.*

WATER CHESTNUTS

Diseases

Black Rot　*Pathogen Involved*　*Cerastomella paradoxa.*

Description   This fungus causes a soft rot that is characterized by an odor similar to pineapple. Fluffy, dark grayish mycelium is evident externally and dark fruiting bodies may occur externally and internally.

Development and Control   Symptoms develop within a few days after infection. Since the fungus enters via wounds, black rot can be inhibited by careful handling of the corms and by curing them 3 days at 100% RH and 30° to 32° C (86° to 90° F) if they cannot be stored as noted under *Commodity Requirements*.

Trichoderma Rot   *Pathogen Involved*   *Trichoderma viride.*

Description   The mycelium is first fluffy and white, but soon turns dark green. Affected corms usually are covered with a dense mass of green tufts of mold. Internally, the tissue is pale yellow and soft, but not liquid as with black rot. The decayed tissue is not sharply outlined and emits a "peculiar" moldy odor, according to Chinese researchers (Anon. 1955).

YAMS

Disorder

Chilling Injury   *Description*   Symptoms of chilling injury differ somewhat among cultivars, but a softening of the tissue is characteristic of all. Initially only patches of tissue are soft, but when they coalesce the entire root softens.

Internally, the normally creamy white tissue appears slightly mottled, grayish, and flecked with reddish-brown in *Dioscorea alata*, but only a dirty buff in *D. rotundata*. In the former, the tissue immediately below the skin is brown.

Prolonged chilling causes complete disintegration and decay of the tissue.

Chilling injury also accelerates weight loss of yams, particularly after removal to a nonchilling temperature, where, as with other chilling-sensitive crops, all symptoms become intensified.

Development and Cause   Yams are obviously chilled after 4 weeks at about 7° C (45° F) or lower, although individual cultivars differ somewhat in this respect. *D. alata* seems to be injured, as determined externally, only at 10° C (50° F) or below, whereas *D. rotundata* is injured even during 5 weeks at 12° C (54° F) (Coursey 1968). However, internal symptoms might have shown up earlier had the roots been transferred to a nonchilling temperature after 1 or 2 weeks of chilling.

Prevention   Yams must never be exposed to temperatures below 13° C (55° F) if chilling injury is to be avoided. Although some cultivars can withstand somewhat lower temperatures, there is no advantage in holding them below 13° C, and 16 ± 1° C (61 ± 2° F) is optimal.

REFERENCES

BULBS

Garlic and Onions

CLARK, C. A., and LORBEER, J. W. 1973A. Symptomology, etiology, and histopathology of Botrytis brown stain of onion. Phytopathology *63*, 1231–1235.

CLARK, C. A., and LORBEER, J. W. 1973B. Reaction of onion cultivars to Botrytis brown stain. Plant Disease Reptr. *57*, 210–214.

DIATCHENKO, V. S. 1974. Methods of controlling carrot and onion diseases under storage conditions. Acta Hort. No. 38, Vol. *2*, 397–410.

GUNKEL, W. W., LORBEER, J. W., KAUFMAN, J., and SMITH, H. A., JR. 1971. Artificial drying—a method for control of Botrytis neck rot in bulk stored onions. New York Farm Elect. Counc. 28th Ann. Progr. Rept. 71–80.

HARROW, K. M., and HARRIS, S. 1969. Artificial curing of onions for control of neck rot (*Botrytis allii* Munn). New Zealand J. Agr. Res. *12*, 592–604.

ISENBERG, F. M., and ANG, J. K. 1963. Northern-grown onions. Curing, storing, and inhibiting sprouting. Cornell Ext. Bull. *1116*.

KAUFMAN, J., HRUSCHKA, H. W., and HARDENBURG, R. E. 1953. Onion prepackaging tests. Pre-Pack-Age 7, No. 1, 9–13.

LIPTON, W. J., and HARRIS, C. M. 1965. Factors influencing the incidence of translucent scale of stored onion bulbs. Proc. Am. Soc. Hort. Sci. *87*, 341–354.

OGATA, K. 1961. Physiological studies on the storage of onions bulb (*sic*). Bull. Univ. Osaka Pref. Ser. B. *11*, 99–119.

RAMSEY, G. B., and BUTLER, L. F. 1928. Injury to onions and fruits caused by exposure to ammonia. J. Agr. Res. 37, 339–348.

SMITH, M. A., McCOLLOCH, L. P., and FRIEDMAN, B. A. 1966. Market diseases of asparagus, onions, beans, peas, carrots, celery and related vegetables. U.S. Dept. Agr. Handbook *303*.

STOW, J. R. 1975. Resistance of 20 cultivars of onions (*Allium cepa*) to rotting and sprouting during high-temperature storage. Exptl. Agr. *11*, 201–207.
VAUGHAN, E. K., CROPSEY, M. G., and HOFMAN, E. N. 1964. Effects of field-curing practices, artificial drying, and other factors in the control of neck rot in stored onions. Oregon Agr. Expt. Sta. Tech. Bull. *77*.
WALKER, J. C., and LARSON, R. M. 1961. Onion diseases and their control. U.S. Dept. Agr. Handbook *208*.
WRIGHT, W. R., and BILLETER, B. A. 1975. Bruising of midwestern storage onions. U.S. Dept. Agr. Mktg. Res. Rept. *1030*.
WRIGHT, R. C., LAURITZEN, J. I., and WHITEMAN, T. M. 1935. Influence of storage temperature and humidity on keeping quality of onions and onion sets. U.S. Dept. Agr. Tech. Bull. *475*.

ROOTS, TUBERS AND OTHER STRUCTURES

Beets

WALKER, J. C. 1939. Internal black spot of garden beet. Phytopathology *29*, 120–128.

Carrots

SEGALL, R. H., and DOW, A. 1973. Effects of bacterial contamination and refrigerated storage on bacterial soft rot of carrots. Plant Disease Reptr. *57*, 896–899.
THORNE, S. N. 1972. Studies of the behaviour of stored carrots with respect to their invasion by *Rhizopus stolonifer* Lind. J. Food Technol. 7, 139–151.

Ginger

AKAMINE, E. K. 1962. Storage of fresh ginger rhizomes. Hawaii Agr. Expt. Sta. Bull. *130*.

Miscellaneous Roots and Structures

ANON. 1955. Studies on the storage diseases of water chestnuts and post-harvest treatments, particularly curing as an effective means of disease control. Phytopathology Lab. Coll. Agr. Nat. Taiwan Univ. Spec. Publ. *I*.
KADOW, K. J., and ANDERSON, H. W. 1940. A study of horseradish diseases and their control. Illinois Agr. Expt. Sta. Bull. *469*.
LIPTON, W. J. 1972. Market quality of radishes stored in low O₂ atmospheres. J. Am. Soc. Hort. Sci. *97*, 164–167.
PARSONS, C. S., and DAY, R. H. 1970. Freezing injury of root crops: Beets, carrots, parsnips, radishes, and turnips. U.S. Dept. Agr. Mktg. Res. Rept. *866*.

SEGALL, R. H., and SMOOT, J. J. 1962. Bacterial black spot of radish. Phytopathology *52*, 970–973.

TAKANO, T. 1966A. Studies on the pithiness of radish. IV. On the process of pithy tissue formation in the radish root. J. Japan. Soc. Hort. Sci. *35*, 152–157.

TAKANO, T. 1966B. Studies on the pithiness of radish. V. On the correlation of the concentration of soluble solids weight of top and root length of inflorescence or the specific gravity of radish roots to the degree of pithiness. (*sic*). J. Japan. Soc. Hort. Sci. *35*, 304–308. (Japanese, English summary)

TAKANO, T. 1967. Studies on the pithiness of radish. VIII. General discussion and conclusions. Studies Lab. Hort. Sci. Fac. Agr. Nagoya Univ. (English summary)

Potatoes

AKELEY, R. V., HOUGHLAND, G. V. C., and SCHARK, A. E. 1962. Genetic differences in potato-tuber greening. Am. Potato J. *39*, 409–417.

BERAHA, L., RAMSEY, G. B., SMITH, M. A., and WRIGHT, W. R. 1959. Effects of gamma radiation on some important potato tuber decays. Am. Potato J. *36*, 333–338.

CROMARTY, R. W., and EASTON, G. D. 1973. The incidence of decay and factors affecting bacterial soft rot of potatoes. Am. Potato J. *50*, 398–407.

DEWEY, D. H., and BARGER, W. R. 1948. The occurrence of bacterial soft rot on potatoes resulting from washing in deep vats. Proc. Am. Soc. Hort. Sci. *52*, 325–330.

DWELLE, R. B., and STALLKNECHT, G. F. 1976. Rates of internal blackspot bruise development in potato tubers under conditions of elevated temperature and gas pressures. Am. Potato J. *53*, 235–245.

FINNEY, E. E., JR., and NORRIS, K. H. 1973. X-ray images of hollow heart potatoes in water. Am. Potato J. *50*, 1–8.

FORSYTH, F. R., and EAVES, C. A. 1968. Greening of potatoes—CA cure. Food Technol. *22*, 48–50.

GRIFFIN, G. J. 1964. Effect of chilling on phenol metabolism and Fusarium infection of cut potato tissue. Phytopathology *54*, 1275–1277.

GULL, D. D., and ISENBERG, F. M. 1960. Chlorophyll and solanin content and distribution in four varieties of potato tubers. Proc. Am. Soc. Hort. Sci. *75*, 545–556.

HARDENBURG, R. E. 1964. Greening of potatoes during marketing—a review. Am. Potato J. *41*, 215–220.

HARVEY, O. A., *et al.* 1970. Preliminary report, potato sequence analysis, phase 2—harvester, Kern district 1969. Potato Growers Assn. Calif. Yearbook *26*, 91, 93.

HORNE, A. S. 1912. Bruise in potato. J. Royal Hort. Soc. *38*, 40–50.

HOWARD, F. D., LORENZ, O. A., and TIMM, H. 1968. A review of internal black spot in potato tubers with special reference to the White Rose variety grown in California. Potato Grow. Assoc. Calif. Yearbook *24*, 50–52.

528   HANDLING, TRANSPORTATION AND STORAGE OF FRUITS AND VEGETABLES

HOWARD, F. D., YAMAGUCHI, M., and KNOTT, J. E. 1962. Carbon dioxide as a factor in the susceptibility of potatoes (*Solanum tuberosum* L.) to black spot from bruising. Proc. 16th Intern. Hort. Cong. 584–590.

HRUSCHKA, H. W., SMITH, W. L., JR., and BAKER, J. E. 1967. Chilling injury syndrome in potato tubers. Plant Disease Reptr. *51*, 1014–1016.

HRUSCHKA, H. W., SMITH, W. L., JR., and BAKER, J. E. 1969. Reducing chilling injury of potatoes by intermittent warming. Am. Potato J. *46*, 38–53.

HUDSON, D. E. 1975. The relationship of cell size, intercellular space, and specific gravity to bruise depth in potatoes. Am. Potato J. *52*, 9–14.

HUDSON, D. E., and ORR, P. H. 1977. Incidence of mechanical injury to potatoes during certain storage-related handling operations in the Red River Valley production area. Am. Potato J. *54*, 11–21.

HUNTER, J. H., and TOKO, H. V. 1965. Control of potato-storage diseases as affected by air flow, temperature and relative humidity. Trans. Am. Soc. Agr. Eng. *8*, 578–580.

IRITANI, W. M., and WELLER, L. 1973. The development of translucent end tubers. Am. Potato J. *50*, 223–233.

ISENBERG, F. M., and GULL, D. D. 1959. Potato greening under artificial light. Cornell Univ. Ext. Bull. *1033*.

KENDRICK, J. B., JR., WEDDING, R. T., and PAULUS, A. O. 1959. A temperature-relative humidity index for predicting the occurrence of bacterial soft rot of Irish potatoes. Phytopathology *49*, 701–705.

LORENZ, O. A., TAKATORI, F. H., TIMM, H., OSWALD, J. W., BOWMAN, T., FULLMER, F. S., SNYDER, M., and HALL, H. 1957. Potato fertilization and black spot studies. Santa Maria Valley—1956. Dept. Veg. Crops, Univ. of Calif., Davis, Veg. Crops Series *88*.

RAMSEY, G. B., WIANT, J. S., and SMITH, M. A. 1949. Market diseases of fruits and vegetables: potatoes. U.S. Dept. Agr. Misc. Publ. *98*.

RICHARDSON, L. T., and BUCKLAND, C. T. 1958. Eradication of ring rot bacteria from contaminated potato bags by moist heat treatment. Plant Disease Reptr. *42*, 241–245.

SAWYER, R. L., BOYD, L. L., CETAS, R. C., and BENNETT, A. H. 1965. Potato storage research on Long Island with forced-air ventilation systems. N.Y. State Coll. Agr. Bull. *1002*.

SCHWIMMER, S., and WESTON, W. J. 1958. Chlorophyll formation in potato tubers as influenced by gamma irradiation and by chemicals. Am. Potato J. *35*, 534–542.

SMITH, W. L., JR. 1976. Non-chemical control of postharvest deterioration of fresh produce. *In* Biodeterioration of Materials, Vol. *3*. John Wiley and Sons, New York.

SMITH, W. L., and SMART, H. F. 1955. Relation of soft rot development to protective barriers in Irish potato slices. Phytopathology *45*, 649–654.

SMITH, W. L., JR., and WILSON, J. B. 1978. Market diseases of potatoes. U.S. Dept. Agr. Handbook *479*.

SPARKS, W. C. 1977. Potato bruising can cost you $. Am. Veg. Grower *25*, No. 1, 14, 16.

TIMM, H., YAMAGUCHI, M., HUGHES, D. L., and WEAVER, M. L. 1976. Influence of ethylene on black spot of potato tubers. Am. Potato J. *53*, 49–56.
WORKMAN, M., KERSCHNER, E., and HARRISON, M. 1976. The effect of storage factors on membrane permeability and sugar content of potatoes and decay by *Erwinia carotovora* var. *Atroseptica* and *Fusarium roseum* var. *Sambucinum*. Am. Potato J. *53*, 191–204.
WU, M. T., and SALUNKHE, D. K. 1972. Control of chlorophyll and solanin formation in potato tubers by oil and diluted oil treatments. HortScience 7, 466–467.

Sweetpotatoes

BUESCHER, W. A., SISTRUNK, W. A., and KASAIAN, A. E. 1976. Induction of textural changes in sweetpotato roots by chilling. J. Am. Soc. Hort. Sci. *101*, 516–519.
COOK, H. T. 1955. Sweetpotato diseases. U.S. Dept. Agr. Farmers Bull. *1059*.
DAINES, R. H., CEPONIS, M. J., and HAMMOND, D. F. 1974. Relationship of chilling to hard core in sweetpotatoes. Phytopathology *64*, 1459–1462.
KUSHMAN, L. J. 1959. Curing of Porto Rico sweetpotatoes at 95° F for prevention of black rot in storage. Proc. Am. Soc. Hort. Sci. *73*, 467–472.
KUSHMAN, L. J. 1967. Preparing sweetpotatoes for market. U.S. Dept. Agr. Mktg. Bull. *38*.
KUSHMAN, L. J. 1975. Effect of injury and curing on weight and volume loss of sweetpotatoes during curing and storage. HortScience *10*, 275–277.
KUSHMAN, L. J., and COOLEY, J. S. 1949. Effect of heat on black rot and keeping quality of sweetpotatoes. J. Agr. Res. *78*, 183–190.
KUSHMAN, L. J., and POPE, D. T. 1968. Procedure for determining intercellular space of roots and specific gravity of sweetpotato root tissue. HortScience *3*, 44–45.
KUSHMAN, L. J., and POPE, D. T. 1969. Influence of curing, variety, size of root, evacuation time, and holding time upon the accuracy of intercellular space measurements of sweetpotato roots. J. Am. Soc. Hort. Sci. *94*, 505–506.
KUSHMAN, L. J., and POPE, D. T. 1970. Changes in pH and total acidity of sweetpotatoes exposed to wet, cold soil conditions before harvest. HortScience *5*, 510–511.
KUSHMAN, L. J., and POPE, D. T. 1972. Causes of pithiness in sweetpotatoes. N. Carolina Agr. Expt. Sta. Tech. Bull. *207*.
KUSHMAN, L. J., POPE, D. T., and MONROE, R. J. 1966. Estimation of intercellular space and specific gravity of five varieties of sweetpotatoes. N. Carolina Agr. Expt. Sta. Tech. Bull. *175*.
LUTZ, J. M. 1945. Chilling injury of cured and non-cured Porto Rico sweetpotatoes. U.S. Dept. Agr. Circ. *729*.
McCLURE, T. T. 1959. Rhizopus decay of sweetpotatoes as affected by chilling, recuring, and hydrowarming after storage. Phytopathology *49*, 359–361.
PATERSON, D. R., SPEIGHTS, D. E., and HORNE, C. W. 1967. Causes of

handling injury and breakdown of sweetpotato roots. Texas Agr. Expt. Sta. Misc. Publ. *840*.

RAMSEY, G. B., FRIEDMAN, B. A., and SMITH, M. A. 1959. Market diseases of beets, chicory, endive, escarole, globe artichokes, lettuce, rhubarb, spinach, and sweetpotatoes. U.S. Dept. Agr. Handbook *155*.

ROSE, D. H., and WRIGHT, R. C. 1944. Freezing injury of fruits and vegetables. U.S. Dept. Agr. Circ. *713*.

WHITEMAN, T. M. 1957. Freezing points of fruits, vegetables, and florists stocks. U.S. Dept. Agr. Mktg. Res. Rept. *196*.

Yams

COURSEY, D. G. 1968. Low temperature injury in yams. J. Food Technol. *3*, 143–150.

20

Protection During Wholesale and Retail Distribution

The most conscientious and tender care provided for fresh produce at harvest, in the packinghouse, in storage, and during transit does not, unfortunately, guarantee that high quality vegetables and melons will be available to the ultimate consumer. Careful handling and optimum environments are largely wasted if vegetables are carelessly handled and exposed to unfavorable temperatures and humidities during the 3 to 10 days required for movement through wholesale and retail channels.

Maintenance of the garden-fresh quality, which today's shopper demands, requires the best possible protection at each step of the complex marketing structure.

HANDLING AT WHOLESALE

Wholesaling of perishable products involves receipt, unloading, and warehousing of van or rail shipments, and subsequent distribution of the products to retail stores. The wholesaler may provide fresh produce to independent grocers and supermarkets within a radius of several hundred miles or, as a chain store supplier, serve as a distribution warehouse under the management and operation of the chain store organization. In either case, the distribution of a carload or truckload of fresh produce may involve as much as a week for the more perishable items and several weeks for hardier items, such as potatoes. Under these circumstances, some refrigerated space is essential for maintenance of product quality.

Facilities at Wholesale

In planning new facilities for a wholesale or chain store distribution warehouse, a number of factors other than protection of the products handled must be considered. Planning should begin with the type of handling equipment to be used. Room design, ceiling heights, floor strengths, and many other factors will be related to choice of handling equipment. Most modern warehouses use power forklift trucks for materials handling, but other types of full-powered, semi-powered, and manually operated equipment are available, and may be entirely practical for the smaller-volume operations.

Other items which must be considered in designing the wholesale warehouse are: (1) direct flow of commodities by location of aisles, doors, and storage areas so that produce received by truck or rail can be moved to storage or packaging areas in the shortest possible distance; (2) platform widths and heights and arrangements of storage and work areas to permit maximum utilization of handling equipment; (3) quality protection of the products by providing insulated, refrigerated rooms with properly designed and located air circulation equipment; and (4) provision for safety and comfort of employees by adequate lighting, safety guards on equipment, and unobstructed passages for foot traffic. Some excellent guides for layout and design for wholesale produce warehouses, with modification for adaptation to climatic conditions in three different areas of the United States, are available in Marketing Research Report *467* (Bogardus 1961).

A study of wholesale markets in Boston (Karitas and Volz 1974) indicates that substantial cost savings occurred when wholesale facilities were moved from crowded urban areas to the New England Produce Center. Old, scattered, often inefficient facilities, were replaced in 1970 with modern facilities. An average saving of $6.53 per 1000 kg ($5.93 per ton) of produce handled resulted from improved labor productivity, adoption of better handling methods, and the use of mechanized handling equipment.

Transferring produce from wholesale storage to retail stores can be done economically by palletizing in the wholesale storage, and using forklift units for loading and unloading. However, the use of pallets for transfer is limited to those retail stores which have facilities for handling them. Manual loading and unloading of the transfer trucks is the most costly method, and the use of mobile carts for shipment was intermediate between palletization and manual handling (Schaffer and Steckler 1974).

Refrigeration Requirements

Many of the older wholesale produce warehouses have only one general purpose refrigerated room. Temperature in such a storage area is usually maintained at a compromise between the 0° C (32° F) needed for leafy vegetables and the 10° C (50° F) or higher desirable for chilling-sensitive vegetables such as cucumbers, sweet peppers, and sweetpotatoes. Since the compromise at 4.5° to 7° C (40° to 45° F) is suitable for neither type of produce, the obvious alternative is separate storage rooms for those products requiring low temperature and those for which intermediate temperatures are best.

Coop (1976) states that probably the greatest problem in wholesale warehouses is inadequate temperature control for maintenance of good shelf-life in fresh fruits and vegetables. He indicates that those warehouses using 5° to 7° C (40° to 45° F) for all fresh produce are not doing an adequate job of quality control. He suggests that the industry work toward reducing the temperature to just above freezing for leafy vegetables and all others which are not subject to chilling injury.

The quality of many green and leafy vegetables is best maintained throughout marketing by the generous use of crushed ice in and around the package. Consequently some produce wholesalers maintain a wet cold storage area at about 0° C (32° F) in addition to a so-called "dry" cold storage at the same temperature. Such vegetables as cabbage, spinach, green peas, and celery are held in wet storage. This may involve only the original package ice or the spreading of crushed ice over the stacked containers. In either case, RH in the wet room should be continuously at 95% or above. Relative humidity in the "dry" room should be maintained at 90% or above to prevent wilting of such items as mushrooms, summer squash, and vacuum-cooled lettuce. Essentially the only difference between the "dry" and "wet" storage areas is the absence of crushed ice and free water in the former. With the present tendency toward fiberboard containers, hydrocooling before packaging, or vacuum cooling after packaging, the need for a separate 0° C (32° F) wet storage is questionable. The small-volume wholesaler is hardly justified in the added investment and even some of the larger wholesale and chain store distribution warehouses operate satisfactorily with only one category of low temperature storage.

A separate storage area operated at about 10° C (50° F) is essential for satisfactory holding of chilling-sensitive products, such as eggplant, cucumbers, sweet peppers, okra and others. This area is also desirable for extending the market life of less perishable items, such as potatoes, dry onions, and Honey Dew melons. Relative humidity in this intermediate temperature area should be maintained at 80% or above, which probably will require the addition of some moisture by floor wetting or mechanical humidifiers.

Bogardus and Lutz (1961) have published recommended temperatures and conditions for maintaining quality of fresh produce in the wholesale warehouse.

Tomato Ripening

A major function of some wholesale produce houses is the sorting, ripening and distribution of tomatoes. The harvesting of "vine-ripe" tomatoes has increased gradually in the 1970s, but a major part of U.S. field-grown tomatoes for fresh market is harvested as mature-greens. A few tomato growing areas, notably Florida, are treating mature-green tomatoes with ethylene to initiate the ripening process before shipment to market. The U.S. standard for tomatoes defines mature as "having reached the stage of development which will insure a proper completion of the ripening process, and that the contents of two or more seed cavities have developed a jelly-like consistency and the seeds are well developed." However, handling practices after harvest are critical for good ripened quality, so harvest at the defined mature-green stage does not in itself guarantee good quality.

Mature-green tomatoes should be transported to market at 13° to 18.5° C (55° to 65° F). In this temperature range ripening will occur, and during transit periods of five days or more some fruits will be showing some pink or red color at arrival at the market. The receiver may be a service wholesaler, a chain store distribution warehouse, or repacking specialist. Whatever the market destination, the tomatoes are usually sorted into color classes at arrival. After preliminary sorting all fruits not ready for immediate repacking are placed in a ripening room.

Optimum ripening environments, and methods for accelerating or retarding ripening of tomatoes, are discussed in Chapter 8. The wholesaler must be knowledgeable in all phases of tomato handling, ripening and packaging to be a successful middleman with this temperamental crop.

Consumer Packaging

Packaging of fresh produce in consumer units is done at all marketing levels from the origin packer to the retail store. Where the product is packaged depends largely on the nature of the product and the costs of such items as labor and facilities. Practically all carrots are retailed in plastic film bags holding 0.5 to 1 kg (1 or 2 lb). These are invariably packaged at point of production because packaging in small units follows logically after topping, washing and hydrocooling; because of weight reduction for transportation; and because the packaged product has a long market life when given continuous refrigeration. On the other hand, the packaging of tomatoes in consumer units is done entirely at or near the terminal market. This is because most field-grown tomatoes require some ripening before retail display, and must be ripened before packaging to obtain reasonable uniformity within the consumer package.

Large volumes of potatoes and dry onions are sold in consumer units, usually paper, mesh, or plastic film bags containing from 1 to 4.5 kg (2 to 10 lb). These products are consumer-packed at all levels from point of production to retail store, but terminal repackers, wholesale warehouses, and chain store distributors package vast quantities, particularly in large urban markets. Packaging at or near the terminal market decreases the chance of product deterioration in the retail store. With mechanization and automation of packaging equipment, the generally higher hourly wages for labor at the terminal market become less important in the per-unit cost of repacking.

Receiving Produce for Repacking

Most of the produce received at wholesale and chain store warehouses is in conventional shipping containers. Burlap or mesh bags are widely used for potatoes and onions. Wirebound veneer crates, wooden boxes, or fiberboard cartons of various sizes are common for tomatoes, celery, artichokes, and other products having net product weights from 18 to 45 kg (40 to 100 lb). When these products are to be repacked at wholesale level, the unloading, dumping, and often disposition of these conventional shipping containers is costly. The most efficient and economical methods of handling shipping containers in wholesale warehouses are discussed by Bogardus and Ferris (1961).

Larger shipping containers for produce intended for terminal repacking are increasingly being considered and tested. Bulk shipment, whether in pallet bins or bulk rail cars or trucks, has great possibilities for cost reduction. Substantial savings are possible in container costs and in labor for loading and unloading (Shaffer 1970). Problems remain in the return of empty bulk bins, and the loading and unloading of bulk cars and trucks, but the growth of bulk handling of produce for repacking appears certain. See also Chapters 13 and 14.

Sorting and Packaging Equipment

A great variety of fine equipment is available for repacking produce into consumer-size units. This ranges from automatic box or bin dumpers, sorting belts, product sizers, and conveyors to automatic scales and bag fillers, tray wrappers and sealers, and heat tunnels for shrinking plastic film. Much of the commercial equipment is automated to an extent that few attendants are required. Detailed description of equipment presently used in wholesale warehouses is published (Shaffer 1970; Karitas 1969). Improvements and changes in equipment constantly occur, so that what is modern today may be obsolete tomorrow. For that reason, no detailed descriptions of repacking equipment are given here.

Loading Out Packaged Produce   Containers for shipment of consumer-packaged produce from the wholesale warehouse to the retail store vary from salvaged shipping containers to returnable thermoplastic boxes which can be nested when empty for compact storage or transport. Several salvage containers are commonly used for delivery to the retail store. The wooden celery box is favored for 1.5 kg (3 lb) bags of onions, and the 24 doz corrugated egg carton for 2.2 and 4.5 kg (5 and 10 lb) bags of potatoes. However, any reasonably sturdy shipping container may be used for delivery, and is often reused 3 or 4 times before discard. The reluctance to discard such containers often causes them to be kept in use after they have been damaged to the point of injuring bagged produce.

Lightweight thermoplastic or fiberglass containers, which nest when empty, are now available. These will last from 3 to 5 years, and are much less likely to damage the packaged produce. Various types of bails or hinged lugs keep the product from bearing the load of stacked containers. Fully returnable wood containers are also used. If these are to be handled manually, size and weight must be kept within manageable limits. Pallet bins are sometimes used for delivery. These are advantageous for moving high-volume items to large stores which have receiving docks and forklift equipment for handling pallets within the store. Bins which are light in weight and collapsible facilitate handling of the empties (Shaffer 1970).

HANDLING AT RETAIL

The retail store is the last link in a long chain of handlers of fresh produce. This is the only place where the consumer has direct contact with the handler of fresh vegetables and melons. If the retail store offers sound and attractive fresh produce, benefits and profits can be reflected all the way back to the original producer. By the same token, unattractive and out of-condition produce in the retail store can cause direct or indirect losses throughout the distribution chain.

In a typical food market, produce accounts for 8 to 12% of the store's sales volume. It usually ranks just below the grocery and meat departments in volume of sales, but because of the perishability of fresh produce, the handling margin is the highest in the store.

The fresh vegetables displayed at retail are often near the end of a long lifeline that began with harvest, perhaps thousands of miles away, and continued through sorting, packing, transport, and sometimes storage. If the chain of refrigeration has been continuous and careful handling has prevailed at each step, the retailer receives sound, salable products. He can do much to protect this quality while it is in his charge.

Maintenance of Quality

Total effort in protecting the quality of produce at retail involves careful handling of containers at unloading and transfer to holding or display areas; trimming some items to enhance appearance and remove inedible parts; display at temperatures and humidity conditions appropriate for the product; constant attention to displays for rotation and replacement; and protection of highly perishable items during nonsales hours.

Unloading and Receiving   If the store has a loading dock, produce can be handled most efficiently by continuous palletization from the wholesale warehouse (Fig. 20.1) to the retail storage or work area. Unloading at stores without a dock is most efficiently done by using wheeled skids with an average capacity of 20 cases. Belt and roller conveyors can be advantageously used when produce is moved directly from the wholesale delivery truck to a refrigerated holding room. Collapsible racks on skids are useful for transferring watermelons, and consumer-bagged potatoes or onions. The same racks can also be used for displaying melons or bagged items (Shaffer and Anderson 1956).

Trimming for Display   Trimming of leafy vegetables before display involves removing damaged outer surfaces, trimming the butt to remove discolored tissue, and, in some cases, removing excess wrapper leaves so that the product can be seen better. Trimming effort usually represents about $1/6$ of total labor in the produce department.

Since trimming constantly involves personal judgment, it does not

From Bogardus and Burt (1959)

FIG. 20.1.   TYPICAL LOADING OF PALLETIZED MIXED PRODUCE IN TRUCK
FOR DELIVERY TO RETAIL STORE

lend itself to mechanization. It is a manual operation so the training of
personnel for the job is critical to success, as is the provision of adequate
space, convenient tables and sinks, sharp knives, and efficient disposal
of waste materials. A detailed study of produce trimming operations in
four supermarkets showed that employee time devoted to actual trimming varied from about 52% at the worst to 66% at the most efficient
operation. The remaining time was used in opening and setting up
containers, handling salvage and garbage, and cleanup (Anderson and
Shaffer 1964).

Facilities and Layout

The principles of design and layout for retail produce facilities are
well established and have been discussed in detail by Anderson *et al*.
(1963). Since these are primarily matters of operating efficiency and
cost control rather than product protection, only those aspects related to
product quality will be discussed.

Protective Facilities and Methods   The fact that most fresh produce
requires continuous refrigeration is now generally accepted by retailers. All of the chain food stores and supermarkets display the more
perishable vegetables in refrigerated cases. In addition, all except the
smallest food stores have walk-in refrigerated space in the back room for

display replenishment and carryover. Mechanically refrigerated display cases are widely used, but small neighborhood stores, with only a few produce items, cannot always justify the investment in mechanical refrigeration. These stores either provide no refrigeration or use crushed ice or water misting to extend display life for wet produce.

Mechanically Refrigerated Cases   Fresh produce must be prominently displayed in the food store for two reasons: (1) good produce, well displayed, provides the most attractive area of the food store, and constitutes a major drawing card for a store; (2) vegetables and melons are often impulse purchase items which would be overlooked without prominent display.

The aesthetic features of produce display are not related to quality maintenance, so we will not discuss them here. However, it has been repeatedly demonstrated that eye-pleasing arrangements of contrasting or blending colors and textures attract customers and increase sales.

Many types of mechanically refrigerated display cases are used for fresh produce. These include open and closed convection (gravity air flow) and forced-air circulation types. The protection provided by open, convection-type cases depends upon the depth of the case and the distance of the produce from the evaporator coils. High temperatures occur in upper layers when produce is piled high in these cases. The products should never be piled above the top front edge of the open convection-type case. False racks should never be placed in an open case since this raises the produce above the desirable temperature level. Lewis (1957) found average product temperatures of 15.5° C (60° F) in an open case with the produce raised on a false rack, whereas average temperatures were a satisfactory 6° C (43° F) when the same quantity of produce was piled on the built-in rack. Stacking of produce on the rack must be such that air can flow freely.

An effective type of forced-air refrigerated case has fans which circulate air past evaporator coils beneath or behind the produce racks and then over and through the produce (Fig. 20.2). The air returns through ducts to the refrigerated coils where it is recooled and recirculated. This type of air movement permits higher, more prominent position of produce in the open case. However, air flow over the produce will cause some wilting of leafy vegetables if the velocity is high. This can be minimized by sprinkling the produce with water several times each day.

Another type of mechanically refrigerated case is the so-called air curtain unit. This is an open display case of conventional appearance but unique air circulation (Fig. 20.3). Refrigeration is supplied within the case by conventional evaporator coils. Air exchange between the

Courtesy of Hussmann Refrigeration, Inc.

FIG. 20.2.   DOUBLE DECK MECHANICALLY-REFRIGERATED DISPLAY CASE WITH FORCED-AIR CIRCULATION UNDER, THROUGH, AND OVER THE PRODUCE

case and store air is essentially prevented by a current of air which moves at an angle downward across the open face of the cabinet. Some air flows from the back of the display case under and through the produce. The remaining air is forced up behind the reflecting mirror, flows out over the top, and returns to the bottom of the case as an air curtain over the display. Visibility and accessibility of the produce are excellent as it can be stacked higher than in display cases without forced air or air movement only below the product.

Nonrefrigerated Display Cases   Some vegetables and melons are not sufficiently perishable to require refrigeration during retail display periods. Among these items are mature potatoes, dry onions, winter squash, and Honey Dew melons. Display cases without refrigeration or mass displays in the original containers are satisfactory for these products (Fig. 20.4). Most retail food stores are now air-conditioned so that product temperatures seldom exceed 21° C (70° F) in nonrefrigerated displays.

Courtesy of The Warren Co.

FIG. 20.3.   MECHANICALLY-REFRIGERATED RETAIL DISPLAY CASE WITH CURTAIN OF COLD AIR FLOWING ABOVE THE DISPLAYED PRODUCE TO PREVENT AIR EXCHANGE

Display of Prepackaged Items   Many of the supermarkets and large chain stores display only prepackaged or unitized vegetables. Such easily damaged products as asparagus, broccoli, and celery hearts are often bunched or banded in 0.5 to 1 kg (1 or 2 lb) units for protection and convenience of price marking. Others, such as green beans, Brussels sprouts, and tomatoes, are commonly displayed in cups, baskets or overwrapped trays. Lettuce and cauliflower are simply overwrapped with permeable or ventilated plastic film. The protection provided by prepackaging varies from product to product, but, at best, provides protection only against moisture loss and customer-handling damage. These products which require refrigeration when displayed in bulk must also be refrigerated when displayed in consumer packages. Vegetables which are packaged "kitchen-ready," such as shredded cabbage, shelled limas, and prepeeled products, are more perishable than the whole product and require constant refrigeration near 0° C (32° F) (Alexander and Francis 1964).

Courtesy of Hussmann Refrigeration, Inc.

FIG. 20.4. AN EFFECTIVE RETAIL DISPLAY OF REFRIGERATED AND NON-REFRIGERATED PRODUCE

Most food stores offer both bulk and prepackaged vegetables in the produce displays. Consumer acceptance studies with a number of fresh produce items have shown that total sales are greater when both bulk and packaged products are available. The stores which offer only prepackaged produce are willing to sacrifice some sales for time savings at the check-out counter derived from prepricing, and the reduction in losses from customer handling of bulk produce.

REFERENCES

Wholesale

BOE, A. A., and SALUNKHE, D. K. 1967. Ripening tomatoes: ethylene, oxygen, and light treatments. Econ. Botany *21*, 312–319.
BOGARDUS, R. K. 1961. Wholesale fruit and vegetable warehouses. Guides for layout and design. U.S. Dept. Agr. Mktg. Res. Rept. *467*.

BOGARDUS, R. K., and BURT, S. W. 1959. Loading out fruits and vegetables in wholesale warehouses. U.S. Dept. Agr. Mktg. Res. Rept. *282*.

BOGARDUS, R. K., and FERRIS, R. T. 1961. Receiving fruits and vegetables in wholesale warehouses. U.S. Dept. Agr. Mktg. Res. Rept. *478*.

BOGARDUS, R. K., and LUTZ, J. M. 1961. Maintaining the fresh quality in produce in wholesale warehouses. U.S. Dept. Agr., Agr. Mktg. *6*, No. 12, 8–9.

CEPONIS, M. J., and BUTTERFIELD, J. E. 1973. The nature and extent of retail and consumer losses in apples, oranges, lettuce, peaches, strawberries and potatoes marketed in greater New York. U.S. Dept. Agr. Mktg. Res. Rept. *996*.

CLOSE, E. G., VARICK, J., and RISSE, L. A. 1971. Comparative methods of handling watermelons—bulk and cartons. Florida Dept. Agr. and U.S. Dept. Agr. *MA 1–71*.

COOP, F. A. 1976. A close look at produce warehousing. The Packer, Annual Review and Outlook Issue—Focus 76–77, 72–73.

KARITAS, J. J. 1969. Packaging produce in trays at the central warehouse. U.S. Dept. Agr. Mktg. Res. Rept. *827*.

KARITAS, J. J., and VOLZ, M. D. 1974. Selected costs of produce wholesaling in old and modern facilities, Boston, Mass. U.S. Dept. Agr. *ARS-NE-50*.

MALLISON, E. D., and SPALDING, D. H. 1966. Use of ozone in tomato ripening rooms. U.S. Dept. Agr. *ARS 52-17*.

MEYER, C. H. 1963. Tomato repacking methods and equipment. U.S. Dept. Agr. Mktg. Res. Rept. *597*.

PARSONS, C. S., and ANDERSON, R. E. 1970. Progress on controlled-atmosphere storage of tomatoes, peaches, and nectarines. *In* United Fresh Fruit and Vegetable Association Yearbook. pp. 175–176, 179–182. United Fresh Fruit and Vegetable Assoc., Washington, D.C.

SEELIG, R. A., and McCOLLOCH, L. P. 1969. Toward better tomatoes. *In* United Fresh Fruit and Vegetable Association Yearbook. pp. 170, 173–174, 176, 178, 180, 182, 185–186, 188, 190, 193–194, 196–198, 200, 202, 205. United Fresh Fruit and Vegetable Assoc., Washington, D.C.

SHAFFER, P. F. 1970. Packaging produce at the central warehouse. U.S. Dept. Agr. Mktg. Res. Rept. *721*.

SHAFFER, P. F., and STECKLER, D. M. 1974. Comparative methods of handling produce from warehouse slots to holding areas of retail stores. U.S. Dept. Agr. *ARS-NE-49*.

WORTHINGTON, J. T., PENNEY, R. W., and YEATMAN, J. N. 1969. Evaluation of light source and temperature on tomato color development during ripening. HortScience *4*, 64–65.

Retail

ALEXANDER, B., and FRANCIS, F. J. 1964. Packaging and storage of pre-peeled rutabagas. Proc. Am. Soc. Hort. Sci. *85*, 457–464.

ANDERSON, D. L., and SHAFFER, P. F. 1964. Improved methods of trimming produce in retail food stores. U.S. Dept. Agr. Mktg. Res. Rept. *192*.

ANDERSON, D. L., SHAFFER, P. F., KARITAS, J. J., and FLYNN, G. 1963. Principles of layout for retail produce operations. U.S. Dept. Agr. Mktg. Res. Rept. *590*.

ANDERSON, D. L., SHAFFER, P. F., and VOLZ, M. D. 1962. Improved methods of displaying and handling produce in retail food stores. U.S. Dept. Agr. Mktg. Res. Rept. *551*.

ASHRAE. 1974. Retail foodstore refrigeration. ASHRAE Handbook Product Direct. Applications *49*, 49.1–49.10.

ASHRAE. 1975. Retail foodstore refrigeration equipment. ASHRAE Handbook Product Direct. Equipment *35*, 35.1–35.6

LEWIS, W. E. 1957. Maintaining produce quality in retail stores. U.S. Dept. Agr. Handbook *117*.

O'NEILL, B. 1976. UPC computerized checkout system increases supermarket efficiency. The Packer, Annual Review and Outlook Issue—Focus 76–77. 119–120.

SHAFFER, P. F., and ANDERSON, D. L. 1956. Unloading and receiving produce in retail food stores. U.S. Dept. Agr. Mktg. Res. Rept. *129*.

SHAFFER, P. F., ANDERSON, D. L., WISCHKAEMPER, P., and KARITAS, J. J. 1958. Packaging and price-marking produce in retail food stores. U.S. Dept. Agr. Mktg. Res. Rept. *278*.

Appendix

PART 1. CONVERSION FACTORS AND EQUIVALENTS

Energy and Related Units

kcal × 3.97 = Btu
Btu × 252 = cal
cal × 1000 = kcal
Btu/lb × 0.55 = cal/g
cal/kg-hr × 86.8 = Btu/ton-day
mg CO_2/kg-hr × 2.55 = cal/kg-hr

Length

cm × 0.394 = in.
m × 3.28 = ft
in. × 2.54 = cm
ft × 0.305 = m
mil (1/1000 in.) × 0.0254 = mm

Mass and Related Units

kg × 2.205 = lb
lb × 0.454 = kg
oz × 28.3 = g
lb/cu ft × 0.016 = g/cu cm

Pressure

1 atm − 760 mm mercury = 29.9 in. mercury
    = 103,300 mm water = 407 in. water
millibar (mb) × 1.02 = g/sq cm; is equivalent to a column of mercury
    0.74 mm or 0.03 in. high; 1000 mb = 1 bar

Temperature

$^\circ$ C = ($^\circ$ F − 32) × 5/9; 1° C = 1.8° F
$^\circ$ F = ($^\circ$ C × 9/5) + 32; 1° F = 0.56° C
(Also see Fig. A.1.)

Fractional Degrees

$^\circ$ C		$^\circ$ F
0.06	0.1	0.18
0.11	0.2	0.36
0.17	0.3	0.54
0.22	0.4	0.72
0.28	0.5	0.90
0.33	0.6	1.08
0.39	0.7	1.26
0.44	0.8	1.44
0.50	0.9	1.62

Volume and Related Factors

liter × 1.06 = qt (U.S.)
liter × 0.881 = qt (Imp.)
gal. (U.S.) × 3.78 = liters
gal. (Imp.) × 4.546 = liters
cu m × 35.3 = cu ft
cu ft × 0.0283 = cu m
bushel (U.S.) × 35.2 = liters
bushel (U.K.) × 36.4 = liters
cu ft/min × 472 = cu cm/sec
cu ft/min-sq ft × 5080 = cu cm/sec-sq m

Refrigerants and Refrigeration

Ton (U.S.) refrigeration × 288,000 = Btu/day
Ton (U.S.) refrigeration × 72,576 = kcal/day

Ice, Dry (Solid CO_2)
Weight-volume: 500 g solid = 0.27 cu m gas at 21° C; 1 lb solid = 8.7 cu ft gas at 70° F; both at 1 atm pressure. Sublimation temperature: −88° C (−190° F)

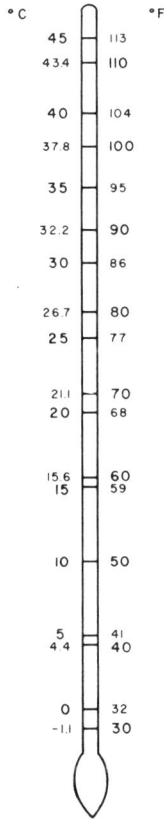

FIG. A.1. THERMOMETER FOR READY INTERCONVERSION OF ° C and ° F, FOR 5° C AND 10° F INTERVALS, RESPECTIVELY

	Cal/g	Btu/lb
Heat absorbed during sublimation	136	247
Heat absorbed from −88° to 2° C		
(−190° to 35° F)	16	29
Total heat absorbed to 2° C (35° F)	152	276
Ice, Water.—Heat absorbed during melting	79	144

Nitrogen, Liquid
Liquid density: 810 kg/cu m (50.4 lb/cu ft)
Weight/liter: 800 g
Weight/gallon: 6.7 lb
Boiling point: −195° C (−320° F)

	Cal/g	Btu/lb
Heat absorbed during vaporization	47	86
Heat absorbed by vapor from −195° to −18° C (−320° to 0° F)	47	85
Heat absorbed by vapor from −18° to 21° C (0° to 70° F)	9	17
Total heat absorbed to 21° C (70° F)	103	188
Heat absorbed by vapor from −195° to 2° C (−320° to 35° F)	49	88
Heat absorbed from liquid at −195° C (−320° F) to vapor at 2° C (35° F)	97	174

Ethylene   1 kg = 0.862 cu m
1 lb = 13.8 cu ft

PART 2. DERIVATIONS AND CALCULATIONS

Derivation of Factor 220

For conversion from quantity of CO_2 (mg per kg-hr) produced during respiration to heat production in terms of Btu per ton-day:

During respiration 673 kcal of energy are released for every 264 g of CO_2 (6 moles) produced. Thus, 2.55 kcal are released per 1 g of CO_2. Converting to mg, we get 2.55 cal per mg, since 1 kcal = 1000 cal and 1 g = 1000 mg.

To get from cal to Btu, we note that 1 Btu = 252 cal. Thus, 2.55 cal = 0.0101 Btu, which is the energy released as 1 mg CO_2 is produced. Further, 1 ton (2000 lb) = 908 kg, and 1 day = 24 hr. Combining the above: 0.0101 × 908 × 24 = 220.

Derivation of Factor 61.2

For expressing mg CO_2 produced per kg-hr in terms of kcal per metric ton-day:

As noted in derivation of factor 220, 2.55 cal are released per mg CO_2. Thus, mg CO_2 per kg-hr × 2.55 = cal per kg-hr; since 1000 cal = 1 kcal, multiplication by the same factor yields kcal per 1000 kg-hr. Finally, 1 day = 24 hr, so that 2.55 × 24 = 61.2.

Note for both derivations: If CO_2 production is given in ml, observe that 1 ml CO_2 weighs 1.9 mg.

Calculation of Q_{10}

When rate (e.g., of respiration) is known, but when temperature difference is not 10° C:

Example 1   A vegetable produces CO_2 at the rate of 54 mg per kg-hr (R_1) when held at 59° F (t_1) and 86 mg per kg-hr (R_2) at 68° (t_2). What is the Q_{10}?

Solution   Convert ° F to ° C: 59° F = 15° C and 68° F = 20° C. Then:

$$Q_{10} = (R_2/R_1) \exp (10/t_2 - t_1)$$
$$= (86/54) \exp (10/20 - 15)$$
$$= 1.6 \exp 2$$
$$= 2.6$$

(Note that we use "exp" to denote exponent to simplify the arrangement: 1.6 exp 2 thus means 1.6 squared, or 3.0 exp ½ means square root of 3.0).

Example 2   Respiration rates as in Example 1, but t_1 is 60° F and t_2 is 71°.

Solution   Convert ° F to ° C: 60° F = 15.6° C and 70° F = 21.1° C. Then, since difference is neither 10° nor 5°, logarithms are used:

$$Q_{10} = (86/54) \exp (10/21.1 - 15.6)$$
$$= 1.6 \exp 1.8$$
$$\log Q_{10} = 1.8 \log 1.6$$
$$= 1.8 \times 0.204$$
$$= 0.367$$
$$Q_{10} = \text{antilog of } 0.367$$
$$= 2.33$$

Calculation of Rate

When Q_{10} is known, but when temperature difference is not 10° C.

Example 3   A vegetable produces CO_2 at the rate of 15 mg per kg-hr (R_1) at 32° F (t_1). The Q_{10} is 3.0. What is the rate at 41°?

Solution   Convert ° F to ° C: 32° F = 0° C and 41° F = 5° C. Then:

$$Q_{10} = (R_2/R_1) \exp (10/t_2 - t_1)$$
$$3.0 = (R_2/15) \exp (10/5 - 0)$$
$$= (R_2/15) \exp 2$$
$$3.0 \exp \tfrac{1}{2} = R_2/15$$
$$R_2 = 15 (3.0 \exp \tfrac{1}{2})$$
$$= 26 \text{ mg } CO_2 \text{ per kg-hr}$$

Example 4   Respiration rate and Q_{10} as in Example 3, but t_1 is 32° F and t_2 is 43°.

Solution   Convert ° F to ° C: 32° F = 0° C and 43° F = 6.1° C. Then, since difference is neither 10° nor 5°, logarithms are used:

$$
\begin{aligned}
3.0 &= (R_2/15) \text{ exp } (10/6.1-0) \\
&= (R_2/15) \text{ exp } 1.6 \\
R_2/15 &= 3.0 \text{ exp } 1/1.6 \\
\log R_2/15 &= 1/1.6 \times \log 3.0 \\
&= 0.477/1.6 \\
&= 0.298 \\
R_2/15 &= \text{antilog of } 0.298 \\
&= 1.986 \\
R_2 &= 1.986 \times 15 \\
&= 29.8 \text{ mg } CO_2 \text{ per kg-hr}
\end{aligned}
$$

CALCULATION OF REFRIGERATION REQUIREMENT DURING HARVEST-PEAK-LOAD IN AN ON-FARM COLD STORAGE (Using British Units)

Problem

Cooling field-cured, fall onions to storage temperature of 32° F over a 15-day period. Cooling is begun when the first onions are placed in storage, and all must be at 32° 15 days after the start.

Conditions

(1) Average temperature of onions at harvest is 70° F.

(2) Pallet boxes are used for pickup after curing and for storage; 2-way pallets; boxes are 40 × 48 in., and 30 in. deep; average net weight of onions is 1200 lb per box; empty boxes weigh 80 lb.

(3) Harvest is at rate of 20 tons per day; 5 days required for filling each 100-ton capacity room.

(4) Two-room storage will require 10 days to fill. Room 1 is completely filled before Room 2 is started.

(5) Refrigeration is started in both rooms 2 days before onions are placed in either room.

(6) Onions in each room must be cooled to 45° in 5 days and to 32° in 10 days.

Facilities

Storage Building   (1) An insulated, mechanically-refrigerated, 2-room storage. Each room opens into a common packing shed, but there is no door between the storage rooms.
(2) Inside dimensions of each room: 24.5 × 32 ft, with a 14 ft ceiling.

Loading Pattern   (1) Pallet boxes are placed 7 × 3 to a layer, on each side of a 6 ft aisle for forklift operation.
(2) Each layer in a room contains 42 boxes.
(3) Boxes are stacked 4 high for a total height of 11 ft, 4 in. (box with pallet totals 34 in.). Space above load is 2 ft, 8 in.
(4) Total capacity of each room is 168 boxes, approximately 100 tons of onions. Total capacity of storage is 200 tons.
(5) A space of 12 in. is maintained along each 24.5 ft room side to permit airflow along the walls.

Refrigeration   (1) Each room has 3 ceiling-mounted blower-coil units. These are evenly spaced along a 24.5 ft outside wall in each room.
(2) Refrigerant for all blower-coil units is supplied from a central compressor-condenser system.
(3) Each cooling unit has a ½-hp fan for circulating air.
(4) Air is ducted from each unit to a point just beyond the work aisle.
(5) Air movement is over the stacked boxes, down the open space at the far wall, back through boxes and pallet openings, and return in the open space on the near wall.

Insulation   (1) Outside walls are insulated with 3 in. of polyurethane, k = 0.16. Mylar film outside of insulation serves as a vapor barrier.
(2) The floor has 4 in. slab polystyrene, laid on polyethylene sheets, and with 4 in. of reinforced concrete as a bearing floor, k = 0.2.
(3) The ceiling has 3 in. of loose mineral wool between the joists, k = 0.27.
(4) The solid partition between the rooms has 2 in. of fiberglass batts between the 2 × 4 studs of the bearing wall.

Calculations

Since only peak load is critical, the calculations for cooling will be for the period when Room 1 has been filled and is cooling from 45° to 32° F, and Room 2 is being filled, and the load is being cooled from 70° to 45° F.

Field or Sensible Heat, Room 1   200,000 (lb onions) × 3 (heat removal per day, ° F) × 0.9 (sp ht) = 540,000 Btu/day
168 pallet boxes at 80 lb = 13,440 lb
13,440 (lb wood) × 3 (removal per day, ° F) × 0.4 (sp ht) = 16,128 Btu/day

Field or Sensible Heat, Room 2   200,000 (lb onions) × 5 (heat removal per day, ° F) × 0.9 (sp ht) = 900,000 Btu/day
13,440 (lb wood) × 5 (removal per day, ° F) × 0.4 (sp ht) = 26,880 Btu/day

Heat Leakage-Transmission via Exposed Surfaces   Outside walls, 2 rooms, 2478 sq ft. 2478 (sq ft) × 0.0534 (U) × 20 (gradient inside-outside, ° F) × 24 (hr) = 63,516 Btu/day
Ceiling, 2 rooms, 1568 sq ft. 1568 (sq ft) × 0.0833 (U) × 25 (gradient, ° F) × 24 (hr) = 78,369 Btu-day
Floor, 2 rooms, 1568 sq ft. 1568 (sq ft) × 0.05 (U) × 15 (gradient, ° F) × 24 (hr) = 28,224 Btu/day

Air Exchange   8 changes per day during filling of Room 2.
10,976 (cu ft air) × 0.75 (Btu/cu ft) × 8 (air changes) = 65,856 Btu/day

Vital Heat, Room 1 (Avg Onion Temp 40°F)   700 (Btu/ton-day at 40°) × 100 (tons) = 70,000 Btu/day

Vital Heat, Room 2 (Avg Onion Temp 60°F)   2500 (Btu/ton-day at 60°) × 100 (tons) = 250,000 Btu/day

Miscellaneous Heat Loads During Filling of Room

Lights   1000 (wh) × 3.42 (Btu/wh) × 10 (hr) = 34,200 Btu/day

Forklift   1 × 4200 (Btu/hr) × 10 (hr) = 42,000 Btu/day

Labor   1 man for 10 hr: 950 (Btu/hr) × 10 (hr) = 9500 Btu/day

Unit Fan Operation, Continuous, 2 Rooms, 6 Units, ½-hp Each   3 (hp) × 2540 (Btu/hp/hr) × 24 (hr) = 182,880 Btu/day

Total Heat Load During Peak Demand	**Btu**
Room 1—Onions, sensible heat	540,000
Room 1—Bins, sensible heat	16,128
Room 2—Onions, sensible heat	900,000

Room 2—Bins, sensible heat 26,880
Heat leakage, walls 63,516
  ceiling 78,369
  floor 28,224
Air exchange, Room 2 65,856
Vital heat, Room 1 70,000
Vital heat, Room 2 250,000
Lights, Room 2 34,200
Forklift, Room 2 42,000
Labor, Room 2 9,500
Fan operation, 2 rooms 182,880
Total per day 2,307,553

$2{,}307{,}553 \div 288{,}000 = 8.0$ tons of refrigeration

Refrigeration Demand After Onions are Cooled to Average of 32° F (outside ambient average 50°)

Heat Leakage

Transmission via Exposed Surfaces.—Outside walls, 2478 sq ft. 2478 (sq ft) × 0.0534 (U) × 18 (gradient, ° F) × 24 (hr) = 57,164 Btu

Ceiling, 1568 sq ft. 1568 (sq ft) × 0.0833 (U) × 18 (gradient, ° F) × 24 (hr) = 56,425 Btu

Floor, 1568 sq ft. 1568 (sq ft) × 0.05 (U) × 10 (gradient, ° F) × 24 (hr) = 18,816 Btu

Air Leakage, 2 Changes per Day   21,952 (cu ft air) × 0.5 (Btu/cu ft*) × 2 (air changes) = 21,952 Btu

Vital Heat   600 (Btu/ton-day at 32°) × 200 (tons) = 120,000 Btu

Miscellaneous Heat Loads

Unit Fans (Avg operation 12 Hr/Day)   3 (hp) × 2540 (Btu/hp/hr) × 12 (hr) = 91,440 Btu

Total Heat Load After Cooling to Storage Temperature

	Btu
Heat leakage, walls	57,164
ceiling	56,425
floor	18,816
Air exchange	21,952

---

* At 50° F outside ambient.

Vital heat	120,000
Fan operation	91,440
Total per day	365,797

365,797 ÷ 288,000 = 1.27 tons of refrigeration

Recommendations   Under the conditions specified, about 8 tons of refrigeration is required during peak loads at harvest and room filling. For assurance of sufficient cooling capacity in seasons of unusually high product and ambient temperatures during harvest, 10 tons of refrigeration capacity should be provided.

Since the refrigeration load is low after initial product cooling, it would be advisable to have an 8 ton unit and a 2 ton unit. Both can be operated if needed at peak load. With decreasing load, only the 8 ton unit will be needed and, during late fall and winter, the 2 ton unit will provide ample refrigeration.

CALCULATION OF REFRIGERATION REQUIREMENT DURING HARVEST-PEAK-LOAD IN AN ON-FARM COLD STORAGE (Using Metric Units)

Problem

Cooling field-cured, fall onions to storage temperature of 0° C over a 15-day period. Cooling is begun when the first onions are placed in storage, and all must be at 0° C 15 days after the start.

Conditions

(1) Average temperature of onions at harvest is 20° C.

(2) Pallet boxes are used for pickup after curing and for storage; 2-way pallets; boxes are 100 × 120 cm, and 75 cm deep; average net weight of onions is 540 kg per box; empty boxes weigh 35 kg.

(3) Harvest is at rate of 18 metric tons per day; 5 days required for filling each 90 metric ton capacity room.

(4) Two-room storage will require 10 days to fill. Room 1 is completely filled before Room 2 is started.

(5) Refrigeration is started in both rooms 2 days before onions are placed in either room.

(6) Onions in each room must be cooled to 7° C in 5 days and to 0° C in 10 days.

Facilities

Storage Building   (1) An insulated, mechanically-refrigerated, 2-room storage. Each room opens into a common packing shed, but there is no door between the storage rooms.
(2) Inside dimensions of each room: 8 × 10 m, with a 4.5 m ceiling.

Loading Pattern   (1) Pallet boxes are placed 7 × 3 to a layer, on each side of a 2 m aisle for forklift operation.
(2) Each layer in a room contains 42 boxes.
(3) Boxes are stacked 4 high for a total height of 3.5 m (box with pallet totals 85 cm). Space above load is 1 m.
(4) Total capacity of each room is 168 boxes, approximately 90.8 metric tons of onions. Total capacity of storage is 181.6 metric tons.
(5) A space of 30 cm is maintained along each 10 m room side to permit airflow along the walls.

Refrigeration   (1) Each room has 3 ceiling-mounted blower-coil units. These are evenly spaced along an 8 m outside wall in each room.
(2) Refrigerant for all blower-coil units is supplied from a central compressor-condenser system.
(3) Each cooling unit has a ½ metric hp fan for circulating air.
(4) Air is ducted from each unit to a point just beyond the work aisle.
(5) Air movement is over the stacked boxes, down the open space at the far wall, back through boxes and pallet openings, and return in the open space on the near wall.

Insulation   (1) Outside walls are insulated with 8 cm of poly-urethane, k = 0.023 w/m° C. Mylar film outside of insulation serves as vapor barrier.
(2) The floor has 10 cm slab polystyrene, laid on polyethylene sheets, and with 10 cm of reinforced concrete above as a bearing floor, k = 0.029 w/m° C.
(3) The ceiling has 8 cm of loose mineral wool between the joists, k – 0.039 w/m° C.
(4) The solid partition between the rooms has 5 cm of fiberglass batts between the 2 × 4 studs of the bearing wall.

Calculations

Since only the peak load is critical, the calculations for cooling will be for the period when Room 1 has been filled and is cooling from 7° C to 0° C, and Room 2 is being filled, and the load is being cooled from 20° C to 7° C.

Field or Sensible Heat, Room 1   90,800 (kg onions) × 1.4 (heat removal per day, ° C) × 0.9 (sp ht) = 114,408 kcal/day
168 pallet boxes at 35 kg = 5880 kg
5880 (kg wood) × 1.4 (removal per day, ° C) × 0.4 (sp ht) = 3292 kcal/day

Field or Sensible Heat, Room 2   90,800 (kg onions) × 2.6 (heat removal per day, ° C) × 0.9 (sp ht) = 212,472 kcal/day
5880 (kg wood) × 2.6 (removal per day) × 0.4 (sp ht) = 6115 kcal/day

Heat Leakage-Transmission via Exposed Surfaces   Outside walls, 2 rooms, 252 sq m 252 (sq m) × 0.2474 (U) × 10 (gradient inside-outside, ° C) × 24 (hr) = 14,962 kcal/day
Ceiling, 2 rooms, 160 sq m 160 (sq m) × 0.4194 × 14 (gradient, ° C) × 24 (hr) = 22,549 kcal/day
Floor, 2 rooms, 160 sq m 160 (sq m) × 0.2495 (U) × 8 (gradient,° C) × 24 (hr) = 7665 kcal/day

Air Exchange   8 changes per day during filling of Room 2.
360 (cu m air) × 6.68 (kcal/cu m) × 8 (air changes) = 19,238 kcal/day

Vital Heat, Room 1 (Avg Onion Temp 4 °C)   194 (kcal/metric ton-day at 4° C) × 90.8 (metric tons) = 17,615 kcal/day

Vital Heat, Room 2 (Avg Onion Temp 16 °C)   695 (kcal/metric ton-day at 16° C) × 90.8 (metric tons) = 63,106 kcal/day

Miscellaneous Heat Loads During Filling of Room

Lights   1000 (w hr) × 0.8605 (kcal/w hr) × 10 (hr) = 8605 kcal/day

Forklift   1 × 1058 (kcal/hr) × 10 (hr) = 10,580 kcal/day

Labor   1 man for 10 hours: 239.4 (kcal/hr) × 10 (hr) = 2394 kcal/day

Unit Fan Operation, Continuous, 2 Rooms, 6 Units, ½ Metric hp

Each 3 (metric hp) × 633.14 (kcal/metric hp hr) × 24 (hr) = 45,586 kcal/day

Total Heat Load During Peak Demand

	kcal
Room 1—Onions, sensible heat	114,408
Room 1—Bins, sensible heat	3,292
Room 2—Onions, sensible heat	212,472
Room 2—Bins, sensible heat	6,115
Heat leakage, walls	14,962
ceiling	22,549
floor	7,665
Air exchange, Room 2	19,238
Vital heat, Room 1	17,615
Vital heat, Room 2	63,106
Lights, Room 2	8,605
Forklift, Room 2	10,580
Labor, Room 2	2,394
Fan operation, 2 rooms	45,586
Total per day	548,587

548,587 ÷ 24 = 22,857 frigories of refrigeration
or = 7.6 tons of refrigeration

Refrigeration Demand After Onions are Cooled to Average of 0° C (outside ambient average 10° C)

Heat Leakage

Transmission via Exposed Surfaces Outside walls, 252 sq m. 252 (sq m) × 0.2474 (U) × 10 (gradient, ° C) × 24 (hr) = 14,962 kcal/day
Ceiling, 160 sq m. 160 (sq m) × 0.4194 (U) × 10 (gradient, ° C) × 24 (hr) = 16,104 kcal/day
Floor, 160 sq m. 160 (sq m) × 0.2495 (U) × 6 (gradient, ° C) × 24 (hr) = 5748 kcal/day

Air Leakage, 2 Changes per Day 720 (cu m air) × 4.45 (kcal/cu m) × 2 (air changes) = 6408 kcal/day

Vital Heat 166.8 (kcal/metric ton-day at 0° C) × 181.6 (metric tons) = 30,291 kcal/day

Miscellaneous Heat Loads

Unit Fans (Avg Operation 12 Hr/Day) 3 (metric hp) × 633.14 (kcal/metric hp/hr) × 12 (hr) = 22,793 kcal/day

Total Heat Load After Cooling to Storage Temperature

	kcal
Heat leakage, walls	14,962
ceiling	16,104
floor	5,748
Air exchange	6,408
Vital heat	30,291
Fan operation	22,793
Total per day	96,306

96,306 ÷ 24 = 4012 frigories of refrigeration
          or = 1.3 tons of refrigeration

Recommendations   Under the conditions specified, about 8 tons of refrigeration is required during peak loads at harvest and room filling. For assurance of sufficient cooling capacity in seasons of unusually high product and ambient temperatures during harvest, 10 tons of refrigeration should be provided.

Since the refrigeration load is low after initial product cooling, it would be advisable to have an 8 ton unit and a 2 ton unit. Both can be operated if needed at peak load. With decreasing load, only the 8 ton unit will be needed and during late fall and winter, the 2 ton unit will provide ample refrigeration.

PART 3. RELATIVE HUMIDITY

Calculations

Relative humidity can be determined in various ways. The most fundamental methods employ equations based on the vapor pressure of water at various temperatures:

$$\%RH = (VP/SVP)_T \times 100$$

where VP = water vapor pressure of air at temperature T, and SVP = water vapor pressure of saturated air at temperature T (after Szulmayer 1969). Or

$$\%RH = 100 \, [(VPD/SVP) + 1]$$

where VPD = vapor pressure deficit (after Williams and Léger 1967).

Practical Determination

The most common method for determining RH utilizes the fact that the degree of evaporation of moisture from a free water surface depends on the quantity of water vapor in the space around the water surface at a given temperature. The evaporation of the water requires energy, and this energy is derived from the water that remains, which thus is cooled. If the reservoir of water is a wet wick around the bulb of a thermometer (the "wet-bulb"), the degree of cooling can be measured and the resultant temperature can be compared with that of a dry thermometer (the "dry-bulb"). The difference between these two, the wet-bulb depression, can then be related to RH. Since the calculations are rather cumbersome, tables and slide rules have been prepared for ready determination of RH from wet-bulb depression readings. These values vary with atmospheric pressure, but for most practical purposes this influence is negligible in the range of 630 to 760 mm (25 to 30 in.) of mercury. These pressures correspond to altitudes of 1525 m (5000 ft) and sea level, respectively.

The principles noted are applied by means of the wet- and dry-bulb hygrometer, which, in practice, most commonly is a sling psychrometer (Fig. A.2). Whirling the instrument through the air with a circular motion lowers the temperature of the wet-bulb due to the evaporation of water, but does not affect the dry-bulb reading. The RH corresponding to the wet-bulb depression is then read on a chart or slide rule, as noted earlier. If the readings from this instrument are to be useful, certain precautions must be followed, as described by Marvin (1941) and Szulmayer (1969):

(1) Use a white and clean "sock" for the wet-bulb that covers the bulb and the lower portion of the thermometer stem. Muslin, a double or triple layer of cheesecloth, or a white shoelace are satisfactory, but the sizing in all fabrics must be washed out before use.

(2) Use only distilled water.

(3) Ventilate the bulbs at a rate of at least 4.5 m (15 ft) per sec.

(4) Keep out of sun and away from cold or warm surfaces.

(5) Sling the instrument for 15 to 20 sec and quickly take a reading. Repeat this procedure until two readings are nearly identical, thus assuring that the lowest temperature has been reached.

If the above suggestions have been adhered to and if the thermometers are precise to within 0.1° C (about 0.2° F), the measured value can be the true value ± 1% RH. However, in most cases, the error will be at least twice as great, and neglect of any one of the precautions can easily render the readings useless.

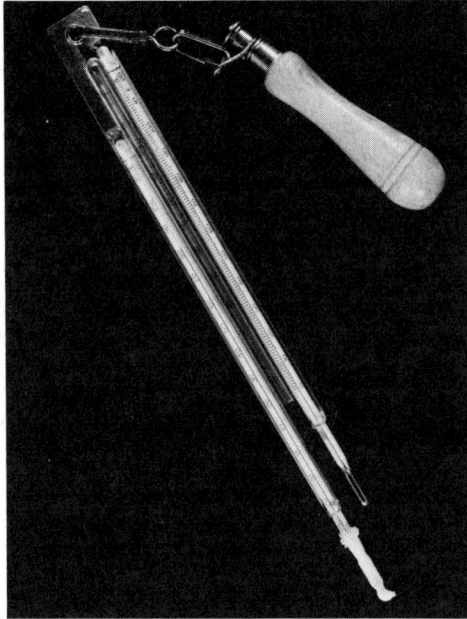

FIG. A.2.   SLING PSYCHROMETER

Tables relating wet-bulb and dry-bulb readings and vapor pressure to dew points and RH have been developed by Marvin (1941) and others, and are contained in various books dealing with refrigeration and air conditioning. Sections of such tables in British and metric units have been extracted for illustration (Tables A.2 and A.3). Psychrometric charts and slide rules are also available for computation of RH and related values.

Further discussion of the principles and theories underlying calculations of RH and related values and of instruments for measuring RH are beyond the scope of this book. Szulmayer (1969) has prepared an excellent brief review of these topics, whereas Wexler (1965) delves more deeply into the subject in a multi-volume work.

PART 4. DEW POINT

Significance

The dew point (dp) specifies the temperature at which the air is saturated with water vapor (100% RH). If the temperature drops further, condensation will occur. While the dp can be used as a basis for calculating RH, it is of particular value in the handling of some vegetables, because it tells when condensation will occur. When onions or potatoes are removed from cold storage prior to being shipped, condensation of moisture on the bulbs or tubers should be avoided, if possible. Occurrence of condensation can be predicted from a knowledge of the dp and of RH.

Determination

Dp can be determined by means of tables that relate dry-bulb temperature and wet-bulb depression to dp. However, once these data are available, RH can readily be determined from tables such as A.2 and A.3, or RH can be measured directly by various instruments, and once RH is known, dp can be read from psychrometric charts. Such charts relate dry-bulb temperature, RH, dp, and other quantities that express the moisture and energy content of air to each other by means of curves and straight lines (Fig. A.3). Slide rules are available for the same purpose.

For example, if potatoes at 5° C (41° F) are transferred to air at 20° C (68° F) and 60% RH, will water condense on the potatoes? Follow the vertical 20° C dry-bulb line on the chart to its intersection with the 60% RH curve. From this intersection draw a horizontal line to the curve labelled "Wet Bulb or Saturation Temperature." The line and the curve intersect just below 12° C (53° F), which is the dp. Thus, moisture would condense on the tubers. Now, at what RH would condensation be avoided? Draw a horizontal line from 5° C wet bulb to its intersection with the vertical line at 20° C (dry bulb). The lines intersect slightly below the 40% RH curve. Thus, RH would have to be below about 38% to avoid condensation.

The chart also can be used to determine direction of moisture migration. When doors of storages are opened, the operator may want to know whether moisture will move into or out of the room. For example, an onion storage is at 0° C (32° F) and 60% RH; the outside air is at 25° C (77° F) and 30% RH. Will moisture move into the storage room when the doors are opened? Draw a vertical line from 0° C to its intersection with the curve for 60% RH, then from this intersection draw a horizontal to intersect with the scale for weight of water vapor, which will be slightly above 0.002kg/kg dry air. Then follow the same procedure by drawing a vertical at 25° C to its intersection with the curve for 30% RH. The horizontal from that intersection leads to about 0.006 kg/kg dry air for weight of water vapor. Thus moisture will move into the storage room.

TABLE A.1.   NET WEIGHTS IN CONTAINERS COMMONLY USED FOR FRESH VEGETABLES AND MELONS

Commodity	Containers	Net Wt (kg)	Net Wt (lb)
Artichokes, globe	18 cm (7-in.) deep carton	9.0–11.5	20–25
Asparagus	Pyramid crate	14.5	32
	Carton, 16 pkgs	11.0	24
	2-layer carton	12.5–13.5	28–30
	1-layer flat	6.5–8.0	14–18
Beans, snap	Wirebound crate	12.5–13.5	28–30
	Carton	12.5–13.5	28–30
	0.035 cu m (bushel) hamper	12.5–13.5	28–30
Beets, topped	Film or mesh bag 0.45 kg (1 lb)	23.0	50
	bags in master	11.0	24
Broccoli	Pony crate	18.0–19.0	40–42
	Carton or crate, 14 bunches	9.0–10.0	20–23
Carrots, topped	Carton or crate with 48 0.45 kg (1 lb) bags	23.0	50
Cauliflower	Bulk in film-lined bag	23.0	50
	Carton, 12 to 16 trim-wrap	8.0–11.0	18–24
	Catskill or wirebound crate	20.5–23.0	45–50
Celery	Florida wirebound crate	25.0–27.0	55–60
	Calif. wirebound crate	27.0–29.5	60–65
Corn, sweet	Wirebound crate	18.0–27.0	40–60
	Mesh or multiwall bag	20.5–23.0	45–50
Cucumbers	0.039 cu m (1-1/9-bu) wirebound crate	25.0	55
	0.035 cu m (bushel) basket or carton		
	Los Angeles lug	21.5–25.0	47–55
		12.5–14.5	28–32
Eggplant	Carton	12.0–13.5	26–30
	0.035 cu m (bushel) basket or carton	13.5–15.5	30–34
	0.039 cu m (1-1/9-bu) wirebound crate	16.0	35
	Los Angeles lug (18–24)	9.0–10.0	20–22
Garlic	Crate and carton	13.5	30
	Sack	23.0	50
Lettuce, head	Los Angeles lug	9.0–10.0	20–22
Melons	Carton	18.0–20.5	40–45
Cantaloups	Jumbo crate	36.5–38.5	80–85
	Standard crate	32.0–36.5	70–80
	Carton (1/2-crate)	17.5–18.5	38–41
Honey Dews	Carton (4 or 5)	13.0–14.5	29–32
	Flat crate	18.0–20.5	40–45
Okra	Jumbo flat crate	20.5–23.0	45–50
	0.035 cu m (bu) basket or crate	13.5	30
	Los Angeles lug	8.0	18
	0.020 cu m (5/9-bu) wire-bound flat	8.0	18

Commodity	Container	Weight (kg)	Count
Onions			
Dry	Sack	23.0	50
	Carton	22.0–23.0	48–50
	Film bags in master	—	—
Green	Carton, 4 doz bunches	7.0–8.0	15–18
	Wirebound crate, 8 doz bunches	16.0–18.0	35–40
Peppers, sweet	Carton	12.5–15.5	28–34
	0.039 cu m (1-1/9-bu) crate	12.5–15.5	28–33
	0.035 cu m (bu) basket or crate	12.5–13.5	28–30
Potatoes	Sack	45.5	100
	Sack or carton	23.0	50
	54.5 kg (10 lb) sacks, baled	23.0	50
	10 2.3 kg (5 lb) sacks, baled	23.0	50
Spinach	0.035 cu m (bu) basket or crate	8.0–11.5	18–25
	Carton, 2 doz bunches	9.0–10.0	20–22
	Wirebound crate	9.0–10.0	20–22
Watercress	Flats, cartons, 2 layers	9.0–10.5	20–23
Squash, small	0.035 cu m (bu) basket or crate	18.0–20.5	40–45
	0.039 cu m (1-1/9-bu) wirebound crate	20.0	44
	0.017 cu m (1/2-bu) wirebound crate	10.0	21
	Carton or Los Angeles lugs	11.0	24
Sweetpotatoes	Carton	18.0	40
	0.035 cu m (bu) basket or crate	23.0	50
Tomatoes Standard	Carton or wirebound crate	18.0	40
	Los Angeles lug	13.5–15.5	30–34
	Lugs and cartons, 3 layers	13.5–15.0	30–33
	8.7 liter (8-qt) basket	4.0–5.0	9–11
	13.0 liter (12 qt) basket	8.0–9.0	18–20
Cherry	12-basket tray	7.0–8.0	16–18
Turnips, topped	Sack	23.0	50
	Mesh or film bag	11.0	24
	Los Angeles lug	13.5	30
Watercress	Carton, 2 doz bunches	—	—

Source: Anon. (undated).

TABLE A.2.   PERCENT RELATIVE HUMIDITY AT VARIOUS DRY-BULB
TEMPERATURES AS RELATED TO DEPRESSION OF THE WET-BULB TEMPERATURE[1]
(° F)

Dry Bulb (° F)	Depression of Wet-bulb Temperature (° F)									
	0.5	1.0	1.5	2.0	2.5	3.0	4.0	6.0	10.0	15.0
					Relative Humidity (%)					
31	95	89	84	79	74	69	58	39	6	
32	95	90	85	79	74	69	60	41	9	
33	95	90	85	80	76	71	61	42	11	
34	95	90	86	81	77	72	62	44	14	
35	95	91	86	82	77	73	64	46	16	
40	96	92	88	84	80	76	68	53	27	
45	96	93	89	86	82	79	71	58	36	2
50	96	93	90	87	84	81	74	62	42	12
55	97	94	91	88	85	82	76	65	47	20
60	97	94	92	89	86	84	78	68	51	27
65	97	95	92	90	87	85	80	70	55	32
70	98	95	93	90	88	86	81	72	58	37
80	98	96	94	91	89	87	83	76	63	44
90	–	96	–	92	–	89	85	78	65	50

[1]For pressure of 29.0 in. Hg (equivalent to 1000 ft altitude).
Source: Data extracted from Table VII of Marvin (1941).

Further, if, during this period, all the air in the room were replaced with outside air that contained 0.006 kg water vapor/kg dry air, the air would have become saturated and have reached the dew point at about 6° C (42° F) (found by drawing a horizontal from 0.006 kg/kg water vapor to the 100% RH curve.

TABLE A.3.   PERCENT RELATIVE HUMIDITY AT VARIOUS DRY-BULB
TEMPERATURES AS RELATED TO DEPRESSION OF THE WET-BULB TEMPERATURE[1]
(° C)

Dry Bulb (° C)	Depression of Wet-bulb Temperature (° C)					
	0.2	0.5	1.0	2.0	5.0	10.0
			Relative Humidity (%)			
−1	96	91	81	62	8	—
0	96	91	81	64	13	—
1	97	92	83	66	17	—
2	97	92	84	68	22	—
4	97	93	85	71	29	—
6	97	93	86	73	35	—
8	97	94	87	75	40	—
10	98	94	88	77	44	—
15	98	94	90	80	53	13
20	98	96	91	83	59	24
30	99	96	93	86	67	39
40	99	97	94	88	72	48

[1]For pressure of 740 mm Hg.
Source: U.S. Department of Commerce (1953).

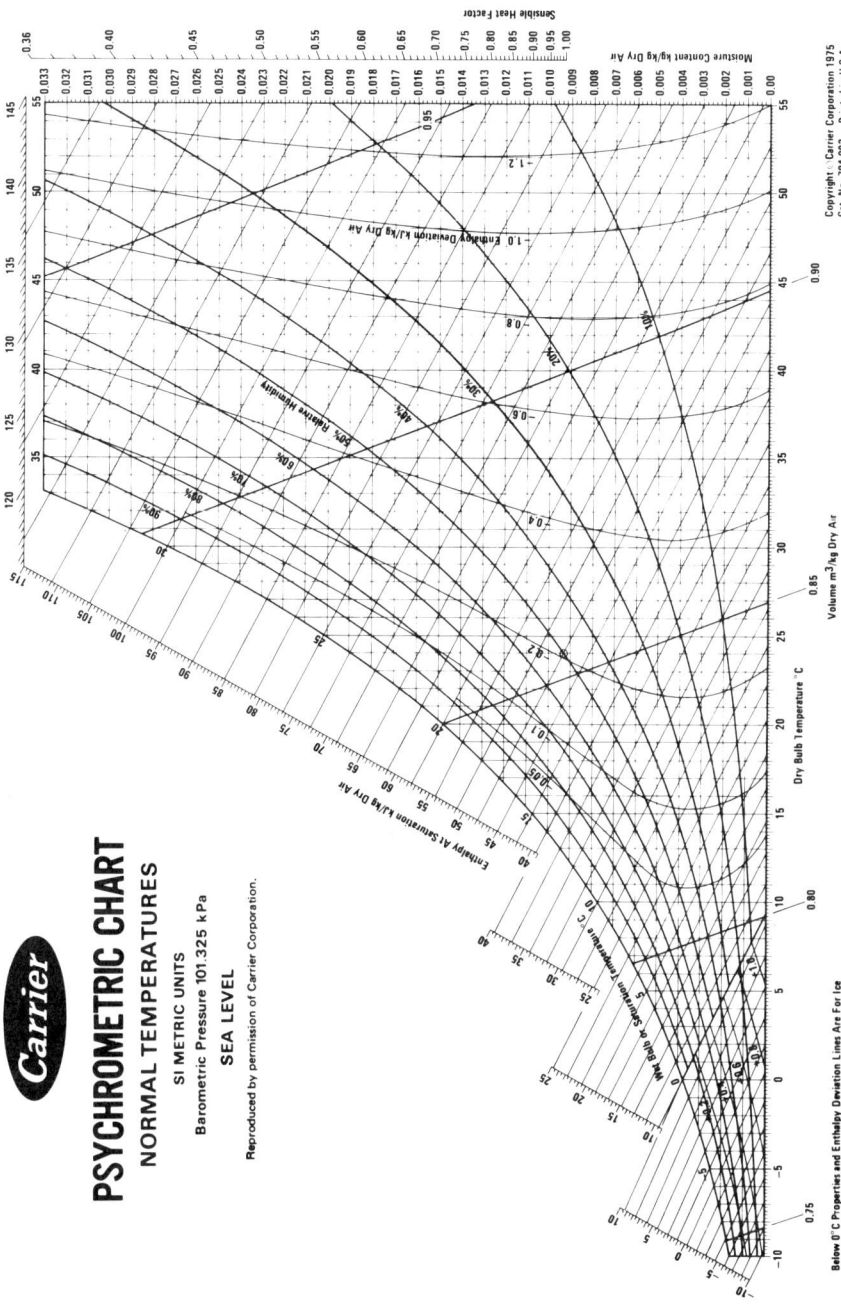

FIG. A.3. PSYCHROMETRIC CHART IN THE INTERNATIONAL SYSTEMS OF UNITS
Pressure given is equivalent to 1 atmosphere.

Courtesy of Carrier Corporation

PART 5. EXCERPTS FROM STANDARDS FOR U.S. NO. 1 GRADE TOMATOES (EFFECTIVE DECEMBER 1, 1973, AS AMENDED NOVEMBER 29, 1973, FEBRUARY 1, 1975, AND APRIL 15, 1976)

Definition

*51.1855 U.S. No. 1.

"U.S. No. 1" consists of tomatoes which meet the following requirements:

(a) Basic requirements:
    (1) Similar varietal characteristics;
    (2) Mature;
    (3) Not overripe or soft;
    (4) Clean;
    (5) Well developed;
    (6) Fairly well formed; and,
    (7) Fairly smooth.
(b) Free from:
    (1) Decay;
    (2) Freezing injury; and
    (3) Sunscald.
(c) Not damaged by any other cause.
(d) For tolerances see *51.1861.

Size

*51.1859 Size.

(a) The size of tomatoes packed in any type container, when specified according to the size designations set forth in Table A.4, shall be within the ranges of diameters specified for the respective designations.

(b) In lieu of specifying size according to the above size designations, the size of tomatoes in any type container may be specified in terms of minimum diameter or of minimum and maximum diameters expressed in whole inches and not less than thirty-second inch fractions thereof, or millimeters, in accordance with the facts.

(c) For tolerances see *51.1861.

(1) In determining compliance with the size designations the measurement for minimum diameter shall be the largest diameter of the tomato measured at right angles to a line from the stem end to the blossom end. The measurement for maximum diameter shall be the

TABLE A.4.   SIZE DESIGNATIONS FOR PACKAGED TOMATOES

Size Designation	Inches		Millimeters	
	Min. Diam[1]	Max Diam[2]	Min. Diam[1]	Max Diam[2]
Extra small	$1^{28}/_{32}$	$2\ ^4/_{32}$	48	54
Small	$2\ ^4/_{32}$	$2\ ^9/_{32}$	54	58
Medium	$2\ ^9/_{32}$	$2^{17}/_{32}$	58	64
Large	$2^{17}/_{32}$	$2^{28}/_{32}$	64	73
Extra large	$2^{28}/_{32}$	$3^{15}/_{32}$	73	88
Maximum large	$3^{15}/_{32}$		88	

[1]Will not pass through a round opening of the designated diameter when the tomato is placed with the greatest transverse diameter across the opening.
[2]Will pass through a round opening of the designated diameter in any position.

smallest dimension of the tomato determined by passing the tomato through a round opening in any position.

Color Classification

*51.1860 Color Classification.

(a) The following terms may be used, when specified in connection with the grade statement, in describing the color as an indication of the stage of ripeness of any lot of mature tomatoes of a red fleshed variety:

(1) **Green**   "Green" means that the surface of the tomato is completely green in color. The shade of green color may vary from light to dark;

(2) **Breakers**   "Breakers" means that there is a definite break in color from green to tannish-yellow, pink or red on not more than 10% of the surface;

(3) **Turning**   "Turning" means that more than 10% but not more than 30% of the surface, in the aggregate, shows a definite change in color from green to tannish-yellow, pink, red, or a combination thereof;

(4) **Pink**   "Pink" means that more than 30% but not more than 60% of the surface, in the aggregate, shows pink or red color;

(5) **Light Red**   "Light red" means that more than 60% of the surface, in the aggregate, shows pinkish-red or red; *Provided,* That not more than 90% of the surface is red color; and,

(6) Red   "Red" means that more than 90% of the surface, in the aggregate, shows red color.

(b) Any lot of tomatoes which does not meet the requirements of any of the above color designations may be designated as "Mixed Color."

(c) For tolerances see *51.1861.

(d) Tomato color standards USDA Visual Aid TM-L-1 consists of a chart containing twelve color photographs illustrating the color classification requirements, as set forth in this section. This visual aid may be examined in the Fruit and Vegetable Division, AMS, U.S. Department of Agriculture, South Building, Washington, D.C. 20250; in any field office of the Fresh Fruit and Vegetable Inspection Service; or upon request of any authorized inspector of such Service. Duplicates of this visual aid may be purchased from The John Henry Co., Post Office Box 1410, Lansing, Michigan 48904.

Tolerances

*51.1861 Tolerances.

In order to allow for variations incident to proper grading and handling in each of the foregoing grades, the following tolerances, by count, are provided as specified:

(a) U.S. No. 1   *(1) For Defects at Shipping Point* [2]   Ten percent for tomatoes in any lot which fail to meet the requirements for this grade; *Provided,* That not more than one-half of this tolerance, or 5%, shall be allowed for defects causing very serious damage, including therein not more than 1% for tomatoes which are soft or affected by decay; and,

(2) For Defects En Route or at Destination   Fifteen percent for tomatoes in any lot which fail to meet the requirements for this grade: *Provided,* That included in this amount not more than the following percentages shall be allowed for defects listed:

(i) Five percent for tomatoes which are soft or affected by decay;

(ii) Ten percent for tomatoes which are damaged by shoulder bruises or by discolored or sunken scars on any parts of the tomatoes; and,

(iii) Ten percent for tomatoes which are otherwise defective: *And provided further,* That not more than 5% shall be allowed for tomatoes which are exclusive of soft or decayed tomatoes.

---

[2] Shipping point, as used in these standards, means the point of origin of the shipment in producing area or a port of loading for ship stores or overseas shipment, or in the case of shipments from outside the continental United States, the port of entry into the United States.

Application of Tolerances

*51.1862 Application of Tolerances.

The contents of individual packages in the lot, based on sample inspection, are subject to the following limitations:

(a) For packages which contain more than 5 lb (2.27 kg), and a tolerance of 10% or more is provided, individual packages shall have not more than 1½ times the tolerance specified, and for a tolerance of less than 10% individual packages shall have not more than double the tolerance specified, except that at least one defective and one off-size specimen may be allowed in any package: *Provided*, That the averages for the entire lot are within the tolerances specified for the grade; and,

(b) For packages which contain 5 lb (2.27 kg) or less individual packages shall have not more than 4 times the tolerance specified, except that at least one tomato which is soft, or affected by decay, and one off-size specimen may be permitted in any package: *Provided*, That the averages for the entire lot are within the tolerances specified for the grade.

Standard Weight

*51.1863 Standard Weight.

(a) When packages are marked to a net weight of 15 lb (6.80 kg) or more, the net weight of the contents shall not be less than the designated net weight and shall not exceed the designated weight by more than 2 lb (0.91 kg).

(b) In order to allow for variations incident to proper sizing, not more than 15%, by count, of the packages in any lot may fail to meet the requirements for standard weight.

Definitions

*51.1864 Similar Varietal Characteristics   "Similar varietal characteristics" means that the tomatoes are alike as to firmness of flesh and shade of color (for example, soft-fleshed, early maturing varieties are not mixed with firm-fleshed, midseason or late varieties, or bright red varieties having a purplish tinge).

*51.1865 Mature   "Mature" means that the tomato has reached the stage of development which will insure a proper completion of the ripening process, and that the contents of two or more seed cavities have developed a jelly-like consistency and the seeds are well developed.

*51.1866 Soft   "Soft" means that the tomato yields readily to slight pressure.

*51.1867 Clean   "Clean" means that the tomato is practically free from dirt or other foreign material.

*51.1868 Well Developed   "Well developed" means that the tomato shows normal growth. Tomatoes which are ridged and peaked at the stem end, contain dry tissue, and usually contain open spaces below the level of the stem scar, are not considered well developed.

*51.1869 Fairly Well Formed   "Fairly well formed" means that the tomato is not more than moderately kidney-shaped, lopsided, elongated, angular, or otherwise moderately deformed.

*51.1870 Fairly Smooth   "Fairly smooth" means that the tomato is not conspicuously ridged or rough.

*51.1871 Damage   "Damage" means any specific defect described in the U.S. Standards; or an equally objectionable variation of any one of these defects, any other defect, or any combination of defects, which materially detracts from the appearance, or the edible or marketing quality of the tomato.

*51.1872 Reasonably Well Formed   "Reasonably well formed" means that the tomato is not decidedly kidney-shaped, lopsided, elongated, angular, or otherwise decidedly deformed.

*51.1873 Slightly Rough   "Slightly rough" means that the tomato is not decidedly ridged or grooved.

*51.1874 Serious Damage   "Serious damage" means any specific defect described in the U.S. Standards; or an equally objectionable variation of any one of these defects, any other defect, or any combination of defects, which seriously detracts from the appearance, or the edible or marketing quality of the tomato.

*51.1875 Misshapen   "Misshapen" means that the tomato is decidedly kidney-shaped, lopsided, elongated, angular or otherwise decidedly deformed: *Provided*, That the shape is not affected to an extent that the appearance or the edible quality of the tomato is very seriously affected.

*51.1876 Very Serious Damage   "Very serious damage" means any specific defect described in the U.S. Standards; or an equally objectionable variation of any one of these defects, any other defect, or any combination of defects, which very seriously detracts from the appearance, or the edible or marketing quality of the tomato.

REFERENCES

ANON. (undated). Net weight of fresh fruits and vegetables in containers delivered to institutions. United Fresh Fruit and Vegetable Assoc., Washington, D.C.

MARVIN, C. F. 1941. Psychrometric tables for obtaining the vapor pressure, relative humidity, and temperature of the dew point from readings of the wet- and dry-bulb thermometers. U.S. Dept. Comm. Weather Bur. *235*.

SHIPTON, J. 1965. Use of liquid nitrogen for food transport, freezing and storage. Australian Refrig. Air Cond. and Heatg. *19*, No. 2, 22–25, 28–30.

SZULMAYER, W. 1969. Humidity and moisture measurement. Food Preserv. Quart. *29*, 27–35.

U.S. DEPARTMENT OF COMMERCE. 1953. Relative humidity-psychrometric tables. Celsius (Centigrade) temperatures. Weather Bureau, Washington, D.C.

WEXLER, A. 1965. Humidity and Moisture. Measurement and Control in Science and Industry, Vol. 1–3. Reinhold Publishing Co., New York.

WILLIAMS, G. D. V., and LÉGER,R. 1967. Vapor pressure deficit, relative humidity, and dew point temperature conversion tables. Can. Dept. Agr. Meteorol. Tech. Bull. *12*.

Glossary

Abaxial In a leaf, the surface facing away from the axis.

Abscission Natural separation of leaves or fruits from the plant.

Adaxial In a leaf, the surface facing toward the axis.

Barometric condenser A condenser in which a partial vacuum can be maintained, despite connection with the outer atmosphere, because a long pipe containing water permits flow out of the condenser into a hot well below while maintaining a vacuum above.

Breakbulk system Loading and unloading ship's cargo by manual handling of individual shipping containers.

Chilling Exposure of a vegetable or fruit to a low, but nonfreezing temperature that injures the item upon sufficient exposure; for most chilling sensitive crops, between 0° and 13° C (32° and 55° F).

Chilling injury Physiological damage inflicted by low, but nonfreezing temperatures.

Cleat A strip of wood, attached to the top ends of a crate to prevent the crate on top from crushing the product in the bulged pack below.

Corm A short, thickened, vertical, underground stem with few scale-like leaves, e.g., water chestnut.

Cultivar A cultivated variety of plant, such as the Tendergreen snap bean; if together with species name, written: *Phaseolus vulgaris* 'Tendergreen.' (See *variety*)

Dew point Temperature at which air is saturated with water vapor. A high dew point indicates moist air, a low one, dry air. If the temperature drops below the dew point, water will condense out.

Disease Symptoms of the destructive effects of various microorganisms.

Disorder   Symptoms of disturbances in the normal metabolism or in the structural integrity of a plant part. No microorganisms are involved as causative agents.

Dormancy   A physiological state of some plant parts during which neither sprouting nor rooting occurs because of unfavorable environmental conditions. (See *rest*)

Dunnage   Wood strips used to separate stacks, rows, or layers of cargo to permit circulation of air through the load.

Epidermis   The skin of various plant organs usually one cell layer thick. (See *periderm*)

Frigorie   European unit of refrigeration capacity: 1 kcal/hr.

Half-cooling time   The interval during which the initial temperature difference between the object cooled and the coolant is halved.

Hardware item   A fictitious produce item that can tolerate physical abuse.

Heat capacity   The quantity of energy required to raise the temperature of a body one degree.

Inoculum   Spores or other structures of microorganisms in the environment that are capable of infecting a plant.

k-factor   A designation of thermal conductivity of a material, expressed in units of W/sq m (° C/m of thickness), or, in the reduced form, W/m° C. The equivalents in British units are Btu/hr sq ft (° F/in.), or Btu/hr sq ft (° F/ft), or in the reduced form, Btu/hr ft ° F. Good insulators have low k-factors. (See *U-factor*)

Krad   A measure of energy used in irradiation: 1000 rad = 1 kilorad (Krad); 1 rad = energy absorption of 100 erg per gram of material.

Latent heat   Change in energy content during a change of state, as in evaporation of water. (See *sensible heat*)

Layer   Each successive vertical increment one container high.

Lenticels   Pores in the skin of some fruits and vegetables through which gas exchange occurs.

Mole   The weight of a substance, in grams, numerically equal to its molecular weight.

Mycelium   Vegetative filamentous growth of fungi.

Periderm   The skin of storage organs, such as roots and tubers; usually several cell layers thick. (See *epidermis*)

Phloem   Portion of the vascular system of plants that primarily conducts products of photosynthesis to various parts of the plant.

Pintles   Rotating strips of rubber with multiple small fingers; used to mechanically scrub vegetables before packing.

Plenum (chamber)   A space (usually above or below the storage room) where air pressure is higher than in the outside atmosphere (the storage room).

Precooling   Removal of a substantial portion of the field heat from a commodity prior to shipment or storage.

Quality evaluation   Subjective evaluations, made as objectively as possible, of various aspects of quality during examination of produce; quantified by use of a rating system. (See *Rating system for quality*.)

Rating system for quality   For general appearance: 9—excellent, no or only very minor defects; 7—good, minor defects that generally are not objectionable and can easily be removed; 5—fair, major defects that can be removed and render the product salable again; 3—poor, product no longer salable, but possibly still usable after removal of defect; 1—unusable. For specific defects: 1—none; 3—generally noticeable only upon inspection by trained personnel; 5—defect readily noticeable and generally objectionable; 7—defect strongly objectionable and seriously detracts from quality; 9—commodity unusable because of specific defect alone. Intermediate values are used, as necessary.

The ratings for general quality and specific defects are inverse, so that the quality rating decreases as defects increase.

Refrigeration capacity   One ton of refrigeration refers to a heat absorbing capacity of 12,000 Btu per hr.

Relative humidity (percent)   The ratio of the actual amount of water vapor in the air to the maximum it can hold at a given temperature, multiplied by 100.

Rest   A physiological state of some plant parts that prevents sprouting or rooting even in an environment conducive to such growth; diminishes with time in storage. (See *dormancy*)

Rhizome   Elongated, horizontally growing underground stems, e.g., ginger.

Row   A single file of piled produce containers lengthwise of the transit vehicle or storage room.

Saturation vapor pressure   The pressure exerted by a vapor in equilibrium with its liquid; i.e., when the rate of escape of vapor from the liquid is exactly equal to the rate of return. In discussions related to refrigeration this quantity is expressed in mm or in. of mercury (Hg).

Scrubbing   Removing a gas, generally CO_2 or O_2, from the storage atmosphere.

Senescence   The period in the life of an organism during which degradative changes predominate.

Sensible heat   Change in energy associated with a change in temperature. (See *latent heat*)

Shook   Individual parts of wood containers before their assembly.

Split   The difference in temperature between the heat exchange surface, e.g., ice or the cold coils of a mechanical unit, and the space being cooled.

Spores Minute reproductive structures of microorganisms, analogous to seeds in higher plants.

Stack A single file of piled produce containers crosswise of the transit vehicle or storage room.

Stolon Stem that grows horizontally on the soil surface.

Sublimation Change in state from solid to gas without passing through liquid state.

Substrate The substance that is chemically changed by an enzyme.

Supercooling Lowering the temperature of a substance below its freezing point without formation of ice crystals.

Tariff A set of published regulations dealing with transport of goods by common carriers.

Ton of refrigeration See *Refrigeration capacity*

Transpiration Loss of water vapor by plants.

Tuber Enlarged, relatively short underground stem, such as a potato.

U-factor Overall coefficient of heat transfer, such as exists between two sides of a wall, expressed in units of W/sq m ° C or Btu/hr sq ft ° F. (See *k-factor*)

Vapor Pressure (of water) The pressure exerted by water vapor at a given temperature, frequently expressed in mm or in. of mercury (Hg) (See *saturation vapor pressure*)

Vapor pressure deficit or differential The difference between the actual vapor pressure and the saturation vapor pressure.

Variety A subdivision in botanical nomenclature, following subspecies in sequence. Formerly applied to cultivated varieties, properly called cultivars. (See *cultivar*)

Xylem Portion of the vascular system of plants that primarily conducts materials from the roots to the tops.

Index

Related AVI Books

AN INTRODUCTION TO AGRICULTURAL ENGINEERING
  Roth, Crow and Mahoney
COMMERCIAL VEGETABLE PROCESSING
  Luh and Woodroof
COMMERCIAL WINEMAKING
  Vine
ENCYCLOPEDIA OF FOOD SCIENCE
  Peterson and Johnson
ENCYCLOPEDIA OF FOOD TECHNOLOGY
  Johnson and Peterson
EVALUATION OF PROTEINS FOR HUMANS
  Bodwell
FOOD AND BEVERAGE MYCOLOGY
  Beuchat
FOOD QUALITY ASSURANCE
  Gould
FUNDAMENTALS OF FOOD FREEZING
  Desrosier and Tressler
HORTICULTURAL REVIEWS, VOLS. 1–4
  Janick
LABORATORY MANUAL FOR ENTOMOLOGY AND PLANT PATHOLOGY
  2nd Edition   *Pyenson and Parké*
NUTRITIONAL EVALUATION OF FOOD PROCESSING 2nd Edition
  Smith
POSTHARVEST: AN INTRODUCTION TO THE PHYSIOLOGY &
  HANDLING OF FRUIT & VEGETABLES   *Wills et al.*
POTATOES: PRODUCTION, STORING, PROCESSING   2nd Edition
  Smith
PRESCOTT & DUNN'S INDUSTRIAL MICROBIOLOGY   4th Edition
  Reed
SMALL FRUIT CULTURE 5th Edition   *Shoemaker*
SOURCE BOOK FOR FOOD SCIENTISTS
  Ockerman